OXFORD STUDIES IN DEMOCRATIZATION

Series Editor: Laurence Whitehead

. . . .

GENDER JUSTICE, DEVELOPMENT, AND RIGHTS

OXFORD STUDIES IN DEMOCRATIZATION

Series Editor: Laurence Whitehead

. . . .

Oxford Studies in Democratization is a series for scholars and students
of comparative politics and related disciplines. Volumes will concentrate
on the comparative study of the democratization processes that accompanied
the decline and termination of the cold war. The geographical focus of
the series will primarily be Latin America, the Caribbean, Southern
and Eastern Europe, and relevant experiences in Africa and Asia.

OTHER BOOKS IN THE SERIES

The Politics of Memory:
Transitional Justice in Democratizing Societies
*Alexandra Barahona de Brito,
Carmen González Enriquez, and Paloma Aguilar*

Citizenship Rights and Social Movements:
A Comparative and Statistical Analysis
Joe Foweraker and Todd Landman

Democratic Consolition in Eastern Europe:
Volume 1. Institutional Engineering
Jan Zielonka

Democratic Consolition in Eastern Europe:
Volume 2. International and Transnational Factors
Jan Zielonka and Alex Pravda

New as paperback

The International Dimensions of Democratization:
Europe and the Americas
Laurence Whitehead

Institutions and Democratic Citizenship
Axel Hadenius

The Architecture of Democracy: Constitutional Design, Conflict Management and
Democracy
edited by Andrew Reynolds

The *United Nations Research Institute for Social Development* (UNRISD) is an
autonomous agency engaging in multidisciplinary research on the social dimensions of
contemporary problems affecting development. Its work is guided by the conviction that,
for effective development policies to be formulated, an understanding of the social and
political context is crucial. The Institute attempts to provide governments, development
agencies, grassroots organizations and scholars with a better understanding of how
development policies and processes of economic, social, and environmental change affect
different social groups. Working through an extensive network of national research
centres, UNRISD aims to promote original research and strengthen research capacity in
developing countries.
Current research programmes include: Civil Society and Social Movements; Democracy,
Governance and Human Rights; Identities, Conflict and Cohesion; Social Policy and
Development; and Technology, Business and Society.
A list of UNRISD's free and priced publications can be obtained by contacting the
Reference Centre, UNRISD, Palais des Nations, 1211 Geneva 10, Switzerland; Phone:
(41 22) 917 3020; Fax: (41 22) 917 0650; info@unrisd.org; http://www.unrisd.org.
UNRISD thanks the governments of Denmark, Finland, Mexico, the Netherlands,
Norway, Sweden, Switzerland and the United Kingdom for their core funding.

Gender Justice, Development, and Rights

. . . .

edited by

MAXINE MOLYNEUX
and
SHAHRA RAZAVI

OXFORD
UNIVERSITY PRESS

OXFORD
UNIVERSITY PRESS

Great Clarendon Street, Oxford OX2 6DP

Oxford University Press is a department of the University of Oxford.
It furthers the University's objective of excellence in research, scholarship,
and education by publishing worldwide in

Oxford New York
Auckland Bangkok Buenos Aires Cape Town Chennai
Dar es Salaam Delhi Hong Kong Istanbul Karachi Kolkata
Kuala Lumpur Madrid Melbourne Mexico City Mumbai Nairobi
São Paulo Shanghai Taipei Tokyo Toronto

Oxford is a registered trade mark of Oxford University Press
in the UK and in certain other countries

Published in the United States
by Oxford University Press Inc., New York

A catalogue record for this title is available from the British Library

Library of Congress Cataloging in Publication Data
Gender justice, development, and rights / edited by Maxine Molyneux and Shahra Razavi.
p. cm.—(Oxford studies in democratization)
Papers presented at an UNRISD workship held in New York on June 3, 2000 to
coincide with the General Assembly Special Session for the Beijing+5 review.
Includes bibliographical references and index.
1. Women's rights—Cross-cultural studies—Congresses. 2. Women's rights—Developing
countries—Congresses. 3. Women—Developing countries—Social
conditions—Congresses. 4. Women—Developing countries—Economic
conditions—Congresses. 5. Developing countries—Social policy—Congresses. 6. Social
justice—Developing countries—Congresses. I. Molyneux, Maxine. II. Razavi,
Shahrashoub. III. United Nations Research Institute for Social Development. IV. Series.

HQ1236 .G4615 2002   305.42–dc21   2002027769

ISBN 0-19-925644-6 (hbk.)
ISBN 0-19-925645-4 (pbk.)

3 5 7 9 10 8 6 4 2

Typeset by Newgen Imaging Systems (P) Ltd., Chennai, India
Printed in Great Britain on acid-free paper by
Biddles Ltd, King's Lynn, Norfolk

Preface

The 1980s and 1990s saw the collapse of authoritarian regimes in many parts of the world. This revitalized the debate over democratic and participatory governance and gave a major impulse to human rights agendas. In this context, women's movements flourished as strong advocates of women's rights and attained a considerable number of legal and institutional advances. And yet the last two decades of the twentieth century also saw the ascendance of neo-liberal agendas in many parts of the world, with regressive social and economic consequences. This has placed significant constraints on the substantiation of human rights in general, and women's rights in particular.

From their diverse regional perspectives, the contributions to this volume reflect on the gender content of the new policy agenda and how it has been translated and contested in disparate local contexts. The volume grows out of a two-year (1999–2001) research project at the United Nations Research Institute of Social Development (UNRISD) in Geneva. Some of the commissioned papers which appear here were presented and discussed at an UNRISD Workshop that took place in New York on 3 June 2000, coincide with the General Assembly Special Session for the Beijing Plus Five Review. At this meeting, six members of the research team, and the editors of the volume, presented their work on issues of gender justice, development, and rights. The immediate output from the Workshop was a short report circulated at the Special Session of the General Assembly. Later, the edited version of the report was published as an issue of the UNRISD Conference News series, Gender Justice, Development and Rights: Substantiating Rights in a Disabling Environment.

Financial assistance for the preparation of this manuscript, and the UNRISD Workshop in New York, was provided by the Swedish International Development Agency (Sida) and UNRISD's core funders, the governments of Denmark, Finland, Mexico, the Netherlands, Norway, Sweden, Switzerland, and the United Kingdom.

Thandika Mkandawire
Director
UNRISD

....
Acknowledgements
....

The editors would like to extend their appreciation to the chapter contributors who responded so positively to the numerous rounds of revision requested. We would also like to thank those who contributed to the Workshop that UNRISD organized in New York (June 2000) to initiate the research project on which this volume is based, especially Gita Sen, Ros Petchesky and Yakin Ertürk. At UNRISD, Caroline Danloy and Cristina Paciello provided valuable support with library searches, checking references, and proof reading. Thanks too to Rachel Sieder and Ann Zammit for editing some of the chapters, and to Yusuf Bangura and Caroline Danloy who provided valuable comments on several chapters. We are also grateful to our respective institutions, the Institute of Latin American Studies (ILAS), University of London, and the United Nations Research Institute for Social Development (UNRISD), for providing us with institutional support.

M. M., S. R.
December 2001

Contents

viii   *Contents*

III. Democratization and the Politics of Gender

IV. Multiculturalisms in Practice

Notes on Contributors

CECILIA BLONDET is Minister for the Advancement of Women and Human Development in Peru. Previously, she served as the General Director of the Instituto de Estudios Peruanos. She is a member of the board of directors of TRANSPARENCIA, a civil association created to oversee the electoral process in Peru. She is also a member of the Steering Committee of the Civil Society Project (Ford Foundation and the IDS-Sussex). Since 1985 her main research area has been gender and politics, on which she has published widely.

DIANE ELSON is Professor of Sociology at the University of Essex, UK. Previously, she worked for the United Nations Development Fund for Women (UNIFEM) and for Manchester University where she was Chair in Development Studies. Her current research and teaching interests are in global social change and the realization of human rights with a particular focus on gender inequality. She edited *Male Bias in the Development Process* (1995); co-edited Special Issues of *World Development* on *Gender, Adjustment and Macroeconomics* (1995); *Growth, Trade, Finance and Gender Inequality* (2000); and the *UNIFEM Report on Progress of the World's Women* (2000).

ANNE MARIE GOETZ is Senior Fellow at the Institute of Development Studies, Sussex, UK. She has written extensively on gender and institutions, including *Getting Institutions Right for Women in Development* (Zed, 1997). She has also done research on the gender implications of credit programmes in rural Bangladesh.

SHIREEN HASSIM teaches Political Studies at the University of the Witwatersrand in Johannesburg, South Africa. She has worked on the South African women's movement for several years, and has lectured and published in this field. During 1999, she was a member of the Gender and Elections Reference Group of the Electoral Institute of South Africa, and co-edited the *Elections* bulletin. She is a member of the Advisory Board of Womensnet, a website for women.

JACQUELINE HEINEN is Professor at the University of Versailles St-Quentin-en-Yvelines and at Sciences Po-Paris. She is Director of the magazine *Cahiers du genre* and a member of the Printemps-CNRS workshop. Her main area of work is on state politics and citizenship in Central and Eastern Europe, with a particular focus on Poland. She is currently directing an international comparative study on gender and local democracy in seven countries of the European Union. Her recent work includes 'Les politiques sociales et familiales' (in *Dictionnaire critique du féminisme, Paris*: PUF, 2000).

AÍDA HERNÁNDEZ CASTILLO has a Ph.D. in Anthropology (Stanford University, 1996) and is Researcher-Professor at the Center for High Studies in Social Anthropology (CIESAS), Mexico City. She has carried out research projects in different regions of the state of Chiapas with Mexican peasants and Guatemalan refugees and published three books and several articles on gender, ethnic identity, legal anthropology, and religion. In 1997, she won a National Prize in journalism for an essay on the impact of the war on indigenous women and one of her books won the Fray Bernardino de Sahagún national prize for the best research in social anthropology.

MAZNAH MOHAMAD is the 2001 Visiting Chair in ASEAN and International Studies at the Munk Centre for International Studies, University of Toronto. At the University of Science Malaysia, she holds the position of Associate Professor in Development Studies. She is also a member of the Board of Directors of the International Women's Rights Action Watch of the Asia-Pacific, a regional NGO monitoring the implementation of CEDAW. Her recent publications include, *Muslim Women and Access to Justice: Historical, Legal and Social Experience in Malaysia* (editor, Penang: WDC, 2000) and 'At the Centre and Periphery: Contributions of Women's Movements to Democratisation' (in Loh and Khoo (eds.), *Discourses and Practices of Democracy in Malaysia*, Curzon Press, 2001).

MAXINE MOLYNEUX is Professor of Sociology at the Institute of Latin American Studies, University of London. She has published widely in the field of gender, politics, and development, and has acted as consultant to the UN and to international and regional NGOs. Her recent books include *Women's Movements in International Perspective: Latin American and Beyond* (Palgrave, 2000); *The Hidden Histories of Gender and the State in Latin America*, ed. with Elisabeth Dore (Duke University Press); and *The Politics of Gender and Rights in Latin America*, ed. with Nikki Craske (Palgrave, 2002).

MARTHA NUSSBAUM is Ernst Freund Distinguished Service Professor of Law and Ethics at the University of Chicago, with appointments in the Law School, the Philosophy Department, and the Center for Gender Studies. Her books include *Cultivating Humanity: A*

Classical Defense of Reform in Liberal Education (1997); *Sex and Social Justice* (1999); and *Women and Human Development: The Capabilities Approach* (2000).

PARVIN PAIDAR works in international development, currently with UNIFEM in Afghanistan. Her research interests include gender and social development issues in developing countries. She has written on Iran and Islam from a gender perspective. She is the author of *Women in the Political Process of Twentieth Century Iran* (Cambridge University Press, 1997).

ANNE PHILLIPS is Professor of Gender Theory at the London School of Economics (LSE), and has served as Director of the Gender Institute at the LSE. Her publications include *Engendering Democracy* (Polity Press, 1991); *Democracy and Difference* (Polity Press, 1993); *The Politics of Presence: The Political Representation of Gender, Ethnicity and Race* (OUP, 1995); and *Which Equalities Matter?* (Polity Press, 1999).

STÉPHANE PORTET is currently working on a thesis in sociology on the gender dimension of part-time work in France and Poland. He is in charge of research at the University of Warsaw for the European network 'Women in European Universities'. He is a member of Sagesse-Simone group at the University of Toulouse-le-Mirail. His work includes 'Le Temps partiel fait-il toujours mauvais genre? La Dimension sexuée du travail à temps partiel en France et en Pologne' (Mémoire de DEA, University of Toulouse-le-Mirail, 1999); 'Intégration de la Pologne à l'Union européenne et rapports de genre' (with Jacqueline Heinen, *Lien social et politique RIAC*, 45, 2001).

SHAHRA RAZAVI is Research Coordinator at the United Nations Research Institute for Social Development (UNRISD), Geneva. She is the editor of the books, *Gendered Poverty and Well-Being (Development and Change*/Blackwells, 2000); *Shifting Burdens: Gender and Agrarian Change under Neoliberalism* (Kumarian Press, 2002); and co-editor with Carol Miller of *Missionaries and Mandarins: Feminist Engagement with Development Institutions* (Intermediate Technology Publications, 1998). She is editing a Special Issue of the *Journal of Agrarian Change*, on Agrarian Change, Gender and Land Rights (Jan./April 2003).

VERÓNICA SCHILD is Associate Professor of Political Science at the University of Western Ontario. Born in Chile, she studied in the United States and Canada, obtaining a Ph.D. in Political Science from the University of Toronto. She is the author of articles on the Chilean women's movement in a time of political transition, and most recently on gendered citizenship formation in neo-liberal Latin American contexts. She is currently working on a book on the women's movement and neo-liberal state formation in Chile.

RAMYA SUBRAHMANIAN is a Fellow at the Institute of Development Studies, University of Sussex working on social policy and gender issues. Her particular focus is on primary education, and the intersections between livelihoods, poverty, and household strategies for investing in education. She is also interested in education policy processes and decentralization of education management. She is the co-editor with Naila Kabeer of *Institutions, Relations and Outcomes: A Framework and Case Studies for Gender-Aware Planning* (Kali for Women 1999; Zed 2000).

AILI MARI TRIPP is Associate Professor of Political Science and Women's Studies at the University of Wisconsin-Madison, USA. Her publications include *Women and Politics in Uganda* (2000); *Changing the Rules: The Politics of Liberalization and the Urban Informal Economy in Tanzania* (1997); and a co-edited volume with Marja-Liisa Swantz, *What went Right in Tanzania? People's Responses to Directed Development* (1996). She is currently writing a book on women and politics in Africa with Joy Kwesiga and has published numerous articles and chapters on the politics of ethnicity and religion in Africa; economic and political reform in Africa; and transformations of associational life in Africa.

Introduction

Maxine Molyneux and Shahra Razavi

The 1990s were a landmark in the international human rights movement and saw many positive changes in women's rights as well as
in human rights more broadly. This collection of theoretical and
empirical studies reflects on these gains, and on the significance
accorded in international policy to issues of rights and democracy
in the post-cold war era. It engages with some of the most pressing
and contested of contemporary issues—neo-liberal policies, democracy, and multiculturalism—and in so doing invites debate on the
nature of liberalism itself in an epoch that has seen its global ascendancy. These issues are addressed here through two optics which cast
contemporary liberalism in a distinctive light. First, by applying a
'gender lens' to the analysis of political and policy processes and,
by deploying the insights gained from feminist theory, this volume
provides a gendered account of the ways in which liberal rights, and
ideas of democracy and justice, have been absorbed into the political
agendas of women's movements and states. Second, the case studies contribute a cross-cultural dimension to the analysis of modern
forms of rule by examining the ways in which liberalism—the dominant value system in the modern world—both exists and is resisted
in diverse cultural settings.

The twelve chapters—whether theoretical and general, or case
studies of particular countries—reflect on a key moment in international policy-making. The collapse of authoritarian regimes in the
Soviet Union and Eastern Europe, in Latin America and other parts
of the world, gave issues of rights and democracy a major impulse,
and simultaneously revitalized debates over development policy. The
cluster of UN summits held in the 1990s provided NGOs with a public forum and stimulated debate, both domestic and international,
over policy. In these various policy arenas, women's movements and
their representatives were active participants. The decade saw the
growing size and influence of an international women's movement,

one linked through regional and international networks and able to collaborate on issues of policy and agenda setting. At the same time, the return to civilian rule in many previously authoritarian states presented women's movements with an opportunity to press for political and legal reform at the national level. By the end of the decade all but a handful of the world's states had signed up to the proposals for gender equity contained in the Beijing Platform for Action, and to the Convention on the Elimination of All Forms of Discrimination Against Women (CEDAW), one of the most significant bodies of international law pertaining to women.[1] In their reports to the United Nations' mid-term review meeting in 2000 to assess progress many governments claimed to have put in place policies that were achieving positive results. Quota systems had brought more women into parliaments; many discriminatory laws had been amended or scrapped; women had attained new rights in the family and assurances that existing rights would be respected. Political reforms such as decentralization had increased local participation and had brought many more women to leadership positions at community and government levels.[2]

In much of the world, however, these advances in political and legal rights were not matched by significant progress in the achievement of greater social justice. Throughout the 1980s and 1990s income inequalities rose in all but a few states, while poverty remained a persistent, even a growing, phenomenon in many countries both developed and developing. The new economic model introduced from the mid-1970s had brought high social costs and a mixed record of economic achievement. This *ambivalent* character of the record of the 1990s lies at the heart of the international policy agenda. This rests on two central elements: the consolidation of a market-led development model; and a greater emphasis on democracy and rights. The extent to which these two elements could be reconciled or came into conflict has been the subject of much scholarly and political debate in the period since. It was the issue that dominated the discussions of the international women's movement at the 1995 global summit on women held in Beijing, and it has continued to perplex participants in subsequent regional mid-term reviews. At these meetings as government representatives reported on the not insignificant progress that had been made in improving women's rights, NGOs and women's movement representatives deplored the disabling economic and social conditions that helped to keep large numbers of women in a state of poverty and deprivation.

This ambivalent character of the new policy agenda forms the backdrop to the chapters in this volume. In much of the world, and with serious social consequences in many poorer countries, the new economic policies have failed to deliver the hoped-for prosperity. Inaugurated under conditions of harsh stabilization and structural adjustment they succeeded in ending hyper-inflation, but at an unacceptable social cost, as incomes, wages, and employment went into sharp decline. While enthusiasm for the 'market fundamentalism' that reigned during the 1980s has waned, and the Washington-based financial institutions as well as many governments apply their economic prescriptions with more caution, the results are hotly contested. A comparison of regional growth rates for the period 1960–80, when developing countries were pursuing *dirigiste* policies with those for the 1980–2000 period, when they were enticed to 'open up' to world markets (Weisbrot *et al.*, 2000), provides little support for those advocating further trade and financial liberalization. Moreover, rising income inequalities, coupled with widespread poverty in many countries, have been accompanied by record levels of crime and violence. Meanwhile states have downsized, abdicating former responsibilities in the domains of economic and social policy, just at the moment when they are most needed to play a coordinating function between public and private provision. Where not starkly inadequate, welfare delivery under the new schemes has been patchy.

By the end of the 1990s therefore, following the financial crises that gripped the former Soviet Union and East Asia, the optimism that accompanied the spread of democracy in the South and in the former socialist economies had begun to ebb. The new millennium entered its first years amidst the unravelling of peace accords, growing communal violence, environmental setbacks, and a global crisis occasioned by terrorism and war. If this was not enough to set back human rights agendas, it had already become apparent that, despite the dynamism of the human rights movement, a wide gulf remained between the articulation of global principles and their application in many national settings. Much the same could be said of democratization; the hopes invested in democracy as the most effective system for the delivery of social justice dimmed when confronted with the uneven trends in the post-authoritarian transitions across different regions. The gap between global principles and outcomes is particularly striking in the case of gender equality, women's rights and access to decision-making power: for all the advances noted earlier, these have been modest when judged against the standard of equality.[3]

Faced with this record, many have come to question the significance of the much-heralded global turn to democracy and human rights. Some have argued that this has represented a new form of Western hegemony, the sweetener for the bitter pill of neo-liberal adjustment and rising inequality; some believe that it amounted to little more than empty rhetoric with little content or effect. This critique, persuasive in regard to welfare and equality, is often linked to a critique of the use of human rights to legitimize policies of 'humanitarian intervention'. But others, both scholars and activists, including many NGOs working with poor communities and with women, have argued that democracy and human rights provided the only effective means to challenge inequality and to advance programmes that would promote greater social justice and more equitable development.

This debate over what has been termed liberal internationalism, whether framed as an engagement with neo-liberalism, the new development agenda, or globalization, continues apace and it is at once evident that many of the questions posed of the record of the last few decades are far from new. Indeed in many ways it represents a contemporary refiguring of a much older concern about the limits and the potential of liberal systems of governance to effect meaningful reform and to promote social justice. Much of course depends on what is understood by liberalism, itself a contested analytic terrain and of variable historical presence. Even what is taken as the founding principle of liberalism, that of individual freedom, has generated argument over its interpretation in the domains of philosophy, economics, and politics. Yet, if liberalism, both political and economic, has achieved a qualified dominance over other values, incorporating all but a few states into an increasingly interdependent global system, this has not resulted in a process of homogenization of legal or political culture, or in institutional arrangements. Western liberal states might share similar conceptions of law and governance that have shaped their institutions accordingly, but history has left its mark on the state–society relations that have evolved in each case, with corresponding variations in the policy domains of welfare and economic management.

Organization of the Volume

This book is divided into four parts. In Part I, which provides a theoretical engagement with some of the principal themes of the volume, Martha Nussbaum, Diane Elson, and Anne Phillips examine different aspects of liberalism and consider some challenges to its neo-liberal or contractarian form. Nussbaum's critique of utilitarian liberalism and Elson's analysis of neo-liberal approaches to state–society restructuring argue for a greater role for the state in public welfare, while Phillips examines the implications for gender equality of multicultural claims to citizenship and democracy. From their distinct disciplinary perspectives in philosophy, economics, and politics respectively, they all address the question of how far liberal rights agendas, whether embodied in national or international legal instruments, have taken account of women's needs and interests. In seeking to draw out the implications for women of the different generations of rights—political, economic, and social—they contribute to the ongoing debates over how gender justice might be advanced.

Parts II, III, and IV of this book consist of case studies which examine three fundamental challenges from the perspectives of economics, politics, and culture respectively, that have been made to prevailing liberal versions of democracy and rights. The chapters in Part II by Jacqueline Heinen and Stéphane Portet, Verónica Schild, and Ramya Subrahmanian, revisit the themes taken up by Nussbaum and Elson. They examine the gender implications of the tensions between orthodox macroeconomic agendas, social rights, and the delivery of welfare. The cases of Poland, Chile, and India show how the dominant economic and social agenda impacts upon gender relations and the 'care economy' and consider how women's capabilities and social rights have been affected in these different regional settings.

Part III considers how women's movements have positioned themselves in relation to states and social movements that claim democracy as a legitimizing principle. Democracy here is understood both in institutional terms and as a value and a practice within civil society, but as the case studies by Parvin Paidar, Cecilia Blondet, Anne Marie Goetz and Shireen Hassim show, the understandings of democracy and their institutional forms are variable, with markedly different implications for women's rights, whether in terms of their political rights to representation or their rights within the family and society at large. The three chapters in this section, on Iran, Peru, and South Africa and Uganda, examine the political arena and the constraints on women's representation in political parties and in national legislatures. They contribute to the reassessment of both the role of national women's movements during periods of regime change, and committment of movements struggling for greater democracy in political life to gender justice.

In Part IV the tensions between universalism and multiculturalism, discussed by Phillips in theoretical terms, are examined in regard to three developing countries, Malaysia, Mexico, and Uganda. Maznah Mohamad, Aída Hernández Castillo, and Aili Mari Tripp challenge us to consider whether the contemporary scepticism over universalism is well founded, and to what extent the debate over multiculturalism as it has developed within Western democracies has an application within quite different political environments.

In what follows we shall consider the issues that arise in relation to each of the four sections of the book in order to place them in a broader policy context.

Rethinking Liberal Rights and Universalism

Since its inception, and for the two centuries that followed, feminism has been engaged in what might be seen as a critical endorsement of Enlightenment principles of universal rights, equality, and individual freedoms. Universal principles of citizenship were generally considered fairer and more inclusive, having been developed in opposition to particularist rights such as those invested in castes, estates, or ethnic groups. While feminists have long sought to expose what in recent debates has been identified as the 'false universalism' of an exclusionary, androcentric liberalism,[4] this critique informed a strategy that sought not to dispense with universalism but to ensure that it was *consistently* applied.[5] Along with other disadvantaged social groups, women have demanded recognition as moral and juridical equals, and have deployed egalitarian arguments to advance claims on the rights associated with citizenship. However, while they claimed that they had the same entitlements to justice and political representation as men, they also insisted that women's 'difference' be recognized as a basis for equal treatment rather than serving to justify discrimination.[6]

In its subsequent evolution in the twentieth century as an increasingly transnational, pluralized, and ethnically diverse social movement, feminism continued to advance claims to equality while at the same time challenging the masculine bias that inhered in the way that universal principles were normatively applied. In recent times feminist critiques of universalism have been extended to the spheres of international law and justice. During and after the UN Decade for Women, international legal instruments came under scrutiny in an effort to identify ways in which they could be made more consistent with their avowed principles while at the same time according recognition to some of the specificities of the female condition. Women's movements protested at the exemption of women in the family and in society at large from universally agreed standards of decent treatment. At the same time such historic demands as the recognition of women's unpaid reproductive labour were joined with more recent and contested claims for the extension of women's human rights to include the right to bodily integrity and for reproductive and sexual choice. Violence against women for example, was reframed as a human rights issue and more exacting criteria for advancing women's rights across a number of spheres—economic, political, and social—were developed (Charlesworth and Chinkin, 2000).

However, while representing a step in the direction of legal equality between the sexes, the real impact of these international instruments on women's lives was limited and variable. Most governments sought to interpret their commitments selectively, and many entered clauses of exemption on cultural or religious grounds, effectively rendering their signature meaningless.[7] Even where governments signed up in full, positive outcomes in the form of appropriate measures and policies depended on political factors and material resources: if political parties and social movements failed to press for implementation, governments were inclined to ignore them. Laws are important in promoting changes in social relations, but they are only as good as the conditions under which they are exercised, politically and otherwise. Where women's new rights were not accompanied by the conditions that allowed them to be exercised, they meant little in practice.

As several contributions to this volume make clear, the period of liberal ascendancy has therefore been associated with some limited advances in women's formal rights, but without sufficient attention being paid to making their rights meaningful or substantive. As many activists in national and international arenas have insisted, the achievement of greater equality between the sexes could not rest on law alone but required a multi-dimensional approach to develop appropriate policies, social and economic, as well as the democratic institutions that would enable women's needs to be voiced and heard.

Capabilities, Rights, and Neo-liberalism

There is therefore a historical and ongoing feminist critique of liberalism on a variety of grounds. It would appear that feminists have been largely justified in their distrust of its 'false universalisms', its masculinist exclusions, its apparent disregard for social justice, and for promoting an equality that is merely formal rather than substantive.[8] These are serious charges. But it is an open question how well these criticisms stand up to scrutiny in what is arguably a changed global context where liberalism's evolution along diverse paths may allow greater scope for accommodating women's demands.

This is a point of departure in Martha Nussbaum's conceptual approach in Chapter 2. She insists on differentiating the diverse historical strands within the Western tradition of liberalism. The idea of 'negative liberty', prevalent in much Western liberalism and reinscribed at the heart of neo-liberalism, suggests that rights are primarily protections against state interference. Neo-liberalism is premised on the freedom of contract as the most basic value. But as both Martha Nussbaum and Diane Elson in Chapter 3 point out, this 'thin' defence of freedom is in reality no defence at all if the subjects of rights lack the conditions and resources on which enjoyment of their rights and freedoms depends. Moreover, as Anne Phillips argues in Chapter 4, if freedom implies a choice of options, the ability to choose itself depends on substantive conditions, which in turn require cultivation. These include, at a minimum, having the political and civil freedoms that enable one to voice an objection, and the educational and employment opportunities that make 'exit' a genuine option. Such criticisms of liberal rights have been shared by many feminist theorists.

However, there is another strand within liberalism, associated with John Stuart Mill and Thomas Hill Green, that insists on an active role for the state in creating the material and institutional prerequisites of positive freedom. This strand can arguably best support human rights agendas by generating positive obligations for state action to support human well-being and develop individual and group capacities. Nussbaum considers this 'the only sort of liberalism worth defending'. At the same time she emphasizes that this implies far more than the standard critique of the thin idea of freedom of contract. Here she advances the idea of a much wider range of human capacities for choice as appropriate goals for development.

In recent engagements with this theme, liberal theorists such as Rawls have placed questions of equality and social justice at the core of liberalism, in ways clearly at variance with more libertarian classical and neo-classical theorists.[9] While Rawls's *Theory of Justice* has been the subject of feminist critique—for presuming that 'individuals' are male household heads, and for assuming that justice prevails within the family—not all liberal engagements with questions of justice share these assumptions. In the writings of Nussbaum in particular, including her contribution to this volume which synthesizes and develops her earlier work, we find a theory of justice that is at the same time liberal *and* feminist, while being attentive to the material preconditions that are necessary if formal rights are to be substantiated.

The capability framework, outlined in the writings of Amartya Sen within the economics discipline and elaborated in philosophical terms by Nussbaum, sets out to identify the 'basic constitutional principles that should be respected and implemented by the governments of all nations, as a bare minimum of what respect for human dignity requires' (p. 49 this volume). The idea of a basic social minimum is provided by focusing on human capabilities, that is, 'what people are actually able to do and to be—in a way informed by an intuitive idea of a life that is worthy of the dignity of the human being' (p. 49 this volume).[10]

In this approach emphasis is placed on the distribution of resources and opportunities *to each person*. Given how often women are treated as members of families, communities, and nations, and their interests subordinated to the goals of these entities, Nussbaum maintains that what they need is more, not less, liberal individualism. They need to be seen, and to see themselves, as autonomous, free human beings capable of making their own choices, rather than being 'pushed around by the world'. When viewed in the light of the substantial body of evidence documenting significant, and sometimes life-threatening, incidences of discrimination against females in the intra-household distribution of resources, and the dangers for women that inhere in group rights and entitlements, it is difficult to disagree with Nussbaum's plea to take individual rights seriously. Perhaps the reservations often expressed in regard to individualism by those supporting more collectivist values has led us to forget the crucial importance to women of being recognized as individuals in their own right (Phillips, 2001).

The objections to liberalism do not, however, end here. Much of the dissatisfaction of the left in particular has centred on liberalism's attachment to formal rights. The point repeatedly made is that equality of rights will generate inequality when it pays no attention to background conditions. As Phillips expresses it, 'grand assertions about all individuals having the equal right to hold on to their property turn rather sour when one individual owns only the clothes she stands up in and another owns the Microsoft empire' (p. 117 this volume). Feminists have joined in this criticism, drawing attention to the problems women encounter in exercising certain formal rights. They have queried, for example, the significance of the 'right to employment', inscribed in constitutions and labour legislation, where childcare facilities are neither widely available nor affordable, and where women's physical mobility is subject to family and community censure or control.

While such criticisms are justly levelled against liberal thinkers championing negative freedoms (e.g. Berlin or Hayek), they do not appear well-founded in regard to Nussbaum's version of liberalism. The capability framework draws attention to what people are actually able *to do* and *to be* with the resources at their command. It is therefore sensitive to interpersonal differences in need, rather than advocating a version of equality that pays no attention to background conditions and differences. Nor does the capability framework fall into the trap of 'physical condition neglect' (Sen, 1985), as utility- or preference-based approaches do. Nussbaum sees preferences as socially shaped (and misshaped). Even if women show a preference for a lower standard of living, she argues, we should not conclude that public policy should not meet the conditions for developing their human capabilities. Whatever questions this may raise about Nussbaum's attachment to the notion of 'choice' (Phillips, 2001), it is indicative of a profound awareness of the substantive conditions under which choice becomes meaningful—an awareness that is not widely shared by liberals.

A related criticism of the liberal interpretation of rights has been its tendency to prioritize some rights (political, civil) over others (economic, social). A product of the politics of the cold war era, prevailing categorizations of rights were separated into different 'generations'—a controversial metaphor for it suggests a hierarchy in the importance of various forms of rights (Charlesworth, 1994). The capability framework, however, embraces both sets of rights or capabilities even though in practice it has tended to concentrate on economic and social rights, such as life expectancy and nutrition, which lend themselves more readily to measurement.

Yet despite the long way that these proponents have come in placing questions of social justice at the core of liberalism, one objection remains unanswered. The central issue is liberalism's neglect of *equality* (Phillips, 2001). Liberalism places individual freedoms at the heart of its analysis, and is driven principally by a commitment to free choice.

If the tradition were as centrally concerned with the equality and distinctness of individuals as Nussbaum's account suggests, it really is difficult to make sense of its tardy appreciation of women's claims. The conundrum becomes less puzzling if we recognize that liberalism is driven by its critique of authoritarian and (later) interventionist government rather than any grand thesis about each individual being of equal worth. (Phillips, 2001: 7)

On the one hand, the capability framework directs attention to chronic failures in the satisfaction of social needs and it has been instrumental in exposing gender inequalities in human capabilities— the '100 million missing women' (Sen, 1992) being a case in point.[11] But, on the other hand, Nussbaum's proposal of a minimum 'threshold' that all governments should be required to provide is open to the charge of evading the issue of inequality. Phillips concedes that attempting to secure such a basic minimum may be good practical politics and probably an effective way to proceed in tackling global poverty, 'but it is also important to recognize how far it moves from a discourse of equality' (2001: 17). The retreat from equality is replicated across the literature on economic development, which is now far more concerned with issues of poverty than of inequality (and redistribution).[12] It is also evident in the recent shift in social policy thinking away from ideas of universal welfare provision aimed at creating a more equal society, towards a residualist emphasis on the provision of *basic* services targeted to the needy and the 'poorest of the poor'. The latter aims to reduce poverty and destitution, but is unconcerned about the overall distribution of income and wealth within society.

Yet, even though inequality may not be central to capability thinking, it is crucial to underline the fundamental differences between capability/human rights thinking and neo-liberal thinking—this is what Elson sets out to do in her contribution to this volume. She examines the contrasting criteria that neo-liberal economic thinking and human rights (and capability) thinking use to measure the effectiveness of resource use procedures. According to human rights and capability approaches, realizing the full set of human rights, or achieving the full set of human capabilities, constitutes the key criterion for judging the effectiveness of resource use. In contrast, the criterion prioritized within neo-liberal policies is 'economic efficiency', which consists of getting maximum output from a set of inputs, where the consumption of output is determined by the preferences of consumers. The operational criterion of success is growth of output; and private enterprise and market relations are presumed to be better, on the whole, at promoting economic efficiency.

Neo-liberalism emerged out of what Ha-Joon Chang (2001: 4) calls 'an unholy alliance' between neo-classical economics, which provided most of the analytical tools, and the Austrian Libertarian tradition represented by Hayek, which provided the political and moral philosophy. Its economic agenda, also referred to as the 'Washington Consensus', centres on strengthening private property, extending profit-driven markets, and reducing the economic and welfare roles of the state. Since the late 1970s macroeconomic policy around the world has been increasingly focused on fiscal restraint, open trade and capital accounts, and privatization. The debt crises of the early 1980s—induced by US-led deflationary policies, and the decisions taken by Western governments to adjust to OPEC-inspired rises in the price of oil via the emerging private international financial market—provided a critical opening for Washington to try to impose this agenda on indebted developing countries. This was facilitated through the so-called 'policy conditionalities' that were attached to IMF and World Bank loans. As noted above, and as elaborated upon in the case studies in Part II with reference to policy reforms in Poland, Chile, and India, the outcomes of these policies continue to be highly contested.

Thus if neo-liberalism exists in tension with some of the broader claims of contemporary human rights discourses, both are derived from the foundational principles of liberalism. There is continuing debate over the interpretation of the application of these principles, even in the case of such apparently essential constituents of liberal-ism as the right to own property. This right, enshrined in Article 17 of the Universal Declaration of Human Rights, can be deployed to argue against state intervention and to allow a range of freedoms in the name of respect for private property, which, it is argued, can con-flict with human rights. While rights discourses have reconfigured development thinking by placing the human person as the central subject and beneficiary of development, critics argue that rights dis-courses can be used to legitimize the opening up of markets to foreign capital, the promotion of unregulated private enterprise, and the realignment of social policies in accordance with market principles. Nussbaum acknowledges that these ambiguities in the meaning of rights can lead to a blurring of the issues whereby all rights struggles are seen as promoting commercial liberalism. She argues that while under certain conditions markets can promote human capabilities, they often do so unevenly. For some capabilities, like those relating to health, education, and nutrition, markets often fail to deliver, and indeed as Elson suggests, free enterprise can flourish at the expense of human capabilities.

Given these ambiguities, should we give up on rights as the lan-guage for making justice claims? The answer to this question must surely be negative. As is clear from some of the other contributions to this volume, the language of rights has considerable rhetorical and mobilizing power; it reminds us that people have justified and urgent claims; rights confer agency and enable women in particular to articulate strong claims for *equality*. If rights have been understood in many different ways, and there are fundamentally different ways of thinking about the connections between human rights and resource use, the terrain of rights is marked by politics and demands engage-ment from those seeking social and gender justice. Elson invites us to think of human rights in terms of ideas of mutuality or solidarity. These express the principle of social and human interconnected-ness. Human rights can then be seen as claims 'to a set of social arrangements—norms, institutions, laws and an enabling economic environment—that can best secure the enjoyment of these rights'. It is the obligation of governments to implement policies to create and uphold such arrangements; and it is also the obligation of citizens to contribute to their observance.

This is a fruitful way of thinking about human rights and about 'rights-based development'. It reinstates a particular form of universalism as entailing both solidarity and redistribution, ideas that have been increasingly marginalized from both policy and research agendas in recent years. It also rehabilitates the state as the principle agent in policy development and implementation. Only the state, argues Elson, can ensure the existence of adequate social arrangements, to which all citizens have a duty to contribute and from which they have a right to demand accountability. While states need not be, and arguably should not be, the sole agencies involved in social and economic management, they must have a coordinating function and ultimate responsibility for the quality and extent of provision.[13]

Universalism and Multiculturalism

If, as argued above, liberalism can accommodate social rights, can it also accommodate cultural diversity and difference in ways that do not violate the principle of equality? If the claims of multiculturalism are accommodated how are women's rights affected? Are feminists such as Moller Okin right to argue that multiculturalism is 'bad for women' because it subordinates women's individual rights to masculine privilege enshrined in group rights that are legitimized by 'culture', 'tradition', and religion (Moller Okin *et al.*, 1999)? In Chapter 4 Phillips revisits the charge that liberal universalism 'erases difference' both in regard to women and in regard to 'other' cultures and considers the areas of conflict and agreement between feminist and multicultural agendas.

An important starting point in this debate is to recognize that the positive import of multiculturalism lies in its challenge to a 'difference-blind liberalism' (Taylor, 1994) that worked with *simpliste* notions of national homogeneity. Multiculturalism instead insists on the hybrid character of modern societies, which have been rendered culturally complex through colonialism, greater global interdependency, and transnational migration. The very term 'multicultural' unsettles crude assimilationist strategies that refuse to accord any positive value to cultural difference. However, there is considerable disagreement among those who support multicultural principles over how culture is itself understood and over what policies should be pursued within a multicultural society. If culture is conceived of as 'tradition' and identified with religious doctrine, the potential for conflict over women's rights is considerable. On the other hand, there are liberal versions of multiculturalism that are arguably compatible with the universal principles contained in the international legal instruments that advance women's rights.

Resistance to universal standards for women's rights has grown in recent years. If this has been led in international arenas by a group of conservative states and largely religious NGOs (Sen and Correa, 1999), it has also gained support from within the scholarly literature with the turn to postmodernism and poststructuralism, evident within feminism itself. From these different positions has come a challenge to the principle of universalism which underlies the human rights movement. These politically diverse tributary currents of multiculturalism unite in arguing that moral standards are culture-bound and that legal pluralism should prevail over universal law. Poststructuralists argue that there is no theoretical or foundational basis for endorsing one set of values over another. Neither humanism nor reason can serve as the basis of law. Reason, the foundation of such claims, is itself a relative concept and can provide no independent referent for justice. A derivative view, shared by conservative nationalist states, is that, as ideas of rights are bound to their Western origins, they have little meaning or application within 'other' cultures. Variants of this position ground their objection to what they term a 'western universalism' in a history of economic and cultural dominance that continues today. Resistance to such dominance is seen as essential to the cultural survival of 'othered' subaltern cultural formations.

As a consequence of the rise of more vocal and self-confident ethnic politics, there have been moves by states and international policymakers to accommodate a greater respect for cultural diversity at both the global and national levels and to accord recognition of cultural rights as a form of human rights. While liberalism is associated with individual rights and legal capacity, the idea that collective rights are necessary for the full enjoyment of individual human rights has gained ground in national and international policy arenas. Here it has been accommodated, albeit not without difficulty, within an overall legal framework that gives primacy to human rights.

One example is the international legislation according rights to indigenous peoples and their cultures originally encoded in ILO Convention 169. On the books since the 1960s, it has been given greater prominence in recent years as a result of the greater strength

and activism of indigenous movements. It commits signing governments to ensuring equality of rights within their jurisdiction and
respect for their customs and laws. The convention however stipu-
lates that customary law should be respected when it does not conflict
with universal human rights; this formulation was incorporated into
a number of state constitutions, notably in Latin America in the
1990s (Sieder, 2002).[14]

Such versions of multiculturalism do not necessarily entail sur-
rendering women's claims on rights and for equality within plural
societies. However, for more radical interpretations, recognizing the
plural character of social formations entails the adoption of a cultural
and moral relativism that is at variance with universal legal standards. It is evident that such positions conflict with women's human
rights in four major ways. In the first place, the kind of feminist
cosmopolitanism that has inspired the demands of the increasingly
internationalized women's movement is committed to 'transversal'
legal principles, applicable in all contexts albeit through a process
of negotiation and translation (Petchesky, 1998). Second, if feminism
has been associated with one principle above others it has been that of
equality, and where difference has been the basis for claims of recognition it has been within the overall terms of an argument for equality.
Third, feminist claims (*pace* dissenters such as Iris Young[15]), have
generally privileged individual over group or cultural rights for the
reasons discussed earlier. Finally, feminism has always questioned
appeals to culture and tradition where these are used to legitimate
female subjugation. The fact that the roles and symbolism associated
with femininity together with patriarchal authority and masculine
privilege are often made into cultural signifiers, places women's individual rights in conflict with those seeking to impose 'traditional',
'authentic', or 'national' customs on their people.[16]

However, while there is clearly a conflict between universalist principles and some versions of multiculturalism, Anne Phillips argues
that the gulf between feminism and multiculturalism is not usefully
characterized as one of simple opposition. She revisits the criticism
that universalism 'erases difference', and argues that this is the
crucial point on which feminism and multiculturalism can agree.
Indeed, she sees a 'close family relationship' between the two bodies
of thought in that both oppose the way that difference (of gender
and/or culture) is taken to signify inferiority. Feminism and multiculturalism unite in sharing a critique of universalism for 'falsely
generaliz(ing) from one sex or one culture'; they both address oppressions that share a common structure and tackle issues of inequality.
Phillips therefore joins those who support multiculturalism in its

demand for a greater respect to be accorded to difference, and suggests that this requires a questioning of the terms and conditions of universalism, while not renouncing it altogether.

Feminist poststructuralists such as Phillips have not, then, entirely given up on universalism. While eschewing the foundationalist claims of human rights, there are those who argue that some qualified forms of universalism are defensible for political or ethical reasons.[17] Phillips therefore calls for a critical and grounded approach to universalism and to its practices, but maintains that universal human rights remain a necessary part of a good global society. They represent values that both traverse particular cultures and have meaning in struggles across continents by those who have claimed them.

Phillips argues that, although the claims made on behalf of women and on behalf of minority cultures are both equality claims, they are different in that cultures are not akin to individual subjects, and they cannot make claims about 'their' rights. Such formulations reify culture into a 'thing' that is independent of political forces, social agency, and historical influences, a point elaborated upon in the case studies in Part IV with reference to Malaysia, Mexico, and Uganda. With these broader theoretical reflections in mind, we turn now to consider the case studies grouped in Parts II–IV.

Social Sector Restructuring and Social Rights

If states have a duty to create the material and institutional prerequisites that can best secure the enjoyment of human rights, as the theoretical reflections by Nussbaum, Elson, and Phillips suggest, then an important arena of positive state action must be that of social provision. Needless to say, the nature and extent of state responsibility for social provision is highly variable, even among the bloc of countries that established welfare states in the twentieth century. Nordic countries and France for example retain a commitment to more universalist, citizenship-based entitlements, while in other parts of continental Europe the welfare state evolved along more corporatist lines where social entitlements derived principally from employment (with its in-built gender bias) rather than from universalist principles of citizenship. Moreover, both contrast with the residualist model that is dominant in the United States where social entitlements derive from proven need. Thus while the post-war Western welfare states expressed rather similar objectives, 'they differ(ed) both in terms of ambition and how they did it' (Esping-Andersen, 1996: 6). Moreover, as these same welfare states seek to adapt to the pressures of globalization, they do so differently, largely because of 'institutional legacies, inherited system characteristics, and the vested interests that these cultivate' (ibid.). A recent ILO research project, for example, found certain 'regional clusters' and marked heterogeneity in recent welfare policy developments, with a striking degree of country-specific variation (Alber and Standing, 2000: 112).

Beyond the institutionalized welfare states, in the developing and post-transition countries, there is again considerable diversity of approach as resource constraints and different political and institutional histories bear upon the policy environment and influence the impact and application of neo-liberal agendas. The three case studies in Part II document how systems of welfare provision are being restructured in very different regional contexts. While a fuller picture of welfare reform in these diverse regions would require far more comprehensive comparative empirical research than is currently available, what is clear even from the existing studies of social policy is the *absence* of a uniform response to the pressures of globalization.

Ironically the region with a history of extensive social policies—Central and Eastern Europe—also appears to be the one where there have been significant policy reversals, even though the authors of the above-mentioned ILO study find the notion of 'social dumping', that is, abandoning welfare commitments, in response to globalization inadequate when it comes to describing the social policy reforms undertaken in the region. They argue that, while there has been some privatization (e.g. education, housing), the social expenditure ratio increased rather than declined in most countries, and that various taxes have been raised. A good number of countries in the region appear therefore to be moving towards different Western European welfare state models rather than towards the residualist, liberal model—the outcomes having been largely determined by political battles in which supranational and national actors were intertwined in various coalitions.

These findings do not take into account how social policy reforms have impacted differently on men and women in the region. This is, however, a common concern running through the case studies in Part II of this volume, which probe the tensions between women's economic and social rights and the ongoing economic and social policy reforms. In some contexts (e.g. Poland, Chile) these are threatening to undermine the gains that have already been made, while elsewhere (e.g. India) they deny even the prospect of the progressive realization of a non-discriminatory system of decent jobs and public services and broad-based social security systems.

In the case of Poland, which is considered by Alber and Standing to be moving towards an 'institutionalised welfare state model', women have experienced a severe erosion of their social rights according to Jacqueline Heinen and Stéphane Portet in Chapter 5. It is appropriate therefore to ask *what kind of* an institutionalized welfare state model is being created in Poland if women's entitlements have been so undermined in the process?

Heinen and Portet document a large number of legal and policy changes introduced in Poland since the transition to democracy and the advent of a market economy that have eroded long-standing social rights that primarily benefited women. These reforms have taken liberal principles of autonomy, individualism, and indeed equality as the justification for stripping women of what in Poland are called their 'special privileges'. At the same time severe cuts in the state budget have dealt a heavy blow to the public provision of infant-care and childcare services, while economic rationalization and privatization have led to the widespread closure of pre-schools and subsidized infant-care facilities previously provided by enterprises. Such 'privileges' as paid leave to take care of sick children and entitlements to free or subsidized childcare services might be considered necessary mechanisms to secure a more 'level playing field' for those who are otherwise disadvantaged.

In the emerging model of welfare, comprehensive access to social rights, particularly to social security, is increasingly dependent on economic status: only those who are economically active, whether as employees or employers, have full access to these rights. But in Poland, as in many other former socialist countries, women's official labour force participation rate has fallen since the collapse of state socialism, while women are by far the most severely affected by unemployment, particularly long-term unemployment—a state of affairs that reflects, among other things, the inadequacy of affordable infant-care and childcare facilities as well as hiring preferences that favour men. This has coincided with an increasing gender gap in wages in many sectors; it is estimated that women earn on average 20 to 30 per cent less than men who have similar educational qualifications and experience. Hence many social benefits (pensions, health insurance, and so on) that used to be universal rights associated with socialist versions of citizenship are now available only to those enjoying direct access to the formal labour market, which, if not directly discriminating against women, indirectly places many at a disadvantage—revealing what has been identified as a male bias in social policy (Lewis, 1992; Elson and Cagatay, 2000; Molyneux, 2000*a*).

The 1999 reform of the Polish social security system, which introduced funded pension plans, has further reinforced the link between the level of income and social citizenship. While previously access to a state pension depended on a system of mutual aid and was an automatic right for both men and women, it now depends much more strictly on past earnings and ability to contribute on a monthly basis to a pension fund. Hence women, who constitute 75 per cent of those who earn below-average wages and the majority of the unemployed, have seen a significant curtailment of their entitlements due to their marginal economic status.

Yet Heinen and Portet's account of social and political citizenship in Poland ends on an optimistic note. There is mounting criticism of the growing inequalities in Poland, including a distinct feminist critique that underscores the dangers of constructing a 'masculine democracy'. Concrete proposals have been put forward to give women a genuine voice and presence in democratic fora, such as a recent legislative bill for establishing quotas for women on electoral slates in anticipation of the 2002 legislative elections. The prohibition on termination of pregnancy was a reminder of how deeply gender-biased liberal principles of individualism, autonomy, and the separation of the public and the private realm can be in their application, yet it may have instilled a sense of urgency about the need to increase women's representation in the political arena. This is all the more necessary if women are not to lose out in the process of democratic consolidation and integration into the European Union, as occurred in the early phase of the transition process.

A somewhat similar trend towards the privatization of social security has been under way in Chile for far longer, as Verónica Schild shows in Chapter 6. The centre-left coalition known as the *Concertación* that came to power in Chile in 1990 and has survived two elections since, was heir to a military dictatorship (1973–89) that launched the first experiment in neo-liberal policies in Latin America. The regime of General Augusto Pinochet, notorious for the human rights violations committed in its efforts to crush opposition, set about implementing a programme of radical social and economic reform that achieved average growth rates of 7 per cent over a decade and a half. The *Concertación* governments continued to pursue integration into the global economy through orthodox macroeconomic policies. These have sustained economic growth but social inequalities have deepened (ECLAC, 1998). There has, however, been a distinct shift in both the language ('growth with equity') and the social policy package since the Pinochet years.

Schild shows how the social policies of the 1990s represent both a change and a continuation of the reforms implemented during the Pinochet era. Perhaps the most significant element of continuity is the retreat from the universalist principles of provision characteristic of the pre-Pinochet period with the turn to targeted social assistance. Developed under the dictatorship, these targeted programmes were judged by many commentators as successful in mitigating the worst effects of the adjustment process (Angell and Graham, 1995). Under the coalition these programmes were refined and extended and, together with employment generation schemes, a 36 per cent rise in the minimum wage, and buoyant growth, a million people were taken out of poverty by 1993. However, the high rates of income concentration have remained constant. Chile is one of the most unequal countries in a region known for its skewed income distribution (ECLAC, 1998). An important lesson from comparative social policy is that the countries which have more equitable income distribution are not only those with high levels of social welfare provision accessible to all, but are also those where the professional and middle classes have a stake in these services, that is, they help fund them through taxation and they use them (Deacon, 2000). Targeting and means-testing separate the 'ultra poor' from the rest of the population, thereby deepening social divisions between the needy and those who are expected to turn to the market for social services (Mackintosh, 2000).

The 'Chilean model' is also associated with an extensive privatization of social security. Initiated under the military dictatorship, the privatization of the public pension system proceeded on the basis of largely unsubstantiated claims about the superiority of the private system compared to all other policy options.[18] The *Concertación* governments did not undertake any major institutional changes in social policy although taxes were raised to increase social expenditure (Huber and Stephens, 2000). As in the case of Poland, a major drawback of the funded pension plan is its in-built gender bias. In a system where benefits are calculated strictly based on contributions, women tend to be at a disadvantage as their incomes are generally lower than men's and their working lives shorter and more interrupted. This is indicative of a broader problem, namely that privatized systems have not favoured redistribution and seem to have exacerbated existing inequalities.

There are some novel features in the Chilean system of social provisioning, in particular the role that NGOs are playing in the delivery of welfare. However, while there clearly are some positive aspects to this involvement, Schild argues that it depends upon an unpaid or poorly paid and unregulated workforce of female 'extension workers'. Ultimately what this means is that claims for more 'efficient' social spending, through a 'partnership' of state and civil society, rely on what Elson refers to as the 'unspoken and invisible safety net of women's unpaid work', whether in their capacity as mothers and wives or as NGO and community workers. Furthermore, there are questions as to the adequacy of the coverage and the quality of service delivered by this patchwork of NGOs, with their poorly paid staff and army of volunteers.

Schild is also pessimistic about the political implications of the new model of social provisioning. Neo-liberalism in Chile has been associated with the demobilization of women's movements. The selective institutionalization of social movements into NGOs competing for government funds, has gone along with an emphasis on individual autonomy, choice, and responsibility. There is little in her account to suggest that the top–down mode of delivering social services has been replaced by an empowering bottom–up or 'demand-driven' process of welfare provisioning over which citizens and communities exercise meaningful control. On the contrary, project choices and designs, she argues, are often decided by officials in SERNAM (the ministry for women) and other government ministries, with standardized programmes that are not always tailored to the wishes or needs of the communities—criticisms that are frequently levelled against government provision. This view finds support in the literature on the new social programmes—whether it considers 'social safety nets' or 'Social Funds' (Vivian, 1995; Tendler and Serrano, 1999; Cornia and Reddy, 2001).

What is not clear, however, is whether the demobilization of women's grass-roots organizing can be entirely attributed to the new roles in which many women's NGOs find themselves. Research shows that social movements have their own life cycles as older members retire from public life or find themselves in new positions inside the new democratic state or legislature.[19] The very success of democratic transition often deprives such movements of a common goal and rallying cry, confronting them with the challenge of having to operate on different terms and in a transformed political landscape. Schild notes that new forms of organizing have emerged which are more consonant with today's 'political grammar', including among them programmes that are being supported by the state agency SERNAM. The extent to which these initiatives can sustain themselves and make a positive impact on public policy and gender inequality remains an open question.

Chapter 7, by Ramya Subrahmanian, examines the issue of female educational deprivation in India, one that must be understood as part of a broader picture of class and gender relations that intertwine with social hierarchies of caste and kinship to produce a formidable challenge for public policy. India never achieved the level and scope of social provisioning that was in place in Chile prior to 1973, let alone what state socialism offered the Polish population. Social security in India is subject to a plethora of laws, and administered through a wide range of specific schemes designed to deliver welfare in crucial areas. While there are some notable exceptions, the states of Kerala and West Bengal being the most widely known, India has a history of poor implementation, low and declining public funding, and inadequate social participation and accountability (Ghosh, 2001; Bardhan, 1999).

The programme of economic reform initiated in 1991 marks a significant shift in policy thinking, aimed at reducing the role of the state in the economy. It has entailed some important welfare reforms, such as the targeting of subsidized food grains through the Public Distribution System (PDS), and greater emphasis on the private provision of welfare services. Although the share of privately managed schools is much smaller than government schools, and its spread uneven across the country, there are indications that private schools are proliferating in many rural areas, and that they are increasingly appealing to poorer households as well.

A notable feature of education policy is the apparent increase in public social expenditure being allocated to *primary* education. Such a focus coincides with the World Bank's minimalist definition of the 'public good' aspect of education in terms of primary education alone, when arguably the entire education system, from pre-primary to tertiary levels, needs to be treated as a whole. This increase in resources for primary education in India has largely come from soft loans from the World Bank and has to some extent reversed the decline in social sector expenditure. To what extent this is sustainable is a matter of debate. It is also not yet clear what kind of education system is being forged. Perspectives on the current state of education reform vary, from celebrations of the increase in available resources for education, to those who warn of the dangers of ignoring some of the deeper trends that are being set in motion. Critics worry that the bringing in of 'para-teachers' who are paid less and trained less than teachers employed in the formal system, and the setting up of a parallel school system through NGOs, may effectively split the 'universal' education system into a patchwork of schools that would continue to penalize the worst-off and do little to correct the inequalities that are endemic within the system. Pragmatists, on the other hand, see such an expansion as necessary to ensure mass literacy, with a view to increasing basic opportunities.

As most of the country's low-income population depends on state provision, the universal right to education remains an important principle informing strategies for education development. In India this right is acknowledged but attendance in school is not compulsory. Decades of agitation have resulted in a concerted civil society approach to making the state take its duties regarding education more seriously. A proposal was first floated in Parliament in 1997 to make elementary education a fundamental right, thereby committing the state to provide free and compulsory education for children aged 6–14—in November 2001 the bill was passed in the Lower House of Parliament to await approval sanction from the Upper House before it becomes a part of the Constitution.

India is unusual for its robust and long-standing liberal democracy, yet it is a country marked by significant social deprivation. The state has been singularly ineffective in extending social rights beyond a small fraction of the population, predominantly its own employees (Herring, 1999). Does this mean that, even if the right to education is made justiciable through civil society agitation, it will amount to little more than empty rhetoric with little content or effect (like the progressive array of labour legislation that is regularly and openly violated)? This is clearly a possibility, and there are significant questions about the real implications of such a policy shift. Can the state be compelled to increase significantly its financial allocation and enforce attendance in schools? Subrahmanian lays out the multiple hurdles that would have to be overcome for the right to education to be substantiated. Securing such a right will depend crucially on securing other rights that are interlinked with the right to education, including those to food and survival, health and personal security.

Subrahmanian is wary of approaches that rely excessively on a legally mandated set of rights as the basis for pushing state accountability. Both rights and capabilities, she claims, are associated with similar problems of translation from normative framework to on-the-ground outcome. A critical issue is the lack of institutional access of socially disadvantaged groups to formal institutions of the state, including to the legal institutions in charge of carrying out justice—the basic requirement of a liberal democratic state. Women, in particular, remain untouched by—and uninformed—about many areas of state legislation and action (Rai, 1996). Indian democracy provides the formal channels and democratic spaces for demanding state accountability, yet deep social divisions of class, caste, and gender impose limits on what can be achieved. The elucidation of a rights discourse is thus merely the first step in the journey; it needs to be accompanied by clearly worked out institutional relationships and the restructuring of incentives to allow for the claims of the poorest to be heard and addressed.

Democratization and the Politics of Gender

The central instrument for the protection of rights has been, and must remain, the state. As women's movements turned their attention in the 1990s to rights issues, they were drawn into an engagement with the state as rights activists and as participants in government. Whether states advance or curtail women's rights cannot be explained in terms of any single variable, although democratic institutions and procedures are generally assumed to allow greater voice and presence to social forces pressing for reform. Yet, while many countries now identify themselves as democracies, and have established institutions of representative government, the degree to which democracy has been consolidated and institutionalized is highly variable. As the case studies in Part III bear out, in some countries even a minimal democracy has yet to be institutionalized. Even where elections have been held, political parties often remain weakly institutionalized, all too often serving as instruments to secure the rule of kleptocratic oligarchies and discriminatory ethnic groups. In much of the world, the institutions for popular participation are weakly embedded in society, civil rights are not protected, and political parties lack strongly articulated social programmes. It is in the context of such states, some semi-authoritarian or 'soft dictatorships', others where institutions of liberal representative democracy are grafted on to highly fragmented societies, that the three case studies are positioned.[20] Yet in these diverse contexts women have in recent years become a visible political force both as individuals and as a social group, even under conditions that deny them full or indeed at times any political voice and representation. Where the latter occurs, however, there is a danger that as women's movements are co-opted by states they lose their ability to represent their constituency and to advance programmes of radical reform.

In Chapter 8 Parvin Paidar analyses the efforts by women's movements in Iran to contest prevailing interpretations of women's rights by the repressive Islamist regime that has been in power for more than two decades. In particular she considers the implications for women of the ways in which the nascent reform movement has sought to democratize political life by strengthening and working through some of the country's existing formal democratic institutions.

The revolutionary Islamist forces that took power through a popular uprising that toppled the ruling monarchy in 1979 very quickly developed into an authoritarian state, annihilating or driving its diverse opponents into exile. In its first decade—the most politically and socially repressive period in twentieth-century Iran—the state took upon itself the task of transforming social and gender relations in conformity with its reinterpreted doctrine of Shii Islam.

The erosion of popular support for the hard-line state was an important factor behind the emergence of the reform movement in 1997. Authoritarianism, economic stagnation, and rising levels of unemployment, corruption, and misappropriation of funds, and the state's zealous attempts to regulate the private and social lives of citizens have combined to erode the support the Islamic Republic initially enjoyed. This had created a crisis of legitimacy for the hard-liners who still control the key apparatuses of the state (the judiciary, the theocratic establishment). The 1980 Constitution of the Islamic Republic combines Islamic theocracy with some forms of democratic accountability: the political stalemate of recent years is in some ways a reflection of the tensions between these two irreconcilable principles that the Constitution has unsuccessfully tried to square.

The embryonic reformist movement had to confront formidable obstacles placed in its way by hard-liners in the regime who used (and abused) all of their constitutional powers to undermine it. Yet it managed in some degree to change the terms of the debate. Paidar argues that, despite the fragility of this coalition, the reform movement had the potential to initiate positive political change. This was in no small measure due to the strength of the movement which was not simply manifest in electoral terms. Across the country, the 'thirst for citizenship and participation' (Najmabadi, 2000) became apparent on an unprecedented scale as a grass-roots movement, both widespread and diffuse, developed, involving a significant participation of women. This diffuseness made it difficult for any particular current to monopolize or to undermine it.

Many of these cultural and social initiatives were, as Paidar shows, gendered and politicized. Yet despite the mushrooming of women's political, cultural, and grass-roots initiatives and the politicization of gender issues that occurred, the women's movement was weakened by internal divisions and factionalism, reflecting long-standing tensions and suspicions between Islamist and secularist currents.

For their part, the reformist forces failed to link their arguments favouring democratic principles to women's rights, and their political and intellectual leadership has been, by and large, impervious to women's concerns. Moreover, before the reform movement had a chance to coalesce into a genuine social movement able to voice and reflect the demands and interests of a wide range of constituents, it became prematurely institutionalized (or co-opted) into the state apparatus (Hajarian, 2001). This helps explain why the reformists have been so unreceptive to the women's issues and concerns emanating from different social groups. Although President Khatami's government set up numerous women's units within the state apparatus and awarded a number of high-profile posts to women, women's independent activism[21] remained controlled by the state and marginalized by the reform movement.

Yet, if the reform movement is to grow and if it is to promote greater democracy in political life, it cannot afford to overlook women's interests and concerns. Democracy is not just a question of how well the institutional arenas perform, but of the quality of democratic life more broadly. This depends crucially on the character of civil society itself, and the extent to which it embraces democratic principles in which notions of gender justice are fully recognized.

In Chapter 9 Cecilia Blondet examines another case where a government sought to co-opt and utilize a social movement, in this instance, the women's movement. If the problem in Iran was that women were ignored, in Peru former President Alberto Fujimori championed the cause of women's rights, while courting the woman's vote and recruiting women to senior positions. Fujimori, unusually for a male head of state, even attended the Fourth World Conference on Women in Beijing, lending his support to the programme of reform that eventuated. His administration saw an emphasis on promoting the rights and opportunities of women, the fine-tuning of legislation, the development of numerous social programmes for women, and the promulgation of quotas for women candidates in the legislature. Yet Blondet questions this record of apparent progress and analyses the Faustian bargain that women's representatives entered into with this increasingly authoritarian state.

President Fujimori came to power through democratic elections in 1990, in the midst of a profound national crisis. Hyperinflation, the demise of political parties, and the absence of state authority combined with terrorist attacks to create widespread social insecurity, disorder, and poverty. As Fujimori set out to reassert state control—a project for which he received sustained popular support—circumstances combined to create a powerful executive branch that placed Peru's weak and fragile democracy under threat.

Blondet provides a detailed analysis of the diverse groups of women from different social strata who entered public office during the Fujimori regime—women whose interests and expectations had previously been ignored and who believed, in a 'pragmatic' way, that the regime held the key to fulfilling their needs. How these women acted and what they achieved raises two sets of issues. First, the mere fact that there was a growing number of women in positions of power and influence, and that they became familiar with the exercise of power, had some positive implications; women's participation in politics had ceased to be unusual but had became part of what Blondet calls the 'new common sense' in society. It also allowed the diverse interests of women to be debated and even acted upon; passage of many of the current laws benefiting women would have been unthinkable without it. However, such gains cannot be abstracted from the social and political context in which they occurred. Many governments aim to capture the female vote for instrumental reasons. In a democratic polity partisan struggle over the organized constituencies and 'vote banks' that the women's movements represent can lead to a readiness to take on board some of their demands. Authoritarian regimes, however, seek to curb the independence of such constituencies and of the individuals associated with them. Blondet argues that Fujimori 'colonized' the social organizations that were useful to him, leaving them submissive and dependent on government patronage. The eruption in 2000 of Peru's own democracy movement, fuelled by the ignominious flight of Fujimori to Japan, testified to the sense of betrayal felt by a population that had traded democracy for favours from a corrupt elite bent on filling its own coffers.

Like Fujimori, President Museveni of Uganda also promoted women's rights and recruited women to his project, resulting in their consistently high presence in representative and appointed posts. In Chapter 10 Anne Marie Goetz and Shireen Hassim provide a comparative analysis of Uganda and South Africa—two African countries that witnessed a dramatic increase in recent decades of the numbers of women in national and local politics. In both countries governments recognized the importance of women as a political constituency. However, it is the difference, rather than the similarities, between these two polities that casts light on the institutional forms that can facilitate more meaningful representation of women's interests.

Museveni came to power in Uganda after a prolonged guerrilla war (1981–6) and his response to this history of sectarianism and ethnic conflict was to institutionalize a 'no-party' system where political participation would be organized through a supposedly all-encompassing movement, called the National Resistance Movement (NRM). Historically hostile to sectarian politics and suspicious of political parties and engagement with the state, significant sections of the women's movement supported Museveni's project. Within a relatively short period of time the NRM had instituted measures to institutionalize spaces for women within the state apparatus and inside the five-tier Resistance Council system, including the Parliament known as the National Resistance Council.

Like Fujimori's regime in Peru, Museveni's slide into authoritarianism was gradual, as steps were taken to entrench the no-party system of government, concentrating power in fewer hands while promising a path of no return to the insecurity and violence of the recent past. The authors argue that the NRM's patronage of the women's movement contributed to its post-conflict recovery. It also facilitated a number of important legislative gains. Even setbacks in promoting gender equity in legislation and policy, such as the stalemate over the spousal co-ownership of land, radicalized the women's movement and intensified its concern about issues such as corruption and the lack of pluralism.

Presidential patronage however came at a price. Without a party system, women were not able to bring membership pressure to bear on party executives to promote gender-equity concerns within the party, in its recruitment, candidate promotion, policies, or leadership. By refusing to call itself a party, the NRM avoided the need to submit to the usual forms of regulation and its organizational procedures remained opaque. Yet it conducted itself as if it were a party, despite its insufficient institutionalization. As Goetz and Hassim argue, the lack of formal structures, lines of authority, or structured approaches to determining policy priorities effectively disabled attempts to render it more gender-sensitive, accountable, and more transparent. Moreover, in the absence of multi-party competition women's movements were also unable to develop political leverage around a gendered voting gap.

Goetz and Hassim do not judge the women's movement too harshly for throwing in its lot with the Museveni government. Nor do they feel that the women's movement should be blamed for rejecting the option of seeking to promote their interests through political parties, when the latter had been so negligent of women's interests in the past. But where the women's movement did commit a strategic mistake, they argue, is in failing to protest the undermining of democracy in the country. This contributed not only to a deepening stagnation and paralysis in the old political parties, but to an erosion of democracy within the NRM itself. The absence of pluralism and of internal party democracy left the women's movement entirely dependent on presidential patronage for access to office and for the promotion of gender-equity policies.

Under what circumstances, then, can women's access to political office and the promotion of gender-equity policies be more favourably institutionalized? Goetz and Hassim explore this question through a comparative analysis of political dynamics in Uganda and in South Africa. In the latter a negotiated transition created a plural democratic political context that opened a space for women activists to extend feminist conceptions of democracy and citizenship. The authors reject the account that is often given for the success of South African feminists, namely, the strength of the women's movement. Instead, they suggest a multi-causal explanation pointing to a number of crucial factors that coalesced to give women activists the opportunity to pursue their demands. In the first place, the fear of ethnic and racialised conflict drove the major negotiating parties to search for democratic mechanisms that would forge a stable, legitimate, and democratic state and would reduce the potential for political mobilizations centred on ethnic affiliation. Citizenship, broadly conceived, and rights-based discourses increasingly displaced nationalism as the new political ideal, and proportional representation (PR) with party lists was institutionalized as the country's electoral system.[22] Second, given the negotiated nature of the transition—one which involved numerous compromises—women became important to the governing ANC as it faced criticisms that it had abandoned its revolutionary ideals. The Party's support for women's rights demonstrated its continued commitment to inclusion and to redressing the substantial inequalities of the past. Third, partly in reaction to the ANC's own history of internal dispute women welcomed cooperation through the Women's National Coalition (WNC) prior to constitutional debates so as to develop views on how democracy should be conceived and to demand inclusion as a right. Finally, pluralism and a dominant party that represented itself as socially inclusive, committed to equality and internally democratic, meant that women could deploy these principles to press their own cause and use electoral processes to exert leverage on behalf of their political and policy ambitions.

In their discussion of the ANC's role in advancing women's rights, Goetz and Hassim question the long-standing ambivalence and hostility that women's movements have shown towards political parties. While political parties have not been hospitable sites for women activists, they remain the central mechanism in democratic systems for channelling political demands. This raises questions about how women can best engage political parties within pluralist liberal democracies. A central issue is the long-term effectiveness of party–movement linkages and the challenge of working 'within and against the party'—of having direct and strong links to political parties and yet avoiding an over-reliance on allies within political parties who can become hostage to a hierarchical and male-dominated party system.

While the authors see little danger to democracy's survival in South Africa, they are nevertheless concerned about the increasing centralization of power within the presidency and a corresponding weakening of the Parliament and its committee system. The decision taken by the Presidency and the Ministry of Finance to place the macroeconomic framework outside of party debate and make it a non-negotiable aspect of ANC policy is a case in point. In this more constrained party context, women MPs and ministers in particular might find it difficult to articulate policy positions that differ sharply from those of the party leadership. Ironically, the very PR system that helped bring large numbers of women into the parliament may be to blame for strengthening vertical accountability.

Multiculturalisms in Practice[23]

The chapters in Part IV examine issues of cultural difference and universalism and give particular consideration to some of the theoretical objections and political obstacles that confront women's rights movements in developing countries. In their different ways they all engage aspects of the debate that has been framed as a conflict between the opposing principles of universalism and multiculturalism. As is evident from the substantial literature on this issue, feminist theorists are themselves divided over which principles to endorse within a broader critique of the common assumptions of both.[24] Efforts to rework these concepts have shown that much depends on what is understood by these terms and, crucially, what politics and practices they are (or have been) associated with.

The three case studies in this section invite us to consider the pertinence for developing countries of debates that to a considerable degree have been conducted in the different conditions of liberal democracies. In the latter the issue has been how to accommodate ethnic minorities' claims for recognition within the terms of liberal principles of equal opportunity, tolerance, and non-discrimination (Barry, 2000). Where these principles are enshrined in law, it is reasonable to expect policies that are consistent with them, and if this does not occur, then the processes of democratic demand making can serve to create or correct them. However, in ethnically segmented societies ruled by authoritarian elites, such legal and political conditions do not normally prevail: here multicultural policies can serve to hinder equality claims rather than to advance them.

Feminism and multiculturalism may converge in their critique of 'difference-blind liberalism' but how far their advocates can accommodate their respective claims is to some degree contingent on the political forces and interpretative powers engaged in the practices of each. In recent years they have brought their often divergent interests to bear on international human rights law and other areas of policy. The points of convergence between these two positions noted by Phillips in Chapter 4 suggest some basis for a productive dialogue. In practice, however, the potential for dialogue is to a large degree contingent on political factors: the ample scope allowed in the interpretation and implementation of these various laws can indeed facilitate a productive dialogue in the formulation of policies, but it can also lead to seemingly irreconcilable conflict over core principles.

The authors in this section take issue with both the poststructuralist and essentialist arguments advanced by different versions of multiculturalism. The case studies of Malaysia, Mexico, and Uganda show how principles such as universalism or multiculturalism can be seized upon by political forces and deployed in ways that contradict the principles themselves. Just as the principle of universalism was traduced by colonial 'liberal' elites in the treatment of indigenous people, so too can some forms of multiculturalism serve to maintain populations in subjection.

Chapter 11 by Maznah Mohamad on Malaysia examines how identity politics together with a form of constitutional pluralism inherited from the colonial period became vehicles through which an increasingly authoritarian and kleptocratic state ensured its rule. Under the post-colonial Constitution recognition was accorded to the laws and customs of certain ethnic groups and institutional mechanisms were provided for their representation. However, this division of the population along ethnic lines favoured a situation in which politics became 'hyper-ethnicized', where political parties served only to articulate narrowly defined 'ethnic interests', thus fatally weakening civil society and the possibility of effective political opposition.

This process was assisted from the 1970s by a reinvigorated Malay national identity that was refashioned in a novel combination of what Mohamad calls 'technocratic modernity with a reconstructed Islam'. Following trends elsewhere in the world, this greater assertiveness of Muslim identity began to impact upon the political process in Malaysia. While the elite presided over an accelerated modernization of the economy, its official version of identity politics was predicated on a rhetorical invocation of 'traditional, authentic' Islam. This version of nationalism gained popular support as a cultural referent with which to oppose what was projected as an alien Western cultural hegemony. As elsewhere in the Muslim world, this combination of discursive elements worked to demobilize campaigns around women's rights by positioning women and the patriarchal family as privileged signifiers of a cultural authenticity legitimized by religion.

Given the divisions that existed within the population as a whole, women's demands, like those of other disadvantaged groups, could find no universal expression. Within the various ethnic groupings themselves, women's scope for contestation was limited by the prevailing constructions of ethnic identity and by the constraints imposed by the dominant interpretations of ethnic politics. For Malay women, the absence of a secular space within which to demand and debate the rights they were accorded by the state, positioned them, as in Iran, as able only to challenge some of the interpretations of Koranic justice advanced by the elite. Some limited cooperation across ethnic lines was achieved from the mid-1980s by small autonomous groups fortified by international networks, and these were able to make some headway on a limited range of issues. But in these circumstances, no inter-ethnic or common platform could be found for expressing women's demands for justice and equality since the very terms of universalism and commonality were rejected and subverted by other claims of solidarity.

This stalemate was broken with the economic crisis of 1997. It was in the conditions of the ensuing political upheaval that popular discontent and women's demands were to find expression in a more universal language of democratic reform. As in democratic conjunctures in Latin America, when authoritarian rule was challenged and reform movements erupted, social movements can acquire some influence over events. In Malaysia the reform or *reformasi* movement signified a partial reconfiguration of politics that allowed women's demands some space of articulation, even among the most conservative Islamist Party, the PAS.

In the new political context, opposition parties found themselves compelled to bury their differences in order to form a united front against the state. As they competed in the electoral process, they also began to use the 'gender card' and women leaders emerged through the party process and made demands on behalf of women's rights. Even the PAS bowed to pressure and allowed women to stand for election for the first time, while the ruling party also declared itself in favour of women's rights. Mohamad's case study can be read as an example of how reform in women's rights depends both on universal values and on democratic politics. The political transition transformed the situation and allowed the discussion of women's citizenship rights to transcend ethnic politics. However, the dangers of co-option for women's representatives were ever present and the scope for advancing real claims of equality were still limited, in a context where political institutions retained an authoritarian cast and where support for conservative religious values remained strong.

In Chapter 12, Aída Hernández Castillo examines the situation of Mexico where, on independence from Spain, a liberal constitution accorded the Amerindian people the same rights of citizenship as the rest of the population.[25] This amounted to what has been called identical rather than equitable treatment (Tully, 1995) in that it stripped the Indian population of some of their former communal land rights while making few concessions to their language and culture. In 1992 however, following a decade of agitation by the growing indigenous movement both in Mexico and worldwide, a constitutional amendment redefined the Mexican nation as a multicultural entity. It signalled the recognition of indigenous cultural identity and customary law and practices (*usos y costumbres*). This was soon followed by changes in the penal code recommending that indigenous cultural norms and practices should be taken into account when judging crimes committed by individuals who belong to an indigenous ethnic group.

These legal reforms raised a number of urgent questions for Indian women. Customary law in Mexico, with few exceptions, denies women rights to land, while political institutions exclude women along with religious minorities. Men are permitted to 'discipline' their wives and children through beating, and acts of violence against women, even those resulting in death, can be condoned. How then could women's human rights and claims for cultural recognition be reconciled? Moreover it was unclear which law—state or customary—prevailed in specific legal cases, given the scope allowed in the interpretation of law and the role played in the legal process by 'expert anthropologists'.

Hernández Castillo considers the conflict over women's rights and customary law in regard to domestic violence and bride abduction and rape, and the attempts to reconcile them made by the revolutionary EZLN, known popularly as the 'Zapatistas'. She highlights the need to see how both liberal and customary rights are understood, translated, and claimed in local contexts, and how the concept of culture is negotiated and contested by Indian women themselves. The EZLN positions itself as the bearer of 'millennial traditions and ancestral customs' but at the same time advocates forms of conflict resolution which draw on elements of national and international law. It also advocates the invention of 'new traditions' in which women have a more active and equal social role. Law, custom, and culture are treated here in terms that allow Indian culture to be reclaimed even as it is redefined.

The 'Women's Revolutionary Law' of 1994 exemplifies the EZLN's attempt to reconcile women's and indigenous cultural rights. In drafting this law, the organization sought to combine the principle of indigenous self-determination with respect for individual rights, including women's rights. The law recognizes the right of indigenous people to their own norms and practices but in such a way that the 'dignity and integrity of women were honoured'. It proposes a number of rights for women, not recognized in customary law, including rights to political representation and to land ownership. Zapatista women presented their struggle for recognition and rights as a critical re-evaluation of customary practices and as a challenge to the authority of tradition and the state in matters of law. In the case of domestic violence they opposed cultural norms in the name of moral principles that are in conformity with women's human rights and which are consistent with the international consensus on domestic violence.

Opposition to these new rights of Indian women has come from those who favour national law on the one hand and from those who argue for more 'authentic' versions of indigenous law on the other. Hernández Castillo argues against these positions and calls instead for a critical stance in regard to both legal systems in order to develop political and legislative strategies that will ensure greater access to justice for those to whom it has been denied. In her review of the debate in Mexico on customary law she argues that both the universalism of the state and the particularism of indigenous cultural claims rest on a common essentialism that dichotomizes Western and indigenous law while misrecognizing the nature of law itself. Such oppositions, commonly deployed to differentiate contract from customary law, have little meaning in modern Mexico. State law and indigenous law are not discrete systems—one based on Western rationality, the other on an essentialized traditional culture. Legal norms in Mexico are heterogeneous, overlapping, and reflexive.[26]

Hernández Castillo therefore affirms a constructivist approach to law and culture; she sees this as helpful for women in claiming their rights since it allows them to escape being positioned as either endorsing national law or indigenous customs. State justice has proven to be a far from adequate guarantor of women's rights and is distrusted by Indian populations. The official projections of the Mexican state regarding the 'right to equality' in practice sought to homogenize the nation. Where a *de facto* recognition of indigenous culture prevailed in certain regions this served all too often as a pretext to justify the economic and social marginalization of ethnic minorities, and to legitimize the rule of pro-government clients among indigenous leaders or *cacicazgos*. In the name of respect for indigenous culture women were denied the right to own or inherit property and access to political power. At the same time, as in Malaysia, a proclaimed respect for indigenous culture was used by the ruling party, the PRI, to impede political alliances across the ethnic divide that could challenge its corrupt forms of rule. The important point here is that *both* difference and equality strategies can eventuate in deepening the marginalization of indigenous people. What determines outcomes is to a considerable degree the power relations at stake within an overall context of domination.

Chapter 13 by Aili Mari Tripp revisits Uganda through an examination of three campaigns by women's movements, concerning respectively women's rights to land, female genital cutting (FGC), and ritual virgin rape. Each involved a confrontation with customary law and practice and a challenge to group cultural rights. Tripp's principal argument is directed against critics of women's rights who not only tend to reify culture, elevating it beyond critique but in so doing also fail to examine the material interests and the political issues at stake in these disputes.

As Goetz and Hassim note in Chapter 9, a divisive ethnic politics prevailed in Uganda prior to the election of Museveni. The Constitution of 1995 is secular but contains clauses respecting cultural diversity and customary law. However, it also provides for equality between the sexes. Women's movement activists used this national legal machinery, along with the international covenants on women that Uganda signed up to (International Covenant on Civil and Political Rights and the African Charter on Human and People's Rights), to press for the recognition of women's human rights in Uganda. They argued that customary laws and practices that harmed women conflicted with the Constitution, the latter superseding customary law and having ultimate legal authority. They also succeeded in inserting a clause that explicitly prohibited 'laws, cultures, customs and traditions which are against the dignity, welfare or interest of women or which undermined their status'.

These legal arguments were not unopposed and, in the three cases of conflict discussed by Tripp, it was argued that women's rights were alien to Ugandan culture and that, if applied, they would put at risk the culture and identity of the nation or of the community concerned. Tripp opposes these claims on some of the same grounds as Phillips and Hernández Castillo, seeing cultural forms and practices as more reflexive and 'malleable' than those who defend a static view of 'tradition' and culture as bounded totality. Like Hernández Castillo she questions the essentialism that underlies the opposition between Western and 'other' cultures and argues that there may be more commonalties than differences in regard to core values. She challenges the idea that there are irreducible tensions between liberal Western and Third World perspectives, as if these were themselves entirely separate, homogenous, or uncontested: the 'West' is made up of a range of diverse cultures, as is the 'non-West'. Moreover, to see civil and political rights as 'belonging' to Western culture is to underestimate the support that exists worldwide for human rights as a result of transnational processes and greater global interdependency. Such commonalities, she insists, can be the basis of a shared politics. The argument that this is more difficult in developing countries, on account of their greater cultural constraints and stronger group identities, confuses the issues. The locus of the struggle in the South, she argues, is not primarily over culture but politics.

Tripp therefore argues that practices that harm women have to be addressed as a political problem and as such are most effectively tackled within the society itself. The strategies adopted need not be overtly political or confrontational and will vary according to circumstance—education can serve as an important vehicle for change, as in the case of FGC—and dialogue between reformers and their opponents is an essential part of the process. Here Tripp insists that the suppression of women's rights is not essential to the uniqueness of a particular cultural group. This raises a crucially important question for women, namely who is authorized to decide what traditions are considered important in preserving the continuity, integrity, and sovereignty of nations? Women are largely absent from the arenas where such questions are deliberated.

The argument that cultural identity does not *have* to depend upon practices that harm women seems to be borne out by Tripp's accounts of female genital cutting and virgin rape. These practices were eventually abandoned or replaced with other rituals that signified some continuity of meaning without harming women. This implies that the meaning of what constitutes an ethnic identity or of what is customary can change. Indeed the idea that culture is always contested and 'tradition' constantly reinvented has gained wide acceptance. Cultural 'continuity' is therefore always relative. Does this mean that women's rights pose no threat to culture at all?

The case of land ownership might suggest otherwise. Here, the granting of women's rights to land has the potential to undermine existing social relations and hence put cultural continuity in jeopardy. The individuation of rights unless offset by new and more egalitarian forms of cooperation can undermine clan and communal property; this was a policy favoured by modernizing states, colonial, capitalist, and socialist, to achieve precisely this end. However, Tripp's insistence on understanding the vested interests at stake among those opposing women's rights to land reformulates the issue as a political and ethical one. In Uganda, these are not altruistic defenders of an unchanging culture but an elite with material concerns which presides over a situation of harsh inequalities in the access to resources. Ultimately both the preservation of culture (and of the social relations that underpin it) and the granting of women's rights come at a price, and they are not always commensurable.

The debate over which is the supreme ethical principle in such cases—equality or cultural continuity—will ultimately find no resolution since the values in dispute are essentially contested. To those involved in struggles for rights, debates over principles can seem overly abstracted and sometimes irrelevant. Some argue that a more pragmatic approach yields greater potential for dialogue over change, but the reconciliation of women's rights with nationalism, culture, or tradition is more difficult when doctrinal interpretations of religion are enforced by political authority. When religious authorities become the spokesmen (and they usually are men) for nations and ethnic communities and determine that the rights of individuals are derived from a particular tradition, there is less scope for contestation let alone for dialogue. Yet, as Phillips states, in deliberations over such matters as rights and culture it is essential that women have both presence and voice. We could add that the usual prerequisites of such a presence, if it is not to be a token one, or as in the case of Peru, a clientelistic one, are a political context in which the values of equality and democracy, together with its institutional forms are guaranteed.

Conclusions

Rights-based strategies, always a central part of feminist campaigns for justice, have acquired a new international pertinence in the twenty-first century. Rights have always been integral to citizenship, and in its modern, global idiom of human rights, the emphasis is upon their multi-dimensional and indivisible character as well as their transnational applicability. The aim of this book has been to promote reflection on the way that these principles operate in and are contested in a variety of socio-political contexts.

The issues raised in this book—social rights and capabilities, democracy and multiculturalism—represent new and not so new challenges to those engaged in movements for social justice. The emphasis on human rights and capabilities within international development policy has encouraged a rethinking of the relations between feminism and liberalism, in ways that recognize some of their commonalities and suggest grounds for a critical accommodation. Many obstacles however remain in the path of such a reconciliation, not least those presented by neo-liberalism, on the one hand, and by some versions of multiculturalism, on the other. It may be argued that liberalism's history and its modern forms of rule are so far from many of the ideals it claims association with that it offers little prospect to those concerned with equality or social justice.

This gulf between the principles and the materialization of liberal governance is, however, the political space within which social movements such as feminism have most often located their demands. As the contributions to this volume suggest, the nature and meaning of rights is contested from a variety of positions, including those within feminism itself. The sites of contestation are as much at the international as at the local and neighbourhood levels; the actors engaged in them are diversely positioned in a multiplicity of political fields. Feminism in its various forms has changed both the discourse and practice of rights in important ways, and women's movements from Latin America to South-east Asia, have owned the language of rights to press as much for social reform as for greater equality.

At the same time, the international debate over liberalism, rights, and democracy cannot be abstracted from its contemporary forms, or from the political forces that both support and oppose it. Neo-liberal appropriations of rights discourses as the guarantors of free enterprise stand in opposition to the idea of social rights contained in the 'second generation' of human rights and affirmed in the support accorded to the principle of the indivisibility of human rights. Women's demands for rights and justice are situated in complex ways in this political field and women's movements have had to manœuvre with considerable caution. As the case studies show, the dangers of co-option are ever present, as rulers seek to deploy women's movements in the service of the state. Social movements cannot know their effects and the outcomes of struggles around rights are unpredictable. But the point made by several of the authors is that rights-based strategies and equality claims depend to an important degree upon democratic values and institutions. If rights are interpreted and contested within conditions of political struggle, political freedom is a condition of their contestation as it is of their realization.

References

Alber, J., and G. Standing (2000) 'Social Dumping, Catch-Up, or Converg-ence? Europe in Comparative Global Context', *Journal of European Social Policy*, 10/2: 99–119.

Alvarez, S., E. Dagnino, and A. Escobar (eds.) (1998) *Cultures of Politics: Politics of Cultures* (Boulder, Colo.: Westview).

Angell, A., and C. Graham (1995) 'Can Social Sector Reform Make Adjust-ment Sustainable and Equitable?', *Journal of Latin American Studies*, 27: 189–219.

Bardhan, P. (1999) 'Democracy and Development: A Complex Relationship', in I. Shapiro and C. Hacker-Cordon (eds.), *Democracy's Value* (Cambridge: Cambridge University Press).

Barry, B. (2000) *Culture and Equality: An Egalitarian Critique of Multicul-turalism* (Oxford: Polity Press).

Benhabib, S. (1995) 'Cultural Complexity, Moral Interdependence, and the Global Dialogical Community', in M. Nussbaum and J. Glover (eds.), *Women, Culture, and Development: A Study of Human Capabilities* (Oxford: Clarendon Press).

Butler, J. (1995) 'Contingent Foundations', in L. Nicholson (ed.), *Feminist Contentions* (London: Routledge).

Chalmers, D. A., C. M. Vilas, K. Hite, S. Martin, K. Piester, and M. Segarra (eds.) (1997) *The New Politics of Inequality in Latin America: Rethinking Participation and Representation* (Oxford: Oxford University Press).

Chang, H. J. (2001) *Breaking the Mould: An Institutionalist Political Eco-nomy Alternative to the Neo-Liberal Theory of the Market and the State* (Programme Paper SPD, 6; Geneva: UNRISD).

Charlesworth, H. (1994) 'What are 'Women's International Human Rights'?', in R. J. Cook (ed.), *Human Rights of Women: National and International Perspectives* (Philadelphia: University of Pennsylvania Press).

—— and C. Chinkin (2000) *The Boundaries of International Law: A Feminist Analysis* (Manchester: Manchester University Press).

Cornia, G. A., and S. Reddy (2001) *The Impact of Adjustment-Related Social Funds on Income Distribution and Poverty* (Discussion Paper No. 2001/1; Helsinki: WIDER, May).

Craske, N., and M. Molyneux (eds.) (2002) *Gender and the Politics of Rights and Democracy in Latin America* (Houndmills: Palgrave).

Deacon, B. (2000) *Globalization and Social Policy: The Threat to Equitable Welfare* (Occasional Paper, 5; Geneva: UNRISD).

ECLAC (1991) 'Nota sobre el desarrollo social en América Latina', in ECLAC, *Notas sobre la economía y el desarrollo*, 511/512 (July, Santiago, Chile).

—— (1998) 'Income Distribution: Determinants and Trends', in ECLAC, *Social Panorama of Latin America 1998*, internet edition, <www.eclac.org>.

Elson, D., and N. Cagatay (2000) 'The Social Content of Macroeconomic Policies', *World Development*, 28/7 (July): 1347–64.

Esping-Andersen, G. (1996) 'Welfare States without Work: The Impasse of Labour Shedding and Familialism in Continental European Social Policy', in G. Esping-Andersen (ed.), *Welfare States in Transition: National Adaptations in Global Economics* (London and Geneva: Sage and UNRISD).

Ghosh, J. (2001) *Globalisation, Export-Oriented Employment for Women and Social Policy: A Case Study of India* (Geneva: UNRISD, Mimeo).

Hall, S., and M. Sealey (eds.) (2001) *Different* (New York: Phaidon).

Hajarian, S. (2001) 'Mardon Khatami ra Tanha Nakhahand Gozasht', *Hayet-e No* (daily newspaper in Farsi, 26 May).

Herring, R. (1999) 'Embedded Particularism: India's Failed Developmental State', in M. Woo-Cumings (ed.), *The Developmental State* (Ithaca, NY: Cornell University Press).

Hirst, P. (1994) *Associative Democracy: New Forms of Economic and Social Governance* (Oxford: Polity Press).

Huber, E., and J. D. Stephens (2000) *The Political Economy of Pension Reform: Latin America in Comparative Perspective* (Occasional Paper, 7; Geneva: UNRISD).

Lewis, J. (1992) 'Gender and the Development of Welfare Regimes', *Journal of European Social Policy*, 3: 159–73.

Mackintosh, M. (2000) 'Inequality and Redistribution: Analytical and Empirical Issues for Development Social Policy', paper presented at UNRISD Conference on Social Policy in a Development Context, Tammsvik, Sweden, 23–4 Sept.

Mesa-Lago, C. (2001) 'Myths and Realities of Pension Reform: The Latin American Evidence', *World Development*.

Miller, C., and S. Razavi (eds.) (1998) *Missionaries and Mandarins: Feminist Engagement with Development Institutions* (London: IT Publications).

Moller Okin, S., J. Cohen, M. Howard, and C. Martha Nussbaum (eds.) (1999) *Is Multiculturalism Bad for Women?* (Princeton: Princeton University Press).

Molyneux, M. (2000a) 'Gender and Citizenship in Comparative Perspective', in J. Cook, J. Roberts, and G. Waylen (eds.), *Towards a Gendered Political Economy* (Houndmills: Palgrave).

——(2000b) *Women's Movements in International Perspective: Latin America and Beyond* (Houndmills: Palgrave).

Najmabadi, A. (2000) '(Un)Veiling Feminism', *Social Text*, 18/3: 29–46.

O' Donnell, G. (1993) 'On the State, Democratization and Some Conceptual Problems: A Latin American View with Glances at Some Postcommunist Countries', *World Development*, 21/8: 1355–69.

——(1998) 'Horizontal Accountability in New Democracies', *Journal of Democracy*, 9/3: 10–126.

Pateman, C. (1988) *The Sexual Contract* (Cambridge: Polity Press).

Petchesky, R. (1998) 'Introduction', in R. Petchesky and K. Judd (eds.), *Negotiating Reproductive Rights: Women's Perspectives across Countries and Cultures* (London: Zed Press).

Phillips, A. (1991) *Engendering Democracy* (Cambridge: Polity Press).

—— (1993) *Democracy and Difference* (Cambridge: Polity Press).

—— (2001) 'Feminism and Liberalism Revisited: Has Martha Nussbaum Got it Right?', *Constellations* 8/2 (June): 249–66.

Rai, S. (1996) 'Women and the State in the Third World: Some Issues for Debate', in S. Ray and G. Lievesley (eds.), *Women and the State: International Perspectives* (London: Taylor & Francis).

Razavi, S. (ed.) (2000) *Gendered Poverty and Well-Being* (Oxford: Blackwell), originally published as special issue of *Development and Change*, 30/3.

Robbins, B. (1998) *Cosmopolitics: Thinking and Feeling Beyond the Nation* (Minnesota: University of Minneapolis Press).

Sen, A. (1985) *Commodities and Capabilities* (Amsterdam: Elsevier Science).

—— (1992) 'More than 100 Million Women are Missing', *New York Review of Books* (Dec.): 61–6.

Sen, G., and S. Correa (1999) 'Gender Justice and Economic Justice: Reflections on the Five-Year Reviews of the UN Conferences of the 1990s', a paper prepared for UNIFEM in preparation for the five-year review of the Beijing Platform for Action.

Shapiro, I., and C. Hacker-Cordon (eds.) (1999) *Democracy's Edges* (Cambridge: Cambridge University Press).

Sieder, R. (ed.) (2002) *Implementing Multiculturalism: Indigenous Rights, Diversity and Democracy in Latin America* (Houndmills: Palgrave).

Taylor, C. (1994) 'The Politics of Recognition', in A. Gutmann (ed.), *Multiculturalism* (Princeton: Princeton University Press).

Tendler, J., and R. Serrano (1999) 'The Rise of Social Funds: What are they a model of?', draft paper for the MIT/UNDP Decentralization Project Management Development and Governance Division, UNDP, New York.

Tully, J. (1995) *Strange Multiplicity: Constitutionalism in an Age of Diversity* (Cambridge: Cambridge University Press).

UNIFEM (2000) *Progress of the World's Women 2000* (New York: UNIFEM).

Vivian, J. (ed.) (1995) *Adjustment and Social Sector Restructuring* (London and Geneva: Frank Cass in association with The European Association of Development Research and Training Institutes (EADI), UNRISD).

Wade, R. (2001) *Is Globalization Making World Income Distribution More Equal?* (Working Paper Series, 01-01; London: LSE Development Studies Institute).

Weisbrot, Mark, Dean Baker, Robert Naiman, and Gila Neta (2000) 'Growth may be Good for the Poor—But are IMF and World Bank Policies Good for Growth: A Closer Look at World Bank's Most Recent Defense of its Policies', draft CEPR briefing paper, Center for Economic and Policy Research, Washington, DC.

Wilson, R. (ed.) (1997) *Human Rights, Culture and Context: Anthropological Perspectives* (London: Pluto Press).

Young, I. M. (1990) *Justice and the Politics of Difference* (Princeton: Princeton University Press).

Yuval-Davis, N., and P. Werbner (eds.) (1999) 'Introduction', in *Women, Citizenship and Difference* (London: Zed Books).

I

Rethinking Liberal Rights and Universalism

Gender Justice, Development, & Rights, (M. Molyneux & S. Razavi, eds.). Oxford: Oxford Univ Press, 2002

·················

2

·················

Women's Capabilities and Social Justice

Martha Nussbaum

> It will be seen how in place of the *wealth* and *poverty* of political economy come the *rich human being* and *rich human need*. The rich human being is ... the human being *in need of* a totality of human life-activities.
>
> (Marx, *Economic and Philosophical Manuscripts of 1844*)

> I found myself beautiful as a free human mind.
>
> (Mrinal, heroine of Rabindranath Tagore's 'Letter from a Wife', 1914)

Development and Sex Equality

Women in much of the world lack support for fundamental functions of a human life. They are less well nourished than men, less healthy, more vulnerable to physical violence and sexual abuse. They are much less likely than men to be literate, and still less likely to have pre-professional or technical education. Should they attempt to enter the workplace, they face greater obstacles, including intimidation from family or spouse, sex discrimination in hiring, and sexual harassment in the workplace—all, frequently, without effective legal recourse. Similar obstacles often impede their effective participation in political life. In many nations women are not full equals under the law: they do not have the same property rights as men, the same rights to make a contract, the same rights of association, mobility, and religious liberty.[1] Burdened, often, with the 'double day' of taxing employment and full responsibility for housework and childcare, they lack opportunities for play and the cultivation of their imaginative and cognitive faculties. All these factors take their toll on emotional well-being: women have fewer opportunities than men to live free from fear and to enjoy rewarding types of love—especially when, as often, they are married without choice in childhood and have no recourse from a bad marriage. In all these ways, unequal social and political circumstances give women unequal human capabilities.

   According to the *Human Development Report 1999* of the United Nations Development Programme, there is no country that treats its women as well as its men, according to a complex measure that includes life expectancy, wealth, and education (UNDP, 1999). Developing countries, however, present especially urgent problems. Gender inequality is strongly correlated with poverty.[2] When poverty combines with gender inequality, the result is acute failure of central human capabilities. In the group of 'medium human development' countries taken as a whole, the male adult literacy rate is 83.3 per cent, as against 67.3 per cent for women; in the 'low human development countries' the rate is 57.2 per cent for males, 35.8 per cent for females. School enrolment percentages (combining all three levels) are, in the medium development countries, 60 per cent for females, 68 per cent for males; in the low human development countries, 33 per cent for females, 44 per cent for males. In terms of real GDP per capita, in the medium development countries women control $2,220 as against $4,414 for men; in the low human development countries, $691 for women, $1,277 for men. We do not yet have reliable statistics for rape, domestic violence, and sexual harassment, because in many countries little attention is paid to domestic violence and sexual harassment, rape within marriage is not counted as a crime, and even stranger-rape is so rarely punished that many women are deterred from reporting the crime.[3]

   If we turn to the very basic area of health and nutrition, there is pervasive evidence of discrimination against females in many nations of the developing world. It is standardly believed that, where equal nutrition and health care are present, women live, on average, slightly longer than men: thus, we would expect a sex ratio of something like 102.2 women to 100 men (the actual sex ratio of Sub-Saharan Africa[4]). Many countries have a far lower sex ratio: India's, for example, is 92.7 women to 100 men, the lowest sex ratio since the census began early in the twentieth century. If we study such ratios and ask the question, 'How many more women than are now present in Country C would be there if they had the same sex ratio as Sub-Saharan Africa?' we get a figure that economist Amartya Sen has graphically called the number of 'missing women'. There are many millions of missing women in the world today.[5] Using this rough index, the number of missing women in South-east Asia is 2.4 millions, in Latin America 4.4, in North Africa 2.4, in Iran 1.4, in China 44.0, in Bangladesh 3.7, in India 36.7, in Pakistan 5.2, in West Asia 4.3. If we now consider the ratio of the number of missing women to the number of actual women in a country, we get the following percentages: for Pakistan 12.9, India 9.5, Bangladesh 8.7, China 8.6, Iran 8.5, West Asia 7.8, North Africa 3.9, Latin America 2.2, South-east Asia 1.2. In India, not only is the mortality differential especially sharp among children (girls dying in far greater numbers than boys), the higher mortality rate of women compared to men applies to all age groups until the late thirties (Drèze and Sen, 1989: 52). In some regions, the discrepancy is far greater than the national average: in rural Bihar, for example, an NGO has counted heads and arrived at the astonishing figure of 75 females to 100 males.[6]

One area of life that contributes especially greatly to women's inequality is the area of care. Women are the world's primary, and usually only, caregivers for people in a condition of extreme dependency: young children, the elderly, those whose physical or mental handicaps make them incapable of the relative (and often temporary) independence that characterizes so-called 'normal' human lives. Women perform this crucial work often without pay and without recognition that it is work. At the same time, the fact that they need to spend long hours caring for the physical needs of others makes it more difficult for them to do what they want to do in other areas of life, including employment, citizenship, play, and self-expression.[7]

The influential human rights approach has a great deal to say about these inequalities, and the language of rights has proven enormously valuable for women, both in articulating their demands for justice and in linking those demands to the earlier demands of other subordinated groups. And yet the rights framework is shaky in several respects. First, it is intellectually contested: there are many different conceptions of what rights are, and what it means to secure a right to someone. (Are rights pre-political, or artefacts of laws and institutions? And what are human rights rights to? Freedom from state interference primarily, or also a certain positive level of well-being and opportunity? Many other questions are raised, as we shall see below.) Thus to use the language of rights all by itself is not very helpful: it just invites a host of further questions about what is being recommended. Second, the language of rights has been associated historically with political and civil liberties, and only more recently with economic and social entitlements. But the two are not only of comparable importance in human lives, they are also thoroughly intertwined: the liberties of speech and association, for example, have material prerequisites. A woman who has no opportunities to work outside the home does not have the same freedom of association as one who does. Women deprived of education are also deprived of much meaningful participation in politics and speech. Third, the human rights approach has typically ignored urgent claims of women to protection from domestic violence and other abuses of their bodily integrity. It has also typically ignored urgent issues of justice within the family: its distribution of resources and opportunities among its members, the recognition of women's work as work. Fourth, the historical association of the rights framework with the influential Western tradition of 'negative liberty' suggests to many users of the idea that rights are primarily protections against state interference, rather than generating positive obligations for state action supporting human well-being—a view eloquently criticized by Diane Elson in Chapter 3. Fifth, and finally, the rights approach is often criticized for being merely Western, and for being insensitive to non-Western traditions of thought. Even if one believes that these criticisms are in many ways mistaken (as I shall argue they are), one might still wish to search for an alternative or at least a supplement to this contested language that would be free of this problem.

I shall argue that the alternative or supplement we need is the capabilities approach, an approach to issues of basic justice and to the measurement of quality of life pioneered within economics by Amartya Sen, put into practice in the *Human Development Reports*, and developed by me in a slightly different way within feminist political theory.

The Capabilities Approach: An Overview

I shall argue that international political and economic thought should be feminist, attentive (among other things) to the special problems women face because of sex in more or less every nation in the world, without an understanding of which problems general issues of poverty and development cannot be well confronted. An approach to international development should be assessed for its ability to recognize these problems and to make recommendations for their solution. I shall propose and defend one such approach, one that seems to me to do better in this area than other prominent alternatives. My version of this approach is philosophical, and I shall try to show why we need philosophical theorizing in order to approach these problems well.[8] It is also based on a cross-cultural normative account of central human capabilities, closely allied to a form of political liberalism; one of my primary tasks will be to defend this type of cross-cultural normative approach as a valuable basis from which to approach the problems of women in the developing world. Finally, I shall also try to show that my version of the capabilities approach, while attractive for many reasons, has special advantages when we are approaching the special problems faced by women: both intellectually and practically, there is a strong link between a concern for gender justice and reasons we might have to turn to the capabilities approach.

The aim of my project as a whole is to provide the philosophical underpinning for an account of basic constitutional principles that should be respected and implemented by the governments of all nations, as a bare minimum of what respect for human dignity requires. I shall argue that the best approach to this idea of a basic social minimum is provided by an approach that focuses on human capabilities, that is, what people are actually able to do and to be—in a way informed by an intuitive idea of a life that is worthy of the dignity of the human being. I shall identify a list of central human capabilities, setting them in the context of a type of political liberalism that makes them specifically political goals and presents them in a manner free of any specific metaphysical grounding. In this way, I argue, the capabilities can be the object of an overlapping consensus among people who otherwise have very different comprehensive conceptions of the good.[9] And I shall argue that the capabilities in question should be pursued for each and every person, treating each as an end and none as mere tools of the ends of others. Women have all too often been treated as the supporters of the ends of others, rather than as ends in their own right; thus this principle has particular critical force with regard to women's lives. Finally, my approach uses the idea of a threshold level of each capability, beneath which it is held that truly human functioning is not available to citizens; the social goal should be understood in terms of getting citizens above this capability threshold.

The capabilities approach has another related, and weaker, use. It specifies a space within which comparisons of life quality (how well people are doing) are most revealingly made among nations. Used in this way, as in the *Human Development Reports*, it is a rival to other standard measures, such as GNP per capita and utility. This role for the conception is significant, since we are not likely to make progress towards a good conception of the social minimum if we do not first get the space of comparison right. And we may use the approach in this weaker way, to compare one nation with another, even when we are unwilling to go further and use the approach as the philosophical basis for fundamental constitutional principles establishing a social minimum or threshold. On the other hand, the comparative use of capabilities is ultimately not much use without a determinate normative conception that will tell us what to make of what we find in our comparative study. Most conceptions of quality of life measurement in development economics are implicitly harnessed to a normative theory of the proper social goal (wealth maximization, utility maximization, etc.), and this one is explicitly so harnessed. The primary task of my argument will be to move beyond the merely comparative use of capabilities to the construction of a normative political proposal that is a partial theory of justice.

The capabilities approach is fully universal: the capabilities in question are important for each and every citizen, in each and every nation, and each is to be treated as an end. Women in developing nations are important to the project in two ways: as people who suffer pervasively from acute capability failure, and also as people whose situation provides an interesting test of this and other approaches, showing us the problems they solve or fail to solve. Defects in standard GNP and utility based approaches can be well understood by keeping the problems of such women in view; but of course women's problems are urgent in their own right, and it may be hoped that a focus on them will help compensate for earlier neglect of sex equality in development economics and in the international human rights movement.

The Need for Cross-Cultural Norms

Should we be looking for a set of cross-cultural norms in the first place, where women's opportunities are concerned? Obviously enough, women are already doing that, in many areas. To take just one example, women labouring in the informal sector, for example, are increasingly organizing on an international level to set goals and priorities.[10] Many other examples are provided by the international human rights movement and international agreements such as CEDAW. But this process is controversial, both intellectually and politically. Where do these normatives categories come from, it will be asked? And how can they be justified as appropriate ones for cultures that have traditionally used different normative categories? Now of course no critical social theory confines itself to the categories of each culture's daily life. If it did, it probably could not perform its special task as critical theory, which involves the systematization and critical scrutiny of intuitions that in daily life are often unexamined. Theory gives people a set of terms with which to criticize abuses that otherwise might lurk nameless in the background. Terms such as 'sexual harassment' and 'hostile work environment' give us some obvious examples of this point. But even if one defends theory as valuable for practice, it may still be problematic to use concepts that originate in one culture to describe and assess realities in another—and all the more problematic if the culture described has been colonized and oppressed by the describer's culture. Attempts by international feminists today to use a universal language of justice, human rights, or human functioning to assess lives like those of Vasanti and Jayamma is bound to encounter charges of Westernizing and colonizing—even when the universal categories are introduced by feminists who live and work within the nation in question itself. For, it is standardly said, such women are alienated from their culture, and are faddishly aping a Western political agenda. The minute they become critics, it is said, they cease to belong to their own culture and become puppets of the Western elite.[11]

We should begin by asking whose interests are served by the implicit nostalgic image of a happy harmonious culture, and whose resistance and misery are being effaced. Describing her mother's difficult life, Indian feminist philosopher Uma Narayan writes, 'One thing I want to say to all who would dismiss my feminist criticisms of my culture, using my "Westernization" as a lash, is that my mother's pain too has rustled among the pages of all those books I have read that partly constitute my "Westernization," and has crept into all the suitcases I have ever packed for my several exiles.' This same pain is evident in the united voice of protest that has emerged from international women's meetings such as those in Vienna and Beijing, where a remarkable degree of agreement was found across cultures concerning fundamental rights for women.

None the less, when we advance a set of universal norms in connection with women's equality, we will also face three more sincere and respectable objections, which must be honestly confronted.

First, one hears what I shall call the *argument from culture*. Traditional cultures, the argument goes, contain their own norms of what women's lives should be: frequently norms of female modesty, deference, obedience, and self-sacrifice. Feminists should not assume without argument that those are bad norms, incapable of constructing good and flourishing lives for women. By contrast, the norms proposed by feminists seem to this opponent suspiciously 'Western', because they involve an emphasis on choice and opportunity.

My full answer to this argument will emerge from the proposal I shall make, which certainly does not preclude any woman's choice to lead a traditional life, so long as she does so with certain economic and political opportunities firmly in place. But we should begin by emphasizing that the notion of tradition used in the argument is far too simple. Cultures are scenes of debate and contestation. They contain dominant voices, and they also contain the voices of women, which have not always been heard. It would be implausible to suggest that the many groups working to improve the employment conditions of women in the informal sector, for example, are brainwashing women into striving for economic opportunities: clearly, they provide means to ends women already want, and a context of female solidarity within which to pursue those ends. Where they do alter existing preferences, they typically do so by giving women a richer sense of both their possibilities and their equal worth, in a way that looks more like a self-realization than like brainwashing—as Tagore's heroine vividly states, telling her husband why she has decided to leave him. Indeed, what may possibly be 'Western' is the arrogant supposition that choice and economic agency are solely Western values!

Another general point should be stressed: cultures are dynamic, and change is a very basic element in all of them. Contrasts between West and non-West often depict Western cultures as dynamic, critical, modernizing, while Eastern cultures are identified with their oldest elements, as if these do not change or encounter contestation. Looking at the relationship between her grandmother's way of life and her own, Narayan comments, 'I find it impossible to describe "our traditional way of life" without seeing *change* as a constitutive element, affecting transformations that become "invisible" in their taken-for-grantedness' (1997: 26). Criticism too is profoundly indigenous to virtually all cultures,[12] but to none more so than to the culture of India, that extremely argumentative nation.[13] To cite just one famous and typical example, Bengali religious thinker Rammohun Roy, imagining the horrors of death, singles out as especially terrible the fact that 'everyone will contest your views, and you will not be able to reply'.[14] This too is Indian culture. In short, because cultures are scenes of debate, appealing to culture gives us questions rather than answers. It certainly does not show that cross-cultural norms are a bad answer to those questions.

Let us now consider the argument that I shall call the *argument from the good of diversity*. This argument reminds us that our world is rich in part because we do not all agree on a single set of practices and norms. We think the world's different languages have worth and beauty, and that it is a bad thing, diminishing the expressive resources of human life generally, if any language should cease to exist. So too, cultural norms have their own distinctive beauty; the world risks becoming impoverished as it becomes more homogeneous.

Here we should distinguish two claims the objector might be making. She might be claiming that diversity is good as such; or she might simply be saying that there are problems with the values of economic efficiency and consumerism that are increasingly dominating our interlocking world. This second claim, of course, does not yet say anything against cross-cultural norms, it just suggests that their content should be critical of some dominant economic norms. So the real challenge to our enterprise lies in the first claim. To meet it we must ask how far cultural diversity really is like linguistic diversity. The trouble with the analogy is that languages do not harm people, and cultural practices frequently do. We might think that threatened languages such as Cornish and Breton should be preserved, without thinking the same about domestic violence: it is not worth preserving simply because it is there and very old. In the end, then, the objection does not undermine the search for cross-cultural norms, it requires it: for what it invites us to ask is whether the cultural values in question are among the ones worth preserving, and this entails at least a very general cross-cultural framework of assessment, one that will tell us when we are better off letting a practice die out.

Finally, we have the *argument from paternalism*. This argument says that when we use a set of cross-cultural norms as benchmarks for the world's varied societies, we show too little respect for people's freedom as agents (and, in a related way, their role as democratic citizens). People are the best judges of what is good for them, and if we say that their own choices are not good for them we treat them like children. This is an important point, and one that any viable cross-cultural proposal should bear firmly in mind. But it hardly seems incompatible with the endorsement of cross-cultural norms. Indeed, it appears to endorse explicitly at least some cross-cultural norms, such as political liberties and other opportunities for choice. Thinking about paternalism gives us a strong reason to respect the variety of ways citizens actually choose to lead their lives in a pluralistic society, and therefore to seek a set of cross-cultural norms that protect freedom and choice of the most significant sorts. But this means that we will naturally value religious toleration, associative freedom, and the other major liberties. These liberties are themselves cross-cultural norms, and they are not compatible with views that many real people and societies hold.

We can make a further claim: many existing value systems are themselves highly paternalistic, particularly towards women. They treat them as unequal under the law, as lacking full civil capacity, as not having the property rights, associative liberties, and employment rights of males. If we encounter a system like this, it is in one sense paternalistic to say, sorry, that is unacceptable under the universal norms of equality and liberty that we would like to defend. In that way, any bill of rights is 'paternalistic' *vis-à-vis* families, or groups,

or practices, or even pieces of legislation, that treat people with insufficient or unequal respect. The Indian Constitution, for example, is
paternalistic when it tells people that it is from now on illegal to use
caste or sex as grounds of discrimination. But that is hardly a good
argument against fundamental constitutional rights or, more generally, against opposing the attempts of some people to tyrannize over
others. We dislike paternalism, in so far as we do, because there is
something else that we like, namely liberty of choice in fundamental
matters. It is fully consistent to reject some forms of paternalism
while supporting those that underwrite these basic values.

Nor does the protection of choice require only a formal defence of
basic liberties. The various liberties of choice have material preconditions, in whose absence there is merely a simulacrum of choice.
Many women who have in a sense the 'choice' to go to school simply
cannot do so: the economic circumstances of their lives make this
impossible. Women who 'can' have economic independence, in the
sense that no law prevents them, may be prevented simply by lacking assets, or access to credit. In short, liberty is not just a matter
of having rights on paper, it requires being in a material position to
exercise those rights. And this requires resources. As Diane Elson
(Chapter 3) argues, the state that is going to guarantee people rights
effectively is going to have to recognize norms beyond the small menu
of basic rights. It will have to take a stand about the redistribution
of wealth and income, about employment, land rights, health, education. If we think that these norms are important cross-culturally, we
will need to take an international position on pushing towards these
goals. That requires yet more universalism and in a sense paternalism; but we could hardly say that the many women who live in abusive
or repressive marriages, with no assets and no opportunity to seek
employment outside the home, are especially free to do as they wish.

To put things in another way: there are two historical strands
within the Western tradition of liberalism. One, now called 'neo-
liberalism', considers adult freedom of contract the most basic value.
Such a neo-liberalism need not take a stand on very many other values, and some of its defenders regard this as an advantage: people
are 'free' to be and do many different things that they choose. But,
as Diane Elson points out, such 'freedom' is a simulacrum, in the
absence of state action that promotes the real abilities of people to
be and to do various things that they choose. And as Anne Phillips
(Chapter 4) points out, even the conditions of choice require cultivation. But these facts suggest that a thin defence of 'freedom', such
as is present in neo-liberalism, is actually no defence at all: it leaves
people not at all free to do many things that they wish, perhaps not

even free to choose. So another strand within liberalism (associated historically with J. S. Mill and T. H. Green) insists that positive state intervention is required to create the material and institutional prerequisites of freedom. I consider this the only sort of liberalism worth defending: but of course it has to take a stand on far more than the thin idea of freedom of contract. It needs to endorse a wider range of human capacities for choice as appropriate goals for development.

The argument from paternalism indicates, then, that we should prefer a cross-cultural normative account that focuses on empowerment and opportunity, leaving people plenty of space to determine their course in life once those opportunities are secured to them. It does not give us any good reason to reject the whole idea of cross-cultural norms, and some strong reasons why we should seek such norms, including in our account not only the basic liberties, but also forms of economic empowerment that are crucial in making the liberties truly available to people. And the argument suggests one thing more: that the account we search for should seek empowerment and opportunity for each and every person, respecting each as an end, rather than simply as the agent or supporter of the ends of others. Women are too often treated as members of an organic unit such as the family or the community is supposed to be, and their interests subordinated to the larger goals of that unit, which means, typically, those of its male members. However, the impressive economic growth of a region means nothing to women whose husbands deprive them of control over household income. We need to consider not just the aggregate, whether in a region or in a family; we need to consider the distribution of resources and opportunities *to each person*, thinking of each as worthy of regard in her own right.

Traditional Economic Approaches to Development: The Need for Human Norms

Another way of seeing why cross-cultural norms are badly needed in the international policy arena is to consider what the alternative has typically been. Prior to the shift in thinking that is associated with the work of Amartya Sen[15] and with the *Human Development Reports* of the UNDP,[16] the most prevalent approach to measuring quality of life in a nation used to be simply to ask about GNP per capita. This approach tries to weasel out of making any cross-cultural claims about what has value—although, notice, it does assume the universal value of opulence. What it omits, however, is much more significant. We are not even told about the distribution of wealth and income, and countries with similar aggregate figures can exhibit great distributional variations. (Thus South Africa always did very well among developing nations, despite its enormous inequalities and violations of basic justice.) Circus girl Sissy Jupe, in Dickens's novel *Hard Times*, already saw the problem with this absence of normative concern for distribution. She says that her economics lesson didn't tell her 'who has got the money and whether any of it is mine'.[17] So too with women around the world: the fact that one nation or region is in general more prosperous than another is only a part of the story: it does not tell us what government has done for women in various social classes, or how they are doing. To know that, we would need to look at their lives. But then we need to specify, beyond distribution of wealth and income itself, what parts of lives we ought to look at— such as life expectancy, infant mortality, educational opportunities, health care, employment opportunities, land rights, political liberties. Seeing what is absent from the GNP account nudges us sharply in the direction of mapping out these and other basic goods in a universal way, so that we can use the list of basic goods to compare quality of life across societies. Thus Diane Elson's trenchant critique in Chapter 3 of neo-liberal approaches converges with the recommendations that Sen and I have been making for a thicker account of the goals of development in terms of a set of fundamental entitlements.

A further problem with all resource-based approaches, even those that are sensitive to distribution, is that individuals vary in their ability to convert resources into functionings. This is the problem that has been stressed for some time by Amartya Sen in his writings about the capabilities approach. Some of these differences are straightforwardly physical. Nutritional needs vary with age, occupation, and sex. A pregnant or lactating woman needs more nutrients than a nonpregnant woman. A child needs more protein than an adult. A person whose limbs work well needs few resources to be mobile, whereas a person with paralysed limbs needs many more resources to achieve the same level of mobility. Many such variations can escape our notice if we live in a prosperous nation that can afford to bring all individuals to a high level of physical attainment; in the developing world we must be highly alert to these variations in need. Again, some of the pertinent variations are social, connected with traditional hierarchies. If we wish to bring all citizens of a nation to the same level of educational attainment, we will need to devote more resources to those who encounter obstacles from traditional hierarchy or prejudice: thus women's literacy will prove more expensive than men's literacy in many parts of the world. If we operate only with an index of resources, we will frequently reinforce inequalities that are highly relevant to well-being. As my examples suggest, women's lives are especially likely to raise these problems: therefore, any approach that is to deal adequately with women's issues must be able to deal well with these variations.

If we turn from resource-based approaches to preference-based approaches, we encounter another set of difficulties.[18] Such approaches have one salient advantage over the GNP approach: they look at people, and assess the role of resources as they figure in improving actual people's lives. But users of such approaches typically assume without argument that the way to assess the role of resources in people's lives is simply to ask them about the satisfaction of their current preferences. The problem with this idea is that preferences are not exogenous, given independently of economic and social conditions. They are at least in part constructed by those conditions. Women often have no preference for economic independence before they learn about avenues through which women like them might pursue this goal; nor do they think of themselves as citizens with rights that were being ignored before they learn of their rights and are encouraged to believe in their equal worth. All of these ideas, and the preferences based on them, frequently take shape for women in programmes of education sponsored by women's organizations of various types. Men's preferences, too, are socially shaped and often misshaped. Men frequently have a strong preference that their wives should do all the childcare and all the housework—often in addition to working an eight-hour day. Such preferences, too, are not fixed in the nature of things: they are constructed by social traditions of privilege and subordination. Thus a preference-based approach typically will reinforce inequalities: especially those inequalities that are entrenched enough to have crept into people's very desires. Once again, although this is a fully general problem, it has special pertinence to women's lives. Women have especially often been deprived of education and information, which are necessary, if by no means sufficient, to make preferences a reliable indicator of what public policy should pursue. They have also often been socialized to believe that a lower living standard is what is right and fitting for them, and that some great human goods (for example, education, political participation) are not for them at all. They may be under considerable social pressure to say they are satisfied without such things: and yet we should not hastily conclude that public policy should not work to extend these functions to women. In short, looking at women's lives helps us see the inadequacy of traditional approaches; and the urgency of women's problems gives us a very strong motivation to prefer a non-traditional approach.

Human Dignity and Human Capabilities

I shall now argue that a reasonable answer to all these concerns—capable of giving good guidance to government establishing basic constitutional principles and to international agencies assessing the quality of life—is given by a version of the capabilities approach.

The central question asked by the capabilities approach is not, 'How satisfied is this woman?' or even 'How much in the way of resources is she able to command?' It is, instead, 'What is she actually able to do and to be?' Taking a stand for political purposes on a working list of functions that would appear to be of central importance in human life, users of this approach ask, 'Is the person capable of this, or not?' They ask not only about the person's satisfaction with what she does, but about what she does, and what she is in a position to do (what her opportunities and liberties are). They ask not just about the resources that are present, but about how those do or do not go to work, enabling the woman to function.

To introduce the intuitive idea behind the approach, it is useful to start from this passage of Marx's 1844 *Economic and Philosophical Manuscripts*, written at a time when he was reading Aristotle and was profoundly influenced by Aristotelian ideas of human capability and functioning:

It is obvious that the *human* eye gratifies itself in a way different from the crude, non-human eye; the human *ear* different from the crude ear, etc. ... The *sense* caught up in crude practical need has only a *restricted* sense. For the starving man, it is not the human form of food that exists, but only its abstract being as food; it could just as well be there in its crudest form, and it would be impossible to say wherein this feeding activity differs from that of *animals*.

Marx here singles out certain human functions—eating and the use of the senses, which seem to have a particular centrality in any life one might live. He then claims that there is something that it is to be able to perform these activities in a fully human way—by which he means a way infused by reasoning and sociability. But human beings do not automatically have the opportunity to perform their human functions in a fully human way. Some conditions in which people live—conditions of starvation, or of educational deprivation—bring it about that a being who is human has to live in an animal way. Of course what he is saying is that these conditions are unacceptable, and should be changed.

Similarly, the intuitive idea behind my version of the capabilities approach is twofold: first, that there are certain functions that are particularly central in human life, in the sense that their presence or absence is typically understood to be a mark of the presence or absence of human life. Second, and this is what Marx found in Aristotle, that there is something that it is to do these functions in a truly human way, not a merely animal way. We judge, frequently enough, that a life has been so impoverished that it is not worthy of the dignity of the human being, that it is a life in which one goes on living, but more or less like an animal, not being able to develop and exercise one's human powers. In Marx's example, a starving person just grabs at the food in order to survive, and the many social and rational ingredients of human feeding cannot make their appearance. Similarly, the senses of a human being can operate at a merely animal level—if they are not cultivated by appropriate education, by leisure for play and self-expression, by valuable associations with others; and we should add to the list some items that Marx probably would not endorse, such as expressive and associational liberty, and the freedom of worship. The core idea seems to be that of the human being as a dignified free being who shapes his or her own life, rather than being passively shaped or pushed around by the world in the manner of a flock or herd animal.

At one extreme, we may judge that the absence of capability for a central function is so acute that the person is not really a human being at all, or any longer—as in the case of certain very severe forms of mental disability, or senile dementia. But I am less interested in that boundary (important though it is for medical ethics) than in a higher one, the level at which a person's capability is 'truly human', that is, *worthy* of a human being. The idea thus contains a notion of human worth or dignity.

Notice that the approach makes each person a bearer of value, and an end. Marx, like his bourgeois forebears, holds that it is profoundly wrong to subordinate the ends of some individuals to those of others. That is at the core of what exploitation is, to treat a person as a mere object for the use of others. What this approach is after is a society in which individuals are treated as each worthy of regard, and in which each has been put in a position to live really humanly. Thus from the start it takes its stand against viewing women as primarily the agents or adjuncts of men, and, by implication, against the 'male-breadwinner bias' described by Diane Elson in Chapter 3.

I think we can produce an account of these necessary elements of truly human functioning that commands a broad cross-cultural consensus, a list that can be endorsed for political purposes by people who otherwise have very different views of what a complete good life for a human being would be. The list is supposed to provide a focus for quality of life assessment and for political planning, and it aims to select capabilities that are of central importance, whatever else the person pursues. They therefore have a special claim to be supported for political purposes in a pluralistic society. They can be regarded as the basis for a set of fundamental constitutional entitlements, in a nation with a written constitution, or as the analogue in a nation without a written document.[19]

The list in its current form represents the result of years of cross-cultural discussion,[20] and comparisons between earlier and later versions will show that the input of other voices has shaped its content in many ways. It remains open-ended and humble; it can always be contested and remade. Nor does it deny that the items on the list are to some extent differently constructed by different societies. Indeed part of the idea of the list is that its members can be more concretely specified in accordance with local beliefs and circumstances. Here is the current version of Central Human Functional Capabilities:

1. Life

Being able to live to the end of a human life of normal length; not dying prematurely, or before one's life is so reduced as to be not worth living.

2. Bodily Health

Being able to have good health, including reproductive health;[21] to be adequately nourished; to have adequate shelter.

3. Bodily Integrity

Being able to move freely from place to place; to be secure against violent assault, including sexual assault and domestic violence; having opportunities for sexual satisfaction and for choice in matters of reproduction.

4. Senses, Imagination, and Thought

Being able to use the senses, to imagine, think, and reason—and to do these things in a 'truly human' way, a way informed and cultivated by an adequate education, including, but by no means limited to, literacy and basic mathematical and scientific training. Being able to use imagination and thought in connection with experiencing and producing works and events of one's own choice, religious, literary, musical, and so forth. Being able to use one's mind in ways protected by guarantees of freedom of expression with respect to both political and artistic speech, and freedom of religious exercise. Being able to have pleasurable experiences, and to avoid non-necessary pain.

5. Emotions

Being able to have attachments to things and people outside ourselves; to love those who love and care for us, to grieve at their absence; in general, to love, to grieve, to experience longing, gratitude, and justified anger. Not having one's emotional development blighted by fear and anxiety. (Supporting this capability means supporting forms of human association that can be shown to be crucial in their development.)

6. Practical Reason

Being able to form a conception of the good and to engage in critical reflection about the planning of one's life. (This entails protection for the liberty of conscience.)

7. Affiliation

(A) Being able to live with and toward others, to recognize and show concern for other human beings, to engage in various forms of social interaction; to be able to imagine the situation of another and to have compassion for that situation; to have the capability for both justice and friendship. (Protecting this capability means protecting institutions that constitute and nourish such forms of affiliation, and also protecting the freedom of assembly and political speech.)

(B) Having the social bases of self-respect and non-humiliation; being able to be treated as a dignified being whose worth is equal to that of others. This entails protections against discrimination on the basis of race, sex, sexual orientation, religion, caste, ethnicity, or national origin.

8. Other Species

Being able to live with concern for and in relation to animals, plants, and the world of nature.

9. Play

Being able to laugh, to play, to enjoy recreational activities.

10. Control over one's Environment

(A) Political: being able to participate effectively in political choices that govern one's life; having the right of political participation, protections of free speech and association.

(B) Material: being able to hold property (both land and movable goods); having the right to seek employment on an equal basis with others; having the freedom from unwarranted search and seizure. In work, being able to work as a human being, exercising practical reason and entering into meaningful relationships of mutual recognition with other workers.

The list is, emphatically, a list of separate components. We cannot satisfy the need for one of them by giving people a larger amount of another one. All are of central importance and all are distinct in quality. The irreducible plurality of the list limits the trade-offs that it will be reasonable to make, and thus limits the applicability of quantitative cost–benefit analysis. At the same time, the items on the list are related to one another in many complex ways. One of the most effective ways of promoting women's control over their environment, and their effective right of political participation, is to promote women's literacy. Women who can seek employment outside the home have more resources in protecting their bodily integrity from assaults within it. Such facts give us still more reason not to promote one capability at the expense of the others. As Elson says (in Chapter 3), we may need to set priorities in actually implementing the items on the list, but we should at all times remember how interdependent they are, and also remember that the goal of creating a minimally just society is not achieved when entitlements in any of these areas are not secured to citizens.

Among the capabilities, two, practical reason and affiliation, stand out as of special importance, since they both organize and suffuse all the others, making their pursuit truly human. To use one's senses in a way not infused by the characteristically human use of thought and planning is to use them in an incompletely human manner. Tagore's heroine, summarizing her decision to seek a life apart from her husband, says, 'I found myself beautiful as a free human mind'. This idea of herself infuses all her other functions. At the same time, to reason for oneself without at all considering the circumstances and needs of others is, again, to behave in an incompletely human way.

The basic intuition from which the capability approach begins, in the political arena, is that human abilities exert a moral claim that they should be developed. Human beings are creatures such that, provided with the right educational and material support, they can become fully capable of these human functions. That is, they are creatures with certain lower level capabilities (which I call 'basic capabilities'[22]) to perform the functions in question. When these capabilities are deprived of the nourishment that would transform them into the high-level capabilities that figure on my list, they are fruitless, cut off, in some way but a shadow of themselves. If a turtle were given a life that afforded a merely animal level of functioning, we would have no indignation, no sense of waste and tragedy. When a human being is given a life that blights powers of human action and expression, that does give us a sense of waste and tragedy—the tragedy expressed, for example, in the statement made by Tagore's heroine to her husband, when she says, 'I am not one to die easily'. In her view, a life without dignity and choice, a life in which she can be no more than an appendage, was a type of death of her humanity.

The capabilities approach considers each person as an end, and thus shares Anne Phillips's (Chapter 4) scepticism about group entitlements, where these are in tension with the fostering of the full set of entitlements for people taken one by one. Thus it will be insufficient to promote the good of 'the community' or 'the family', where that leaves intact gross asymmetries of capability among community or family members. Women are especially likely to be the losers when the good of a group is promoted as such, without asking about hierarchies of power and opportunity internal to the group. The capabilities approach insists on pressing that question. What the approach is after is a society in which persons are treated as each worthy of regard, and in which each has been put in a position to live really humanly. (That is where the idea of a threshold comes in: we say that beneath a certain level of capability, in each area, a person has not been enabled to live in a truly human way.) The capabilities sought are sought for *each and every person*, not, in the first instance, for groups or families or states or other corporate bodies. Such bodies may be extremely important in promoting human capabilities, and in this way they may deservedly gain our support: but it is because of what they do for people that they are so worthy, and the ultimate political goal is always the promotion of the capabilities of *each person*.[23]

We begin, then, with a sense of the worth and dignity of basic human powers, thinking of them as claims to a chance for functioning, claims that give rise to correlated social and political duties. And in fact there are three different types of capabilities that play a role in the analysis. First, there are basic capabilities: the innate equipment of individuals that is the necessary basis for developing the more advanced capability, and a ground of moral concern. Second, there are internal capabilities: that is, states of the person herself that are, so far as the person herself is concerned, sufficient conditions for the exercise of the requisite functions. A woman who has not suffered genital mutilation has the internal capability for sexual pleasure; most adult human beings everywhere have the internal capability for religious freedom and the freedom of speech. Finally, there are combined capabilities, which may be defined as internal capabilities combined with suitable external conditions for the exercise of the function. A woman who is not mutilated but who has been widowed as a child and is forbidden to make another marriage has the internal but not the combined capability for sexual expression (and, in most such cases, for employment, and political participation) (Chen, 1995, 2000). Citizens of repressive non-democratic regimes have the internal but not the combined capability to exercise thought and speech in accordance with their conscience. The list, then, is a list of combined capabilities. To realize one of the items on the list entails not only promoting appropriate development of people's internal powers, but also preparing the environment so that it is favourable for the exercise of practical reason and the other major functions.

Functioning and Capability

I have spoken both of functioning and of capability. How are they related? Getting clear about this is crucial in defining the relation of the 'capabilities approach' to our concerns about paternalism and pluralism. For if we were to take functioning itself as the goal of public policy, a liberal pluralist would rightly judge that we were precluding many choices that citizens may make in accordance with their own conceptions of the good. A deeply religious person may prefer not to be well-nourished, but to engage in strenuous fasting. Whether for religious or for other reasons, a person may prefer a celibate life to one containing sexual expression. A person may prefer to work with an intense dedication that precludes recreation and play. Am I declaring, by my very use of the list, that these are not fully human or flourishing lives? And am I instructing government to nudge or push people into functioning of the requisite sort, no matter what they prefer?

It is important that the answer to this question is no. Capability, not functioning, is the appropriate political goal. This is so because of the very great importance the approach attaches to practical reason, as a good that both suffuses all the other functions, making them fully human, and also figures, itself, as a central function on the list. The person with plenty of food may always choose to fast, but there is a great difference between fasting and starving, and it is this difference that we wish to capture. Again, the person who has normal opportunities for sexual satisfaction can always choose a life of celibacy, and the approach says nothing against this. What it does speak against (for example) is the practice of female genital mutilation, which deprives individuals of the opportunity to choose sexual functioning (and indeed, the opportunity to choose celibacy as well).[24] A person who has opportunities for play can always choose a workaholic life; again, there is a great difference between that chosen life and a life constrained by insufficient maximum-hour protections and/or the 'double day' that makes women unable to play in many parts of the world.

Once again, we must stress that the objective is to be understood in terms of combined capabilities. To secure a capability to a person it is not sufficient to produce good internal states of readiness to act. It is necessary, as well, to prepare the material and institutional environment so that people are actually able to function. Women burdened by the 'double day' may be internally incapable of play—if, for example, they have been kept indoors and zealously guarded since infancy, married at age 6, and forbidden to engage in the kind of imaginative exploration of the environment that male children standardly enjoy. Young girls in poor areas of rural Rajasthan, India, for example, have great difficulty learning to play in an educational programme run by local activists, because their capacity for play has not been nourished early in childhood. On the other hand, there are also many women in the world who are perfectly capable of play in the internal sense, but who are unable to play because of the crushing demands of the 'double day'. Such a woman does not have the combined capability for play in the sense intended by the list. Capability is thus a demanding notion. In its focus on the environment of choice, it is highly attentive to the goal of functioning, and instructs governments to keep it always in view. On the other hand, it does not push people into functioning: once the stage is fully set, the choice is theirs.

In other words, to return to a contrast I have stressed in discussing Elson and Phillips, the approach is liberal, emphasizing choice as a good. But it is not neo-liberal, because it holds that choice has material and institutional necessary conditions, and that it is the duty of political action to provide these to all citizens.

Capabilities and Care

All human beings begin their lives as helpless children; if they live long enough, they are likely to end their lives in helplessness, either physical or also mental. During the prime of life, most human beings encounter periods of extreme dependency; and some human beings remain dependent on the daily bodily care of others throughout their lives. Of course putting it this way suggests, absurdly, that 'normal' human beings do not depend on others for bodily care and survival; but political thought should recognize that some phases of life, and some lives, generate more profound dependency than others.

The capabilities approach, more Aristotelian than Kantian, sees human beings from the first as animal beings whose lives are characterized by profound neediness as well as by dignity. It addresses the issue of care in many ways: under 'life' it is stressed that people should be enabled to complete a 'normal' human lifespan; under 'health' and 'bodily integrity' the needs of different phases of life are implicitly recognized; 'sense', 'emotions', and 'affiliation' also target needs that vary with the stage of life. 'Affiliation' is of particular importance, since it mentions the need for both compassion and self-respect, and it also mentions non-discrimination. What we see, then, is that care must be provided in such a way that the capability for self-respect of the receiver is not injured, and also in such a way that the care-giver is not exploited and discriminated against on account of performing that role. In other words, a good society must arrange to provide care for those in a condition of extreme dependency, without exploiting women as they have traditionally been exploited, and thus depriving them of other important capabilities. This huge problem will rightly shape the way states think about all the other capabilities.[25]

The capabilities approach has a great advantage in this area over traditional liberal approaches that use the idea of a social contract. Such approaches typically generate basic political principles from a hypothetical contract situation in which all participants are independent adults. John Rawls, for example, uses the phrase 'fully cooperating members of society over a complete life'.[26] But of course no human being is that. And the fiction distorts the choice of principles in a central way, effacing the issue of extreme dependency and care from the agenda of the contracting parties when they choose the principles that shape society's basic structure. And yet such a fundamental issue cannot well be postponed for later consideration, since it profoundly shapes the way social institutions will be designed.[27] The capabilities approach, using a different concept of the human being, one that builds in need and dependency into the first phases of political thinking, is better suited to good deliberation on this urgent set of issues.

Capabilities and Human Rights

Earlier versions of the list appeared to diverge from approaches common in the human rights movement by not giving as large a place to the traditional political rights and liberties—although the need to incorporate them was stressed from the start. This version of the list corrects that defect of emphasis.[28] The political liberties have a central importance in making well-being human. A society that aims at well-being while overriding these has delivered to its members an incompletely human level of satisfaction. As Amartya Sen has written, 'Political rights are important not only for the fulfillment of needs, they are crucial also for the formulation of needs. And this idea relates, in the end, to the respect that we owe each other as fellow human beings'.[29] There are many reasons to think that political liberties have an instrumental role in preventing material disaster (in particular famine: Sen, 1981), and in promoting economic well-being. But their role is not merely instrumental: they are valuable in their own right.

Thus capabilities as I conceive them have a very close relationship to human rights, as understood in contemporary international discussions. In effect they cover the terrain of both the so-called 'first-generation rights' (political and civil liberties) and the so-called second-generation rights (economic and social rights). And they play a similar role, providing the philosophical underpinning for basic constitutional principles. Because the language of rights is well-established, the defender of capabilities needs to show what is added by this new language.[30]

The idea of human rights is by no means a crystal-clear idea. Rights have been understood in many different ways, and difficult theoretical questions are frequently obscured by the use of rights language, which can give the illusion of agreement where there is deep philosophical disagreement. People differ about what the *basis* of a rights claim is: rationality, sentience, and mere life have all had their defenders. They differ, too, about whether rights are prepolitical or artefacts of laws and institutions. (Kant held the latter view, although the dominant human rights tradition has held the former.) They differ about whether rights belong only to individual persons, or also to groups. They differ about whether rights are to be regarded as side-constraints on goal-promoting action, or rather as one part of the social goal that is being promoted. They differ, again, about the relationship between rights and duties: if A has a right to S, then does this mean that there is always someone who has a duty to provide

S, and how shall we decide who that someone is? They differ, finally, about what rights are to be understood as rights *to*. Are human rights primarily rights to be treated in certain ways? Rights to a certain level of achieved well-being? Rights to resources with which one may pursue one's life plan? Rights to certain opportunities and capacities with which one may make choices about one's life plan?

The account of central capabilities has the advantage, it seems to me, of taking clear positions on these disputed issues, while stating clearly what the motivating concerns are and what the goal is. Bernard Williams put this point eloquently, commenting on Sen's 1987 Tanner Lectures:

> I am not very happy myself with taking rights as the starting point. The notion of a basic human right seems to me obscure enough, and I would rather come at it from the perspective of basic human capabilities. I would prefer capabilities to do the work, and if we are going to have a language or rhetoric of rights, to have it delivered from them, rather than the other way round. (Williams, 1987: 100)

As Williams says, however, the relationship between the two concepts needs further scrutiny, given the dominance of rights language in the international development world.

When we think about fundamental rights, I would argue that the best way of thinking about what it is to secure them to citizens is to think in terms of combined capabilities. The right to political participation, the right to religious free exercise, the right of free speech—these and others are all best thought of as realized only when the relevant capabilities have been achieved. To secure a right to citizens in these areas is to put them in a position of combined capability to function in that area. (Of course they may have a right to good treatment in this area that is not yet secured: people have a right to religious freedom just by virtue of being human, even if the state they live in has not guaranteed them this freedom. I shall shortly return to this important feature of rights language.) By defining the securing of rights in terms of combined capabilities, we make it clear that a people in country C do not really have an effective right to political participation just because this language exists on paper: they really have been given this right only if there are effective measures to make people truly capable of political exercise. Women in many nations have a nominal right of political participation without having this right in the sense of capability: for example, they may be threatened with violence should they leave the home. In short, thinking in terms of capability gives us a benchmark as we think about what it is really to secure a right to someone.

We see here a strong advantage of the capabilities approach over understandings of rights that derive from the tradition within liberalism that is now called neo-liberal. Often fundamental constitutional rights have been understood as prohibitions against interfering state action, and that is all: the state has no more affirmative task. (Much of the wording of the Bill of Rights in the US Constitution derives from this tradition, although centuries of interpretation has to some extent broadened the understanding. The Indian Constitution's section of Fundamental Rights takes a more affirmative approach, and the securing of fundamental rights is explicitly understood to involve affirmative state action.) Thus the capabilities approach fits well with Phillips's emphasis (Chapter 4) on creating the conditions of choice for women by affirmative state action. Measures such as the two recent constitutional amendments in India that guarantee women one-third representation in the local panchayats, or village councils, are strongly suggested by the capabilities approach, which directs government to think from the start about what obstacles there are to full empowerment for all citizens, and to devise measures to address these obstacles. Thus it supports Phillips's emphasis on securing conditions of political participation, while it also supports her scepticism about a simple majoritarianism where fundamental entitlements are at issue.

A further advantage of the capabilities approach is that, by focusing from the start on what people are actually able to do, it is well set up to notice and foreground inequalities that women suffer inside the family: inequalities in resources and opportunities, educational deprivation, the failure of work to be recognized as work, and, of course, insults to bodily integrity. It is no accident that these feminist issues have been central to the approach since its inception: conceptually, the approach is well suited to their recognition to making recommendations for their amelioration.

The language of capabilities has one further advantage over the language of rights: it is not strongly linked to one particular cultural and historical tradition, as the language of rights is believed to be. This belief is not very accurate: although the term 'rights' is associated with the European Enlightenment, its component ideas have deep roots in many traditions.[31] Where India is concerned, for example, even apart from the recent validation of rights language in Indian legal and constitutional traditions, the salient component ideas have deep roots in far earlier areas of Indian thought—in ideas of religious toleration developed since the edicts of Ashoka in the third century BC, in the thought about Hindu–Muslim relations in the Mughal Empire, and, of course, in many progressive and humanist thinkers of the nineteenth and twentieth centuries, who certainly cannot be described as simply Westernizers, with no respect for their own traditions.[32] Tagore portrays the conception of freedom used by the young wife in his story as having ancient Indian origins, in the quest of Rajput Queen Meerabai for joyful self-expression. The idea of herself as 'a free human mind' is represented as one that she derives, not from any external infusion, but from a combination of experience and history.

So 'rights' are not exclusively Western, in the sense that matters most; they can be endorsed from a variety of perspectives. None the less, the language of capabilities enables us to bypass this troublesome debate. When we speak simply of what people are actually able to do and to be, we do not even give the appearance of privileging a Western idea. Ideas of activity and ability are everywhere, and there is no culture in which people do not ask themselves what they are able to do, what opportunities they have for functioning.

If we have the language of capabilities, do we also need the language of rights? The language of rights still plays, I believe, four important roles in public discourse, despite its unsatisfactory features. First, when used as in the sentence 'A has a right to have the basic political liberties secured to her by her government', this sentence reminds us that people have justified and urgent claims to certain types of urgent treatment, no matter what the world around them has done about that. This role of rights language lies very close to what I have called 'basic capabilities', in the sense that the justification for saying that people have such natural rights usually proceeds by pointing to some capability-like feature of persons (rationality, language) that they actually have on at least a rudimentary level. And I actually think that without such a justification the appeal to rights is quite mysterious. On the other hand, there is no doubt that one might recognize the basic capabilities of people and yet still deny that this entails that they have rights in the sense of justified claims to certain types of treatment. We know that this inference has not been made through a great deal of the world's history. So appealing to rights communicates more than does the bare appeal to basic capabilities, which does no work all by itself, without any further ethical argument of the sort I have supplied. Rights language indicates that we do have such an argument and that we draw strong normative conclusions from the fact of the basic capabilities.

Second, even when we are talking about rights explicitly guaranteed by the state, the language of rights places great emphasis on the importance and the basic role of these spheres of ability. To say, 'Here's a list of things that people ought to be able to do and to be' has only a vague normative resonance. To say, 'Here is a list of fundamental rights', is more rhetorically direct. It tells people right away that we are dealing with an especially urgent set of functions, backed up by a sense of the justified claim that all humans have to such things, in virtue of being human.

Third, rights language has value because of the emphasis it places on people's choice and freedom. The language of capabilities, as I have said, was designed to leave room for choice, and to communicate the idea that there is a big difference between pushing people into functioning in ways you consider valuable and leaving the choice up to them. But there are approaches using an Aristotelian language of functioning and capability that do not emphasize liberty in the way that my approach does: Marxist Aristotelianism and some forms of Catholic Thomist Aristotelianism are illiberal in this sense. If we have the language of rights in play as well, I think it helps us to lay extra emphasis on the important fact that the appropriate political goal is the ability of people to choose to function in certain ways, not simply their actual functionings.

Thus in many ways the capabilities framework and the human rights framework are complementary. One cautionary note is, however, suggested by some current uses of rights talk. The historical connection of the rights framework with 'negative liberty' and an absence of state interference has led to its increasing use in connection with opening markets to foreign capital. The connection of these putative economic rights with the promotion of a wide range of human capabilities for all citizens of a nature is difficult to trace: complex empirical questions are involved. Markets sometimes do promote human capabilities. Sometimes, however, they do so very unevenly. And there are some capabilities, for example those related to health and education, that markets do not deliver well to people; other forms of state action are required.

To some degree the ambiguities I have described in the language of rights can lead to a blurring of these issues: people may come to believe that there is a clear conceptual connection between 'promoting human rights' in the sense of opening markets and 'promoting human rights' in the sense of promoting each citizen's capabilities. Using rights language without capabilities language thus seems unwise, particularly at a time of rapid economic globalization.

Capabilities as Goals for Women's Development

I have argued that legitimate concerns for diversity, pluralism, and personal freedom are not incompatible with the recognition of cross-cultural norms, and indeed that cross-cultural norms are actually required if we are to protect diversity, pluralism, and freedom, treating each human being as an agent and an end. The best way to hold all these concerns together, I have argued, is to formulate the norms as a set of capabilities for fully human functioning, emphasizing the fact that capabilities protect, and do not close off, spheres of human freedom.

Used to evaluate the lives of women who are struggling for equality in many different countries, developing and developed, the capabilities framework does not, I believe, look like an alien importation: it squares pretty well with demands women are already making in many global and national political contexts. It might therefore seem superfluous to put these items on a list: why not just let women decide what they will demand in each case? To answer that question, we should point out that the international development debate is already using a normative language. Where the capabilities approach has not caught on—as it has in the *Human Development Reports*—a much less adequate theoretical language still prevails, whether it is the language of preference-satisfaction or the language of economic growth. We need the capabilities approach as a humanly rich alternative to these inadequate theories of human development.

Of course the capabilities approach supplies norms for human development in general, not just for women's development. Women's issues, however, are not only worthy of focus because of their remarkable urgency. They also help us see more clearly the inadequacy of various other approaches to development more generally, and the reasons for preferring the capabilities approach. *Preference-based approaches* do not enable us to criticize preferences that have been shaped by a legacy of injustice and hierarchy: men's preferences for dominance and for being taken care of, women's preferences for a low level of attainment when that is the only life they know and think possible. The capabilities approach, by contrast, looks at what women are actually able to do and to be, undeterred by the fact that oppressed and uneducated women may say, or even think, that some of these capabilities are not for them. *Resource-based approaches*, similarly, have a bias in the direction of protecting the status quo, in that they do not take account of the special needs for aid that some groups may have on account of their subordinate status: we have to spend more on them to bring them up to the same level of capability. This fact the capabilities approach sees clearly, and it directs us to make a basic threshold level of capability the goal for all citizens.[33] *Human rights approaches* are close allies of the capabilities approach, because they take a stand on certain fundamental entitlements of citizens, and they hold that these may be demanded as a matter of basic justice. In relation to these approaches, however, the capabilities approach is both more definite, specifying clearly what it means to secure a 'right' to someone, and more comprehensive, spelling out explicitly certain rights that are of special importance to women, but which have not until recently been included in international human rights documents.

The capabilities approach may seem to have one disadvantage, in comparison to these other approaches: it seems difficult to measure human capabilities. If this difficulty arises already when we think about such obvious issues as health and mobility, it most surely arises in a perplexing form for my own list, which has added so many apparently intangible items, such as development of the imagination, and the conditions of emotional health. We know, however, that anything worth measuring, in human quality of life, is difficult to measure. Resource-based approaches simply substitute something easy to measure for what really ought to be measured, a heap of stuff for the richness of human functioning. Preference-based approaches do even worse, because they not only do not measure what ought to be measured, they also get into quagmires of their own, concerning how to aggregate preferences—and whether there is any way of doing that task that does not run afoul of the difficulties shown in the social choice literature. The capabilities approach as so far developed in the *Human Development Reports* is admittedly not perfect: years of schooling, everyone would admit, are an imperfect proxy for education. We may expect that any proxies we find as we include more capabilities in the study will be highly imperfect also— especially if we need to rely on data supplied by the nations. On the other hand, we are at least working in the right place and looking at the right thing; and over time, as data gathering responds to our concerns, we may expect increasingly adequate information, and better ways of aggregating that information. As has already happened with human rights approaches, we need to rely on the ingenuity of those who suffer from deprivation: they will help us find ways to describe, and even to quantify, their predicament.

Women all over the world have lacked support for central human functions, and that lack of support is to some extent caused by their being women. But women, like men—and unlike rocks and trees and even horses and dogs—have the potential to become capable of these human functions, given sufficient nutrition, education, and other support. That is why their unequal failure in capability is a problem of justice. It is up to all human beings to solve this problem. I claim

74 *Martha Nussbaum*

that the capabilities approach, and a list of the central capabilities, give us good guidance as we pursue this difficult task.

References

Agarwal, Bina (1994) *A Field of One's Own: Gender and Land Rights in South Asia* (Cambridge: Cambridge University Press).

Alkire, Sabrina (1999) 'Operationalizing Amartya Sen's Capability Approach to Human Development: A Framework for Identifying Valuable Capabilities', D.Phil. dissertation, Oxford University, Oxford.

Aman, K. (ed.) (1991) *Ethical Principles for Development: Needs, Capabilities or Rights* (Montclair: Montclair State University Press).

Anand, S., and C. Harris (1994) 'Choosing a Welfare Indicator', *American Economic Association Papers and Proceedings* 84: 226–49.

Bardhan, Kalpana (ed.) (1990) *Of Women, Outcastes, Peasants and Rebels: A Selection of Bengali Short Stories* (Berkeley, Calif.: University of California Press).

Basu, K., P. Pattanaik, and K. Suzumura (eds.) (1995) *Choice, Welfare, and Development: A Festschrift in Honour of Amartya K. Sen* (Oxford: Clarendon Press).

Boserup, Esther (1970) *Women's Role in Economic Development* (New York: St Martin's Press; 2nd ed. Aldershot: Gower Publishing, 1986).

Chakraborty, Achin (1996) *'The Concept and Measurement of the Standard of Living'*, Ph.D. thesis, University of California at Riverside.

Chen, Martha A. (1983) *A Quiet Revolution: Women in Transition in Rural Bangladesh* (Cambridge: Schenkman).

—— (1995) 'A Matter of Survival: Women's Right to Work in India and Bangladesh' in Martha Nussbaum and Jonathan Glover (eds.), *Women, Culture and Development: A Study of Human Capabilities* (Oxford: Clarendon Press).

—— (2000) *Perpetual Mourning: Widowhood in Rural India* (Delhi and Philadelphia: Oxford University Press and University of Pennsylvania Press).

Dasgupta, Partha (1993) *An Inquiry into Well-Being and Destitution* (Oxford: Clarendon Press).

Desai, Meghnad (1990) 'Poverty and Capability: Towards an Empirically Implementable Measure', *Suntory–Toyota International Centre Discussion Paper* 27 (London School of Economics Development Economics Research Program).

Drèze, Jean, and Amartya Sen (1989) *Hunger and Public Action*, (Oxford: Clarendon Press).

—— (1995) *India: Economic Development and Social Opportunity* (Delhi: Oxford University Press).

Folbre, Nancy (1999) 'Care and the Global Economy', background paper for *Human Development Report* (1999).

Harrington, Mona (1999) *Care and Equality: Inventing a New Family Politics* (New York: Knopf).

India Abroad (1998) 'Special Report on Rape' (10 July).

Kittay, Eva (1999) *Love's Labor: Essays on Women, Equality, and Dependency* (New York: Routledge).

Kniss, Fred (1997) *Disquiet in the Land: Cultural Conflict in American Mennonite Communities* (New Brunswick, NJ: Rutgers University Press).

McMurrin, S. (ed.) (1980) *Tanner Lectures on Human Values*, i (Cambridge: Cambridge University Press).

Narayan, Uma (1997) *Dislocating Cultures: Identities, Traditions, and Third World Feminism* (New York: Routledge).

Nehru, Jawaharlal (1990) *Jawaharlal Nehru: An Autobiography* (Oxford: Oxford University Press).

Nussbaum, Martha (1988) 'Nature, Function, and Capability: Aristotle on Political Distribution', *Oxford Studies in Ancient Philosophy*, supplementary vol. 1: 145–84.

—— (1990) 'Aristotelian Social Democracy' in R. B. Douglass, G. R. Mara, and H. R. Richardson (eds.), *Liberalism and the Good* (New York: Routledge).

—— (1992) 'Human Functioning and Social Justice: In Defense of Aristotelian Essentialism', *Political Theory*, 20: 202–46.

—— (1993) 'Non-Relative Virtues: An Aristotelian Approach', in M. Nussbaum and A. Sen (eds.), *The Quality of Life* (Oxford: Clarendon Press).

—— (1995a) 'Aristotle on Human Nature and the Foundations of Ethics', in J. E. J. Altham and Ross Harrison (eds.), *World, Mind and Ethics: Essays on the Ethical Philosophy of Bernard Williams* (Cambridge: Cambridge University Press).

—— (1995b) 'Human Capabilities, Female Human Beings', in M. Nussbaum and J. Glover (eds.), *Women, Culture, and Development* (Oxford: Clarendon Press).

—— (1997a) 'The Good as Discipline, the Good as Freedom', in David A. Crocker and Toby Linden (eds.), *Ethics of Consumption: The Good Life, Justice, and Global Stewardship* (Lanham, Md.: Rowman & Littlefield).

—— (1997b) 'Capabilities and Human Rights', *Fordham Law Review*, 66: 273–300.

—— (1997c) 'Religion and Women's Human Rights', in Paul Weithman (ed.), *Religion and Contemporary Liberalism* (Notre Dame, Ind.: University of Notre Dame Press).

—— (1998a) 'Public Philosophy and International Feminism', *Ethics*, 108: 770–804.

—— (1998b) 'Still Worthy of Praise', *Harvard Law Review*, 111: 1776–95.

—— (1999) *Sex and Social Justice* (New York: Oxford University Press).

—— (2000a) 'Why Practice Needs Ethical Theory: Particularism, Principle, and Bad Behavior' in S. Burton (ed.), *The Path of the Law in the Twentieth Century* (Cambridge: Cambridge University Press).

Nussbaum, Martha (2000b) *Women and Human Development: The Capabilities Approach* (Cambridge and New York: Cambridge University Press).

—— (forthcoming) 'Rawls and Feminism', in Samuel Freeman (ed.), *The Cambridge Companion to John Rawls* (Cambridge: Cambridge University Press).

—— and J. Glover (eds.) (1995) *Women, Culture, and Development* (Oxford: Clarendon Press).

—— and Amartya Sen (eds.) (1993) *The Quality of Life* (Oxford: Clarendon Press).

—— —— (1989) 'Internal Criticism and Indian Rationalist Traditions', in Michael Krausz (ed.), *Relativism: Interpretation and Confrontation* (Notre Dame, Ind.: University of Notre Dame Press).

Pattanaik, Prasanta (1998) 'Cultural Indicators of Well-Being: Some Conceptual Issues', in UNESCO, *World Culture Report: Culture, Creativity, and Markets* (Paris: UNESCO Publishing).

Rawls, John (1996) *Political Liberalism*, expanded paper edn. (New York: Columbia University Press).

Sen, Amartya (1981) *Poverty and Famines: An Essay on Entitlement and Deprivation* (Oxford: Clarendon Press).

—— (1982) *Choice, Welfare, and Measurement* (Oxford and Cambridge, Mass.: Basil Blackwell and MIT Press).

—— (1984) *Resources, Values, and Development* (Oxford and Cambridge, Mass.: Basil Blackwell and MIT Press).

—— (1985a) *Commodities and Capabilities: Lectures in Economics Theory Policy*, vii (Armsterdam: Elsevier Science).

—— (1985b) 'Well-Being, Agency and Freedom: The Dewey Lectures 1984', *Journal of Philosophy*, 82/4: 169–221.

—— (1992) *Inequality Reexamined* (Oxford and Cambridge: Clarendon Press and Harvard University Press).

—— (1994) 'Freedoms and Needs', *New Republic*, (10–17 Jan.): 31–8.

—— (1997a) 'Human Rights and Asian Values', *New Republic*, (14–21 July): 33–41.

—— (1997b) 'Tagore and his India', *New York Review of Books* (26 June).

Stewart, Frances (1996) 'Basic Needs, Capabilities, and Human Development' in Avner Offer (ed.), *In Pursuit of the Quality of Life* (Oxford: Oxford University Press).

Taylor, Charles (1999) 'Conditions of an Unforced Consensus on Human Rights', in Joanne R. Bauer and Daniel A. Bell (eds.), *The East Asian Challenge for Human Rights* (Cambridge: Cambridge University Press).

Tinker, Irene (ed.) (1990) *Persistent Inequalities* (New York: Oxford University Press).

Tsui, Amy O., Judith N. Wasserheit, and John G. Haaga (eds.) (1997) *Reproductive Health in Developing Countries* (Washington, DC: National Academy Press).

United Nations Development Programme (UNDP) (1993) *Human Development Report 1993* (Oxford and New York: Oxford University Press).

—— (1994) *Human Development Report 1994* (Oxford and New York: Oxford University Press).

—— (1995) *Human Development Report 1995* (Oxford and New York: Oxford University Press).

—— (1996) *Human Development Report 1996* (Oxford and New York: Oxford University Press).

—— (1999) *Human Development Report 1999* (Oxford and New York: Oxford University Press).

Williams, Bernard (1987) 'The Standard of Living: Interests and Capabilities', in G. Hawthorne (ed.), *The Standard of Living* (Cambridge: Cambridge University Press).

Williams, Joan (1999) *Unbending Gender: Why Family and Work Conflict and what to Do about it* (New York: Oxford University Press).

....
3
....

Gender Justice, Human Rights, and Neo-liberal Economic Policies

Diane Elson

There is widespread and deepening attention to the promotion of democracy and the fulfilment of human rights in ways that recognize the importance of gender justice. But there is also widespread and deepening concern that neo-liberal economic policies are creating a disabling environment for women's enjoyment of human rights. This chapter explores the interconnections between neo-liberal economic policies and women's substantive enjoyment of human rights and develops some ideas on what a 'rights-based approach to development' might mean for women. It looks at the intersections of two different discourses—that of human rights and that of economic efficiency—and examines the experience of women, especially poor women, in the era of neo-liberal economic policies. It considers alternative approaches to economic policy that would provide a more enabling environment for social justice for poor women.

Human Rights and Economic Resources

The Universal Declaration of Human Rights makes the moral claim that human rights belong equally to everyone by virtue of being human, and sets out the content of these rights, as recognized by the members of the United Nations. Moreover, in Article 28, the Declaration states that 'Everyone is entitled to a social and international order in which the rights and freedoms set forth in this Declaration can be fully realized'. In practical terms, human rights can be seen as claims to 'a set of social arrangements—norms, institutions, laws, an enabling economic environment—that can best secure enjoyment of these rights' (UNDP, 2000: 73). It is the obligation of everyone to contribute to such a set of arrangements. As Article 29 of the Universal Declaration of Human Rights puts it, 'Everyone has duties to the community in which alone the free and full development of his personality is possible' (where 'his' of course must be read to include 'her'). Ratification of a human rights treaty stemming from the Declaration places a government under a specific obligation to protect, promote, and fulfil the rights specified in that treaty.

All human rights require resources for their fulfilment. This is just as true of the rights specified in the Covenant on Civil and Political Rights (such as the right not to be held in slavery, subject to torture, subjected to arbitrary arrest or arbitrary interference), as of those specified in the Covenant on Economic, Social, and Cultural Rights (such as the right to social security and an adequate standard of living). Enjoyment of so-called negative freedoms depends on well-resourced systems of law and order, financed by taxation, just as much as enjoyment of so-called positive freedoms, such as the right to education, depends on well-resourced educational systems, financed by taxation. Resources, however, are not unlimited. Moreover, they can be used in a variety of alternative ways. So any human society has to have ways of setting priorities for resource use and of judging the desirability of alternative ways of using resources, recognizing that in many circumstances there are trade-offs between achievements of different goals within a limited period of time. Economists of all persuasions have emphasized this and have stressed that attention has to be paid to the effectiveness of different ways of using resources to attain human goals, including the realization of human rights.

Human rights discourse does not focus on issues of priorities and trade-offs. Instead it emphasizes the indivisibility of human rights (see, for instance, statement by Mary Robinson, UN High Commissioner for Human Rights, UNDP, 2000: 113). So there is often a gap in communication. However, the *Human Development Report 2000* on human rights and human development (UNDP, 2000) suggests it is possible to bridge that gap if we can agree that the idea of the indivisibility of human rights should not be seen as a claim that setting priorities and recognizing trade-offs do not apply to the realization of human rights. Rather, it should be seen as a claim that there is no hierarchy of human rights as ultimate goals: they are all equally valuable and mutually reinforcing. The idea of indivisibility is also an assertion that the procedures for setting priorities for resource use and for judging the effectiveness of resource use must incorporate principles of respect for all human rights. They should be procedures that take as their starting point Article 1 of the Universal Declaration of Human Rights 'All human beings are born free and equal in dignity and rights. They are endowed with reason and conscience and should act to one another in a spirit of brotherhood' (understanding 'brotherhood' to mean 'human solidarity'). The indivisibility of human rights means that measures to protect, promote, and fulfil any particular right should not create obstacles to the protection, promotion, and fulfilment of any other human right.

It is easier to bridge the gap between discourses of human rights and resource allocation if we bear in mind that the fulfilment of human rights is a complex process unfolding over time, not a single legislative act at a moment in time. The Preamble to Universal Declaration of Human Rights recognizes this in its references to 'progressive measures, national and international, to secure their universal and effective recognition and observance'. The Covenant on Economic, Social, and Cultural Rights further elaborates the idea of realization over time, using the phrase 'with a view to achieving progressively'. It is sometimes thought that 'progressive realization' only applies to economic, social, and cultural rights, but I would suggest that the fulfilment of civil and political rights can also be seen as a process of progressive realization, even though this wording is not found in the Covenant. For instance, periodic elections with universal suffrage and secret ballots are a prerequisite for the realization of the right to take part in the government of your country, directly or through freely chosen representatives. But they do not ensure that every citizens' concerns are equally included. Achieving a situation in which 'the will of the people shall be the basis for the authority of government', rather than, say, the will of powerful transnational corporations, is much more complex. Human rights treaties place governments under an obligation to end violations of human rights immediately as far as possible; and to set in motion arrangements that will lead to clear reductions in violations and a deepening of the enjoyment of human rights over time. This applies as much to arrangements that govern the allocation of resources as to those that ensure equality before the law. The Declaration of Human Rights, and the treaties stemming from it, make it clear that governments and all other organizations and individuals have a duty to contribute to the creation of an enabling economic environment for the enjoyment of human rights.

The Neo-liberal Economic Environment

The neo-liberal agenda, which began in the 1970s, and came to dominance from the early 1980s, presumes that the best way to give substance to human rights is to reduce the role of the state, liberate entrepreneurial energy, achieve economic efficiency, and promote faster economic growth. Some governments, notably the US government led by Ronald Reagan and the UK government led by Margaret Thatcher, embraced this agenda of their own volition; but many governments in the South had it thrust upon them as the condition for more loans from the IMF and World Bank in the context of the debt crisis of the early 1980s. The neo-liberal economic agenda centres on strengthening private property and profit-driven markets and retrenching the state. Almost everywhere in the world, the rising trend in the ratio of public expenditure to national income has come to an end since the mid-1980s (World Bank, 1997). It has marginally increased in OECD countries and Sub-Saharan Africa; fallen in the Middle East and Latin America; and stayed more or less the same in East Asia. In Latin America and Africa, shares of expenditures on health and education in national budgets fell in the 1980s. Moreover in those regions, public expenditure levels in the 1980s also fell significantly in real terms and, in countries with rapid population growth, there was a decline in real expenditure per person. Such cutbacks led to deterioration in social programmes in many countries (UN, 1999: 52). The emphasis in fiscal and monetary policy was 'sound' finance, irrespective of social costs. Public assets were transferred to private ownership (although they were often run by the same social elite, now operating as business people rather than as officials). Throughout the world, the regulation of markets was changed to permit businesses to move goods, services, and finance around the world much more easily and speedily. At the same time permanent labour migration declined, in large part because of increased restriction by developed countries against labour mobility from developing countries. New forms of impermanent migration, offering reduced rights, developed, and there was an increase in undocumented migration (UN, 1999: 31).

The neo-liberal policy regime is described by its proponents as an agenda of liberalization and stabilization—persuasive words, for it is hard to get a hearing for economic agendas which say they will promote authoritarianism and instability. But critics charge that the underlying effect has been to assert new disciplines on those who do not own capital (see Gill, 2001). Very high rates of inflation are indeed an important problem for poor people, but so are very low rates of inflation, which generally denote stagnant employment opportunities. Moreover, inflation can be brought under control in a number of ways, with a varying balance between cutting expenditure on public services important to poor people and raising taxation on the incomes of rich people. (For more discussion, see Taylor, 1991).

It is important to distinguish between two kinds of advocates of neo-liberalism: fundamentalists and pragmatists. Fundamentalists, such as Hayek, believe that the state is inevitably the key threat to liberty; that free enterprise is good in itself, not only for the growth it will bring; that markets are realms of freedom, and that promotion of entrepreneurship and innovation is not only key to efficiency and growth but is also good in itself. Taxation is a kind of expropriation and must be minimized (along with public expenditure). Government budgets should be balanced. There should be no discretion in fiscal and monetary policy. Rather such policies should be governed by rules built into the constitution, such as the requirement to ensure that the government budget is always in balance and that the money supply does not expand faster than a stipulated rate (see Gill, 2001). For fundamentalists, empirical evidence on outcomes is less relevant because neo-liberal policies are good in themselves. Neo-liberalism widens opportunities. Everyone can be an entrepreneur if they so choose.

Pragmatists emphasize 'optimality' rather than entrepreneurship. 'Optimality' consists of getting maximum output from a set of inputs, with the composition of output determined by the preferences of those who will consume the output ('consumer sovereignty'). Human labour is treated as an input, on the same footing as machinery, raw materials, and land. The operational criterion of success is the rate of growth of output. Private enterprise and market relations are judged to be better, on the whole, at promoting this kind of efficiency. The majority of mainstream economists are pragmatists.

In principle, pragmatists recognize that both states and markets can fail to achieve economic efficiency, but during the 1980s and early 1990s, state failure was identified by many mainstream economists as the more serious problem (for more guidance to the relevant literature, see Toye, 1987). Pragmatists tend to believe that the macroeconomic policy framework should be determined by well-trained technocrats. They are responsive to evidence that policies are not producing growth, that financial crises are occurring, and that poverty is deepening, but dispute about whether this is really the result of the polices or of failure to implement them properly, or external events like bad weather. Pragmatists are willing to allow the importance of public goods and a bigger role for the state.

Evidence of the shift to pragmatism at the World Bank can be seen in the changing stance on fees for public education. In the mid-1980s, World Bank economists developed an economic model showing that, where there is excess demand for education, charging fees at all levels of education would be good from both an equity and efficiency perspective (Psacharopoulos *et al.*, 1986). Introduction of such charges for primary education was made a condition of loans to several countries. Subsequently the Bank distanced itself from such charges and the emphasis has switched to community participation in the provision of education (Fine and Rose, 2001: 167). Community participation also comes at a price: in many poor countries, it means spending time to construct school facilities or growing crops to finance the teachers' salaries.

The World Bank has so far been more pragmatic than the International Monetary Fund (Elson and Cagatay, 2000). But both strongly support 'free enterprise' globalization, and a policy of 'grow first, redistribute after'. Both organizations talked in the late 1990s about the importance of citizen participation in decision-making, about local level allocation of public expenditure (here citizens are allowed to discipline officials and politicians), but not in the determination of the parameters of macroeconomic policy (e.g. how much public expenditure there should be in total). At this level, citizens, officials, and politicians must all be disciplined by market forces and bow to the technocratic economic consensus about what will promote growth of GDP and economic efficiency (Bakker, 2001; Elson and Cagatay, 2000).

The main intersection between neo-liberal economic discourse and that of human rights is in terms of Article 17 of the Universal Declaration of Human Rights: 'Everyone has the right to own property alone as well as in association with others. No one shall be arbitrarily deprived of his property'. The right to own property is construed in neo-liberal thinking as entailing the right to sell your property; and the right to use it to make a profit by employing other people. In some strands of neo-liberal thinking, taxation and government regulations that reduce profits are interpreted as arbitrary deprivations of property. Concerns about poverty and inequality can be dealt with, neo-liberals assume, by encouraging better-off people to give to the poor and by encouraging governments to introduce measures to redistribute some output, being careful to ensure that they do not jeopardize incentives for economic growth. Thus there is no direct link between most of the rights specified in the Declaration of Human Rights and the neo-liberal criteria for judging resource allocation arrangements. The best resource allocation arrangements from a neo-liberal viewpoint are those that maximize economic growth and encourage private enterprise. This will, it is supposed, indirectly support the right to an adequate standard of living (Article 25) by increasing the availability of resources. It is proposed by pragmatic neo-liberals that links can be created between greater availability of resources and the enjoyment of human rights by setting targets for poverty reduction and for enjoyment of health and education; and by drawing up plans to achieve these targets with the participation of poor people. However, the post-Washington consensus emphasis on participation in public expenditure planning has been argued to be shallow and superficial, focusing only on consultation about how to allocate additional funds between different services, and not on consultation about the overall macroeconomic strategy (Cheru, 2001; Elson and Cagatay, 2000).

The neo-liberal objective has been to reduce poverty through participation in markets wherever possible; and to provide social safety nets for those who fall out of market-based prosperity (a common thread in the World Bank *World Development Reports* 1990 and 2000). Access is privatized in the sense that the main way in which people are expected to obtain the resources required to support human life is via private production for sale and the purchase of the goods and services they need. Access to a livelihood is privatized in several ways—privatization of public enterprises, contracting out of public services, reduction in the social rights of employees in the name of flexibility and efficiency, dissolution of social arrangements for sharing agricultural work under the pressure of commercialization, privatization of land. Access to publicly provided services such as health, education, and water is made dependent on ability to pay through the introduction of fees for use. Provision for old age and ill health is privatized through privatization of insurance—a privatization of risk. Credit is privatized through financial 'liberalization' both nationally and internationally. There is a less visible privatization that comes from transferring costs of providing care from the public sector to households and communities. Neo-liberal policies find it hard to take account of non-monetary costs and benefits of any policy change. Fiscal and monetary policy (which is a key determinant of the incomes generated by market exchange) is privatized, in the sense that the arbiters of policy are private financial institutions buying and selling government bonds, rather than elected representatives and social partners (such as trade unions, farmers associations, community organizations). All relies on the unspoken and invisible ultimate safety net of women's unpaid work (see Bakker, 2001; Elson, 2001; *World Development*, special issue, 28/7, 2000).

Alternatives to the Neo-liberal Agenda

The optimism about the neo-liberal agenda has been challenged by many researchers and NGOs. UNICEF was in the forefront in sponsoring studies that investigated the social impact of this agenda, with a particular focus on the well-being of poor children. Widespread evidence was found of deterioration of the nutritional status of children in poor countries (Cornia *et al.*, 1987). Moreover, neo-liberal economic polices have in many cases not delivered improved economic growth. Economic growth in the 1980s and 1990s has been much lower in most regions than that achieved in the 1950s and 1960s in the era of regulated markets and Keynesian macroeconomics (Singh and Zammit, 2000). In the poorest countries per capita GDP has actually declined. A recent study comparing the annual average growth rate in the period 1980–2000 with that in the period 1960–80, for the countries that were poorest at the beginning of the two periods, reveals a change to a decline of 0.5 per cent a year in the later period, compared to an increase of 1.9 per cent in the earlier period (Weisbrot *et al.*, 2001). The same study found that progress in increasing life expectancy, reducing infant mortality, and enrolling children in school all slowed down, comparing the later period with the earlier period.

One response to such evidence is to argue that, despite the negative impacts of the neo-liberal agenda, there was no alternative set of policies that was economically sustainable. If countries had massive debts which they were unable to service, and were on the verge of bankruptcy, then they had to cut government expenditure, goes the argument. Raising taxes, it is suggested, would have discouraged the foreign investment they needed. Neo-liberal policies were a necessary response to the unsustainable policies of the 1970s, which had resulted in widespread economic crisis.

An alternative reading, on which this chapter is premised, is that the debt crisis itself was a result of the neo-liberal agenda rather than a response to the neo-liberal agenda. The roots of the debt crisis lie in the decisions taken in the 1970s about how to adjust to the huge OPEC-inspired rises in the price of oil in 1973 and 1979. One possibility was to recycle the massive additional dollar earnings of oil-exporting countries to oil-importing countries via a low-conditionality facility at the IMF. Such a facility did operate in 1974 and 1975, enabling countries with oil-related balance of payments difficulties to borrow from the IMF at below market rates of interest, with few strings attached (Killick, 1984: 135). Indeed, in the years 1973–4, almost two-thirds of the resources provided by the IMF involved only low conditionality (Killick, 1984: 160). However, under pressure from the USA, the main emphasis was placed on recycling via the emerging private international financial market, to the enormous benefit of US, European, and Japanese banks.

This international market turned out to be very different from the competitive market depicted in neo-classical economics textbooks and the over-selling of loans by private banks was a major factor in the evolution of the debt crisis (Loxley, 1997). A further factor was the monetary policies of the Reagan and Thatcher governments which deepened the recession of the early 1980s, depriving indebted countries of markets for their exports. Moreover, when the debt crisis broke in the early 1980s, the strategy for managing it, heavily influenced by the US Treasury, was designed primarily to meet the needs of private creditors: 'a lender-of-last-resort function designed to keep the Northern banking system stable' (Devlin, 1989). In addition, the strings attached to IMF loans were tightened and by 1980 more than three-quarters of IMF lending was high-conditionality lending (Killick, 1984: 160). There were always critics pointing out that the oil price rises and the debt crisis were collective problems and needed internationally equitable solutions. One of the most prominent, the Canadian economist Gerry Helleiner, raised the issue of the risks involved in recycling petrodollars through the private market as early as 1977; and urged that contingency plans against a recession be prepared (Loxley, 1997: 140). His warnings went unheeded.

Helleiner, and other heterodox economists, repeatedly proposed alternative ways of dealing with the debt crisis, including alternative ways of restructuring economies of debtor countries (for further discussion, see Cornia *et al.*, 1987; Culpeper *et al.*, 1997). But instead of a reduction in the exposure of indebted countries to private international financial markets, this exposure was increased. Opening up the domestic capital market to foreign lenders (capital account liberalization) became a standard condition of IMF lending, in the mistaken belief that this would promote efficient resource allocation. Moreover governments of indebted countries were encouraged to take responsibility not only for public external debt but also for the external debt of the country's private firms. Take the case of Chile, analysed by Meller (1991), where almost two-thirds of the Chilean external debt in the early 1980s belonged to the private sector, especially to Chilean banks. When the debt crisis hit Chile in 1983, foreign banks pressured the government into providing a government guarantee for the debts of Chilean banks, bailing out both the foreign creditors and high-income Chilean bank shareholders, at an annual cost of about 4 per cent of GDP in 1982–5. At the same time there were sharp cuts in public expenditures that benefited poorer groups, with expenditure on health, housing, and education reduced by 20 per cent per capita.

The Chilean case also illustrates another key feature of the implementation of the neo-liberal agenda in the years since the debt crisis: a propensity to preserve the position of the rich at the expense of that of lower income groups. Research by the UN World Institute for Development Economics Research has shown a widespread pattern of widening inequality in household incomes in many countries in the 1980s and 1990s (WIDER, 1999). Alternative responses to the debt crisis have repeatedly been suggested by heterodox economists since the early 1980s (e.g. Killick, 1984; Helleiner, 1986; Cornia *et al.*, 1987). They typically call for less deflationary macroeconomic policies, with more external financing and a longer period for adjustment; and a broad redirection of a country's resources to support the production and consumption of poorer social groups. Such alternatives require changes at both national and international levels. They are economically feasible. The problem has been building political support for them in a climate dominated by the neo-liberal agenda and the interests of private financial institutions. They have typically been framed in terms of equity rather than in terms of human rights. The analysis that follows here is predicated upon some such alternative, but is framed to make a stronger connection to human rights. Equity objectives may be treated as optional, but respect for human rights is obligatory. A human rights framework may thus offer new opportunities for changing the agenda. In a widely cited article on economic and social rights, Beetham (1995) has suggested that the enjoyment of economic and social rights has indeed been made more precarious from the early 1980s onwards by the displacement of collective choice by market forces, and the growing influence of sentiment in financial markets. He also points to the fact that human rights language provides a more authoritative and urgent discourse than 'welfare' discourses and 'identifies the deprived themselves as potential agents of social change, as active claimants of rights'. It is in the hope that a human rights focus may make a difference that the analysis here is presented.

Women's Enjoyment of Human Rights in the Neo-liberal Era

There has long been criticism of the implications of neo-liberal economic polices for poor women in poor countries, much of it with an emphasis on World Bank and International Monetary Fund stabilization and structural adjustment programmes (see reviews of the empirical literature by Beneria, 1995; Summerfield and Aslanbeigui, 1998; Elson, 1995*b*; for important case studies, see Moser, 1992;

Brown and Kerr, 1997; for critiques of the underlying economic theory, see Elson, 1991, 1995a).

There are many problems in assessing the impact of particular policy programmes on women as compared to men. There is still a lack of timely, reliable, sex-disaggregated statistics for many parts of the world. Moreover, it is intrinsically difficult to examine causal links between policies and events that follow their introduction. The policy may not have been fully implemented. Generally there are also other significant events taking place at the same time—such as changes in social and political forces and changes in the weather. It is hard to allow for the effects of these. Economists often try to construct a 'counterfactual' as a benchmark; this is a 'best guess' about what would have happened if the policy had not been introduced. But this is a matter of judgement, not an exact science. Should the counter-factual be the continuation of the debt crisis which often precipitated the introduction of neo-liberal economic policies in countries in the South, or should it be the improvements which could have been intro-duced by an alternative set of economic polices which hypothetically could have created a more enabling environment? Not surprisingly, neo-liberal economists tend to choose the former, and those who are critical of neo-liberal policies, the latter. There is also disagreement about what should be regarded as parameters and what should be regarded as variables. An individual country may have to take debt repayment as an inescapable obligation but the creditors have more scope for choice about whether to exact repayments. Interpretations of the results of empirical studies are also influenced by the theor-etical framework used. Neo-liberal economists who use an economic theory which does not take into account gender differences within households, or the role of unpaid care work in creating and sustain-ing the labour force, or the cultural persistence of gender divisions of labour, tend not to see any reason why neo-liberal polices should have an adverse impact on women (Elson, 1991, 1995a).

Pragmatic neo-liberal economists are becoming more aware of the importance of gender in economics, as demonstrated in the World Bank report, *Engendering Development* (World Bank, 2001). This report focuses mainly on charting the relationship between gender inequality and economic development, arguing that reducing gender inequality promotes economic development, and promoting economic development promotes gender equality. It devotes only a few pages to considering the implications of neo-liberal policies for women, focusing on the impact of structural adjustment policies in Sub-Saharan Africa and Latin America and the Caribbean. It reviews some arguments and evidence on how these policies harm gender equality and also some arguments and evidence on how adjustment promotes gender equality. It concludes: 'While there is evidence to support both sides of the debate about the impact of structural adjustment, on balance the evidence suggests that females' absolute status and gender equality improved, not deteriorated over the adjustment period' (World Bank, 2001: 215).

This conclusion is based on the argument that over the adjusting period girls' schooling generally rose relative to boys; that female life expectancy continued to rise, with the exception of Sub-Saharan Africa; and that the gender gap in wages has decreased in Latin America and Sub-Saharan Africa over the adjustment period. It also claims that in Sub-Saharan Africa and Latin America and the Caribbean gender equality of rights either stayed the same or improved between 1985 and 1990.

It is to the credit of the report that it does raise the issue of links between economic polices and women's rights, but it does so in a very cursory way. The report discusses gender equality in rights in its first chapter, comparing gender equality in rights in 1985 and 1990, using data from Charles Humana's *World Human Rights Guide* (Humana, 1986, 1992). Humana presents evaluations of the enjoyment of forty dimensions of human rights, including political and legal equality for women; social and economic equality for women; and equality of men and women in marriage and divorce proceedings. He does this by collecting human rights information from the United Nations and other international institutions, governments, NGOs, research institutions, and the media for as many countries as possible. On the basis of this he makes a judgement about the extent to which the right in question is violated in that country. This judgement is then represented as a grade on a 0–3 scale. A '0' represents a constant pattern of violation of human rights; while a '3' represents unqualified respect for human rights. The grades were not available for any other years at the time of the World Bank research. The World Bank report uses these grades to look at gender equality in rights on a regional basis, weighting the grade for each country by its population (World Bank, 2001: 4, 38–41). No region enjoys the highest grade for any of the three gender-sensitive dimensions of human rights under consideration.

With respect to gender equality in political and legal rights, the report finds that gender equality is highest in the OECD countries and has not changed in the period 1985–90. Next highest is Europe and Central Asia (formerly centrally planned economies), but in this region there was a deterioration over the period to levels comparable with South Asia. Latin America and the Caribbean, in contrast, have enjoyed an increase over the period to almost the same level as the OECD. South Asia has seen virtually no change. After South Asia in terms of levels of rights, as judged by Humana, comes Sub-Saharan Africa, where there has been an increase in gender equality. Middle East and North Africa come next, and are judged to have experienced a deterioration. Last in the ranking is East Asia and the Pacific, where gender equality is judged to have improved somewhat over the period. So the picture is mixed, with two regions apparently staying the same, three regions improving, and two regions deteriorating.

Turning to gender equality in social and economic rights, Humana's gradings shows a different pattern, both in terms of rankings and changes over time. The OECD again ranks highest and has not experienced any change. Next comes East Asia and the Pacific, which has shown a small increase. The formerly centrally planned economies of Eastern Europe and Central Asia have fallen from second place to more or less the same level as Latin America and the Caribbean, where there has been only a slight increase. Middle East and North Africa are judged to come next and to have experienced a deterioration. Then comes Sub-Saharan Africa, with no change, and finally South Asia, with a small increase. The World Bank report sums this up by saying 'there was little, if any, improvement in gender equality in these rights between 1985 and 1990' (World Bank, 2001: 38). Since these are the rights most directly linked with neo-liberal economic polices, one might have expected more attention to be paid to the deterioration of these rights in two regions which have introduced neo-liberal policies—Eastern Europe and Central Asia and Middle East and North Africa. But since the World Bank assessment in Chapter 5 is limited to structural adjustment policies in Latin America and the Caribbean and Sub-Saharan Africa, the regions of deterioration are ignored. There are in any case a number of problems with Humana's system of evaluating women's human rights, which are discussed below.

Equality in marriage and divorce rights appears to vary across the regions more than gender equality in the other two categories of rights. There are judged to have been improvements in the OECD (which has the highest ranking); a deterioration in Eastern Europe and Central Asia, which nevertheless still ranks second; a big increase in Latin America and the Caribbean, which ranks third; no change in East Asia and the Pacific, which ranks fourth. There have apparently been improvements in the other regions, which now rank as follows, fifth, Sub-Saharan Africa; sixth, Middle East and North Africa and, seventh, South Asia. So in relation to marriage and divorce rights, most regions have apparently seen an improvement.

Overall, the most striking change in the second half of the 1980s is judged to have been in the formerly centrally planned economies, where gender equality is judged to have fallen from its formerly high level on all the three indicators. The second important pattern shown by the indicators is that gender equality in economic and social rights is apparently lower than for the other two types of rights and has shown only slight improvements in only two regions.

There are, however, many problems in using Humana's grades in this way. Humana's grading system is inherently problematic because it reduces complex and multi-dimensional social practices to a single scale, on the basis of subjective judgements using information which is not revealed. Humana does not discuss exactly what statistics and other evidence he uses; nor how he weights different aspects of the rights he considers. For instance, in his comments on the grades assigned for equality in economic and social rights, he sporadically mentions education, employment, and earnings, and female circumcision; but there is no indication of how he weights these components or how reliable the evidence is about them or what thresholds he uses. Nor is there any discussion of why female circumcision is singled out for attention when other forms of gender-based violence are not mentioned. In addition, it is not clear how he treats the issue of how far a formal legal right is actually enjoyed in practice by the majority of women in a country. The inherent problems of Humana's grading system are compounded by the World Bank in using them to construct population-weighted regional averages. Such averages are dominated by the grades assigned to the biggest countries and obscure government responsibility for ensuring there is no discrimination against women.

In any case, indicators of gender equality in rights do not reveal whether an improvement in gender equality has been achieved as a result of equalizing up, so that women's position comes closer to that of men; or equalizing down, so that men's position comes closer to that of women. There have been concerns expressed that neo-liberal economic policies lead to harmonizing down, especially in the labour market. We need information not only about the gap between men and women in their enjoyment of rights, but also the level of rights they enjoy.

It is clear that changes in the enjoyment of specific human rights needs to be investigated using empirical research for specific countries, and if possible for specific groups of men and women. There is reason to be concerned that it is poor women who are particularly adversely affected by neo-liberal policies, either directly in the present, or in terms of adversely affecting the prospects for the progressive realization of their economic and social rights. Unfortunately, available empirical evidence of changes over time is rarely systematically disaggregated by gender and class. Here we look at women's enjoyment of the economic and social rights specified in Articles 23–6 of the Universal Declaration of Human Rights in the 1980s and 1990s, the neo-liberal years. We make considerable use of two recent publications, a report on progress towards realization of women's rights issued by United Nations Development Fund for Women (UNIFEM, 2000) and a report called *Social Watch*, prepared for an international network of NGOs and edited by Roberto Bissio of the Instituto Del Tercer Mundo, Uruguay (Bissio, 1999). Where possible we investigate whether trends indicate sustained progress towards a full enjoyment of these rights. This rests on the judgement, explained earlier, that there was nothing inevitable about the emergence of the economic crisis of the early 1980s; and in particular, nothing inevitable about the measures taken to deal with the debt burden of countries in the South. What happened was in large measure due to decisions of key players on how to govern the international economy, and alternative ways of governing the international economy were always available (for more discussion of this see, for instance, Culpeper *et al.*, 1997).

   Article 23 of the Declaration of Human Rights deals with employment rights. It begins by stating that 'Everyone has the right to work, to free choice of employment' (reflecting the prevailing gender relations of the mid-twentieth century, it does not recognize unpaid care work as work). It is clear that women's participation in the labour force has increased in most parts of the world in the 1980s and 1990s (UN, 1999: 8). Of course, this was happening in many countries in the 1950s, 1960s, and 1970s before the major turn to neo-liberal polices. However, there is evidence that the trend was strengthened in countries which introduced structural adjustment programmes (Cagatay and Özler, 1995). In particular, there have been dramatic increases in countries which have reoriented their manufacturing industries to the world market and the service sector has continued to absorb large numbers of women. In a very wide range of countries, women's share of paid employment in industry and services increased in the period 1985–97 (UNIFEM, 2000: 73–5). The exception is Eastern Europe, where the transition from central planning to market-based allocation of resources has been accompanied in many countries by falls in female participation rates, though this may partly reflect an 'informalization' of women's work and reduced visibility in labour force statistics (UNIFEM, 2000: 73).

Women's increased participation in the labour force does not necessarily mean that women enjoy various rights specified in Article 23, such as 'just and favourable conditions of work', 'protection against unemployment', 'the right to equal pay for equal work', 'the right to just and favourable remuneration ... supplemented by ... social protection', and the 'right to form and join trade unions'. The lack of all of these rights in many export-oriented factories has been well-documented (UN, 1999).

In industry and services, women on average typically only earned about 78 per cent of what men earned in the late 1990s (UNIFEM, 2000: 92). There is some evidence that the gap has narrowed in a number of countries during the 1980s and 1990s. Data from the ILO suggest the gap has fallen in twenty-two out of the twenty-nine countries for which the ILO has data (UNIFEM, 2000: 94). Of these, none are in Africa and eleven are in Latin America. Studies listed in the report on *Engendering Development* (World Bank, 2001: appendix 3) suggest a fall in two countries in Africa and eight countries in Latin America. As is clear from this, these two publications do not always agree on the countries in which this has happened. The UNIFEM report has the gender gap widening in Chile and Venezuela, while the World Bank report indicates that it has narrowed. The UNIFEM report cautions that data on the gender wage gap in developing countries is likely to reflect mainly the earnings of those in full-time 'formal' employment, as much informal employment is not captured by statistical surveys in many countries. It reports that studies by the international network, Women in Informal Employment Globalising and Organising, suggest that the gender wage gap is likely to be higher in informal employment. The evidence does not seem sufficiently robust for the weight placed on it by the World Bank report, as an important piece of evidence that structural adjustment has not had an adverse effect on gender equality in Latin America and Africa. In so far as the gap has been narrowing, it is more likely to reflect mainly the experience of better-educated and better-off women than that of poor women. Rapid economic growth is not necessarily associated with a lower gender wages gap. In East and South East Asia, the countries with the fastest growth have had the biggest gender wages gaps (Seguino, 2000).

Many women in all parts of the world have lost employment, through displacement by cheaper imports (as a result of trade liberalization), or recession, or financial crisis (UN, 1999; Lim, 2000; Kucera and Milberg, 2000) and governments have typically given priority to the problems of unemployed men. Many jobs have been reorganized to make them more 'flexible', but 'flexibility' has turned out to mean a weakening of labour standards rather than a better balance between work and life (Standing, 1999). There has been 'feminization' of employment not only in terms of increases in women's overall share of paid employment but also in the sense that the labour market conditions of men have deteriorated and become more like the precarious labour market conditions that have typically characterized many 'women's jobs'. There has been a decline in the proportion of jobs that have security of employment, rights against unfair dismissal, pension rights, health insurance rights, maternity rights. There has been rapid growth in 'informal employment' which lacks social protection. It is estimated that well over half of the urban jobs in Africa and Asia are informal, and a quarter in Latin America and the Caribbean. The share is higher for new jobs, with as many as 83 per cent of new jobs in Latin America and 93 per cent in Africa being informal (Charmes, 1998). Women's share of informal employment is typically higher than their share of formal employment.

Women's increased participation in the labour market does mean that barriers which formerly excluded women from paid employment are crumbling. And that women's right to paid work is increasingly being recognized, but one must be cautious in interpreting this as evidence that women have 'free choice of employment'. The choices that poor women make are constrained by the pressures of poverty. Case studies document the way that neo-liberal policies have forced poor women in poor countries to accept whatever paid work they could get, despite deteriorating pay and conditions, in order to feed and clothe their families in the context of rising prices and falling male employment (González de la Rocha, 2000; Moser, 1996).

Article 24 of the Declaration states that 'Everyone has the right to rest and leisure, including reasonable limitation of working hours and periodic holidays with pay'. The impact of neo-liberal policies on women's enjoyment of free time has been a major area of concern. Very long hours of work and enforced overtime have been documented in many export-oriented factories in developing countries. Moreover there is reason to expect that the time that has to be spent in poor families on unpaid work caring for family members will have to be increased to compensate for cutbacks in expenditure on public services. This will be intensified by strategies to reduce expenditure as prices of food and other basic goods rise as a result of cutbacks in subsidies and devaluation of the currency. Shopping around and buying unprocessed food (which is cheaper but takes more time to prepare) both take up more time. Unless men and boys increase their participation in unpaid care work in poor families, the time that poor women and girls have for rest and leisure is likely to fall. This is hard to document since the collection of time use data is in its early stages in most developing countries. Case studies in a range of countries have documented the time pressures that poor women in poor countries face and the way in which neo-liberal policies intensify those pressures (Floro, 1995; Moser, 1992; Elson, 1995*b*; Zohir, 1998). The squeeze on the time of adult women may mean that demands on daughters' time intensifies—with adverse implications for their schooling (see Moser, 1992; Senapaty, 1997). There is no sign of these pressures leading to men playing a substantially greater role in unpaid care work in households.

The right to an adequate standard of living is addressed by Article 25, which makes specific reference to health, food, clothing, housing, medical care, and social services. It also specifies that everyone has a right to social security in the event of 'unemployment, sickness, disability, widowhood, old age or other lack of livelihood'; and states that 'motherhood and childhood are entitled to special care and assistance'. One important dimension of an adequate standard of living is money income. The World Bank produces statistics on the number of people living on less than one US dollar a day. In 1987 there were 1,227 million people in this position; by 1993 the number had increased to 1,314 million (Bissio, 1999: 43). Of course, population as a whole has been growing at the same time. Overall, the proportion of people living in extreme poverty fell only slightly over this period, from 30.1 per cent to 29.4 per cent. In three regions the proportion rose: in Latin America and the Caribbean from 22.0 to 23.5 per cent; in Sub-Saharan Africa, from 38.5 per cent to 39.1 per cent; in Europe and Central Asia from 0.6 per cent to 3.5 per cent (Bissio, 1999: 43). During this period the proportion living in extreme poverty in Asia declined somewhat, but this changed in the late 1990s, as financial crisis hit living standards: 'progress slowed temporarily in some Asian countries in the late 1990s, and ground to a halt or reversed in others' (IMF *et al.*, 2000: 6). There are no comprehensive statistics on what proportion of these poor people are women and girls, making it hard to come to conclusions on the degree to which there has been a feminization of income poverty. There has been a growth in the proportion of households which are female-headed, but the evidence is mixed on whether these households are disproportionately poor. There are ways of measuring the degree to which women and girls are over-represented among poor people, using data from household surveys, but neither the World Bank nor national statistical offices have attached any priority to producing such measures (for further discussion, see UNIFEM, 2000: 95–6).

Access to social services is another important dimension of the right
to an adequate standard of living. There is widespread agreement
that health workers with midwifery skills are key to reducing maternal mortality. Data by region on the proportion of births attended
by skilled health personnel in 1988 and 1998 shows little progress
in Latin America and the Caribbean (from 70 to 77 per cent) and in
Asia, excluding Indian and China (from 29 to 32 per cent). In the
Middle East and North Africa progress was more substantial (from
48 to 61 per cent) but in Sub-Saharan Africa, the proportion fell
(from 50 to 46 per cent) (IMF *et al.*, 2000: 14). Country-level data
covering all regions suggest that, in just over one-third of 132 countries in the world, there was a reduction in the proportion of births
attended by skilled health personnel from around 1990 to around
1996 (calculated from Bissio, 1999: 31–2). There has also been a
fall in access to health care in general in the same period in a wide
range of countries. In twenty developing countries out of forty-three
for which data is available, the proportion of the population with
access to health services fell (calculated from Bissio, 1999: 29). Such
a fall is likely to imply more burdens for poor women, as they have
the main responsibility for maintaining the health of other family
members. Problems in maintaining family health are compounded
when safe drinking water is unavailable. In fifteen out of sixty-two
developing countries for which data are available, the proportion of
the population with access to safe drinking water fell in the period
from around 1990 to 1995 (calculated from Bissio, 1999: 38). Poor
nutrition compounds health problems. Data from the Food and Agriculture Organization suggest that national-level food availability fell
in sixty-seven of 159 countries in the same period (calculated from
Bissio, 1999: 26–7). Child malnutrition has also increased in a third
of sixty developing countries for which data is available for the period
1990–6 (calculated from Bissio, 1999: 28). When the price of food or
health care rises, girls may be more at risk than of having their needs
unmet. A review of quantitative studies for Pakistan, India, Ghana,
Peru, Malaysia, and the Philippines concludes that 'the demand for
investment in women and girls tends to be more sensitive to changes
in prices (or costs) than demand for investment in men and boys'
(World Bank, 2001: 165).

Many people have suffered loss of livelihood in circumstances
beyond their control and have not enjoyed any social security, in contravention of Articles 22 and 25 of the Declaration. In many parts of
Sub-Saharan Africa, women farmers have been particularly hard hit
by privatization of land, as Western-style private property regimes
have been introduced at the expense of non-market systems of land

tenure. 'By conferring formal ownership on land and water, privatization has in general strengthened the control of already powerful groups over these resources to the detriment of small-scale farmers, particularly women's rights and access to resources' (UN, 1999: 40). In South-east Asia many women lost their jobs as a result of the financial crisis of the late 1990s but measures to help workers regain a livelihood were directed mainly at men.

Article 26 refers to the right to education. The enjoyment of this right is best measured in terms of educational outcomes. However cross-country data on short-run changes in the number of boys and girls, men and women, with particular types of skills and qualifications are scarce. The best that can be done is to look at enrolment rates. During the period 1980–94 the gap between girls' enrolments and boys' enrolments at primary level did indeed narrow in developing countries but in Sub-Saharan Africa this was a result of a fall in the enrolment of both boys and girls, with boys' enrolment falling further (Colclough *et al.*, 2000: 8). This evidence of equalizing down in primary education in Sub-Saharan Africa calls into question the validity of the conclusions of the World Bank's *Engendering Development* report on gender and structural adjustment. As discussed above, one of the pieces of evidence invoked to justify the conclusion that on balance females' absolute status and gender equality improved during structural adjustment was that girls' schooling rose relative to boys between 1985 and 1990 in Sub-Saharan Africa and Latin America and the Caribbean. In Sub-Saharan Africa, according to UNESCO data, the gross primary enrolment rate for girls was 68 in 1980 and 66 in 1990, while that for boys was 87 and 79 respectively (Colclough *et al.*, 2000: 8). The gap indeed narrowed—but not in a way that was consistent with the realization of the right to education of either boys or girls. It is essential to look at absolute levels of enrolment of girls, as well as at the gender gap if we want to evaluate how far girls have enjoyed the right to education in the neo-liberal era.

The World Bank report on *Engendering Development* does provide some analysis for Sub-Saharan Africa which looks at both gender gaps and absolute levels of primary and secondary enrolment, comparing so-called 'adjusting' and 'non-adjusting' countries, defined by whether the country ever took a structural adjustment loan from the World Bank. It claims that the trends are similar in both groups of countries, on the basis of population-weighted trends, implying that 'adjustment' has had no particularly adverse impact. However, there are two important limitations to this analysis. The first is that a country does not need to take a loan from the World Bank in order to introduce some neo-liberal policies. The second is that use of population-weighted averages obscures the accountability of governments for the realization of rights. The outcomes for the 'adjusters' group in Sub-Saharan Africa is dominated by what happens in Nigeria, which has by far the biggest population in that group.

If we examine progress at the country level, with respect to girls' enrolment in secondary school, the picture is far from encouraging for about a quarter of countries. UNESCO data show that girls' net enrolment in secondary school declined between 1985 and 1997 in ten out of thirty-three countries in Sub-Saharan Africa; seven out of eleven countries in Central and Western Asia; two out of twenty-one countries in Asia and the Pacific; six out of twenty-six in Latin America and the Caribbean; and six out of nine in Eastern Europe (UNIFEM, 2000: 69–71).

Overall, the picture with respect to women's enjoyment of specific rights in the neo-liberal era is not encouraging. The evidence reviewed above suggests that there has been regress rather than progress in the realization of economic and social rights in many countries, even though in some countries progress has been made.

Article 28 of the Universal Declaration of Human Rights suggests we need to go beyond an examination of individual rights to examine whether an enabling environment for the realization of rights is being constructed. Article 22 reinforces that point, stating that 'Everyone, as a member of society, has the right to social security and is entitled to the realisation, through national effort and international cooperation and in accordance with the organisation and resources of each State, of the economic, social and cultural rights indispensable for his dignity and the free development of his personality'.

The most recent *World Survey on the Role of Women in Development* (UN, 1999: ch. 5) argues that neo-liberal economic polices have transformed the public policy environment in ways that are detrimental to women. Three aspects of this are singled out for comment: a deflationary bias in macroeconomic polices; an increase in economic instability; a reduction in the ability of the state to raise resources for redistribution and social protection (i.e. social security). Deflationary bias refers to the way in which governments are pressured by financial markets to cut spending and maintain high interest rates, keeping employment and output growth below their potential. This pressure constrains policy in any country with liberalized capital markets, irrespective of whether it is in receipt of stabilization and structural adjustment loans from the IMF and World Bank. Evidence from across the regions is cited in the *World Survey* showing that low growth has more negative effects on women's 'formal' employment than on men's. Increased volatility in capital flows has resulted in 'booms' followed by financial crises in East Asia, Eastern Europe, and Latin America. Women have typically born the brunt of managing household adjustment to these crises and of cushioning their societies against the disintegrative impact of these financial shocks (Singh and Zammit, 2000; Lim, 2000; Floro and Dymski, 2000; Elson, 2001). Governments have been constrained in their ability to provide social protection because of trade liberalization, which reduces import and export taxes; and pressure from mobile capital to reduce corporate, capital gains, and income taxes. To keep budget deficits within reasonable bounds, public expenditure has had to be reduced and public services have deteriorated. There has been a 'commodization bias' in which it has been assumed that provision by the private sector is inherently better than provision by the public sector for many goods and services (Elson and Cagatay, 2000). Neo-liberal policies have increased the need for social security against market risks and at the same time reduced the capacity of states to finance this. As a result there has been a retreat (discussed elsewhere in this volume) from the objective of providing universal forms of social security to the objective of providing only narrowly targeted 'social safety nets'.

It may be objected that for the poorest women in poor countries nothing much has changed, since they have never enjoyed the benefits of good public services, stable employment, and universal social security. Moreover the systems of social protection which did exist were frequently biased in favour of men, who were assumed to be the 'breadwinners'. Women were assumed to be 'dependants' of men, and accessed benefits through husbands or other male relatives (UN, 1999; Elson and Cagatay, 2000). However, the changing direction of public policy means that the poorest women in poor countries have been deprived of even the prospect of the progressive realization of a non-discriminatory system of decent jobs and public services and broad-based social security systems. That is no longer the object of public policy in most countries. Neo-liberal economic thinking suggests that this goal is no longer attainable because of resource constraints. While there are indeed real resource constraints on the full achievement of such objectives, the impact of these is much exaggerated. Successive *Human Development Reports* have shown how much more could be done within the constraints of existing resources. It is the constraints on the raising and spending of public money which are the immediate barriers, but these are socially constructed constraints. It is the political, not the natural environment, which inhibits debt cancellation. It is free-market fundamentalism that insists on capital market liberalization.

Creating an Enabling Economic Policy Environment
for the Realization of Women's Economic
and Social Rights

One way to assist the creation of an enabling environment would
be by making a more direct link between economic and social rights
and economic policies, rather than treating economic growth as the
intermediary. A one-sided focus on economic growth obscures the fact
that there can be better realization of economic and social human
rights in countries with slow growth than those with fast growth (for
examples, see UNDP, 2000). In thinking this through, we might draw
upon the ideas of entitlements and entitlement failures developed by
Amartya Sen (1981, 1984). These ideas were developed in his work
on famine and hunger, but have a wider application, not only for
the individual but also for social systems (Elson and Cagatay, 2000;
Fine, 1997).

The Universal Declaration of Human Rights repeatedly states that
all human beings are entitled to the rights described therein. The
Declaration is a statement of moral entitlements, of rightful claims.
There is of course a huge gap for millions of people between their
moral entitlements and their practical entitlements, the entitlements
they actually enjoy. Sen gave the term 'entitlement' an economic
twist by defining a person's entitlements in terms of the resources
over which they have command: for example, 'Entitlement refers
to the set of alternative commodity bundles that a person can command in a society using the totality of rights and opportunities that
he or she faces' (Sen, 1983: 18). Sen (1981) explains how entitlements depend upon rights to inherited and legally acquired assets,
including health, strength, and skills, and property; and rights to use
this 'endowment' to produce for one's own consumption or for sale;
and rights to goods, service, and financial transfers from the state.
These comprise a system of entitlement relations. He excludes non-
entitlement transfers such as theft, pillage and plunder, and charity.
Sen's concept of entitlements thus includes both production and distribution, both market transactions and provision by the state. It is
thus a statement about entitlements that actually exist, rather than
a normative statement of moral entitlements.

Command over resources is important to Sen because of its importance to capabilities, to what people are actually able to do and be: 'On
the basis of this entitlement, a person can acquire some capabilities,
i.e. the ability to do this or that (e.g. be well-nourished), and fail
to acquire some other capabilities' (Sen, 1983: 18; see Nussbaum,

Chapter 2, for an extended discussion of capabilities). The over-arching idea is the capability to live a dignified human life, the same goal as is expressed in the Universal Declaration of Human Rights.

Sen argued that many deaths in famines occurred not because there was an overall insufficiency of food in the country as a whole but because some people were excluded from obtaining food because they could not produce it themselves, could not pay for it in the marketplace, and had no institutionalized claim on the state to provide food for them. They died because of entitlement failure. As Sen put it: 'Most cases of starvation and famines across the world arise not from people being deprived of things to which they are entitled, but from people not being entitled, in the prevailing legal system of institutional rights, to adequate means for survival.' Although entitlements were defined by Sen on an individual (micro) basis, he also gave the idea a social systemic (macro) dimension, referring to a 'network of entitlement relations' (Sen, 1981: 159). Famine occurred because entitlement failures were endemic in the prevailing social arrangements, so that episodes of bad weather or economic recessions led to a needless loss of people's ability to live a well-nourished life, which would have been prevented by a better system for sharing resources. A one-sided focus on the fall in food output obscured this important fact.

While Sen has used the idea of entitlement failure only in relation to food and the capability to be well-nourished, the concept clearly encompasses the idea of a person's inability to acquire as of right a set of goods and services that enables them to function at a basic minimum level. More generally, we might extend the idea of entitlement failures to cover all occurrences when the resources a person can obtain as of right are not sufficient to enable that person to avoid deprivation of basic capabilities. Sen himself has not defined such a list but he has referred to poverty as 'a deprivation of basic capabilities' reflected in 'premature mortality, significant undernourishment, persistent morbidity, widespread illiteracy and other failures' (Sen, 1999: 20). He argues that criteria for evaluating the enjoyment of capabilities should be generated by an open public discussion (ibid. 81). This is congruent with the approach being developed by the UN Committee on Economic, Social, and Cultural Rights, which monitors the implementation of the International Covenant on Economic, Social, and Cultural Rights (one of the key treaties which put into effect the Universal Declaration of Human Rights). In 1990, the Committee issued a General Comment on the obligations of states that are party to the covenant, stating that:

The Committee is of the view that a minimum core obligation to ensure the satisfaction of, at the very least, minimum essential levels of each of the rights is incumbent upon every State party. Thus, for example, a State party in which any significant number of individuals is deprived of essential foodstuffs, of essential primary health care, of basic shelter and housing, or of the most basic forms of education, is prima facie, failing to discharge its obligations under the Covenant. (UN, Committee on Economic, Social, and Cultural Rights, para. 10, 1990)

The UN Commission on Human Rights has urged states to 'consider identifying specific national benchmarks designed to give effect to the minimum core obligations' (UN, Commission on Human Rights, 1993). The specification of such benchmarks in open and democratic debate would provide a framework for setting priorities for resource allocation. Analysis of the system of entitlement relations would permit an identification of potential entitlement failures in relation to these benchmarks. This would form the basis for identifying measures that might be used to avoid such failures, so as to enhance the capabilities of deprived individuals. This is not so ambitious as the approach advocated by Nussbaum (Chapter 2) in terms of the capabilities to which priority attention is directed, but it is an approach which helps to focus attention on the system of rights to resources and obligations to secure these rights which must underpin any prospect of widespread enjoyment of basic capabilities.

Sen's entitlement approach has been criticized for putting too much weight on formal legal rights and not paying enough attention to the problems people with little power have in exercising their legal rights (Gasper, 1993). It has also been criticized for leaving out the informal gifts of income and property within families and kinship networks, to which people may feel they have moral entitlements (Gore, 1993). Scepticism has also been expressed about the absence from Sen's concept of entitlements of the domain of interpersonal care, for which the time and energy is mainly given by women (Staveren, 1996).

A key issue relevant to all these comments is the importance of examining the processes through which people articulate and claim their entitlements and recognize their responsibilities, both legal and moral. But in doing this it is important not lose sight of the core idea of the exercise of rights, and the dignity that comes from this. To have an entitlement implies access to an accountable process in which the discretion of decision-makers is limited. If my access to a resource is at the arbitrary discretion of a public official or dependent on the favour of a patron or the goodwill of a husband, or the price-fixing power of a monopoly supplier, then I do not get that resource as of right. Here it is useful to refer to a recent statement adopted by the UN Committee on Economic, Social, and Cultural Rights on poverty and human rights:

Critically, rights and obligations demand accountability: unless supported by a system of accountability, they can become no more than window dressing. Accordingly, the human rights approach to poverty emphasises obligations and requires that all duty-holders, including States and international organisations, are held to account for their conduct in relation to international human rights law. In its General Comment No. 9, the Committee remarks upon mechanisms of legal accountability for States parties. As for other duty-holders, they must determine which accountability mechanisms are most appropriate to their particular case. However, whatever the mechanisms of accountability, they must be accessible, transparent and effective. (UN, 2001: para. 14)

This statement usefully reminds us that rights do imply duties. These duties are clearly specified for states which are party to the Declaration, and the human rights treaties stemming from it. They are obliged to protect, promote, and fulfil human rights. They are held to account through the mechanisms of the UN Commission on Human Rights and other UN mechanisms. The problem with moral rules on interfamilial transfers, for instance, is that there may be no such clearly specified duties and no clear accountability mechanism, so although one family member may feel they have a moral right to a transfer of income, if other family members do not feel the moral obligation to make this transfer, there is no redress available. This is a particularly important issue for women who are often in a very weak position to exercise 'moral rights'. One way in which entitlement failure occurs is through 'male breadwinner bias', a bias which occurs when men are assumed to be providing for dependent women and children (Elson and Cagatay, 2000). Where this bias prevails, women are not entitled to resources in their own right, but only by virtue of their relationship to an adult male. This may fail to provide them with the necessary resources, both because of their reluctance to ask or to take, and the unwillingness or neglect of the relevant men. Some kind of formal or informal public process (which could involve the local community rather than the national government) seems essential for an entitlement to have substance. Any such process must meet the criteria of accessibility, transparency, and effectiveness.

The idea of entitlement failures (rather than market failures and bureaucratic failures) offers an alternative normative criterion for

Diane Elson

judging the effectiveness of procedures for resource allocation from a human-rights perspective. This criterion is particularly (though not only) relevant to the fulfilment of core obligations to ensure the satisfaction of at least minimum essential levels of economic and social rights. The Committee on Economic, Social, and Cultural Rights has begun to identify the core obligations arising from the minimum essential levels of the rights to food, education, and health, and it has confirmed that these core obligations are 'non-derogable'. In other words there is an obligation to fulfil these obligations right now, on the part of states and any others 'in a position to assist'. It is not permissible to 'trade off' provision of the goods and services required to fulfil these rights against an increase in the provision of some other goods and services.

In judging the effectiveness of an economic policy regime, we can examine how far the system of entitlement relations that it promotes has adequate safeguards against entitlement failures. Entitlement relations that operate through buying and selling in competitive 'liberalized' markets seem to have several advantages: if the market is competitive, access is relatively open and prices are relatively transparent. Moreover, transactions in competitive markets seem to avoid the problem of social dependence. However, the independence that markets seems to provide is an illusion, masking a many-sided dependence on many other people scattered far and wide, whose only social bond is the market. Moreover, such markets are inherently risky and volatile. There is absolutely nothing to guarantee that the prices a person gets for the goods or services they sell (including their labour) will be high enough to enable them to purchase the minimum levels of food, education, and health, let alone the requirements for a well-functioning life. Moreover, if the prices are too low, it is not clear who in the market can be held accountable. Responsibility is diffused through many buyers and sellers, none of whom has an overview of the market system; and different decisions made by any one of them acting alone will make no perceptible difference to the outcomes. Everyone can say with truth that they are merely offering the 'going rate' for the good or service in question. This diffusion of responsibility gives rise to the illusion that the outcome is a result of ineluctable market forces acting beyond human control, whereas the outcome is in fact the result of human decisions to establish a set of entitlement relations that have no provision for mutual scrutiny of interactions of individual decisions and mutual assurance of social security. The only kind of security that markets offer is through the purchase of private insurance—which is beyond the means of those who need it most. This private security is in turn subject to the inherent risks of markets. Of course other kinds of entitlement relation are also subject to risk, but they tend to be less volatile. Moreover, responsibility for changes tends to be easier to identify.

From women's point of view, there is a further disadvantage with markets. Since markets cannot recognize the value of goods and services which have no price, they cannot take into account the unpaid work that is mainly done by women in caring for families and reproducing the labour force. Market-based entitlements are thus inherently male-biased and women are penalized because much of their work is non-market work.

Markets can be made less risky and participants in them can be held accountable through appropriate forms of democratic social regulation, enforced by states; and through 'socialized' markets in which the cash nexus is embedded in democratic social networks between market participants (Elson, 1988, 2000). Minimum wage regulations and controls on the international movement of short-term financial capital are two important examples of appropriate social regulation. However, the main thrust of the neo-liberal policy agenda has been against such regulations, in the name of 'efficiency'. It is true that many systems of market regulation have protected the interests of the better-off and the socially powerful (including men as compared to women) and disadvantaged poor people, especially poor women in poor countries. But this is a reflection of the balance of political power that has shaped the regulations, not an inevitable characteristic of regulations. A different policy agenda would have focused on reshaping market regulation to produce democratically enforced regulations designed to promote the human rights of poor people, women equally with men. But even the best markets have to be complemented by other kinds of entitlement relation.

A pragmatic neo-liberal might object that regulations that might appear to benefit poor people in fact disadvantage them, if the operation of the market economy as a whole is taken into account. Minimum wage legislation is often argued to be likely to 'price poor people out of a job'. What seems to make sense at the individual level looks different at the systemic level. The force of this argument depends on what is assumed about the regulation of the system as a whole. Poor people are much more likely to be priced out of jobs by effective minimum wage regulation in a situation where demand for their labour is low and declining. This tendency can be counteracted by the state in several ways: offering an alternative source of labour demand in the public sector, limiting the ability of businesses to move jobs to another country, and avoiding deflationary bias in macroeconomic policies. The regulatory system has to be looked at as a whole, at both macro and micro levels.

Pragmatic neo-liberals do recognize that competitive markets are risky, which is why they advocate state provision of targeted social safety nets. But there are several problems with this kind of residual provision. There may be no minimum standards. Access is determined by public officials operating means tests of various kinds; criteria are often complex and difficult to understand; public officials may exercise such discretion that the claimant has very few, if any rights, so that the provision is not properly described as an entitlement. The effectiveness of such provision in meeting needs is limited by the unwillingness of the better-off to pay taxes to finance services that they do not themselves make use of; and by the stigmatization of those claiming such provision, so that they become less willing to make those claims.

A safety-net system accords greater moral value to making claims for resources on other people (outside one's family) via the market rather than via the state. This depends on the illusion (noted above) that exercising entitlements via the market constitutes providing for oneself, being independent, not being a burden on others; whereas making claims via the state entails being dependent. This ideological dimension of the neo-liberal agenda has considerable social power and may result in a sense of social exclusion on the part of those who have recourse to the safety net. It also results in many people not claiming the resources to which they are legally entitled.

Universal state-based entitlements which are equally available to all members of a society are likely to be more accessible, more transparent, and more effective. Claiming such entitlements is not stigmatizing. It is not taken as a sign of failure or dependency. Universal entitlements are more secure than narrowly targeted safety nets or market entitlements. They can be changed by the political process and their real value may be eroded by rising prices, but the majority of citizens have a stake in maintaining them, not just poor people. It is clear that the government has responsibility for these entitlements and must be held accountable for them. Such entitlements are a form of mutual assurance against entitlement failure and symbolize citizenship as a social bond. Of course such entitlements do demand a society willing to pay taxes, but this willingness is more likely to be forthcoming if everyone stands to gain; and they do raise issues of individual work incentives to produce the goods and services which are required to make them a reality. But they are essential in ensuring sufficient supply of public goods.

Public goods are goods whose benefits spill over to those who do not directly utilize them—education is clearly one important example, and so are many health services, such as those directed to improving maternal health or reducing the incidence of infectious diseases. But the category of public goods is broader than this. The public service ethos could be considered a public good, since its cultural values of mutuality and obligation, which are vital for the realization of human rights, spill over into areas of life beyond the public sector itself and inform the whole political culture. Of course, not every public sector is imbued with a public service ethos; many public services have been run for largely the private benefit of public-sector workers. But an alternative policy agenda would be concerned with nurturing and promoting such an ethos rather than minimizing its potential field of activities.

Support for the production of public goods is often deficient from the point of view of women's rights because one of the most important public goods in any community is not recognized because it is produced in private. This public good is the unpaid care and socialization of children, whose benefits spread well beyond the individual children who receive the care, to employers, neighbours, and indeed permeate the whole society (Folbre, 1994). Investment in public provision of a range of complementary services (clean water, sanitation, electricity, paved streets, health services, as well as childcare itself) is important to ensure that those caring for children on an unpaid basis have adequate resources to ensure that they and the children enjoy a progressive realization of their human rights, and that society as a whole benefits from generations of children who have been well cared for. Instead there has been a 'reprivatization' of this work of social reproduction (Bakker, 2001).

An enabling system of well-regulated and socially responsive markets and universal entitlements for all members of society, designed to avoid male breadwinner bias and commodification bias, depends not only on micro-level policy, but also on macro-level fiscal and monetary policy. Fiscal and monetary policy set some of the parameters which constrain individual entitlements. If fiscal and monetary policies are inappropriate there can be macro-level entitlement failure, in which macro policy leads to multiple entitlement failure in both markets and public provision. The neo-liberal policy agenda prioritizes the danger of systemic entitlement failure through high rates of inflation. 'Sound' policy is policy which minimizes this risk. But it downplays the risk of systemic entitlement failure through deflationary bias resulting in high levels of unemployment and under-employment. It embraces a miserly macroeconomics in which budget surpluses (or speedy deficit reduction) are seen as the top priority, and lower levels of taxation and public expenditure are typically preferred (Elson and Cagatay, 2000). Of course, hyperinflation does erode entitlements, but hyperinflation is usually the result of 'populist' policies which fail to place sufficient emphasis on increasing revenue. The avoidance of hyperinflation does not entail massive reductions in public provision. It requires building the social capacity to finance adequate levels of public provision. As Amartya Sen has put it:

Financial conservatism has good rationale and imposes strong requirements, but its demands must be interpreted in the light of the overall objectives of public policy. The role of public expenditure in generating and guaranteeing many basic capabilities calls for attention; it must be considered along with the instrumental need for macroeconomic stability. Indeed, the latter need must be assessed *within* a broad framework of social objectives. (Sen, 1999: 141).

A major problem in doing this is that macroeconomic policy is constructed in the neo-liberal agenda as something beyond social dialogue and public debate. The fundamentalists want to take it beyond debate by writing rigid rules for balanced budgets into state constitutions (Gill, 2001). The pragmatists organize it as a technocratic exercise in short-term balancing of financial flows, with key decisions increasingly handed over to 'independent' central banks which have little political accountability. Bakker describes a 'high priesthood' of economists wielding mathematical models, carrying the same message to every country 'as if the truth were carved in stone' (2001: 5). The World Bank recently produced a Comprehensive Development Framework which was supposed to promote dialogue and coordination among a range of social actors, but the dialogue did not include macroeconomic policy which instead was treated as a parameter (Elson and Cagatay, 2000). The IMF refers to the importance of the 'national authorities' explaining the economic reform programme to the public and building a 'national consensus' to support the programme; which sounds much more like 'selling' a preformulated programme than involving the public in creating the programme (Elson and Cagatay, 2000). These suspicions are confirmed by a recent report to the Human Rights Commission (Cheru, 2001) on the implementation of the Highly Indebted Poor Countries Initiative. The report concludes that the IMF and World Bank staff involved in the preparation of the Poverty Reduction Strategy Plans (PRSPs), which must be developed in order to qualify for debt relief, see the process as 'essentially technocratic'. It notes that: 'While civil society groups have been invited to participate extensively in discussions on the social policy-planning component of the I-PRSP, they have effectively been excluded when it comes to discussions on the content of macroeconomic policy choices' (Cheru, 2001: 14). It further notes that 'there is still a tendency to design macroeconomic policy with a focus on market-based criteria and financial concerns. This tendency always leads to a situation where social and human development and equity concerns take a back seat to financial considerations' (Cheru, 2001: 15). The PRSPs reviewed in the report mainly emphasize down-sizing the public sector and introducing cost-recovery measures such as user charges, and fail to show how such measures will reduce poverty. The picture that emerges indicates that the macroeconomic policy process associated with HIPC does not conform to the accountability criteria set out by the Committee on Economic, Social, and Cultural Rights (UN, 2001: para. 14). It is not accessible, transparent, and effective in realizing human rights.

Some pragmatic neo-liberal economists see a little more room for manœuvre than do IMF economists. Bevan and Adam (2000), for instance, are concerned to identify what scope there is for consultation and participation in macroeconomic policy in poor indebted countries. They do find some scope for participation in determining the composition of government spending and the extent of the net resource inflow from donors, but not in determining the structure and level of tax rates and the size of the domestic budget deficit and its financing. With respect to taxes, they state that 'a powerful consensus has developed as to the appropriate design of tax systems... [including] not only the structure of taxes, but also the level of tax rates. This conventional wisdom is probably pretty soundly based, and so to refuse to subscribe to it would be imprudent as well as incurring disapproval from the IFIs.' It seems an extraordinary weakening of democracy to leave the determination of taxes to a 'powerful [Washington] consensus': social dialogue about taxation is surely a key part of any democratic polity. Bevan and Adam do agree that there is scope for choice in many countries about the size and financing of the budget deficit but 'it does not seem appropriate to see this as a participatory issue rather than as a technical judgement by government' (2000: 3). Nor do they consider participation in setting macroeconomic targets. They take it for granted that there will be an inflation target: 'the target rate of inflation is fundamental to the macroeconomic framework'. Other targets typically include net foreign exchange reserves, money supply, domestic credit to the private sector, and the budget deficit. Poverty reduction is brought into the macroeconomic framework through growth rates.

Much more innovative approaches are being developed in a number of NGO initiatives on participatory development of alternative national budgets and budget processes (Cagatay *et al.*, 2000). In Bangladesh, the Institute for Development Policy Analysis at Proshika has conducted a participatory study of people's understanding of budget issues and the impact of the budget on their livelihoods. Subsequently it has made recommendations on participation in the production of the Bangladesh budget, including the democratization of priority setting; pre-budget consultations with civil society; gathering public feedback on expenditure choices from citizen juries; and strengthening the capacities of parliamentary budget committees. In Canada an Alternative Federal Budget has been prepared each year since 1995 through consultation between a wide range of labour, social, and community organizations. It includes alternative taxation and monetary policy to achieve a range of social goals including gender equality and the protection of human rights. It aims to improve the entitlements of a wide range of disadvantaged people, focusing not only on market-based entitlements through growth and full employment, but also on universal gender-equitable state-based entitlements through public services and public income transfers.

Gender equality is being addressed through a wide range of gender budget initiatives in both developed and developing countries, some organized outside government and some inside government (Budlender, 2000; Sharp, 1999; see also www.gender-budgets.org). These initiatives have been particularly concerned to analyse the gender distribution of budget benefits and burdens; and ensure that government budgets are more oriented to the needs and priorities of women, especially poor women. Many of them, especially those involving parliamentarians and members of women's organizations, also emphasize the right to information about budgets, and promote measures to make budget processes more accountable to women. They exchange information and experiences across international boundaries and promote more open dialogue about economic policies. They resist the idea that a market calculus is the final arbiter of policy and insist on the democratization of economic policy.

Such gender budget initiatives offer scope for making a direct link between economic policy and the realization of women's rights. They could promote an analysis of the effects of government tax and spending on women's entitlements, both on entitlements to state services and transfers, and on market-based entitlements. They could highlight the areas of entitlement failure and put forward alternative polices to prevent entitlement failure. They offer the opportunity to capitalize upon the gains that women have made in civil and political rights to begin on the work of transforming the economic policy agenda. They are limited, it is true, by the external constraints placed upon each country by its positioning in the international financial system. But they also have the potential to contribute to the loosening of these constraints by rebuilding confidence in the possibility of well-organized, fair, and accountable public finances and services; and by mobilizing women to demand that prevention of entitlement failure has to take precedence as the goal of international financial policy.

References

Bakker, I. (2001) '*Who Built the Pyramids? Engendering the New International Economic and Financial Architecture*', paper presented to the International Studies Association Annual Conference, Chicago, Feb.

Beetham, D. (1995) 'What Future for Economic and Social Rights?', *Political Studies*, 43: 41–60.

Beneria, L. (1995) 'Toward a Greater Integration of Gender in Economics', *World Development*, 23/11: 1839–50.

Bevan, D. L., and C. S. Adam (2000) '*Poverty Reduction Strategies and the Macroeconomic Policy Framework*', draft guidance note (London: Department for International Development).

Bissio, R. (ed.) (1999) *Social Watch* (Montevideo: Instituto del Tercer Mundo).

Brown, L. R., and J. Kerr (eds.) (1997) *The Gender Dimension of Economic Reforms in Ghana, Mali and Zambia* (Ottawa: The North–South Institute).

Budlender, D. (2000) 'The Political Economy of Women's Budgets in the South', *World Development*, 28/7: 1365–78.

Cagatay, N., and S. Özler (1995) 'Feminization of the Labor Force: The Effects of Long-Term Development and Structural Adjustment', *World Development*, 23/11: 1883–94.

——M. Kelik, R. Lal, and J. Lang (2000) *Budgets as if People Mattered: Democratizing Macroeconomic Policies* (New York: UNDP).

Charmes, J. (1998) 'Informal Sector, Poverty and Gender: A Review of Empirical Evidence', background paper for *World Development Report 2000* (Washington, DC: World Bank).

Cheru, F. (2001) *The Highly Indebted Poor Countries (HIPC) Initiative: A Human Rights Assessment of the Poverty Reduction Strategy Papers (PRSP)*, report to Commission on Human Rights, E/CN.4/2001/56 (Geneva: UN).

Colclough, C., P. Rose, and M. Tembon (2000) 'Gender Inequalities in Primary Schooling: The Roles of Poverty and Adverse Cultural Practice', *International Journal of Educational Development*, 20: 5–27.

Cornia, Andrea, R. Jolly, and F. Stewart (eds.) (1987) *Adjustment with a Human Face* (Oxford: Clarendon Press).

Culpeper, R., A. Berry, and F. Stewart (eds.) (1997) *Global Development Fifty Years after Bretton Woods* (London: Macmillan).

Devlin, R. (1989) 'Options for Tackling the External Debt Problem', *CEPAL Review*, 37: 27–34.

Elson, D. (1988) 'Socialization of the Market', *New Left Review*, 172: 3–44.

—— (1991) 'Male Bias in Macro-economics: The Case of Structural Adjustment', in D. Elson (ed.), *Male Bias in the Development Process* (Manchester: Manchester University Press).

—— (1995*a*) 'Gender Awareness in Modelling Structural Adjustment', *World Development*, 23/11: 1851–68.

—— (1995*b*) 'Household Responses to Stabilisation and Structural Adjustment: Male Bias at the Micro Level', in D. Elson (ed.), *Male Bias in the Development Process*, 2nd ed. (Manchester: Manchester University Press).

—— (2000) 'Socializing Markets, Not Market Socialism', in L. Panitch and C. Leys (eds.), *Necessary and Unnecessary Utopias: Socialist Register 2000* (Rendlesham: Merlin Press).

—— (2001) *International Financial Architecture: A View from the Kitchen'*, paper presented to the International Studies Association Annual Conference, Chicago, Feb.

—— and N. Cagatay (2000) 'The Social Content of Macroeconomic Policies', *World Development*, 28/7: 1347–64.

Fine, B. (1997) 'Entitlement Failure?', *Development and Change*, 28: 617–47.

—— and P. Rose (2001) 'Education and the Post-Washington Consensus', in B. Fine, C. Lapavitsas and J. Pincus (eds.), *Development Policy in the Twenty-First Century: Beyond the Post-Washington Consensus* (London: Routledge).

—— C. Lapavitsas and J. Pincus (eds.) (2001) *Development Policy in the Twenty-First Century: Beyond the Post-Washington Consensus* (London: Routledge).

Floro, M., and G. Dymski (2000) 'Financial Crisis, Gender, and Power: An Analytical Framework', *World Development*, 28/7: 1269–83.

Floro, M. S. (1995) 'Economic Restructuring, Gender and the Allocation of Time', *World Development*, 23/11: 1913–29.

Folbre, N. (1994) *Who Pays for the Kids?* (London: Routledge).

Gasper, D. (1993) 'Entitlements Analysis: Relating Concepts and Contexts', *Development and Change*, 24/4: 679–718.

Gill, S. R. (2001) *'Constitutionalizing Inequality'*, paper presented to the International Studies Association Annual Conference, Chicago, Feb.

González de la Rocha, M. (2000) *Private Adjustments: Household Responses to the Erosion of Work* (New York: UNDP).

Gore, C. (1993) 'Entitlement Relations and "Unruly" Social Practices: A Comment on the Work of Amartya Sen', *Journal of Development Studies*, 29/3: 429–60.

Helleiner, G. (ed.) (1986) *The IMF and Africa* (Washington, DC: IMF).

Humana, C. (1986) *World Human Rights Guide*, 2nd ed. (London: Hodder & Stoughton).

——(1992) *World Human Rights Guide*, 3rd ed. (New York: Oxford University Press).

International Monetary Fund, Organisation for Economic Co-operation and Development, United Nations, World Bank Group (2000) *A Better World for All: Progress Towards the International Development Goals* (New York, Paris, and Washington, DC: IMF *et al.*).

Killick, T. (ed.) (1984) *The Quest for Economic Stabilisation: The IMF and the Third World* (London: Gower).

Kucera, D., and W. Milberg (2000) 'Gender Segregation and Gender Bias in Manufacturing Trade Expansion: Revisiting the "Wood Asymmetry" ', *World Development*, 28/7: 1191–210.

Lim, J. Y. (2000) 'The Effects of the East Asian Crisis on the Employment of Women and Men: The Philippine Case', *World Development*, 28/7: 1285–306.

Loxley, J. (1997) 'International Capital Markets, the Debt Crisis and Development' in R. Culpeper, A. Berry, and F. Stewart (eds.), *Global Development Fifty Years after Bretton Woods* (London: Macmillan).

Meller, P. (1991) 'Adjustment and Social Costs in Chile during the 1980s', *World Development*, 19/11: 1545–61.

Moser, C. (1992) 'Adjustment from Below: Low-Income Women, Time and the Triple Role in Guayaquil, Ecuador', in H. Afshar and C. Dennis (eds.), *Women and Adjustment Policies in the Third World* (London: Macmillan).

——(1996) *Confronting Crisis. A Comparative Study of Household Responses to Poverty and Vulnerability in Four Poor Urban Communities* (Environmentally Sustainable Development Studies and Monographs Series, 8; Washington, DC: World Bank).

Psacharopoulos, G., J.-P. Tan, and E. Jimenez (1986) *Financing Education in Developing Countries* (Washington, DC: World Bank).

Seguino, S. (2000) 'Gender Inequality and Economic Growth: A Cross-Country Analysis', *World Development*, 28/7: 1211–30.

Sen, A. (1981) *Poverty and Famines: An Essay on Entitlement and Deprivation* (Oxford: Clarendon Press).

——(1983) 'Development: Which Way Now?', *Economic Journal*, 93; reprinted in K. Jameson and C. Wilber (eds.), *The Political Economy of Development and Underdevelopment* (New York: McGraw-Hill).

——(1984) 'The Right Not to be Hungry', in G. Fløistad (ed.), *Contemporary Philosophy: A New Survey* (The Hague: Martinus Nijoff).

——(1999) *Development as Freedom* (Oxford: Oxford University Press).

Senapaty, M. (1997) '*Gender Implications of Economic Reforms in the Education Sector in India: The Case of Haryana and Madhya Pradesh*', Ph.D. thesis, University of Manchester.

Sharp, R. (1999) 'Women's Budgets', in J. Peterson and M. Lewis (eds.), *The Elgar Companion to Feminist Economics* (Cheltenham: Edward Elgar).

Singh, A., and A. Zammit (2000) 'International Capital Flows: Identifying the Gender Dimension', *World Development*, 28/7: 1249–68.

Standing, G. (1999) 'Global Feminization through Flexible Labor: A Theme Revisited', *World Development*, 27/3: 583–602.

Staveren, I. V. (1996) *'Amartya Sen's Entitlement Approach and Women's Poverty'*, paper presented at the FENN Seminar 'Countering the Feminization of Poverty', Utrecht, 7 June.

Summerfield, G., and N. Aslanbeigui (1998) 'The Impact of Structural Adjustment and Economic Reform on Women', in N. P. Stromquist (ed.), *Women in the Third World: An Encyclopedia of Contemporary Issues* (New York: Garland Publishing).

Taylor, L. (1991) *Varieties of Stabilisation Experience: Towards Sensible Macroeconomics for the Third World* (Oxford: Clarendon Press).

Toye, J. (1987) *Dilemmas of Development* (Oxford: Blackwell).

United Nations (1990) *The Nature of States Parties Obligations, General Comment No. 3*, adopted 13–14 Dec., Committee on Economic, Social and Cultural Rights, 5th Session, 49th and 50th meeting, UN Doc. E/C.12/1990/8.

—— (1993) Commission on Human Rights, Resolution 1993/14.

—— (1999) *1999 World Survey on the Role of Women in Development: Globalization, Gender and Work* (New York: UN).

—— (2001) *Substantive Issues Arising in the Implementation of the International Covenant on Economic, Social and Cultural Rights: Poverty and the International Covenant on Economic, Social and Cultural Rights*, statement adopted by the Committee on Economic and Social Council, E/C.12/2001/10 (Geneva: UN).

UNDP (2000) *Human Development Report 2000* (New York: Oxford University Press).

UNIFEM (2000) *Progress of the World's Women 2000* (New York: UNIFEM).

Weisbrot, M., D. Baker, E. Kraev, and J. Chen (2001) *The Scorecard on Globalisation 1980–2000: Twenty Years of Diminished Progress* (Washington, DC: Centre for Economic and Policy Research).

WIDER (World Institute for Development Economics Research) (1999) *WIDER Angle*, 2: 12.

World Bank (1997) *World Development Report 1997* (Washington, DC: World Bank).

—— (2001) *Engendering Development* (New York: Oxford University Press).

Zohir, S. C. (1998) *'Gender Implications of Industrial Reforms and Adjustment in the Manufacturing Sector in Bangladesh'*, Ph.D. thesis, University of Manchester.

Multiculturalism, Universalism, and the Claims of Democracy

Anne Phillips

Feminism is about change. It challenges the existing pattern of relations between the sexes, wherever these are characterized by sub-ordination and inequality. In doing so, it necessarily takes issue with the customs and practices of existing societies. Feminists have pur-sued different priorities, disagreed over short-term strategies and, often enough, in their formulations of long-term goals. But whatever conclusions have been reached about the conditions for a sexually egalitarian society, most have seen these as applying beyond the con-fines of their own immediate world. If certain things are necessary for men and women to be equal in one society, then surely the same things must be necessary for men and women wherever they are?

This suggests that feminism is committed to a strongly universal-ist discourse of rights and equality—and if cultural relativism were the only alternative to universalism, this suggestion would surely be right. I take cultural relativism to be the view that norms of justice are always relative to the society in which they are formed, reflect-ing values and practices that vary enormously from one society to another; that there is no 'truth' outside these various local stand-points; and that it is therefore inappropriate to take the norms that emerge within one society as the measure against which to assess the practices of another. The value of this position is that it cap-tures the situated nature of any principles of justice, the way ideals like equality or autonomy or democracy become more or less prom-inent depending on historical conditions, and the way the previously unthinkable becomes possible as these conditions change. To take just the more obvious examples, there was a long period of time when people found it almost impossible to conceive of slaves as sharing a common humanity with freemen, or of women as entitled to the same rights and consideration as their male counterparts; one reading of this, most notably by Marx, is that it was only as the evolution of market society made people more interchangeable that it became possible to think of them as in some sense equals. Whatever we make of this particular reading (which I find rather plausible), ideals are always formed in a context, and that context shapes and limits what people are able to conceive.

But while cultural relativism grasps at a truth about the contextual nature of principles of justice, it does so in a way that seriously overstates the incommensurability of the discourses that arise in contemporary societies, and wrongly represents the difference between cultures as a difference between hermetically sealed, internally self-consistent wholes. As Seyla Benhabib (1999) has argued, it gives the impression that a 'culture' coincides with a society, which in turn coincides with a nation (or nation of origin). In doing so, it ignores the multiplicity of cultures with which any one person is associated, some of which will be very locally circumscribed, others associated with their political identifications or occupational positions, while others still (like religion) extend way beyond the boundaries of a single nation-state. Cultural relativism suggests a degree of mutual insulation between 'us' and 'the others' that is very far from the realities of the contemporary world. It also encourages us into a troubling suspension of judgement when competing principles collide.

From a gender perspective, this last is a particularly pressing concern, for norms of justice are not formulated under conditions of gender equality. The 'society' that generates and authorizes existing norms is never an innocent subject; on the contrary, since no society yet operates under conditions of gender justice, what is considered to be right and just within any given society must always be open to critical scrutiny. We do not have to hypothesize a standpoint outside all society (the famous 'view from nowhere') to see how this process can occur. Sometimes the criticisms arise internally, from what are perceived to be inconsistencies between rhetoric and reality, or the failure to extend to one group of citizens rights and possibilities that have been regarded as entirely appropriate for others. In a world of rapid and extensive global communication, many of the criticisms will be provoked by comparison with principles endorsed elsewhere. We often draw on the experiences and values of other groups and societies to scrutinize prevailing understandings and formulate alternative norms.

Cultural relativism is not a useful ally for feminism, but the very reasons that make cultural relativism so unattractive have posed problems for universalism as well. If feminists have been peculiarly sensitive to the dangers in elevating existing cultural understandings to the status of unquestioned norms, they have been equally (and rightly) sensitive to the way these cultural understandings shape what are then presented as universal principles of justice and truth. Much of the work of feminist philosophers and political theorists over the last fifteen years has been devoted to exposing the 'false' universalisms of mainstream theory: the elevation of a self-owning (masculine) individual as the supposed subject of liberal contract theory (Pateman, 1988); the association of universality with impartiality, and the injunction this places on subordinated social groups to put their own 'partial' needs to one side (Young, 1990); the cultivation of conceptions of rationality and justice that expel any element of emotion or care (Gilligan, 1982; Benhabib, 1987). In some cases, the object of the argument has been to develop a different understanding of universalism that detaches it from its masculine provenance. In others, there has been a more trenchant critique of the very possibility of universal theory or norms. In all cases, feminists have raised problems about the way the norms and perspectives of particular social groups (largely male) come to claim the authority of 'universal' truth. I do not intend to rehearse these more philosophical arguments here. The point to stress is that those concerned with gender justice have good reason to distrust what currently pass as 'universal' principles and norms.

Since one of the problems that arises in discussion of this is that universal discourses of rights and equality often fail to engage adequately with difference, there is an obvious area of overlap between the problems encountered in achieving gender justice and those posed by justice between different cultures. One of the critiques of universalism is that it looks to a common core of humanity behind all the (supposedly contingent) differences of class, gender, ethnicity, religion, or race, that in doing so it tends to equate equality with sameness, and thereby leaves untouched systemic inequalities in power. Part of this (the least problematic part) restates an older objection associated with socialist critiques of liberalism to the effect that an equality of rights will generate inequality when it pays no attention to background conditions. Grand assertions about all individuals having the equal right to hold on to their property turn rather sour when one individual owns only the clothes she stands up in and another owns the Microsoft empire. In similar fashion, asserting the equal right of women and men to employment can end up pretty empty when the prevailing arrangement of familial and domestic responsibilities prevents most women from exercising this right. When understood as a claim about the basic human rights to which all human beings are entitled, universalism then promises more than it can deliver. In extending to all the same set of rights and guarantees, it obscures (and may in some circumstances reinforce) those background inequalities that continue to generate inequalities of power.

This first part of the argument points to hugely contentious political questions, but is not, at a philosophical level, such a devastating critique. The political implication is that some groups may need different rights or guarantees from others in order to achieve the same kind of equalities: that there is not a single list of entitlements that should be applied in the same way to all individuals, and often a compelling case for local variation. To link this to one of the other issues discussed in this collection (and returned to later in my argument), it may be that societies need to introduce specific guarantees for the political representation of women—perhaps reserved seats for women, or a minimum quota for women candidates—in order to combat the background inequalities that would otherwise exclude women from political influence and power. Or it may be that societies need to provide additional resources and opportunities for minority ethnic groups, in order to combat a history of marginalization; and that in doing so, they may have to modify what would otherwise be universally applicable regulations for entry to university or the civil service.

This is politically contentious, but not yet at odds with universalism *per se*. The proposed remedies may well involve interim modification of universal rules and practices—no simple schedule of universal rights and equalities, perhaps differential rather than identical rights—but the overall objective may still be that all groups and individuals should end up with the same conditions. The argument reminds us that universalism has to be nuanced by a better understanding of disparities in income or power, and suggests that one way of dealing with these disparities is to treat different groups differently. It does not otherwise take issue with the idea that the same rights should be universally enjoyed by all.

A second, more challenging objection is that there are some differences that will always be there, and that many of these are differences we value and want to sustain. At one level, this is so obvious it is hard to see how anyone could have overlooked it. No conceivable scenario for social change is going to eliminate in their entirety all the differences between women and men (and for those of a heterosexual disposition, there would be little reason to desire such a scenario). That this obvious point was so long overlooked reflects the dominance of class in previous critical thinking, for when one focuses on class as the central measure of inequality, it becomes more plausible to think of processes of elimination or suspension that either remove the difference or make it irrelevant to the distribution of rights and power. When extended to gender, race, or sexuality, this approach becomes less compelling. Women do not want their acceptance into the world of equals to be made conditional on others not noticing whether they are female or male (as if the femaleness is something to be ashamed of); and the same clearly goes for those whose skin colour or sexuality marks them out as a minority group within their society. An equality that depends on others ignoring or overlooking key features of our identity is not an acceptable option. It has to be possible to be both different and equal.

Here too, the tension with universalism may be more apparent than real (universalism is more closely associated with the idea that all individuals should have the same rights or protections or entitlements than the idea that all individuals should end up the same), but it is at this point that we edge into parallel arguments that have been developed in relation to cultural subordination. Sexual difference has almost always been associated with inequality: what marks women as different from men is also taken to mark them as of lesser value. The history of cultural difference is in some ways less depressing, already throwing up occasional examples of that more egalitarian respect for difference that has mostly evaded the relationship between the sexes. We often find ourselves intrigued, and sometimes positively impressed, by what we discover to be the different practices associated with different cultures, and there is a long history of individuals seeking to embrace cultures that are very different from their own.[1] But cultural difference, like sexual difference, still resonates with images of superiority and inferiority (and, indeed, those who do try to embrace a different culture sometimes end up in a patronizing relationship to their new-found communities, feeling that those born into the cultures do not sufficiently appreciate or understand the strengths of their own way of life).

Cultural difference is more often read as cultural hierarchy than cultural variation. There are said to be 'better' and 'worse', 'more advanced' and 'more backward' cultures. Given this history, the deployment of universal principles as a measure for judging the practices and values of other cultures begins to look rather suspect: yet another case of those 'false' universalisms that draw on the practices and values of one group for the delineation of supposedly universal rules, refuse to recognize the legitimacy of difference, and seek to impose the practices of the dominant group. Many feminists will sympathize with this suspicion, noting the parallels with their own experiences of gender. The twist in this case is that one of the key

Anne Phillips

measures currently employed to differentiate 'better' and 'worse', 'more advanced' and 'more backward' cultures is their treatment of women: whether they practise forms of genital mutilation that deny women (but not men) the enjoyment of their sexuality; whether they allow men (but never women) to have multiple marriage partners; whether they insist on the confinement of women to the home or the veiling of women when they go out in public; whether they insist on the segregation of the sexes in education or religious worship.

This is the issue that has surfaced in recent debates on the tensions between feminism and multiculturalism. Some feminists (myself included) perceive a close family relationship between feminism and multiculturalism: see these as linked, not just because both tackle issues of inequality and oppression, but more deeply, because the oppressions they address share a common structure. In each case, the failure to recognize people as equals seems to be bound up in some way with the inability to accept difference: it is assumed that those marked by difference (and it is always the people on the margins who get marked by their difference while the others are somehow seen as the norm) should bring themselves into line with the others in their society in order to be included as full members.

This generates a strong coincidence of concerns between those pursuing sexual and those pursuing cultural equality, linked to a shared critique of the universalisms that have falsely generalized from one sex or one culture, and a shared perception that equality may depend on greater respect for/recognition of difference. For many feminists, the coincidence of concerns is reinforced by the knowledge that Western feminism too often read the world off the experience of white middle-class women, a knowledge learnt through a lengthy period of internal critique and reassessment which revolved around the very different experiences and priorities of women depending on their class, race, ethnicity, religion, or nationality. These shared concerns have fostered what might otherwise seem an unlikely alliance of feminism and multiculturalism. But when this alliance makes it impossible for women identified with one culture to criticize what they regard as the sexually oppressive practices of another, this can lead to a form of cultural relativism that is not, I have suggested, compatible with feminist politics. So how are we to deal with this issue? Can feminists working in international organizations confidently draw up a schedule of basic women's rights that they then present as a requirement for all societies? Can feminists from the majority culture in a multicultural society take it on themselves to criticize what they see as the sexually inegalitarian practices of minority cultural groups? Can feminists from a minority culture take it on themselves to challenge the practices of the majority group?

Despite my earlier reservation about treating cultural difference as a matter of 'us' and 'the others', I have posed this as a question about the critics from 'outside'. This is because it seems to me too easy to resolve the tension by pointing to the many women inside each 'culture' contesting its understandings of women's position. In those parts of Africa where genital mutilation is most widely practised, there are many women's groups that have campaigned long and hard to get the practice declared illegal, and then campaign equally long and hard to get their governments to enforce the legislation. There are women activists across India working to publicize instances of dowry murder, campaigning for the employment rights of secluded women, and battling against the heavy weight of cultural practices that tie women's existence to oppressive notions of family honour and legitimate continuing sexual violence. In Britain, groups like Southall Black Sisters work inside as well as outside Islamic communities to challenge the power differential between men and women; and there are women within all the churches and religions organizing for greater equity between the sexes in the practices of their religion. This history of internal contestation reinforces what should be the starting point for thinking about issues of multiculturalism: that cultures are not monolithic, are always in the process of interpretation and reinterpretation, and never immune to change. But I do not think we should rely on these observations to close off discussion of the 'hard case' scenario of external critique—as if criticism is legitimate when we can identify internal critics but not otherwise allowed.

Tensions between Sexual and Cultural Equality

In the most influential recent statement of the conditions for multicultural citizenship, Will Kymlicka (1995) argues that the case for minority cultural rights is entirely consistent with universalism so long as it is conceived on a relatively weak model. His first point is that the claims of minority cultures are justified precisely through reference to the universal rights of individuals, for if all individuals are to have the same rights and capacities for choosing how to lead their lives, and culture provides (as he argues) the context within which individuals can make meaningful choices, then members of minority cultures need the security of their own cultures in order to enjoy the same individual rights as others. The second point is that we should distinguish between the stronger self-government rights of indigenous peoples who have been involuntarily incorporated into a larger unit by conquest or colonization, and the lesser 'polyethnic' rights of immigrant groups that have voluntarily uprooted themselves; the case for the former does not spill over into a case for the latter.[2] His third point is that we should distinguish between the 'external protections' that may prove necessary to secure the rights of minority cultures *vis-à-vis* other cultural groups, and the 'internal restrictions' that illegitimately constrain individual members. Multicultural accommodation, in this view, does not mean that groups are to be allowed to discriminate amongst their members on the grounds of sex, race, or sexual preference.

At first glance, this would seem to resolve any tensions between sexual and cultural equality. In their pursuit of equal citizenship, societies need to recognize more fully the rights of minority cultures, but any resulting policies of accommodation should be curtailed by reference to standard liberal guarantees on the rights of individuals. Whatever powers are delegated to the group in question, these must not be such as to violate the rights of its women members. So far, so good, but on closer examination Kymlicka's solution looks less satisfactory. First, it is not always so easy to distinguish between the legitimate 'external protections' and the illegitimate 'internal restrictions'. As Ayelet Shachar has argued (1998, 1999, 2001), one of the main concerns of identity groups *vis-à-vis* other groups or the state is to retain the authority to decide who is a group member: to decide, for example, who counts as a Jew, or who is to be recognized as a member of a particular indigenous group. This authority operates primarily through family law, which can then involve significant restrictions on the rights of women members; and in many cases, the criteria for membership have been self-evidently discriminatory, as when Indian tribes in North American reservations have recognized the children of men who marry outside the group as full members, but not the children of women who marry outside. It is not always possible to draw a line between the external rights of the group and the internal rights of its members, and depending on how generously we interpret the first, they may well conflict with the second.

The further problem arises when Kymlicka considers the conditions in which the state could reasonably act against discrimination within a cultural group. 'Obviously,' he notes, 'intervention is justified in the case of gross and systematic violation of human rights, such as slavery or genocide or mass torture and expulsions' (Kymlicka, 1995: 169); and in the case of newly arriving immigrant groups, he does not think it wrong 'for liberal states to insist that immigration entails accepting the legitimacy of state enforcement of liberal principles, so long as immigrants know this in advance and none the less voluntarily choose to come' (Kymlicka, 1995: 170). This still leaves a very large area open to debate. At this point, Kymlicka backs away from what might be conceived as a coercive imposition of liberal principles on minority groups, arguing that if there is a consensus within the community on the legitimacy of restricting individual rights, it may not be appropriate for governments to intervene. The theoretical protections for women then dissolve in the face of worries about imposition, and it seems that only the 'gross and systematic violations' will qualify for action. We know, however, that much of the discrimination against women will fail this test, being of its nature more informal, 'private', and covert. Much of it, moreover, will have become 'naturalized' over the years, to the extent where even those most discriminated against may accept their conditions as legitimate and just. As Condorcet remarked in his *Essay on the Political Rights of Women*: 'Custom may familiarize mankind with the violation of their natural rights to such an extent, that even among those who have lost or been deprived of these rights, no one thinks of reclaiming them, or is even conscious that they have suffered any injustice.'

It is in this context that Susan Moller Okin poses the question: 'Is multiculturalism bad for women?'[3] The questions she raises are primarily addressed to the internal politics of societies made up of a number of cultural groups (questions of cultural respect within countries, rather than between them); and the aspect of multiculturalism that most concerns her is the claim that minority cultures or ways of life are not sufficiently protected by guaranteeing the individual rights of their members, but should also be protected through special group rights or privileges. Examples include the decision of the French government in the 1980s to extend the normal understanding of marital dependant so as to enable immigrant men (from certain cultures) to bring multiple wives into the country; and the exemption of minority groups in Britain from a variety of legal regulations that might otherwise be construed as imposing a discriminatory burden on them. (The most quoted of these is the exemption of turban-wearing Sikhs from safety regulations that require motorbike riders to wear a helmet.) Further examples would include the recognition of customary (religious) law in countries like India, where worries about the political effects of imposing standardized legislation on Muslim and Hindu alike produced a range of religion-specific Acts to regulate marriage, divorce, and succession arrangements for the different religious communities; or the delegation of marriage and divorce affairs in Israel to the autonomous courts of the different religious communities.

In these cases, sensitivity to ethnic or religious difference has meant a modification of what would otherwise be universally applicable regulations and rules. Often enough, these exemptions allow for greater inequality between women and men. Okin argues that 'we—especially those of us who consider ourselves politically progressive and opposed to all forms of oppression—have been too quick to assume that feminism and multiculturalism are both good things which are easily reconciled' (Okin *et al.*, 1999: 10). In her analysis, there are more often tensions than compatibilities, and we then have to decide whether to prioritize cultural group rights or women's equality. 'What we need to strive toward is a form of multiculturalism that gives the issues of gender and other intragroup inequalities their due—that is to say, a multiculturalism that effectively treats all persons as each other's moral equals' (Okin *et al.*, 1999: 131). Though this final statement might seem a pretty good summary of what is necessary for gender justice, reactions to Okin have been mixed—including reactions from other feminists.[4] I note here three recurrent objections.

1. Appealing to Principles that are Also Negated by Western Societies

One objection is that the criticism of minority cultural practice appeals to principles of equality and autonomy that are also being negated by practices in the majority culture; that Western societies have a poor record on women's rights and equalities; and that one should put one's own house in order before trying to sort out anyone else's. The critique of polygamy or forced marriages or the enforced seclusion of women gives the impression that all is well in the heartlands of liberal democracy. Since women in the most developed societies continue to suffer from inequalities of pay and employment, from gross violations of their bodily integrity through rape and domestic violence, and a persistent devaluation of their sex as reflected in cultural and political representation, the implied contrast with majority cultural practice is deeply disingenuous.

I think there are circumstances in which this would be a valid complaint. I have often been struck by the dishonesty of those who draw on the language of sexual equality to characterize Muslim communities in Europe and elsewhere as alien, backward, pre-modern—but otherwise exhibit no interest in sexual equality. In such circumstances, one cannot but think that the real agenda is racism rather than a high-minded concern for the rights of Muslim women. The complaint is hardly valid, however, as applied to feminists who have spent most of their lives campaigning against what they see as gender injustices in their own society. Nor, to push this further, is it so obvious that people must 'earn' the right to speak out against injustice by first demonstrating their track record closer to home. If they have not done so, we may query their complacency; we may doubt their grasp of gender issues; and may sometimes want to question their real agenda. But even in the worst instances, where highlighting injustice elsewhere is primarily about claiming the superiority of one's own society or group, there may still be an injustice to address.

2. Appealing to Principles that are Themselves Open to Critique

This second objection returns us to the worries about universalism, and whether the principles employed to criticize the cultural practices of others are just a glorified version of the principles that underpin one's own. Prioritizing the rights of individuals over the rights of groups, for example, may reflect a particular conception of the relationship between the individual and his/her community that values personal autonomy and mobility over the ties of family or community, sees freedom as 'freedom from' the constraints of tradition, and attaches little weight to the sense of belonging to a particular community or group. This conception of human freedom has been linked historically to the evolution of market society, which values individuals by their contribution to production rather than their status in the social order, and often requires them to detach themselves from family, community, or country in their pursuit of work. The detached and autonomous individual then becomes the focus for liberal ideals of freedom and equality, but it may be that the high value liberals attach to autonomy illegitimately takes what has become a central preoccupation of Western cultures and turns it into a universal norm.[5]

This problem surfaces even in the most promising versions of liberal thought. In setting out her case for the capabilities approach, Martha Nussbaum argues that the language of capabilities is less strongly linked to a particular cultural and historical tradition than the language of rights, and is not therefore so vulnerable to complaints about cultural specificity. Yet the more content she puts into the notion of capabilities (see the list in her essay in this collection), the less plausible this claim appears; while the centrality she attaches to ensuring the conditions for individual choice still leaves it open to the standard complaint. Whether we operate with a language of capabilities or a language of rights, questions of historical provenance will continue to arise; I would argue, however, that we should see these questions as cautioning us against the dogmatic presumption to exclusive truth, not as ruling certain principles out of court because of the context in which they arose. That principles of rights or justice emerge and change through time is, I think, beyond question. That they often express and legitimate the partial experiences of particular societies—and as many feminists would add, of particular groups within particular societies—also seems to me beyond question; and one consequence of this is that all principles of justice have to be regarded as open to contestation, revision, and critique. But questions of historical provenance do not settle which norms are the most defensible, and there are certain elements in the liberal conception of freedom and equality—including, as Nussbaum (1999) has noted, its insistence on the separateness of each individual and the dangers of subsuming the needs of women under the 'greater good' of the family or community or state—that feminists would be ill-advised to abandon.

My own view is that the liberal tradition is still deeply flawed by the priority it gives to choice over equality, by its uncritical endorsement of what can be a coercive notion of autonomy, and its all too frequent conception of the individual as 'owner' of his/her self.[6] But the debate on this continues within what are regarded as liberal cultures as well as those regarded as non-liberal; and if it would be mistaken on the one side to dismiss liberalism as just the local prejudice of the West, it would be equally mistaken to treat it as a foreign import that has no purchase in Africa or Asia or the Middle East. The issue we should be focusing on is the tension between sexual and cultural equality: whether the requirements of gender justice (however we come to define these) come into conflict with the requirements of justice between cultural groups and, if so, whether we have to resolve this by giving priority to one over the other. Displacing this onto a debate about liberalism—one side defending its superior conception of justice, the other pointing out its incipient tendencies towards cultural imperialism—is not the best way to promote such a discussion. On the contrary, it may unwittingly reinforce what Richard Bellamy (1999: 3) describes as 'a widespread liberal prejudice that pluralist objections to liberalism derive solely from illiberal throwbacks miraculously marooned in the modern world'. While doubts about liberalism are often justified, I would advise against turning the debate on gender and cultural justice into a debate that places feminism/liberalism on the one side and multiculturalism on the other. In this context, the source of the ideals is less pressing than whether they provide adequate guides to policy.

3. Failing to Understand the Social Meaning of Different Practices

A third objection levelled at Okin is that her understanding of the practices she criticizes is constrained by her 'outsider' status and that, particularly in her critique of the religious practices that segregate women from men and enforce their subordination, she overstates the patriarchalism of what she describes. I am not primarily concerned with whether this is a fair criticism of Okin, but more with the underlying issue about who is in the best position to understand.

There are three sub-issues here. The first relates to the observation in the last section about misreading objections to liberalism as 'illiberal throwbacks miraculously marooned in the modern world'. Against this perception, I find it more compelling to read contemporary assertions of cultural, religious, or ethnic identity, and their associated demands for recognition, as a quintessentially modern phenomenon. One only has to think of the recent movements against secularism in India, the Islamist revival of the last twenty years, or the 'rediscovery' of ethnic and religious identities in the former Yugoslavia to recognize that cultural and religious identities have come to matter in a new way over recent decades. Within Europe, one might also look at the tensions that arise between first- and second-generation migrants, and the bewilderment of parents who worked hard to assimilate with the dominant culture when their children (and not only their boy children) now reject this. Global migration is intensifying problems of group inequality within countries, often along the faultline of ethnic or religious difference; while between countries, globalization and its associated 'sharp shocks' have generated counter-movements that frequently mobilize along cultural and religious lines. Within this, women are often significant players. In Turkey, the mobilization of Islamist women was one of the major contributors to the electoral success of the Welfare Party in the local elections of 1994 (Arat, 1998), and their challenge to the secular dress codes that denied 'covered women' access to the universities or professions has been one of the most explosive political battles in recent years. If we fail to understand these developments as features of *contemporary* politics, we will end up with an oversimplified picture of ancient patriarchy tussling with modern principles of sexual equality. This would be a reassuring picture—making the issues considerably easier than they really are—but it is not in accord with reality.

The second point is that we do not understand social practices unless we understand the social meanings with which they are invested, and that critics from outside a particular cultural setting are often too ready to dismiss what they do not understand. I have never heard a plausible version of this that makes me less critical of genital mutilation, and I have found it hard to sympathize with the explanations of polygamy when these invariably explain why men should have multiple wives rather than women having multiple husbands. But I can see that the critique of arranged marriages often fails to differentiate between marriages that are forced on unwilling partners and marriages arranged by parents concerned with their children's best interests; and that veiling sometimes contests the sexual commodification of women even while confirming unveiled women as sexually loose. A number of respondents to Okin's essay have stressed what they see as her lack of sympathy for religion, and that gulf between believers and non-believers—even greater, it often seems, than the gulf between those who follow different religions—is indeed one of the more difficult ones for the social critic to bridge. There are limits to what we can ask of the social critic: we clearly cannot insist that people engage in a particular practice or embrace a particular set of beliefs before venturing any judgement. But differences in culture and religion have provided a particularly fertile ground for misunderstanding, and it is likely that many of the initial judgements will prove too simple or too harsh.

Against both these points is a third issue that concerns the tendency of all human beings make the best of a bad job (Condorcet's point). It must surely be that 'insiders' can claim a deeper understanding of their social meanings and social practices, but they may also be so thoroughly subordinated by their conditions that they are unable to recognize any injustice. Though this edges disturbingly close to notions of 'false consciousness', I would defend it as an indispensable component in feminist thought. Sexual oppression is not justified by the generations of women who have put up with it; nor is it justified by them saying that the silencing of women in public or the unequal division of domestic labour is 'natural' and right. We know that people living in unjust or impoverished conditions adjust their expectations downwards in order to survive and remain sane; we know that women can live their lives by images of femininity that do immense damage to their self-esteem; we know that people living in relations of domination often find it hard to imagine themselves living under anything else. Perceptions of what is desirable are always shaped and constrained by perceptions of what is possible, and the fact that a woman living in a society where women have always taken the responsibility for children and household may think it unnatural for men to take an equal share does not require us to suspend our critique of the sexual division of labour. Similarly, the fact that women living in societies where girls are considered unmarriageable if they freely enjoy their sexuality may insist on the genital mutilation of their daughters does not require us to regard the practice as what they freely 'choose'. Choices are made within particular social constraints, and much of the time we are not even aware that other choices were possible. If so, this suggests that those most subordinated may also be those least able to recognize the injustice of their position. It may then be the outsiders not insiders who are best placed to judge.

This is not a comfortable conclusion, and clearly has to be moderated by the earlier points about the tendency to misrepresent current tensions as episodes in the battle between modernity and tradition, and the likely misreading of social practices and values by those who can only view them from outside. In most cases, the starkness of the conclusion is further moderated by the presence of internal critics who do not accept their conditions as either natural or just, but I have argued that this last cannot be the decisive consideration. Criticism will certainly be better informed when there are internal as well as external critics, and the resulting dialogue may well lead to a different understanding of values and rights. We should not, however, conclude that there is nothing to be said about abuses of women's rights until these abuses have been challenged from inside. We should not, as Martha Nussbaum observes, allow the fears of a 'do-gooder colonialism' to block initiatives towards gender justice (Nussbaum, 1999: 32).

Equalizing Women's Power

All the above is by way of preamble and clarification: setting out the reasons for anticipating both alliance and tension between feminism and multiculturalism; identifying the dangers of cultural relativism but also the legitimate concerns about universalism; challenging the paralysis that sometimes sets in when we are confronted with cultural claims. Let me restate some key points:

1. Cultural relativism, understood as the belief that norms of justice are relative to the society in which they are formed, and that it is inappropriate to take the norms that emerge within one society as the measure against which to assess the practices of others, is not a useful way forward.

2. At the same time, principles of justice are always formed in a particular historical context, and often reflect the preoccupations of more powerful groups. This does not prevent such principles from having a universal application, but it does mean they must always be regarded as open to contestation, reformulation, and change.

3. Cultural reification, understood as the belief that 'cultures' are monolithic, internally self-consistent, and externally sealed off from other influences, is not a plausible way of understanding the world.

4. The social meaning and significance of cultural practices is best understood by those who engage in them, and it is all too easy for 'outsiders' to misread them.

5. At the same time, the social construction of preferences and aspirations suggests that those most oppressed by a particular practice may also be the least well equipped to recognize its inegalitarian character. Evidence of internal support or consensus is not decisive, and a 'hands-off' approach to cultural difference can end up capitulating to unjust social power.

Since principles of justice are always potentially skewed by the conditions of their formulation, and the understanding of social practices is always open to reinterpretation in the light of new knowledges and experience, one important implication from the above is that principles and policies should be worked out with the fullest possible involvement of all relevant groups. So it is not just 'global citizens' who should work to define human rights or principles of justice, nor yet the religious and cultural leaders representing the principles of 'their' culture or religion, but also the more hidden constituencies with what may be their very different experiences and perspectives and concerns. In seeking to establish which rights should be regarded as inalienable or which practices are inimical to equality between women and men, it is not possible to rely on simple deduction from supposedly universal principles. We always need the maximum possible dialogue to counter the false universalisms that have so dogged previous practice, as well as the 'substitutionism' that has allowed certain groups to present themselves as spokespeople for the rest. The persistent under-representation of women in most of the forums in which these issues are addressed then emerges as a particularly pressing problem. This leads us to what I have elsewhere described as a 'politics of presence' to ensure full participation of all those concerned (Phillips, 1995).

I do not mean by this that matters of basic principle are to be settled by majority vote, and I shall return shortly to reasons why democratization alone is not enough of an answer. But it is only in relatively rare circumstances that policy disagreements involve fundamental issues of principle—pitting equality, for example, against inequality, or the right to life against the right to kill. More commonly, disagreements revolve around competing interpretations of such principles, as in the famous disputes about when a foetus becomes a human being, and whether it has an independent right to life. Even if we start (as I would recommend) from an unashamed commitment to equality, this often turns out to settle surprisingly little. It can be argued, for example, that equality means desegregation: no separate spheres for men and women, no separate enclaves for white and black. But there is often a compelling egalitarian case for segregation, as when people suggest that, in the context of current gender relations, girls will get more equal attention from their teachers and a more equal opportunity to advance their education if they are taught in single-sex schools; or that in a context of racist attacks, ethnic minority groups will enjoy more equal security when they are able to concentrate in the same neighbourhood rather than being dispersed throughout a wider community. The French 'affaire des foulards' (when Muslim schoolgirls were banned from wearing headscarves in school) was argued in competing discourses of equality: on the one hand, that all citizens should be equally bound by the same principles of secularism; on the other, that it was unfair to prevent Muslim students from wearing a symbol of their religion when Catholic schoolgirls were permitted to wear the crucifixes that symbolized their own.

The requirements of equality are rarely transparent, and sorting them out is not just a matter of the depth of one's commitment or the clarity of one's thought. It also matters where one is coming from, what kind of experience one brings to bear on the issue, and from what kind of position one speaks. Perspectives matter for, consciously or not, all of us draw on local knowledge and past experience in making our political judgements, and we often reach contrasting conclusions depending on our location in hierarchies of power. When national governments contest what they see as the intrusiveness of international agencies, they often make the point that schedules of rights have been drawn up by the more powerful nations and do not adequately reflect their own rather different experiences. They rarely, however, go on to recognize the further implication about the way their own understandings have been formed: the dominance of particular groups in defining what counts as 'traditional' culture, and the persistent under-representation of women's voices in identifying what is defensible and fair. Social customs that reflect patterns of male dominance are often wrongly represented as part of what 'the society' wants to sustain. Where this happens, cultural claims can become a vehicle for maintaining the subordination of women.

The case for equalizing women's access to decision-making arenas is therefore closely bound up with the issues explored in this chapter. Women need equality of political and policy representation for a whole range of reasons: as a straightforward matter of fairness between the sexes; so as to provide more vigorous advocacy for interests that would otherwise be overlooked; so as to challenge the infantilization that regards women as better looked after by the (supposedly) more knowledgeable men. All these are substantial reasons in themselves. The crucial addition is that societies cannot confidently establish which policies are most just without the equal involvement of women and men, young and old—of the less as well as the more powerful members of the society. Basic principles are often very basic, not really saying much about how they are to be interpreted and applied. The safe translation from principle to policy is heavily dependent on local knowledge and differences of perspective, and policy prescriptions that are arrived at without the full involvement of all social groups are always open to doubt. When women are excluded from (or just significantly under-represented in) decision-making assemblies and forums, we cannot but suspect the supposed universalism of the policies that then emerge, and this applies a fortiori to the self-defined voices of any 'community' or 'culture'. Equalizing the power of men and women in the processes of policy formation and decision-making has to be seen as central to resolving the tensions discussed here.

Consider, in this context, the issues that arose in the constitutional disputes in Canada leading up to the referendum on the 1992 Charlottetown Accord.[7] The Accord promised to strengthen the self-government powers of Aboriginal peoples and the province of Quebec, and Aboriginal leaders argued that one measure of this self-government was that they should have the power to suspend the provisions of the 1982 Charter of Rights and Freedoms. They argued that the Charter had been developed without the equal involvement and consent of Aboriginal peoples; that its schedule of rights had been drawn up in relation to preoccupations and experiences that differed from their own; and that the principles enshrined in it reflected an adversarial approach to rights conflicts that was at odds with their own values and traditions. Since one of the key provisions of the Charter was the protection it offered to women seeking legal equalities with men, this threatened to set up a stark conflict between Aboriginal self-determination on the one hand and sexual equality on the other. Sexual equality figured in the arguments about sovereignty as an illegitimate imposition. For some participants, it was an alien imposition that was at odds with their community's traditions; for others, it was said to be a legitimate enough objective, but more appropriately dealt with by policies devised by Aboriginal governments themselves.

Since the objections to the Charter seem to conform to my own argument about policies deriving from an unrepresentative gathering tending to overlook certain preoccupations or concerns, this might seem to place me in a quandary: if I think policies have to be worked out with the full and equal involvement of all those affected, how can I then defend what was an imperfectly derived charter of rights and freedoms and allow it to override self-government concerns? Fortunately for my argument—and rather more to the point, for the many Aboriginal women who had benefited from the sex equality provisions—other organizations also entered the arena. 'In the light of entrenched forms of discrimination against them by leaders of their own communities, some women argued that they could not trust their local band chiefs or indeed national leaders to guarantee their sex equality rights at the local reserve level or to include such protections in proposed Aboriginal consitutions' (Deveaux, 2000: 528); and a number of native women's groups, including most notably the Native Women's Association of Canada, argued that future Aboriginal governments should continue to be bound by the Charter's provisions.

Though women were still imperfectly represented in the subsequent public debate, there was enough space for their different interpretations of self-determination and equality to be aired; and, significantly, this developed not just as a debate between supporters and opponents of self-government but as an internal argument between groups that were equally committed to self-government goals. In the event, a surprising majority of Aboriginal peoples living on reserves voted against the self-government provisions of the Accord, and this outcome has been partly attributed to the issues raised about sexual equality. As Monique Deveaux puts it, 'the sense that it exposed a serious rift among Aboriginal associations was not insignificant to the accord's ultimate defeat' (2000: 531).

Democracy scores rather well in this example. It enabled different groups to articulate competing understandings of cultural group rights and sexual equality, and thereby generated a more nuanced debate that complicated the initial rather stark alternative between protecting cultural traditions and securing women's equality. It would be overly complacent, however, just to leave things here. There is an understandable tendency among those tussling with issues of universalism and cultural specificity to look to the democratization of debate as the solution, to insist that principles must be formulated in dialogue, that women's participation will be crucial in challenging monolithic representations of cultural traditions, and that competing voices must be heard. My argument so far falls broadly within this pattern, but I do not want to suggest that democratization is enough of an answer, or that we should drop the philosophical meanderings about universality and concentrate on getting more women involved.

There is always an element of utopianism in appealing to democratic participation to solve all our problems, for who in her wildest dreams expects the right kind of egalitarian democracy to occur? If we set the conditions at too high a level—only recognizing as legitimate, for example, what emerges from the full and equal participation of men and women, young and old, more and less powerful across the globe—we will end up in precisely the kind of paralysis I want to argue against. We would probably be unable to recognize the legitimacy of *any* cultural rights, for there would always be issues about whether the voices of the community or culture in question were genuinely representative. Nor would we be able to settle *any* policies for sexual equality, for there would always be a question mark about the inclusiveness of the decision-making process through which the policies emerged. This is not where I want to end up. We have to aim at a 'good-enough' democracy, rather than paralysing ourselves with an impossible ideal, and my argument should be seen as a case for more extensive consultation—and more equal representation—rather than a statement about the only conditions under which gender justice could emerge.

The further complication derives from the 'on the one hand/on the other hand' pairing that notes the insights 'insiders' will bring to the social meaning and significance of their cultural practices, but sets this against the social construction of preferences and aspirations that can make it hard for those most oppressed by a particular practice to recognize it as unfair. I think it highly unlikely that a discussion conducted on genuinely inclusive lines would fail to throw up evidence of internal opposition to practices that constrained women's freedom or subjected them to arbitrary male power; and I think this particularly unlikely in the light of what I have argued about the interpenetration of different cultures and different ethical ideals. I also believe (and have argued elsewhere[8]) that the very process of inclusion encourages people to stretch their sense of what is desirable and possible, enabling them to articulate previously repressed interests and concerns. But what if all this is too starry-eyed? What if there still turns out to be no internal contestation, or the dissident voices that are raised turn out to be regarded as unrepresentative by the vast majority of women? Should 'outsiders' then reassure themselves with the notion that practices are legitimate because hardly anyone engaged in them states an objection? Should they restrict themselves to condemning only policies that are being actively contested from inside?

Modesty is not always a virtue, and important as it is to challenge the arrogance of those who believe they can settle everything from first principles, this line of inaction would be taking modesty too far. I do not, that is, think we can close off discussion of what I have termed the 'hard case' scenario of external critique. Democratization should be regarded as a crucial element in tackling tensions between multiculturalism and women's equality, but democratization sometimes becomes indefinite postponement, and is better regarded as part, rather than all, of the solution. Despite the questions I have raised about the shaky basis on which supposedly universal principles get formed, there is no getting away from guiding principles as a way of identifying which practices are most indefensible and most at odds with sexual equality concerns.

The ones I offer here are not particularly original: harm is one; equality a second; and whether people enjoy substantive conditions for choice is a third. Though the harm that is done to people by the various practices enjoined on them is always contestable—what I regard as harmful will not always coincide with what you think most damaging to a person's well-being or self-esteem—this contestability should not blind us to questions of degree. Harm varies in grievousness and reversibility: this is presumably what Will Kymlicka has in mind when he identifies the 'gross and systematic violations' of slavery, genocide, or mass torture as legitimating external intervention, and intimates a range of lesser violations that liberal societies might have to condone. My own list would be somewhat longer and would certainly include the irreversible violation of bodily integrity involved in rape or genital mutilation, or the sometimes reversible but still gross harm of being forced into a marriage against one's will. There are certain harms that are sufficiently grievous to override worries about the legitimacy of any one person's understanding, and do not allow for indefinite postponement until full consultation has occurred. In the messy world of real politics, it is important to retain a sense of scale, for even if all harms are philosophically contestable, some are patently more compelling than others. Here, too, we should aim at 'good-enough' discriminations, and not set the standards of rigour so high as to paralyse any kind of action.

Harm addresses the content of a practice; the equality principle asks whether it is permitted for both women and men. One might set aside, for example, the question of whether it is better for people to have one or many (or no) marriage partners, or whether this is something that can be usefully discussed by any except the individuals involved. If the laws of a society permit men to have multiple marriage partners but do not extend the same latitude to women, there is still a prima-facie case for complaint: something is being presented as acceptable for one sex but entirely illegitimate for the other. In this context, the formality often associated with the equality principle (and criticized as such by many feminists) works to its advantage, for it is not always necessary to take up a position on the content of the practice, only whether it applies equally to both women and men.

The third principle addresses an issue that has recurred through my argument, which is whether we can take consent as evidence that there is no problem, or should also be considering the substantive conditions that enable people to choose. Political theorists sometimes refer to the distinction between 'voice' and 'exit' as different ways of getting at people's preferences and choice: so sometimes we explicitly voice our approval or dissatisfaction, perhaps through voting or writing or participating in a political campaign; other times we show what we think by getting up and going away. Either can be taken as evidence that certain practices are consensual, for if no one has either objected or left, there cannot be very much of a problem. As applied to the situation of many women around the world (and I include here some of the most developed liberal democracies), this offers far too rosy a vision, for neither voice nor exit is an easy option if you live in daily fear of physical abuse and see no prospect of earning a living outside your present community. So while it is hardly appropriate for one person or group to dictate to another what they 'ought' to be choosing, it can also be inappropriate to take silence as evidence of consent. Choice depends on substantive conditions. These include, at a minimum, having the political and civil freedoms that enable one to voice an objection, and the educational and employment opportunities that make exit a genuine choice.

With each of these principles, of course, the devil is in the detail, and there is an (entirely defensible) circularity that returns us to the democratic agenda. As the harm continuum stretches out, for example, beyond the more extreme cases of grievous bodily harm, there will be numerous instances where the issues are far from obvious—either because there is genuine uncertainty over the harm involved, or because its scale seems too indecisive to justify sacrificing other values. I have already mentioned the case of segregated education, which is arguably something that harms girls and boys by restricting their communication with members of the opposite sex and encouraging an ideology of separate spheres, but is also arguably of benefit to both in promoting more favourable conditions for learning. Or consider the harm that is done to women whose religion denies them the opportunity to serve as priests or rabbis. I might feel that this is unquestionably a harm, or might suspend judgement on the content of the harm and simply note the inequality that permits to men an opportunity it simultaneously denies to women. But I might still want to weigh these considerations against the harm done to religions if they are forced by legislative intervention to standardize their arrangements for worship and comply with equal opportunities law.[9]

The uncertainties thrown up in the application of general principles to specific cases bring us back to the necessity for inclusive participation, for these uncertainties are best resolved when all relevant groups are fully engaged in the decision-making process. Cultural claims matter: they are themselves important claims about equality, and not to be arrogantly dismissed by reference to a pre-ordained list of universal rights. But cultural claims are too often framed by a monolithic understanding of 'culture' that overstates the internal consensus and misrepresents social customs that sustain male dominance as practices 'the society' wants to sustain. The best protection against this lies in the mobilization of alternative voices, which will often throw up more nuanced readings of the tension between cultural and sexual equality, and may well modify the understanding of both. The full representation of women in discussion and decision-making is a crucial condition for settling the troubled relationship that is developing between multiculturalism and the defence of women's rights. It is important, however, not to be too starry-eyed about democracy, and not postpone action until that ideal democracy occurs.

References

Arat, Yesim (1998) 'Feminists, Islamists, and Political Change in Turkey', *Political Psychology*, 19/1: 117–31.

Bellamy, Richard (1999) *Liberalism and Pluralism* (London: Routledge).

Benhabib, Seyla (1987) 'The Generalized and Concrete Other', in S. Benhabib and D. Cornell (eds.), *Feminism as Critique* (Cambridge: Polity Press).

——(1999) ' "Nous" et "les Autres" ' in C. Joppke and S. Lukes (eds.), *Multicultural Questions* (Oxford: Oxford University Press).

Deveaux, Monique (2000) 'Conflicting Equalities? Cultural Group Rights and Sex Equality', *Political Studies*, 48/3: 522–39.

Gilligan, Carol (1982) *In a Different Voice* (Cambridge, MA: Harvard University Press).

Kymlicka, Will (1995) *Multicultural Citizenship* (Oxford: Oxford University Press).

Nussbaum, Martha (1999) *Sex and Social Justice* (Oxford: Oxford University Press).

Okin, Susan Moller (1998) 'Feminism and Multiculturalism: Some Tensions', *Ethics*, 108/4: 661–84.

—— Joshua Cohen, Matthew Howard, and Martha Nussbaum (eds.) (1999) *Is Multiculturalism Bad For Women?* (Princeton: Princeton University Press).

Parekh, Bhikhu (2000) *Rethinking Multiculturalism: Cultural Diversity and Political Theory* (Basingstoke: Macmillan).

Pateman, Carole (1988) *The Sexual Contract* (Cambridge: Polity Press).

Phillips, Anne (1995) *The Politics of Presence* (Oxford: Oxford University Press).

—— (2001) 'Feminism and Liberalism Revisited: Has Martha Nussbaum Got It Right?', *Constellations*, 8/2: 249–66

Saharso, Sawitri (2000) 'Female Autonomy and Cultural Imperative: Two Hearts Beating Together', in Will Kymlicka and Wayne Norman (eds.), *Citizenship in Diverse Societies* (Oxford: Oxford University Press).

Shachar, Ayelet (1998) 'Group Identity and Women's Rights in Family Law: The Perils of Multicultural Accommodation', *Journal of Political Philosophy*, 6: 285–305.

—— (1999) 'The Paradox of Multicultural Vulnerability: Individual Rights, Identity Groups, and the State', in C. Joppke and S. Lukes (eds.), *Multicultural Questions* (Oxford: Oxford University Press).

—— (2001) *Multicultural Jurisdictions: Cultural Differences and Women's Rights* (Cambridge: Cambridge University Press).

Young, Iris Marion (1990) *Justice and the Politics of Difference* (Princeton: Princeton University Press).

II

Social Sector Restructuring and Social Rights

Political and Social Citizenship: An Examination of the Case of Poland

Jacqueline Heinen and Stéphane Portet

The fall of the Berlin Wall brought the re-establishment of democratic freedoms in East European countries, along with civil and political rights characterizing a state based on the rule of law. But at the same time, the logic of profit and the austerity policy accompanying the development of the market economy meant that most of the social gains of the former system were put into question—and women appear most often to have been losers on all counts in the social field. How far do new democratic rights have a different meaning for men and women, and how far do they contribute to building a gendered model of citizenship? Taking into account the changes which have occurred over the past decade, this chapter through concrete examples, will analyse the articulation between public and private realms in Poland and the way it affects women's status at all levels of society—economically, socially, and politically.

The demise of 'real socialism' has been viewed as a triumph for democracy. It was hoped that people living in the former Soviet bloc and in Poland in particular would regain the rights they had been deprived of for decades: freedom of expression, freedom to travel, freedom of opinion and of religion, etc. Twelve years later, these rights seem to have, at best, only a formal existence for many inhabitants (e.g. the right to travel, which is severely limited by low incomes). But Poland, unlike other Eastern bloc countries,[1] has managed to institute a democratic system based on the rule of law. As in other countries that are candidates for membership in the European Union, freedom prevails in Poland and representative democracy has become the norm. Thus, the Poles have achieved status as citizens.

As in the developed, capitalist countries, this citizenship is not, however, the same for women and men. While all individuals have acquired new civil and political rights associated with the establishment of a democratic system, unequal circumstances have created a situation in which men and women do not have the same degree of access to full citizenship. Furthermore, the market economy has severely eroded old social rights that primarily benefited women, often in their role as mothers. Marginalized in the labour market and widely affected by the pauperization of part of the population, they have paid the highest price in the transition. Thus, unless one subscribes to the most liberal view of citizenship (limited to civil and political rights), one must conclude that the advent of democracy in Poland, as well as in other Eastern European countries, while bringing positive social changes, has led to a series of setbacks.

After having stressed how, both under communism as well as today, individual rights are shaped by or defined in function of one's social group or gender, the chapter will concentrate on the difference in status assigned to men and women in Poland. In a country where the weight of the Church is so important, the relationship each has with the public sphere is very much influenced by the dominant culture and is largely the result of the societal role of family. What, then, will be the effects of Poland's prospective entry into the European Union? This question will be considered below, relying on recent examples of legal changes affecting employment, reproduction, and political representation, with emphasis on the reactions these changes have provoked among Polish feminists eager to reverse historical social patterns concerning gender.

Yesterday and Today: Different Types of Rights

Access to citizenship, democratic rights, and social and political participation are often viewed as a single phenomenon. Classical analyses of citizenship propose a highly universalist concept, in which citizenship is the prerogative of every individual within a democratic regime—a regime that tautologically defines itself as a political system in which all individuals are citizens. Constitutionally, democracies are based on the equality of citizens before the law. The corollary to such a postulate is that everyone, regardless of gender or ethnicity, is a citizen. However, this approach to citizenship prevents a full understanding of the different 'degrees' of citizenship enjoyed by different social groups. The question is not simply one of knowing whether one is a citizen or regards oneself as a citizen—and hence part of the social and political environment. Rather, it is a matter of the degree to which one is, or feels oneself to be, an active participant in that environment. Not all people enjoy the same status; not all are considered full citizens. This is the case with immigrants deprived of political rights, or women, whose civil rights are often curtailed. How can one separate citizenship from the norms and values that govern legitimate male–female relationships? (Pfau-Effinger, 1999).

The approach formulated by T. H. Marshall after the Second World War, when there was a perceived need to redefine citizenship in the context of the advent of the welfare state, appears useful as a basic scheme for identifying the rights denied to certain social groups in so far as it disaggregates various elements of citizenship.[2] Marshall's typology[3] is strongly influenced by the English environment of the period (particularly as regards full employment) and takes no account of differences in the legal and social circumstances of men and women. Leaving aside such criticisms, the analysis he proposes is helpful in the case of Poland and of the Central and Eastern European countries more generally. His *method* can help us think about the status of individuals who are *not* recognized as full citizens; it facilitates identifying rights that existed under the communist regime, as well as new, currently emerging citizenship rights, the way these rights intertwine and how far they define the social status of individuals, in particular among the poorest layers of society (on this point, see Chapter 3).

Under communism, civil and political rights were largely formalistic, unlike social rights, which were universal and assured people certain minimum conditions, regardless of their circumstances. Guaranteed employment and the associated benefits, free provision of most services, and government subsidies in areas such as housing, health, transportation, and basic nutrition made the 'socialist' state similar, in certain respects, to the welfare state.[4] Nevertheless, an intense distrust among the population of anything akin to state intervention precluded an appreciation of the social advantages communism provided. It should be noted that the general malfunctioning of the society and the waste in the economy were visible in the inefficiency of many social services, which fell far short of Western standards—an assessment that understates the situation, when one considers, for example, the health care system. Suffice it to say that these social policies were not viewed in a positive light.

On the contrary, there were extremely high expectations of the market economy, and the implosion of the communist system after 1989 only reinforced the illusion that economic and political change would be accompanied by increased and higher quality social services.

It has become clear, however, that free enterprise and individual liberties do not necessarily go hand in hand; in fact, free enterprise may create strong tensions between civil and social rights. The magnitude of the economic crisis, combined with pressure from international organizations such as the IMF has, in fact, led successive Polish governments to reduce their budgets drastically and to question statutory provisions and structures deemed to be too costly or contrary to the logic of a market economy, as will be seen later in this chapter.

In the move from universalist to residualist rights in the forms of social protection adopted, there is a strong trend towards limited access to benefits for the poorest members of society in present-day Poland, as in most other Eastern European countries: only Polish families with per capita income below one-fourth of the average wage are entitled to benefits.[5] This 'decivilizing' trend, to use Ferge's term (1998), has much to do with the conditionality imposed on these countries by international bodies providing financial assistance.[6] The state's concern to reduce spending brings with it a reconsideration of universal welfare provisions: currently, only the most impoverished segments of the population are eligible for cash benefits. Hence the utility of Marshall's typology in identifying the types of rights involved, the way in which they are affected by the public–private relationship, and the degree to which they affect the social and political definition of citizenship. As Anne Phillips states: 'Democratization remains an empty promise unless it pushes on to address power relations between rich and poor, white and black, women and men' (2000: 100). Dissociating the various levels and nature of rights helps in the scrutiny of what is the social status[7] of men and women facing the outcome of the ongoing changes in Eastern Europe—that is to say, how far they are in a position to *exercise* their (old and new) rights. In this sense, the notion of 'entitlement failures' proposed by Elson (Chapter 3) is quite useful 'for judging the effectiveness of procedures for resource allocation'.

In the specific case of Poland, the emergence of full citizenship for women clashes with the problematic definition of an ideal citizenship based on gender equality in both the public and private spheres. In its definition of citizenship, Polish democracy ranges from a highly universalist concept of citizenship (particularly in regard to political rights) to a differentialist approach (in the area of social rights). When it comes to citizenship, it is the men who are 'citizens', while women are merely 'wives' or 'mothers'. This view is rooted in the centrality of the family, and in the particularity of the public–private relationship under communism.

Continuity/Restructuring of the Public–Private Relationship

In both East and West, the family plays a primary and multi-faceted role as intermediary between the individual and the state. First, it is a source of solidarity, protecting individuals from the outside world and often against state interference. Second, it is inseparable from the reproductive function of women, namely 'their' task of caring for dependent persons within the family. Third, the family serves as a reason for modulating certain rights, particularly social rights that are based on family income.

The first of these functions is especially sensitive in countries with bureaucratic or dictatorial governments. In the Soviet-type societies of Eastern Europe in particular, the private sphere consisted almost exclusively of the family unit, which served as protection against adversity. For both economic and political reasons, this role became increasingly important over the years. Shortages of all sorts, as well as the increasing gap between the state and those living under the yoke of communism, only increased the importance of domestic life, which served as the foundation of the very limited individual autonomy.[8] The second function occupied an especially important place in these societies. As a result of the patent inability of government to satisfy people's need for goods and services, women assumed even greater responsibility, on the domestic front, for ensuring the well-being of their families. While enhancing the value placed on the private sphere and on family solidarity, this situation helped to obscure gender inequalities within the family. The third function of the family played a role analogous to that which it plays in the West, with the level of social services almost always dependent on family income, not on individual rights.

In the case of Poland, the centrality of the family also has its roots in the country's history of martyrdom and in the influence of the Catholic Church. The family was a major factor in resisting outside forces seeking to occupy the country, particularly in the nineteenth century, and served as a vehicle for transmitting the language, cultural memory, and religion of the people. The Matka-Polka myth was rooted in the family—the 'Polish Mother', resisting the occupier, embodying the continuity of the nation, and inheriting the task of 'raising the defenders of the fatherland'. Under the socialist regime, the family retained its status as a refuge and form of resistance, becoming a decisive resource for dealing with the vicissitudes of everyday life (Golinowska, 1995). Today, as in the past, the value of family remains central to two-thirds of the population. While the size of the Polish family is on the decline—the fertility rate dropped from 2.32 in 1985 to 1.43 in 1999 (World Bank, 2000)—family structure is more intact than in the highly developed countries. Material constraints have been a contributing factor,[9] the family helping to withstand the changes imposed by the passage to a market economy, in other words, the 'assaults of another modernity' (Molnar, 1990). Thus, the family has continued—and continues—to occupy a place of honour within the culture. This is all the more so as the rightist nationalist and religious movements occupy a significant place on the political scene. They recycle, for their own purposes, certain nineteenth-century 'communitarian' theories, emphasizing the central role of the home, a notion which is implicit in these theories. Placing the mother on a pedestal, they consider the emancipation of women to be one of the prominent (and despised) features of so-called socialist societies and Western capitalist economies.

This explains in part the high value that both society and women themselves place on women's role in the domestic realm. Such a view is the vector by which women's exclusion from the 'vita activa'—to use Hannah Arendt's term (1958)—is constructed. It also reinforces the concept of dual citizenship, which relegates women to the home. In 1997, 74 per cent of Polish men and women said that they believed women should take care of the house and children, and 67 per cent were convinced that children were harmed by women working (Siemienska, 2000a). According to recent surveys, 78.8 per cent of males and 70.4 per cent of females believe that a mother with young children should not work (Domanski, 1999).[10] While, in the case of men, 'citizen' is generally equated with the elected official, the voter, the producer, or the consumer, the 'female citizen' is not so much a citizen as she is a mother or a wife. Thus, status defined by gender is both a characteristic of the preceding historical period and a reformulation of different facets of citizenship that reinforces the marginal condition of the vast majority of women. As a matter of fact, the role assigned to men and women within the family remains quite different, as can be seen from the sexual division of work: in 1994, women dedicated 4 hours and 30 minutes each day to housework, and men only 53 minutes (IPISS, 1997: 28).

The Polish nurses' strike of October–November 2000 illustrates the continuing view that a woman's place is in the home. The strikers demanded an increase in wages, which in some cases were below the poverty line.[11] The arguments put forward by male politicians against a pay rise demonstrated the fact that low wages were a consequence of society's view regarding nursing—namely, that it is an expression of women's selflessness and 'natural' sense of devotion. As emphasized by Longina Kaszmarska, secretary of the Mazowie nurses' and midwives' union, after one of the demonstrations, 'the government is not really scared, nor is Parliament. If we were men—given our numbers—the barriers would crumble'.[12] Her remark was intended to emphasize the fact that the nurses' strike had been perceived above all as a women's strike, that is, a matter of secondary importance. During the same period, there were a number of miners' strikes opposing the restructuring of the mining industry. These two sets of strikes were treated very differently, both by the government and by the press. Nurses, who were poorly paid under the previous regime, have been one of the losers in the transition. Indeed, most of those who lost out in the transition were women, precisely because of their link to the private sphere.

New Citizenship Opportunities But Growing Marginalization of Women

In Poland, the line between the private and public spheres, on the one hand, and between the social and political spheres on the other, plays a major role in determining the form of citizenship, which is defined today in the most traditional liberal terms. This view holds that individuals are born free and equal, reducing citizenship to a matter of legal status involving the rights of the individual vis-à-vis the state (Mouffe, 1993). As a matter of fact, along with democracy the rule of law was imposed. As Mary Dietz puts it:

Not only does the concept of rights reinforce the underlying liberal principles of individual freedom and formal equality; it also sets up the distinction between 'private' and 'public' that informs so much of the liberal perspective on family and social institutions. Individual rights correspond to the notion of a private realm of freedom, separate and distinct from that of the public. (1992: 65–6)

Thus, citizenship is only definable in the public context, and the 'natural' relegation of women to the private sphere acts as a constraint on their access to the public sphere and on their status as full citizens.

This dynamic is all the more pernicious in a country in which the public sphere enjoys enhanced prestige—a result of the democratization of political life and of the increased importance of economic life. Thus, there has been an emergence of political and economic elites. These elites, consisting primarily of men, embody change, experience, and, above all, 'success', and have come to represent a new form of active citizenship—a break with the passive citizenship of the previous period. More than ever, citizenship is being expressed in the public sphere, which, operating under new rules, has gained increased legitimacy. Society, however, has only scant means of expressing its discontent.

In sharp contrast with the period of Solidarność in the 1980s, these eagerly awaited forms of democracy and of market economies are not subject to the filter of social criticism (as is presently the case in the West). Indeed, as demonstrated by the return to power, in 1993, of the successor of the POUP (Communist Party), the Poles rather quickly expressed, through their votes, dissatisfaction with the social effects of the transition. But while politicians have been criticized harshly for lack of competence and widespread corruption, there is no attempt to question the prevailing forms of representative democracy or of the market economy. The traditional relationship between those governing and those governed, based on the principle of delegation of authority, has been imposed as a model, and has been extended to the business sector, where previous forms of employee participation could have led to new types of professional relationships. Indeed, in Poland, references to self-management, which at a certain point was advocated by one segment of Solidarność, were abandoned rather quickly in favour of a more traditional conception of the employer–employee relationship, based on the contractual subordination of the workforce.

The poor reception given to unions by the workers is quite illuminating in this sense.[13] On the one hand, Solidarność quickly lost much of the ground it had gained under martial law, as it proved unable to defend workers' interests during the very difficult first years of the transition, when unemployment rose dramatically. On the other hand, the other so-called 'branch' trade unions, formally linked to the POUP under the Communist regime, lacked credibility although they tried harder to resist the effects of liberalization. This situation illustrates the problems most individuals currently face in criticizing the new socio-political environment—a reluctance that is perhaps the result of a lack of perspective or the result of economic constraints, particularly unemployment.[14]

This renegotiation of the public sphere presents a new concept of citizenship, one from which women are largely excluded. It is supposedly an inclusive form of citizenship involving all individuals, but it is far from universal, as it seems only to apply to males. This concept of universal interests thus obscures the reality of unequal power relationships between social groups, whether based on class or on gender:

> The promise of democratic equality continues to be subverted by stark differences in access to income and wealth, and deep structural differences in position in the social division of labour; and if we think of democracy not just as a mechanism for generating governments but as a deeper claim about the equality of citizens, there is necessarily a tension between the universalism of political equality and the persistence of inequality and domination in social and economic life. (Phillips, 2000: 101)

A rhetoric that purports to champion equal opportunity masks a situation of equality of rights based on inequality of conditions and can only lead to relationships characterized by increased domination. The political citizenship of women is hindered by the fact that they are relegated primarily to the domestic sphere, thus limiting their ability to participate in political life and further restricting the legitimacy of their actions as citizens. In short, social citizenship is nowadays increasingly linked to economic resources. Complete access to social rights, particularly social security, depends on economic status: only those who are economically active—whether employees or employers—have broad access to these rights.

Indeed, today the 'citizen' is defined, above all, as the consumer, and social integration is accompanied by rapid and profound economic differentiation. Economic capital plays an increasing role in access to political and social citizenship and, in today's world, is replacing those elements that, in the past, were central to the existence of social inequalities, such as the workplace and membership of the Communist Party. The figure of entrepreneur has gained much prestige and, for very concrete reasons, it is seldom associated with women.[15] In addition, the wage gap between men and women and the marked feminization of unemployment and poverty pose significant challenges to women's ability to achieve full social citizenship.

Inequalities in the Right to Work

Since 1989, and particularly since applying for membership of the European Union, Poland has modified its legal structure to create greater equality between the sexes. Equality in the labour market is enshrined in the 1990 Constitution,[16] Article 33, which not only provides that 'men and women in the Republic of Poland have equal rights in the family, and in political, social and economic life', but that 'men and women have equal rights, specifically in regard to education, work, and job promotion, and they have the right to equal pay for work of equal value. They have equal rights as regards social security'.

Under the communist regime, Poland ratified a number of international conventions concerning the equality of men and women in the labour market, including ILO Convention 111 (adopted in 1958). However, while the Polish Constitution of 1952 asserted the principle of respect for the equality of men and women in society as a whole, there was a huge gap, not only between principle and practice, but also between the Constitution itself and other legal provisions. The Labour and Civil Codes contained a number of clauses directly contrary to the principle of equality: access to childcare leave for parents, to take but one example, was highly restrictive for men, while women were excluded from a number of professions, this prohibited list extending to approximately ninety professions, including truck driver, bus driver, and so on. Such discrimination persists in a formal sense in the current Labour Code. Article 176 excludes women from working in particularly uncomfortable or unhealthy professions. However, the list was sharply reduced in 1996.

Poland has by now ratified most of the international conventions and treaties dealing with equality in the labour market.[17] However, the Labour Code made no reference to the issue until 1996, when provisions were introduced to guarantee equality of opportunity in employment and in childhood education.[18] In the context of Poland's accession to the European Union, the country plans to incorporate, between 2001 and 2002, the *acquis communautaire* (the totality of EU legislation) regarding equality of the sexes.[19]

Feminists view these ratifications and the adoption of EU regulations as a means of consolidating the legal framework for the effective implementation of provisions for equal treatment (Nowakowska and Swedrowska, 2000). The implementation of policy stipulations on equal pay and equal treatment in the workplace, as well as in regard to training and promotion, requires monitoring mechanisms to enforce the rules. The principal defect of Polish labour legislation is the absence of sanctions for indirect discrimination.[20] The Labour Code also fails to include rules guaranteeing the principle of equal pay for equal work. In case of conflict, the Constitution is the only recourse available. However, such an approach is not consistent with the tradition of defending individual rights in Poland. The incorporation of European guidelines in Polish law should correct what seems to be a limitation regarding the effectiveness of the law. Specifically, Poland will be obliged to incorporate in its Labour Code the principle of equal pay, the notion of indirect discrimination, and the prohibition of references to gender in employment advertising.

A long tradition underlies this highly significant situation. It is only very recently that employment offices ceased to categorize job offers by gender. Even more important, the classified job advertisements in the press are systematically pervaded by sexism, and are full of job offers explicitly mentioning the gender and age of the person being sought (especially young men in the 30 to 35 year range). When a woman is sought, the required attributes frequently refer to physical appearance (Fuszara and Zielinska, 1995).

Above all, this will make it necessary to facilitate easier resort to legal remedies, widening the authority of labour tribunals to include discrimination cases, and placing the burden of proof on the defence—in most cases the employer. In short, the incorporation of European Union guidelines will extend work-related protection to the hiring phase, which is the most important point at which discrimination occurs. Besides eliminating any mention of gender in job offers, this will make it possible to protect women from discriminatory practices associated with potential motherhood, or with their responsibility for caring for young children.

Despite this progress, the application of European Union standards will not eradicate all legally sanctioned discrimination, such as the continuing differences in retirement ages (65 for men, 60 for women). The proposal to change this provision was rejected in 1997, after debate in the Parliament. As a result, women's pensions average only 60 per cent of those of their male counterparts. The consequent difference in pensions contributes to a precarious economic situation for older women, and limits the career advancement of women, particularly for women over the age of 50.

Changes in maternity leave are also a case in point. In the context of its 'pro-family' policy, the Polish government recently decided to increase maternity leave. This plan provoked a unified response from feminist organizations, which denounced it as an additional barrier to the hiring of women. They also demanded that fathers be given a share of maternity leave. A law providing for the prolongation of maternity leave from sixteen to twenty-six weeks and to thirty-nine weeks for multiple births (instead of twenty-six) was finally integrated into the labour code adopted on 1 May 2001. The law also allows the mother to choose to take as little leave as sixteen weeks (the standard period prescribed by Polish law, as of 1972). Also, after a very heated debate, the Parliament (the Polish Diet), and finally also the Senate, approved a provision allowing men to take up a portion of the maternity leave.

This being said, while the title of the new chapter (Chapter VIII) of the Labour Code has been changed from 'Women's job protection' to 'Job protection for women and men raising children', the principal focus of the law remains the protection of mothers, indeed, protection of the mother's role in her children's education. The wording of the law makes it clear that this task is assigned almost exclusively to women. Thus, while Polish law tends to conform, in a general way, to international standards regarding equal treatment of men and women in employment, it nevertheless continues to contain measures which, in the guise of protecting women, are primarily designed to compel women to assume basic responsibility for infant care. Employers use this to justify their preference for male workers. At the same time, other social measures tend to aggravate this situation further.

The Importance of Unemployment and Limitations on Social Rights

In addition to legal measures, which constitute the statutory framework for citizenship, there is a need to update current practices in the Polish labour market—practices which, at present, fall far short of true equality. The degree of occupational segregation in Poland—45 per cent[21]—is one of the highest in the region (UNICEF, 1999: 36).[22] Also, as in all of the former 'socialist' countries, with the exception of Hungary, women are by far the most severely affected by unemployment, particularly long-term unemployment. Women represent 54 per cent of the unemployed and 57 per cent of the long-term unemployed (GUS, 2001), though they constitute only 46 per cent of the economically active population. The proportion of women in the latter category declined with the drop in unemployment rates between 1997 and 1999, but it rose once again following the subsequent increase in unemployment (as of January 2001, 15.8 per cent of the economically active population was unemployed). This situation reflects hiring preferences favouring men, especially when jobs become more scarce.

At the same time, many sectors show an increase in wage differentials, reflecting the lower value put on women as active participants in the economy. The wage gap has remained more or less stable since 1989, with women earning an average of 20 to 30 per cent less than men with the same educational level and experience. Within that ten-point range, the figure varies according to the economic sector and segment of the labour market. It has increased sharply among blue-collar workers and among the most highly educated wage earners: the latter have lost ten points compared to men within a decade (Heinen, 1999a).[23] Moreover, this job discrimination is exacerbated by the low proportion of women working in the private sector where salaries are higher,[24] and specifically by the greater difficulty women face when becoming self-employed and starting up their own business—for example, being penalized when it comes to obtaining bank loans, given their lower incomes.[25]

As emphasized earlier, professional activity is one of the essential means of gaining access to social citizenship, in the sense of access to the various social rights that are attached to the latter. Reform of the Polish social security system, which began in 1999, has introduced funded pension plans. In so doing, it has contributed to reinforcing, to an extreme degree, the link between the level of income and social citizenship. Although rather poor, previous pension schemes were based on a system of mutual aid to which women and men had an automatic right. Now the level of pension depends much more strictly on (a) the amount of the previous salary and whether the recipient was unemployed or not for a given period; and (b) the ability of the person to contribute monthly to a pension fund based on the principle of capitalization. Thus, women—who represent 75 per cent of those receiving below-average wages and the majority of the unemployed—pay a high price in terms of access to social rights, due to their marginal economic status. This situation is further aggravated by the efforts of successive Polish governments to reduce public spending in order to satisfy conditions for Poland's entry in the European Union.[26]

As a result of these budgetary restrictions, many structures and legal provisions are considered to be too onerous and have been called into question, as has occurred throughout Eastern Europe. The protective laws of the old regime, which provided special entitlements for mothers of young children (childcare leave for parents, leave to care for a sick child) and for single mothers (priority access to childcare and pre-school for toddlers, and twice the standard family or childcare benefits) were among the first to be questioned. This applies, particularly, to childcare leave. Today, while this leave still exists in theory, it is a mere shadow of what it was under communism. Then, the fact that a person had a right to return to his or her job following leave was one of the system's major attractions. Today, though this leave has been extended to fathers without restriction (a change from the previous system), due to the elimination of the right to return to one's job following leave, it has lost any real significance. This change occurred in tandem with group lay-offs and business closures. Hence, between 1990 and 1996, the proportion of women availing themselves of maternity leave dropped by two-thirds[27] (Balcerzak-Paradowska, 1997: 58). In terms of leave to care for a sick child (sixty days per year, with 80 per cent pay[28]), very few women currently take advantage of this benefit, for fear of losing their jobs. One employer states bluntly: 'Someone who is absent too many times gets fired. ... We expect women to limit the time they take off to care for a sick child' (Zylicz, 1999: 5). The pay for days taken as childcare leave in particular was already grossly inadequate, and pay for both childcare leave and maternity leave has been cut drastically. Under the current system, only families whose per capita income is less than one quarter of the average wage are entitled to benefits. This low level of benefits proves a strong disincentive to mothers and, to an even greater extent, to fathers.

Severe cuts in the state budget have also dealt a blow to the publicly provided infrastructure for infant care, while the policy of providing childcare free of charge has been abandoned, as has been the case throughout Eastern Europe.[29] Thus, many infant care facilities and pre-schools provided by the municipality have had to close, the number of infant care facilities falling by almost two-thirds, and by close to one-third for pre-schools between 1989 and 1996 (IPISS, 1997: 60). Furthermore, economic rationalization and privatization have been responsible for the elimination of non-essential social spending, with the result that two-thirds of the pre-school facilities provided by the productive sector have been closed, as have almost all the employer-subsidized infant-care facilities. In the latter case, either they disappeared in the context of industrial restructuring that involved the liquidation of unprofitable firms, or they closed for economic reasons, with managers seeking the maximum reduction of costs not directly associated with production. Thus the number of infant-care facilities provided by employers dropped from 236 in 1990 to two in 1997 (Siemienska, 2000a).

In addition, the prices charged by public institutions have increased considerably. The monthly cost for one child in a childcare centre can be up to one third (sometimes even half) of an average salary. For many families, the prohibitive cost discourages the use of outside childcare, all the more so since allowance must be made for various additional expenses such as food and special activities. As an expert put it: 'We have seen a tendency for the children from the least comfortable and most impoverished environments to be removed, when a stay in a childcare centre can help put the conditions of their development on an equal footing' (Balcerzak-Paradowska, 1997: 59). The private facilities now available in order to compensate for the lack of public provision only benefit the higher socio-economic groups, since the cost of such services is prohibitive for the families most in need of them (particularly single-parent and large families).[30] These changes represent a huge step backward for a great many families, and particularly for women, who are already penalized in the job market (Heinen, 2001).

Indeed, these measures affect women first and foremost. They tend to limit their mobility and restrict their chances of finding a job and establishing a degree of autonomy. More particularly, they affect specific social segments, including single mothers, who comprise a disproportionate percentage of persons living below the poverty line,[31] as the legal provisions guaranteeing them state protection were eliminated during the first round of reforms.[32] Thus, in terms of social citizenship, women have lost much during the past decade. It might be suggested that this new lack of security is the price of increased access to civil and political citizenship. In reality, however, women have few of the advantages enjoyed by men. Moreover, their subjugation in the social realm has a very explicit counterpart in the civil domain, namely, the elimination of the right to abortion.

Prohibition on Termination of Pregnancy

Reconsideration in 1993 of the right to abortion and the passing of legislation introducing its almost complete prohibition demonstrates clearly that, in regard to civil citizenship, Polish democracy discriminates against women and treats them as minors. Indeed, the law prohibiting termination of pregnancy was adopted even though polls and surveys carried out in connection with the bill (which was supported by the Catholic Church) showed repeatedly that the majority of the public, especially women, were hostile to legislation depriving women of the right to decide whether or not they wished to have a child (Heinen and Matuchniak-Krasuska, 1995; Zielinska, 1999). Thus the law incorporated standards and values that, from the perspective of current social practices, were antiquated.[33] This is one more indication that, in the government's view, the quintessential Polish woman is, above all, a mother or potential mother, whose primary purpose should be procreation.

It should be noted that, in the 1990s, opinion on abortion varied widely according to age group and that the Church's determined campaign against abortion finally scored some success in the overall population. While close to 60 per cent of adults interviewed in the early 1990s opposed criminalizing abortion, this figure was only 20 per cent among those under 18 years of age, who had been more exposed to Church indoctrination. Today, this is an even more sensitive issue, with the catechism again becoming mandatory in schools— where priests have the status of ordinary teachers—and with the elderly becoming less liberal on the issue. In 1995, Parliament adopted an amendment to the 1993 law on abortion, expanding the circumstances under which a woman could terminate a pregnancy, by recognizing the validity of certain 'social' factors. However, at this point a little less than half of the Polish population favoured provisions which, under the laws in effect during the communist regime, permitted women to justify abortion based on material considerations (insufficient income, inadequate housing) or for psychological reasons (Federacja, 1996).[34]

At the time, voluntary termination of pregnancy was authorized only in cases of rape, malformation of the foetus, or when the life of the mother was in danger. These exemptions cover barely 5 per cent of voluntary terminations that have been reported.[35] Though women resorting to extralegal voluntary terminations merely risk a fine, doctors performing the procedure are subject to a two-year prison sentence. The Polish government takes great pride in the low number of legal abortions—151 for the entire year 2000. As emphasized, however, in a report published by the Federation for Family Planning (Nowicka and Tajak, 2000), this figure fails to give a realistic picture of the situation, since it does not take account of the 80,000 to 200,000 abortions performed clandestinely in Poland or obtained abroad, primarily in Belarus, the Ukraine, or Germany. Government hypocrisy is beyond imagination: 'gynaecological travel agencies', which have proliferated in the last ten years, are often well-established businesses that, with impunity, place small newspaper advertisements with slogans such as 'All services guaranteed. Absolutely all'.

Thus, in reality, the law is not being enforced. The few prosecutions of gynaecologists on charges that could lead to prison sentences, of travel agents whose advertisements openly defy the law, or of women accused of abandoning or killing their children have stalled or ended in dismissal. The defendant goes free, with no determination of guilt or innocence, as if the institutions responsible for enforcing the law could not decide to impose 'order' on the situation. This non-interventionist approach, in effect, openly questions the appropriateness of norms that underlie the prohibition on abortion, and it illustrates the problem of defining abortion as a crime: there is a flagrant contradiction between the severity of the required sentences and prevailing public opinion, which opposes the current legislation for its repressive dimension. This is all the more true due to the fact that the primary reasons women give for ignoring the law involve a lack of material resources. This fact can hardly be ignored in a country in which there is considerable ongoing debate and intense press coverage on the economic problems experienced by the majority of families. The authorities—the police, the judiciary, and especially political entities—run the risk that active attempts to enforce the law could backfire, leading to a further loss of credibility.

Nevertheless, the right to abortion itself is being denied, despite the fact that it is central to a woman's autonomy. The right includes various important elements of citizenship, and emanates not only from civil rights, but also from political and social rights. In reality, it consists of: (*a*) a political right that became, in the West, part of the feminist agenda seeking to affirm a collective feminine identity; (*b*) a civil right, inasmuch as reproductive freedom involves an individual's right to physical integrity; and (*c*) a social right, since the legal termination of pregnancy depends on treatment in a public facility and therefore involves public health policy (Marques-Pereira, 1995, 2000).

This prohibition demonstrates—in Poland, better than anywhere else—that the liberal concept of the separation between the public and private realms is less than absolute and is applied differently to men and women. By opposing women's control over their fertility, in the name of protecting the 'conceived child' (the name given to the foetus in the 1993 law regarding termination of pregnancy),[36] the Polish political authorities are claiming that they can legitimately intervene in the private lives of women and subordinate their bodies to a particular concept of life—a concept intimately linked to their determination to effect an increase in the birth rate. The denial of the right to abortion is emblematic of the politicization affecting the private sphere in numerous areas—a form of politicization, however, that does not extend to issues of domestic violence or the sharing of household tasks, subjects presumed to be purely private matters.

Thus, the democratic dynamic emphasizing the individual, along with personal autonomy, is not assigned the same value for men and women in modern-day Poland. Despite the country's efforts to restore civil rights that were denied or effectively gutted of any real meaning under the Soviet regime, the denial of women's personal liberties demonstrates that 'citizenship' has a strong gender dimension. How far does the prospect of integration into the European Union reinforce such a process or otherwise?

European Integration: A Wind of Change?

As mentioned above, the integration process has a rather limited impact when it comes to equal opportunities between men and women (Heinen and Portet, 2001). This is due to several reasons.

First, the implementation of European directives on gender equality does not involve a rupture with the very traditional conception of gender supported by the Polish government, all the more as the rightist political current exerts a significant influence among the intelligentsia (which includes the experts involved in current negotiations with the European Union). This has been shown both through debates on the integration of Poland into the European Union and through recent legal and political developments covering a range of social issues.

The recent parliamentary debate on maternity leave provides an illustration of the persisting power of the traditional model. Secondly, the type of negotiation itself does not imply a radical evolution of the gender contract legitimated by Polish society. The integration of European directives into Polish law appears more as an obligation or formality, rather than as a sign of real willingness. During the UN Special Session of the General Assembly 'Women 2000: Gender Equality and Peace for the Twenty First Century' (5–9 June 2000, New York), the chief of the Polish delegation stressed this fact by expressing the desire to preserve the Polish cultural exception until integration with Europe is implemented. By stressing the relative compliance of the Polish law *vis-à-vis* the European rules, the political powers tend to minimize the scope of the coming changes. A leaflet concerning the equal opportunities chapter in the European integration process, published by the Committee for European Integration[37] in 1999, offers an edifying illustration of such a discourse. The case of Ireland, which despite being a member state maintains a very traditional policy towards reproductive rights, is presented as a model for Poland. The leaflet stresses the non-compulsory character of most of the European dispositions and makes it clear that the aim is to make the Polish law conform to European demands without modifying fundamental aspects of the gender contract. For example, the leaflet says that 'whatever value Polish society attributes to family and to traditional domestic roles, we will have to accept that women's work should not be perceived as bad and women as less important [than men]' (Komitet, 1999: 26). Or, 'the Christian-democrat majority in the European parliament let us think that the way of thinking of the European legislators will be closer to the traditions of Polish society. This will help us to defend the values supported by the majority of Polish citizens' (1999: 28). Finally, the document presents three controversial questions for Polish society: 'Will entry into the European Union impose a quota of 40 per cent of women in political and administrative institutions?', 'Will entry into the European Union impose changes in the anti-abortion law?', 'Will entry into the European

Union mean accepting legislation supporting the right to marriage for homosexuals?' Obviously, the answer to these three questions is no. These issues are not compulsory and each member state has full sovereignty to decide for itself (1999: 39–40).

Beyond this ideological resistance, the effects of the integration process are narrowed by two institutional mechanisms: the weakness of the means of control and of penalties and the *mainstream* paradigm. Concerning the first point, the implementation of European law faces the same limits as that of Polish law when it comes to control and penalties. This weak point of the system is stressed in the 1999 screening report presented by the European Commission.[38] Second, the enlargement process is based, as is the whole European equal opportunities policy, on the paradigm of the mainstream, and all parts of the negotiations have to respect the principle of equality between men and women. Positive in many respects, such an approach can, however, appear quite inadequate in a case like Poland, when no added specific programmes for equal opportunities exist. Of course, the mainstream strategy does not exclude such a possibility,[39] but nor does it imply it automatically. As Agnes Hubert argues, this global approach could 'contribute to neutralizing the problem by successive dilution' (1998: 118), in particular when the administration is not wholly convinced of the legitimacy of equal opportunities policies.

Participation in Political Life

The fact that women are poorly represented in the nation's political life reinforces this situation. Since the last legislative election (September 2001) the proportion of women is 20 per cent in Parliament and 23 per cent in the Senate. However limited, these results represent a turning point. Since 1989, women comprised no more than 13 per cent of members of Parliament in Poland, as opposed to approximately 30 per cent during the previous period.[40] Renata Siemienska correctly points out that, in the earlier period, Parliament performed a merely 'decorative' function, with real power residing in the hands of the leaders of the Communist Party (POUP) and certain governmental bodies, from which women were effectively excluded.[41] Nevertheless, with the Senate and Parliament gaining a pivotal role and making decisions that would ultimately determine the rights and interests of different social groups, including women's groups, this decline in the number of women elected to the country's highest decision-making bodies[42] assumed symbolic significance.

Until recently, women affected by this situation have largely remained silent in the face of their blatant exclusion from decision-making spheres. This passivity is explained by several factors. First, the egalitarian rhetoric of communist officials, who proclaimed women's emancipation to be an achievement of 'real socialism', combined with the way the quota system was applied,[43] have, over a period of time, tended to discredit the importance of sexual equality in politics. Second, material concerns cause most women to focus their attention on the family unit. This, reinforced by the rhetoric of nationalist movements, which urge women to give priority to their role as mothers, tends to promote acceptance of the traditional public–private dichotomy. Finally, the lack of transparency in the decision-making apparatus, the prevalence of organized crime, and problems in instituting a democratic system that accommodates the aspirations of the majority have merely aggravated the sense of disillusionment with politics in Poland, as in neighbouring countries. The tendency to regard politics as something 'dirty' is particularly evident among women, many of whom also consider it a 'male game'. These feelings seem to have a negative effect on women's desire to invest energy in public affairs, leading to an inclination—even more pronounced than in the West—to remain in the periphery.

Nevertheless, not all women eschew involvement with political parties, as indicated by the recent demand for parity. In March 2001, joint efforts by feminists groups and female members of Parliament resulted in a legislative bill proposing that 40 per cent of seats be reserved for women. Though the bill was defeated, it prompted an important discussion about women in politics. The issue of parity is popular in Poland. In 1999, 63 per cent of the Poles were in favour of a reserved percentage of seats for female candidates (Fuszara and Zielinska, 1998).[44] However, the biggest problem women face in running for political office is that of getting selected for inclusion on a party slate. The nature of this selection process tends to be determined by the very structure of political life in Poland. For the most part, parties are grouped in large coalitions, and individual slates must first of all represent each of the organizations involved in a given coalition. Since the main (male) leaders of this collection of small parties must be given places on the slates, the opportunities for women are minimal. Furthermore, as demonstrated by the sexism typically found in political bodies and by the impunity with which some male members of Parliament interrupt their female colleagues with cries of 'Talk less and make more children!' (Graham and Regulska, 1997), many men would prefer to banish women from the political scene altogether, convinced that women belong elsewhere—namely, at home.

In the legislative elections of 1997, the percentage of women among the candidates for office ranged from 25 per cent (in the case of the leftist Union for Labour) to 11 per cent (in the rightist Electoral Solidarity Alliance, linked to Solidarity), and they generally were at the bottom of the lists. A strong tradition is at work, and women encounter numerous obstacles to gaining access to the political arena. Thus, there is a paradox and, to some extent, a contradiction. On the one hand, there is the behaviour of the majority of women (who are always reticent about becoming personally involved in politics) and the rejection faced by women candidates within the political system. On the other hand, especially among women, there is a positive evolution regarding the importance attached to the presence of women candidates.

Thus the Pre-electoral Coalition (Przedwyborcza Koalicja Kobiet)—a platform of feminist organizations—launched a campaign supporting female candidates in the legislative election of September 2001 in the hope of increasing the number of women elected. The coalition proposed training for women candidates and put pressure on the political parties. A number of newspapers reported these efforts, which appeared to be a real success. The proportion of women candidates became a new variable in party-political campaigning, above all for the left. Most left-wing and centre-left parties tried to achieve more than 30 per cent of women in their candidates' list. The Social Democrat coalition list included 34.6 per cent of women and Unia Wolności (Union of Freedom, centre-left) had 30.03 per cent, while the right-wing Electoral Solidarity Alliance had only 12 per cent of women in its candidates list. The victory of the left, with 44 per cent of the votes, increased the number of female deputies in the Parliament by 35 per cent and in the Senate by 48 per cent, compared with 1997.

These figures reflect the fact that, over the last ten years, the difference of opinion between men and women regarding women's abilities as politicians has increased, with men increasingly sceptical and women somewhat more confident. Men's conservative reflex is an expression of their view regarding the new era, based on a number of years of experience. In a context of social differentiation, where there has been a levelling of the conditions for choosing 'players' in the political and economic arena, women appear to be increasingly viable as competitors in a race where there are fewer places on each party slate.

Thus, in 1992, in the view of 35 per cent of men and 45 per cent of women, men were not deemed more suitable for political life than women, while in 1998, 27 per cent of men and 49 per cent of women expressed a similar opinion—showing, in both instances, a well-entrenched scepticism concerning the competence of women. The difference is greatest, however, among the young. In 1997 a 'mere' 30 per cent of women under 29 years of age still considered men more able than women, 57 per cent of men of the same age held this opinion (Siemienska, 2000*b*). Thus, as is true with employment, the younger generations of women tend to be more keen on participation and autonomy, calling for a renegotiation of the contract between the sexes and a change in the traditional model of the family, in the direction of greater equality.[45] This trend is demonstrated particularly in increased voting among women, with each successive election manifesting a narrowing of the gap between men's and women's participation.[46] This suggests that there is a growing awareness of the importance of politics in the new socio-economic framework, despite the fact that a large segment of the population distrusts politics.

Although the impact of the European integration process is very limited in practice, it has played quite a significant role in promoting equality between men and women in Poland, at least in terms of ideas and in encouraging women's social and political activity. European standards are a definite point of reference for those Polish non-governmental organizations (NGOs) defending women's rights and for groups claiming to be feminist. Activists receive European Union financial support but above all the EU gives their activities and discourse legitimacy, and these groups have had a decisive impact on the current change in representation. This is a factor which to some extent corrects the rather pessimistic picture of gender relations presented above.

NGOs and Feminist Groups Open New Perspectives in the Political Field

Over the last ten years, NGOs have increasingly played a key role, assuming responsibility for issues that national or local government have neglected or failed to address adequately. Moreover, consideration of their activities can hardly be undertaken without considering the involvement of Polish women in these organizations, since they constitute the majority of active members. The involvement of these independent organizations in issues of general concern (employment, assistance to the poorest segment of the population), as well as in issues of specific interest to women, implies participation in the public sphere, which is not confined to governmental or well-established institutions, but encompasses the entire range of citizen initiatives.

Family planning organizations, for example, have a social dimension (training of specialists, distribution of contraceptives), as well as a political one (debate on abortion legislation). It would be absurd to refuse to label them 'political' on the pretext that they are not part of an established political structure, or because they have no immediate connection with the circles of power.

Although not necessarily perceiving themselves as feminist, such initiatives, which are a response to the shortcomings of government, facilitate women's access to the public/political realm. They have also the merit of ending the passivity inherited from communism. As leading players in negotiations with the state, members of NGOs are active political citizens, playing an important role *vis-à-vis* international organizations (UNESCO, ILO, etc.) and in the process of European integration.

Second, the general tendency to marginalize women has not gone unopposed. Kazimierz Kapera, Poland's former Minister of the Family, in maintaining in 1999 that 'Poland is not a country where women suffer discrimination' (cited by Warsaw Women's Rights Centre, 2000), provoked the anger of many feminist activists, who spoke out in the nation's press. In the words of Agnieszka Graff (1999), 'The French have cheese, the English, their Queen, and the Poles, discrimination against women', while Magda Sroda (1999) commented, with irony, that 'Poland's greatest success was the period of "de-emancipation"'. Observers attentive to the question of gender relationships in Poland point to a new feminist critique emanating from activist groups which, though modest in numbers, occupy an increasingly prominent place in the media. They also note a revival of research on social relationships between men and women, due to the creation of a number of centres in Polish universities dedicated to gender studies, especially in Warsaw and Łódź.

Some of the NGOs mentioned here claim to be feminist. This is a change compared to the period of the 1980s, the time of political opposition, when the Solidarity movement rather ignored women's issues. Since the fall of the Berlin Wall in 1989, the landscape of activities regarding women's interests has changed considerably. If *Liga kobiet* (Women's League) the major women's association and mass movement linked to the Communist Party continued to have some influence at the beginning of the transition, currently it has a very limited role on the public scene. On the other hand, several feminist organizations emerged in the early 1990s, particularly during the struggle against the anti-abortion law.[47] With the help of international bodies (EE, UN, etc.) and foundations (Friedrich–Erbert Stiftung, Foundation Stefan Batory, etc.), many organizations promoting and defending women's rights were founded in Poland. That is the case of the already mentioned Federation for Family Planning, an umbrella of several organizations, which is fighting for women's reproductive rights; the Warsaw Women's Right Centre, which offers juridical support and training to women to improve their employment prospect; the centre for promotion of women, supporting women seeking a job or who want to be self-employed. There are now almost 200 organizations of this type, including information centres such as the highly active Oska centre in Warsaw. These organizations are important in lobbying national institutions and are attracting increasing attention from international institutions. Some publish important reports on the situation of women in Poland which tend to be major sources for international recommendations. Beyond these activities, which give priority to institutional action, more and more active radical groups have also emerged involving young women. One part of these feminist groups (like *Emancipunx* in Warsaw) is linked to the rising anarchist movement in Poland, and the other is managed by students in gender studies (*Speculum*). These organizations give priority to public demonstrations, generally 'happenings', and focus their action against social stereotypes.

It is revealing that today Polish feminists dedicate a considerable part of their efforts to political activities. In doing so, they rely on the experience of women's movements in the West (or some of them, at least) since, little by little, these movements have found it necessary to re-evaluate their relationship with institutions, giving high priority, as in the case of France, to women's political participation. The year 2000, in particular, was marked by a series of offensives designed to improve the lot of women in Polish democracy, as can be seen in the case of the legislative bill on parity. Though the bill was defeated, the initiative demonstrates that women—who were big losers in the transition—are beginning to claim some of its benefits. It is symbolic that one of the first major battles after that lost on abortion rights in the early 1990s aimed at the very heart of Poland's political life, with demands for increased representation of women in elected offices. This highlights once again the central role of politics in citizenship matters.

Conscious of the dangers of constructing an exclusively male political world, Polish feminists have decided to react. In order to make their voices heard, and to combat the backlash against the legitimate presence of women in Parliament—at the very time when Parliament is undertaking a wide-ranging refashioning of legislation—the majority have opted to engage in lobbying, a tactic necessitated by the relatively small number of individuals in the movement.[48] The road is not an easy one, as feminists have had to overcome the painful experience of March 1999, when Parliament rejected a bill on equality of the sexes.[49] Inspired by a Norwegian law, the bill proposed a framework for intervention, based on practices within the European Union that offer a systematic approach to equality through mainstreaming—a policy incorporating all spheres of society. Reference to European legislation and practice was central, both in developing the language and the arguments, as its authors stress in pointing out that equal status is a new concept in Poland (Fuszara and Zielinska, 2001). The proposal was intended to incorporate the *acquis communautaire*—European Union legislation in its entirety—giving national legislation a certain sense of equality.

Of course, it cannot be concluded from the adoption of such an approach that integration into the European Union is a miracle cure. Polish feminists understand this quite well. This is expressed by, among others, Wanda Nowicka, President of the Federation of Women and Family Planning, who writes 'The Union will not solve all the problems. It will not force Parliament to adopt the principle of parity, provide for equal retirement ages for men and women, or liberalize abortion, but standards of reference in other countries of the Community will influence Polish legislation.'[50]

Whatever the limits set by the negotiating framework, it has established the context for the current struggle aimed at establishing a 30 per cent quota for women on electoral slates, in anticipation of the legislative elections of 2002. Though efforts to change the law have, to date, been unsuccessful, a number of parties, including the SLD, the majority party of the left, are committed to increasing the number of women in the ballots. Most important, perhaps, is the fact that this initiative by feminist organizations has paved the way for a public debate on the intensely male character of Polish democracy. Though the debate has failed to reverse the course of affairs for the moment, it has created an opening and helped clarify the positions held by the advocates of gender equality and by those adhering to the traditional model—with the latter being compelled to acknowledge the extent to which such a model involves excluding half of the Polish population from the decision-making process.

Conclusion

At the start of the process of economic change, many Poles dreamt of the social-democratic model prevalent in Scandinavian countries. The road to such a reality is, however, a long one, especially as regards women's rights. Many feminists see the process of European integration as providing powerful leverage for improving the existing situation, and it is true that the gender equality perspective espoused by the European Commission is very progressive by Eastern European standards.

However, while from a formal point of view and in terms of the law, the process of integration leads to positive change, the criteria for 'good economic management' required of countries seeking membership are inimical to *progressive* social policy. Although a struggle seems to be developing concerning the respective roles of men and women in the new Poland, the current trend remains geared towards marginalizing women and consolidating their status as second-class citizens. Once again, in the integration process—as was true in the earlier transition process—women run the risk of ending up among the losers.

Despite this somewhat sombre picture, there are grounds for hope. There is mounting criticism regarding the growing inequalities, which tend to impede social cohesion and hence weaken the process of economic change. Women are participating in the debate, as are other social groups. Women still represent a minority in this discussion, and most of those involved are from the upper social strata. However, in the current legislative campaign, women's issues tend to be considered as more and more important, as politicians have come to understand that women comprise half the electorate. Even the President of the Republic recently took part in the public debate by publishing an article about the need to accord women a place in the new Polish society.[51] Such an attitude constitutes a break from the spirit prevailing during the Solidarity period, when, during the massive strikes in 1980, one could read on the walls of the Gdansk shipyards, 'Women, do not disturb. We are fighting for Poland'. The fact that nearly 60 per cent of women and 50 per cent of men in Poland now believe that a feminist movement is necessary[52] seems to indicate a certain renewal, with marked differences from the earlier period.

References

Arendt, H. (1958) *The Human Condition* (Chicago: University of Chicago Press).

Balcerzak-Paradowska, B. (1997) 'Publiczne instytucje społecznych a rodzina' (Public Social Institutions and the Family), in IPISS, *Partnerstwo w rodzinie i na rzecz rodziny* (Partnership in the Family and on Family Issues) (Warsaw: IPISS).

CBOS (1999) *Młodzież i Dorośli o aborcji* (Young People and Adults on Abortion) (Warsaw: CBOS).

Del Re, A. (1994) 'Droits de citoyenneté: Une relecture sexuée de T. H. Marshall', in Eliane Vogel-Polsky (ed.), *Women Studies: Manuel de Ressources*, (Brussels: ULB).

Dietz, M. (1992) 'Context is All: Feminism and Theories of Citizenship', in Chantal Mouffe (ed.), *Dimensions of Radical Democracy. Pluralism, Citizenship, Community* (London and New York: Verso).

Domanski, H. (1999) *Zadowolony niewolnik idzie do pracy* (The Happy Slave Goes to Work) (Warsaw: IFIS/PAN).

European Commission (1999) *Regular Report from the Commission on Poland's Progress towards Accession* (Brussels: European Commission).

—— (2000) *Communication from the Commission: Towards a Community Framework Strategy on Gender Equality (2001–2005)* (Brussels: European Commission).

Federacja na rzecz Kobiet i Planowania Rodziny (1996) *Skutki ustawy antyaborcyjnej* (Consequences of the Anti-Abortion Law), Report No. 2 (Warsaw: Federacja).

Ferge, Z. (1998) 'L'évolution des politiques sociales en Hongrie depuis la transformation du système', *Revue d'études comparatives Est–Ouest*, 29/3: 35–59.

Fraser, N. (2000) 'Rethinking Recognition: Overcoming Displacement and Reification in Cultural Politics', *New Left Review* (May–June).

Fuszara, M. (1995) 'Obstacles and Barriers to an Equal Status Act in Poland', in Renata Siemienska (ed.), *Women: the Past and the New Roles* (Warsaw: Centre for Europe, Warsaw University).

—— (2001) 'O Kobietach w parlamencie raz jeszcze' (On Women in Parliament, Again), *Buletyn Oska*, 2: 17–19.

—— and E. Zielinska (1995) 'Obstacles and Barriers to an Equal Status Act in Poland', in *Women: The Past and New Rules* (Warsaw: Centre for Europe, Warsaw University).

—— —— (1998) 'Krótka acz zawiła historia ustawy równościowej' (Brief but complicated story of the law on equality), *Buletyn Oska*, 4/98: 12–14.

Golinowska, S. (1995) 'Family Formation in Poland: Brief Historical Approach', in IPISS, *Families in Poland* (Occasional Papers, 7, Warsaw: IPISS).

Graff, A. (1999) 'Patriarchat po seksmisji' (Patriarchy after Seksmisja), *Gazeta Wyborcza* (19–20 June).

Graham, A., and J. Regulska (1997) 'Expanding Political Space for Women in Poland: An Analysis of Three Communities', *Communist and Post-Communist Studies*, 30/1: 65–82.

GUS (1998) *Earnings Distribution in the National Economy as of September 1997* (Warsaw: GUS).

GUS (2001) *Miesięczna informacja o bezrobociu w Polsce w lutym 2001 roku* (Monthly information on Unemployment in Poland, February 2001) (Warsaw: GUS).

Haney, L. (1997) ' "But we are Still Mothers": Gender and the Construction of Need in Post-Socialist Hungary', *Social Politics: International Studies in Gender, State and Society*, 2: 208–44.

Heinen, J. (1995) *Chômage et devenir de la main-d'œuvre féminine en Pologne: Le coût de la transition* (Paris: L'Harmattan).

—— (1997) 'Public/Private: Gender, Social and Political Citizenship', *Theory and Society*, 26/4: 577–97.

—— (1998) 'Women in Local and National Politics in Central and Eastern Europe', in Council for European Municipalities and Regions (CEMR), *Men and Women in European Municipalities* (Paris: CEMR).

—— (1999*a*) 'East European Transition, Labour Markets and Gender. In the Light of Three Cases: Poland, Hungary and Bulgaria', *Polish Population Review*, 15: 106–25.

—— (1999*b*) 'La question sociale en Pologne: Un processus de polarisation qui modèle les rapports de genre', *Matériaux pour l'histoire de notre temps*, 53: 41–52.

—— (2001) 'Children Collective Keeping in Poland', in Mahon Rianne and Sonya Michel (eds.), *Child Care and Welfare State Restructuring: Gender and Entitlement at Cross Roads* (London: Routledge).

—— and A. Matuchniak-Krasuska (1995) 'Abortion in Poland: A Vicious Circle or a Good Use of Rhetoric', *Women's Studies International Forum*, 18/1: 27–33.

—— and S. Portet (2001) 'Intégration de la Pologne à l'Union européenne et rapports de genre', *Lien social et politiques—RIAC*, 45.

Hubert, A. (1998) *L'Europe et les femmes: Identités en mouvement* (Rennes: Apogée).

IPISS (1997) *Partnerstwo w rodzinie i na rzecz rodziny* (Partnership in the family and on family issues) (Warsaw: IPISS).

Komitet Integracji Europejskej (1999) *Informator Unia Europejska—Kobiety* (Warsaw: Komitet Integracji Europejskej).

Marques-Pereira, B. (1995) 'Citoyenneté et liberté reproductive: L'approche de T. H. Marshall est-elle pertinente?', communication at the second ESA Conference, Budapest, 23–5 Aug.

Marshall, T. H. (1992) *Citizenship and Social Class* (London: Pluto Press).

—— (2000) 'Citoyenneté', in H. Hirata *et al.* (eds.), *Dictionnaire critique du féminisme* (Paris: PUF).

Molnar, M. (1990) *La Démocratie se lève à l'Est: Société civile et communisme en Europe de l'Est* (Paris: PUF).

Mouffe, C. (1993) *The Return of the Political* (London and New York: Verso).

Nowakowska, U., and A. Swedrowska (2000) 'Kobiety na rynku pracy' (Women in the labour market), in *Polskie Kobiety w latach 90* (Warsaw: Warsaw Women's Rights Centre).

Nowicka, W., and M. Tajak (2000) 'The Effects of the Anti-Abortion Act', in *The Anti-Abortion Law in Poland* (Warsaw: Family Planning Federation).

Pfau-Effinger, B. (1999) 'Welfare Regimes and the Gender Division of Labour', in J. Christiansen, P. Koistinen, and A. Kovalainen (eds.),

Working Europe: Reshaping European Employment Systems (Aldershot: Ashgate).

Phillips, A. (2000) 'Identity Politics: Had we Now Had Enough?', Communication at the GEP International Conference 'New Challenges to Gender, Democracy, Welfare States', Vilvorde, Denmark, 18–20 Aug.

Siemienska, R. (2000*a*) 'Factors Shaping Conceptions of Women's and Men's Roles in Poland', in M. E. Domsch and D. H. Ladwig (eds.), *Reconciliation of Family and Work in Eastern European Countries* (New York and Oxford: Peter Lang Verlag).

——(2000*b*) *Nie mogą, nie chcą, nie potrafią? O postawach i uczestnictwie politycznym kobiet w Polsce* (Are they Unable, are they Unwilling, are they Incapable? Attitudes and Political Participation of Women in Poland) (Warsaw: Scholar).

Sroda, M. (1999) 'W patriarchalnej sieci', *Gazeta Wyborcza* (12 July).

UNICEF (1999) *Women in Transition: The Monee Project* (Regional Monitoring Report, 6: Florence: UNICEF).

Warsaw Women's Right Centre (2000) *Women in Poland in the 1990s* (Warsaw: Warsaw Women's Right Centre).

World Bank (2000) *World Bank Data Base*, internet website <www.worldbank.org>.

Zielinska, E. (1999) 'Recent Trends in Abortion Legislation in Eastern Europe, with Particular Reference to Poland', *Criminal Law Forum*, 4/1: 47–93.

Zylicz, B. (1999) 'Społeczne efekty prywatyzacji: Wywiady z dyrektorami przedsiębiorstw'(Social Effects of Privatization: Interviews with Heads of Enterprises), Communication at the Conference on the Results of Privatization with Respect to the Situation of Women in Poland, Warsaw, 22 Apr.

Engendering the New Social Citizenship in Chile: NGOs and Social Provisioning under Neo-liberalism

Verónica Schild

For the past decade, the centre-left coalition Concertación de Partidos Por la Democracia governing Chile has built on the radical economic and institutional restructuring successfully undertaken during the period of military rule to pursue a two-pronged development or mod-ernization agenda of 'growth with equity'. This agenda is premised on a notion of the state as enabling or facilitating, and constitutes an extension of the market rationality put in place through the reforms of the 1970s and 1980s to the social domain of government, centrally among them that of social intervention. The programme of privatiz-ations and deregulations, and down-sizing of the state, undertaken by countries in Latin America in the name of a more effective and efficient state, known also as the neo-liberal model, has already been successfully completed in Chile. Since 1990, and particularly since 1994, the two elected Concertación governments have actively pur-sued an agenda of intensified global economic integration at the same time as a political programme focused on greater equity, claiming to be making a concerted effort to reduce poverty. This programme has relied on increased levels of social investment in the face of the coun-try's glaring problem of poverty and inequality. If the completed first phase of neo-liberal reforms succeeded in altering the rules of the eco-nomic game in Chile, this second, more subtle, phase of institutional reforms has entrenched the values and premises of the marketplace associated with neo-liberalism as the dominant political grammar and rationality of government.[1]

The state intervenes today in a coordinating capacity, as one part-ner in social development, in conjunction with 'civil society', or the private sector broadly understood to include business and non-governmental organizations (NGOs), and with clients themselves.

More importantly, it claims to do so in the name of promoting active citizen participation and rights. The rationality of government no longer depends on the principle of 'subsidiarity' which guided state down-sizing during the period of military rule in the 1970s and 1980s.[2] Subsidiarity entailed the premise of near-total reliance on market forces as the driving force in the export-led development process, and saw the state, in the words of then Minister of the Interior Sergio Fernandez, as 'responsible only for those activities which by their nature individuals, families and private organizations are not capable of carrying out adequately' (quoted in Austin, 1998: 314).[3] Today's rationality of government recognizes a greater role for the state in development, including increased social responsibilities as a central component of the post-dictatorship project of social and political integration.[4] Yet, it should be clear that this present project marks a profound departure from those of the post-Second World War period, which shaped national consensus for the Import Substitution Industrialization, or state-led development strategy, and which oversaw profound social reforms in the decade 1960–70. Tackling the legacy of inequalities and poverty—or the so-called 'social cost' of Chile's transformation—has not, therefore, meant a return to the principles of universality guiding social provisioning, and more broadly, the needs-based projects of social and political integration under the older *Estado de Beneficiencia* (welfare state).[5] Instead, the redefined social aims of government, and the rights and obligations of clients, are today themselves defined in market terms.

In defining the recent social agenda, and the project of social and political integration more generally, the governments of Aylwin and Frei have appropriated the rights-based discourse developed in the non-governmental organizations (NGOs) which gained prominence during the period of authoritarian rule. This discourse emphasized the basic rights of individuals and social justice, and stressed self-development, empowerment, and autonomy. Indeed, the social policy field has come to rely heavily on the capacities, personnel, and approaches of the NGO sector. Furthermore, in Chile as elsewhere, women have been at the centre of initiatives to reduce poverty, both as staff members implementing them, and as their direct or indirect clients. The organized efforts of relatives of the disappeared and the Church's Vicariate of Solidarity in the aftermath of the coup in 1973, as well as the work of NGOs with poor communities around issues of economic and political empowerment, contributed significantly to the elaboration of a discourse of rights in Chile. However, it is the women's movement which must be credited with making the most sustained contribution. Indeed, in 1989, in the context of the

political negotiations under way to set up the parameters for the
country's first civilian government in nearly seventeen years, a group
of prominent feminists, high-profile professional and party women,
and women's movement activists—by far not the majority but certainly the most vocal and visible group within the Chilean women's
movement—came together as the Concertación Nacional de Mujeres
por la Democracia (National Coalition of Women for Democracy)
and presented key demands to the future government.[6] Once elected
into office, the Aylwin government relied heavily on the professional
expertise of the NGO sector, and on women employed by the NGOs,
many at either nominal or volunteer-level fees. For middle-class professional women, the social agenda of the subsequent Concertación
governments has meant new employment possibilities in both the
state and the private sector. The recently elected third Concertación
government, headed by Socialist Ricardo Lagos, has also committed
itself to this rights-based agenda of social intervention.[7]

The goal of new social programmes is to enable marginal groups in
society as rights-bearing subjects to access the means to meet their
own needs. Embedded in these programmes is a reconfigured notion
of social citizenship, or 'market' citizenship. Of course, this is not
unique to Chile. The ethos of neo-liberal politics embeds the values,
norms, and language of market rationality—with its focus on individual choice, control over one's own fate, personal responsibility, and
self-government—in state restructuring and policy-making discourse
worldwide.[8] What makes the present model of social provisioning
innovative is the involvement of non-governmental organizations as
active partners and the application of tools and experiences perfected by these organizations in their pedagogic work with the poor.
In Chile this has meant not only making it possible for NGOs, having met prior criteria of accreditation, to act as executors of social
programmes, but also for agencies of the state to recruit vast numbers of professionals from the NGO world. Thus, ironically, the
long-standing legacy of critical popular education, extending back
to the late 1950s and formative for an entire generation of activists
and professionals, has itself helped shape the innovative social policy
agenda and the new grammar of citizenship which is at the centre of
Concertación's social-political integration project.[9]

Although women have always been the main targets of social
programmes, since 1991 they have also become explicit clients. Beginning with Patricio Aylwin's government (1990–4), and in response
to both international commitments and the demands of the Concertación de Mujeres por la Democracia, Concertación governments
have committed themselves to a strategy of integrating women into

development efforts outlined in the UN Convention on the Elimination and Discrimination Against Women (CEDAW) which was ratified in 1989 by the outgoing military government. The Servicio Nacional de la Mujer (SERNAM), or National Women's Bureau, the government agency created in 1991 to address women's needs and rights as an integral part of the Chilean democratization process, is by law charged with overseeing the implementation by the national government of CEDAW's objectives and measures. In addition to proposing legal reforms, advising other relevant ministries on gender-sensitive policies, and initiating educational campaigns, SERNAM channels government funds and foreign aid to gendered social programmes intended to integrate women fully into the development process.

Judging by the critical voices that have been heard for some time, the goal of integrating women through a gender equity strategy has faced serious difficulties. For example, a recent follow-up report by a CEDAW Committee set up to study Chile's adherence to the Convention, concluded that, despite some advances, the government had failed to address important limitations on women's rights in the areas of family law, health and reproduction, political participation, and work and social security.[10] Similar concerns were raised in SERNAM's own comprehensive report presented at the meeting Beijing+5 in New York in June 2000.[11] Moreover, the Group Iniciativa Mujeres (Group Women's Initiative), an umbrella organization representing twelve women's NGOs and private research centres, and the Red de Organizaciones Sociales de Mujeres (REMOS), the umbrella organization representing poor and working class women's organizations, both of which were also present at the Beijing+5 meeting in New York, presented their own critical reports. The report of Grupo Iniciativa Mujeres was backed by the results of a national survey on 'opinions and attitudes of Chilean women on their gender condition' which they conducted in thirty-four communes of Santiago and in twenty-one cities throughout the country, with a sample of 1,800 people, 1,250 women and 550 men, of different socio-economic backgrounds and ages. One of the main conclusions of this survey, which focused primarily on family law, reproductive health, and other social issues, is that the importance given by women to issues such as divorce and abortion are not reflected in the priorities as defined by opinion leaders and politicians.[12] The critique of REMOS emphasized, among other things, the distance between the gender equity agenda as defined and articulated by the government in Chile (for example, in areas like health) and what working-class women themselves consider priorities in those areas.[13] Frustration and disappointment with the achievements of the decade-long effort to pursue a comprehensive gender justice agenda in Chile does, of course, extend beyond these visible and internationally recognized groups.

Sympathetic critics of SERNAM, including many who were architects of the institutionalization of the feminist agenda in Chile, point to the difficulties in advancing on an agenda that was never only about helping women but also about engendering rights more comprehensively.[14] One major obstacle, critics point out, is those lingering authoritarian legacies manifested, for example, in the organization of the structures of the state bureaucracy (Molina, 1998: 132–3). These critics argue that the Chilean democratization process has been constrained by the constitutional, legal, and institutional framework left in place by the outgoing regime.[15]

These critics are correct to highlight various institutional legacies limiting democratic reform and equity agendas. However, overcoming such legacies at some point in the future is not going to be the answer. The active pursuit during the past decade of a strategy of development which is premised on global economic integration and framed in the terms and principles of the marketplace is generating new forms of exclusion and inequality which pose a serious challenge to any meaningful gender justice agenda. Furthermore, the international pressures to which the Chilean national state is exposed as a result of this strategy should not be seen as a passive subjection of state action to external dictates. Rather, the Chilean nation-state has actively and willingly been involved in the restructuring of production and the redefinition of social relations in the name of the 'modernization' which the external world now dictates.

Neo-liberal restructuring never really entailed merely 'shrinking' the state as such. After all, as Hector Schamis reminds us, market-oriented reforms are about 're-forming' the state, that is, about 'state crafting' (Schamis, 1996: 130). Shrinking the state, in other words, is not a mere matter of fiscal and budgetary adjustments which have no sociological or ideological import. It is most centrally a process of institutional transformation aimed at changing the very forms of the state, or of redefining the rationality of government by reconceptualizing the domains government attends to, thus rearticulating the terms of the relation between state and society (Rose, 1999: 26–8). Schamis highlights this process for Latin America by suggesting that 'reforms such as the privatization of public enterprise or the recommodification of welfare provisions, let alone the reorganization of state agencies... consolidate new institutional arrangements— rules, norms, and organizations' (Schamis, 1996: 127). Furthermore, the actions of the state are not limited to the socio-economic realm but extend to those domains of culture and politics which are critical for building consensus for the development model as presently conceived. A key dimension of that pertains to the definition of the very terms of belonging in the 'national community'. Central to this is the redefinition of citizenship embedded in the social policy agenda.

Chile's radical economic liberalization programme introduced by the Pinochet government in the late 1970s and early 1980s, was accompanied by a broad programme of social reforms known as the social 'modernizations'. This programme of privatizations and commodification of welfare provisions 'transferred to the market and private sector the task of providing goods and social services previously offered by the state' (Vergara, 1994: 238–9). These privatizations entailed a reorganization of state agencies, and reconfiguration of institutional forms which resulted in the consolidation of a new governmental rationality. The transformations begun three decades ago have been embraced and legitimated by the three centre-left coalition governments that have ruled Chile since 1990. Indeed, the Concertación's institutional reforms of the past decade have been framed in terms of the main premises and values of neo-liberalism.[16] Today, the language and norms of market rationality, forcefully introduced during the military regime to dismantle the welfare state, shapes the very terms of economic and institutional modernization, spells out the terms of state–society relations, and sets the parameters of social policy reform, including those of the gender equity agenda. Indeed, the policy agenda of all Concertación governments sees the market as the mechanism for incorporating the poor to modernity. More generally, welfare provisions once defined as entitlements integral to a meaningful citizenship for which the state took responsibility are, under their present market definition, commodities available for purchase by individual citizens in the marketplace.

The present discussion takes this socio-economic and cultural-political context as the starting point in its attempt to evaluate critically the implications of the decade-long experience of NGO participation in social provisioning in Chile for the advancement of gender justice. It suggests that there is a fundamental contradiction between the rights-based agenda of present social democratic programmes and the requirements and limitations of a globalized economy and their negative effects on the lives of the majority of people. For feminists, in particular, the experience of NGO participation in social provisioning of the last decade poses a serious challenge: are the present efforts to integrate certain categories of women, that is, the poorest of the poor, into the development process an advancement in women's rights? Furthermore, what are the effects of the development process on the majority of women? Or, rather, are these efforts a sign of complicity with an order that relies on the cheap labour of women, and one which seems, of necessity, to prevent most women from exercising meaningful citizenship?

I begin with an overview of the social development strategy pursued by the two Concertación governments since 1990 in the name of 'growth with equity', and focus on the innovative social programmes implemented through a partnership between NGOs and government agencies (including SERNAM). I then turn to a detailed discussion of the gendered impact on people's working lives and communities from the processes and effects of intensified global economic integration and argue that these social programmes fail to address these impacts. Finally, I outline the implications of a gender equity agenda which aims to integrate women fully as subjects of rights into the development process but which does so by relying on the volunteer-like work of women, and which targets only those who are the poorest of the poor in a context of increasing, generalized social vulnerability.

The 'Growth with Equity' Agendas of the Concertación

For the past decade, Concertación governments have pursued an agenda of economic and institutional modernization premised on growth with equity. This has meant pursuing the goal of promoting an export-led development strategy by actively seeking integration in the global economy through regional trade agreements and laws that have consistently favoured the competitive needs of Chilean businesses over the needs and demands of workers. In addition, it has meant entrenching the institutional reforms of the previous government in the social arena, while also increasing social spending to address the needs of the poor relative to such spending during Pinochet's government. The military regime (1973–89) abandoned social programmes framed by the principles of universality which, by 1973, covered most of the population. It also reduced social spending and privatized and decentralized the provision of health, education, social security, and social services. It developed a targeted approach to address poverty, intervening only in those areas where the private sector either could not or would not intervene.

At the time of the first democratic elections in 1990, macroeconomic indicators were a source of much optimism for the victorious centre-left coalition. For many, the possibility of Chile joining the ranks of developed nations suddenly seemed very real. However, poverty rates told a different, nastier story. Those living below the poverty line had reached 45 per cent of the total population in 1987 and lingered around 39 per cent when Patricio Aylwin came to power in 1990.[17] Aylwin's 'growth with equity' programme and Eduardo Frei Jr.'s 'promotion of opportunity and quality of life' were strategies of social spending within the parameters set by the broader macroeconomic context that attempted to combat this legacy of widespread poverty left by the military regime.

According to official sources, levels of poverty have been reduced over the past ten years, from 38.6 per cent of the total population in 1990 to 21.7 per cent in 1998. This has been attributed in great part to the consistent application of targeted social policies and also to job creation. However, we should be cautious about this self-evaluation of the effectiveness of targeted social policies. The system of poverty measurement on which poverty reduction figures are based only takes into account 'monetizable dimensions of material consumption' and leaves untouched other dimensions of poverty, including those material and non-material ones that affect people's capacity to embark on life projects which are congruent with the present modernization, and cultural ones that condemn large numbers to a kind of *pobreza ciudadana* (citizen poverty) (Salazar, 1995: 25–6). Moreover, as recent national and regional studies make clear, profound inequality and generalized social vulnerability have not diminished over the past decade but have, in fact, become more acute.[18] Before the 1973 coup Chile had become one of the countries in Latin America with the least degree of relative inequality and the strongest index of social development (Munoz Goma, 1991: 23). Today, it is one of the most unequal places not only in the region but in the world. Poverty today, in the more comprehensive sense described above, is directly linked to employment and to the quality of jobs, and it is associated with the transformations in the development model itself in the last ten years. New 'winners' and 'losers' have emerged, predominantly in formal employment, and are related to what is now referred to openly in Chile as the 'feminization' of labour (Fundación and UNDP, 2000).

ECLAC's recent report, *Social Panorama of Latin America, 1999–2000*, has documented what it calls the growing sense of being threatened, vulnerable, and at risk affecting most of the region's people today, and it views this widespread perception as a result of 'trends in the labour market, the State's pulling back from some areas of action, new institutional structures for providing access to social services, the decline in traditional expressions of social organization, and difficulties facing micro and small companies' (ECLAC, 2000b). The study estimates that 50 per cent of Latin America's urban workforce is engaged in precarious employment in both formal and informal job markets. The numbers are even higher in rural areas.[19] Moreover, it points out that, regardless of higher social spending during the last decade, social vulnerability is also evident in the social services area, especially in education, health care, and social welfare.[20] Despite impressive levels of economic growth for most of the decade—until the devastating effects of the Asian crisis in 1997— Chile has one of the most regressive income distributions rates in the world, ranking number six (number two in Latin America after Brazil) according to World Bank figures.[21] Wages, adjusted for inflation, are still below the level reached in 1972, although productivity has increased by 60 per cent in the same period (Riesco, 1999: 125).

For the past decade, the two successive Concertación governments have followed a social policy agenda that has not reversed these trends. Social policy has followed strategies which, although framed in terms of solidarity and equity, continue to have a distinctive neo-liberal bias.[22] In this perspective, the state assumes responsibilities for specific initiatives needed to break the structural limitations preventing the integration of vulnerable groups into the process of development. It does so within the parameters set by macroeconomic considerations and, thus, by spending effectively, claims to promote equal opportunities for all to participate in the market as producers and consumers. Concretely, this has meant developing a panoply of programmes to prepare individuals to compete in the market through skills and job training schemes, community self-development, social service initiatives in health and education, or to do so through the support of small economic initiatives, for example, microenterprises, small businesses, and microcredits. The thrust of these policies is to integrate marginal sectors of the population by educating them to become active and autonomous citizens, or as I would claim, to become 'market citizens'.

Social policy design and implementation have been framed within the so-called 'new social policy' which is rapidly becoming the norm throughout Latin America.[23] The new social policy discourse articulates a reconfiguration of state social responsibilities which varies drastically from the older, post-Second World War conceptions. States are seen as only one partner in the delivery of social services and social assistance, with a greater emphasis on the involvement of so-called civil society, or the private sector broadly understood to include business and NGOs. The role assigned to clients of social services is central in this reconceptualization. They are seen as consumers who are active participants in social service delivery, and are contrasted with older notions of clients as passive and dependent on government largesse. The present government promises to continue with this model of social provisioning.

The ethos of neo-liberal politics shaping the social policy field gives new content to the terms of social exclusion and marginality, and, more specifically, to the problem of poverty—the focus par *excellence* of social policy. It views the poor as those individuals, and by extension communities, who because of lack of skills or opportunities, are excluded from participating in the market. The thrust of social policy, therefore, is to help individuals and communities become active, autonomous participants in the market.

President Ricardo Lagos, in power since March 2000, has committed his government to continue with the innovations introduced by his predecessors (Gobierno de Chile, 2000). Social spending is an important part of the government's agenda, although Lagos has made it clear that increases will not be made at the expense of economic growth. In his words, 'Without affecting investment, savings and growth, we need to produce a society a little more just with less of a gap in the inequality of opportunity'.[24] In his programmatic speech of 21 May 2000, he outlined the social goals of his government in the present era of global integration as 'widening the freedom and entrepreneurial and innovative capacity of persons, families and communities; never extend the paternalism of another time' (Gobierno de Chile, 2000).

The social spending of the last ten years represents both a change, and also an important continuation, of reforms implemented during the period of military dictatorship. As before, poverty is defined in narrow economic terms as the effects of exclusion from the market and measured primarily in terms of income levels.[25] Empowerment, a critical dimension seen as necessary for overcoming poverty, is above all understood as empowerment for the market. Techniques and technologies developed during the previous regime for identifying the most vulnerable sectors of the population, and for targeting social spending effectively—the Encuesta de Caracterización Socioeconómica Nacional (CASEN) (Survey of National Socioeconomic Characterization) and the Ficha de Clasificación Social (Ficha CAS) (the Social Classification Index)—have been perfected further since 1990. The categories of affected people have been expanded to include youth, indigenous people, women, the ageing population, and the disabled. Economically depressed regions are also singled out for targeting. These additions notwithstanding, the tools of poverty measurement are used to target those considered most needy within those categories for social spending (that is, those in situations of extreme poverty). Vast numbers of poor people are excluded by this targeting approach.[26] Other critics of targeting have shown that forcing the working poor and the middle class into the private sector leads to an erosion of political support for social services.[27]

The much celebrated, though until recently woefully underfunded, government agency Fondo de Solidaridad (FOSIS) has been Chile's showcase of the new social policy.[28] It was set up with the explicit mandate of elaborating and testing innovative social programmes and was staffed by professionals and technical experts from the NGO world. Its programmes have centred around technical and financial support for microenterprises, community self-development, and youth community initiatives. The agency develops the broad lines of social programmes, and makes funds available for them, but it relies on the participation of NGOs to execute them. FOSIS, however, is not the only agency following this new approach to targeted social spending. In fact, every ministry in the social field assigns a portion of its spending to *fondos concursables*, funds which can be accessed through competition by NGOs and potential beneficiaries. The new social policy as developed and implemented by these agencies, particularly by FOSIS, does not have a gender-sensitive approach, nor does it target women explicitly. However, existing figures suggest that women are the primary beneficiaries. For example, women constitute 60 per cent of the microfinancing programme, and 45 per cent of the Chile Joven programme, the two best-known FOSIS programmes (Fundación and UNDP, 2000: 93).

The National Women's Bureau, SERNAM, does have a specific mandate to develop gender-sensitive social policy, and has done so quite successfully. SERNAM was established by the first Concertación government in response to pressure from Concertación de Mujeres por la Democracia.[29] This group brought together that sector of the women's movement, by no means the majority of the women's movement but certainly its most prominent and vocal segment, which joined in the political discussions of the late 1980s to set the terms of the future Concertación government. It pressured the government for the creation of a state agency to address women's needs and rights as an integral part of the democratization process.[30] SERNAM's goals and objectives were shaped by the demands articulated by the Concertación de Mujeres, and by the objectives and measures outlined by the UN Convention on the Elimination of Discrimination against Women (CEDAW), which the outgoing military government signed in 1989. The explicit aim of SERNAM is 'to design and coordinate public policies at sectoral and interministerial levels' in the pursuit of greater equality for women, and more generally to work for the full integration of women into the development process (SERNAM, 1994: 15–16). By law, its mission also includes the overseeing of policies, plans, and proposals elaborated nationally to meet the objectives of CEDAW. In practice, SERNAM has promoted legal reforms, developed educational campaigns, and has coordinated social spending targeted at women. Women's NGOs and NGOs dealing with 'women's issues' have become partners in the pursuit of women's full integration into the development process.

Since 1990, NGOs working on women's issues have played a critical role as partners in gendered social provisioning in Chile. NGOs emerged in Chile, first in response to human rights abuses after the coup in 1973, and then to the devastating impact of economic policies pursued by the military regime. They provided technical and financial support to the initiatives for economic survival by organized people in poor areas.[31] Moreover, they relied on a legacy of previous involvement in social-action projects in Chile's rural and urban areas during the 1960s and early 1970s.[32] The collaboration between professionals in NGOs and members of social organizations in poor areas, shaped by notions of poverty as disempowerment broadly understood and also of the value of participatory development, resulted over time in initiatives in areas as diverse as health care and nutrition, housing, and employment.[33] By the late 1980s, NGOs had evolved into a diversified network of organizations, some focusing on policy research and others on social action.

NGOs' specific focus on women and development can be dated to the United Nations Decade for Women, initiated with the conference in Mexico City in 1975. 'Gender', which meant typically 'poor women' and their issues, soon became a required component of development grants, and Chilean NGOs, like those in the rest of the region, learned to accommodate to this new donor demand. This accommodation was neither smooth nor easy, to say the least, but by the late 1980s 'poor women' had become objects of funding in their own right and action research had come to include explicitly feminist concerns.[34] A study conducted in Chile in 1989, for example, indicated that eighty-seven NGOs of an estimated total of 400 dealt with women's issues, and seven NGOs were composed of 'women that work almost exclusively with women' (Arteaga and Largo quoted in Loveman, 1995: 130).

Since the return to civilian rule in 1990, the financial and institutional context in which NGOs operate has changed significantly. Aid to Chile from bilateral agencies and private foundations had in any case begun to decline in the late 1980s, and after 1990 the remaining flow of aid was directed to the incoming Concertación government's social spending initiatives. An estimated one billion dollars in international aid flowed to the new government between 1990 and 1993, half of which was in the form of donations.[35] In the case of SERNAM, the agency received some funds from public expenditure, while much of its operating budget came directly from foreign funds (Matear, 1996: 159). Furthermore, the government took explicit steps to control relations with foreign funding sources and established a new agency, the International Cooperation Agency (AGCI). Today, then, government agencies, not international donors, are the main direct source of funding for NGOs. In fact, NGOs have become a key actor in the government's design, delivery, and evaluation of social programmes, and funds are channelled to them in their new capacity as instruments of government social action.[36]

To refer exclusively to NGOs and their role in implementing social policy agendas in today's context, as far as the activities of SERNAM are concerned, is to simplify unnecessarily a process which has become very complex. As I have argued in another context, feminist professionals and activists, as well as women committed to gender-related work, who were housed in NGOs during the dictatorship, formed a vast web of contacts and friendships which extended to include their clients, namely organized women in poor areas. This web, which I call a 'symbolic network', became a conduit for the circulation of important information, and for cementing a pattern of popular education work with a feminist content with working-class women.[37]

With the return to civilian rule, this network was expanded as many professionals found employment in the various ministries and agencies of the state, as well as in university programmes. Moreover, as NGOs struggled to survive, a number retooled themselves and formed *Consultorias* (consulting companies) which also belong now to the network. SERNAM's work, then, relies on this NGO sector, broadly understood, to develop its agenda. It needs to be said, however, that this network, like Chilean society in general, is stratified along class lines, and is therefore exclusionary. Not all women's NGOs have had equal access to the various activities outsourced by this agency.[38] In fact, some NGOs are not at all in the loop through which information about project bids circulates, while others, particularly those that have been involved in popular women's organizing, tend to be tapped as sources of ready-made clients for SERNAM's projects.[39]

SERNAM, in collaboration with experts from the NGO sector, has developed a number of programmes on behalf of women. For one thing, the Plan de Igualdad, which offered a blueprint for social action in connection with an equity agenda, was itself commissioned from one of the leading women's NGOs. Furthermore, policy-related research needed for identifying potential areas of social action for women, as well as background research for legal reform proposals, are regularly commissioned from experts based in NGOs and in universities. In addition to the highly visible Programa de Violencia Intrafamiliar (Programme of Intrafamily Violence), Programa Para Adolescentes Embarazadas (Programme for Pregnant Teenagers), SERNAM developed the Programa Jefas de Hogar (Programme for Women-Headed Households), the Programa de Microempresas (Microenterprise Programme), and the Programa de Capacitación Laboral (Employment Training Programme). These last three programmes are targeted at the poorest of the poor, and rely on a prior identification of the specific problems affecting these women's entry into viable forms of employment.[40]

Thus in present-day Chile, institutional initiatives to transform women into subjects of rights are framed in the discourse of neoliberal modernization. SERNAM defines a gendered perspective as taking into account the characteristics, peculiarities, wants, and the practical and strategic needs of women and their families in relation to the opportunities of men in similar situations (SERNAM, 1994). Gendered social policy, SERNAM proposes, needs to support women's efforts to overcome their poverty by recognizing their particular needs and guaranteeing them equal opportunities and access to resources and public services. This means enabling women to become subjects of rights by educating those who are excluded, namely the poorest of the poor, to become responsible, autonomous, self-governing agents in the market.

However, despite claims as to the newness of this social policy agenda, there are some troubling old patterns at work. The state's redefinition of responsibilities for social spending, in the name of a redefined active citizenship, continues to be accomplished on the backs of women. During Pinochet's dictatorship, vast numbers of women, mostly wives of military men and other right-wing supporters, organized themselves as Damas de Colores (Ladies in Colour) to volunteer their labour to fill the vacuum left by a drastically retreating state. They also joined *on a volunteer basis* the new agency created by the state to address family and women's issues, the Secretaria de la Mujer.[41]

Furthermore, women and their efforts—what I would call a volunteerism of the left—were at the centre of the much celebrated social activities of the opposition during the 1970s and 1980s. For example, not only was women's involvement, as professionals, experts, and as extension workers in the field, at the core of the Catholic

Church's human rights and social agenda, it was also central for the myriad action research projects developed by the NGOs. Thousands of women, working and middle class, who had been employed by Allende's Popular Unity government, or who had been actively involved in politics before 1973—young university graduates, health practitioners, educators, social workers, and activists—and who had then either resigned from their jobs or been fired, imprisoned, or sent into internal or external exile immediately following the coup, joined the volunteer and quasi-volunteer activities of NGOs and the Catholic Church. Over a period of nearly two decades, they were joined by younger graduates and activists looking for work that was politically meaningful.

This trend of relying on women's volunteer labour continues today. To begin with, SERNAM itself relies heavily on a staff of experts who do not belong to the core of the civil service but who are paid on an honorarium basis.[42] Furthermore, NGOs continue to operate with uneven income scales, and to rely on the success of project competition for their economic survival. Moreover, just as before, these organizations rely on extension workers or *promotores(as)*, previously called *monitores(as)*—who remain invisible in studies of the new social policy, just as they are in discussions about NGOs more generally—who in effect are responsible for 'translating' programmes on the ground.[43] This veritable army of volunteers, of underpaid and overworked and highly dedicated individuals, is predominantly made up of women.[44] Clearly, then, Chilean women's undervalued labour and well-developed volunteer spirit is what lies beyond abstract references to civil society's involvement in innovative models of social provisioning.

There is a further problem with this trend in social provisioning. Implicit in this innovative framework for policy-making as a modernizing force in the social policy field, both in Chile and beyond, and endorsed today by bilateral and multilateral aid agencies like the World Bank, are some very old, gender-biased notions about the private–public divide that discriminate against poor women. For claims for more effective and efficient social spending, through a partnership of state and civil society organizations, take for granted that communities and households can take up the slack for what the state no longer invests in. Ultimately, this means that women, who have traditionally been responsible not only for the well-being of family members but also of their communities, pick up where the state leaves off. Thus, the new social policy refers back to a notion of the private which is attached to the unencumbered individual, rather than the family household. In other words, it ignores gender and, thus, the extra burdens placed specifically on women who are overwhelmingly the clients, now active clients, of social programmes.

SERNAM's mandate, to make visible the specific conditions of inequality women face, and to identify women's particular needs, within a broader project of engendering the policy process more generally, is of necessity transmuted into programmes which follow the logic of the new social policy. Programmes help women cope with the extra burdens of their expanded responsibilities in the private, domestic sphere, while nudging them onto the market as ostensibly self-governed, responsible citizens. Implicit in programmes aimed at women, for example, the female single heads of households, is the assumption that women need to be helped to 'develop their potential so that they can solve their problems themselves'. The national coordinator of the programme explains that 'the point of this program is not to give you a handout. You're taught things and given tools so that you can get ahead' (Chile News, 2000). Individual effort in the marketplace, then, translates into meaningful participation for women, rather than in passive acceptance of government largesse. Clearly, what is taken for granted in such efforts is the view that women can and should aspire to being competitive individuals in the marketplace. Despite claims to the contrary, this reflects what Diane Elson (1998, 1995) and other feminist economists have highlighted as the deep gender categories of classical economic categories. Having said this, we need to ask, does women's insertion in the labour market as active economic agents translate into the 'meaningful participation' gender-sensitive programmes envision?

The Impact on Women of 'Growth with Equity' Policies

'What are we doing to this country when women who work in the hospitals must spend their lunch breaks selling used clothes in a flea market?' demanded Gladys Marin, the Communist Party's presidential candidate during the campaign in early December 1999.[45] She was right to choose women as her example of the drama poor working people face in Chile's successful economy. Three decades of economic restructuring have fundamentally changed the way people work and live in Chile and these transformations have affected women's lives in very distinct and detrimental ways.

Many more women than ever before have become economically active, although by regional standards Chile still lags behind other countries. Women's participation in formal employment has increased considerably since 1970, from 22 per cent to 36 per cent in 2000.[46] Having said this, women suffer consistently higher rates of unemployment than men, and the jobs they manage to get are of very poor quality.[47] A recent study, by the Chamber of Commerce of Santiago, revealed that 79 per cent of the total number of women active in the formal labour force are engaged as factory workers or in the service sector, both areas characterized by highly precarious work conditions.[48] Moreover, the latest census data suggests that it would be mistaken to assume that women's lack of education or skills is at the root of their inability to access good jobs. Over 40 per cent of women engaged in domestic activities, for example, have completed elementary schooling, and even some additional years of schooling. Indeed, 146,000 women engaged in this type of work have finished high school (Fundación and UNDP, 2000: 24).

The lack of good jobs has serious implications for women in today's Chile. Quality education, health, and pensions, once social goods inherent in the social rights of citizenship for which the state was responsible, are now commodities available in the marketplace for a price. Moreover, it is a price which the overwhelming majority of women workers cannot afford. Workers' real wages fell sharply after 1973 and only began to improve beginning in 1988. However, the steady increases in wages in the last decade or so only means that they have recuperated to 1970 levels.[49] Moreover, the impact of the Asian crisis of 1997 is a reminder of just how precarious this recovery is.[50] In other words, Chile has experienced unprecedented levels of growth without comparable increases in real wages, and this lies at the root of the present predicament of poor working people. Indeed, as Barrera remarks, in terms of real wages, 'poor workers have become poorer than all other workers combined' (Barrera, 1998: 134). These trends are corroborated by a number of recent studies. A study by the United Nation's Economic Commission for Latin America and the Caribbean, ECLAC, *The Equity Gap: A Second Look*, published in early 2000, included Chile in its conclusion about widespread poverty and inequality in the region. According to ECLAC, today, even being employed in a 'large-sized company is no guarantee of being above the poverty line'.[51] In fact, today, the majority of the poor are urban dwellers occupied in activities in the formal sector of the economy. They are the so-called working poor, people whose work does not command a living wage.

SERNAM's programmes have left the specific situation of women in formal sector employment virtually untouched. According to a survey commissioned by the Secretaria Técnica de la Mujer (Technical Women's Secretariat) of the CUT, Central Unitaria de Trabajadores, or the Chilean Labour Council, women face a range of severe problems. Among them are: temporary contracts that prevent them from having access to basic benefits such as maternity leave, sick pay, or pension coverage; wages which are lower than those of men in comparable activities; pregnancy tests as a condition of hiring; lack of childcare provision by employers who deliberately ignore the law; and sexual harassment.[52]

Most waged workers work in small firms, of twenty or less employees, with irregular work contracts. Women workers are found overwhelmingly in such firms, many of which are subcontracted by larger ones (Fundación and UNDP, 2000: 24). A great proportion of these workers are not able to contribute to Chile's well-publicized private pension system. Although by law all workers have to be enrolled in this system imposed during the Pinochet regime in 1981, fully half of the workforce does not pay the monthly fees into it.[53] Furthermore, another 25 per cent pays very small instalments and cannot hope to reach a minimum pension on their own. In fact, it has been estimated that only 25 per cent of affiliates will ever receive more than the minimum pension (Riesco, 1999: 109).[54]

Women workers face specific forms of discrimination by privatized social security. Their particular work cycles and low wages translate into lower or even no pensions. On average, women's taxable income is 20 to 30 per cent lower than men's. Women also take time off to have children, and care for them, and their legal retirement age is lower than men's. The conclusion of one study of women and these much celebrated pension schemes is that the privatized social security system discriminates against women in ways that the old, public system did not (Arenas de Mesa and Montecinos, 1999).[55]

Women workers are also discriminated against in the privatized insurance schemes, ISAPRES, in very concrete ways. Women of reproductive age are considered *mal negocio* (bad business) for the private insurers, and a significant number who try to join are rejected. When they are accepted, they face the possibility of having benefits which are considerably lower than benefits for men of the same age and in the same income situation—one fourth the benefits according to some estimates—because they alone must finance the cost of maternity.[56]

Discrimination against women workers also extends to their conditions of work. Despite some advances in labour legislation affecting women specifically, women face often harsh conditions. We should not forget that the devastating effects of the loss, twenty years ago, of progressive labour rights have also been felt by women. In addition, women have had to endure the loss of protective legislation that guaranteed them some basic gender-specific rights. The two initiatives proposed since 1990 to reverse some of the most egregious abuses concerning the rights of labour, which were enshrined in the regressive labour code in place since 1980, have been rejected in Parliament.[57] Moreover, although SERNAM has spearheaded legal reforms on behalf of women and their special needs, for example, around pregnancy and maternity issues, employers continue to ignore them. For example, a new law passed in November 1998 made it illegal for employers to demand pregnancy tests of potential female employees; however, employers continue to flaunt it. In a recent, well-publicized case involving the country's largest copper company, the state-owned National Copper Corporation (CODELCO), the workers' union brought a case against the company for the wrongful dismissal of a pregnant employee. In addition, it denounced publicly the routine practice of forcing job applicants to undergo medical exams that include a test designed explicitly to predict pregnancies with a high degree of accuracy (Mujer/Fempress, 1999*b*).

Employers are adamantly opposed to maternity benefits for workers. For example, on the eve of the vote to ratify the ILO Convention this past June, business leaders headed by the president of the Confederation of Production (Confederación de la Producción) asked the government not to vote in favour of the Convention. Ratifying the Convention would mean regulating maternity benefits and this, the powerful organization argued, 'would imply introducing rigidities into legal legislation and would prevent more women from finding employment because it would become too expensive to hire them' (Mujer/Fempress, 2000*b*). Clearly, then, women may be joining the labour market in unprecedented numbers but they are also strongly discriminated against in the areas of access to paid employment, quality of jobs, and recognition of labour rights. Theirs is a subordinate and exploited integration into development.

In addition, poor working women are the real-life casualties of the 'modernization' of labour through its casualization or flexibilization. With the exception of the copper sector, the pattern of flexibilization predominates in three of the so-called four pillars of Chile's dynamic, 'modern' economy, namely forestry, fruit, and fisheries. This flexibilization or cheapening of labour is gendered (and racialized), and women invariably occupy the lowest rungs of the production process. Women, mostly young, often with low qualifications, working for poor pay, without benefits or access to social security, make up a vast number of 'flexibilized' workers (Martinez and Diaz, 1996). This is not surprising, for, as feminist economists have made clear, 'the combination of high productivity and low wages which characterizes women's work, offers the lowest cost per unit of production demanded by rational management following commercial rather than sexist or discriminatory logic' (Pearson, 1998: 173).[58] Flexibilization has also become the norm in the service sector, one of the expanding sectors in which women predominate (Martinez and Diaz, 1996). In addition, it characterizes the new jobs found in the drastically down-sized older industrial areas like textiles and leather where women have traditionally found employment. Thus, not only is precarious, unregulated formal work one of the more relevant characteristic of Chile's new economic and labour order, so is the increasing presence of women in its cheapest forms (Martinez and Diaz, 1996). This means that women are not only the poorest of the poor, but most importantly, the poorest of the poor workers.

The majority of women earning a living have typically done so through informal activities, like domestic work and other forms of service-sector self-employment, and they continue to do so. Today, however, they are also increasingly involved in areas of what has been called the 'new informality'. These are precarious and poorly paid activities which are functional to the dynamic, 'modern' sectors of Chile's new economy.[59] Policies implemented to make Chilean production internationally competitive, including labour laws enshrined in the regressive Labour Code of 1981, the Plan Laboral, in combination with innovations to production within firms, have led to important changes in the structure of employment, remuneration levels, and labour relations.[60] The expanding, dynamic sectors of the export economy, for example, agriculture, mining, and manufacturing (in particular, the garment industry) have been subjected to an aggressive process of segmentation of production and subcontracting, geared to cheapening labour costs.[61] Chile, once an example of progressive labour legislation, has become an instance of extreme forms of labour flexibilization, and making women's labour cheap is at the heart of the country's much touted economic modernization.

Women make up the majority of those engaged in self-employment and in other income-generating activities which are unregulated and, more often than not, difficult to measure and (until very recently) invisible beyond the poor areas where they took place.[62] A newly established working group, Mujer-Trabajo (Woman-Work), an initiative of the Consejo de Dialogo Social, headed by SERNAM's new director, will bring together representatives from Chile's Labour Council (Central Unitaria de Trabajadores), CUT, and from small and medium business, plus the Confederation of Production and Commerce (Confederación de la Producción y Comercio), to discuss this and other issues pertaining to women's work. The informal employment sector is the second largest form of employment, after waged employment, and has grown fast.[63] Moreover, this is a region-wide trend, as shown by the *Social Panorama of Latin America, 1999–2000* (ECLAC, 2000*b*). This report has concluded that employment became more precarious during the 1990s in the region as a whole, and that 'the percentage of people employed in informal or low-productivity sectors rose to almost 50 per cent of the workforce in urban areas and even higher percentages in rural areas' (ECLAC Press Release, 2000*c*).

Many of the activities women are involved in are not marginal to the formal economy, and are not, therefore, a sign of economic backwardness, of the failure of individuals to become integrated into regulated forms of economic activity. They are, in fact, linked functionally to the formal economy (Martinez and Diaz, 1996). Women account for 34 per cent of those employed in companies with fewer than five employees—or microenterprises—or among the self-employed.[64] This phenomenon has been referred to as the 'new informality'. The garment industry is a case in point. The industry has undergone a process of restructuring, relying heavily on down-sizing and subcontracting.[65] Today, women in poor areas of Santiago, for example, are finding new economic opportunities by subcontracting to do piecework out of their own homes for the garment industry. Others, however, are having to accept this type of work after losing full-time positions. A long-time labour organizer in the garment industry, who is now director of a labour NGO, was made redundant in December 1997 by her employer, the Arrow Shirt Company, where she had worked for twenty years. Part of her severance package consisted of a sewing machine and a commitment to be part of the pool of women subcontracted for piecework. Thus, many women like this labour activist are the casualties of down-sizing who are swelling the ranks of the new poor, workers whose lives are made precarious after enjoying a modicum of stability and the security of full-time employment.

The prevalence of piecework in the vast poor areas of the city's southern periphery has led local activists and labour activists to dub it the 'maquila' of Chile. As labour activists point out, this type of work does offer women the opportunity of earning an income. However, neither the women themselves nor activists are under the illusion that this work represents a genuine economic opportunity. The conditions under which women toil are unregulated and harsh. Indeed, they are reminiscent of the exploitative, inhuman conditions prevailing at the turn of the century, which feminist labour activists fought so hard to overcome.[66] Working hours are long, sometimes stretching up to eighteen hours per day, as women rush to outdo themselves to increase their production quotas. The piece rate does not take into account expenses women incur, for example, consumption of electricity, sewing machine needles, and supplies such as thread. Moreover, the impact of piecework on women's health and on women's families, particularly school-age children, is a serious concern for organizers. Not only are women having to recruit their children, often as young as 6 or 7 years of age, to help with the work, but they are exposing themselves to injuries and to emotional exhaustion and stress from long hours of monotonous work at their sewing machines, combined with domestic chores for which they remain responsible. In the long term, this income-generating strategy is likely to be, in the words of a solidarity NGO representative working in the area, a veritable 'time bomb' for women. Not only will the toll on their bodies be very high, but nor will women be in a position to access the social services necessary to cope and will have to face the consequences on their own.[67]

Women engaged in the widespread and ever popular microenterprises which have become the focus of government support through loan schemes, technical training and other offers, typically translate for women into working conditions that parallel those of piecework. The overwhelming majority of microenterprises are family enterprises run out of people's homes. These women are 'reluctant entrepreneurs', to borrow a term used by Marguerite Berger, Chief of the Women and Development Unit at the Inter-American Bank, to refer to women who create their own businesses out of a lack of other alternatives (Berger, 1995: 211–19). They would rather have 'real' jobs, with living wages, and proper work conditions, including regular hours, and access to childcare, but know that their chances of obtaining such work are virtually non-existent.

Women in the maquilas fall through the cracks of Chile's targeted social programmes. Because they earn an income, and have been enterprising enough to seek their way out of their own condition of unemployment, they are considered among the economically successful. In addition, if they are successful at recruiting the free labour of other family members, as is commonly done, their family incomes disqualify them from social programmes targeted at the poorest of the poor.

The economic policies of the past two decades have had a profound impact on labour relations, and, more specifically, on union organization. Unionization reached a peak, during the Allende years, of 34 per cent of the workforce. Since 1991, levels of organization have fluctuated, but have not reached beyond 20 per cent (Riesco, 1999: 114). Attempts to reform the regressive Labour Code of 1980 have been stalled in Parliament, and most recently a watered-down bill was vetoed by the outgoing president himself. Thus, workers continue to have individual contracts with employers and the existing law makes it extremely difficult to organize in certain sectors, especially those defined as 'temporary labour'—which includes construction and agricultural workers. Moreover, organizing has become more, not less, difficult for some categories of workers. Since 1997, public employees in Chile have been barred from forming unions and 'can only join associations that do not engage in collective bargaining or go on strike' (IWRAW, 2000). Despite these difficulties, a new awareness about the need to reach workers, especially women who are particularly difficult to organize, is emerging in the labour movement. In part this is due to a new generation of powerful women leaders within the union movement. Seasonal workers in the fruit-growing areas, or *temporeras*, have scored some victories. The most difficult women to reach remain, of course, those engaged in subcontracted work.[68] Workers in the formal employment sector, however, have been and continue to be defenceless *vis-à-vis* their employers, who have the law on their side.

Furthermore, poor working women return home daily to face the challenges of a double burden in settings which have been shaped by Chile's crumbling social infrastructure. Some two decades of neoliberal 'modernizations' have had a profound impact on the quality of life of the majority of Chileans.[69] The privatization of health and pensions, and the decentralization of social services and education, have resulted in a veritable apartheid. For those Chileans who have the means, life has reached levels of comfort unimaginable a generation ago. The vast majority, however, must do without the modicum of well-being offered by an earlier, now officially much-maligned, welfare state.

The stated commitment of the Concertación governments to increase social spending as part of their growth with equity strategy has not had an effect on the deteriorated conditions in which a large proportion of the population live their lives. To begin with, actual social spending during the 1990s did not increase across the board but actually declined in some areas, like pensions, education, and housing, in relation to spending levels reached during the 1980s, while in others, like health, it has increased moderately.[70] The Lagos administration, even before the end of its first year in power, and faced with a persistent economic downturn, had to downplay its commitment to growth with equity. The Concertacion governments' commitment to push ahead on the global integration of the economy through a strategy of neo-liberalism with a human face, then, has not stemmed the further deterioration of the quality of life for Chileans, but seems instead to have contributed to it. The cumulative effect of these nearly three decades of unequal distribution of resources, of the flexibilization of labour with its concomitant erosion of wages, the loss of benefits, the unequal access to quality health, old age protection, affordable housing, and education, impact the particular conditions of life in which the urban poor exist.

Not surprisingly, those living in poor urban areas are the most affected. Although the issue of *seguridad ciudadana* (citizenship safety) has been made into a national concern, and became a focus in the recent presidential elections, it is one that overwhelmingly affects poor sectors. Recent studies on crime reporting and on the impact of the widespread problem of drug trafficking confirm the widespread fear about urban safety and the lack of generalized trust in the police, a particularly acute problem in poor areas. According to one study, although crime reporting is more common in well-off areas, the actual levels of crime are much higher in poor areas. However, these crimes are grossly under-reported. Only one in three incidents is ever reported to the police, for example (Afani, 1999). Inhabitants of poor areas do not trust the police, whom they consider to be ineffective and corrupt.[71]

Widespread drug trafficking and drug consumption, and the violence associated with these activities, exacerbate the sense of insecurity and fear in poor neighbourhoods. A recent study conducted by the Association of Chilean Municipalities identified forty-one communes in the Metropolitan Region of Santiago with neighbourhoods that were no longer controlled by the police but lived under law imposed by drug traffickers. This means that an estimated one million inhabitants, all in the poorest municipalities of the city, or one-fifth of the total population of Santiago, live by rules imposed by bands of traffickers with no police protection.[72]

Drug trafficking has also, without question, become a means of 'getting by', or for some even a means of 'making it', in the current economic conditions. Poor areas became centres of drug supply in the 1980s, particularly of the cheap *pasta base*, a highly addictive residue of coca paste. Women have become increasingly involved as suppliers of drugs, and they and their families have prospered from their illicit entrepreneurship in very visible ways. Over the past nearly fifteen years of doing ethnographic research in the poor areas of Santiago's southern periphery, I have gauged this impressive infusion of drug-related money by the boom in fancy homes, as well as by the demise of old-established retail outlets, with the appearance of brand-new and bigger establishments. Retail money tends to be invested overwhelmingly in liquor stores, and in dry goods as a distant second. These successful predatory entrepreneurial activities of some, however, occur at the cost of new problems in the neighbourhoods. Alcoholism and the perpetuation of addiction predominantly, but not exclusively, among the young, and the theft and prostitution that go along with it to maintain the habit, contribute to an overall climate of fear and insecurity.

The bands controlling the traffic of drugs do not rule simply by violence, though it undoubtedly plays an important role. They also rely on family relations, and long-time acquaintanceships, to ensure loyalty, or at the very least, silence. Moreover, they also garner local support by promoting social activities that benefit their worse-off neighbours. According to Angela Cereceda, a council member from San Joaquin, who is in charge of the Commission for Citizenship Safety (Seguridad Ciudadana) of the Chilean Association of Municipalities: 'The *narcos* promote activities that benefit their Communes. If someone dies, they make resources available for the burial. They permanently offer aid, they contribute food parcels. This is why, though neighbours fear them, they also consider them their godfathers' (quoted in Espinoza, 1999).

The recent economic downturn and massive unemployment precipitated by the effects of the 1997 Asian crisis on Chilean exports has made visible the limitations of the exclusionary Chilean development model.[73] The exclusive focus of redistributive policies on the poorest sectors, in addition to the continuing weakened status of unions, has left vast sectors of working people—the working poor and parts of the middle class—vulnerable to the vagaries of the open economy. The impact of the Asian crisis, for example, revealed yet another dimension of the vulnerability which characterizes the lives of poor working people. During the first trimester of 1999, a total of 400,000 people, roughly 200,000 plus their dependants, moved from the private health insurance schemes ISAPRES to the under-funded, unpopular public service FONASA. While some moved as premium holders, the majority did so as indigents. Most belonged to low-income groups who lost their incomes or saw them reduced, and thus were unable to afford any of the health plans offered by ISAPRES.[74] Even before the Asian crisis, approximately 24 per cent of patients covered by the private health insurance scheme had to rely on the dilapidated public clinics and hospital care because they could not afford the co-payments required by their plans.[75]

The Concertación governments have pursued a social development strategy centred on active, self-governing citizens in their communities, against this backdrop of increased vulnerability. As this discussion makes clear, this means that while the poorest of the poor—namely a few poor and working-class women—have been the beneficiaries of innovative social provisioning, the majority are left without protection. We need to ask, then, what are the implications of a gender equity agenda, committed to enabling women to become subjects of rights, which is pursued within this economic and institutional framework?

A New Social Citizenship?

The last decade has ushered in a new political period in Chile, one emphasizing neo-liberal democratic politics and a renewed interest in citizenship. As I have argued in a different context, this has entailed the redefinition of citizenship, particularly social citizenship, away from its earlier welfare state conception as resting on a notion of universal rights to basic public goods as necessary for meaningful citizenship. The reconfigured social citizenship rests on a notion of citizens as empowered clients, who as individuals are viewed as capable of enhancing their lives through judicious, responsible choices as consumers of services and other goods. This shift in social citizenship has given rise to new ways of governing subordinate populations.[76] More broadly, Chileans have recovered certain basic civic and political rights, though the continued violation of basic labour rights and women's continued subordinate position in key areas are reminders of the profound shortcomings of Chilean democracy. People's social rights, however, have been radically undermined. In the name of personal responsibility, autonomy, and accountability, individuals are left to fend for themselves and to bear on their own the responsibility for not making it in the market.

The model of social provisioning prevalent today, including its gender-sensitive variants which are promoted in the name of advancing the gender equity agenda, is a mechanism for integrating the poor marginal sectors as 'market subjects of rights'. In effect, it constitutes a form of social restructuring that aims to integrate broad categories of people—including technocrats, professionals, civil servants, scholars, political activists, and many others who in one way or another are involved in designing, implementing, and evaluating these programmes—by educating them to behave in new ways. Whether or not this effort succeeds remains to be seen.

One implication of the pursuit of market citizenship, with its individualistic focus on individuals and communities, is the erosion of the means used by women to participate collectively in the articulation of their own demands, and quite possibly of alternative gender-rights agendas. These developments are particularly worrisome in the case of poor and working-class women, for they threaten the very possibility of participating democratically in deliberations about their own needs and wants.

One dimension of the possible long-term implications of economic and political restructuring, and, by extension, of SERNAM's project, is the historically accumulated experiences of collectivist organizing of peoples in communities. It is important to remember that women and their community-based activities, either in the name of the well-being of their families, or as women, have been the predominant force in the nearly forty years of working-class community-based activism in Chile. Certainly, men often took the visible, politically important posts, and caught the imagination first of the New Left in the 1960s and early 1970s and then of the disenchanted left in search of popular movements as new historical actors in the 1980s. Women, however, have historically been the unsung backbone of day-to-day neighbourhood-based organizing, acting as handmaids to these various projects of popular integration or popular emancipation, which have resulted in a rich, accumulated collectivist experience. Though they and their activities only became visible in the 1980s, when the particular political circumstances of the military coup led them to mobilize—and when their activities captured the imagination of feminists in Chile and beyond—it is a grave mistake to assume that their day-to-day earlier activities, rooted in a maternalist discourse and confined to their neighbourhoods, made them somehow passive players in everyday politics of poor urban areas. What they were, of course, were largely invisible players.

What seventeen years of dictatorship did not manage to undermine, the cumulative effects of some two decades of neo-liberal restructuring, economically, politically, and culturally, are threatening to achieve rapidly. Local activists and women themselves point out that it is difficult today to keep organizations going because women simply cannot afford the time, or energy, to take part in them.[77] On the one hand, women's incomes are critical for the well-being of the household; on the other, they have greater economic opportunities today than during the 1980s. Moreover, as the small improvements in poor households indicate (for example, increased numbers of the latest electronic gadgets, from microwave ovens to electric kettles, and wide-screen TVs), women and their families are not only 'reluctant entrepreneurs' but also eager consumers. The ethos of neo-liberal politics, then, with its individualistic emphasis on individual self-development, is enacted daily through social programmes, labour relations, the experience of work more generally, not to mention the culture and practice of consumerism with its concomitant widespread and high levels of personal indebtedness. As one community activist from La Pintana put it, 'when creditors come to impound someone's possessions, this person—a neighbour or friend—suffers in silence. His poverty is a sign of personal failure, of deep shame'.[78]

Poor women have not been passive receivers of these transformations. New forms of organizing have emerged which are shaped by the political grammar that characterizes 'normal times' politics today. Take the example of REMOS, the umbrella organization which coordinates over forty women's organizations in poor communities, which aims to make international agreements known to women from popular sectors and to ensure that these are met—or, as they put it, to *ejercer control ciudadano* ('exercise citizen control'). In addition, women participating in programmes for female heads of households have begun to meet—with the support of SERNAM—to discuss their specific situation and to explore their needs.

Given this context, it remains to be seen whether the emerging forms of organized activity, within the new political grammar, open up new possibilities for genuine democratic participation, or whether they constitute initiatives structured in a certain way, which leave intact what the Chilean historian Gabriel Salazar calls the basic dominant consensus of the present, namely, that poverty can be eradicated 'without modifying any of the fundamental bases of the neo-liberal economic and political model' (Salazar, 1995: 15).

Conclusions

In this chapter I have argued that the very ethos of neo-liberal politics at the centre of today's institutional 'modernization' is a central element to consider when exploring critically the implications of pursuing a gender justice agenda through innovative models of social provisioning, framed within the new policy agenda. This policy agenda exacerbates inequalities and itself contributes to the creation of new 'winners' and 'losers', and thus can neither promote nor guarantee meaningful gender justice.

Advancing a gender-rights agenda through the new social policy means, by definition, having to settle for a discursive resource which offers a very narrow range of possibilities for translating women's needs and demands into social action. Indeed, in the present context, this rights-based agenda, as implemented in practice, seems to be more a tool for a hierarchical and exclusionary project of social integration which is functional to the 'modernization' restructuring project more generally, than it is a means for enabling the meaningful citizenship of the majority of poor women. For middle-class professional women, it has offered new venues for remunerated employment, both in agencies like SERNAM and other ministries and government agencies, as well as in private consulting firms and universities. Its overwhelming characteristic, however, is that it relies on the cheap work—and volunteer spirit—of vast numbers of women, mostly lower-level civil servants, and poor and working-class community activists, to get the job done. Moreover, the programmes that flow from it, with their focus on targeting the poorest of the poor in a context of generalized social vulnerability which is a direct result of two decades of restructuring, themselves contribute to the exclusion of the majority of women from meaningfully exercising their citizenship. The danger, as I see it, is that these programmes, articulated through a neo-liberal policy discourse with its focus on individualized relations to the market, are contributing—in the name of the advancement of gender justice—to the erosion of collective practices and spaces where poor and working-class women have historically learnt to exercise meaningful democratic and critical participation. While the implicit gendered market citizenship that is now being promoted through social programmes may enable some women to acquire producer and consumer capacities, or to become enterprising individuals as subjects of market rights, one needs to ask whether or not such a narrow conception and practice of citizenship is something feminists should settle for.

References

Afani, Paula (1999) 'Temor a Denunciar Subestima Cifra de Delitos', *La Tercera*, 25 Nov., internet edition, <www.tercera.cl>.

Aguayo de Sota, Carmen Gloria (1982) *Des Chiliennes* (Paris: Des femmes).

Alvarez, Sonia (1999) 'The Latin American Feminist NGO "Boom"', *International Feminist Journal of Politics*, 1/2 (Sept.): 181–209.

Arenas de Mesa, Alberto, and Veronica Montecinos (1999) 'The Privatization of Social Security and Women's Welfare: Gender Effects of the Chilean Reform', *Latin American Research Review*, 34/3: 7–37.

Austin, Robert (1998) 'The State, Literacy and Popular Education in Chile, 1964–1990', Ph.D. dissertation, La Trobe University.

Barrera, Manuel (1998) 'Macroeconomic Adjustment in Chile and the Politics of the Popular Sectors', in Phillip D. Oxhorn and Graciela Ducatenzeiler (eds.), *What Kind of Democracy? What Kind of Market?* (Philadelphia: Pennsylvania State University Press).

Beneria, Lourdes (1996) 'The Legacy of Structural Adjustment in Latin America', in Lourdes Beneria and Mary Jo Dudley (eds.), *Economic Restructuring in the Americas* (Occasional Paper Studies, 3; Dec.; New York: Cornell University), 3–30.

—— and Martha Roldan (1987) *The Cross-roads of Class and Gender: Industrial Homework, Subcontracting, and Household Dynamics in Mexico City* (Chicago: University of Chicago Press).

Berger, Marguerite S. (1995) 'Poverty, the Environment, and Women in the Work Force', in Jorge A. Lawton (ed.), *Privatization Amidst Poverty* (Coral Gables, Fla.: North–South Center Press at the University of Miami).

Bienefeld, Manfred (1997) 'La Economía Política de la "Nueva Political Social"', in Maria Cristina Rojas de Ferro and A. Delgado Gutierrez (eds.), *Política Social: Desafíos y Utopías* (Bogota: Edición de la Facultad de Ciencias Politicas y Relaciones Internacionales de la Pontifica Universidad Javeriana).

Boron, Atilio A. (1998) 'Faulty Democracies? A Reflection on the Capitalist "Fault Lines" in Latin America', in Felipe Aguero and Jeffrey Stark (eds.), *Fault Lines of Democracy in Post-Transition Latin America* (Coral Gables, Fla.: North–South Center Press at the University of Miami).

Chile News (2000) 'Women Heads of Household: Getting by on Sheer Determination', internet edition, <www.segegob.cl>.

Corrigan, Philip (1990) *Social Forms/Human Capacities: Essays in Authority and Difference* (London: Routledge).

—— and Derek Sayer (1985) *The Great Arch: English State Formation as Cultural Revolution* (Oxford: Basil Blackwell).

Deacon, Bob (2000) *Globalization and Social Policy* (UNRISD Occasional Paper, 5; Geneva: UNRISD).

Di Marco, Graciela (2000) 'Políticas Publicas, Genero y Ciudadanía', paper presented at the 22nd International Congress of the Latin American Studies Association, 16–18 Mar., Miami.

ECLAC (2000a) *Proyecciones Latinoamericanas 1999–2000*, internet edition, <www.eclac.org>.

—— (2000b) *Social Panorama of Latin America, 1999–2000*, internet edition, <www.eclac.org>.

—— (2000c) *The Equity Gap: A Second Look*, internet edition, <www.eclac.org>.

ECLAC Press Release (2000a) 'Details of Poverty in Latin America and the Caribbean', internet edition, <www.eclac.org>.

—— (2000b) 'Perceptions of Threat and Vulnerability', internet edition, <www.eclac.org>.

—— (2000c) 'Social Panorama of Latin America 1999–2000', internet edition, <www.eclac.org>.

Elson, Diane (1995) 'Male Bias in Macro-economics: The Case of Structural Adjustment', in Diane Elson (ed.), *Male Bias in the Development Process*, 2nd edn. (Manchester: Manchester University Press).

Elson, Diane (1998) 'Talking to the Boys: Gender and Economic Growth Models', in Cecile Jackson and Ruth Pearson (eds.), *Feminist Visions of Development* (London: Routledge).

Espinoza, Guillermo (1999) 'Santiago Esta Perdiendo la Batalla contra Narcos', *La Tercera*, 11 Nov., internet edition, <www.tercera.cl>.

Foucault, Michel (1991) 'Governmentality', in Graham Burchell, Colin Gordon, and Peter Miller (eds.), *The Foucault Effect: Studies in Governmentality* (Chicago: Chicago University Press).

Franklin, Jonathan (1999) 'Recession Puts Chileans in the Mood to Punish Coalition at Polls', *Guardian* (10 Dec.): 21.

Fundación Nacional para la Superación de la Pobreza and UNDP (2000) 'Mujer y Pobreza', mimeo.

Galleguillos, Nibaldo (1998) 'From Confrontation to Friendly Persuasion: An Analysis of Judicial Reform and Democratization in Post-Pinochet Chile', *Canadian Journal of Latin American and Caribbean Studies*, 23/46: 161–92.

Garcia, Alvaro (1993) 'Social Policy and International Cooperation', in Marcelo Garcia (ed.), *Beyond Chile's Borders: Institutional Framework and International Cooperation Policy in Chile, 1990–1994* (Santiago: Editores Asociados and Paulina Castro).

Garcia, Marcelo (ed.) (1993) *Beyond Chile's Borders: Institutional Framework and International Cooperation Policy in Chile, 1990–1994* (Santiago: Editores Asociados and Paulina Castro).

Gaviola, Edda, Eliana Largo, and Sandra Palestro (1994) *Una Historia Necesaria: Mujeres en Chile, 1973–1990* (Santiago: Aki & Ahora).

Gobierno de Chile (2000) 'Mensaje Presidencial del 21 de mayo del 2000', internet edition, <www.presidencia.cl/cuenta/index.htm>.

Graham, Carol (1995) 'From Emergency Employment to Social Investment: Alleviating Poverty in Chile', in Jorge A. Lawton (ed.), *Privatization Amidst Poverty: Contemporary Challenges in Latin American Political Economy* (Boulder, Colo.: Lynne Rienner).

Gutiérrez, Pamela (2000) 'La Pobreza Escondida que No Recogen las Encuestas', *La Tercera*, 2 Apr., internet edition, <www.tercera.cl>.

Huber, Evelyne, and John D. Stephens (2000) *'The Political Economy of Pension Reform: Latin America in Comparative Perspective'* (UNRISD Occasional Paper, 7; Geneva: UNRISD).

Hutchison, Elizabeth (1995) 'Working Women of Santiago: Gender and Social Transformation in Urban Chile, 1887–1927', Ph.D. dissertation, University of California at Berkeley.

Instituto Nacional de Estadísticas (2000) *Índice de Remuneraciones por Hora*, Aug., internet edition, <www.ine.cl>.

IWRAW (2000) *IWRAW Country Reports: Chile*, internet edition, <www.igc.org/iwraw>.

Kay, Stephen J. (2000) 'Recent Changes in Latin American Welfare States: Is there Social Dumping?', *Journal of European Social Policy*, 10/2: 185–202.

Krauss, Clifford (2000) 'A Chilean Socialist in the Clinton–Blair Mold', *New York Times* (18 Jan.): A3.

Lechner, Norbert, and Susana Levy (1984) 'Notas Sobre la Vida Cotidiana III: El Disciplinamiento de la Mujer' (Material de Discusión, 56; Santiago: FLACSO).

Leiva, Fernando (1995) *Los Limites de la Actual Estrategia de Lucha Contra la Pobreza y el Dilema de las ONGs* (Serie de Documentos de Análisis, 7; Santiago: Taller de Reflexión, PAS).

—— (1998) 'The New Market Discipline', *Connection to the Americas*, 14/4: 1–6.

Loveman, Brian (1995) 'Chilean NGOs: Forging a Role in the Transition to Democracy', in Charles A. Reilly (ed.), *New Paths to Democratic Development in Latin America: The Rise of NGO–Municipal Collaboration* (Boulder, Colo.: Lynne Rienner).

Martinez, Javier, and Alvaro Diaz (1996) *Chile: The Great Transformation* (Washington, DC, and Geneva: Brookings Institution and United Nations Research Institute for Social Development).

Matear, Ann (1996) 'Gender, the State, and the Politics of Transition in Chile', Ph.D. dissertation, University of Liverpool, Liverpool.

Mayer, Carrie A. (1999) *The Economics and Politics of NGOs in Latin America* (Westport, Conn.: Praeger).

Molina G., Natacha (1998) 'Women's Struggle for Equality and Citizenship in Chile', in Geertje Lycklama a Nijeholt, Virginia Vargas, and Saskia Wieringa (eds.), *Women's Movements and Public Policy in Europe, Latin America, and the Caribbean* (New York: Garland).

Montecino, Sonia, and Josefina Rossetti (eds.) (1990) *Tramas par un Nuevo Destino: Propuestas de la Concertación de Mujeres por la Democracia* (Santiago: Arancibia Hermanos).

Montecinos, Veronica (1994) 'Neo-Liberal Economic Reforms and Women in Chile', in N. Aslanbeigui, S. Pressman, and G. Summerfield (eds.), *Women in the Age of Economic Transformation* (London and New York: Routledge).

Mujer/Fempress (1999a) *Chile en el Banquillo*, 213, Aug., internet edition, <www.fempress.cl>.

—— (1999b) *Despiden a Trabajadora Embarazada*, 213, Aug., internet edition, <www.fempress.cl>.

—— (1999c) *Encuesta Nacional: Las Chilenas de Fin de Siglo*, 211, June, internet edition, <www.fempress.cl>.

—— (2000a) *Deteriorada Condición Laboral de las Mujeres*, 226, Sep., internet edition, <www.fempress.cl>.

—— (2000b) *Exigen Ratificar Fuero Maternal*, 219, Mar., internet edition, <www.fempress.cl>.

Muñoz, Alejandra (1999) 'Crisis Económica Expulsa a 400 Mil Personas de ISAPRES', *La Tercera*, 8 Oct., internet edition, <www.tercera.cl>.

Munoz Goma, Oscar (1991) 'Estado, Desarrollo y Equidad: Algunas Preguntas Pendientes', *Colección Estudios CIEPLAN*, special issue, 31: 23–30.

Orford, Anne, and Jennifer Beard (1998) 'Making the State Safe for the Market: The World Bank's *World Development Report 1997*', *Melbourne University Law Review*, 22: 191–216.

Paley, Julia (2001) *Marketing Democracy: Power and Social Movements in Post-Dictatorship Chile* (Berkeley, Calif.: University of California Press).

Pearson, Ruth (1998) ' "Nimble Fingers" Revisited: Reflections on Women and Third World Industrialisation in the Late Twentieth Century', in Cecile Jackson and Ruth Pearson (eds.), *Feminist Visions of Development* (London: Routledge).

Petras, James, and Fernando Ignacio Leiva (1994) *Democracy and Poverty in Chile* (Boulder, Colo.: Westview).

Portes, Alejandro, Manuel Castells, and Laurent A. Benton (1989) *The Informal Economy: Studies in Advanced and Less Developed Countries* (Baltimore: Johns Hopkins University Press).

Raczynski, Dagmar (1995) 'Programs, Institutions and Resources: Chile', in Dagmar Raczynski (ed.), *Strategies to Combat Poverty in Latin America* (Washington, DC: Inter-American Development Bank).

Riesco, Manuel (1999) 'Chile, a Quarter of a Century on', *New Left Review*, 238: 97–125.

Rose, Nikolas (1999) *Powers of Freedom* (Cambridge: Cambridge University Press).

Salazar, Gabriel (1995) *Los pobres, los intelectuales y el poder, Chile, 1989–1995* (Serie de Documentos de Análisis, 6; Santiago: Taller de Reflexión, PAS).

Schamis, Hector (1996) 'The Politics of Economic Reform in Latin America: Collective Action, Institution Building and the State', in Lourdes Beneria and Mary Jo Dudley (eds.), *Economic Restructuring in the Americas* (Conference proceedings, Latin American Studies Program; New York: Cornell University Press).

Schild, Verónica (1995) 'NGOs, Feminist Politics and Neo-Liberal Latin American State Formations: Some Lessons from Chile', *Canadian Journal of Development Studies*, special issue, pp. 123–47.

—— (1998a) 'Market Citizenship and the "New Democracies": The Ambiguous Legacies of Contemporary Chilean Women's Movements', *Social Politics* (Summer): 232–49.

—— (1998b) 'New Subjects of Rights? Women's Movements and the Construction of Citizenship in the "New Democracies" ', in Sonia Alvarez, Evelina Dagnino, and Arturo Escobar (eds.), *Politics of Culture/Cultures of Politics* (Boulder, Colo.: Westview).

—— (2000) 'Neo-liberalism's New Gendered Market Citizens: The "Civilizing" Dimensions of Social Programmes in Chile', *Citizenship Studies*, 4/3: 275–305.

SERNAM (1994) *Plan de Igualdad de Oportunidades para las Mujeres 1994–1999* (Santiago: SERNAM).

—— (2000) *Informe del Gobierno de Chile sobre el Cumplimiento de los Compromisos Contraídos en la Cuarta Conferencia Mundial de la Mujer,*

Igualdad, Desarrollo y Paz, Beijing, 4–15 de septiembre de 1995, conten-idos en la Plataforma de Acción de Beijing (Santiago: Servicio Nacional de la Mujer, Departamento de Relaciones Internacionales y Cooperación; Apr.).

SERNAM Press Release (2000) 'SERNAM impulsa plan de apoyo al empleo femenino en la región' (14 Aug.).

Steinmetz, George (ed.) (1999) *State/Culture: State Formation After the Cultural Turn* (Ithaca, NY, and London: Cornell University Press).

Vergara, Pilar (1990) *Políticas Hacia la Extrema Pobreza en Chile 1973–1988* (Santiago: FLACSO).

—— (1994) 'Market Economy, Social Welfare, and Democratic Consolidation in Chile', in W. C. Smith, C. H. Acuna, and E. A. Gamarra (eds.), *Democracy, Markets, and Structural Reform in Latin America* (Coral Gables, Fla.: North-South Center Press at the University of Miami).

Waitzkin, Howard, and Celia Iriart (2000) 'How the United States Exports Managed Care to Third-World Countries', *Monthly Review*, 55/1: 21–35.

Weisbrot, Mark, Dean Baker, Robert Naiman, and Gila Neta (2000) 'Growth may be Good for the Poor—But are IMF and World Bank Policies Good for Growth?', draft, Center for Economic and Policy Research, internet edition.

World Bank (1997) *World Development Report 1997: The State in a Changing World* (New York: Oxford University Press).

Engendering Education: Prospects for a Rights-Based Approach to Female Education Deprivation in India

Ramya Subrahmanian

Introduction

Female education deprivation in India remains high despite recent efforts to improve the overall quality of and access to education in order to achieve universal elementary education. The reasons for these high levels of deprivation are commonly explained in terms of complex intersections between social and cultural norms that devalue female education and create disincentives at household and community level for investment in female well-being, on the one hand, and economic deprivation and the wider discrimination embedded in structures of labour and capital markets, on the other. However, the struggle to bring education into the realm of state-guaranteed rights has added a new dimension to efforts to universalize education. The right to education, usually spoken of rhetorically within education policy efforts, has started assuming a greater role in actions and policies of civil society groups as well as some multilateral agencies (Irvine, 2000).

This chapter will focus on two challenges to the promotion of the right to education: the economic and education policy context within which such an approach is being attempted, and the gender perspective being employed to make the case for a focus on women's education. Women enter the education policy picture as the stated priority of education policy interventions and international development targets.[1] The development of women is seen as the best vehicle for advancing the basic needs of other groups such as children and securing progressive rates of development across a range of human well-being indicators. Drawing on recent developments in India, the chapter will place the rhetoric of the importance of female education in the context of, first, education policy reforms; second, policy discourses juxtaposed with micro-level analysis of the dynamics of female education; and finally recent developments in the promotion of the right to education. Although rights discourses are in their infancy, and do not as yet find reflection in the policy frameworks that guide education provision in India, the prospects and struggles beyond underpin the discussion. Questions are also raised about the value of rights discourses beyond the symbolic, and the challenges posed in making them 'real' for people who need them most.

The proliferation of rights seen as essential for development has expanded the traditional area of civil and political liberties into a wider programme addressing economic, social, and cultural rights. In particular the rights approach offers a strategic common ground for articulating people's claims and states' obligations. Huq, for instance, points to the strategic value of rights-based approaches, arguing that they allow women 'to contest notions of unequal worth embedded in many cultures and given statutory recognition in their laws; and to demand that notions of citizenship be extended to women and be re-conceptualised accordingly' (2000: 74). She notes that for feminist activists working in the south, international frameworks of rights strengthen local strategies to make visible the neglect of women in a wide array of policies; demand redress of disparities in resource allocation; counter local traditions that impinge on women's fundamental freedoms and rights; and claim accountability from states to their citizens (ibid.).

However, challenges still remain in terms of the substantive elaboration of rights and how they may be made operational. Problems of hierarchy and prioritization surface where equally important rights vie for attention,[2] and where the basic entitlements of people to function even with minimal human dignity have not been met. The argument that certain rights are preconditions for others, and that indeed the language of rights may be a luxury where basic survival is a daily challenge, provides a reminder to proponents of the rights discourse of the achievements yet to be made in substantiating rights in a meaningful way. Further, the capacity of individuals to claim rights provided to them within constitutions or policy frameworks remains contingent upon the construction of a more 'universal' notion of citizenship, where other forms of identity do not intervene in a manner that locates people within hierarchies of inequality and disprivilege.

The promotion of the right to education is further likely to be complicated by its relational complexity with other goods, entitlements, and resources. The importance of opportunity and aspiration in positively influencing investment in education, as people see others around them gaining new skills and access to new resources through literacy and education, cannot be overemphasized. Thus the 'right to education' needs to be placed within the context of wider socio-political rights, and prospects for its realization, for both women and men, assessed in terms of the challenges posed by gendered constructions of social and economic opportunities and obligations.

In this chapter, the capabilities framework (Nussbaum, 2000) is used to distinguish rights-based approaches to social development from the more conventional policy debates in the education sector, which tend to focus on access in terms of a descriptive state rather than a more substantive concern with inclusion and citizenship. The human capabilities approach, outlined in the work of Amartya Sen and Martha Nussbaum, but most notably in relation to gender inequalities in the work of Nussbaum, sets out an approach towards identifying the universal basic social minimum that allows for 'a life that is worthy of the dignity of the human being', arrived at by focusing on central human capabilities, that is, 'what people are actually able to do and to be' (Nussbaum, 2000: 5). This approach rests on the conception of each individual 'as an end' rather than as a mere tool of the ends of others (2000: 5) and provides a normative base upon which claims for justice and rights can be grounded in struggles for survival with dignity and improved quality of life. The approach seeks to avoid prescribing desirable achievements in absolute terms, preferring instead to conceptualise capabilities in terms of 'thresholds' or minimum basic levels beneath which 'it is held that truly human functioning is not available to citizens' (2000: 6). Ambitiously, the framework developed seeks to provide both 'cross-cultural norms of justice, equality and rights, and at the same time [be] sensitive to local particularity, and to the many ways in which circumstances shape not only options but also beliefs and preferences' (2000: 7).

Within this framework, literacy, not education *per se*,[3] is seen as a central component of interlocking capabilities, 'critical in giving women greater access to goods they are already pursuing', and strategically important 'in supporting a wide range of other human capabilities' (Nussbaum, 2000: 295–6). As part of an interlocking basic minimum basket of social goods, literacy becomes both a means to enhancing capabilities as well as a desired outcome of enhanced capabilities. This opens up possibilities for seeking out the different pathways and conditions under which rights can be made operational. The chapter concludes with a brief assessment of applying the capabilities approach to the arguments for the right to education.

Education Policy Reform in the Neo-liberal Context

The challenge of achieving rights is posed against a macroeconomic environment that is perceived widely as potentially disabling for groups that have been historically deprived of opportunities that would help them take advantage of rapidly changing economic landscapes. Despite the rhetoric of policy documents which club together the various rationales for investing in education, particularly female education—ranging from positive externalities such as better child health and survival rates, lower maternal mortality, lower fertility, greater focus on children's well-being, among other things—trends and achievements in the recent history of education have belied such predictions of the rewards of investment in education. Investment levels have continued to fall short of the required rates, both on the part of governments as well as on the part of donor agencies (Bennell and Furlong, 1997). Household behaviour, especially in contexts of impoverishment, continues to fail to live up to the optimism of projected returns. Intra-household gender discrimination persists in the absence of the scale of structural change that would promote the value of girls and women both in the public and private domains. Policy attention to female education has seen an increase, but on the basis of narrowly framed concerns, which by and large obscure real attention to reversing processes of devaluation and discrimination.

A significant factor in the persistence of inequitable outcomes in education is the continuing economic pressure that prevents poor households from gaining easy access to schooling institutions. Despite significant reforms in education provision, focusing on the 'supply side', the ability of poor households to trade off current consumption requirements against future gains has not been strengthened. Evidence from around the world has shown the significant damage done to education investment and reform by both economic decline as well as harsh economic solutions imposed in the course of structural adjustment (Colclough, 1997; Malhotra, 2000), although to varying degrees in different regions. There is widespread consensus, however, that Sub-Saharan Africa has been particularly affected by structural adjustment policies. While some countries saw reversals to their achievements in education, others were unable to move from low education attainment, both on account of cuts to public expenditure, particularly social-sector expenditure, as well as the debilitating impact on the ability of households to survive and invest in their futures.

The call to put a human face onto structural adjustment yielded some result in terms of a new focus on human resource development, particularly education. The 1990 Jomtien Conference on Education for All is hailed as a turning point in global consensus on the import-ance of basic education.[4] However, despite the greater subsequent attention paid to education, it is a matter of debate whether the policy framework, and the neo-liberal[5] assumptions upon which it was founded, has undergone much change. The continuing domin-ance of human capital theory as the underlying framework of the policy debate led by the Bank has been highlighted most notably by Fine and Rose (2001). Apparent discursive reversals, however, include the re-emergence of the state after years of neo-liberal rejec-tion of any role for the state beyond the minimum, a focus on human development, rights, and equality, supposedly as equal partners to the focus on economic growth, and a focus on 'community' as opposed to the individualism of earlier policy approaches. However, to what extent have these reversals really taken effect?

External funding for education has largely taken the form of external debt, through the provision of soft loans by the World Bank to governments for promoting education reform. In India, for example, the apparent increase in resources for education has largely come as soft loans from the World Bank, although aid money from other sources also contributes to the financing of education (Kumar *et al.*, 2001). Despite the trenchant critiques mounted on the 'rates of return' arguments used to justify a range of cost recovery and other financial policies, not least on account of their negative impacts on class and gender equity in education, the belief that education yields high financial returns continues to dominate financing policies of the Bank, which is the largest single source of external funding on education. The concern with securing efficiency of education reform continues to dominate equity considerations (see Subrahmanian, 2000, for a discussion), upholding the central neo-liberal concern with achieving economic growth as a primary policy objective (Colclough, 1991).

In the Indian context, the influx of resources through external funding has largely come to the primary education sector and has, to some extent, reversed the decline in social-sector expenditure. To what extent this is sustainable is a matter of debate. While the central government extends 85 per cent of support for the District Primary Education Programme (DPEP), the vehicle through which primary education sector reform is taking place, states are meant to main-tain their current levels of expenditure and contribute the remaining 15 per cent (Kumar *et al.*, 2001). However, evidence from the early years[6] of India's economic reform period indicates that real per capita social sector expenditure declined for many states, at a higher rate than the decline in real per capita total expenditure (Prabhu, 2000). Social-sector investment (around 3.2 per cent of GDP) has tended to remain far below the levels identified by numerous commissions and policy texts (6 per cent of GDP), and significant reforms that would sustain the financing of primary education by altering policies towards the funding of higher education, the traditional beneficiary of education investment, are yet to be seen (Prabhu, 2000).

Despite the recognition of the important role for states in securing equitable and universal education (see Colclough, 1997, for a discussion), the challenge of financing universal education continues to emphasize the need to raise revenue through levying fees and recovering costs. While the ideological extremes of neo-liberal faith in markets may have shifted somewhat in terms of defining the policy agenda, the practicalities of financing education have led to a continued emphasis on how best to raise revenues from the use of education services. This debate, as Tilak (1997) notes, is marked by numerous shifts, with the Bank itself changing its position on cost recovery in the form of user fees, from simultaneous opposition and support, to its subsequent distancing from this particular policy approach, particularly with regard to primary education. Malhotra describes the continuing economic efficiency focus of debates on policy reform as stemming from the 'minimalist' definition of the 'public good' aspect of education by the Bank in terms of primary education alone (2000: 366), when in reality the education system, from pre-primary to tertiary levels and adult education, needs to be seen as a whole.

The changes made to levels of social-sector expenditure, represent only one aspect, albeit a crucial one, of the challenge of universalizing education. Kumar *et al.* (2001) note that the impacts of the new equations of donor investment on state capacity and state–citizen relations have been little discussed, largely on account of the 'benign image' of primary education.

As Bordia notes:

People assume that education in developing countries will reduce inequalities by enhancing the knowledge and skill levels of the disadvantaged. In reality, education perpetuates and widens inequalities. The privileged and the rich have access to a range of educational facilities that equip them to strengthen their hold over resources. Conversely, the poor and marginalised have access to a kind of education that demotivates them, creates hurdles for its completion, and even if they do continue their education, it rarely qualifies them to make a real change in their social and economic status. (2000: 313)

Poor households are expected to make the trade-offs required to send children to school at the expense of their current consumption in an economic climate that seems on course to perpetuate if not widen existing income disparities, in some cases along new fissures of inequality. Discussions on cost recovery also omit to recognize that, in practice, poor households are already paying a high price for investment in education, even where it is described as 'free' in policy rhetoric[7] —Tilak cites economic data from India that indicate that the share of household expenditure in total national expenditure in 1985–6 was as high as 50.3 per cent. Further, the emphasis on enrolling children into school has obscured from rigorous disaggregated analysis and policy debate questions regarding the extent to which the entry of more children into public schooling is facilitating the exit of others into the unregulated, private schooling sector, and related impacts on equity (Kumar *et al.*, 2001).

Perspectives on the current state of education reform vary from celebrations of the increase in available resources for education to the perspective of ' "we have no choice" pragmatists' (Shah *et al.*, 1994: 145), to those who warn of the dangers of ignoring some of the deeper trends that are being set in motion (Kumar *et al.*, 2001). Kumar *et al.* point to the way in which primary education is being treated as part of a 'safety-net' approach, in a bid to 'humanize' economic reform. This they see as leading to an approach which sees a rolling back of the state, not in terms of commitment to education, but in the way in which education systems are designed. They point to the increasing trend of bringing in para-teachers, paid less and trained less than teachers employed in the formal system, and the setting up of 'alternate schools' in hitherto unserved habitations, which have minimal infrastructure and hence possible quality implications. Such an approach, they argue, in effect sees the public system being abdicated by the better-off, who have the option of moving into private schools, effectively splitting the 'universal' education system into a hierarchy based on differing levels of quality. Leaving those already education-deprived within the poor-quality public system and under-resourced alternative schools will do little to correct the inequalities that are endemic within the system.

The question, however, remains whether the universal provision of services is a prerequisite for promoting inclusive citizenship and fulfilling rights, or whether an inclusive notion of citizenship needs to be promoted in order that public services perform more equitably.[8] The proliferation of rights is particularly ironic in situations where rampant marketization has been encouraged, with states cutting back more and more of the essential services they are obliged to provide to meet the rights of their citizens. Thus while the much-criticized top–down mode of delivering services to 'beneficiaries' has been challenged fairly successfully in rhetoric if not in practice,[9] the shift to meeting the needs of 'citizens' seems to have been overridden by the shift to servicing the 'consumer' in the case of many 'public' services.[10]

In the Indian context, the articulation of rights as citizens remains an important requirement of strategies for education development, largely on account of the fact that, for most of the country's excluded populations, state provision remains the best chance for getting relatively 'free' education. Private education remains accessible to a relatively small proportion of the population, overwhelmingly an urban elite. However, indications are that private schooling is growing, encouraged by a state that is far from achieving its goal of providing universal elementary education. Table 7.1 indicates the spread of private education.

As Sudarshan (2000) notes, the data reflect the management of schools, and not the funding of schools—government expenditure has actually risen relative to other sources of funding, largely on account of increasing donor assistance for elementary education programmes. Although the share of privately managed schools is much smaller than government schools (including the category under local bodies), and its spread uneven across the country, there are indications that private schools are proliferating in many rural areas, and that they are increasingly appealing to poorer households as well (Kingdon, 1996). Further, many of these schools are not recognized by the state, so official data will not reveal an accurate picture of the expansion of the private sector. The weak regulation of these schools indicates that the rights of parents and children as 'consumers' of education are also

Table 7.1. *Educational institutions by management type 1992–1993 (%)*

	Government	Local bodies	Private
Higher Secondary (Grade 12)	40	2	58
High School (Grade 10)	36	9	55
Middle (Grade 8)	44	32	24
Primary (Grade 5)	48	45	7
Pre-primary	46	38	16
Total	46	38	16

Source: Sudarshan, 2000.

not institutionalized, and thus a broader framework of citizenship-based rights is essential to protect all children.

Ascertaining the equity effects of private schooling is complex. While private schools are biased towards urban or semi-urban areas, and towards boys rather than girls, it has also been noted that they are likely to be more accountable and responsive to parents than government schools (Sudarshan, 2000).[11] However, the view that public schooling alone can provide equitable access for marginalized groups can be opened to question. National survey[12] data cited by Sudarshan (2000) found that a higher proportion of children from minority groups, and the Scheduled Caste and Scheduled Tribes groups, attended private schools, relative to other Hindu groups. This suggests possible alternative explanations: either that for traditionally disadvantaged groups private schooling may be more equitable, as it uses ability to pay as the entrance criterion, or that private schools may be those run by community associations that cater to particular social groups. The latter point may pertain particularly to religious minorities. Aggregate data, however, need to be backed up by micro-level studies. For instance, Srivastava (2001) found in rural Uttar Pradesh that private school enrolment is more concentrated among upper castes, Sikhs, and to a lesser extent, Muslims, and low for girls. However, there were differences in the spread and access by social group to private schooling between districts.

It is too early to predict the consequences of the range of changes that are taking place in several policy arenas in India. NGO interventions, empowerment programmes, the activities of the different strands of the women's movement, juxtaposed with the very obvious inclination towards marketization and privatization in many spheres of economic life, are throwing up a range of opportunities and constraints which are changing the social and economic configurations within the country. However, the extent to which the 'right' to education is likely to be made real through an active and responsive public policy environment needs to be assessed, particularly in relation to the situation of those disadvantaged in education. Further, to what extent are women likely to be in a position to take advantage of new opportunities in education, whether provided by the state or the market? In the next section I turn to the question of gender deprivation in education, and an examination of the policy space for constructing a rights approach, as well as a micro-level consideration of the complexities of women's rights to education in the Indian context.

Contours of Female Education Deprivation in India

Statistical Contours

Gender-disaggregated data on education are widely available in India, and the patterns of discrimination are well-known. Inequalities are exacerbated by level of education, by geographical location (rural over urban), by social group (by caste and ethnicity, with Scheduled Castes and Scheduled Tribes[13] trailing significantly behind higher status social groups), and by occupation.[14] A succinct summary of the broad axes of exclusion from/inclusion into schooling is provided by Vaidyanathan and Nair:

> In general, children of the upper castes, the economically better-off families, families dependent on non-agricultural occupations, parents who are better educated, and villages that have easier access to schools, are more likely to be enrolled ... The larger the number of infants and old people in the household ... the smaller are the chances of children getting enrolled in school. (2001: 33)

The gender gap intersects with these broader social and economic inequalities. Data suggest that, although there has been an increase in female enrolment in school over time, the trends indicate that the gender gap (between boys and girls) remains constant. Further, enrolment data are notoriously unreliable (Dreze and Sen, 1995; Subrahmanian, 2000a) and tell us little of the quality of participation to be useful beyond purely satisfying statistical interest.[15] As Sudarshan notes, 'qualitative understanding is essential to interpretation of statistics', given the lack of correlation observed between data on the facilities provided by the state and literacy outcomes, amongst others (2000: 46). Table 7.2 provides a glimpse into the statistical representations of educational inequality in India, based on data from 1996.[16]

Data indicate that literacy levels and school enrolment ratios are lowest, and discontinuation rates highest, for Scheduled Castes,

Table 7.2. *Education profile of India by social groups (%)*

	Literacy (aged 7+)	Enrolment (6–14)	Discontinuation rates (6–14)
SCs and STs	40.8	61.8	7.1
Other Hindus	59.4	77.4	5.5
Muslims	49.4	61.6	6.9
Other minorities	65.2	83.5	5.2

Table 7.3. *Education profile 1994 (%)*

	All groups		ST		SC		Muslims		Other Hindus	
	M	F	M	F	M	F	M	F	M	F
Rural India	65.6	40.1	51.4	26.0	53.4	28.2	64.7	46.4	72.3	45.0

Note: Figures for ST, SC, Muslims, and Other Hindus represent per cent of the population of each of those groups.

Scheduled Tribes, and Muslim children, with non-SC Hindus faring better, and other minorities (including, notably, Christian) faring the best. What this says about the complex issues of identities of religion, caste, and ethnicity, and the nature of education provision and participation requires deeper investigation, beyond the scope of this chapter. However, the gender gap across all these groups remains significant. Sudarshan (2000) shows the consistency of the gender gap across the various social groups (albeit drawing on different statistical indicators from those in Table 7.2), as presented in Table 7.3.

The aggregate gender gap (across all groups) in rural India stands at 25.5 percentage points. Although the data are drawn from 1994, the progress made over the last few years is unlikely to have made a significant change in this scenario.

Pathways to Enhanced Capabilities

Conventional policy wisdom has emphasized the returns gained to societies as a whole from investments in female education, and implicitly suggests that these translate in some (unspecified) way into gains for individual women as well.[17] Statistical analyses often point to the indisputability of correlations between female literacy and fertility decline, especially in comparison with other possible explanatory factors such as urbanization, poverty reduction, and male literacy (Dreze and Murthi, 2000). Indeed, Dreze and Murthi argue that 'female education plays a key role in the social development approach [to fertility decline]' (2000: 2). However, the issue of the 'pathways' that lead to the link drawn between increases in female literacy and declines in fertility remains contentious. Some pathways, such as the effect of female education on delaying the age of marriage and improving access to information and basic reproductive and contraceptive health services, are not the subjects of dispute. Others, such as the claim, implicit or otherwise, that it is the impact of education on female autonomy that results in greater control exerted by women over their fertility and other crucial life decisions, remain a matter of debate.

Critics of the latter argument term it 'instrumentalist', particularly when it is used to provide the policy case for investing in women's education. They argue, among others, that although social returns may provide a compelling reason to educate women, they tell us little of the actual gains that women make from being educated, in terms of achieving their own aspirations, and securing a better quality of life for themselves. The work of Roger and Patricia Jeffery (1998, 1994) in particular offers a consistent and persuasive attack on the often misleading ways in which statistical correlations are expanded upon to imply that changes can be attributed to the enhanced autonomy of women. They note that the question 'education for what?' provides sharper insight into the gendered outcomes expected from investment in education, particularly the strengthening of women's prospects within conventional marriage markets. Further, claims made about women's gains in terms of enhanced autonomy and agency at household level as a result of education, and in terms of their better access to public resources including employment, have been met with evidence that gendered ideologies shaping both the labour market and the family are most often not challenged by the education institutions and processes to which the majority of women have access. As Kabeer (1999a) argues, a focus on 'access' to different resources tells us little or nothing of the choices that access to the resource in question enables people to make, particularly in relation to the achievement of their well-being.

Causal links drawn between education and a range of other outcomes suffer often from unverifiable statistical correlations and problematic arguments. Important questions are also raised about the basis of instrumentalist claims about the developmental benefits of investing in women's education, particularly in relation to fertility decline (Jeffery and Basu, 1996b). Many scholars argue that, in South Asia, primary schooling alone is inadequate to effect a significant change (see articles in Jeffery and Basu, 1996a). Vatuk (1994) notes in her study of education among Muslim households in South India that the spread of schooling for girls began at a time when age at marriage had *already begun* to rise, rather than the former resulting in this change. As Jeffery and Basu (1996b) note (citing Mason), there are several hypotheses that can be argued as explaining the links between education and fertility decline, none of which are implausible, yet whose accuracy may be questionable given the unreliable and often problematic nature of the data upon which they are based.

It is clearly impossible to speculate on the pathways between education and employment, on the one hand, and education, employment, and a range of other resources on enhancing women's capabilities. Education is also not the only means through which access to employment for women is made possible, and nor does equitable participation in education necessarily secure labour-market opportunities for women and men. The emphasis on waged labour as an outcome of education may in turn be misplaced, where formal-sector job opportunities are limited, and employment restricted largely to agriculture, as in a large part of India. Evidence and their interpretations remain highly context-specific, which indicates that generalized claims made about links between investment in education and well-being outcomes need to be more closely investigated.

While education is clearly an important influence on women's ability to gain access to waged employment, it is not, however, the only means through which women's agency can be enhanced, or well-being outcomes achieved. Dreze and Sen (1995), for instance, note that *both* female education (and literacy) and female labour-force participation are correlated with positive improvements in female child survival. Citing the case of two Indian states, Kerala and Manipur, they note that female literacy, prominence of women in influential social and political activities, and the tradition of matrilineal inheritance were *all* important factors contributing to the more egalitarian gender relations in these states, which enjoy a much higher level of social development than most other parts of India. Debates on the influence of education and employment on women's autonomy are not clearly resolved in the absence of consolidated data from specific areas over time. While Kabeer (1999*b*) argues further that female employment has a much more direct effect on female well-being than education, Sen (1999) argues from a case study in Calcutta city that educated women had a far better chance of dealing with violent husbands than women who were employed. Citing the dismal conditions under which women gain employment, she notes that 'employment is not necessarily a positive or enriching experience' (1999: 83). On the other hand, 'access to secondary stages of education may have an important contributory role in enhancing women's capacity to exercise control in their lives', through the combination of literacy and numeracy skills, and enhanced self-esteem (ibid.).

Contextual factors in the case of different studies making these diverse claims constitute an important set of variables, thus preventing generalizability beyond a point. However, issues like access to social networks and via them a range of choices other than those offered by often oppressive kinship structures, may also play a role in determining the extent to which options are made available to women through which they can gain access to education. The single lesson perhaps to be drawn from such a wide array of debates and findings is that the range of means essential for women to arrive at a basic quality of life (incorporating the critical notions of freedom and choice) cannot be compromised, but require concerted action. There has been a tendency in policy circles to emphasize education as a 'magic' or 'silver' bullet (Jeffery and Jeffery, 1998; Whitehead and Lockwood, 1999), with little interest in how gains can be translated more meaningfully into enhanced capabilities.

The key issue is that of the basis for evaluating change. If female education is treated as a means to a range of externalities resulting from education investment, then perhaps the pathways through which gender equality in education is achieved are not of importance. However, if we see education as a means to ends relating to greater autonomy, choice, and bargaining power for women, then the evaluative framework needs to be specified.[18] Concern purely with the effects of education on other developmental indicators would result in a lack of interest in whether the pathways are those that enhance autonomy and agency en route to securing a better quality of life. Erwer (1998) points this out in relation to Kerala, much celebrated for its achievements in promoting female education in particular, and social development more generally. She notes the 'gender paradox' in a state where female education is high yet women's participation in politics has been dismally low.[19] If concerns are with education serving as a means to empower women and enhance their freedoms to participate in a range of institutions that will enhance their position in society, then evaluations have to be based on the wider framework of capabilities.

'Between Cultures and Markets':[20] Gender and Education Deprivation

As Mukhopahdyay and Seymour note, the 'ongoing tension between macro-structurally-generated pressures that increase the desirability of education for women and micro-structurally-generated pressures that constrain women's education' (1994: 3) provides the locus for focusing attention on gender discrimination in education. Despite increasing awareness about gender issues within the policy arena, the gender gap has not been adequately addressed in practice

(Wazir, 2000). Analysis of why such discrimination persists has been fairly consistent with the picture portrayed of gender relations in India and the overall constraints which prevent females from gaining equitable access to development resources relative to men. These factors have been widely discussed (see, for example, Sudarshan, 2000; Khan, 1993), and bear just a brief summary in this chapter.

Broadly, a gendered analysis of relative female education deprivation would need to be located within an understanding of the gender-differentiated structures of aspiration and expectation on the one hand, and claims and obligations on the other, which influence household decisions on how much to invest in which children. This 'investment settlement' is likely to change over time and with the impact of wider changes in social arrangements surrounding work, marriage and family, and kinship structures, as Seymour (1995) notes in her ethnographic and longitudinal study of female education in Orissa. Further, she notes that, overall in India, these linkages can be viewed as 'patterned', having 'been affected in regular ways by systems of social stratification and family organisation' (1995: 83). For instance, she notes that changes have been negligible in low-status families that rely on female labour from an early age; more controlled for middle and upper status families where girls reside in large joint families within caste-based neighbourhoods, and more dramatic where more class-based stratification operates, mounting challenges to the patrifocal family structure and ideology (ibid.)

The importance of kinship structures and family organization have been emphasized in the work of many scholars, particularly in explaining the regional disparities evident in the data on female deprivation in general. Dasgupta *et al.* (2000) argue, drawing on Dyson and Moore's influential study (1983), that the integration of kinship structures and social norms with labour-market variables together help explain why patterns of disprivilege are more acute in northern states than in the southern states of India.[21] For example, they cite Agarwal's argument that kinship norms in northern India are likely to influence the (lower) expectations of transfers that parents have of their daughters, relative to households in southern India. Lower expectations are thus seen to translate into limited rationales for investment and the strategic preference for boys' over girls' education.

While structures of kinship and ideology shape differentials in expectations and aspirations for girls and boys, claims and obligations that structure the parent–child relationship provide a different though not entirely unrelated lens through which to view the ways in which parents invest in children's futures. As Kabeer notes:

The essence of the intergenerational contract is that parents look after their children when they are young and expect to be looked after by them in their old age: 'looking after' in this context extends to emotional as well as material support. However, it is both socially and individually recognised that this inter-temporal asymmetry in the nature of the contract carries risks. Parents carry out their obligations in anticipation of future returns; children in recognition of past benefits. The contract therefore requires an act of faith on the part of parents who sacrifice current consumption for future security that their children will survive, will become economically productive and, most important, will be willing to honour their side of the contract when parents have become old and dependent. (2000: 465)

Normative understandings of the differential roles played by girls and boys in securing parental futures, and the transitional role the female child is seen to play in her parents' future limits parental expectations of the female child in the intergenerational bargain or contract, thus giving rise to gender-differentiated claims and obligations from a young age. Gender ideologies associated with the dominant patrifocal family structure, with its emphasis on the subordination of individual goals and interests to the welfare of the larger family, have particularly emphasized the centrality of males to the continuity of the family and kin group, and the marginality of females who are seen to belong to the marital family once marriage has been transacted (Mukhopadhyay and Seymour, 1994).[22] This has translated into the relative devaluation of females as a source of support for parents in old age, and thus compromises the amount that families, particularly those facing economic hardship, are willing to invest in female education. Seymour also notes that enhanced educational opportunities have benefited middle- and upper-class urban families more than lower-status ones, arguing that for the latter, 'female employment is not a potential benefit of education but a handicap of it' as girls' labour is called upon within the family from an early age (1995: 83).

The dual constraints of gendered labour markets and the structure of the marriage market combine in overlapping ways to prevent aspirations for enhancement of girls' and women's prospects from moving significantly beyond the basic minimum of literacy and numeracy. Wider community norms within which households manage their investment decisions also play a crucial role in influencing decision-making—particularly where girls' behaviour in public is subject to the strictest of scrutiny in line with norms of chastity, and where aspersions on a girl's moral character are often sufficient to severely hamper her chances in relation to marriage (Subrahmanian,

2000*a*). The gender division of labour, particularly the early socializ-ation of girls into the undervalued and often invisible reproductive work of their mothers, leads to more intensified work patterns for female children relative to boys (although the work contributions of the latter are far more visible), and the more deleterious impact on the quality of their participation in schooling.

The importance of family and marriage cannot be overemphas-ized in the Indian context, across social class. Derne (1994) notes that marriage alliances remain crucial for supporting family prosper-ity, protecting family honour, and expanding its network of social ties. The 'social capital' effects of marriage make it a powerful insti-tution that is hard to bypass in the quest for promoting female autonomy. Recent research with *sangha*[23] women in Karnataka, exploring women's views on the institutions of marriage and fam-ily, revealed that marriage and family were viewed by women as 'the essential truths of life': 'It gives you an identity in relation to others. It enables you to enact multiple roles. It brings a sense of belonging and owning: my husband, my child, something in the world that is mine' (cited in Dave and Krishnamurty, 2000: 25).

Further, women interviewed by Dave and Krishnamurty indicated that marriage, rather than education, jobs, asset creation, or inherit-ance, was valued as a source of security 'in a society replete with institutionalised threats: caste, hierarchy, poverty and powerless-ness' (2000: 26). These views were articulated by women whose views on changing gender relations within the family indicated a desire to improve the quality of gender relations within the home, and revealed the development of an 'expanded notion of self'. Thus belief in the importance of marriage and family was not presented as incompat-ible with the women's recognition of the importance of a notion of 'self', and coexisted with exertions to ensure that girls went to school, among other ideas.

Economic insecurity surfaces as a crucial parameter informing household decisions on investment in education. Security of liveli-hoods plays an important role in determining both the opportunity costs of children's time as well as the willingness of parents to invest in the short term in a good whose economic returns may be unre-liable in the medium to long term.[24] The promise of high economic returns are not necessarily enjoyed by the rural poor, where access to formal employment, the focus of aspirations for economic mobility,[25] is mediated by considerations of caste and gender, and often demands considerable outlays of cash in the form of bribes, in situations where the demand for formal employment outstrips supply.[26] Different social groups are often engaged in relations of competition for access, resources, credentials, and opportunities, especially in situations of scarcity and inequality. How education figures in the politics of competition requires analysis and assessment in diverse contexts. For instance, caste-disaggregated empirical data show that there are changing patterns of employment and occupation for different social groups, with some groups moving into salaried jobs, professions, and businesses while others remain in agriculture (for some examples on Uttar Pradesh, see Srivastava, 2001). This competition can be particularly pronounced between Scheduled Castes and backward castes, where state reservation policy in employment and higher education may be benefiting the former.

Economic vulnerability has been exacerbated by the rise in casualization of the labour force since the onset of reforms (Duraisamy, 2000) and this has different, and possibly contradictory, effects for the education investment of different households. On the one hand, it can put pressure on households to engage in multiple livelihoods, drawing particularly on the labour of children to manage diverse economic strategies including migration (Subrahmanian, 2000a). On the other hand, it could push households into non-traditional occupations for which some investment in education is considered necessary (see Dyer and Choksi, 1998).

A particular concern has been that women would lose out from structural economic changes as they become 'pitted against increasingly desperate groups of male workers who have the advantage of greater mobility and better access to skills and education' (Banerjee, 1996: 134). In 1987–8, over 88 per cent of the female workforce working outside of agriculture were employed in the unorganized sector (ibid.). Indications are that this has not changed much. Based on data reviewing changes in work participation rates between 1973 and 1994, Duraisamy (2000) notes that the regular wage/salaried sector accounts for only 16.7 per cent and 6.2 per cent of men and women workers respectively. Further, 29.6 per cent of men and 37 per cent of women are casual labourers, with the proportion of casual labourers increasing by ten percentage points for men and six percentage points for women over the specified time period (ibid.). In the agricultural sector it has been noted that, despite the tendency towards great feminization of the workforce, women are still confined largely to growing traditional crops and excluded from opportunities relating to new techniques and new market relations (Banerjee, 1996).

Banerjee (1996) cautions, however, against viewing these findings as representing a static picture of a gendered labour market under a capitalist model of development, and instead suggests that in the Indian context they need to be located within the wider analysis of the role of ideology spanning all institutions of society. For instance she argues that the ideology of chastity and control over female sexuality is responsible for the phenomenon of women entering the labour market after marriage and the birth of their children, which impedes their mobility (ibid.). Denial of property rights further curtails women's ability to venture into productive activities. However, she notes that, given the hold that households exert over women's labour, incentives offered by economic growth have resulted in changes for those women (largely urban and middle-class) who have gained access to education and employment in the modern sector.[27] Seymour (1995) concurs with evidence from Orissa, where she found that education and employment opportunities were fast changing the internal dynamics and structures of families, where some degree of economic independence was making it possible for women to leave unhappy marriages, and where greater equality was being promoted within the home.[28]

Despite the enormous influence exerted by the dual structures of labour and marriage market on the choices and aspirations for women held by households, it is clear that, with changing employment opportunities, growing urbanization, the influence of the media, and different catalysts with whom communities come in contact, including female teachers, the dynamics of investment in female education are open to change. In some situations, economic uncertainty may result in families investing in female education, given that the prospects for boys are not necessarily as secure as was once perceived. However, the quality of education received by women relative to men is likely to need continuing attention. Many studies show that, even where girls are sent to school, belief in the superior value of boys' education may result in greater supervision paid to boy's schooling, greater investment in providing support such as extra tuition, and the greater vulnerability of girls' school attendance to the demands of the household. The pernicious effect of gendered practices of teaching, biases within the curriculum, and the attitudes of male teachers and fellow students have also been identified across many contexts and countries as constituting reasons why girls are not necessarily encouraged to feel that school is an institution they can claim as their own. Violence *within* schools is also increasingly becoming an issue for concern, especially at secondary level, and alerts us to the need to pay attention to the impact of larger numbers of girls entering public institutions on a wide range of social norms, including those relating to sexuality.

Recognition of the long history of marginal attention paid to female education in policy as well as within households remains necessary despite the evidence of more positive trends beginning to emerge in relation to female education. Seymour (1995) notes that the positive trends may coexist with continuing parental control over choice of marriage partner, dowry, and other forms of practice that perpetuate the construction of female subordination to male authority. Sharieff and Sudarshan (1996) also note that high value for girls' education is often voiced in rural contexts in relation to the hope that it will help women later if they experience problems in their married lives. Where female education is promoted or seen as valuable in relation to the demands of other institutions, such as marriage or the labour market, gains are likely to remain vulnerable to changes in the external environment surrounding schools and employment. Uncertainty of returns to female education—'will it help, will it hinder?' (Sharieff and Sudarshan, 1996: 60)—and its impacts—will it enhance a daughter's marriageability or complicate it? (Seymour, 1995)—continue to render private decisions vulnerable to considerations of wider social position. Rationales and justifications that seek to create 'carrots' for the investment in females remain unlikely to deliver on the broader vision of promoting women's ability 'to be and do'.

Visioning and Realizing Rights: Tackling Female Education Deprivation in India

The 93rd Constitutional Amendment Bill and the Right to Education in India

The poverty of public policy efforts to tackle education has been lamented widely, most notably by Myron Weiner (1991) in his slim but powerful book attacking the failure of Indian elites and policy-makers to secure meaningful rights and opportunities for the vast numbers of working, out-of-school children. Other commentators have not been far behind with sharp critiques of public policy failure, in terms of low resource allocation as well as policy and institutional neglect of rural schools in particular (Dreze and Sen, 1995; PROBE, 1999; Bhatty, 1998; Guhan, 1985). Decades of criticism have resulted in a concerted civil society approach to making the state take its duties in education more seriously, most notably with the recent attempt to shift constitutional attention towards education from the Directive Principles of State Policy (Part IV) to the section on Fundamental Rights (Part III of the Constitution). A proposal was first floated in Parliament in 1997 to make elementary education a fundamental right, thereby committing the state to provide free and compulsory education for children aged 6–14. In November 2001, the 93rd Constitutional Amendment Bill was passed in the Lower House of Parliament, and is, at the time of writing, awaiting sanction from the Upper House, before it can become a part of the Constitution.

The 93rd Constitutional Amendment Bill was proposed in the context of two specific developments. First, was the widely hailed Supreme Court verdict in 1993 in *Unnikrishnan v. State of Andhra Pradesh* (1SCC/645/1993), where the judgment concluded that education 'is at once a social and political necessity' and that the right to life needed to be read in the expanded sense of living 'with human dignity', explicitly including education as a part of this vision. Several subsequent Supreme Court judgments followed this line. As the Supreme Court judgment is binding on all courts within the territory of India, education was effectively declared a Fundamental Right. Nothing was done to translate this into a legislative programme until it was used by CSOs to exert pressure for a constitutional amendment to be enacted. A second development was the election of the United Front Government which saw the Right to Education as a fundamental component of their developmental programme, titled the Common Minimum Programme (National Alliance for the Fundamental Right to Education, 1998).

The fundamental right to education, when passed, has significant implications for the policy framework of education in the country. First, it suggests that all the comprehensive changes being made to education policy strategies, planning and management as laid out in the National Policy on Education 1986 and subsequent policy statements will be eventually translated into legislated commitment at the state level, within the overall framework of a constitutionally guaranteed fundamental right. Therefore, policy commitments relating to the norms for school buildings and equipment, teachers and supportive inputs for UEE will possibly be made justiciable[29] commitments at the state level. This is a staggering proposal in the context of a history of policy ambivalence and non-achievement of stated goals. However, there are significant question marks that remain about the real implications of this policy shift. Is the justiciability of this right alone sufficient to transform a situation marked by wide regional disparities, poverty, and livelihoods uncertainties? Can the state be compelled significantly to increase its financial allocation and enforce attendance in schools? Issues relating to the 'right'[30] are analysed below, in terms of conceptual and technical aspects, as well as the broader issues around state and citizen capacity to enforce claimed rights.

Definitional and Other Challenges

At its core, the right to education refers to the legal right of an individual to seek and receive education, and a corresponding duty on the state to provide such opportunities. However, the real challenges to making the right to education meaningful lie outside the framing of the rights and duties of citizens and states. Mehendale (2000, 1998, n.d.) raises specific concerns about the ways in which the 'right' has been defined in the Indian context. First, the right has been defined with reference to a particular age-group, children aged 6–14, as per the proposed bill, rather than irrespective of age, as is the case in international law. This is in part linked to the state's obligation to provide 'free' education—the Supreme Court judgment has deemed that, after the age of 14, the right will be circumscribed by the economic capacity of the state. Second, and following on from this age-based logic, the scope of the right is restricted to schooling, rather than education as a set of wider lifelong learning processes, excluding from its purview adult literacy programmes, for instance, or early childhood education. This can be linked to the fact that, until now, the common understanding of law on education has been with reference to 'rights within education institutions', largely meant to protect the interests of students, teachers, and the standards of education itself.[31]

Second, the proposed constitutional amendment permits exclusion of private schools from the responsibility of providing free and compulsory education to children, thus emphasizing the divergence between state and private schools, and the exemption of the latter from public policy goals. As Mehendale (n.d.) notes, the exemption of these institutions is particularly problematic, given that in many cases they receive government subsidies and tax exemptions. Further, it implies the state's minimal interest in regulating private schools in relation to the achievement of its own policy goals.

Third, the right to education bill will conflict with existing labour and education policies, which have historically treated the working child with a great degree of ambiguity. The existing legislative framework consists of laws prohibiting and regulating forms of child labour, and compulsory education acts in force to varying degrees in different states. Contrary to the emphasis on universal education for children aged 6–14, child labour laws and policies focus largely on children working in 'hazardous' enterprises, and exclude from consideration children working within family enterprises or within the home, a group which numerically outstrips children working in formal or informal sector enterprises. Further, compulsory education laws have historically excluded large numbers of children by providing 'reasonable excuses for non-attendance' (Mehendale, 2000), including absence of a school within the prescribed distance, when religious instruction in the school is not approved by the parents, when the child is receiving instruction in some other manner, when the child has a physical or mental 'defect', or any other compelling circumstances. Categories of exclusion are also applied to the state's own enforcement of its compulsory education laws—for instance, certain states permit compulsion to be selectively notified for children in specific geographical areas or sexes (ibid.).

In fact, as Weiner (1991) notes, backtracking on commitments is evident in all earlier attempts to make education compulsory at state level. Existing state compulsory education laws all qualify the provision for compulsion with the words 'may' and 'shall', providing state level officials with the discretion over whether to apply the law, or not. In other words, state legislation is an 'enabling legislation that permits local authorities to make education compulsory, but does not compel them' (Weiner, 1991: 56). Safeguards are built into the state legal provisions so that, while elaborating on the range of mechanisms that can be used to deal with non-enrolment or non-attendance, the law does not get over-zealously and inappropriately applied in areas with low enrolment and attendance. Such safeguards include the provision that two-thirds of those present or one-half of the local authorities should approve the proposal, with the state government then providing final authority (ibid.). Weiner observes that 'there are no enforcement authorities, no provisions for the compulsory registration of names and birth dates of children, no enumeration registers, no procedures for issuing notices to parents and guardians whose children are not attending school, and no penalties for failing to send children to school' (ibid.). Prospects for change in this situation are as yet unclear.

While the constitutional amendment would provide the basis for a comprehensive overhaul of the legislation to ensure compatibility of different provisions, it is also possible that it will continue with the encouragement of 'permissive compulsion', which would allow states to proceed in a manner dictated by its financial resources. A committee instituted to look into the implications (financial, primarily) of making education a fundamental right, recommended that states should provide for 'permissive compulsion' which would enable them to enforce the law 'selectively in a phased manner' (Government of India, 1997: 17). Although the committee noted that the 'compulsion contemplated ... is a compulsion on the state rather than on parents', thus 'advocating a consensual approach to motivate parents and children' (1997: 5), states are recommended to identify grounds on which exemption from compulsory attendance may be granted, and asked to identify the minimum and maximum punishment for defaulting parents. This particular recommendation contradicts the definition of compulsory education noted above and this contradiction can also be read as representing the view that the state is presenting itself as helpless in the face of the embedded socio-economic factors that cause parents to compromise children's education in favour of their economic contributions (Weiner, 1991). However, exempting those excluded from education as a result of economic constraints from the purview of compulsory education provisions serves largely to render the purpose of the 'right' meaningless. This would not challenge the exclusionary exemptions that compulsory legislation now rests upon, and also continue to qualify state responsibility within the financial limitations of its fiscal and social policy, which is precisely the approach that CSOs supporting the bill are seeking to challenge. Further it will perpetuate the authority and discretionary powers of the state, and not empower the citizen, thus again diluting the purpose of moving towards a rights-based policy approach.

The fourth challenge, relating to the above is the critical issue of enforcement, which is linked to the question of accountability structures in relation to education provision. With such weak and contradictory policy frameworks, it is not feasible to expect coherent approaches to implementation and mechanisms for enforcement that will make rights meaningful. The legal implications of making elementary education a justiciable fundamental right require careful thought. As Deshpande asks: 'Would this mean that government can punish the guardians of a child for not sending him or her to school? ... Conversely, can a guardian sue the authorities for not providing school facilities in the child's neighbourhood?' (1997: 2382). An overly narrow focus on a regime of penalties that may be imposed appears untenable in the face of the far-from-complete agenda of investment, infrastructure, and service provision with which it is still confronted. Further, the onus of levying penalties has been placed on district and subdistrict panchayat bodies, without any discussion on why or how it is in the interest of these bodies to levy penalties on community members.[32] This also appears to be in conflict with the earlier quoted observation that the objective of policy is to 'motivate' parents using a 'consensual' approach, with the onus borne by the state rather than parents.

Legal challenges to state failure to provide adequately through policy and financial allocations are presented as the primary strategy associated with the formalization of the right to education, central to the notion of justiciability. Ramachandran (2000) suggests that there is scope for public interest litigation (PIL) to be filed by civil society groups in defence of the rights of the education excluded who may otherwise not have the means to exercise their claims. The scope for legal action includes: filing a writ petition in the High Court of Supreme Court in the case of violation of a fundamental right either as an aggrieved party, or in the form of a PIL; issuing of a writ by a High Court against violation of Fundamental Rights; direct moving of the Supreme or High Court by a citizen for the enforcement of Fundamental Rights (National Alliance for the Fundamental Right to Education, 1998). So far, however, jurisprudence is weak, and there has been poor application of law through litigation (Mehendale, 1998).

The dangers of relying excessively on a legally mandated set of rights as the basis for pushing state accountability relate to the lack of institutional access of the poor and rights-deprived to formal institutions of the state. As Houtzager notes, law is often one of many 'sometimes competing and sometimes complementary regulatory orders' influencing people's lives (2001: 9). He notes that, while legal rules are not self-enforcing, people usually interact with 'interpretations of what constitutes enforcement of, and compliance with, these rules' (2001: 11). In his view, legislation that is not enforced falls outside the definition of law as an institution, and laws can be considered institutionalized only when reproduced over time so as to 'acquire a degree of "solidity" for people, allowing them to adjust expectations and plan future actions around them' (ibid.). Where the right to education is perceived to conflict with the need for food, clothing, and shelter, or where the use of the law to effect accountability from state institutions is relatively nascent, the legality of the right is in itself likely to remain insufficient for making conditions for participation real.

Laws are not just regulatory orders, but also normative frameworks, with the scope to enforce normative conceptions of the good, as well as shape them. From the perspective of tackling deprivations that are part of the fabric of social structure, such as those relating to female education highlighted earlier in this chapter, the role and capacity of legal institutions becomes harder to evaluate. As Mukhopadhyay notes:

the problematic of the state... seems to be the difficulty of distinguishing women, as citizens and subjects with individual rights, from women as gendered subjects enmeshed in social relations. ... Men are also enmeshed in social relations but the constitution of the citizen/subject takes men's position in social relations as the norm and herein lies the difference. (1998: 187)

Drawing on case studies of women claiming inheritance rights, she notes that rights-based claims are locked into sets of obligations for women, where considerations of duties towards other members of family or elders in the community constrain women's own motivation for pressing their claims. Similarly with the right to education, if women's understandings of their entitlements are shaped by different priorities imposed by considerations of obligation and responsibility to the social actors and institutions that structure their lives, then their claims are likely to be muted. Where and how education can fit into women's vision of their capabilities and the pathways they choose to take towards this vision remains an enticing research question. Some evidence, such as Dave and Krishnamurthy (2000) and the experience of Mahila Samakhya with adult women (see n. 23) suggests that, in the struggle for rights, education plays an important but not primary role. In developed societies, delinking the achievements of rights from the ability to read and write may be hard to imagine. However, although the ability to read and write enhances social status and enables men and women to reduce relations of dependence, challenging exclusion from basic services may require the prior assertion of voice and internalization of a sense of entitlements for groups who have long been excluded from basic services.

Concluding Thoughts: Moving From the Formal to the Substantive Rights Agenda in Education

As Nussbaum notes, central to the capabilities framework and its central focus on freedoms and liberties are concepts of rights and choice, as is the importance of 'being in a position to exercise those rights' and choices (2000: 54). The *process* of achieving greater freedoms and capabilities may enable many women to rework existing prioritization of rights, especially in seeking better prospects for their own daughters' lives. Working towards the threshold of the minimum basic basket of goods will require the creation of conditions and universally supported norms for the realization of basic rights. These include 'material and institutional resources, including legal and social acceptance of the legitimacy of women's claims' (ibid.). Creating those conditions through work with parents, particularly mothers, can help to shift the boundaries of aspiration and transform the cycle of deprivation that has held back prospects for female education in India.

Rights-based frameworks are important because they ensure that funding and management policies are not just based on limited calculations of returns that are possibly erroneously calculated in the first instance, and which also present a very limiting vision of the potential inherent within education as a tool for promoting rights. Clearly without a conception of rights, or entitlements, little progress is possible in a way that privileges the perspectives and interests of the most powerless and disadvantaged. However, elucidation of a rights discourse is merely the first step in the journey; it needs also to be accompanied by clearly worked out institutional relationships and the restructuring of incentives to allow for the claims of the poorest to be heard and redressed.

While institutionalizing the legal right to education represents a progressive step in relation to the rhetoric of policy that has traditionally accompanied inadequate public policy in education, there are limitations to it serving as a framework that has meaning for those excluded from education. While the supply of education clearly requires significant improvements, the conditions under which education is provided need substantively to address the wider contexts of economic vulnerability as well as powerlessness that characterize groups with a historical disadvantage in gaining access to quality education. How a rights framework is made meaningful requires significant investment, largely through civil society mobilization, in securing numerous rights that are interlinked with the right to education, including those to food and survival, health, and personal security. While rights have a particular resonance in relation to the political and civil liberties of individuals, the application to the economic, social, and cultural arena has been more contentious. The intersection of rights with citizenship points to one potential problem with using a rights framework on its own—its power as a discourse may be undermined by the non-existence, or paucity, of spaces within which these rights can be claimed, particularly where formal institutions of the state are required to confer recognition upon claimants of rights. Bureaucratized notions of 'citizenship' that rely on red tape and very particular forms of conferring recognition can serve to reinforce exclusion through their routinized practices.

Recasting issues conventionally understood to constitute the realm of human 'need' (such as basic entitlements of food and shelter) in terms of human rights is a strategic move to prevent the conflation of basic services with welfare programmes targeting beneficiaries through handouts and not economic redistribution. The notion of 'capabilities' is useful here, given its concern with identifying such an integrated minimum basket of goods considered to constitute a universal minimum set of goods that will allow human beings to live with the basic freedom to achieve basic human functionings

(Nussbaum, 2000). Thus, while rights identify desirable ends for humans to aspire to and on which they can claim their entitlements, capabilities go one step further by suggesting what we should be looking for and measuring in a more tangible way. Both together provide a powerful normative framework; both suggest goals, envisage mutuality and reciprocity between states and citizens, and chalk out forward-looking agendas.

However, both rights and capabilities have associated with them similar problems of translation from framework into realized outcomes. Rights and capabilities also rely on the individual as the central unit of concern, particularly important in the case of women, whose basic well-being is often traded off against the interests or needs of others around them, but also particularly problematic because of the nature of trade-offs involved in the institutions to which women are primarily confined in many societies in India. While both rights and capabilities are concerned with outcomes specified for each individual, capabilities in particular allow for a sense of values that are shared across a society, aimed at ensuring the well-being of each and every individual. Although Nussbaum argues passionately for the importance of focusing on the individual as the goal, the implementability of the capabilities framework in a context where family and other institutional ideologies (such as caste) may provide normative frameworks stipulating the opposite creates a challenge that needs addressing. Further, the interconnectedness of different means to enhancing people's capabilities (of which education is just one, albeit important, means), leaves us with the very real problem of how to judge or value people's differential priorities. Where decisions to invest in education are collectively, rather than individually, undertaken,[33] as is the case with decisions for female education in India (Mukhopadhyay and Seymour, 1994), individually articulated rights or claims may be insufficient to transform collective norms. Where membership of a group provides a sense of belonging and identity, the shift to individually articulated rights *vis-à-vis* the state may be less easy to achieve. While Nussbaum persuades us that a capabilities framework is an essential constitutional project, it is less clear how it can be implemented as a framework owned and exercised by those whose entitlements have been bypassed. Pressures to conform in particular are hard to address, without a simultaneity of efforts aimed at different social institutions.

The challenge lies in 'rights' being accepted as a normative framework that is widely valued and promoted through a range of institutions. Frameworks of international cooperation and national governments can set the tone by agreeing a common approach based on promoting rights across a range of entitlements, which national and local CSOs can further use to ensure translation of promises into realities. Both instrumentalist discourses about women's value to development and the lack of concerted attention to the unintended and intended consequences of particular economic policies serve to disable attempts to secure rights with equity for women and men.

References

Aruna, R. (1999) 'Learn Thoroughly: Primary Schooling in Tamil Nadu', *Economic and Political Weekly* (1 May).

Banerjee, N. (1996) 'The Structural Adjustment Programme and Women's Economic Empowerment', in N. Rao, L. Rurup, and R. Sudarshan (eds.), *Sites of Change: The Structural Context for Empowering Women in India* (New Delhi: FES and UNDP).

Bennell, P., and D. Furlong (1997) *'Has Jomtien Made Any Difference?: Trends in Donor Funding for Education and Basic Education since the Late 1980s'* (Working Paper, 51; Brighton: Institute of Development Studies).

Bhatty, K. (1998) 'Educational Deprivation in India: A Survey of Field Investigations', *Economic and Political Weekly* (4 and 11 July).

Bordia, A. (2000) 'Education for Gender Equity: The Lok Jumbish Experience', *Prospects: Quarterly Review of Comparative Education*, 30/3 (Sept.).

Colclough, C. (1991) 'Structuralism versus Neo-liberalism: An Introduction', in C. Colclough and J. Manor (eds.), *States or Markets? Neo-Liberalism and the Development Policy Debate* (Oxford: Clarendon Press).

—— (1997) 'Education, Health, and the Market: An Introduction', in C. Colclough (ed.), *Marketizing Education and Health in Developing Countries: Miracle or Mirage?* (Oxford: Clarendon Press).

Cornwall, A., and J. Gaventa (2000) 'From Users and Choosers to Makers and Shapers: Repositioning Participation in Social Policy', *IDS Bulletin*, 31/4: 50–62.

Dasgupta, I., R. Palmer-Jones, and A. Sengupta (2000) *Between Cultures and Markets: An Eclectic Analysis of Juvenile Gender Ratios in India* (CREDIT Research Paper, 00/15, University of Nottingham).

Dave, A., and L. Krishnamurthy (2000) 'Home and the World. Sangha Women's Perceptions of 'Empowerment': Some Reflections', Alarippu, New Delhi, mimeo.

Deacon, B. (2000) 'Globalisation: A Threat to Equitable Social Provision?', *IDS Bulletin*, 31/4: 32–41.

Derne, S. (1994) 'Arranging Marriages: How Father's Concerns Limit Women's Educational Achievements', in C. Mukhopadhyay and S. Seymour (eds.), *Women, Education and Family Structure in India* (Boulder, Colo.: Westview).

Deshpande, J. V. (1997) 'Elementary Education as Fundamental Right', *Economic and Political Weekly* (20 Sept.).

DFID (2000) *Poverty Elimination and the Empowerment of Women: Strategies for Achieving the International Development Targets* (London: Department for International Development).

Dreze, J., and M. Murthi (2000) 'Fertility, Education and Development: Further Evidence from India', *DEDPS*, 20 (London School of Economics, STICERD).

—— and A. Sen (1995) *India: Economic Development and Social Opportunity* (New Delhi: Oxford University Press).

Dugger, C. (2001) 'Abortion in India is Tipping Scales Sharply Against Girls', *New York Times*, 22 Apr., internet edition, <www.nytimes.com>.

Duraisamy, P. (2000) *Changes in Returns to Education in India, 1983–94: By Gender, Age-Cohort and Location* (Center Discussion Paper, 815, Economic Growth Center; New Haven: Yale University Press).

Dyer, C., and A. Choksi (1998) 'Education is like Wearing Glasses: Nomad's Views of Literacy and Empowerment', *International Journal of Educational Development*, 18/5: 405–13.

Dyson, T., and M. Moore (1983) 'On Kinship Structure, Female Autonomy and Demographic Behaviour in India', *Population and Development Review*, 17: 517–23.

Erwer, M. (1998) 'Development beyond "the Status of Women": The Kerala Model from a Gender Perspective', unpublished licentiate thesis, PADRIGU, University of Gothenburg, Sweden.

Fine, B., and P. Rose (2001) 'Education and the Post-Washington Consensus', in B. Fine, C. Lapavitsas, and J. Pincus (eds.), *Development Policy in the Twenty-First Century: Beyond the Post-Washington Consensus* (London: Routledge).

Goetz, A. M., and R. Jenkins (1999) 'Accounts and Accountability: Theoretical Implications of the Right-to-Information Movement in India', *Third World Quarterly*, 20/3: 603–22.

Government of India (1997) *Report of the Committee Reviewing the Proposal to Make Education a Fundamental Constitutional Right* (New Delhi: Ministry of Human Resource Development, Department of Education).

Guhan, S. (1985) 'Towards a Policy for Analysis', in R. S. Ganapathy, S. R. Ganesh, R. M. Maru, Samuel Paul, and R. M. Rao (eds.), *Public Policy and Policy Analysis in India* (New Delhi: Sage).

Haq, M., and K. Haq (1998) *Human Development in South Asia 1998* (Karachi: Oxford University Press).

Houtzager, P. (2001) ' "We Make the Law and the Law Makes Us": Some Ideas on a Law in Development Research Agenda', *IDS Bulletin*, 32/1: 8–18.

Huq, S. (2000) 'Gender and Citizenship: What does a Rights Framework Offer Women?', *IDS Bulletin*, 31/4: 74–82.

Irvine, J. (2000) 'South Asia and Basic Education: Changing UNICEF's Strategic Perspectives on Educational Development and Partnerships', *Prospects: Quarterly Review of Comparative Education*, 115: 297–311.

Jeffery, P., and R. Jeffery (1994) 'Killing my Heart's Desire: Education and Female Autonomy in Rural North India', in Nita Kumar (ed.), *Women as Subjects: South Asian Histories* (Calcutta: Stree).

——— (1998) 'Silver Bullet or Passing Fancy? Girls' Schooling and Population Policy', in C. Jackson and R. Pearson (eds.), *Feminist Visions of Development: Gender Analysis and Policy* (London: Routledge).

Jeffery, R., and A. M. Basu (eds.) (1996a) *Girl's Schooling, Women's Autonomy and Fertility Change in South Asia* (Thousand Oaks, Calif., and London: Sage).

——— (1996b) 'Schooling as Contraception?', in R. Jeffery and A. M. Basu (eds.), *Girl's Schooling, Women's Autonomy and Fertility Change in South Asia* (Thousand Oaks, Calif., and London: Sage).

Kabeer, N. (1999a) 'Resources, Agency, Achievements: Reflections on the Measurement of Women's Empowerment', *Development and Change*, 30/3: 435–64.

——— (1999b) *The Conditions and Consequences of Choice* (Discussion Paper, 108; Geneva: UNRISD).

——— (2000) 'Intergenerational Contracts, Demographic Transitions and the "Quantity-Quality" Trade-Off: Parents, Children and Investing in the Future', *Journal of International Development*, 12: 463–82.

Khan, S. (1993) 'South Asia', in E. M. King and M. Anne Hill (eds.), *Women's Education in Developing Countries: Barriers, Benefits and Policies* (Baltimore and London: Johns Hopkins University Press).

Kingdon, G. G. (1996) *Private Schooling in India: Size, Nature and Equity-Effects* (Development Economics Research Programme; London: Suntory–Toyota International Centre for Economics and Related Disciplines, University of London).

Kumar, K., M. Priyam, and S. Saxena (2001) 'Looking beyond the Smokescreen: DPEP and Primary Education in India', *Economic and Political Weekly* (17 Feb.), 560–8.

Leach, F., and P. Machakanja (2000) *A Preliminary Investigation into the Abuse of Girls in Zimbabwean Junior Secondary Schools* (DFID Education Research Report, 39; London: DFID).

McMahon, W. (1999) *Education and Development: Measuring the Social Benefits* (Oxford: Oxford University Press).

Malhotra, K. (2000) 'Educational Priorities and Challenges in the Context of Globalization', *Prospects: Quarterly Review of Comparative Education*, 30/3 (Sept.).

Mehendale, A. (n.d.) 'Education and the Law', *Voices*, 2/3.

——— (1998) Right to Education: Examining the Rhetoric (Bangalore: Centre for Child and the Law, National Law School of India University, mimeo).

——— (2000) 'Child Rights, Child Labour and Education: A Study of the Legal Regime', paper presented at the National Seminar on Child Labour

Realities and Policy Dimensions, 5–7 Dec., VV Giri National Labour Institute, India.

Mendelsohn, O., and M. Vicziany (1998) *The Untouchables: Subordination, Poverty and the State in Modern India* (Cambridge: Cambridge University Press).

Mukhopadhyay, C., and S. Seymour (eds.) (1994) *Women, Education and Family Structure in India* (Boulder, Colo.: Westview).

Mukhopadhyay, M. (1998) *Legally Dispossessed: Gender, Identity and the Process of Law* (Calcutta: Stree).

Nambissan, G. (2000) 'Identity, Exclusion and the Education of Tribal Communities', in R. Wazir (ed.), *The Gender Gap in Basic Education: NGOs as Change Agents* (New Delhi: Sage).

National Alliance for the Fundamental Right to Education (1998) *Frequently Asked Questions on the Fundamental Right to Education* (Bangalore: Centre for Child and the Law, National Law School of India University).

Nussbaum, M. (2000) *Women and Human Development: The Capabilities Approach* (Cambridge: Cambridge University Press).

Prabhu, K. S. (2000) 'Structural Adjustment and Social Sector Expenditure in Indian States', in Centre for Women's Development Studies (ed.), *Shifting Sands: Women's Lives and Globalization* (Calcutta: Stree).

PROBE Team (1999) *Public Report on Basic Education in India* (New Delhi: Oxford University Press).

Ramachandran, V. K. (2000) 'Educational Deprivation and the Right to School Education in India' (Geneva: UNRISD, mimeo).

Sen, P. (1999) 'Enhancing Women's Choices in Responding to Domestic Violence in Calcutta: A Comparison of Employment and Education', *European Journal of Development Resesarch*, 11/2 (Dec.).

Seymour, S. (1995) 'Family Structure, Marriage, Caste and Class, and Women's Education: Exploring the Linkages in an Indian Town', *Indian Journal of Gender Studies*, 2/1, (Jan.–June).

Shah, N., S. Gothoskar, N. Gandhi, and A. Chhachhi (1999) 'Structural Adjustment, Feminization of Labour Force and Organisational Strategies', in N. Menon (ed.), *Gender and Politics in India* (New Delhi: Oxford University Press).

Sharieff, A., and R. M. Sudarshan (1996) 'Elementary Education and Health in Rural India: Some Indicators', in N. Rao *et al.* (eds.), *Sites of Change: The Structural Context for Empowering Women in India* (New Delhi: Friedrich Ebert Foundation and UNDP).

Srivastava, R. (2001) 'Access to Basic Education in Rural Uttar Pradesh', in A. Vaidyanathan and P. R. Gopinathan Nair (eds.), *Elementary Education in Rural India: A Grassroots View* (New Delhi: Sage).

Subrahmanian, R. (2000a) 'Co-producing Universal Primary Education in a Context of Social Exclusion: Households, Community Organisations and State Administration in a District of Karnataka, India', unpublished Ph.D. thesis, Open University, Milton Keynes.

Subrahmanian, R. (2000*b*) 'Gender and Education: A Review of Directions for Social Policy' (Geneva: UNRISD, mimeo).

—— (forthcoming) ' "Community" at the Centre of Universal Primary Education Strategies: An Empirical Investigation', in N. Kabeer, G. Nambissan, and R. Subrahmanian (eds.), *Child Labour and the Right to Education in South Asia. Needs versus Rights?* (New Delhi: Sage).

Sudarshan, R. (2000) 'Educational Status of Girls and Women: The Emerging Scenario', in R. Wazir (ed.), *The Gender Gap in Basic Education: NGOs as Change Agents* (New Delhi: Sage).

Tilak, J. B. G. (1995) *How Free is 'Free' Primary Education in India?* (NIEPA Occasional Paper, 21; New Delhi: National Institute for Educational Planning and Administration).

—— (1997) 'Lessons from Cost Recovery in Education', in C. Colclough (ed.), *Marketizing Education and Health in Developing Countries: Miracle or Mirage?* (Oxford: Clarendon Press).

Vaidyanathan, A., and P. R. Gopinathan Nair (eds.) (2001) *Elementary Education in Rural India: A Grassroots View* (New Delhi: Sage).

Vatuk, S. (1994) 'Schooling for What? The Cultural and Social Context of Women's Education in a South Indian Muslim Family', in C. Mukhopadhyay and S. Seymour (eds.), *Women, Education and Family Structure in India* (Boulder, Colo.: Westview).

Wazir, R. (ed.) (2000) *The Gender Gap in Basic Education: NGOs as Change Agents* (New Delhi: Sage).

Weiner, M. (1991) *The Child and the State in India* (New Delhi: Oxford University Press).

Whitehead, A., and M. Lockwood (1999) 'Gendering Poverty: A Review of Six World Bank African Poverty Assessments', *Development and Change*, 30/3: 525–55.

III

Democratization and the Politics of Gender

Encounters between Feminism, Democracy and Reformism in Contemporary Iran

Parvin Paidar

Introduction

This chapter provides a critical analysis of the interface between the movement for women's rights and the reform movement that has gained momentum in the Islamic Republic of Iran since the mid-1990s.[1] The process of democratization in Iran, as in many other countries, has been an uneven one, marked by numerous obstructions and setbacks. The historical reasons for this are well documented (Abrahamian, 1982; Paidar, 1995) and will not be repeated here. Suffice it to say that democratic movements have had a substantial place in the political history of twentieth-century Iran and have led to the establishment of various formal democratic institutions. However, neither during the Pahlavi monarchy (1925–79) nor in the Islamic Republic (1979–) has the existence of such formal institutions acted as a guarantor of democratic rights for the Iranian people. Indeed, as far as a minimalist freedom of expression, association, and press were concerned, these were only achieved during brief episodes in which, for one reason or another, absolute power slipped through the tight grip of the reigning monarch or ayatollah (e.g. during and immediately after the Constitutional Revolution of 1905–11, in the late 1940s and early 1950s, during the Revolution of 1979, and since the election of President Khatami). These were also periods during which, not surprisingly, women's independent movements flourished. The Pahlavi monarchs did establish themselves as the champions of women's liberation in the twentieth century. However, this was achieved through firm control of the national women's movement by the secular patriarchal state. The Islamic Republic has facilitated the development of an Islamist women's movement, but again under the tight control of the Islamist patriarchal state (Paidar, 1995).

Given the limited scope of democratic institutions in Iran, I have decided to focus this chapter on two aspects of the interface between processes of democratization (including its setbacks and deficits) and the struggle for gender justice. First, rather than dwelling on the severe limits of the existing democratic institutions in Iran and the constraints this poses for a meaningful exercise of citizenship by women in particular, I focus on the opportunities that women have created and used to enact their rights within the existing authoritarian context. The Iranian experience can thus be taken as one more illustration of the paradox of weak democratic institutions and active female citizenship, which has been observed in many other countries as well. The second dimension that the chapter focuses on is the new window of opportunity that has been opened through the ongoing dialogue between and within the democratization and women's rights movements. The new strands of political thought and discourse and the dialogue between them, I believe, present more emancipatory potential for women's rights than democratic institutions have had in Iran since their inception.

It is also important to clarify at the outset what the two movements convey in the current Iranian context. The democratization movement, often used interchangeably with such terms as the civil society movement, reform movement, and reformism (*eslahtalabi*), refers to the oppositional movement inside Iran (comprised of Islamic and secular followers) led by moderate Islamists against the reign of hard-line Islamists. This movement came to prominence with the election of the first reformist president, Mohammad Khatami, on 23 May 1997. The characteristics of the democratization movement will be discussed in different parts of the paper, particularly in the section on 'The Gender Boundaries of Reformism'.

Contrary to reformism, the term feminism, used interchangeably with the term women's equal rights movement, does not have a Farsi (Persian) equivalent and is widely used as a Western import into Farsi. In the Iranian context, the definition conveyed by feminism depends on the sympathy of the user, and there is substantial diversity in the meaning given to the term even by those who are sympathetic to it. But the most common messages conveyed by feminism are those of support for women's equal rights and struggle against patriarchy and male domination.

Both terms are widely used in this chapter.[2] The main reason is that in no other historical period in Iran have women's issues had a higher political profile and displayed higher potential for women's mobilization, albeit around varied and sometimes contradictory agendas. The absence of some of the characteristics of twentieth-century women's movements (such as clear leadership and agreed political agenda) in contemporary Iran is largely due to political repression. Furthermore, despite the fact that many Islamist women leaders have only recently publicly referred to themselves as feminists and it is still common among women to reject feminism for various reasons, in fact in no other historical period has feminism been accepted by so many Iranian women (inside and outside the country) as part of their identity. The characteristics of the feminist movement will be discussed at some length in the third major section of the chapter.

This chapter is presented in three parts. The first part, 'Women and the Democratic Institutions in Iran', briefly sets the historical background and explains the nature of democratic rights and institutions in the Islamic Republic. It proceeds to a discussion of the ways in which women have played their citizenship role, and concludes by explaining the recent social and political trends that have contributed to the strengthening of the democratization and women's rights movements.

The second part, 'The Gender Boundaries of Reformism', focuses on the conceptual contribution of the democratization movement to gender politics since the mid-1990s. It analyses the gender emancipatory potential and limitations of the most influential current Islamist reformist strands. This is followed by a discussion of the feminist contribution to Islamist reformism.

The third part of the paper, 'The Dawn of Pragmatic Feminism', describes the recent debates within the feminist movement. The positions of the two broad categories of secularist and Islamist feminisms are presented and the emergence of 'pragmatic' feminism discussed.

Women and Democratic Institutions in Iran

The revolutionary leadership established the Islamic Republic through a three-pronged process: the establishment of what they considered as 'Islamic' political institutions, the Islamization of gender relations, and the annihilation of secular and Islamic political opposition.

The state and the way it represents the populace have specific features in the Islamic Republic. With the overthrow of the secular Pahlavi dynasty, Ayatollah Khomeini (the supreme leader of the Revolution) established an Islamic theocratic state based on his own particular articulation of the 'governance of the jurisprudent' (*velayat faqih*) in Shiism (the branch of Islam dominant in Iran). The Constitution of the Islamic Republic combines Shii theocracy with democratic accountability by assigning different degrees of power and accountability to different layers of the state pyramid. At the top of the pyramid is the Supreme Leader of the Revolution, a male cleric, who is selected by a constitutional body (*majles khobregan*) comprised of high-ranking clerics (who are themselves elected, but screened by the Council of Guardians), and who has absolute power with accountability only to God. The Supreme Leader is the head of the armed and the security forces, controls the media, and is able to dissolve the Parliament and intervene in the affairs of the executive (e.g. determine foreign policy) and the judiciary (e.g. give amnesty to those convicted by courts) when he deems appropriate. The second layer of the pyramid consists of a number of constitutional and judicial bodies occupied by male clerics, selected by, and accountable to, the Supreme Leader. The Council of Guardians (*shoraye negahban*) is one such body in charge of approving the Islamic credentials of election candidates and judging the Islamic compatibility of the laws passed by the Parliament. Various special courts (such as the court that deals with dissident clerics) are other examples.

Popular accountability and relative gender equality only feature in the bottom layer of the state pyramid, which consists of the executive and the legislature. The President, the members of Parliament and the members of local councils are elected by the electorate from a list of candidates approved by the Council of Guardians. The office of presidency is not open to women, but women can elect and be elected for the Parliament and the local councils.

The setting up of the institutions of the Islamic Republic was combined with the articulation of the Islamist position on woman. This led to major reversals in women's rights. The combination of revolutionary populism, anti-Americanism, and internal power struggles constituted the cornerstone of the Islamization policies of the state on all fronts, and determined which concepts and policies on women were defined as 'Islamic' and which were regarded as 'un-Islamic'. Two years on from the Revolution, sexual segregation outside the home and women's *hejab*[3] were in full force—if women were to have a presence in the public arena it had to be desexualized to protect the Islamic nation from corruption. Women were barred from becoming a judge or president; they could not study or work in certain fields (such as mining), and travel or enter educational establishments and employment without the consent of their male guardian (e.g. father, husband); they lost the rights that they had gained in the mid-1970s to initiate divorce, get custody of their child, and choose abortion for social reasons, and so on. With the revoking of the Civil Code of 1936—which was established by Reza Shah Pahlavi based on the traditional Shii jurisprudence *(feqh)*—as the main family law of the Islamic Republic, the total supremacy of men over women within the domestic sphere was legalized once more. The Bureau for Combating Corruption (the morality police) was set up to cleanse society from the manifestations of 'Westernized' gender relations. Sex outside marriage and homosexuality were pronounced public offences punishable by stoning to death. These policies resulted in a horrifying atmosphere of state and domestic violence against women, which has claimed the lives of many female victims and made a lasting impact on gender relations in Iran.

The consolidation of the Islamic theocracy was also facilitated by driving the secularist and Islamist left and the secularist women's movement into exile. Exclusion from power was then extended to the moderate liberal and cultural nationalists who had shared power with Ayatollah Khomeini during the immediate post-revolutionary transitional period (as the Provisional Government). The next group to be alienated from power were Islamist intellectuals turned technocrats who played an important role in consolidating the hard-liners' power in the early post-revolutionary years. But the excessive anti-Western and pro-Islamization zeal of the hard-liners managed to alienate them too. They gradually left their official positions and took up intellectual pursuits, taking forward the Islamist debate on the nature of Islamic society behind the scenes. They produced dissident political and intellectual figures, such as Mohammad Khatami (the current President) and Abdolkarim Sorush (a professor of Islamic philosophy), who emerged as public figures in the mid-1990s, when the conditions were ripe, to haunt the hard-line Islamists. They and many others like them laid the ground for the reformist movement that aimed to empower the civil society.

The Challenge of Women's Citizenship

The gradual erosion of popular support for the hard-line state was one of the most important factors behind the strengthening of the democratization movement (hereafter reformism). The reasons for this included economic stagnation, war, authoritarianism, corruption, and misappropriation of funds, as well as the state's attempts to regulate the private and social lives of its citizens. These factors gradually eroded the mass support for the Islamic Republic and amounted to a crisis of legitimacy for the hard-liners controlling the key apparatuses of the state.

With the erosion of support for the hard-line state and no opposition to speak out, women and young people found themselves carrying the mantle of the opposition in the politically harsh decade of the 1980s. This made a tremendous contribution to the survival of the ideals of reformism and feminism. This was not a surprise development, though, with women taking the main brunt of state repression and with 65 per cent of the population being under the age of 25. Political repression, the legacy of eight years of war with Iraq and the death and destruction caused by it, the mismanagement of the economy, the decreasing educational opportunities and rising inflation and unemployment, all resulted in the alienation of the youth from the hard-liners in power. Moreover, the hasty Islamization of women's position resulted in the alienation of many groups of women.

In this atmosphere, women and young people took up spontaneous individual action to protect their identity against the onslaught of Islamization. A spontaneous 'movement' of civil disobedience against the morality police developed. During the first decade of the Islamic Republic, which can be regarded as the most politically and socially repressive period in twentieth-century Iran, secular middle-class women demonstrated their objection to forced *hejab* on a daily basis and irritated the authorities over the colour, size, and shape of their *hejab* to no end. Secular middle-class youth in Western fashion outfits fought daily battles on the streets with the anti-corruption police. The subjugation of women and youth became the main preoccupation of the authorities, who every now and then gave up their street battles with half-covered women and young men mixing in public, but resumed it when they went too far. Such scenes were by no means confined to the capital and were reported from most cities. Reports also spread about incidents of bystanders beating off the anti-corruption police who tried to arrest women for not wearing proper *hejab*, and people warning young people in public places about the presence of the police in the area.

But women's opposition did not only take a secular form. Women who were once strong supporters of the Islamic leadership joined in the protest in their own ways. One of the most effective forms of spontaneous protest by Islamist women in the 1980s and 1990s was the publicity generated by women's magazines and women parliamentarians about gender-based injustices against individual women from social categories that were grass-roots supporters of the Islamic Republic. The stories of war widows whose children were being forcefully taken away from them by their paternal guardians were particularly effective. Where there was no possibility of oppositional collective action on gender or any other ground, such publicity helped to soften the state's gender policies to some extent and nurtured a collective consciousness among women. These examples of resistance were supported by the Iranian exile communities abroad.[4]

This demonstrated that, although the Islamic Republic seriously undermined women's position and violated their human rights, it gave its female supporters the opportunity for social participation and a sense of righteousness and self-worth. Despite the limited nature of democracy and democratic rights offered by the Constitution, women used all available avenues to enact their citizenship.[5] The central role given to the clergy in the Constitution (without them being accountable to anyone) had been made possible by the mass support of men and women. Women's political participation was thus regarded to be an essential safeguard for the survival of the regime. It legitimized the gender policies of the state and created an image of popular support and stability, both internally and internationally. For these reasons the hard-liners in power harnessed women's tremendous mobilization potential as best they could, for example through their involvement in the Iran–Iraq War which raged for most of the 1980s.

But women also participated in great numbers in protests against the unaccountable constitutional powers of the clergy for as long as this was tolerated inside the country, and later in exile. Women's mass support was also channelled into strengthening the democratic institutions of the Islamic Republic's Constitution and women's electoral participation was considered of prime importance to the populist image of the Islamic Republic. Later, women's electoral participation played an important role in shifting the balance of power in favour of reform and change.

Another impressive achievement by women has been their participation in educational institutions. Female literacy that stood around 36 per cent in 1976 rose to 80 per cent by 1999 (the ratios for rural women were 17.4 per cent and 62.4 per cent respectively). The ratio of female to male students in secondary education rose from 66 per cent in 1976 to 90 per cent in 1999; by 2000 almost 60 per cent of university students were women. But women's employment record has remained dismal, with their share of total employment being 14.3 per cent in 1999. This is, however, partly due to the absence of appropriate mechanisms for accurate assessment of women's economic contribution in both rural and urban areas (Rostami-Povey, 1999). Women's mass participation in politics and education can be considered as the most significant dimension of citizenship that they have exercised in the Islamic Republic. To some extent this was made possible through 'purifying' the public space through *hejab* and the imposition of the state's authority over traditionalist families (Hoodfar, 1997). Many issues remain to be tackled in making women's participation meaningful and equal to that of men, but there can be no dispute about the Islamic Republic's ability to bring out those categories of women who had remained untouched by, or resistant to, the monarchy's modernization project. These were women from a range of backgrounds, including urban and rural women from low-income households who had been exposed to the uneven and contradictory impact of state-led modernization; women who had strong religious beliefs and attended mosques; women whose family members had been subjected to human rights abuses; women from traditionalist families who were unable or unwilling to assume a public role in a society that was moving towards free association between men and women; women who felt discriminated against in the public arena for wearing the *hejab* (the Pahlavi states opposed women's *hejab*); and so on. The exposure of these women, who were isolated and alienated from public life during the Pahlavi era, to the outside world changed not only themselves but also helped to change the state and the society, and with these Islam itself (see the next section).

Less extensive, but still impressive, has been women's presence in the state machinery as well as in the Parliament in the Islamic Republic. The history of women's collective action in twentieth-century Iran points to statist feminism playing a significant role within the women's movements (Paidar, 1995). It also points to a tradition of women's involvement in formal politics, as elected and selected politicians, civil servants, and critics of the state. These traditions were initiated by the Pahlavi states, which encouraged a degree of controlled participation by women in formal politics and implemented their gender policies through the statist women's organization. The policy suited not only the state but also women who used family and state connections as an opportunity to enter into formal politics and influence social policy. However, women's activism before and after the Revolution differed in significant ways. While in the former period women's activism had been scripted by the opposition, secular or Islamist, as a discredited venture at the service of the state or as foreign colonial importation, it became authenticated during the Revolution, opening new possibilities for the development of all kinds of activism including through formal politics.

Furthermore, the gradual disillusionment of Islamist women activists in formal politics created an oppositional force within the state apparatus itself. The disillusionment arose from the realization that, far from supporting women's high status in 'true Islam', the Islamic Republic granted second-class status to women under the influence of 'traditional Islam'. These women considered the failures of 'traditional Islam' to be rooted in the male dominant culture with its distorted interpretations of the Koran and Islamic laws. Further-more, the earlier expectation that they would receive support and recognition from the state and play a meaningful role in the formu-lation of the state's gender policies had not been realized. Women in official positions, whether as politicians or as civil servants, were given limited opportunity to enter top decision-making positions and faced tremendous difficulties in influencing gender policies (Mossaffa, 1996, 2000; Kar, 1998). The Islamization policies of the state went in the opposite direction to what they had aspired for. As far as the hard-line Islamists who occupied the state machinery were concerned, there was no need for free debate on women's issues and no place for an independent women's movement to promote it.

Women's presence in formal politics had taken a turn for the worse immediately after the Revolution as many secular women were purged from the state. In later years women with a secular orientation were replaced by women with Islamic disposition in the state apparatuses. Women did not, however, make it to the cabinet level until recently when President Khatami appointed Masumeh Ebtekar as the vice-president on environment and women's issues, and Zahra Shojai as his adviser and the head of the coordination body on women, Centre for Women's Participation (Markaz Mosharekat Zanan), which is part of the President's office and is headed by a cabinet member. Women's role as civil servants and politicians, their power relations with male colleagues, and the strategies that they have adopted in pushing the women's rights agenda forward are under-researched areas. But the existing evidence points to a tre-mendous amount of male resistance and ignorance within the state machinery towards gender issues. This has been particularly prob-lematic since the election of President Khatami in a context in which the reformist government has had to respond to the dual pressures of grass-roots women's expectations and demands, as well as the international calls for progress on gender equality.[6]

Over the past four years President Khatami's government has responded to these diverse pressures by engendering the state struc-ture in ways that do not challenge the dominant and politically charged policy of gender segregation. The 'institutional approach to women's advancement' has included the setting up of separate women's units in almost all government departments and exec-utive agencies. The judiciary, the legislature, and the executive now have special institutions to advise them on women's issues (UNDP, 1999). Women have also been included in the decentraliz-ation policies of Khatami's government. The government's decent-ralization programme has apparently envisaged a twelve-member committee of women for each province, which effectively adds a total of 336 women's seats to current ones in government decision-making levels.[7]

Women have filled the state's women's units and embraced the international links.[8] The refusal of the High Council of the Cultural Revolution, which is dominated by the hard-liners, to sign up to CEDAW has created heated debate among the hard-liner and reformist factions of the state. Reformist women of both Rafsanjani (president for the previous eight years) and Khatami eras have strongly argued for acceding and, meanwhile, developed indicators and other planning and monitoring tools for measuring women's advancement in Iran against CEDAW (Habibi and Beladi-Musavi, 1998). The process of engagement with CEDAW has proved an empowering one for reformist women within the state who are now heavily engaged in the international development debates. Participation in the Beijing process has inspired many initiatives, such as measures to prevent violence against women, which are currently under consideration and which include establishing police stations staffed by women (UNDP, 1999).

Women's presence in the Parliament has gone down substantially since the Revolution: 7 per cent in 1976–9 compared to 1.5 per cent in 1979–83, and 3.7 per cent in 1996–2000 (Hoodfar, 1999; Esfandiari, 1994). This constitutes a major challenge to the credibility of reformist political parties. Indeed, the February 2000 parliamentary elections, in which the reformists won the majority of parliamentary seats for the first time, produced two women members of Parliament (eleven altogether) less than the previous Parliament in which the hardliners held the majority of seats. But women fared better in the February 1999 elections for the city and village councils throughout the country—an election that the reformists forced upon the reluctant hard-liners. Women candidates constituted just over 2 per cent of the total candidates but successful women candidates constituted more than 10 per cent of the total elected representatives.

Women members of Parliament have played an important role in the direction that the Islamic Republic's gender legislation has taken. These women have found themselves in the precarious position of, on the one hand, being elected by a constituency of men and women, and on the other, being expected by their male parliamentary colleagues, the women's lobby, and women's grass-roots constituency to focus on women's issues because nobody else would. This is partly due to the culture of segregation and partly because of the limited representational opportunities open to women. Under pressure to represent women's interests and through taking up concrete women's issues, some of these women have developed gender awareness and a feminist point of view that they did not have when they first assumed their parliamentary role. Some use this awareness in a reformist direction, while others have given support to the hard-liners (Afshar, 1998). Therefore, not all of the laws passed pertaining to women's rights have been reformist and women members of Parliament have not always succeeded in preventing the passing of discriminatory bills that the hard-liners (male and female) have been determined to push through.

But it can be said with certainty that no progressive laws have been passed on women's rights without women members of Parliament initiating them. There are also many examples of earlier discriminatory measures being reformed through the efforts of these women. These touch upon education (reversal of the earlier ban on women studying 'male' subjects such as agriculture and mining), professions (reversal of the earlier ban on women becoming judges and police-women), marriage (standard marriage forms which enable women to negotiate the terms of the marriage contract), alimony (revaluation of the alimony set at the time of marriage in line with inflation at the time of divorce), divorce (the reinstatement of women's conditional right to divorce which used to be part of the Pahlavi Family Protection Law), and so on.

Emergence of New Political Space

In addition to women's active citizenship, another significant contributor to the emergence of reformism should be mentioned that might not have been so tangible before the presidential election of 1997. This was the merging of the social currents of Islamization and secularization that had been moving in parallel since the Revolution. These processes eventually met up and created a 'middle ground' polity, referred to as the civil society. The Islamization process that started in the immediate aftermath of the Revolution with women's position and engulfed the society made a lasting impact on the Iranian society. It reinforced the traditionally prevalent social conservatism, which had existed before the Revolution during the Pahlavi era (perceived as a secular political era) and drove secular social groups towards common language and thought with moderate Islamists. On the other hand, a parallel current of secularization ran counter to Islamization. The influence of the secularization process opened many windows in Islamism and brought many supporters of the Islamic Republic closer to secularists. Eventually the merging of these two processes created new opportunities for political development.

But what were the driving forces of the process of secularization? This process has been commented upon in the Iranian studies literature as significant to the understanding of Islamist reformism and feminism. This process has involved both external and internal factors. The external factors included, briefly speaking, the influence of global forces and developments that neither the population nor the state in Iran could be 'protected' from, and the close links between Iranians inside and outside the country. The most significant internal factor was the exposure of the men and women of religion to political power, which is worth expanding on here. Many examples have been given in Iranian studies literature of how the different categories of Islamists of the revolutionary era (such as the ultra conservative clerics or radical anti-American youth of the early 1980s) have now changed their Islamist outlook due to their exposure to concrete power and authority. Mir-Hosseini has argued that 'When they were in opposition, the clerics, as guardians of Islam, could deal with practical issues at an abstract and generalised level, leaving it to the conscience of the believer to interpret and carry out the appropriate practices' but 'when *Sharia*[9] becomes part of the apparatus of a modern nation state, its custodians may have to accommodate, even seek novel interpretations. This opens room for change on a scale that has no precedent in Islamic history' (1999: 7, 273).

Others have shown how the wide range of issues faced by the Islamist elite as state functionaries, for which no ready-made *Shariah* answers exist, have had a secularizing effect on them (Boroujerdi, 2001; Kian-Thiebaut, 1998; Schirazi, 1997). Adelkhah has described the impact of the exercise of power by Islamists and noted the reformulation of their social role as a result: 'Defence of their special corporate identity no longer seems a crucial issue, since an increasing number of men of religion participate fully not only in the exercise of power but much more widely in the life of society as doctors, journalists, deputies, mayors, military personnel, even television producers' (2000: 101). Hoodfar (1998) has described the unintended consequences of governmental projects that depend on mobilizing women, in this case volunteer health workers. Women selected from neighbourhoods by Community Health Centres of the Ministry of Health, trained as health workers, gained not only self-confidence and neighbourhood recognition; they learnt to expect betterment of their daily lives from the government and they learnt to become campaigners and activists for local change. It is from among these activists that some of the reformists and their supporters have emerged.

Other examples of how exposure has fed into the secularization process can be given in relation to women. The Islamic Republic's ability to bring out those categories of women who had remained untouched by, or resistant to, Pahlavi modernization has had significant consequences for society. As was mentioned earlier, these women came from a range of backgrounds. Their exposure to the outside world changed not only themselves but also the state and the society, and with these Islam itself. Furthermore, the flourishing of women's intellectual and cultural production has been very impressive. In literature, cinema, and the arts, women have produced a flurry of work in the past two decades, all highly gendered, politicized, and marked by issues of presentation and representation of women. This has no doubt acted to bring women of various social groups closer in identity and interest. The more oppositional women's politics and the more independent their activism became, the more it became possible for moderate Islamist and secularist feminists to work with each other. Throughout the Islamic Republic, the moderate Islamist and secular women activists inside Iran have acted as the conscience of society, giving a 'formal' and public voice to the changes that have affected women and society. Some of the Islamist women have taken their opposition to the state's gender policies as far as formulating 'feminist' alternatives. There have been many locally generated pragmatic examples of collaboration among feminists with Islamic and secular tendencies. Indeed, despite its limited nature, it is surprising how much collaboration has taken place between these women under such harsh political suppression.[10] Islamist feminists have also embraced international collaborations and participated in UN events, which has exposed them to secular influences.

The new 'middle ground' polity created by the merging of Islamization and secularization processes found an opportunity to burst into the open in May 1997. The mass support of women and young people for the presidency of Khatami, who promised democracy and the 'rule of law', was the first open display of the quiet and spontaneous opposition of ordinary people to the Islamist hard-line state. It was the proof of the birth of the new public space in Iranian politics, that is, the civil society. By voting for President Khatami, women and young people established themselves as the founding forces of a new civil society. This display of 'womanpower' against the establishment through the ballot box, a first in Iranian politics of normal times, was no doubt made possible by the precedence of women's mass participation in the Revolution. But in a society that had been traditionally dominated by elder statesmen, the reality of women and young people bringing presidents and parliaments into power proved a shock and made the new political space all that more novel. This was another major contribution by women to the emergence of reformism in the Islamic Republic.

The Challenge of Reform

The ongoing battle that ensued between the reformist and the hard-line factions of the state took the reform agenda through many victories and setbacks. The reformists controlled the presidency and the government, and the hard-liners controlled all other organs of the state. During the early years of reformist presidency, government policies helped to develop the reform agenda in at least two ways: first, the conceptual development of the new political space, particularly in relation to freedom of expression; second, the extension of the reformist power base by gaining control of the legislature.

Conceptually, the new political space was shaped as a universalist, democratic, and pluralist space in which the boundaries of secularism and Islamism merged and the divisions between 'insiders' and 'outsiders' (so obsessively maintained by Islamist hard-liners) got blurred. It was also perceived as a gender-neutral space in which the political interests of men and women were equally represented.[11] The new political space gave rise to a repertoire of oppositional political vocabulary such as 'civil society', 'rule of law', 'social justice', 'human rights', 'citizenship rights', 'popular sovereignty', 'participation', 'empowerment', and so on. Such terms appeared on the lips of ordinary people unexpectedly and gained rapid currency through the efforts of the reformist press. They articulated a whole range of concrete concerns by ordinary people from loss of livelihoods, lack of dignity, security, and freedom of expression, to the arbitrary and unjust nature of the rule of the hard-liners and the role of the Shii jurisprudence in the Constitution of the Islamic Republic. The new terms that gave expression to these concerns were regarded as neither Islamic nor secular but universal principles of humanity applicable to Muslims and non-Muslims alike.

The early years of reformist presidency also gave rise to the mushrooming of the oppositional press and a vocal student movement. The government was handsomely rewarded by the citizens for its policy of freedom of expression when reformists attempted to extend their power base into the legislature. The elections of the local councils (the first since the Revolution, despite the existence of this provision in the Constitution) and the sixth post-revolutionary Parliament were won over by the reformists amid a huge process of resistance and obstacle-creation by the hard-liners.

But these successes made the hard-liners determined to turn the tide by using (and abusing) all of their constitutional powers. There- fore, the second half of the reformist presidency was characterized by the reversals and paralysis of the gains made in the first half. Response from the hard-liners to the development of the reform agenda took two directions. The predominant response was to create barriers at every stage against the revered symbols of reformism. The courts closed down the reformist press and jailed reformist journ- alists (with over forty-five newspapers/magazines closed and over fifteen journalists in jail so far); those who talked to foreign media and took part in conferences in Western countries were arrested, jailed, fined, or threatened (some of them women activists); lawyers defend- ing human rights were harassed and prevented from practising (including one prominent woman human rights lawyer); the student movement was crushed and its leaders jailed; the Islamist moderate nationalist party (The Freedom Movement of Iran) that had formed the first post-revolutionary provisional government and had been allowed to operate in a low-key manner, was crushed and its leaders arrested; many reformist candidates for the local council and par- liamentary elections were disqualified and fourteen parliamentary seats were left unoccupied to prevent more reformists being elected; popular government ministers such as Mr Mohajerani (Minister for Culture and Islamic Guidance who was behind the mushrooming of the oppositional press) were removed from their posts under pres- sure; President Khatami's aide faced assassination attempts; and so on. All this was achieved by the hard-liners on the strength of the extreme and arbitrary powers accorded to the Supreme Leader Ayatollah Khamenei by the Constitution. The political manipulation of the judiciary enabled the courts to convict anyone they did not like and the direct intervention of the Supreme Leader in the affairs of the legislature prevented the sixth Parliament from passing reform- ist laws. The screw was so tightened by the hard-liners that by the end of the first reformist presidency even the Parliament stopped being a safe forum of expression for reformists. By the end of its first term, the presidency of Khatami and the policy and practice of the reformist government had reached total stalemate.

Whether President Khatami's inability to carry out even his basic constitutional responsibilities resulted in a serious loss of popularity for him and his reformist government would only be gauged after the presidential election of 1 June 2001. However, despite the lim- ited nature of the reforms achieved, there can be no doubt that the reformists managed to shift the arena of political struggle fundament- ally and determine the terms of the political debate in the Islamic

Republic. For this reason, a second response to reformism emerged among the hard-liners that envisaged survival in caution and compromise. With such massive loss of legitimacy, which had left their ranks in disarray and its leaders at a loss as to what else to try to prevent power slipping from their hands, some hard-liners attempted to narrow the gap with the reformists and reach a stable power-sharing arrangement through negotiation with President Khatami. The President was reported to be using this opportunity to negotiate guarantees for his constitutional powers if he was to stand for a second term.

The depth of change that has affected the politics of the Islamic Republic in recent years, despite the continuity of the Constitution and the political system, is obvious when one compares the terms of the political debate before and after the first reformist presidency. The experience of the exposure of men of religion to power and the emergence of the new political space has made the boundaries between a 'hard-liner', 'reformist', 'Islamist', 'secularist', and so on, very flexible and created a great deal of ideological overlap despite sharp political differences—so much so that it is difficult to fit the student movement, the protesting crowds, or the intelligentsia into the ideological labels of Islamists and secularists. There is no clear dividing line between the state and civil society either. The government of President Khatami has effectively acted as an opposition inside the state. The dividing line on gender has been blurred too. Some hard-liners in positions of power have demonstrated better understanding of women's issues than some reformists. The experience of the past few years has also raised more questions than answers about the future. With many tests still ahead for the fragile power relations within this diverse reformist movement, the future of Islamist reformism in Iran and its gender boundaries remain an open question. But what is clear is that in the current political context Islamist reformism has the best chance of initiating and carrying through positive political change, albeit of an unpredictable degree. It is therefore important to assess the potentials and limitations of reformist political thought on gender as manifested in the past few years.

The Gender Boundaries of Reformism

The broad alliance of reformists occupying the middle ground of politics in opposition to Islamist hard-liners is comprised of a range of pragmatic Islamists and secularists inside and outside Iran. Among the host of individuals and groups that have contributed conceptually to the cause of Islamist reformism in Iran in the past few years, three loosely grouped, interconnected intellectual and political currents can be regarded as key contributors. Together, these groups have presented a fairly comprehensive set of Islamist alternatives to the Islamic Republic's gender vision.

Emancipatory Potential of Islamist Reformism

One of the influential oppositional views has come from the heart of the establishment—the clerics. This is another unintended consequence of the exposure of Shiism to state power. The Shii jurisprudence (*feqh*), which is the traditional sphere of power and authority for the clergy, has formed the basis of state polices in Iran. The crisis of legitimacy of the clerical rule, and the fact that the *Shariah* did not have ready-made answers for the social issues faced by the clerics, resulted in the alienation of many clerics and strengthened the growth of what has been referred to as 'alternative' jurisprudence. Dynamic jurisprudence (*feqh puya*), as opposed to traditional jurisprudence that the state clerics adhere to, is among the most credible alternatives.[12] Dynamic jurisprudence is about shaking off the traditional rigidity of jurisprudence and opening it to innovative solutions for new problems. As a result of it taking hold, Shii jurisprudence and its underlying gender perceptions have started to change in novel directions. As an example of the views held by the proponents of dynamic jurisprudence, one can quote Ayatollah Sanei stating that, since the situation of women has changed in modern society, 'so the civil law should change too. Our current civil laws are in line with the traditional society of the past, whereas these civil laws should be in line with contemporary realities and relations in our own society' (Mir-Hosseini, 1999: 160). He puts emphasis on the duty of the Islamic state to protect women's rights against male discrimination and abuse (1999: 147–69). The younger generation of clerics taking this approach, such as Hojatoleslam Saidzadeh, have an even more radical approach. In his view, 'women's gender roles are defined and regulated more by familial and social circumstances than by nature and divine will' (1999: 249). In his lecture to an audience of secular feminists in 1995 in the United States, Saidzadeh talked about the reconcilability of feminism with Islam. He defined feminism 'as a social movement whose agenda is the establishment of women's human rights. Feminism endeavours to free women from an unwanted subordination imposed on them by androcentric societies; it recognises that women are independent and complete beings, and puts the

emphasis on the common humanity of the sexes, not their differences'
(1999: 249).

Another influential oppositional group within the civil society
movement are the 'religious intellectuals' (*roshanfekran dini*). The
best-known representative of this position is Abdolkarim Sorush
who is British-educated and who has lectured extensively in Iran
and abroad about his special brand of Islamism. The emancipatory
potentials of Sorush's theory of Islam arise from a number of interventions on the fundamental tenets of the Islamic Republic.[13] His
most influential one is about the separation of religion from religious
knowledge. He considers the core Islamic texts (the Koran, hadith
and the teachings of the Shii Imams) as the divine and unchange-
able 'religion'. He argues that the divine is only accessible to human
beings through 'religious knowledge', which is a changeable human
product. Religion as understood by human beings has to be time- and
context-bound and the divine can be reinterpreted infinitely on the
basis of the religious knowledge of time and place. Therefore, any religious ideology that aims to prevent religious innovation and change
is bound to fail. The gender implication of this is that everything that
is considered 'Islamic' about women's position is subject to change,
depending again on time and place. He considers debate and dialogue
between religious and extra-religious discourses as the main source
of innovation and change in religion and society.

Another important intervention by Soroush is his rejection of
Islamic jurisprudence as the basis for law (including on women's position) in an Islamic society. He argues that the Islamic jurisprudence
(*feqh*) is not 'divine' but religious knowledge and as such subject to
change, depending on contextual factors. He goes even further than
this by suggesting that it should be discarded altogether. In the modern world, he argues, the state should seek solutions to social issues
in social science and religious values of the society and not in Islamic
jurisprudence. He therefore refuses to get engaged in debates on
women's rights in Islamic jurisprudence. In his view, in the modern world extra-religious rights and concepts (e.g. human rights,
women's rights, justice, freedom, democracy) have become part of
the meaning of humanity and found their way into religious knowledge through coexistence. He considers these the legitimate sources
of law in modern society rather than Islamic jurisprudence.

A third set of interventions by Sorush is about the place of democracy and human rights in Islam. He tries to show the fallacy of
imposing a theocratic model of governance on a complex society and
is critical of the Islamic Republic for basing its policies on Islamic
jurisprudence. He believes that the concept of democracy and its

associated rights have to be accepted by religion as the basis for the legitimacy of a religious state. He aims to replace the top–down imposition of religious ideology on people with a bottom–up reflection of people's religious values in the state and its policies: the only legitimate form of Islamic (as opposed to Islamist, i.e. ideological) government is one which is elected by a nation with religious values out of free choice in a pluralist political environment; one that is based on the accountability of those in the position of power. He considers democracy and human rights to be universal concepts, thereby rejecting their Western origin and arguing that they are also central to Iranian culture. Indeed, he believes, Iranians to be heirs to three cultures: pre-Islamic, Islamic, and Western. He considers cultures heterogeneous and open to change and argues that cultural growth requires borrowing from others, including the West.

The third influential reformist strand is comprised of the key politicians and oppositional spokespeople who have promoted broader political participation (*tarafdarane toseeh siasi*) in the Islamic Republic. This category is a 'rainbow coalition' of numerous reformists (hereafter the Coalition), formed in 1997 to support Khatami's first presidential campaign. It was strengthened by Khatami's presidency and was the main force behind the mushrooming of the pro-reform press and the development of the student movement. The demand for democracy, pluralism, and freedom of speech and association increased with the elections for local councils in February 1999 and that of the sixth post-revolutionary Parliament in February 2000. The Coalition supported the reformist candidates and won the overwhelming majority of the councils as well as 72 per cent of the parliamentary seats. However, as was noted earlier, women occupied a smaller proportion of seats in the reformist-dominated Parliament compared to the previous hard-liner-dominated one.[14]

Democracy and political and cultural pluralism were the cornerstones of President Khatami and the Coalition's discourse. The agenda of the pro-Khatami Coalition for the sixth Parliament was: to institute uniform legal procedures and to eliminate duplicate centres of authority; to reform electoral laws and allow political parties to flourish; initiate legislation defining 'political crime' and establish procedures and means for jury selection of political crime; initiate legislative reforms on the freedom of press; remove discriminatory rules and regulations which limit access to information; remove discriminatory rules for employment of individuals which constitute a barrier to equal opportunity employment; initiate legislation which fosters equal rights for both men and women; legislate laws to attract foreign capital thus clarifying laws pertaining to private investment; initiate a comprehensive programme of social welfare; decentralization of government and economic activity (Vatandoust, 2000).

However, due to resistance by the hard-liners, Khatami and the Coalition did not have a chance to prove that their actions matched their words. The only policies that they managed to implement partially were the freedom of the press and expression, and the establishment of the local councils. Since they believed men and women equally benefited from freedom, they did not take special measures to increase women's candidacy for elections or to develop and support women's press and publication. The only special measure taken for women by Khatami was further development of President Rafsanjani's 'institutional approach to women's advancement', to which reference has already been made. President Khatami's Centre for Women's Participation continued the previous state policy of channelling women's activism away from independent NGOs and into the state-supported grass-roots collective activities, probably to compete with the hard-liners on the mobilization of grass-roots women. But it only partially succeeded in doing this as the reformist political environment gave women the courage to resist the traditional pattern of state control over women's movement (which has been state practice in Iran since the early twentieth century) much more openly than before (Ahmady-Khorasani, 1999). So, although the reformist government made serious efforts in the direction of engendering the state structure and putting women in decision-making positions, it did so in a way that reinforced the segregation of women's issues to women, and fell short of creating an enabling environment for women's independent organizations.

Due to the subversive implications of their views, the above three reformist strands have faced tremendous pressure from the hard-line establishment, but this has only increased their popularity among women and young people. Sorush's views have found their way into the thinking of the two other categories of reformism. His separation of religion from religious knowledge has allowed the radicals of the dynamic jurisprudence such as Saidzadeh to call for the abandonment of the traditional interpretations of Koran and Islamic jurisprudence in favour of interpretations that are based on time and context (Mir-Hosseini, 1999). His rejection of jurisprudence-based Islamic state in favour of the state giving expression to religious values of people is reflected in President Khatami's 'another model of democratic life' based on 'spirituality and morality'. But there are also tensions between the views of the three groups, a major point of contention being about the role of jurisprudence in the discourse of reformism. The rejection of jurisprudence as an arena for gender politics by religious intellectuals, and the insistence of the dynamic jurisprudence on the compatibility of jurisprudence and women's equality have created duality of thought that the men of religion have not yet been able to overcome.

Gender Limitations of Islamist Reformism

Although many of the underlying concepts of the above three Islamist reformist positions cannot stand up to feminist scrutiny, nevertheless these views have, together, managed to open up the political space for Islamist gender activism in a way that had not been possible before. Therefore, the issue here is not the validity or otherwise of these theories but their emancipatory potential at the current political juncture in Iran.

However, when it comes to gender issues, the 'theory' and 'politics' of reformism (both Islamist and secularist) are not necessarily harmonious. For example, by rejecting jurisprudence as an arena for gender politics altogether, religious intellectuals have undermined the efforts of Islamist women activists to change the legal status of women here and now, rather than waiting for the ideal society to arrive where Islamic jurisprudence does not influence the state's gender policies. Another example is the promotion of democracy in Islam on the one hand, and the conceptualization of democracy as a gender-neutral concept on the other. These limitations have been challenged by feminists. Islamist feminism has transformed reformist theories by taking forward their gender potential and challenging their limitations. Some of the issues highlighted by this strand of feminist thought are discussed below.

Feminist Bridge between Jurisprudence and Theology

Women have taken up the challenge of gender intervention in both theology and jurisprudence through a number of complementary strategies.[15] One strategy has been the reinterpretation of core religious texts. Although the history of interpretive attempts within Islam to deal with questions posed by modern transformations of Islamic societies (including gender) goes back to the mid-nineteenth century, the current interpretive ventures by women are novel and do not have precedence. Whereas the dominant method of interpretation on gender by reformists has been to use more woman-friendly sources from an already-existing set of authoritative exegetical texts, in these recent attempts women have engaged in direct interpretations in their own right. Women have argued that the domain

of interpretation should be open not only to every Muslim but even
to non-Muslims, as a matter of expertise rather than a question of
faith, and that interpretation should not only take into consideration
the needs of the time but also the contemporary schools of philosophy
and thought.

Another strategy with a notable consequence is the one that is
fundamentally different from the familiar reformist historicizing and
contextualizing in order to delimit the effective field of Koranic verses
to particular time and circumstances. Women's strategy has been to
carry out their interpretative ventures in a different social space:
in the printed pages of a women's journal—in a public space, rather
than the private chambers of a religious scholar. They speak as 'public
intellectuals', rather than as private theology teachers. Their audience is other women (and men) as citizens, rather than theological
students and other clerical commentators. They write not in order to
command the believers into obedience, but, as they put it, in order
'to awaken women' so that they would proclaim their rights. Furthermore, on the issue of rights, women have made another worthy
leap, from the pages of their magazines to the seat of the Parliament
and the floor of the family courts. As members of Parliament and
lawyers, women have taken important initiatives on women's group
rights through legislation and managed to influence the opinion and
judgments of the male judges (clerics) in Islamic courts on women's
individual rights through jurisprudence-informed defence.

A third strategy has been intervention in jurisprudence on the issue
of equality of rights. Whereas almost all mainstream Islamist discourses on women (traditional or dynamic) have grounded their case
for differences of rights and social responsibilities in differences of
women and men in creation/nature, some Islamist feminists have
at last severed this widely accepted connection. They argue for the
social construction of gender, a debate that is similar to, and informed
by, the debates within Western feminism. This has enabled Islamist
feminists to draw vastly different conclusions (from male Islamist
scholars) about gender relations in an Islamic society. Instead of
beginning with creation as a narrative of origins for women's rights
and responsibilities, they place individual woman, in her contemporary social concreteness with her needs and choices, in the centre
of their arguments.

The last strategy to comment on is bringing together 'religious'
and 'extra-religious' knowledge, and more specifically the bringing together of 'Islam' and 'feminism'. For this, women writers
and activists had to go beyond the conventional Iranian attitude
towards feminism. Attacking feminism out of gender conservatism

and Westphobia—that is, distancing oneself from any identification with feminism as threatening and as Western—is still a fairly common response among Iranian women, both Islamists and secularists. However, a different response is taking hold among women activists of both persuasions that is based on the affiliation of Islam with feminism. Islamist journals now freely translate from Western feminist writers whatever they judge useful to their readership, and women members of Parliament publicly identify themselves with feminism. As will be noted in the final part of the paper, the introduction of the individual woman's needs and autonomy into an Islamist discourse, and the increasing association by the Islamist women activists with international feminism has opened up a productive space for pragmatic feminism.

The feminist bridge between jurisprudence and theology has produced a radical decentring of the men of religion from the domain of interpretation and reformism, and placed women as interpreters and their needs as grounds for reformism, at the centre of a feminist revisionist effort. That women have now positioned themselves as public commentators of jurisprudence promises that the process of democratization of politics would not remain an exclusively masculine preoccupation. This is also a serious challenge to religious intellectuals and reformist politicians who have by and large left the legal sphere to the clerics of the dynamic jurisprudence. The fact that they are not theologically trained (as claimed by a prominent reformist Mohammad Javad Kashi) or that the discourse of rights is limiting to their intellectual pursuits (as claimed by religious intellectuals) cannot be a credible reason for the reformist avoidance of gender any more (Noorbakhsh, 2000).

Engendering Democracy

The feminist critique has also addressed a number of serious shortcomings in the reformist conceptualization of democracy and human rights. The conceptualization of democracy as a gender-neutral process has acquired many dimensions.[16] One aspect of reformist thinking on democracy has been its silence on gender. Taking the well-known reformist journal *Kian* that had become one of the most important sites of critical rethinking for religious intellectuals, it is not possible to find a woman writer or an article that deals with gender issues. Asked in an interview about the reason for this, Sorush responded by explaining that religious intellectuals were preoccupied with other pressing issues and believed that women's journals could take care of the gender issues (Mir-Hosseini, 1999: 243).

A related aspect of reformist thinking on democracy is the perception that democracy and democratization affect men and women in the same way. Abbas Abdi, a prominent writer and editor echoed the widespread reformist perception that the general struggles for citizenship rights would naturally be inclusive of women.[17] While a great deal of rethinking and realignment has been taking place on women's issues among Iranian feminists of diverse outlooks in the 1990s, gender seems to be all but non-existent as a category of thinking among some Islamist reformists (Najmabadi, 2000*a*). This is not, of course, something that is specific to Islamist reformism. As the experience of feminists during the Revolution and in exile has demonstrated, some sections of the secular opposition are, and have been, equally gender-blind (Najmabadi, 1999).

The third conceptual inadequacy has been the perception of 'human rights' as a set of rights that have priority over 'women's rights'. This has parallels with the perception that the democracy movement is the 'main' struggle and the women's movement a 'deviation'. Abbas Abdi articulated this view and concluded that, although it was acceptable that groups would organize for and around their special group rights, one would have to be careful that these special group activities would not come into conflict with the broader and more general struggles for democracy. In response, women have objected to the idea that there is a hierarchy in rights and pointed out that women's rights are an indispensable part of human rights and hence of the democratization process (Moti', 2000).

Finally, the common fear of women losing womanhood revealed yet another weakness in the reformist gender analysis. Imad-ul-din Baghi drew the attention of women activists to what he called the danger of wanting to replace androcracy with gynocracy,[18] and Sorush expressed concern that 'women should remain women and men should remain men', and that 'one must not impose regulations that would push women outside the circuit of womanhood and men outside the circuit of manhood'.[19] These concerns and fears aim to postpone, if not oppose outright, equal rights sentiments and activism emerging among women Islamists (Farhi, 2000).

But feminism has begun to make inroads into reformism. Some reformists have admitted that, even though Islamist reformism has been ready to embrace sociological and philosophical notions from Europe, it has never seriously engaged with feminism, except in gestures of repudiation.[20] Indeed, in the domain of individual and social liberties, and especially when it comes to issues of gender, Islamist reformism continues to revert to 'traditionalist' views that hold women responsible for the upkeep of norms.

The Dawn of Pragmatic Feminism

Having explored the interface between feminist and reformist political thought, the chapter will now focus on the diversity within Iranian feminism, especially its secular and Islamist strands. The emergence of a new category of what I have called 'pragmatic feminism', which cuts across secularism and Islamism, will be highlighted. The threads that run through the discussion below are key debates in the post-revolutionary Iranian feminism. Two sets of debates have proved particularly persistent within the Iranian (and indeed, Middle Eastern) women's studies, namely, the compatibility of Islam and feminism and the universality of women's rights. These issues have surfaced frequently in secularist and Islamist feminist literature, and all key players in Iranian feminism have gone through evolution of thought on these issues.

Secularist Feminism

Secularist feminism is a broad umbrella category used for identifying a range of feminisms that revolve around a 'secularist' as opposed to a 'secular' identity. The difference between these two categories is that a 'secularist identity' is a consciously chosen political identity that constructs secularism as the main political dividing line in Iranian feminist politics. Many monarchist and socialist secularists are as ideologically committed and extreme in their secularism as are Islamist fundamentalists in their Islamism. A 'secular identity' in the context of Iran, on the contrary, is a much looser and more flexible social identity that can mix with a range of political positions that do not necessarily revolve around secularism.

Secularist feminists cover a wide range of views, often in opposition to each other, and follow diverse political agendas (including socialist and monarchist). Each of these labels covers a variety of hard and soft positions. However, the common secularist identity held in opposition to Islamism has brought close some of the most divergent of these feminisms, such as the more sophisticated forms of socialist and monarchist feminisms, on issues such as the compatibility of Islam and feminism and the universality of women's rights. Since socialist feminism has presented a more articulate position among secularist feminists, it will be drawn upon more than the others here. Particular reference will be made to the works of Hideh Moghissi (1996, 1999) who presents one of the more sophisticated versions of socialist feminism.

The debate on the compatibility of 'Islam' with 'feminism' started in the immediate aftermath of the Revolution, with many secularists agreeing, for different reasons, that Islam and feminism were incompatible. It became a secularist preoccupation to identify the limits that Islam placed on women's position and advancement. The repressive nature of the post-revolutionary state in Iran and its rapid and forced Islamization policy confirmed the age-old theory that Islam was the cause of women's oppression. This conception inspired a wave of feminist opposition to Islam in the 1980s. One of the old theories that this helped to revive was the 'modernization theory' that had underpinned US support for the Pahlavi modernization project in Iran. It conceptualized the political history of Iran, particularly in relation to women, in terms of the battle between the forces of 'tradition' represented by an essentialized Islam, and the forces of 'modernity' represented by the Pahlavi state (Beck and Keddie, 1978; Paidar, 1995). The socialist critique of Islam coincided with the 'modernization theory' by arguing that 'the struggle between secular modernism and Islamic revival is fundamentally a struggle about secular democracy, economic justice, and the liberation of women, ultimately a claim to replace existing society with a modern, secular society' (Moghissi, 1999: 61).

Socialist feminism believed that it was best placed to represent women's interests and tended to dismiss other forms of feminism. Islamist feminism was dismissed on the ground that it is connected 'with the question of the compatibility of feminism with Islamic teaching and scripture, and the social and legal frameworks which have evolved in Islamic societies' (Moghissi, 1996: 126). But 'how could a religion which is based on gender hierarchy be adopted as the framework for struggle for gender democracy and women's equality with men?' (ibid.) As far as socialist feminists were concerned, Islam and Islamism were unified categories. They spent a great deal of energy on refuting the work of any secular feminist who analysed gender politics in Iran on the basis of differentiation within, and deconstruction of, these categories. Such secular feminist analyses were regarded as confused (Moghissi, 1996: 133) and their authors were accused of being 'professional opportunists' guilty of 'virtual capitulation ... to the demands of the religious text' (Moghissi, 1996: 135, 143). The treatment given to Islamist feminist activists by some socialist feminists was even worse. Women who were invited for conferences and lectures from Iran and appeared with the *hejab* for personal or political reasons were often shouted down and subjected to insult by socialist (and monarchist) women in the audience.

As for the debate on the universality of women's rights, too, social-ist and monarchist feminists proved to be the most ardent supporters of universalism, which they regarded to be the oppositional bin-ary of cultural relativism advocated by the Islamists. The basis for universalism was identified to be patriarchy:

We still may not have a cross-cultural definition of feminism or a feminist framework wide enough to identify women's oppression in diverse socio-historic contexts. This, however, does not alter the fact that the basis of women's oppression everywhere is patriarchal structures and relations. Des-pite diverse forms, they have the same content. Feminist paradigms and frameworks are as useful for understanding and theorising gender relations in non-Western societies as they are in the West. (Moghissi, 1996: 17–18)

The aim of universalism was regarded to be an 'international and unitary [feminist] ideology to cut across national and cultural barriers, to go beyond political systems and economic divisions' (Sanasarian, 1982: 155).[21]

But despite its total rejection of Islamist feminism as a credible feminist politics, socialist feminism paradoxically shared some of its basic theoretical premises with the more sophisticated versions of Islamist feminism. These included heavy reference to the concept of patriarchy as 'the basis of women's oppression everywhere', the belief in the universality of women's rights, and the same concep-tualization of the 'equality versus similarity of rights'. As Moghissi put it, 'feminism's core idea is that women and men are biologic-ally different but this difference should not be translated into an unequal valuation of women's and men's experience; biology should not lead to differences in legal status, the privileging of one over the other' (1996: 140). Another source of similarity in the situation of socialist and Islamist feminisms was that both were identified with oppressive political systems: Islamism with the Islamic Republic and socialism with the Soviet Union and other authoritarian socialist regimes. Both have had to obtain credibility by distancing themselves from authoritarianism and demonstrating the existence of variation of political thought and agenda within their ideology. Both have had recourse to the argument that women's position in 'true' Islam or 'true' socialism is different from that in the actually existing Islam or socialism.

However, it is important to emphasize the evolution of thought that has occurred within Iranian socialist feminism since the Revolution. This movement should be credited with moving away from a starting point in which it was not much more than the 'cheer leader' of this or that Marxist-Leninist or Maoist male-dominated organization, to a point where it has articulated its own feminist theory and acquired a cherished political independence. This evolution demonstrates the developmental potential of socialist feminism for the future.

Islamist Feminism

The term Islamist feminism was first used within the Iranian women's studies in the West to demonstrate the diversity of the post-revolutionary women's movement (Paidar and Tabari, 1982). In later years it found a place among the Islamist women activists who had revised their original resistance to the concept of feminism and wished to express the specificity of their feminism through the Islamic adjective. However, political considerations made it difficult for these women publicly to use the term Islamist feminism. Whilst many of them privately identified with this term, and in the past few years many have made their allegiance to feminism and their definition of it public, until recently none used the term 'Islamist feminist' publicly. This was partly because putting the adjective 'Islamist' next to the term 'feminist' had the potential of causing more trouble (from the hard-liners) than using the term feminist on its own.

Islamist feminism is a broad category comprised of all feminists who hold 'Islamist', as opposed to Islamic or Muslim, identity. The difference between these two categories is that an 'Islamist identity' is a consciously chosen political identity that constructs Islamism as the main political dividing line. An 'Islamic or Muslim identity', on the contrary, is a much looser and more flexible social identity that can mix with a range of political positions that do not necessarily revolve around Islamism.

Islamist feminism represents different shades of reformist politics and there has been no collective presentation or assertion of the principles and agenda of 'Islamist feminism' in public. There are numerous reasons for this, but self-censorship is bound to feature as a major one. The public statements of Islamist feminists often have to be more conservative than their actual beliefs if they are to avoid the wrath of the hard-liners. While far more research is required to understand the Islamist feminist thoughts and beliefs, it is nevertheless possible to present a collection of ideas and positions from their writings, public statements, and, more importantly, private conversations in the past few years. The claim is not that these views are held by all Islamist feminists or even the majority of them, or that any of them accept all of the views represented, but that the following views have found their way into Islamist feminist thought in Iran.[22]

Islamist feminists are devout believers and practise the basic tenets of Islam by personal choice, but they hold a variety of views on the relationship between Islam and the state. Many of them follow the religious intellectuals in basing the legitimacy of politics in pluralism of thought and a democratic mandate (from the people). They consider equality of rights in the family and the social sphere more broadly to be compatible with their 'modern Islam', but incompatible with the Islam represented by the hard-liners (that is, the 'traditional Islam' being practised by the Iranian state). They believe that many of the gender positions attributed to Islam are not in fact Islamic but arise from patriarchy. Their effort is focused on proving this and detaching Islam from its patriarchal heritage. Their goal is to bring Islam in line with the requirements of modern women through interpretive ventures. Their emphasis is on stretching the gender boundaries of Islam to accommodate what women need for a modern life, as opposed to changing women's position to bring it in line with Islam.

On women's role within the family, Islamist feminists believe that the biological differences between men and women should not give rise to inequality of rights. They believe in equal rights as well as additional positive rights for women because of their childbearing role. They have campaigned on increasing the age of marriage for women and against the institution of arranged marriage wherein women do not assert a free choice. Many have spoken out against polygamy and 'temporary marriage' which is a Shii-specific practice (Haeri, 1989). They have advocated divorce laws that are based on women's autonomy, choice, and economic security, and custody laws that are based on the best interests of the child and the mother. They have campaigned for recognition of housework as paid work to increase housewives' independence and influence in family affairs. They have also supported family planning and greater involvement of men in housework and child rearing to release women for social activities. On abortion, it has been stated that the mother's health and control are paramount, but further research is required to establish the range of Islamist feminist views on abortion.

Many Islamist feminists have condemned state and family-based violence and abuse against women, but again further research is required on the range of views on the infamous Law of Retribution (*qanun qesas*), which has legalized punishment such as stoning to death for women and men convicted of adultery and homosexuality. Research is also required to establish the range of views on sexual freedom and homosexuality. It would be useful to establish the degree of choice and individuality that Islamist feminists are prepared to advocate on sexuality. The more liberal of them have kept quiet about these issues but chosen to endorse and celebrate the sexually expressive poetry of Forough Farrokhzad who is an icon of female individual freedom in sex and whose brother was a well-known homosexual. Others have expressed public views that reject sexual freedom and homosexuality (Rahnavard, 1995).

On women's social role, Islamist feminists have almost unanimously supported it and advocated positive action to ensure women's equal participation in all decision-making processes, at all levels, and in civil society, including education and employment. Many have rejected the hard-line Islamist view that gives less value to women's testimony and prohibits women's judgeship, and advocated equality between men and women in these matters. Many do not consider *hejab* an Islamic practice but a patriarchal one, and reject it as a prerequisite for women's participation in social life. They do practise *hejab* themselves but many have advocated education on 'public modesty' for both men and women, leading to choice in adopting it and in the form of *hejab* adopted (Hashemi, 1982; Sherkat, 2000).

On the issue of the compatibility of Islam with feminism, the Islamist feminist position, like those of socialist and monarchist feminists, started with the proposition that Islam is incompatible with feminism. The initial response of Islamist feminists was to treat the issue of women's rights and feminism separately. While it was agreed that Islam had all the credentials to support women's rights, not many believed that feminism was compatible with Islam. Many Islamist feminists, however, have revised their position on feminism and accepted that feminism, as the 'theory of universal patriarchal oppression of women' is relevant to the understanding of women's position in Iran (Rahnavard, 1995). Some now regard themselves as feminists struggling to overcome patriarchy and achieving equality of rights for women (Abasgholizadeh, 2000).

This interest in feminism has coincided with the general interest in democratization as a universal necessity. Nayereh Tohidi (2001) has traced the trajectory of Islamism on the issue of universalism. Proud of international adoration for the success of the Iranian Revolution, the post-revolutionary Islamist women activists argued that women's emancipation was only possible within Islam and therefore the Islamist vision of womanhood was universal (Paidar and Tabari, 1982). In parallel to the emphasis on the universality of women's position in Islam, the Islamists followed an argument on the cultural relativism of women's position in the West (Tohidi, 2001). But in later years, many of the statist and independent Islamist feminists converted to the idea of the universality of women's rights. Tohidi (2001) argues that (in addition to the delegitimization of the hard-liners and the secularization trend in Iran) two main developments have contributed to this trajectory. First, the failure of the 'Islamic model of womanhood' propagated by the Iranian government to gain international recognition and following. Second, the international condemnation of the Islamization policies of the government and the pressure on Iran to conform to the international standards on women's human rights (mainly through the United Nations and other international fora).

Islamist feminism (even in its sophisticated mode) suffers from serious theoretical inadequacies that it needs to address urgently. These include the essentialization of both Islam and the West, and the theoretical vacillation between cultural relativism and universalism, both with their own dangers for women's rights. There is an urgent need for a fundamental rethinking of the concepts of Islam and patriarchy, and the issues of difference and multiculturalism. However, Islamist feminist politics should be commended for developing substantially from where it started twenty-two years ago. The move to patriarchy and the universality of rights as a mode of analysis, although theoretically as problematic as cultural relativism, have in the context of the isolationism of the established Islam and the reformist–hardliners' rivalry in Iran politically strengthened the Islamist feminist movement by linking it to the democratization movement inside Iran and the UN-supported international women's movements. Islamist feminists, like most other Iranian feminisms, have emphasized social responsibility as opposed to individual rights. Indeed, looking back at Iranian history over the past century, ideas of individuality, autonomy, and choice have not been part of the political discourse (of the state, the opposition, or the women's movement) until relatively recently. Even the Iranian secularist feminisms of today fall short of the ideal on these principles. In this context, it is fair to acknowledge that Islamist feminists have moved a long way towards liberal feminism on issues of individual rights, choice, and autonomy (Najmabadi, 1998, 2000a, 2000b).[23] All this shows that the 'identity' expressed by many Islamist feminists is in fact quite complex and rather individualized.[24] It often incorporates not only elements of what they call 'true Islam' but also what they regard as the egalitarian and non-exploitative elements of Western political and social thought and feminist history (Tohidi, 2001). Islamist feminism has moved from a passionately religious movement two decades ago to one which is a mixture of social conservative, culturalist, and liberal feminism. The Islamist feminism of today has successfully dissociated itself from the Islamist hard-line positions represented in many of the key apparatuses of the state. It has taken up a credible oppositional stand on behalf of women in Iran.

Pragmatic Feminism

One of the impacts of the twin processes of Islamization and secularization on feminism has been the emergence of a new category of feminism that I have referred to as pragmatic feminism. This emerging category has cut across secularism and Islamism, which were once regarded as self-contained categories of feminism. Pragmatic feminism has attracted a range of women with secular and Islamic, Muslim identities. The political orientation of pragmatic feminists tends to be moderate centre ground, ranging from social-democratic and liberal nationalism to culturalist nationalism and reformist Islamism.

Pragmatism is not an ideology, in the sense that Islamism and socialism are. It is rather a political culture and approach that many Iranian feminists have adopted spontaneously. It advocates a pragmatic approach to the issues of difference and multiculturalism rather than a theoretical/political position on either side of the fence on the debates on 'Islam versus feminism' or 'universalism versus cultural relativism'. The pragmatist approach in feminism has spread not through a conscious feminist campaign but through sporadic collaborative ventures and contributions to the Iranian women's studies literature inside and outside the country. It is a concept that has only recently been developed, and whether it will continue to be used in the future is an open question. But it represents a trend that has been growing within Iranian feminist politics (Keddie, 2000).

As a political culture, pragmatic feminism is about creating an enabling and empowering environment in which feminisms can be encouraged and supported to stretch their boundaries and bring out their full potential rather than corner each other into entrenched positions. Feminism is, of course, about competing theories and which theory and politics can achieve women's goals sooner and better. Moreover, women's interests and priorities are constructed differently by competing feminisms. However, it is exactly for these reasons that the quality of the political culture can be regarded as the key determinant in the overall success of the feminist movement in Iran.

Surely, within any balance of power between the state and the opposition, an enabling feminist political culture would have a better chance of increasing the overall influence of the broad and diverse feminist collective action in Iran. An important element of an empowering feminist culture is recognition of, and respect for, difference. This entails the understanding that feminisms can learn from each other and that none can be free from theoretical shortcoming and political miscalculation.

As a political approach, pragmatic feminism advocates collaboration across feminisms, irrespective of their perceived limitations, on gender issues where interests meet and collaboration can yield results. The kind of alliance-building that it is about is based on recognition of difference, not for the purpose of setting limits and drawing lines, but in order to build across them. It tries to overcome the authoritarianism and sectarianism that have dominated feminist politics in Iran over the past two decades. What is referred to is the state of affairs where each feminism lives a secluded life in its own enclave, spending its energy attacking the other's perceived limitations, while women's rights are abrogated by the Islamist hard-liners, and when the majority of the secularist and Islamist male reformists inside and outside the country conceptualize democratization, at best, as a gender-neutral process.

It tries to do this by differentiating defending or believing in Islam, from appreciating and supporting the potentials of Islamist feminism from a secular standpoint. It also tries to overcome the fear of loss of identity and ideology, which has made so many feminisms disengaged and marginalized. Many secularist feminisms cannot conceptualize women holding multiple identities or conceive of situations in which women from different ideologies can engage in coalitional politics while maintaining their identity and ideology. That is why pragmatic feminists often face the contradictory charge of being Islamic or Western apologists.

However, the political reality of Iran is that an alliance between secularists and Islamist feminists over specific issues at specific junctures is not a theoretical luxury but a political necessity. Since the early 1980s, increasing numbers of pragmatic feminists have tried to create an enabling feminist political culture to increase the overall effectiveness of the feminist movement. The effort has taken a number of directions, such as presenting the efforts of the Islamist feminists and reformists to stretch the boundaries of Islamism in favour of women's rights, or countering the essentialist perceptions of 'women's position in Islam' during the post-revolutionary period, as well as creating a network of women activists and scholars inside and outside the country, and promoting the value of collaboration across ideological boundaries. The journal *Nimeye Digar* (The Other Half) that was published in the United Kingdom and United States by a group of pragmatic feminists started this process in 1983 and continued it until recently when it became possible for the Islamist and secularist women's magazines to carry the mantle inside Iran. There is now an international network of pragmatic feminists and pro-feminist men in place, which has proved active in campaigning against human rights abuses in Iran. These efforts are pointing to the dawn of feminist coalitional politics in Iran despite many pitfalls and challenges.

The goal of feminist solidarity has eluded many feminist movements worldwide.[25] However, there also exist many examples of women taking collective action under particular circumstances and over specific rallying issues, such as the suffrage movement in Britain and the post-revolutionary anti-Islamisation protest movement in Iran. Feminist theory has made serious inroads into understanding both the barriers against, and the possibilities for, achieving feminist alliances. These should be acknowledged and understood if feminists are to overcome marginalization. This is a more urgent requirement in the context of Iran where a particularly vicious attack has been waged on almost all aspects of women's lives, and where the only tangible internal opposition is Islamist-based. In today's Iran the political choices open to secularist, and Islamist, feminists are limited and unsatisfactory. None the less a choice has to be made by feminists of both persuasions between withdrawal or engagement. If engagement is the answer, then collaborative efforts between Islamists and secularists over specific issues are inevitable.

Conclusion

This chapter focused on two aspects of gender and democracy in Iran: first, the political spaces and opportunities that women have created and used to enact their citizenship rights within the constraints of an authoritarian Islamic regime; second, the rise of the reform movement and the movement for women's rights in recent years, and the dialogue between and among them. The chapter attempted to demonstrate the paradox of weak democratic institutions and active female citizenship in the Islamic Republic before proceeding to analyse the male bias and emancipatory potential of the different strands of Islamic reformism. A number of developments and trends in contemporary reformism and feminism were highlighted: the rise of the democratization movement; the troubled relationship between the two broad and diverse movements of feminism and reformism; and the developments and debates within the broad feminist movements and the emergence of pragmatic feminism. The historical rift between secularist and Islamist feminisms has manifested itself in passionate debates over the compatibility of Islam and feminism and the universality of women's rights. These debates have proved both testing and healing for contemporary Iranian feminism. Testing, because they have brought into the open the underlying lack of tolerance of difference and thus resulted in peer pressure against collaborative feminist politics. Healing, because they have made feminists face difficult issues and seek firm grounds on which to base future collaborations.

References

Abasgholizadeh, Mahbube (2000) 'Interview', *Zanan*, 69 (Nov.): 10–13.

Abrahamian, Ervand (1982) *Iran between Two Revolutions* (Princeton: Princeton University Press).

Adelkhah, Fariba (2000) *Being Modern in Iran* (New York: Columbia University Press).

Afshar, Haleh (1998) *Islam and Feminisms: An Iranian Case Study* (Basingstoke: Macmillan).

Ahmady-Khorasani, Nooshin (1999) 'Tashakolhaye zanan: barrasi jayegah va amalkard anan', *Jens Dovom*, 4: 55–62.

Beck, Lois, and Nikki Keddie (1978) *Women in the Muslim World* (Cambridge, MA: Harvard University Press).

Boroujerdi, Mehrzad (1994) 'The Encounter of Post-Revolutionary Thought in Iran with Hegel, Heideger and Popper', in S. Mardin (ed.), *Cultural Transitions in the Middle East* (New York: E. J. Brill).

—— (2001) 'The Paradoxes of Politics in Post-Revolutionary Iran', in J. Esposito and R. K. Ramazani (eds.), *Iran at the Cross-roads* (New York: St Martin's Press).

Esfandiari, Haleh (1994) 'The Majles and Women's Issues in the Islamic Republic of Iran, 1960–90', in M. Afkhami and E. Friedl (eds.), *In the Eye of the Storm: Women in Post-Revolutionary Iran* (London: I. B. Tauris).

Farhi, Farideh (2000) 'Ejaze bedahid beguyam kodam masaleh zan!', *Zanan*, 58 (Nov.): 41–2.

Foreign Policy Journal (1995) *Special Issue on Women*, 9 (Summer).

Habibi, S., and S. Beladi-Musavi (1998) *Mabnaye barnameh rizi ba ruykarde jensiati* (Tehran: Iran Chaap)

Haeri, Shahla (1989) *The Law of Desire: Temporary Marriage in Iran* (London: I. B. Tauris).

Hashemi, Fereshteh (1982) 'Women in an Islamic versus Women in a Muslim View', in Paidar Parvin and Azar Tabari (under the pen name of Nahid Yeganeh), *The Shadow of Islam: Women's Movement in Iran* (London: Zed Press).

Hashemi-Rafsanjani, Faezeh (1999) *Zan dar ruznameh zan: Majmou'eh maghalat montashershodeh dar ruznameh zan* (Tehran: Golleh Publishers).

274 *Parvin Paidar*

Hoghughe Zanan (2000) no. 16 (July): 26–9.

Hoodfar, Homa (1997) 'The Veil in their Minds and on our Heads: Veiling Practices and Muslim Women', in L. Lowe and D. Lloyd (eds.), *The Politics of Culture in the Shadow of Capital* (Durham, NC: Duke University Press).

—— (1998) *Volunteer Health Workers in Iran as Social Activists: Can 'Governmental Non-Governmental Organisations' be Agents of Democratisation?* (Occasional Paper, 10, Dec., Grables: Women Living Under the Muslim Laws).

—— (1999) *The Women's Movement in Iran: Women at the Crossroads of Secularisation and Islamisation*, (Grables: Women Living Under the Muslim Laws).

Jackson, Cecile, and Ruth Pearson (eds.) (1998) *Feminist Visions of Development: Gender Analysis and Policy* (London: Routledge).

Jakobsen, Janet (1998) *Working Alliances and the Politics of Difference, Diversity and Feminist Ethics* (Bloomingdale, Ind.: Indiana University Press).

Kadivar, Mohsen (1999*a*) *Bahaye Azadi: Defaiyat Mohsen Kadivar Dar Dadgah Rohaniyat* (Tehran: Nashr Ney).

—— (1999*b*) 'Interview', *Rah Now*, 1/2: 16–21.

Kar, Mehranguiz (1998) 'Mosharekat siasi zanan vagheiyat ya khial', *Zanan*, 47 (Oct.): 10–11.

Keddie, Nikki (2000) 'Women in Iran since 79', *Social Research*, 67/2 (Summer): 405–38.

Kian-Thiebaut, Azadeh (1998) *Secularisation of Iran: A Doomed Failure? The Middle Class and the Making of Modern Iran* (Paris: Diffusion Peeters).

—— (1999) 'Political and Social Transformations in Post-Islamist Iran', *Middle East Report*, 212 (Fall): 12–16.

Miller, Carol, and Shahra Razavi (eds.) (1998) *Missionaries and Mandarins: Feminist Engagement with Development Institutions* (London: Intermediate Technology Publications in association with UNRISD).

Mir-Hosseini, Ziba (1999) *Islam and Gender: The Religious Debate in Contemporary Iran* (Princeton: Princeton University Press).

Moghissi, Hideh (1996) *Populism and Feminism in Iran* (Basingstoke: Macmillan).

—— (1999) *Feminism and Islamic Fundamentalism: The Limits of Postmodern Analysis* (London and New York: Zed Books).

Mohanty, C. T. (1991) 'Under Western Eyes: Feminist Scholarship and Colonial Discourses', in A. Mohanty and K. Davis (eds.), *Third World Women and the Politics of Feminism* (Bloomingdale, Ind.: Indiana University Press).

Molyneux, Maxine (1998) 'Analysing Women's Movements', in Cecile Jackson and Ruth Pearson (eds.), *Feminist Visions of Development: Gender Analysis and Policy* (London: Routledge).

—— (2001) 'Gender and Citizenship in Latin America: Historical and Contemporary Issues', in Maxine Molyneux (ed.), *Women's Movements in International Perspective: Latin America and Beyond* (London: ILAS/Palgrave).

Mossaffa, Nasrin (1996) *Mosharekat siasi zanan* (Tehran: Moaseseh chaap va entesharate vezarat omur kharejeh).

—— (2000) 'Mosharekat Zanan, Interview', *Hoghugh Zanan*, 17 (Sept.): 28–9.

Moti', Nahid (2000) 'Zanan moatal dar saf democracy', *Zanan*, 62 (Apr.): 37–8.

Najmabadi, Afsaneh (1998) 'Feminism in an Islamic Republic: Years of Hardship, Years of Growth', in Y. Haddad and J. Esposito (eds.), *Islam, Gender and Social Change* (Oxford: Oxford University Press).

—— (1999) 'Bartarihaye mard bar zan dar sokhan siasi nogerayi', *Zanan*, 52 (May): 24–8.

—— (2000a) 'Democracy faregh ast ya roshanfekran ghafel?', *Zanan*, 59 (Jan.): 40.

—— (2000b) '(Un)Veiling Feminism', *Social Text*, 18/3: 29–46.

Nakanishi, Hisae (1998) 'Power, Ideology, and Women's Consciousness in Postrevolutionary Iran', in H. Bodman and N. Tohidi (eds.), *Women in Muslim Societies: Diversity within Unity* (Boulder, Colo.: Westview).

Noorbakhsh, Safura (2000) 'Masaleh Mardiha na Masaleh zan', *Zanan*, 61 (Mar.): 64–5.

Paidar, Parvin (under the pen name of Mina Modares) (1981) 'Women and Shi'ism in Iran', *M/F: A Feminist Journal*, 6–7.

—— (under the pen name of Nahid Yeganeh) and Azar Tabari (eds.) (1982) *In the Shadow of Islam: Women's Movement in Iran* (London: Zed Press).

—— (under the pen name of Nahid Yeganeh) (1984) 'Jonbesh zanan dar Iran', *Nimeye Digar*, 2: 7–28.

—— (under the pen name of Nahid Yeganeh) (1993a) 'Women, Nationalism and Islam in Contemporary Political Discourses in Iran', *Feminist Review*, 44 (Summer).

—— (under the pen name of Nahid Yeganeh) (1993b) 'Zan va zananegi dar farhange dini va donyavi Iran', *Nashriyeh Bonyad pazhuheshhaye zanane Iran*, 3: 23–40.

—— (1995) *Women in the Political Process of Twentieth Century Iran* (Cambridge: Cambridge University Press).

—— (1996) 'Feminism and Islam in Iran', in Deniz Kandiyoti (ed.), *Gendering the Middle East* (London: I. B. Tauris).

—— (2001) *Gender of Democracy: The Encounter between Feminism and Reformism in Contemporary Iran* (Programme Paper 6; Geneva: UNRISD).

—— (under the pen name of Nahid Yeganeh) and Nikki Keddie (1986) 'Sexuality and Shi'i Social protest in Iran', in J. Cole and N. Keddie (eds.), *Shiism and Social Protest* (New Haven, Conn.: Yale University Press).

Perseram, Nalini (1994) 'Politicising the Feminine, Globalizing the Feminist', *Alternatives*, 19: 285–313.

Peyvand's Iran News (2000) 'Iranian Delegation in the UN Conference–Women 2000', (14 June).

Price, Masumeh (2000) 'Meeting Faeze: The Rise and Fall of a Talented Woman', www.iranian.com, 5 October.

Rahnavard, Zahra (1995) 'Zan, Eslam va Feminiasm', *Special Issue on Women's Studies, Foreign Policy Journal*, 9 (Summer).

Razavi, Shahra (2000) *Women in Contemporary Democratization* (Occasional Paper, 4; Geneva: UNRISD).

Rostami-Povey, Elahe (under the pen name of Maryam Poya) (1999) *Women, Work and Islamism: Ideology and Resistance in Iran* (London: Zed Books).

—— (2001) 'Feminist Contestations of Institutional Domains in Iran', *Feminist Review*, 69: 44–72.

Sanasarian, Eliz (1982) *The Women's Rights Movement in Iran* (New York: Praeger).

Schirazi, Asghar (1997) *The Constitution of Iran: Politics and the State in the Islamic Republic* (London: I. B. Tauris).

Sherkat, Shahla (2000) 'Sokhanrani dar conference Berlin', in Lili Farhadpour (ed.), *Zanane Berlin* (Tehran: Me'raj).

Tohidi, Nayereh (2000) 'Jensiyat, moderniyat va democracy', *Jens Dovom*, 3: 10–21, 4: 26–42.

—— (2001) 'The International Connections of Women's Movement in Iran in Iran and the Surrounding World', in N. Keddie and R. Matthee (eds.), *Interactions in Culture and Cultural Politics* (Seattle: University of Washington Press).

—— and H. Bodman (eds.) (1998) *Women in Muslim Societies: Diversity within Unity* (Boulder, Colo.: Westview).

UNDP (1999) *Human Development Report of the Islamic Republic of Iran* (Tehran: UNDP).

UNRISD (2000) *Gender Justice, Development and Rights: Substantiating Rights in a Disabling Environment* (Report of the UNRISD Workshop, New York, 3 June) (Geneva: UNRISD).

Vahdat, Farzin (2000) 'Post-Revolutionary Discourses of Mohammad Mojtahed Sahbestari and Mohsen Kadivar: Reconciling the Terms of Mediated Subjectivity', *Critique*, 16: 31–57.

Vakili, Valla (1996) *Debating Religion and Politics in Iran: The Political Thought of Abdolkarim Soroush* (New York: Council on Foreign Relations).

Vatandoust, Gholamreza (2000) 'President Khatami and the Sixth Majles: Prospects and Expectations', *Journal of Iranian Research and Analysis*, 16/1 (Apr., CIRA).

Yusofi Eshkevari, Hasan (2000*a*) 'Eslam eslahtalab Va jame'eh modern', *Iran Emruz* (Apr.): 7–11.

—— (2000*b*) 'Noandishi dini va kolligari darbareh zanan', *Zanan*, 62 (Apr.): 36–7.

The 'Devil's Deal': Women's Political Participation and Authoritarianism in Peru

Cecilia Blondet

Introduction

Peru provides a unique case for analyzing a series of questions and debates relating to the growing participation of women in national political and economic decision-making. During the last decade, under the undemocratic[1] regime of President Alberto Fujimori (1990–2000), a considerable number of women occupied senior public positions as executives, technocrats, and members of Parliament and advisors. The increased presence of women in public office contributed to a fine-tuning of existing legislation on domestic violence; the promulgation of an electoral quotas law designed to ensure the participation of women as political candidates; the development of reproductive health programmes; and the promotion of credit, training, and employment programmes for women from low-income sectors. Despite the prevailing climate of political authoritarianism, these advances seemed to signal that Peruvian women had finally secured their status as full citizens.

Fujimori's official line was that under his government women would be able 'to determine their own destinies'. However, his assertions have not been borne out by reality. Illiteracy, primarily a problem among women and the indigenous population, affects more than 25 per cent of rural women; adolescent pregnancy and alcoholism among young people have increased due to the lack of educational and employment opportunities; and the high drop-out rate in schools, combined with the poor quality of education, continues to be a serious problem. Large sectors of future generations will lack knowledge of computers and the Internet, with many unable even to perform elementary arithmetic. The manipulation of statistics by a government intent on total control and on retaining power indefinitely managed to conceal from Peruvian society, and from the world, the lack of development and persistent poverty affecting the majority of women in the country.

The persistence of inequality between different groups of women in Peru suggests two seminal questions regarding the importance and nature of women's participation in government:

1. Is the emergence of women in public life effective in promoting the rights of women and in making gender issues part of the national political agenda? To what extent is such promotion determined by the type of political regime and by the level of institutional development? In other words, is the mere presence of women in government desirable, even when they are primarily responding to the interests of an authoritarian, personalistic regime?

2. Do women constitute a discrete social group that can be represented as such? To what extent can 'women's interests' supercede ethnic, political, economic, and social differences?

This article addresses both of these questions, exploring the ways in which women from different social and political groups assumed national prominence during the last decade in Peru, becoming major social and political figures in the Fujimori dictatorship. It is argued here that the political interests of the all-powerful President led to greater contact with a wide range of professional women and social leaders whose interests overlapped with his. These women learned to operate within the confines of the authoritarian regime and indeed became a constituent part of it. In a political context characterized by disorder and weak institutions, they came to serve as important players. Their conduct in government, however, was far from democratic, honest or transparent. In addition to these women leaders, hundreds of thousands of women from the poorest sectors remained loyal to the President as long as they were given assurances on specific issues, such as food aid, clothing, schools, and as long as more general concerns about authority, law and order, and the stability of the country were addressed—issues highlighted in the propaganda of the Ministry of the Presidency[2] and perceived as vital to their children's future.

After briefly presenting the context in which the Fujimori regime emerged and consolidated its hold on power, the points of convergence and divergence between the government's goals and women's needs is analyzed in an attempt to understand the variety of political identities, behaviour and performance of different groups of women participating in public life. The conclusions consider the political challenges facing Peruvian women and men as they emerge from the turbulent decade of Fujimori's rule and assess the impact of women's political participation in a non-democratic context, highlighting the limitations of approaches based on an essentialist conception of women's interests.

The Political and Economic Context of the 1990s

Between 1989 and 1993 Peru was plunged into a profound and all-encompassing crisis: the economy experienced uncontrolled hyper-inflation and political authority all but collapsed as a consequence of the State's retrenchment and loss of legitimacy. In addition the country experienced the demise of the party system and a generalized social crisis caused by the brutal terrorist campaign of Shining Path guerrillas in the countryside and the cities, particularly Lima. Illicit drug trafficking on the part of entrenched organized criminal groups was widespread within the military and local structures of power. Other factors also contributed to the overall vulnerability, insecurity, disorder and anxiety that typified Peruvian life during this period. These included the country's isolation from the international economic system and a pervasive sense of mistrust towards the law that also manifested itself in social relations in general, contributing in turn to the further erosion of already fragile institutions. Daily life became untenable; motherhood, surrounded as it was by anxiety, was threatened by the uncertainty of an unknown future. While mothers were not the only people affected by the crisis, they felt particularly threatened by the almost complete absence of effective authority.

Elected for the first time in the democratic elections of 1990, Fujimori systematically set about re-asserting state control over national security and establishing order. Strategic alliances were established both domestically and internationally. Programmes of structural adjustment and state reform were implemented, resulting in economic stabilization and integration into the international economic community, together with pledges of support for the President by international officials and entrepreneurs. The United States government also lent its support in response to Peru's commitment to combat drug trafficking. Peruvians welcomed the stability and security thus achieved, expressing their gratitude to the President through sustained support of his administration. Fujimori's alliance with the armed forces and the intelligence service was consolidated following the 'self-coup' (*autogolpe*) of April 1992 and the subsequent capture of the main ringleaders of the Shining Path. These circumstances combined to create an extremely powerful executive branch, an executive that posed serious dangers to a weak and precarious democracy (Shifter, 2000).

The costs of economic stabilization, the restoration of state authority, and the pacification of the country were high. They resulted in: (1) the concentration and personalization of Presidential power; (2) corruption, blackmail, and threats, which were used as an instrument of social and political control; and (3) poverty, lack of independent public institutions, and the gradual erosion of the rule of law in Peru. All of this occurred with the implicit consent of President Fujimori's allies.[3]

The process of stabilization and the new domestic order was not based on the law or the strength of state institutions, but rather on the President himself. With the support of the armed forces and the national intelligence service, and thanks to a highly sophisticated control of the media, Fujimori appeared to be the very embodiment of order and stability. Dovetailing perfectly with the nation's sense of frailty, he became a trap from which the country found it hard to extricate itself. Whenever the President's popularity in public opinion polls waned, some event or other would send a shock wave through the country, and the President—stepping onto the scene with the firm hand of authority—would restore stability, as promised by the government's rhetoric.[4]

Within such a context, women—whether professionals or politicians in executive positions, or women who benefited from government assistance programmes—represented pieces in a chess game for Fujimori. Surveys conducted in December 1997 by the Institute of Peruvian Studies (IEP), found widespread public approval for women holding positions of power. Women in politics and in government in general were seen to perform their duties with integrity; specifically, they were viewed as being more honest, more dedicated to social issues and less authoritarian than men. Their presence therefore helped to reinforce the image of respect, order, stability and good governance necessary for the President to remain in power. Because their own interests were also at play, many women, independent of their ideological position, eulogized the President, attributing to him desirable qualities that were lacking in the government. Despite accusations of corruption—which were invariably minimized—they presented Fujimori as honest and socially concerned, emphasizing his populist practices. At the same time, they justified and defended the arbitrary and authoritarian measures that Peruvians had become accustomed to.

In addition to women leaders, mothers—whether from the highest or lowest socio-economic classes—were ideal pawns in Fujimori's political game. They expressed almost unshakeable gratitude to the President for having eradicated hyperinflation and terrorism and were therefore willing to forgive him almost anything. As one community kitchen manager stated months before Fujimori's final demise: 'the President is unresponsive to our concerns, not because he wants to be, but because he is uninformed, because no one lets him know what is happening to us . . . '.[5] It was not Fujimori, but rather those who surrounded him that were at fault.

Fujimori provided women with security and won them over with proactive measures and a discourse centred on issues of interest to them. Women, for their part, in what amounted to a cost-benefit calculation, decided to trust and support the President—perhaps because there was little to lose and much to gain from what he offered. The historic failure of Peruvian governments to address the problems of the poorest women favoured the acceptance of Fujimori's promises—finally it seemed that women were being addressed as citizens with rights. An additional factor was the long-standing culture of dependence on state assistance and clientelism, which reinforced subordination to the President. Poor women and rich women alike bought into the official rhetoric: women from the most prosperous sectors of society also suffered from subordination and discrimination, albeit in a different manner from poor women in the cities and rural areas (Barrig, 1998; Blondet, 1995). How did Fujimori manage to captivate and control women members of Congress, professionals, civil service officials and journalists? These women soon became his most vigorous supporters—as faithful and loyal as the women in the Shining Path's leadership who protected Abimael Guzmán up to the last moment before his arrest.

Women in the Fujimori Decade: A New Common Sense

Fujimori saw in women an attractive source of votes and the chance to enhance his international reputation under the banner of anti-*machismo* and equity. In order to consolidate their support he implemented a series of measures that specifically targeted different women's groups, affording them a level of attention never before seen. At the same time, through his Machiavellian handling of the media, Fujimori capitalized on major social changes that had occurred as a result of modernization, on the achievements of women's struggles at the national and international levels and on the fact that they were both willing and eager to enter the public sphere. This combination of factors ultimately gave rise to a new 'common sense' in Peruvian society regarding the numerous roles women play. This new perspective altered the views of society and of women themselves on politics and power and partly, at least, explains the phenomenon of women's political participation during the 1990s (Blondet, 1999).

The Current Situation of Women

Among the many changes undertaken in Peru since 1990, Fujimori opened the doors to women to participate in the public arena. The presence of women in official circles of power was conspicuous. Throughout the decade Fujimori's personal interest in appointing women to high positions and, on a larger scale, in addressing their problems, became clear. This was evident in the creation of new institutions and the promulgation of certain gender-targeted social policy measures.

One example was the group of eight women who headed different ministries, and the more than twenty female deputy ministers who served over the course of the decade, as well as the women heading high-level public agencies, such as the Consumer Protection Institute (INDECOPI); the Office for the Promotion of Peru (PROMPERU); the National Superintendency of Customs (SUNAD) and the Office of the Comptroller-General of the Republic; the credit development project for microenterprises (MIBANCO), and the State Reform Project, which in many instances was designed for and led by women. A woman served on the Constitutional Court; the Office of the Attorney General of the Nation was headed by a succession of women, and the former Attorney General headed the Public Ministry's Reform Commission. A gradual increase occurred in the number of women serving as judges and magistrates; a woman served as Peru's Ambassador to the Organization of American States, while another woman served as Ambassador to France; and for the first time in the nation's history, an Ombudswoman in charge of women's rights was appointed.

Between 1995 and 2000, thirteen of the 120 members of the national Congress (10.8 per cent) were women, of whom seven were from the governing party. In the Congress elected in 2000, as a result of the Quotas Law[6] passed in 1997, the number of female deputies increased to 26 (21.7 per cent). Despite the fact that men outnumbered women in Congress, the Bureau of the Congress was made up of two women and one man and, in the final term of the Fujimori government, by four women. In the municipalities, the increased participation of women was significant: in 1995, for example, the number of district councilwomen was 7 per cent, increasing to 24.8 per cent in 1998, following the promulgation of the Quotas Law (Blondet, 1999). In 1996 three top-level entities were created to address women's issues: the Ministry for the Advancement of Women and Human Development (PROMUDEH); the Women's Rights Division within the Office of the People's Ombudsman; and the Commission of Women, Human Development and Sports in the national Congress. Among the most important laws passed during the decade were the law against domestic violence, the law against rape, and the Quotas Law. In the 2001 elections, a woman campaigned for the presidency for the first time—running in a field of eight candidates—and finished among the top contenders.[7]

A New Common Sense

The will and interest of the President were clearly important factors in explaining the strong presence of women in politics. But other factors were also significant. One opinion poll on the participation of women in politics[8] indicated that approximately 70 per cent of the population believed that women's opportunities for choosing an occupation were equal to or better than those of men, and that women were on an equal footing with (60 per cent) or had an advantage over (9 per cent) men. This appeared to be part of a broader 'common sense' that women are capable of performing numerous roles, including those involving leadership positions at the highest levels.

While the favourable opinion of women was shared by both sexes, the fact that women were more likely to support a woman implied that women had greater confidence in their own abilities and were therefore more willing to demand rights and assume responsibilities. Interestingly, lower-income women have been most emphatic and optimistic in this regard. It seems that the experience these women gained in social and political organizations and trade unions over the last fifteen years was vital in building a self-image of efficiency, developing self-esteem and gaining confidence in their ability—and that of other women—to assume positions of public responsibility. A similar phenomenon occurred with women from middle and upper socioeconomic classes, who also had a highly favourable view of women's participation in politics and of the benefits this provided both for the country as a whole and for women in particular, believing that women's participation should increase. While suggestive differences emerge from a breakdown of the figures by social class or gender, opinion among young people was fairly uniform. Equality of opportunity appeared to be more internalized in this age group, although young women believed that women's participation should increase.

A particularly interesting indicator of the change that has occurred in society in recent decades is the widespread willingness of the electorate to vote for candidates to political office without regard to gender, something that would have been unthinkable years ago. For 72.5 per cent of Lima residents, a candidate's gender was of no importance—a sentiment shared by young men (80 per cent) and young women (75 per cent).[9] When the question related to specific offices, slightly more than 45 per cent of the population believed that either a man or a woman could serve as a member of Congress, minister, or district mayor. Among the remaining 55 per cent, opinion actually favoured women over men for those offices, with women once again more willing than men to see women serve in these positions. However, when it came to electing individuals to political positions such as that of President, 42 per cent believed a man should occupy the post; for provincial mayor, 26 per cent preferred a man, while 21 per cent preferred a woman; for Minister of the Economy, 28 per cent preferred a man, while 23 per cent preferred a woman. Overall, a preference existed for men—a situation that is not unique to Peru.[10]

For many people in Peru politics is something dirty, unfair, degrading, corrupt (or inclined to be corrupt), and unprincipled. While these are evidently generalizations, political action itself often reinforces opinions of this type. Unlike men, who are traditionally associated with professional politics, women involved in politics enjoy a favourable image. Is it possible that women could change traditional views by behaving differently in positions of power? Or could it be that in coming years, as the number of women in politics increases and as they gain experience and skill, they will be regarded similarly? For the moment, we can only hypothesize on the basis of the views reflected in the 1997 survey.

When male and female politicians were compared, women were considered more honest (64 per cent), more concerned about the poor (58 per cent), better administrators (49 per cent), more capable (23 per cent) and, most encouraging, women were perceived to be less authoritarian than men. In fact, despite the examples of authoritarian women during the Fujimori government, men were perceived as more authoritarian (62 per cent) than women (16.4 per cent). Among those interviewed, only those in the middle and upper socioeconomic classes viewed men as less authoritarian (43.5 per cent), while in the lower socioeconomic classes this figure was actually higher (69 per cent). Clearly, political culture at the end of the century is changing and women are occupying new positions in the national political imagination. As representatives they receive high marks for performance and more and more people appeared willing to support a female candidate. Contrary to the view that Peru has an exclusive, rigid and closed society, it is clear from the survey that despite the existence of racial and cultural discrimination and profound economic inequalities, significant examples of integration and gender tolerance exist. How did this new common sense regarding the participation of women in politics come about?

Women's Ascent to Power

One decisive element in building the new common sense and in women's attitudes towards power was the discourse and pressure emanating from international organizations. The United Nations World Conferences on Women were instrumental in placing the issues of discrimination and violence on the public agenda. They also formulated proposals to governments to incorporate into the political agenda issues that were previously considered to be private matters, of interest only to women. In addition, the women's movement played a key role: feminism skilfully and patiently encouraged women of widely differing social classes and from distinct backgrounds to employ the new language of rights and contributed to creating a favourable current of opinion regarding equality between men and women (Craske, 1999).

Peruvian women's experience in the public sphere is also of fundamental importance. In contrast to other junctures in the nation's history, when women contributed to politics by providing logistical support, today women have gained an awareness of power and public action. Their participation in different arenas and distinct types of organization has gradually transformed roles and models for women's action, bringing about changes in values, attitudes and political practices. In the 1930s and 1940s, for example, women from the *Aprista* and Communist parties played an important part in national political life, building parties, leading solidarity committees, caring for prisoners, dealing with complaints from those who had suffered persecution and exile—at the same time as raising and educating their children, most of whom would become activists in the future. All of these activities were essential to ensuring the survival of the parties. However, women and party leaders alike regarded this as part of women's normal work as mothers and wives. Their activism was seen more as a mother's duty, motherhood extending to politics. Yet most of these women did not seek to become leaders, nor did they compete with men for recognition and power. Belonging as they did to subordinate segments of the population (indigenous peoples, people of African or Chinese descent), they knew their place and remained within those confines, not questioning male hegemony.[11]

In the mid-1950s, during the country's belated and incomplete process of socio-economic modernization, a major change occurred in women's participation in politics and in women's perception of themselves as citizens with rights. Education, birth control, and entry into the labour market helped accelerate the process of emancipation for certain sectors of the female population, transforming their traditional roles and raising new questions concerning power. Toward the end of the 1960s, this phenomenon assumed a political expression in the competition for leadership among party activists. Dissatisfied with preparing meals, doing secretarial work, or selling newspapers, women sought to assume other positions in the party hierarchies. This period saw the birth of the first feminist groups, as well as the appearance of young women leaders in the political parties. At the same time, the massive enrolment of women in universities and higher education institutes during the 1970s led to a major presence of professional women in the labour market and in public life some twenty years later. Young professional women began to enter the country's political arena with apparent ease (Blondet and Montero, 1994).

As a result of the crisis of the 1980s, which prompted the creation of numerous women's social organizations, many women from lower-income sectors were able to learn the intricacies of local politics, to vote and be elected within their organizations. Many women assumed leadership roles on a metropolitan and even national scale. However, the general debacle that the country experienced toward the end of the 1980s interrupted this process, leaving women powerless in a context where politics was chaotic and lacking in legitimacy, much like the situation at the beginning of the present decade.

Educated, professional middle-class women of different generations, together with thousands of organized women from lower socioeconomic classes with experience as grassroots leaders, today constitute an important sector of women ready to enter the public arena and be called into action by the government. One characteristic common to female professionals, lower-income and young women is the *absence* of party ties and of significant partisan loyalties. Their commitment is rather to public action as a means of gaining recognition, distinguishing themselves, serving the community and achieving self-realization.

Without under-estimating the importance of the modernization process, the social movements of the 1980s, or the actions of international organizations, it would be true to say that a particularly favourable—albeit precarious—set of circumstances existed in Peru during the 1990s that accounts for the increased participation and visibility of women in the country's social and political life. These circumstances related directly to the particular interests of the President and to the national political context he engendered.

Presidential Interests

Throughout the decade, major decisions regarding national policy were made and implemented on the basis of the interests and decisions of the President.[12] The personalistic and centralist style—embodied by Fujimori ever since he was first elected—that typified Peruvian politics excluded other types of institutional mediation. Contributing to this were the weakening and delegitimisation of political parties, which failed to provide a channel for women's demands and interests, and a weak civil society, unable to express itself, much less effectively scrutinize the government's actions.

President Fujimori's personal decision to bring together certain sectors of powerful and lower-income women 'from above' can be viewed in a number of ways: as a mechanism for political manipulation of the female electorate, through strategies of selective and segmented inclusion; as an intelligent concession to international organizations that were pressuring governments to address gender issues; as a result of the fact that the President, due to his Japanese ancestry and working-class background, identified with sectors suffering the greatest discrimination; or as related to the fact that he trusted the honesty and loyalty of women and, in his highly personalised politics, believed that, as a direct consequence of the attention they gained, or based on a cost-benefit calculation, they would become his unconditional allies. These explanations are not mutually exclusive and all of these factors contributed to women gaining an undisputable presence in positions of power and influence—whether elected, or appointed from above—and to the new attention given to women's issues.

The Government's Point of Encounter with Women

The Fujimori regime welcomed into its fold women from social groups that had been structurally and historically disadvantaged, women whose interests and expectations had been ignored and who believed that the Fujimori regime held the key to fulfilling their needs. This was exemplified in both governmental discourse and practice and in the expectations of women from different socioeconomic groups. The government, for its part, conveyed an image of strength and employed a rhetoric that emphasized order and security. Individual effort, the value of property and competition were extolled; the importance of promoting the rights and opportunities of women as citizens was proclaimed; and democracy was interpreted as a set of actions culminating in tangible results.

In line with the rhetoric, the government's actions (highly targeted social programmes, public works, loans, titling, identity documents) and those of ad hoc public institutions dedicated to women's issues addressed women as individuals, rather than as groups, unions, or social organizations. Laws and social assistance programmes were not the result of negotiations, nor did they include institutional dialogue with collectives: rather, they were decisions handed down from above. Because of the ways in which they were presented, however, they were often viewed as a more efficient means of incorporating the claims of collective organizations, while—importantly—controlling the organizations themselves at the same time.

Women with numerous and wide-ranging unmet needs and few channels for participation constituted the social counterpart to governmental discourse and practice. For a wide range of reasons women felt themselves to be 'summoned' by the Fujimori regime. In addition to those who were directly involved in positions of power due to ideological affinity, there was a general willingness on the part of women in a variety of circumstances to support the regime. Surprisingly, women from both the upper socioeconomic classes and the poorest sectors—i.e., the extremes of society—viewed the rhetoric on order and security as the basis for supporting *Fujimorismo*. Middle-class women professionals and intellectuals were interested in influencing the social and political restructuring of the country, using existing channels and institutions to expand and ensure women's rights and thus empower other women to claim their rights. Others merely aspired to work, earn money and gain power—as professionals, public administration provided them with acceptable opportunities. Women from lower-income groups were brought together through targeted social policies: they were given direct assistance—nutrition, family planning, loans and social infrastructure (water and drainage systems, medical clinics, health centres, schools, community centres) and economic infrastructure (electricity, roads, small irrigation projects).

In addition, it appears that pragmatic calculations also encouraged women's political participation. In the 1980s organized women's groups played an important role, but were largely invisible, due to the influence and practices of a male-dominated party system that systematically blocked women's participation. In the 1990s, by contrast, women gained greater visibility, insofar as the traditional means of participation and political expression were delegitimised and unable to serve as instruments for representation. Politics ceased to be an attribute of parties and Fujimori—a political outsider—opened up opportunities. The weakness and absence of political parties— traditional male bastions of politics—played a key role in bringing women into the public sphere. The electorate lost confidence in the parties and their ability to mediate between the government and the people declined over the course of the decade—hence, the proliferation of independent players as a key feature of national politics. Women expanded their opportunities for action in tandem with decreased regulation and formality in the political scene and decreased confidence in typically male politics.

Women in the Political Arena: Major Differences

In the 1990s women arrived on the political scene in Peru and lost their fear of power. What implications did this have in terms of their political behaviour? Can it be said that the presence of women ensures women's rights? Does it ensure democracy? Based on their performance, can one speak of a new way of engaging in politics? Through consideration of specific cases this section examines the diversity of women's political behaviour.

Women Leaders from Lower Socio-Economic Groups

Lower-income women played a major role in Peru's May 2000 general elections. Some, perhaps a majority, supported the President's proposals and candidacy for re-election, albeit passively or opportunistically. In a rush to leave behind their community kitchen aprons, they opted instead to attend political meetings and receive free gifts or certificates of attendance. At the same time, a much smaller group of women leaders marched and protested under the banner of Women for Democracy[13] or of regional defence coalitions. These women were prepared to resist pressures and threats in order to oppose the growing popular support for an authoritarian regime that was using populist bribes to win a third term[14] without having made good on its previous promises.

When municipal elections were held in 1998 a similar phenomenon occurred, foreshadowing a more complex situation. Faced with the possibility of assuming a leading role in local politics, women leaders of so-called 'subsistence organizations'[15] fought amongst themselves and negotiated individually with the political parties for positions in local government, rather than agreeing common agendas to present their demands. Ultimately, they lost the capacity to represent their movements as well as their ability to guarantee the support of their own social constituencies. Despite the advantages provided by Quotas Law, women fared poorly in comparison with men in terms of garnering support to run as candidates and, subsequently, in the number of positions they gained and the functions they were assigned— particularly compared to what they might have achieved had they presented a unified front. The most skillful amongst them who managed to negotiate better positions within the municipal structures found that they were alone, without experience or the counsel of the priests, feminists, and politicians which they had become accustomed to during their time as social leaders.

There is little doubt that women created opportunities in public life, particularly within the local sphere. After decades of sustained work in subsistence organizations, today they represent an identifiable and, to a certain extent, recognized social force. Women heading these organizations learned to interact with each other, their husbands, local authorities and public officials and directors of social assistance programmes. They attended hundreds of training courses on leadership and self-esteem, classes on making pies or decorating dolls; they learned about raising guinea pigs, about vegetable gardens; about infant malnutrition and use of contraception, and so on. They also established links, though on a very unequal basis, with the political parties and with government.

However, despite this training and the extensive experience acquired, women social leaders have still not managed to connect effectively with the political structure. Is it possible or desirable to do so? Must they be united and have the same agenda? Clearly their demands and interests could have a greater social impact and achieve more effective results if they had a well-focused programme. However, it seems that those women who were elected and assumed local decision-making positions in municipalities occupy a no-man's land. They do not represent their grass-roots constituencies, which, far from applauding them, are often their harshest critics. Aside from the question of political positions favouring one party or another, these internal discrepancies are indicative of three core problems: the fragility of social institutions; the effective absence of a party system; and the nature of the authoritarian regime. In other words, it points to the weakness of once-powerful social organizations, which for various reasons became less unified, losing their common purpose and capacity to negotiate, as well as their political representativeness. Despite attempts on the part of feminist NGOs, the Church, and international cooperation, this type of association based on assistance and dependency was ultimately and inevitably colonized by the state for what were clearly clientelistic ends.[16]

In addition, although some women experienced a process of emancipation as community social leaders, they have not yet found a means of translating this experience into effective political leverage, due to their limited training and the prevailing nature of Peruvian politics. The absence of political parties has limited the channels for participation that could lead to a career in politics. Thus, although important in different local contexts, these women have been unable to capitalize politically on their ability to mobilize people.

Lastly, the authoritarian government was extremely astute in using its control of institutions, food aid, and resources such as basic staples and other products to gain the support of women who were recognized social leaders, taking advantage both of their experience and their status as institutional 'orphans'. The quid pro quo was straightforward: they would only be able to gain support for their community efforts and their own leadership if they joined the ranks of the government. These grass-roots leaders thus became caught up in a powerful political machine that afforded them a role in exchange for their autonomy.

How can this situation be explained? What factors were instrumental in blocking the ability of female social leaders to exert greater influence? Peru is a typical example of a post-conflict society and it is precisely within this context that the local crisis in women's leadership must be understood. In the late 1980s and early 1990s the terrorist activities of Shining Path, together with hyperinflation and drug trafficking produced a severe crisis that led to the loss of authority by the state, the collapse of the political system, the weakening of institutions, and social breakdown, anomie, and extreme fragmentation. While this situation affected all Peruvians, organized working-class women in the community kitchens, mothers' clubs, and the 'glass of milk' committees became a major target for different political interest groups. This was because their organizations were dynamic and appeared able to withstand the crisis and attacks from Shining Path, but also because hyperinflation attacked the domestic economy head on, leading in the most extreme cases to the near-collapse of the poorest households, particularly in the cities.

The crisis allowed organized women to gain a greater presence within their communities, recognition, and legitimacy. However, although conditions of poverty, violence, and social vulnerability brought women out of domestic isolation and propelled them into local public life, these same conditions subsequently provided the government with the means to co-opt and demobilize them during the period of reconstruction, once the armed conflict had been over-come and a degree of economic stability was achieved (Barrig, 1998; Blondet, 1996). Between 1989 and 1993 working-class women lead-ers and their popular organizations provided a safety net for those living in conditions of poverty and violence in poor neighbourhoods and remote communities, even though these movements were less articulated than they had been in the mid-1980s. It was only in the late 1990s that these movements suffered a decline. As a result of the violence, many NGOs withdrew from the poor neighbourhoods. Once the Shining Path had been disbanded, the Fujimori regime launched new programmes promoting microenterprises and individual initiat-ive, rejecting previous models based on social solidarity and collective action and advancing a new development rhetoric based on neo-liberalism and structural adjustment. Women leaders, accustomed to an organizational rather than a market-based logic, made great efforts to understand the new development paradigm, but with lim-ited success. At the grass-roots level, women were captivated by the promise of having their own businesses and in exchange for miniscule loans they disengaged themselves from social organizations based on principles of collective solidarity. During this process, a new genera-tion of leaders of grass-roots organizations emerged, displacing the majority of the historic leaders. They were generally younger, more urban, and more educated, with expectations of becoming involved with donor agencies, rather than with NGOs as had been the previ-ous pattern. They also had a more individualistic modus operandi, establishing links with the state based around new concepts such as credit and business. 'Politics' was viewed with certain distaste.

One of the most pernicious and enduring effects of the violence was the loss of security, the internalized fear of unrest and instability and lack of trust between people. Added to this was the new offi-cial discourse based on individualism and personal achievement; on reinstituting the principle of authority by centralizing power in the person of the President (and the armed forces, under the command of the National Intelligence Service); and on the disappearance of autonomous institutions. The country that rose from the ashes was disorganized, mistrustful, disorderly, and depoliticized.

In 1995, Peru re-elected Fujimori by a massive margin. That same year women social leaders took stock. Collective action had provided them with little success in recent years and many were prompted to participate in municipal elections, competing for positions as city councilors on the slates of the centre-left parties (since the left had disappeared from the electoral map). However, their success was relative, in part because of the characteristics of the women leaders themselves, but also because of the lack of electoral clout and influence of the parties that welcomed them into their ranks. Thus, in contests for city council positions, they achieved only 8.7 per cent of all the available city council positions. By 1998, when new municipal elections were held, women from subsistence organizations had learnt that the most effective tactics were pragmatic ones. Hence many women leaders volunteered for whichever slate offered the best material and electoral prospects, reasoning that the ends justified the means. The slates of 'independent' candidates grew rapidly and were quickly absorbed by the governing party. When it came to political control, whoever had the tiger by the tail got the whole tiger, so to speak. These women were provided with opportunities and united with a populist project that demanded no clarity on policy matters. Instead they were given a simple script, which they quickly made their own, willingly joining the governing ranks.

In the most recent elections, as a result of the Quotas Law and the willingness of many women to enter politics, the percentage of women city councillors increased to 24 per cent, with the number of women holding such office increasing from 940 in 1995, to 2,258, in 1998—a significant gain (Blondet, 1999). And although social organizations may criticize their counterparts on the city councils, it is clear that they have much greater room for manœuvre and greater influence now that these women occupy decision-making positions in municipal government.

Over the last two decades, the dynamism of social organizations such as the mothers' clubs, the community kitchens, and the 'glass of milk' committees meant it became important to control this sector of organized women for electoral purposes. However, despite the advantages enjoyed by these leaders, many factors hindered their ability to negotiate, making many of them prisoners to irresistible offers and subjecting them to a pragmatic government rhetoric of welfare assistance. Only President Fujimori was presented as able to provide economic security and the prospects for individual economic betterment (through small business initiatives and the like). The notions of security, order, and stability that the Fujimori government manipulated during the entire campaign turned out to be the key to winning over this female majority.

Must we believe, then, that things are black and white? Or are they relative? Perhaps 'ambiguity' is a category that needs to be

considered when analysing the political behaviour of women leaders from lower income groups. Not all are either Fujimoristas or
democrats. They have learnt from pragmatic politics and have their
own agendas, which they negotiate with numerous other players.
This process of political organization and participation is a relatively new phenomenon and the learning process is slow and difficult.
The enormous efforts women have been making towards emancipation and claiming their rights will only yield results in the medium
term. Adjustments and fluctuations are symptomatic of the current context, in which fixed identities are more a problem than
a virtue.

'Beauties', Politicians, and 'Asians': Women in the Fujimori Government

Those women who came to hold positions of power and influence in
the 1990s were a very heterogeneous group, marked by significant
social, ideological, and generational differences. The interests that
brought them to power were wide-ranging, and while some related
directly to the President and enjoyed his trust, others were quite
ambivalent towards the government. Very close to the President
was a small group of young professional women from upper class
families—lawyers, business managers, bankers, or journalists who
had been educated and resided abroad, returning only later to Peru,
thanks to the Fujimori government. Hence their loyalty to the
President, whom they considered to be Peru's saviour until the
myth was dispelled.[17] They had no party affiliation or experience
and formed part of the new bureaucracy as officials, advisers, or consultants to the chief executive. Their legitimacy in power was based
on a liberal discourse promoting modernization and on their close
ties with international organizations, which allowed them to mobilize and channel resources of all kinds. In addition to accompanying
the President to Beijing, they took charge of organizing 'road shows'
on Peru in business circles throughout the world, selling shares of
the Peruvian telecommunications company on the New York financial market, and developing loan programmes for the poor, based
on schemes promoted in India and Bangladesh. At the same time,
they were able to bring new people into the fold and build bridges
with certain circles of feminist intellectuals, specialists on women's
issues, and leaders in the social movements. This dual link with international organizations and with women meant they were extremely
useful to the regime, at the same time as ensuring that they would
not be entirely dependent on the President.

Close to the President, along with the 'beauties', were those women politicians who were his unconditional supporters. Due to ethnic affinities, family relationships, or friendships forged over many years, they formed part of the President's inner circle and held high positions in Parliament or in the state apparatus. Dependent on the President, their tenure was ensured only to the extent that Fujimori remained in power and they remained close to him, as evidenced by events in the wake of Fujimori's flight to Japan in 2000. Within this group, two sectors can be distinguished. On the one hand, there were university-educated congresswomen, ministers, and vice-ministers from middle-class families who were career civil service employees, lawyers, engineers, and well-qualified teachers, women in technical fields, and professionals. In power these women were by turns authoritarian and obsequious.[18] Another group of women loyal to the President were those of Asian descent, of which little is known other than that they were placed in key (though second-tier) positions. They were reported to be the 'eyes and ears' of the President. Given the extent of their responsibilities and their low profile, these appear to have been the women in whom the President came to place the greatest trust. They did not necessarily play a public role: unlike the first group, they were reserved and austere. They never played the seduction game, nor did they aspire to public leadership. They were, in effect, the regime's stewards.

In addition to the 'beauties', politicians, and 'Asians' who were Fujimori's unconditional supporters, a secondary tier of power included a group of women intellectuals, professionals, and specialists on gender issues, many of them feminists from NGOs. This group lacked a close relationship or ties to the President and in the last two years of the regime many women from this sector joined social movements promoting democracy, although few participated in the 2001 elections as parliamentary candidates. It appears that disillusionment has turned them away from political activity, at least for the time being.

The creation of women's institutions in the executive and legislative branches opened up opportunities for many professional women, female lawyers and, particularly, social scientists, who were personally called upon to participate in designing, formulating, and implementing social policy, as well as in the presentation and processing of laws and in preparing operational plans for these institutions. Anxious not to isolate themselves from decision-making and to ensure that new policies were of as high a quality as possible, benefiting the majority of women, these feminist intellectuals and professionals were prepared to collaborate with the government. They provided advice and served as a link between the leaders from lower income groups and congresswomen, women officials, and, eventually, the business sector. They significantly contributed to energizing local leadership and women in the provinces and in the poor sections of Lima.

There were also women members of the opposition in Parliament, lawyers, economists, and journalists, who had no relation at all to the President. Given the differences among them in terms of interests, background, and education, they did not represent a politically unified group. Some had a very low profile, while others were major figures in the opposition, for example Lourdes Flores Nano, presidential candidate in 2001; Anel Townsend, the young congresswoman known for her audacity in criticizing the Fujimori government; and Beatriz Merino, a prominent lawyer who headed the first Congressional Commission of Women.[19]

Lastly, in the public sphere, women judges and prosecutors represented an important sector. The continual constitutional violations and lapses in the administration of justice on the part of politicians and government officials were reined in by a group of honest and upright women judges in the Public Prosecutor's Office and the judicial branch. Their defence of democracy and human rights often made them the object of dismissals, transfers, or disciplinary measures.[20]

Women, Our Sisters

Did this heterogeneous group of powerful women come to act as a feminine bloc, allied in the face of conflict and confrontation? Can they be viewed as a sisterhood transcending ethnic, social, and political differences? The present section deals with two major issues that emerge from the case of Peru and which merit examination: (1) essentialism, that is, women's 'natural' altruism and inclination to seek consensus and co-operation; and (2) the political representation of women as a discrete group (Dietz, 1994; Mouffe, 1993; Scott, forthcoming). These two issues are explored through the analysis of three examples from Peru that highlight the challenges of women's participation in present-day Latin American politics.

The Domestic Violence Law

In 1993, the Domestic Violence Law was passed in Peru, followed, in 1996, by the modification of a series of its articles. On both occasions women in the national Congress played a vital role, providing the bill with the support of feminist organizations and debating the subsequent passage of the law. All the women deputies in Congress voted in favour of the proposal, regardless of party differences. Domestic violence was seen as an issue of direct interest to women and served as a model for encouraging an essentialist feminist discourse that was riddled with stereotypes: women were portrayed as capable of leaving aside political, ideological, and any other differences in order to reach consensus. Public comments on this question became increasingly frequent and enthusiastic, to the point that it was claimed that certain gains were achieved *because* women were involved, because women did not fight, because they resolved their differences and conflicts by talking, and because they acted differently in politics. In other words, women make good legislators because they are essentially peaceful and consensus-building, unlike men, who are combative, aggressive, competitive, and incapable of agreeing. Over time this rhetoric of female virtuousness has undoubtedly been played down. However, Fujimoristas—those who disseminated the 'official rhetoric' and had an overwhelming presence in the media—are today more than ever making indiscriminate use of such arguments in order to present themselves as champions of democracy, the feminist frontline, and national unity. This caricature of feminine perfection could prove counterproductive to the processes of democratization by strengthening historical forms of discrimination against women.

The Quotas Law
When the bill for the Quotas Law was presented to Congress in December 1997, the situation was less than ideal. While female opposition deputies and some members of the governing party supported the proposal as a first step towards addressing discrimination against women in politics, other Fujimoristas openly opposed such legislation. The debate was strident and those opposing the bill questioned the entire notion of positive discrimination, arguing that it was little more than thinly disguised paternalism. Female deputies who supported Fujimori and opposed the bill felt threatened by the proposal and argued strongly against it. However, in the subsequent congressional session, to the surprise of the assembled Congress, the Quotas bill was presented anew and this time every member of the governing party gave it their vote. The bill was passed unanimously. Rather than evidencing a collective change of heart by those deputies opposed to affirmative action, the explanation for the volte-face lay in the instructions issued by President Fujimori that his party vote in favour of the bill. Fujimori viewed women as a tempting prize to capture and control in the political marketplace and measures of this nature, together with clientelistic policies targeting women of lower

socio-economic levels, would allow him to consolidate and increase his support base.

It could be argued that affirmative action is an issue of interest to women in general, even though women might—and, as it turned out, did—have differing positions. However, the outcome depended not on the merits of the argument, but rather on the decision and interests of the hegemonic leader. Those women in the governing bloc who disagreed with the measure chose loyalty to the President rather than opting to raise their voice in discontent. Evidently not every issue related to women is of equal interest to women in positions of power.

In addition, another dilemma arose related to the Quotas Law itself. Clearly some politicians aimed to implement pro-women legislation and social policy in order to 'capture' target groups for their own political benefit. However, while the intention was to win women's commitment to the government in exchange for favours granted, in practice the Quotas Law held out the possibility in the medium term of *reducing* the government's control over women. This issue provoked extensive debate and controversy among different feminist groups in Peru. Some believed that the Quotas Law should be embraced as an opportunity to expand women's political presence and democratize gender relations, despite their differences with the Fujimori regime. However, others argued that this type of tactical alliance with the government would harm democracy and strengthen authoritarianism in the long run. This second group also doubted whether the Quotas Law would ensure greater changes, given the political context in which it was to operate. Furthermore, by 1998 the openly authoritarian nature of the regime was evident and political polarization became acute. The government increasingly dominated state institutions and imposed its decisions in an arbitrary fashion, while opposition forces were fighting hard to maintain minimal democratic spaces. Hence the need for Fujimoristas to act as a monolithic bloc—any breach was seen as disloyalty to their leader. This context also explained the insistence by democratic feminists on keeping their distance from the government, even when its proposals seemed favourable to women's interests in general.

The Bureau of Congress

After the fraudulent elections of May 2000, Fujimori ignored the protests of broad sectors of Peruvian society and national and domestic political opinion and began his third term, appointing a new Bureau of Congress.[21] For the first time in the history of Peru—and indeed in Latin America—the leadership of Congress was placed in the hands of four women. The decision was made by the President himself who ignored hierarchy and constitutional protocol, personally appointing them following a series of disagreements among the different groups within his political bloc.

By this point the monolithic front of the regime had begun to crumble and the struggles for power amongst the leaders of each subgroup within the Fujimori camp became increasingly manifest. The President chose to place women from each faction in leadership positions within the unicameral Congress, rather than the men who were the leaders of the different factions. This was done in order to mediate conflicts, teach the contentious men a lesson, and show the public that his political bloc was united, while at the same time signalling that women deputies sought consensus and avoided divisive politics. The four women accepted the challenge and played the communion-and-sisterhood game. The government delighted in escaping its internal crisis so creatively, extolling the virtues of 'the ladies', as they were repeatedly referred to, and praising the fact that Peru had a modern, forward-looking government that recognized the value of women. At the same time, however, the differences between women in the public sphere also became more profound. Women who were not Fujimori supporters—and many that were—showed no great enthusiasm for this initiative. Instead, a sense of discomfort or open discontent was evident in the responses of many female commentators. Women's groups who were increasingly organized and united in defence of democracy, for example, within Women for Democracy (MUDE), were indignant at the blatant manipulation of gender-based discourse by the government. Yet views differed: some feminists, albeit a minority, said they would rather have four authoritarian women leading Congress than four authoritarian men. However, in effect the four women were engaged in little more than a pragmatic and mutually beneficial exchange: by suppressing their differences and presenting themselves as united they gained an important foothold which they hoped could be capitalized on at a later date.

Fujimori was forced to cut short his third term after just two months following the exposure of corruption, arms trafficking, and blackmail by high-level government officials in order to ensure a majority in Congress and the regime's hold on power.[22] A group of members of Parliament disassociated themselves from the governing party, leaving Fujimori's supporters in the minority in Congress for the first time in ten years. A motion censuring the Bureau of Congress once again revealed the complex relations between women in the governing bloc and those from the democratic sectors, as

well as between women and men. Political interests, rather than
gender, determined the vote. There was not a single woman from the
opposition forces who even considered voting against censure simply
because those in question were four women. The authoritarian
regime in Peru disintegrated with unexpected speed at the end of 2000
as Fujimori fled the country and his top adviser, Vladimir Montesinos,
became a fugitive from justice. Within only a few months, Peruvians were party to open disputes among the Fujimoristas, with the
Fujimori women (paradoxically) in the forefront. During Fujimori's
tenure they had been united by their pledges of loyalty to the President. By the 2001 elections only a few female stalwarts remained loyal
to Fujimori's legacy in an attempt to gain an electoral advantage
against male Fujimoristas.

More 'Fujimorista' than Fujimori

Recent events in Peru indicate that women are no more honest
than men. However, they do seem to have a different relation to
power, immorality, and corruption. While Fujimorista women were
responsible for anti-democratic behaviour, as yet no video has surfaced showing women receiving bribes. Might this be because women
gave their loyalty to the President for free? Female members of the
regime showed a surprising degree of loyalty and deference to their
leader, strenuously defending and protecting him to the point of the
absurd. Their sectarianism echoes that of the fanatical women who
surrounded Abimael Guzmán, or nuns dedicated to preserving their
order, rather than emancipated women who enter politics of their own
free will. When Fujimori announced his desire to leave the presidency,
Luz Salgado, a member of Parliament from the Cambio 90-Nueva
Mayoría party, remarked to the press:

The President has taken a major step with a detachment that is an example
to all politicians. I do not believe that any leader would have given up power
so easily, particularly with the solid support obtained in the first and second
electoral rounds. He is a model of dignity and courage that is a source of
pride to all Peruvians.

When Fujimori had already fled to Japan, Martha Chavez, a
former congressional Chair and a Fujimorista member of Parliament,
observed: 'These days, I have learned to appreciate him even more.
Such is his nobility that he has asked us not to risk ourselves on his
behalf. Not only the cowardly, but also the brave are fleeing.' These
women were capable of justifying some of the worst acts in pursuit
of supposedly honourable ends, accepting cover-ups and violations

of the law by Fujimori in the name of 'the national interest'. Once Fujimori fled they were disoriented and abandoned, anxiously awaiting his return. Finally, when it was clear he was not coming back, they forgave him. Four female Fujimoristas headed the Cambio 90-Nueva Mayoría party's parliamentary slate of candidates in the 2001 elections, continuing to lead the defence of Fujimori's legacy.

Conclusions at the End of the Battle[23]

Before drawing the lessons of the Peruvian case, it is worth remembering the principal factors that conditioned the experience of women's participation in the Fujimori government:

The Culture of Fear

In the face of hyperinflation, terrorism, and the crisis in leadership and authority that occurred at the beginning of the decade, people lost any sense of security and found in Fujimori a protector deserving of unconditional devotion. The country's physical and moral exhaustion, together with the desire to restore order and stability at any cost, laid the foundation for the citizenry's subordination and surrender to the executive branch. The threat that the country would return to a state of chaos became a powerful weapon of social control.

Weak State Institutions

Although always a feature of Peruvian reality, the accelerated weakening of state institutions in recent decades allowed for the concentration and personalization of power, the absence of procedures and controls, the volatility of political loyalties and identities and the fragmentation and disorganization of society. Without political parties, unions, or legitimate social organizations, power was personalized and concentrated in the hands of the governing bloc.

Distorted Commitment of Elite Groups

Business people, the armed forces, and international organizations constituted a tripod on which the highest levels of government rested and on which the politics of 'anti-politics'[24] and 'efficient governance' were developed. In addition to individual, personal interests, these sectors shared a commitment to the regime guided by a sense patriotism, national reconstruction, and salvation. Well-targeted blackmail and pressure tactics mitigated any criticisms business people and army officers might have of the government. International organizations, for their part, endorsed a 'democratically elected' government that met the minimum acceptable requirements and had an exemplary record in regard to debt repayment.

Peru, a Complex, Culturally Diverse and Unequal Country

Vast educational and ethnic differences in access and communication, together with poverty and unequal distribution of wealth, pose serious problems in terms of social inclusion and equity. For a third of Peruvian citizens, justice, government, and public and private institutions are remote. Their active participation in society, and their ability to call rulers to account, is thus severely limited.

In the light of these factors, then, how are we to understand the experience of women's participation in the Fujimori regime throughout the 1990s? Irrespective of their political affiliation, did their presence in politics contribute to improving the situation of women's rights? Were all women equally represented by a political regime in which some women occupied a key role? It is argued here that the mere fact that a growing number of women occupy positions of power and influence has positive implications for women in general, independent of what they actually achieve when in power. Women's participation in public life becomes, in effect, part of the new common sense. In symbolic terms, new models for womanhood are being constructed and disseminated which include women's active participation in power and public decision-making. In this way, womanhood is expanded, diversified, and enriched. The old stereotypes, which place women in traditional roles of serving their husbands, the people, or the country, are being broken down. Today, the range of participation of women, who often assume highly controversial positions, signals their virtues and defects, demonstrating the differences that exist among women and the different positions women adopt in exercising power, helping to end the myth of an idyllic 'sisterhood of women'. In practical terms, the presence of women in power during the 1990s generated a discussion of issues and bills related to the promotion of women's rights. The passage of many of the current laws benefiting women would have been unthinkable had it not been for the presence of women in different positions of power. Curiously, this interest in women's issues was not associated with feminist or democratic affiliations. This is precisely because it was understood that women are a heterogeneous group.

The Peruvian experience underlines the fact that the social, economic, and political context is fundamental to an analysis of the effects of women's political participation. It is understandable that governments wish to gain the votes of female citizens, since it legitimizes their rule. Women represent a major and relatively new form of electoral capital and are of particular interest to political players. In a democratic government, political parties act as channels for expressing and mediating citizens' interests; social institutions, in turn, act as venues for articulating particular interests and exerting pressure in order to draw attention to their demands and bring social issues into the political arena. Authoritarian regimes, however, limit the independence of institutions and of individuals connected with them, blocking the citizenry's channels of expression or using them to channel people's choices in a given direction. The case of former President Fujimori is paradigmatic in this respect.

Fujimori colonized social organizations and relegated them to a strictly welfarist role, leaving them totally submissive and dependent. When women from subsistence organizations sought to express their concerns, they were excluded from food distribution or subjected to blackmail and intense pressure. Women in power repeated the same scheme: as long as Congresswomen or women officials meekly accepted the government's proposals and kept any differences of opinion to themselves, they were part of the power apparatus; any questioning of the word of the President was rejected and admonished. The women who supported Fujimori were incapable of engaging in a discussion of the government's policies or questioning procedures and results.

The history of Fujimorismo and indeed of women's experience in the Shining Path indicates that authoritarian proposals do not ensure the free participation of women in the public arena. They can serve as pawns used to carry out orders and expand the base of support, or can even participate in the highest levels of decision-making, albeit always subordinate to the leader, to whom they are expected to show total loyalty. Such patterns serve to strengthen machismo by offering a false and distorted rhetoric on gender. However, it should also be noted that women played a major role in the new 'civil society' which emerged during the last year of Fujimori's rule and which contributed to his downfall. Along with young students, intellectuals, artists, and human rights advocates, they became the leaders of the democratic resistance movement.

Today it remains essential to analyse critically supposedly absolute truths and identities, notions of total sisterhood, unconditional loyalties, and lofty rhetoric. The 'woman half' of humanity, as the Spanish writer Elena Soriano calls the female 50 per cent, is not homogeneous and is not representable as such. The category of 'women' does not supersede ethnic, social, political, and economic differences. It is impossible to speak on behalf of all women because women have many faces: black or indigenous; illiterates and professionals; those from Quispillacta, in Ayacucho, or from Prague and Cairo; Quechua, gypsies, or Maoris; democrats, authoritarians, or indifferents, and the list goes on. Thus, women *qua* women do not constitute a group—they can be as varied as the different interests that bring them together, that motivate them to coordinate demands and elect representatives. We should guard against the resurgence of 'womanism' as a political rallying call.

It is true that certain issues that have traditionally been marginalized from the political agenda tend to unite women. Among these are family violence, reproductive health, and related issues concerning women's sexuality: abortion, motherhood, and the raising of children, all of which are considered to limit women's participation in the labour market and their economic emancipation. Other 'women's issues' are those relating to discrimination against women in decision-making roles and, more generally, the unequal access and treatment women experience because they are women. Lastly, poverty, although not unique to women, generates conditions of inequality and discrimination which are intrinsically linked to patriarchal principles.

The structural position of women in Peru has undoubtedly improved since the mid-twentieth century. Although the process of socio-economic modernization was staggered and incomplete, it did allow women to obtain an education, access to health and family planning services, paid work, and the vote. The crisis of the 1980s and 1990s also broke down traditional patterns and forced women to seek paid work in order to contribute to family budgets. In addition, the women's movement created a favourable climate of public opinion regarding equality between men and women. International organizations—intent on making issues of non-discrimination and non-violence part of the public debate—formulated proposals for governments, issues that previously had been considered to be private matters.

However, more immediate issues influenced the new role of women in Peru. Two elements stand out here: women themselves who, today, are highly qualified and competitive; and the encouragement provided by the last two governments, which showed a concerted interest in installing women in positions of power. This contributed to expanding the images and models of what a woman in power should and could do. Beyond the question of whether or not one agrees with the political positions adopted by these women, their presence and leadership role in national politics undoubtedly had a significant impact. Finally, we should ask to what extent the Quotas Law, other changes in legislation, and policies targeting women actually improved the lives of ordinary women in Peru? This question is central to evaluating the effects of women's presence in politics and policies targeting women. Why does the number of women suffering extreme poverty continue to be so high despite legislative changes and targeted policies? In short, can the dichotomy—so common in Latin America—between formal democracy and substantive democracy be overcome?

References

Barrig, Maruja (1998) 'Female Leadership, Violence and Citizenship in Peru', in Jane S. Jaquette and Sharon L. Wolchik (eds.), *Women and Democracy: Latin America and Central Eastern Europe* (Baltimore: John Hopkins University Press).

Blondet, Cecilia (1995) 'Out of the Kitchen and onto the Streets: Women's Activism in Peru', in Amrita Basu and C. Elizabeth McGrory (eds.), *The Challenge of Local Feminism: Women's Movements in Global Perspectives* (Boulder, Colo.: Westview).

——(1996) *In No-Man's Land: Poor Women's Organizations and Political Violence in Lima's Neighborhoods* (Los Angeles: UCLA Latin American Center Publication).

——(1999) *Las mujeres y la política en la década de Fujimori* (Working Document, 109, Sociology and Politics Series, 26, Lima: IEP).

——and Carmen Montero (1994) *La situación de la mujer en el Perú, 1980–1994* (Working Document, 68, Gender Studies Series, 1, Lima: IEP).

Craske, Nikki (1999) *Women and Politics in Latin America* (Oxford: Polity Press).

Degregori, Carlos Iván (2000) La década de la antipolítica: auge y huida de Alberto Fujimori y Vladimiro Montesinos (Ideología y política, 13) (Lima: IEP).

Dietz, Mary G. (1994) 'Ciudadanía con cara feminista: El problema con el pensamiento maternal', *Debate Feminista*, 10, pp. 45–65.

Mouffe, Chantal (1993) 'Feminismo, ciudadanía y política democrática radical', *Debate Feminista*, 7, pp. 3–22.

Scott, Joan W. (forthcoming) 'Género y representación paritaria. "La querelle des femmes" a finales del siglo XX', *Debate Feminista*.

Shifter, Michael (2000) '*The Fault Line of Latin American Democracy*', Inter-American Development Bank, Washington, paper presented at the conference: Politics Matter: A Dialogue of Women Political Leaders.

In and Against the Party: Women's Representation and Constituency-Building in Uganda and South Africa

Anne Marie Goetz and Shireen Hassim

This chapter explores women's relationship to political parties in two African countries: South Africa and Uganda. It seeks to examine processes and consequences of transitions from authoritarianism on women's political participation in representative institutions. The relationship of women to parties and politics in the transition and post-transition periods, and the conditions under which, in Waylen's terms, 'conventional political activity' is reconstituted remain relatively under-explored in Third World feminist literature (Waylen, 1994: 340). Given that access to and power within representative institutions is the key to the advancement of the policy demands of social groups, this is a troubling lacuna. Although the experiences of South Africa and Uganda are divergent, the stress each government has put on representation as a key response to women's movement demands for democratization begs examination of the extent to which women in political office can facilitate changes in gender power relations.

We take as our starting point the rich base of research that explores women's organization and experiences of national liberation movements. The following pattern appears to typify their engagement: a period of male-defined and identified political activity; women's challenge for inclusion, often accompanying a triumphalist phase of women's participation as guerrillas and activists; and finally a post-independence period in which women are 'redomesticated'—when their domestic roles are reasserted and political power returns to being the domain of men.[1] The pattern suggests that the transition from liberation movement to party-in-government impacts negatively on women's participation and representation, and that the reshaping of gender relations which might have accompanied exile and warfare are eroded when politics is 'normalized'. In many African post-liberation contexts, there has also been a closing of spaces in which to build constituencies autonomous from the ruling party, to articulate oppositional positions, and from which to hold elected leaders accountable. In many cases, localized opposition tends to be centred on powerful traditional authorities exercising powers inherited from the earlier (colonial) era, with little interest in the democratic values of equality that would allow for the insertion of women's demands.

A common means for restoring some of this lost political space is to create a 'national machinery' for women, a set of special mechanisms and institutions inside government to channel women's political and policy demands. While these have functioned to create bureaucratic representation for women, they have generally failed to act as institutional openings for *feminist* politics, understood here as the struggle against inequalities in power between women and men. In part this is because such structures were created in contexts where women's organizations have been institutionally and politically weak. Even where women's organizations have tried to use opportunities presented by the national machineries (e.g. in Zimbabwe), they have found both ideological and institutional resistance to be an intractable barrier to the advancement of a feminist agenda.

Women in South Africa and Uganda appear to have escaped this pattern, at least in part. One of the characteristics of transitions from authoritarianism in both South Africa and Uganda has been a dramatic increase in the numbers of women in national and local politics, in numbers far outstripping most Western democracies. In both countries, the ruling political parties have recognized the importance of women as a political constituency and the importance of women's representation as a key component of deepening citizen participation. However, it is the differences, rather than the similarities, between the two polities that are instructive for an understanding of the institutional forms that could facilitate more effective representation of women's political and economic interests, and the political conditions under which representational politics might be used to advance a feminist agenda. In South Africa, women appear to have made the transition from liberation to party-competitive politics in the mould of Western representative democracy in such a way as to retain and indeed consolidate feminist policy ambitions. In Uganda, where a 'no-party' system is in operation, the political gains women have made have been impressive, yet highly dependent on presidential patronage. This chapter explores these differences by looking at variations in the relative autonomy of the women's movement in relation to the liberation governments in the two countries. We also explore the implications for women's impact in politics of various other features of the political infrastructure: the framework for political competition, the discourses used for including marginalized groups, and the degree of internal democracy in the main political parties.

We can posit two reasons for the lack of attention to a gendered analysis of political parties in newly democratizing countries. First, women's movements around the world have shown a marked ambivalence towards political parties, because they are often seen as (and often are) 'old boys' clubs' which are indifferent to women's political ambitions. Feminist research in the West confirms this profound male bias in political parties (for instance, Lovenduski and Norris, 1993), a bias which is exacerbated by the way the rules of political competition—including electoral systems, means of campaigning, and party funding, recruitment, and leadership systems—can exclude women (Rule, 1987; Haase-Dubosc, 2000; Vengroff and Fugiero, 2000). Not only have parties been hostile to supporting women and promoting their interests, but in authoritarian systems, parties have actively repressed women's autonomous associational life in the interests of co-opting women to the legitimation projects of the single ruling party. These experiences produce a profound mistrust of parties and politics and a tendency to seek disengagement from the state and from politics (Tripp, 1994). This has obvious implications for women's capacities to carry through the political gains they make in a liberation struggle into changes in political institutions in order to facilitate better representation of their interests (Jaquette and Wolchik, 1998).

Second, in many developing countries, parties may be too weakly institutionalized to provide the democratic internal rules which can give women sufficient purchase to exert leverage and make demands for inclusion. In many developing country contexts, particularly in authoritarian states, parties may be such blatantly hollow vehicles for kleptocratic families or ethnic groups, lacking any but the flimsiest organizational structures, decision-making processes, and ideologies, that there is simply nothing there for women to engage with. There may be no discernible party platform, if politics is a matter of appealing to ascriptive loyalties rather than broad ideas and programmes. Party systems, and the ruling party, may be insufficiently institutionalized for women to begin to start challenging rules which exclude women—simply because there are no firm rules and rights, only patronage systems and favours. Alternatively, where a military or theocratic power structure bolsters ruling parties, there is little scope for women's engagement because the rules of these institutions explicitly deny women's right of participation.

Women's ambivalence towards political parties and politics produces what Waylen calls the dilemma of:

autonomy versus integration. Should women's movements work with the new institutions and parties and risk being co-opted and losing autonomy, or should they remain outside, preserving their independence but risking marginalisation and loss of influence as power shifts toward the political parties? No definitive answer has emerged. (1994: 339–40)

But for most women's movements in Africa, there is little choice about whether to work with political parties. Liberation movements—precursors to parties—have been the primary vehicles for women's political participation. In the post-liberation period, whether they institutionalize as parties, as in South Africa, or cling to the more amorphous 'movement' form, as in Uganda, they remain the central mechanism for channelling political demands. Rarely are women activists—or oppositional social movements in general—able to build a successful movement outside the ruling party, and where they do it is against enormous resistance from the party. As Hope Chigudu and Wilfred Tichagwa ask 'Do [women] have an alternative power base [to the party]? Would they survive if they relied solely on the alternative power base? To both questions the answer is probably no!!' (1995: 2). But parties have not been comfortable homes for women activists. As the two case studies below show, internal democracy and responsiveness have been difficult to create in both Uganda's National Resistance Movement (NRM) and South Africa's African National Congress (ANC). Political parties in Africa, as elsewhere, have been male-dominated institutions, and liberationist discourses and agendas do not automatically challenge sexist biases.

This situation poses a number of dilemmas for women activists in South Africa and Uganda. How can *feminists* gain access to influential positions within the party and within Parliament? How do feminists within political parties balance the often contesting aims of women's advancement and party loyalty? How can women's movements mitigate the perverse consequences of demands for greater representation of women in elected office: in particular, the emergence of elite women leaders with relations of dependency to parties rather than to constituencies of women? This chapter addresses these questions by examining the strategies and discourses used by the women's movements in Uganda and South Africa for inclusion in the dominant parties. We assess the effectiveness of the effort to increase numbers of women in politics in terms of its impact on gender equity in parties, and in national policies.

We also consider how features of party and state organization can affect the capacity of the women's movement to sustain a relationship of solidarity with women politicians which at the same time includes demands for accountability to a female constituency. Equally import-ant is the extent to which these moments of transition can be used by women to recruit support from *men* who support substantive equal-ity within the party. We are also concerned with the extent to which *feminists* find spaces within these parties through processes in which women's demand for representation (understood as descriptive rep-resentation) can allow for the emergence of women politicians who have a feminist agenda. From this point of view, the tendency in the literature to consider descriptive and substantive representation of women as different kinds of strategies is misleading;[2] rather, the 'minimal' demand for a numerical increase in women's representa-tion can become the grounds upon which a deeper struggle may be fought.

South Africa

The 'success story' of the South African women's movement in the transition to democracy is by now a familiar one to feminist scholars and activists. Between 1990 and 1996, women activists were able to demand a place at the multi-party negotiating table, and use that place successfully to advance a number of claims: increased polit-ical representation, a constitutional clause on equality supported by a further clause legitimating affirmative action, and an array of institutions inside and outside the state to promote and safe-guard the implementation of these principles in both the public and the private sectors. The election of a 'critical mass' of women into the National Assembly in 1994 indicated that women activists—and political parties—had taken the need for representation seriously. Furthermore, the record number of women MPs selected for Cabinet positions, four (of twenty-seven Ministers) in 1994, and eight (of twenty-nine Ministers) in 1999, suggested a concern with qualitat-ive representation. By the end of the first democratic Parliament in 1999, path-breaking legislation had been passed in several areas of concern to gender activists.

What accounts for these gains in the early 1990s? Analysts have emphasized the role of the women's movement in driving a feminist agenda (Meintjes, 1996; Cock, 1997). Yet, by the 1990s, women's organizations which had occupied a central role in mass struggles during the mid-1980s were in decline. Their leadership core had been decimated during two states of emergency, and their energies had been diverted from organizing women *per se* to keeping alive the United Democratic Front, a coalition of anti-apartheid organizations. In exile, the ANC Women's Section had made huge advances in gaining formal recognition within the liberation movement for women's increased participation and representation, but still had little power in the movement's decision-making structures. Feminism—defined in its broadest terms as the struggle for gender equality—had a contested status in the liberation movement, and within women's organizations, activists were wary about using the term to describe their aims or their ideology. The conditions for the women's movement's success in the transitional period were by no means apparent in 1990.

These considerations suggest the need for a more precise explanation. Three key factors are apparent. First, the nature of opportunities for the women's movement to pursue its claims at a national political level changed dramatically with the beginning of a process of negotiated transition to democracy. The successful demand by women activists for places at the highest levels of decision-making has been well documented elsewhere (Albertyn, 1995; Meintjes, 1996). Here we wish to draw attention to a more neglected aspect, the ways in which the *nature* of that transition—the creation of a liberal democratic state in which citizenship was accorded irrespective of race, gender, or ethnicity—unexpectedly offered opportunities for feminists to articulate an agenda of equality that unseated nationalist formulations of women's political roles. Second, the creation of the Women's National Coalition (WNC) provided the strategic and organizational basis for women activists to articulate claims for inclusion and representation *independent* of the ANC. Furthermore, it was able to exert pressure for accountability in a way that could not be contained by the internal mechanisms of party discipline and loyalty. Its autonomy was therefore a primary source of strength.

However, as a coalition of organizations that were vastly different in organizational content and ideological orientation, the WNC itself had to contain its demands within a manageable framework—in this case, relatively minimal demands for representation within a liberal democratic state. Radical constitutional demands such as the inclusion of a socio-economic rights clause, and recognition of women's reproductive rights, were pursued more successfully *within* the ANC than within the women's movement. Nevertheless, this strategy worked primarily because of a third factor, the slower process

of internal transformation of decision-making processes and representational structures to include women that had taken place within
the ANC over the course of a decade.

From Nationalism to Citizenship Rights: Women's Demands for Inclusion in the Transition Process

As Waylen (1994) has pointed out, the form of transition is important
to the outcomes of women's politics. In South Africa, the negotiated
transition, involving consensus among the major political parties
and liberation movements, produced a rights-based discourse that
opened a space for women activists to extend feminist conceptions of
democracy. There was an inherent tension in constitutional debates
about democracy: on the one hand, the liberal notion of equality had
considerable attraction as a framework within which to supersede
apartheid's race-based mechanisms for organizing political representation. Democratic mechanisms needed to be found to ensure that
ethnic mobilization was not carried over (and reinstitutionalized)
into democratic South Africa. On the other hand, the ANC was an
organization with a strong socialist component; for large elements
of its supporters it was synonymous with an anti-capitalist, anti-
liberal struggle. Indeed, the process of transition itself was seen by
some members as a 'sellout' of the revolutionary ideals of the movement (Adler and Webster, 1995). Through its alliance with the trade
union movement (and in its role as the political arm of the workers' struggle) the movement was acutely aware of the class conflicts
that shattered racial unity. The use of a liberal discourse—and particularly the stress on *rights*—was therefore by no means an easy
one. The transition was not a revolutionary victory, but a carefully
worked-out compromise in which the ANC had to balance the need
for 'peace' with its commitment to social justice.

Within this debate, 'women' came to occupy a peculiar status as
the proving ground for the extent to which the new order would be
inclusive, participatory, and permeable to socially excluded groups.
Responsiveness to this constituency was thus assured, at least in
the short term. The fact that many of the demands of women—
political inclusion, a strong national machinery, an equality clause,
etc.—could be *relatively* easily accommodated within the crafting of
democratic institutions facilitated this political process.

The shift away from discourses of nationalism was highly significant for feminist activists. Feminist activists and scholars had long
been concerned about the constraints of nationalism on women's
political agency, even within the liberation movement (Walker, 1990;

Charman *et al.*, 1991; Horn, 1991; Hassim, 1993). Women's struggles were treated as subordinate to and defined by the larger national struggle, women's roles were confined to a narrow spectrum of movement activities based on stereotypical assumptions about women's interests and capabilities, and feminism was delegitimized as a model of liberation. The undermining of nationalism in the transition, however, occurred less because of feminist interventions than from the recognition by the major negotiating parties of the dangers of right-wing nationalism to the establishment of a stable, democratic, and unitary state.[3] If the idea that the primary mechanism of political mobilization and organization centred on ethnic affiliation were to be institutionalized, it would open the door to both right-wing Afrikaner and Zulu claims to some degree of special power in the new order or possibly even of special territorial control. In the event, women delegates to the Multiparty Negotiating Process, bolstered from outside by the Women's National Coalition and the Rural Women's Movement, were successful in ensuring that the constitutional clause on the status of customary law was subject to the clause on gender equality. However, as Mbatha and Goldblatt point out, the nature and extent to which rights to culture would be subject to rights to equality was not clearly spelt out (1999: 102).[4]

Citizenship, broadly conceived, displaced nationalism as the new political ideal and the political language through which the aspirations of subordinate groups were expressed. Within this framework, women were able to articulate claims for strong equality. Citizenship offered a more enabling framework because the rights-based discourses that accompanied it allowed for the use of feminist mobilizing language of women's power and autonomy. Unlike nationalism, citizenship as articulated by the ANC during the transition placed emphasis on the individual-in-community rather than primarily on the community. While some political parties wanted to limit citizenship to formal equality and political rights, the strong ANC tradition of social justice was hard to override.[5] As even women within the National Party and Democratic Party conceded, a strong emphasis on the individual would not allow for the creation of programmes and strategies to overcome the historical imbalances of gender relations and of apartheid: the predominance of women among the dispossessed rural populations, the legacies of inequalities in access to education, employment, and control over land. On the other hand, the notion of 'community' had long been criticized in South Africa for its tendency to elevate the concerns of the elite within the community over those of the politically weak (Thornton and Ramphele, 1988). From a feminist perspective, as Yuval Davis (1997) has shown, an emphasis on community (or 'nation') hides inequalities *within* the nation, particularly those of gender.

Because the ANC itself conceived of citizenship in substantial rather than formalistic terms, the new discourse allowed for women to place themselves at centre as the marker of whether the elite-driven negotiated transition would be inclusive of poor and excluded people. By the time the constitutional negotiations began, women's organizations had already debated the nature of mechanisms in the state and processes in civil society that would be conducive to advancing gender equality. Gender activists pushed hard for socio-economic rights and reproductive rights, and establishing a constitutional basis for affirmative action and for a widened notion of social citizenship. These ideas gained broader political legitimacy when the Women's Charter for Effective Equality was finalized in 1994, after considerable debate within the Women's National Coalition.

'We've Got the Future Looking at Us': Finding an Organizational Form for a Fragile Constituency

In order to push for an expanded notion of democracy, however, women activists needed an organizational base. The form of the transition—pacts, roundtables, and negotiating fora—privileged those groups who were organized, could claim constituencies, and who could send representatives to such discussions. However, it was by no means clear that women were organized, a constituency, or had formal leaders. There had been little public space since the early 1980s for the emergence of an independent women's movement. Experienced women activists inside the country had located the UDF as their political home, while in exile women's struggles were inextricably tied to the ANC. In 1990, when the ANC was unbanned, women's organizations that had existed under the banner of the UDF voluntarily disbanded and their members were encouraged to join the ANC Women's League (although not without considerable debate). Yet, long experience of activism within the ANC had taught that there were limits to the party's responsiveness to demands for women's emancipation. In an immediate illustration of these limits, the Women's League failed at the 1990 Congress to get agreement for a quota of positions on the National Executive Committee (NEC) for women, the movement's highest body.[6] It was to be a salutary lesson; as Secretary-General of the League, Baleka Kgositsile, pointed out, 'we've got the future looking at us... It showed that we have to prepare, educate and organize at a grassroots level... It also proved that even when you are promised support from senior leadership, it doesn't mean that you will get it' (*Speak*, 1991). The Women's League began to debate a broader platform from which it could articulate its demands—one that went beyond the ANC.

The impetus for the formation of the Women's National Coalition in April 1992 was inadvertently provided by political parties: in the first round of negotiations, not one women was included in any party's negotiating team—not even that of the ANC. This exclusion—and apparent disdain for a decades-long struggle for representation of women—provided a common ground of protest for women from opposing political parties. Within the ANC, the demand for inclusion 'was a strategic thing ... It was about finding common women's issues to make inroads into other political parties. It broadened the mass base—by including women who would support feminism but may not support the ANC—and got support for a progressive women's agenda'.[7]

The Women's National Coalition was not a product of the organic development of the women's movement but a strategic and opportunistic[8] intervention by women activists frustrated with the pace and nature of institutional transformation within the ANC and concerned about their exclusion from decision-making in the new political system. The organizational base of the WNC remained relatively weak, largely because the widely divergent interests and ideologies of its members precluded the development of a cohesive grass-roots structure. To compound this problem, no substantial organizational consolidation could take place in the context of a rapid and demanding process of national-level political negotiation. Despite this, the value of a coalition instead of women's wings of particular political parties was that the WNC was able to claim a broad constituency across party and race lines, and it was able to mobilize women within political parties to exert internal pressure on their party leaderships. The WNC's claim to speak on behalf of a wide range of organizations—backed up by its extensive membership list—gave it political clout and made it difficult to dismiss. This synergy between expertise—both political and technical—and political authority was not feasible for any single women's organization to effect.

The WNC's Women's Charter of Equality was intended to be both a mobilizing and educating tool, as well as a concrete set of demands to be used at the level of national politics. This strategy provided a constituency-linked basis for interventions in the rights discourses that were emerging in national debates. The WNC articulated the need for gender representation, and broadened it beyond the liberation movements. It brought the notion of gender equality into the mainstream of public discourse and placed it at the heart of the discussions about the values that were to underpin the new democracy. Although it operated on a limited mandate, it exposed the extent to which, despite all the formal commitments by parties such as the ANC, parties failed *even in their own limited terms* to acknowledge women's citizenship rights. The WNC was able to exploit this credibility gap to question the very terms on which the new democracy was being negotiated.

There is no doubt that, thin as the ANC's commitment to gender equality was, it assumed the political high ground here. This was in large measure due to the slow but important changes that had been taking place within the movement in the 1980s. This period saw significant institutional transformation forced in part by the rapid increase in the number of assertive young women activists in exile after 1976. Women's demands for greater power and relative autonomy within the movement resulted in an increase in the number of women representatives of the movement at international fora and a restructured relationship between the Women's Section and the National Executive Committee. The debate over how autonomy was to be understood in the movement loosened the rigid centralized control within the movement.[9] Several policy statements were issued by the ANC during the 1980s that recognized the need for gender equality and for the organization and participation of women. From the late 1980s, when the movement began to plan for a post-apartheid future by debating appropriate policies in a range of sectors, women were better placed to consider how government policy could address the needs of women. Women's demands inside the movement revealed the internal political culture of the ANC as a contested terrain, where the terms in which debate was conducted, the nature of what was 'political', and the accepted hierarchies of 'voice' and authority were disrupted. The process of shifting, disrupting, and reconstructing *inside the liberation movement* laid the basis for a radically new perspective on democracy and gender equality in the 1990s.

The outcome of these processes, even those statements of intent that may be considered 'rhetorical', had knock-on effects on other parties represented within the Women's National Coalition, because they raised the political stakes of gender sensitivity. The most obvious measure of this sensitivity was the extent of women's representation in the different parties. The involvement of women's sections of political parties was the key to the success of the WNC. However limited in power and scope, these structures had access to the negotiators in ways that non-party women's organizations did not, and women party activists had strong career interests in ensuring the involvement of women in national political processes. They were also more skilled at utilizing the technical expertise of lawyers and academics, recognizing the need for concrete alternatives to be offered at the negotiations. The success of the WNC in influencing the constitution-making process and the institutional design of the post-apartheid state was thus dependent on its link to political parties and not just on the strength of the women's movement external to the parties. While the broad range of affiliates provided an important sense of a constituency, it masked the central role played by a small number of feminist activists whose skills had been honed within political parties (and particularly within the ANC) and whose primary target was male decision-makers within parties.[10]

Into the State: From 'Making History' to Making Policy

It was no surprise that, for these women, the natural progression in the period of consolidation was not to stay in NGOs and civil society, but to move into elected and bureaucratic positions within the state. The increase in women MPs was due to the choice of an electoral system based on a proportional representation with party lists. The choice of the PR system was dictated by non-gender considerations: the need to provide incentives for minorities to pursue political mobilization within the formal political system as well as to encourage larger political parties to seek support outside of their traditional constituencies.[11] Gender activists in the ANC welcomed the opportunity the PR system offered to override traditional sentiments against women's election, particularly in combination with the ANC's voluntary adoption of a 30 per cent quota for women candidates on its list.[12] So effective is this combination of a PR system with quotas of women candidates that the PR component in local government elections has been increased from 40 per cent in 1996 (with the remaining 60 per cent of councillors elected through direct ward representation) to 50 per cent in the 2000 elections.[13]

Despite this success, the difficulties of working in a male-dominated terrain,[14] the extra burdens of committee work on the relatively few women MPs, and a deepening rift between women MPs and women's organizations worried many activists. In one of the first studies conducted on the experience of women MPs, Hannah Britton (1997) found high levels of stress and suggested that many women MPs might not stand for election again.[15] As ANC MP Thenjiwe Mtintso points out, 'the quota was seen as a double-edged sword: providing opportunities but also adding burdens for women representatives' (1999: 53). Mtintso's own research, conducted in the latter part of the first Parliament, found that women MPs had overcome some of the cultural and institutional constraints on their participation. MPs she interviewed reported greater confidence, support, and commitment as a result of experience with the technical processes (Mtintso, 1999: 56). She reports that the women 'developed excitement and confidence when tracing what could be attributable to their own participation and contribution. She can proudly say at the end, "this is mine. I did it for this country, for myself and for the women"' (Mtintso, 1999: 57).

The cultural and institutional difficulties described above had real impacts on the effectiveness of women MPs. While political parties, particularly the ANC, trumpeted the large number of women in Parliament, their underlying ethos was that party loyalty, rather than loyalty to constituencies such as women, was primary. Women MPs were in any case not all committed to feminist ideals, and under party leadership pressure and belittling of the importance of gender,[16] many did not identify openly with feminist agendas. The establishment of a multi-party women's caucus (the Parliamentary Women's Group) failed to provide either a support structure or a lobbying point for women MPs. The ANC Women's Caucus, by contrast, acted as the key pressure point within Parliament, along with the Joint Standing Committee on the Improvement of the Quality of Life and Status of Women.[17] Suzanne Vos, an Inkatha Freedom Party MP, comments that male dominance and patronage inhibits the articulation of feminism.

There is no doubt that the PR/list system ensures that all politicians must remain popular with (mostly male) party bosses to survive. Male leadership also invariably selects which women are promoted within party structures and within parliament. They decide who sits on what committee and who gets speaking time in the House, on what and when... Survival instincts triumph... Men are the game, they control the game. (Vos, 1999: 108–9)

These constraints made it difficult for feminist MPs to define strategies for legislative intervention. However, the Joint Standing Committee on the Quality of Life and Status of Women, under the experienced chair of Pregs Govender,[18] established an institutional form within which to identify a set of legislative priorities and begin to lobby for policy changes. Three far-reaching pieces of legislation were passed in the first term. The Termination of Pregnancy Act of 1996 provides women with access to abortion under broader and more favourable conditions than previously. The Domestic Violence Act of 1998 provides protection against abuse for people who are in domestic relationships, regardless of the specific nature of the

relationship (i.e. whether marital, homosexual, or family relationships). The Maintenance Act of 1998 substantially improves the
position of mothers dependent on maintenance from former partners.
In addition, a number of policy programmes, such as free health care
for pregnant women and children, are explicitly directed at improving women's position (Parliament of South Africa, 1999). However,
the three pieces of legislation were only placed on the parliamentary
calendar in 1999, the last year of the first Parliament, and only after
high-level lobbying by the ANC Women's Caucus with the support of
progressive men MPs, including, by some accounts, President Mbeki.
The legislation then had to be 'fast-tracked' through the National
Assembly so that the first Parliament would be seen to be concerned
with gender equality as a substantive issue.

In the first five years of democracy the national machinery for
women has not been very influential in setting the policy agenda
(Albertyn 1999). Lack of resources, institutional resistance, and, not
least, the reluctance of the leadership in the Office of the Status
of Women to challenge openly the ruling party, undermined the
effectiveness of the government machinery (Hassim, 1999). Unlike
Uganda, however, in South Africa this tendency in the bureaucratic
sphere was countered by the strong core of feminists in Parliament
and in civil society, which in many cases bypassed the machinery
to ensure legislative and policy change. As Albertyn *et al.* argue,
' "gender sensitive" women and men holding diverse positions of
power and influence in state institutions were far more important in
ensuring that gender issues were placed on the policy agenda' (1999:
149). In particular, they found that the ability of feminist politicians
to lobby successfully within the ruling party, and their networking
capacities outside of government, outweighed the role of structures
such as the Office on the Status of Women.

However, even these capacities and networks were limited. Despite
their numbers and their presence in the highest fora of Parliament,
women Cabinet Ministers were unable to question or even facilitate debate within the ruling party on key areas of government
policy. During the first Parliament, the ANC shifted from a redistributive Reconstruction and Development Programme (the RDP, the
party's election manifesto in 1994) to a policy of fiscal constraint (the
Growth, Employment and Redistribution policy, GEAR). This shift
removed the enabling discursive environment within which women's
policy demands could be articulated. The RDP had been drafted
with extensive participation of women in the ANC, and provided
detailed proposals for the integration of gender into most sectors
of government policy. The shift away from the RDP represented

in some measure both a less participatory approach to policy formulation and the narrowing of decision-making in the policy arena to an elite within government. 'Cabinet loyalty' precluded open opposition to the new macroeconomic policy that, arguably, dramatically constrained the government's ability to implement effectively policies outlined in the RDP, many of which required increasing expenditure. In part this was a consequence of the decision by the presidency and the ministry of finance to place the macroeconomic framework outside of party debate and make it a 'non-negotiable' aspect of ANC policy. The weak response of women MPs (and most male MPs) to this centralization and hierarchization reflects the extent to which a PR system can undermine both internal party accountability as well as accountability to voter constituencies.

By the end of the first term of Parliament, the issue of accountability of women MPs to the women's movement began to resurface at meetings and conferences, with some activists even questioning whether a reform of the much-vaunted PR system was required to allow for stronger accountability to voters rather than parties (Gender Advocacy Programme, 2000).

Institutionalizing Representation: Political Parties Post-1994

With the advent of representative democracy, experienced feminist activists turned to Parliament as the new terrain of struggle. This opened questions of how electoral politics, institutional restructuring (of Parliament as well as party), and constituency/interest group mobilization could be made to work in women's interests. Although the *number* of women in Parliament was significant, reshaping legislative priorities and reform measures was the work of *feminists*, MPs with a political commitment to gender equality. The weakness of the multi-party structure for women parliamentarians revealed the shallowness of common interest among women from different parties.

Aside from the ANC, parties lacked a history of internal party struggle around equality. Gender work in the Democratic Party, for example, tended to be focused externally; inside the party the mainstreaming approach led to the effective invisibility of issues of gender equality. In the New National Party, the women's structure has not moved beyond its traditional role of tea parties and fundraising to raise issues of power inside the party. Neither the Democratic Party nor the New National Party have women's caucuses in Parliament. As a result, women in the ANC take the lead on issues of gender equality in Parliament, while other parties are reactive and sometimes resentful of the perceived dominance of the ANC MPs.[19]

But even within the ANC, the form of party institutionalization has not always been conducive to the articulation of feminist claims. Centralist elements within the party have been strengthened as power within the party has increasingly come to be a stepping stone to power within the government. The ANC's Deployment Committee makes key decisions on which senior members of the party will be moved into key posts such as provincial premiers, mayors, and heads of parastatal organizations. The leadership of the movement is able to use the PR electoral system to shift MPs around according to party leadership dictates.[20] In this more constrained party context, women MPs and ministers might find it difficult to articulate policy positions that differ sharply from those of the party leadership. The tendency of the PR system to favour accountability to the party rather than to particular constituencies may hamper rather than facilitate the development of substantive representation over descriptive representation in the long term.

One avenue through which internal party accountability to its women supporters might be pursued is through its women's section—the ANC Women's League (Kemp *et al.*, 1995). The League has automatic representation on the ANC's highest decision-making body, and has the formal responsibility of representing women within the party. However, aside from the brief period of the WNC when the League articulated a strong feminist position, it has not managed to break free of its 'tea-making' role. Despite the fact that the League's president, Winnie Madikizela-Mandela, is an outspoken critic of the ANC's leadership (on issues other than gender), the League has not taken a consistent position on gender issues or assumed any leadership role in the women's movement. The League's long period of exile hindered the development of an organized constituency among women, and after 1994 it put very little energy into building branches and consolidating its membership base. In 1995, young feminists who were frustrated with the internal difficulties within the League resigned their membership of key positions and put their energies into the party as a whole. Within a very short space of time, the League returned to its more familiar role as auxiliary to the party, having little capacity to offer political leadership within the women's movement.

The failures of the League, as well as the women's sections within other parties, highlight the vacuum that can be created when institutional channels for representation of women's interests within political parties are weak. Without feminist-driven women's sections within parties, women representatives can be overburdened with the multiple tasks of committee work, party responsibilities, and gender activism and may lack a sense of direct accountability to women supporters of the party. Even where women politicians might take seriously their representative roles—as the first cohort of women in the South African Parliament did—the task of *building* constituencies cannot be done by individuals.

One long-term positive outcome of struggles for political representation is that political parties are being forced to consider women as an important voting constituency. Research conducted by the Commission on Gender Equality prior to the 1999 election showed that all parties had identified women as 'voting populations' (Seedat and Kimani, 1999: 140). Parties emphasized the need to recruit women and to increase women's participation in party structures, not least because women form the majority of supporters of the two largest political parties in the country (CGE and PWG, 1999: 177). The Democratic Party's audit of party membership indicates that 40 per cent of its branch chairpersons and 33 per cent of its local councillors are women (CGE and PWG, 1999: 102), although only 18 per cent of its MPs are women. The party's leading feminist, Dene Smuts argues that this shows that quotas are unnecessary: 'it's automatic. If there is a good candidate, she will be elected. People do not think twice about it now' (CGE and PWG, 1999: 102). The United Democratic Movement and the New National Party are also opposed to quotas, with the UDM arguing that quotas are 'an insult to women' (Gender Advocacy Programme, 2000: 16).

Long-Term Effectiveness: Party–Movement Linkages

The Women's National Coalition did not survive the transition. Despite expectations that it would continue to act as the umbrella body for the women's movement, the external rationale for uniting a diverse and ideologically fractured organization no longer existed. Debates in the Coalition after 1994 emphasized the need for a structure that was autonomous of political parties, and it was decided that women who represented political parties could no longer hold office in the Coalition. This proved to be an ill-considered decision; the Coalition deprived itself of its driving force and its link to national politics. In the absence of experienced political leadership, it struggled to define a new role as a civil society watchdog. The nature of civil society itself changed as NGOs became more stratified, specialized, and professionalized in order to meet the demands of a participatory policy process set up by the ANC government (Hassim, 1999).

Despite the strong efforts by the parliamentary committee on women to develop linkages between women MPs and women's organizations around specific areas of policy (Parliament of South Africa, 1999), the sense of purposeful and united action that had characterized the early 1990s now seems absent. For some commentators, engaging with the state had led to a demobilization of civil society (Ginsburg, 1996; Meer, 1999). However, it is simplistic to read demobilization into the decline of the WNC. While the idea of a national constituency of women with a clear set of demands may no longer exist, a disaggregated and issue-based women's movement appears to have taken its place. Towards the end of the first five years of democratic government, women's issue-based networks were either defending the gains that had been won or challenging the government's position on key policy issues. Among these are the New Women's Movement's campaign against the child maintenance grant proposals of the Department of Welfare (Hassim, 1999), the Reproductive Rights Alliance's successful defence in the High Court of the Termination of Pregnancy Act, and the Network Against Violence Against Women's ongoing campaign for better legislation and policy in the Ministry of Justice.

However, an over-reliance on feminists within the party has many limitations. As Vos (1999) has pointed out, they are hostage to a hierarchical and male-dominated party where the gender ticket is not the route to party power. In Cabinet they are bound by loyalty and are dependent on the leadership for their ministerial positions. These concerns are heightened by indications that the 'consolidation' phase of democratization in South Africa is characterized by the increasing centralization of power within the presidency (Marais, 1998), and by a seeming attack on the role of Parliament and particularly the committee system which is the key forum through which executive accountability is measured. The degree of robust debate in Parliament and the public sphere suggests that there is no fundamental threat to democracy, but the tendency of central party leadership to reassert control indicates a weakening of the ANC's internal democracy.

In this context the weakness of the WNC has had consequences for the depth and quality of representation. Key NGOs and even the Commission on Gender Equality are in danger of becoming new avenues for party advancement rather than avenues for bottom–up articulation of policy needs or constituencies to which parties must be accountable.[21] Parties—The Party (ANC)—remain dominant even in civil society. These concerns highlight the need for greater and deeper constituency-building within and outside the party. As Dahlerup (1986) has suggested, feminists are most effective in the representative arena when there is a constituency outside the state both to hold them to account as well as to provide them with a power base so that they are not speaking as individuals but truly as *representatives*. The South African case suggests that, without moral and political pressure from outside Parliament, there is a danger that women MPs are unable (or increasingly unwilling) to represent adequately the various interests of women. Without strong mechanisms inside and outside political parties for upholding accountability, the danger always exists that representation carries little power to advance the agenda of gender equality.

Uganda

Ethnic conflict and neo-patrimonial authoritarianism has been a dominant characteristic of post-independence politics in Uganda. Unlike South Africa, Uganda had no mass nationalist or liberation struggle through which to forge a cross-sectarian emancipatory project. The main political parties—the Catholic and Southern Uganda-based Democratic Party (DP), and the Protestant and Northern Uganda-based Uganda People's Congress (UPC)—have never transcended exclusionary ethnic politics. The National Resistance Movement (NRM), in power since it won the 1981–6 guerrilla war, has responded to this sectarianism and the poor record of party politics not by beginning a process of democratizing parties, but by forbidding their engagement in electoral processes (without banning them outright[22]), and promising a new approach to organizing political participation, free of parties.

The NRM has made a strategic appeal to the most visible and well-funded part of the Ugandan women's movement—namely, the urban feminist groups and women's development NGOs—to support the spirit of 'neutralising ethnicity' through no-party politics (Muhereza and Otim, 1997). The NRM recognized that women as a constituency, in spite of great differences between women, could be constructed as a non-sectarian political grouping, and was therefore of use in building non-ethnic models of citizenship and political participation. This is one reason why women have been directly courted by and recruited to Museveni's legitimation project, and the result is their consistently high presence in representative and appointed posts. For instance, in mid-2000, women were 18 per cent of representatives in Parliament, 30 per cent of local councillors, and held over 20 per cent of senior administrative posts (FOWODE, 2000, cited in Babihuga, 2000: 6).

The means of achieving this female presence in office have been affirmative action measures and direct presidential appointments.

This patronage towards the female constituency has been dispensed at the cost of politically internalized safeguards on these gains. Without institutionalized parties, and without a discernible party structure even within the NRM, women have not been able to assert their rights—as they have done in South Africa—to consistent party support for their candidatures in elections. Without a party system, they cannot bring membership pressure to bear on party executives to introduce gender sensitivity in the staffing of party posts. Nor can they use the dynamic of multi-party competition to develop political clout around a gendered voting gap. Instead their dependence on presidential patronage risks the discredit of the entire project of representing women's interests in the political arena, should the present system collapse.

Women in Civil Society: The Legacies of Authoritarianism

As noted in the South Africa section, the nature of a political transition away from authoritarianism determines the way civil society groups can influence the political system that follows. In Uganda's post-independence years of repressive authoritarianism (1967–86), the women's movement had developed a deep suspicion of parties and engagement with the state. As Tripp shows, in common with other African neo-patrimonial states, engagement with the state in Uganda had meant the co-optation of women's groups to ruling party support functions (2000: 80). This, combined with deep poverty and years of violent conflict, has slowed the development of a strong, politically independent, and broad-based women's movement in the country. Although Uganda now boasts a large number of urban feminist associations and women's development NGOs, and rural women are very active in self-help associations, some would dispute that they constitute, together, a coherent 'women's movement'. When that term is used in the rest of this chapter, it refers mainly to the increasingly coordinated and effective urban women's associations.

Transition to the current system in Uganda was a violent, not a negotiated process, presided over by a tiny political group with a very narrow social base. Urban and rural women's groups, like many other sectors of civil society, were not centrally engaged in this liberation struggle. However women in combat areas in the centre and south of the country did give marked support to Museveni's guerrilla movement. Not only were rural women supporting the struggle by providing logistical back-up, but a few women fought alongside the men. In the liberated areas, rural women were engaging in the new local government system—the Resistance Councils—set up by the

National Resistance Army, through the one seat for a secretary for women reserved for them in village councils.

For all their importance to the struggle, there were no measures to include women as a group in decision-making in the nascent National Resistance Movement (the political arm of the National Resistance Army, set up in 1981) (Museveni, 1997: 133). Nor did the NRM's ten-point programme, its manifesto for the country, make any mention of women's political participation. The few women directly involved in the NRA and the NRM in the bush war had not formed a distinct constituency within the movement. At the time of coming to power in 1986, the NRM/A was primarily a guerrilla army, given coherence by its overwhelming loyalty to the person of Museveni and its one priority of getting rid of Obote. It had started out as a fighting force of a little over thirty men, and by the 1986 victory, controlled just 20,000 soldiers, with no branch structure, no system for electing leaders, and no political base beyond the army and the ethnic group of the Banyankore in the south, and the allies it had gained among the Baganda in the Luwero triangle.

The Transition and Other Opportunities for Pressing Women's Political Demands

At the outset of the NRM's rule, women were in a strong enough position neither within the NRM nor in civil society to press for inclusion in the liberation government. The gradually reviving women's movement in urban areas, mainly Kampala, did however try from the start to press for women's inclusion in the new order. Shortly after the January 1986 take-over, a small group of urban women's and feminist organizations approached the new president to demand that women be appointed to leadership positions. Museveni, interested in cultivating new constituencies, responded quickly and appointed women who were strong NRM supporters to very prominent positions.

According to Tripp (2000), it took about a year for women's associations to begin to rally around an agenda for gender equity in the new regime. One group which had been created in late 1985, Action for Development (ACFODE), a Kampala-based group of thirty intellectuals and development professionals, generated, with support from other women's organizations, a list of demands to present to the new government (Tripp, 2000: 70). This hastily compiled women's manifesto called for the creation of a women's ministry, for every ministry to have a women's desk, for women's representation in local government at all levels, and for the repeal of the 1978 Amin-era law linking the National Council of Women (an umbrella body for women's organizations) to the government.

Most of these demands were met, starting with the 1988 creation of a Ministry of Women in Development. A seat for a woman was assured at all levels of the now five-tier Resistance Council (RC) system: and a seat for a woman representative to the national assembly for each district was created. Election to this position was to be determined not by popular suffrage, but by an electoral college composed of leaders (mostly male) of the five levels of the RC system. This measure was largely responsible for producing the 1989 National Resistance Council (Parliament) in which 17 per cent of members were women.

A critical opportunity for women to insert their concerns to the institutions and politics of the country was presented by the extended period of preparing a new (and fourth) constitution for the country between 1989 and 1995. The two women lawyers on the constitutional commission (which prepared drafts between 1989 and 1993) introduced clauses on matters of importance to women, and the women's ministry organized a nation-wide consultation exercise to set out women's interest in seeing the repeal of legislation which discriminates on the basis of sex. Fifty-two women, or 18 per cent of delegates, participated in the Constituent Assembly (CA) debates of 1994–5.

The large number of women in the CA enabled them to act as a negotiating and voting block. Most of them joined a non-partisan Women's Caucus, which was strongly supported by urban women's associations. By this time (1994–5), a women's movement had coalesced in urban areas, much encouraged by the years of peace and by a rush of donor funding, and was able to articulate key concerns for the Constitution (although it is unclear how far rural women's concerns were represented, or how far important ethnic and other differences between women were confronted at this time). The Women's Caucus represented women's interests in the Constituent Assembly, and was able to ensure that a number of women's concerns were included in the Constitution, particularly principles of non-discrimination on the basis of sex; equal opportunities; and preferential treatment (affirmative action) to redress past inequalities.

One of the most contentious issues defended by the Women's Caucus at that time was the use of the principle of affirmative action to reserve one-third of local government seats for women. Many male CA members objected to this on the grounds that it violated the principle of equal rights in the Constitution. Women delegates countered that participatory democracy did not deliver equal participation of women without specific instruments to enable women to attain representative office, particularly at the local level (Ahikire, 2000: 13).

The Women's Caucus in the CA did not take a stand on the country's political system—the most important issue in the Constitution. As the Caucus was deliberately non-partisan, it did not enter into a relationship with the multi-party caucus in the CA, and took no position on the decision to entrench the no-party 'Movement' system of government in the Constitution. Unlike in South Africa, women's engagement in the Constitution-writing process was not a struggle that unfolded in tandem with their efforts to gain better representation in the leaderships of their parties and assert stronger influence over their party programmes. Nor were Ugandan women able to enter into a debate about creating a new electoral system which might favour women or minority parties. There was, for instance, little debate over the electoral system, and the old Westminster-inspired, single-member constituency, first-past-the-post system was retained with little discussion of its implications for exacerbating ethnic conflict.[23] Though the option of a system of proportional representation, known for its potential to ease ethnic tensions, was aired at the time, the fact is that it made little sense once political party competition had been ruled out.

The Non-Party Movement: Problems of Institutionalization and Consequences for Women

In 1997 a 'Movement Act' was passed which was intended to institutionalize the NRM's 'no-party' system. Membership in the 'Movement'[24] is mandatory for all Ugandans. The Act creates a new set of local council structures paralleling the existing system, culminating in a National Movement Conference and a permanent Secretariat, whose costs are paid for by the state. All members of Parliament are obliged to be members of the National Movement Conference. It is very hard to see anything but a semantic difference between this 'no-party' set-up and a one-party system.

There is little doubt that the Movement system functions as a ruling party (while denying that it is a party at all), in the sense that it carefully controls the access to power of other groups. However, from the point of view of women, the problem is that the Movement is not sufficiently institutionalized as a party, and lacks internal rules and structures that could be made more gender-sensitive, let alone more democratic. This section will discuss the consequences for women—and indeed any Movement member unconnected to significant patronage systems—of the following features of Movement organization (or lack of organization): support to candidates for local and national elections, organization of the local 'Movement Councils', selection and role of the National Executive, role of the Movement Secretariat, and the lack of a Movement policy statement.

Because the Movement is not a party, it has always claimed that it neither cultivates nor promotes particular candidates in local and national elections. It does not put a limit on the numbers of people who can compete on the basis of 'individual merit'. There is no system for deciding between the many people who may put themselves forward as 'Movementists'.[25] This means that there is no way for women to insist that the Movement provide backing to a quota of women candidates in the way that their South African sisters so successfully did in the ANC.

There has been no structured approach to encourage women's engagement in setting policy priorities within the movement. The Movement has one official system for articulating and aggregating interests, and that is through the 'Movement Councils' parallel to all local councils—in effect a rural party branch system. These Movement Councils are intended, at least formally, to act as a form of caucus for debating policy-making in the Local Council meetings. There are no measures to ensure parity in the participation of women in these Movement Councils, nor to ensure their participation in the leadership of these Councils. The Movement has no women's wing, but it has set up a national network of 'Women's Councils' to parallel the 'Movement Councils'. These have provided some women with a political apprenticeship, typically moving from the 'Women's Council' system to nomination for the position of woman District Representative to Parliament. This system has the worrying effect of creating a double burden of political duty for women, segregating them both from the Local Councils and the Movement Councils. They have not proven particularly attractive to women interested in politics, and in many areas are inactive.

There are other organs for policy-making in the Movement: the National Executive Committee of the Movement, elected at the Movement's National Conference, and the Movement's Parliamentary Caucus. More important still are the decision-making arenas in government: the Cabinet, and the informal and shifting collection of friends and advisers around the President. Elections for the 150 posts on the National Executive Committee took place in July 1998 at the first National Movement Conference. These 150 positions include a few seats for representatives of special interest groups (five are for women), while the rest are filled by the forty-five District chairpersons (all men), and one MP chosen from each district (most of whom are men). According to one of the few women MPs on the NEC, there has been no discussion since 1998 about gender issues, nor mention of any need for the Movement to offer women special support in elections.[26]

The Movement Secretariat is legally charged with ensuring that legislative activity is in line with the Movement's policy. Its directorates for legal affairs, development, information, mobilization, and so on, monitor and occasionally review legislation even before it is seen by Parliament.[27] The NEC is supposed to appoint these directors, but in practice, it is the President who personally nominates them. There are sixteen directors in the Secretariat, three of whom are women. The sub-directorate for gender, labour, and development has not made a marked effort to ensure that the government is enacting the legislation previewed in the Constitution to protect women's rights—such as the Equal Opportunities Commission, the Domestic Relations Bill, or protection of married women's rights to property, particularly land.

There is no comprehensive statement of Movement policy, and it would be difficult to put a single label on the Movement's ideology. The NRM used to be a socialist organization, but it abandoned its ideals in quick order after coming to office and recognizing the country's urgent need for assistance from the World Bank and the International Monetary Fund. Its values are summarized in a thin 1999 document that updates the NRM's 1986 ten-point programme into a fifteen-point programme. Gender is mentioned at point 14, which endorses affirmative action as a means to encourage political, social, and economic participation of marginalized groups (Movement Secretariat, 1999: 46). The terms 'gender equity' or 'equality' are never used, nor are any measurable goals mentioned, in terms of aiming for parity in women and men's political or economic engagement. According to a member of the four-person committee in the directorate which wrote the fifteen-point programme, this 'gender' point was not raised by the one woman on the committee, nor was it a submission by the Secretariat's gender sub-directorate. Instead, it was put there by other directors conscious of the importance of consolidating the Movement's success with the female constituency.

The Cabinet is not significantly closer to providing a forum for debating policy. Although there are six women ministers in Cabinet, none of them is close to real decision-making. Research by the Forum for Women in Democracy (FOWODE) has shown that these women control small budgets, in low-visibility ministries, with few staff (FOWODE, 2000: 10). The Vice-President has been sidelined, described by one woman MP as 'just an errand girl for the

President'.[28] She is ostensibly the chair of Cabinet but this function
is usually usurped by the President. In any case, the Cabinet is not
the real locus of decision-making for the Movement. Insiders say that
most decisions are debated by a very tight circle of close army comrades of the President's: friends on the Army Council, the President's
brother Salim Saleh, and a few senior Movement stalwarts in the
Cabinet.

By shunning the status of a party, the Movement can continue to
remain ill-defined at its very top levels, where decisions are taken
by the President and a tiny group of key friends. There has never
been any move to elect the Movement's top leaders, and no popularly
elected body within the Movement votes on policies (Kasfir, 1998: 61).
There have occasionally been efforts to democratize the movement
from within, but each individual who has dared to challenge abuses of
power has lost their position within the Movement. The latest of these
was Winnie Byanyima, a prominent feminist politician, who lost her
post as Director of Information at the Movement Secretariat in early
1998 when it became clear that this appointment had failed to silence
her protests at official corruption. Two years later she was roundly
booed at the Movement's National Conference when she pointed out
that the endorsement of Museveni as the Movement's sole presidential candidate was in contravention of the policy of allowing anyone
to stand for any position on the grounds of individual merit (*Sunday
Vision*, 2000).

Discourses of Inclusion

Women's arguments and strategies for admission to representative
politics and to policy-making are all framed by one key feature of
the current institutional framework: the suppression of parties. It is
easy to see what the appeal of women was to Museveni in this context. Not only were they a relatively uncaptured vote bank, but when
considered as a group defined by their gender, women were not associated with ethnic rivalry and particular parties. This is not to say
that women were not active in ethnic associations and the old political parties—they were and are. But many women, particularly urban
professionals and feminists, have wished to help forge a non-sectarian
approach to politics, and Museveni has been able to work with these
women in order to appeal to larger numbers of women voters outside
of urban centres and associations.

Yet Museveni's instrumental interest in women as a constituency
has often left the independent women's movement in a reactive,
rather than proactive, position when it has come to strategizing for

inclusion. His approach to women has been similar to his approach to other interest groups such as traditional leaders and ethnic groups. It is based on a politics of patronage. All of his gestures: the affirmative action district seats and administrative offices, the new one-third provision in local government, and new Cabinet positions (women hold 33.3 per cent of new 'Minister of State' positions which have bloated the Cabinet), have created a new female clientele for state patronage. These gestures are based upon expanding access to the political pie, rather than unseating any incumbent politician or any entrenched interests. They do not make space for the suggestion that women may have a set of interests which may change the orientation and beneficiaries of these institutions.

This point relates to the meaning of women's presence in public space, the justification for their inclusion, and the relationship between women in office and those in the women's movement. The terms for the inclusion of women have been determined from the top, not by women in politics or civil society. These terms put the stress on women's social 'difference'; as a group they have been historically excluded, so as a group they are to be included through affirmative action politics. Thus their gender, not their politics, becomes their admission ticket. The practical methods used to incorporate women in politics reveal how the stress on difference has produced a separate and often under-legitimate place for women politicians who are in affirmative action seats. This is revealed by an examination of the mechanics of the 30 per cent reservation for women in local government.

The one-third reservation of local government seats has not been applied to existing seats, but rather, the number of seats on local councils (save at the village level) have been increased by a third to accommodate women. These 'women's seats' are cobbled out of clustering existing wards, in effect at least doubling the constituency which women are meant to represent, compared to 'normal' ward representatives, who represent just one. Elections for the women's seats are held as an afterthought, a good two weeks after the ward elections. In the 1998 local government elections, irritation with this unwieldy system, as well as voter fatigue, resulted in failure to achieve quorum for electing women to reserved seats all over the country. After several attempts to rerun these ballots, the results from suboptimal voter turn-outs were accepted, undermining the legitimacy of the women who won the seats. Women now in these seats say they are very often sidelined by the 'real' ward representatives, with whom local people engage more often than with the women representatives (Ahikire, 2000).

Women have resisted some aspects of the NRM's efforts to create a separate political space for them, particularly where this is obviously aimed at co-opting women's political energies to serve the Movement. This resistance is clearest in the low level of engagement in the National Women's Council system, mentioned in the previous section, which parallels the country's five-tier local government system, and is designed to mobilize rural women into political and development work (and to act as a proxy women's wing for the Movement).

The mechanism of incorporating women to the state in Uganda has been based on a principle of extending patronage to a new clientele, without troubling male privilege. The women's movement has used two strategies to respond to this. One strategy has been to take advantage of opportunities for inclusion, and to use new spaces within the state as the thin edge of the wedge for inserting gender-equity concerns. But without a strong women's movement to hold women politicians and bureaucrats to account, there is a great risk of co-optation. By the late 1990s, a second strategy emerged, where women's associations began to focus more closely upon the outcomes of this form of 'bureaucratic representation': the gender-friendly legislation and gender-equitable development policy which they had expected to emerge from women's presence in the state. Setbacks in the passage of such legislation and policy have made certain parts of the women's movement more concerned with the quality of politics in the country, and more aware of how the absence of pluralism may limit women's leverage on the state.

Nevertheless, women in civil society have been slow to take up two important recent opportunities for mobilizing electoral dynamics to support women's demands. The first was the July 2000 referendum. Women's organizations did not step in to protest the suppression of engagement by opposition parties, or to review whether the NRM's achievements merited a vote for an indefinite continuation of no-party rule. Some women's organizations were engaged in donor-funded civic education programmes for the referendum, but they could not, by virtue of the nature of the exercise, take sides. The second opportunity was the run-up to the mid-2001 presidential elections. Women's organizations by and large failed to take this opportunity to review the democratic fairness of these elections. However, one umbrella women's organization, the Uganda Women's Network (UWONET), spearheaded an initiative bringing together several NGOs, members of the Domestic Relations Bill Coalition, and Local Council leaders, to promote a gender-sensitive 'People's Manifesto' for the elections. This is one of the few places in which the need to improve women's engagement *within* the NRM is stressed (UWONET, 2000).

The women's movement should not be judged harshly for throwing in its lot so whole-heartedly with the first post-independence government in Uganda to bring stability and growth. Nor could it have made much headway in pressing for party development in an institutional framework so hostile to parties. Nor should it be blamed for rejecting the option of seeking to promote women's interests through political parties that had been so abusive of women's interests in the past. But the failure to keep a critical eye on the undermining of democracy in the country has contributed not only to a deepening stagnation and paralysis in the old political parties, but to an erosion of democracy within the NRM itself. By neglecting questions of party development, the women's movement has failed to scrutinize the position of women within the NRM, and has done nothing to promote the institutionalization of gender-equity concerns within the party; in its recruitment, candidate promotion, policies, or leadership.

On the other hand, by working with the NRM, the women's movement has made important gains, which may eventually produce a more critical standpoint on the country's political system. For a start, the NRM's patronage of women has contributed to the post-conflict recovery of the women's movement. Second, as will be shown below, setbacks in promoting gender equity in legislation and policy are radicalizing the women's movement and intensifying its concern about issues such as corruption and the lack of pluralism.

Women in Politics and Gender-Friendly Legislation

One measure of the institutional security of women politicians anywhere, and of their relative autonomy from male or party interests which are hostile to a gender-equity agenda, is their capacity to promote gender-equity legislation, and to retain their positions in high office even when they threaten the existing status quo in gender relations. On this score, the record of women in politics in Uganda has been mixed. To begin with, as a group they are not primarily drawn from women's or feminist associations, and do not therefore share even a broadly defined gender-equity agenda. Though there have been some notable successes in promoting legislation of great importance to women, there have been even more notable failures to promote overdue legislation to bring family law up to date, or to secure married women's property rights. Some very vocal and prominent women advocates of women's rights amongst MPs were neutralized once they accepted a Cabinet position, while other key women politicians, such as the Vice President and the Minister of Gender, have actively opposed or stalled the legislative agendas currently pushed by the women's movement. The Women's Caucus in Parliament has been largely inactive, having met just twice since 1996.

The women MPs in affirmative action seats are not necessarily people who may appeal to a wider women's constituency. Indeed, in many districts, professing a commitment to women's rights might well constitute a disqualification in the eyes of the electoral college. However, it should not be assumed that affirmative action women MPs are necessarily diffident about the gender-equity agenda. One of the most outspoken feminists in Parliament is Miria Matembe, who has twice been the affirmative action representative for her district.

Members of the women's movement in Uganda profess deepening frustration with the lack of responsiveness of the majority of women parliamentarians to the campaigns of women in civil society for legislative change.[29] This is not to say, however, that some women parliamentarians have not made heroic efforts to promote a gender-equity legislative agenda. In 1990, women MPs were instrumental in passing an amendment to the penal code that made rape a capital offence. Since 1995 some women have struggled to get Parliament to pass, within deadlines set by the Constitution, provisions for new institutions and laws to protect women's rights. Observers of women parliamentarians note that the majority of their interventions in Parliament relate to concerns about women's rights or gender relations (Tamale, 1999: 80; Tripp, 2000: 75–6). But since the CA debates, and particularly in the run-up to the mid-2001 elections, there has been a notable flagging of energy around a gender-equity agenda. At least two important efforts to promote women's rights—in relation to land and family law—have quite clearly foundered because of this.

The most dramatic example of Movement hostility to women's concerns, and indeed, direct presidential sabotage, was the way the 'spousal co-ownership' amendment to the 1998 Land Act was quashed in Parliament. This is discussed in detail in Chapter 13 below. The point to note here is the way assiduous lobbying by women's groups, and fairly broad support from women MPs (but not three of the then five women in Cabinet, who remained opposed), which resulted in the tabling and passing of the amendment, was undone by direct interference by the President. He excised the amendment from the Act on the grounds that it belonged more appropriately to the pending Domestic Relations Bill.

This as good as extinguished the amendment altogether, because of the political near-impossibility of passing the Domestic Relations

Bill (DRB)—the second area in which gender-equity legislation has stalled. Various drafts of the DRB have been languishing on the statute books since 1964. Since 1995 the need for legislation to bring family laws in Uganda into conformity with the guarantee of sexual equality in the Constitution has become urgent, but the DRB has not even been tabled in Parliament. The bill covers aspects of gender relations in the family, aiming to protect women's rights in relation to polygamy, bride-wealth, child custody, divorce, inheritance, consent in sexual relations, violence, and property ownership. This kind of legislation, which challenges men's rights to control women and children in the family, is inevitably deeply counter-cultural in a sexually conservative society. The item in the bill which has aroused the most ferocious objections from many men relates to the criminalizing of marital rape. In addition, the Muslim community has objected to the restrictions on polygamous unions in the bill. Already burdened with these 'unpassable' clauses, the DRB can hardly act as a vehicle for pushing through the spousal co-ownership clause.

The bill has no champion among women MPs—even those who are vocal on women's rights have not wanted to risk their political careers on such unpopular legislation so close to parliamentary elections. The objections of the Muslim community have meant that the Minister of Gender, Janat Mukwaya, herself a Muslim, has refused to be associated with it. The criminalization of marital rape has made the bill hard for the Minister of Justice to stomach. A politician from the old Bugandan party, he has exhibited marked indifference to gender-equity legislation, and has admitted to members of the women's movement that he has had trouble presenting this bill to Cabinet because he simply cannot understand the concept of marital rape.

Another sign of the failure of women politicians to act in concert to promote a gender-equity agenda is the non-appearance of the Equal Opportunities Commission. All of the other government commissions foreseen in the Constitution have been created (commissions on human rights, law reform, elections, and judicial service). It is the responsibility of the Ministry of Gender to ensure that the Equal Opportunities Commission is set up. But since an initial costing exercise in 1998, no further effort has been made by the Ministry, and again, the issue has no particular champions in Parliament.

There is, however, one noticeable contribution which women MPs have made: some of them are beginning to constitute an anticorruption lobby. Winnie Byanyima is the most outspoken critic of government corruption, spearheading the first censure motion in Parliament against the MP Brigadier-General Muhwezi, and subsequently Sam Kutesa. Other MPs such as Salaamu Proscovia

Musumba have joined in with efforts to pass a Budget Bill which would impose much greater transparency and disaggregation in the presentation of budgets for ministries and also for districts. In the Ministry for Ethics and Integrity, which is the focal point for all anti-corruption bureaucracies and campaigns, the Minister is the important woman's rights activist, Miria Matembe.

For women within the Movement, it may be that raising issues of corruption is the only way in which to make an implicit critique of its lack of internal democracy. Figures who have been targeted in Byanyima's censure motions are in fact key members of the privileged clique around Museveni. Women MPs have concentrated more closely on corruption than any other group in Parliament, save for the group of new/young parliamentarians between 1996 and 1999, after which key leaders among them were neutralized by being made Ministers of State in the Cabinet.

Conclusion: In and Against the Party

Women's strategies for political inclusion in South Africa differ markedly from parallel processes in Uganda. At heart, the difference comes down to a contrast in the basics of institutional design in these countries. Both countries are faced with a similar dominant dilemma of political management: the challenge of accommodating ethnic and racial differences and preventing ethnic conflict. South Africa tackled this through an electoral system and political infrastructure that enables representation of minority interests at the national level, and some power-sharing with traditional authorities at the local level. Counteracting the pull to sectarian politics is the need for parties to campaign around the country if they are to build any challenge to the ANC, and the great electoral success of the ANC's own non-racial and non-sexist party ideology itself encourages parties to act on programmatic, rather than particularistic, lines. In Uganda, a central institutional choice has been the suspension of multi-party competition on the grounds that parties are incapable of competing on the basis of different programmes, as opposed to ethnic differences. By ruling out pluralism, the NRM has emasculated the development of accountability mechanisms outside of the Movement, and by extending an ever-widening net of patronage, it has neutralized oppositional energies, including those of women pushing for a legislative agenda which would challenge male rights within gender relations.

There are some surface similarities between the ways in which the dominant parties in these two new democracies have responded to women's ambitions for political participation. In both South Africa and Uganda, the dominant liberation parties deliberately courted women as part of their search for new national constituencies. There are differences in the basis on which these ruling parties sought to appeal to women, and these differences have implications for the terms and mechanics of women's incorporation. In South Africa, women were important to the ANC to demonstrate its continued commitment to inclusion, and to the redress of social inequities, in the face of criticism that it had abandoned its revolutionary ideals. In Uganda, the NRM hoped that the incorporation of women as a new political group would demonstrate possibilities of non-ethnic models of group identification and political participation. In South Africa, the ANC's stress on equality of participation by all social groups, and the stand against social inequality, left the party exposed to women's demands for changes in gender relations—within the party and in society—and encouraged the women's movement to seek to hold women politicians accountable for their performance as feminists. In Uganda, the stress on women's difference has meant that they have been treated as a new and separate group in politics, not incorporated as equals within the party or in government, and not necessarily seen as legitimate representatives by voters.

Both the ANC and the NRM have been receptive to using affirmative action mechanisms for increasing the numbers of women in formal politics. But these measures have been installed in different institutions: in South Africa, they have been introduced at the party level, on a voluntary basis. In Uganda, a range of new parliamentary and local government seats were created for women-only competition, thus separating women's political engagement from the mainstream of political competition. In both cases, centralized leadership has been key to the effectiveness of these measures, which would otherwise have fallen victim to opposition from traditional interests within both parties to women's presence. However, centralism can also have negative consequences, reinforcing the power of party elites over weaker constituencies within the party. Even where there is a democratic ethos within the party, as in the ANC, 'democratic centralism' can erode the ability of feminists to challenge policies and processes that hamper equality, and can make women hostage to the goodwill of particular individuals in the party's higher echelons.

There are a number of important differences in the two experiences that relate, first, to the length and depth of engagement by the

women's movement with and within each party, and second, to features of the internal organization of each party. In South Africa, the
struggle to get the ANC to recognize women's interests and provide
for their representation in the party leadership and on party candidate lists had a long history which predates the party's ascension
to power. The urban women's movement was able to coalesce prior
to constitutional debates in such a way as to develop views on how
democracy should be conceived. It also had the opportunity to clarify
for itself some of the issues about the means and meaning of women's
accession to formal representative positions—in other words, linking
the presence of women representatives to the project of representing
women's interests. In Uganda, the women's movement was caught on
a back foot, still fragmented from the years of authoritarian repression under previous regimes. By the time it recovered, the NRM had
pre-empted a number of its demands for inclusion by introducing
affirmative action and creating new political seats for women.

These differences in the role of the women's movement in directing the terms of women's inclusion have important implications for
the capacity of women in civil society to act as a constituency holding the dominant party to account. In South Africa, the women's
constituency is considerably more autonomous from and critical of
the ANC than women in Uganda are of the NRM. In South Africa,
women demanded inclusion as of *right*; in Uganda, inclusion has
been extended as a *favour*. This has obvious implications for women's
influence both within and outside of the party.

The second key contrast in the two cases is in the different levels
of institutionalization and internal democracy in the two parties.
The ANC is an older and more deeply institutionalized party than
the NRM. The ANC has an established rural branch structure for
mobilizing participation and generating new leadership, clear lines of
authority, and structured forms of participation within the party both
for individuals and different interest groups. This has enabled women
within the party, first, to establish their importance as an internal
constituency, and second, to use connections to the women's movement, to assert an 'autonomous' position for feminists and feminist
policy goals in the party (not that this has been easy, of course).

In contrast, the NRM's top levels are completely impervious to
democratic pressures, as indeed are many other levels of the party.
The only arena in which democratic forces are allowed relatively
free play is the one arena in which the Movement is better institutionalized: local government—the institutional bed-rock of the
'no-party' system. Ironically, however, the considerable local political duty expected of ordinary Ugandans has worked as a means of

containing and limiting autonomous associational energy in the country and within the Movement. Mamdani has argued that local councils operate to postpone the evolution of interest-based or broader programmatic patterns of political association. Because rights to participation are based on residence, limits are placed on the capacity of outside interest groups to engage in local politics and generate enthusiasm for non-local issue-based politics. Because competition for office is based on 'individual merit', campaigns inevitably and ironically become personality-based rather than programme-based, resulting in appeals to clan or religious loyalties, rather than interests and ideas (Mamdani, 1988, 1994, cited in Tripp, 2000: 66).

In South Africa, women were ready at the right moment to make an impact, and were able to introduce notions of women's rights to participation on the grounds of their equal citizenship. In Uganda, they were pre-empted by a powerful political association that made considerable electoral mileage out of stressing women's difference as a group. These contrasting discourses of equality and difference, and the differences in the strengths of the women's movements in the two countries, go some way in explaining the differences in the ways women have gained access to representative positions, and influence over policy-making.

Beyond these discourses of inclusion, this chapter has argued that equally important have been the party systems and institutional contexts within which these discourses have been aired. Pluralism in South Africa and a dominant party which is socially inclusive and committed to fighting social inequalities have meant that women can use electoral processes to build leverage behind their political and policy ambitions. The lack of either pluralism or internal party democracy in Uganda means that women are dangerously dependent on presidential patronage for access to office and for promoting gender-equity policies. As summarized by a feminist lawyer engaged in law reform in Uganda: 'If there was pluralism here, there would be space for women to influence political structures. Right now, no political organisation has affirmative action internally. That would give women leverage. Women are captive to the Movement now.'[30]

References

Adler, Glenn, and Eddie Webster (1995) 'Challenging Transition Theory: The Labour Movement, Radical Reform and Transition to Democracy in South Africa', *Politics and Society*, 23/1: 75–106.
Ahikire, Josephine (2000) 'Gender Equity and Local Democracy in Contemporary Uganda: Addressing the Challenge of Women's Political

Effectiveness in Local Government', paper presented at a workshop on Strengthening Democratic Governance in Conflict-Torn Societies, 7–10 Dec., Jinja, Uganda.

Albertyn, Catherine (1995) 'National Machinery for Ensuring Gender Equality', in S. Liebenberg (ed.), *The Constitution of South Africa from a Gender Perspective* (Cape Town: David Philip).

—— (ed.) (1999) 'Engendering the Political Agenda: A South African Case Study', unpublished INSTRAW report.

ANC (1990) *May 2 1990 Declaration on Women by the National Executive Committee of the ANC* (Johannesburg: ANC).

—— (1994) *The Reconstruction and Redevelopment Programme: A Policy Framework* (Johannesburg: Umanyano Publications).

Apter, David (1997) *The Political Kingdom in Uganda: A Study in Bureaucratic Nationalism* (London: Frank Cass).

Babihuga, Winnie (2000) 'Women's Paths to Political Participation and Decision-Making', paper presented during ACFODE Week Public Dialogue, 17 Nov., Uganda.

Basu, Amrita (ed.) (1995) *The Challenge of Local Feminisms: Women's Movements in Global Perspective* (Boulder, Colo.: Westview).

Britton, Hannah (1997) 'Preliminary Report on Participation: Challenges and Strategies', Syracuse University, unpublished report.

CGE and PWG (1999) *Redefining Politics: South African Women and Democracy* (Johannesburg: CGE).

Charman, Andrew, Cobus De Swardt, and Mary Simons (1991) 'The Politics of Gender: Negotiating Liberation', *Transformation*, 15: 40–64.

Chigudu, Hope, and Wilfred Tichagwa (1995) *Participation of Women in Party Politics* (Discussion Paper, 9; Harare: Zimbabwe Women's Resource Centre and Network).

Cock, Jacklyn (1997) 'Women in South Africa's Transition to Democracy', in J. Scott, C. Kaplan, and D. Keats (eds.), *Transitions, Environments, Translations: Feminism in International Politics* (New York: Routledge).

Dahlerup, Drude (1986) 'Introduction', in D. Dahlerup (ed.), *The New Women's Movement: Feminism and Political Power in Europe and the USA* (London: Sage).

FOWODE (Forum for Women in Democracy) (2000) *From Strength to Strength: Ugandan Women in Public Office* (Kampala: FOWODE).

Gender Advocacy Programme (2000) 'Gender Politics at Local Level', *Agenda*, 45: 13–17.

Ginsburg, David (1996) 'The Democratisation of South Africa: Transition Theory Tested', *Transformation*, 29: 74–102.

Haase-Dubosc, Danielle (2000) 'Movement for Parity in France', *Economic and Political Weekly*, 35/43–4 (28 Oct.).

Hassim, Shireen (1993) 'Family, Motherhood, and Zulu Nationalism: The Politics of the Inkatha Women's Brigade', *Feminist Review*, 43: 1–25.

Hassim, Shireen (1999) 'Institutionalising Gender: An Examination of State-Led Strategies for Gender Equality', paper prepared for DAWN project Political Restructuring and Social Transformation, November, Cape Town.

Horn, Pat (1991) 'Post-Apartheid South Africa: What about Women's Emancipation?', *Transformation*, 15: 26–39.

Jaquette, Jane S, and Sharon L. Wolchik (eds.) (1998) *Women and Democracy: Latin America and Central and Eastern Europe* (London: Johns Hopkins University Press).

Kasfir, Nelson (1998) ' "No-Party Democracy" in Uganda', *Journal of Democracy*, 9/2, (Apr.): 49–63.

Kemp, Amanda, Nozizwe Madlala, Asha Moodley, and Elaine Salo (1995) 'The Dawn of a New Day: Redefining South African Feminism', in Basu Amrita (ed.), *The Challenge of Local Feminisms: Women's Movements in Global Perspective* (Boulder, Colo.: Westview).

Lovenduski, Joni, and Pippa Norris (1993) *Gender and Party Politics* (London: Sage).

Mamdani, Mahmood (1988) 'Democracy in Today's Uganda', *New Vision* (16 Mar.).

—— (1994) 'Africa was Highly Decentralised', *New Vision* (20 Dec.).

Marais, Hein (1998) *South Africa: Limits to Change* (London: Zed Books).

Mbatha, Likhapha, and Beth Goldblatt (1999) 'Gender, Culture and Equality: Reforming Customary Law', in Cathi Albertyn (ed.), 'Engendering the Political Agenda: A South African Case Study', unpublished INSTRAW report.

Meer, Shamim (1999) 'The Demobilisation of Civil Society: Struggling with New Questions', *Development Update*, 3/1: 109–18.

Meintjes, Sheila (1996) 'The Women's Struggle for Equality during South Africa's Transition to Democracy', *Transformation*, 30: 47–64.

Monitor (2000) 'Museveni Declared Mot. Sole Candidate' (25 Nov.).

Movement Secretariat (1999) *Movement Fifteen Point Programme* (Pamphlet, Kampala).

Mtintso, T. E. (1999) 'The Contribution of Women Parliamentarians to Gender Equality', unpublished MA thesis, University of the Witwatersrand, South Africa.

Muhereza, Frank Emmanuel, and Peter Omurangi Otim (1997) 'Neutralizing Ethnicity under the NRM Government in Uganda', Nov., Centre for Basic Research, Kampala, mimeo.

Museveni, Yoweri Katunga (1997) *Sowing the Mustard Seed* (London: Macmillan).

Parliament of South Africa (1999) *Annual Report of the Joint Standing Committee on the Improvement of the Quality of Life and Status of Women, 1998–1999* (Cape Town: Parliament of South Africa).

Phillips, Anne (1995) *The Politics of Presence* (Oxford: Oxford University Press).

In and Against the Party 343

Rule, W. (1987) 'Electoral Systems, Contextual Factors, and Women's Opportunity for Election to Parliaments in Twenty-Three Democracies', *Western Political Quarterly*, 40/3: 477–98.

Seedat, Fatima, and Lilian Kimani (1999) 'Gender Profile of Parties', in CGE/PWG, *Redefining Politics: South African Women and Democracy* (Johannesburg: Commission for Gender Equality).

Speak (1991) 'We've got the Future Looking at Us', 36: 8.

Sunday Vision (2000) 'Movt Delegates Boo Byanyima' (26 Nov.).

Tamale, Sylvia (1999) *When Hens begin to Crow: Gender and Parliamentary Politics in Uganda* (Kampala: Fountain Publishers).

Thornton, Robert, and Mamphele Ramphele (1988) 'The Quest for Community', in Emile Boonzaier and John Sharp (eds.), *South African Keywords: The Uses and Abuses of Political Concepts* (Cape Town: David Philip).

Tripp, Aili Mari (1994) 'Gender, Political Participation, and the Transformation of Association Life in Uganda and Tanzania', *African Studies Review*, 37/1: 107–33.

—— (2000) *Women and Politics in Uganda* (Oxford: James Currey).

UWONET (2000) 'The People's Manifesto', Kampala, mimeo.

Vengroff, Richard, and Melissa Fugiero (2000) 'Electoral Systems and Gender Representation in Meso-Level Legislatures', paper presented at the international Political Studies Association Conference, Quebec City, Canada, Aug.

Vos, Suzanne (1999) 'Women in Parliament: A Personal Perspective', in CGE and PWG *Redefining Politics: South African Women and Democracy* (Johannesburg: CGE).

Walker, Cherryl (ed.) (1990) *Women and Gender in Southern Africa to 1945* (Cape Town: David Philip).

Waylen, Georgina (1994) 'Women and Democratization: Conceptualizing Gender Relations in Transition Politics', *World Politics*, 46 (Apr.): 327–54.

Women's National Coalition (1994) *Women's Charter for Effective Equality* (Johannesburg: Women's National Coalition).

Yuval Davis, Nira (1997) *Gender and Nation* (London: Sage).

IV

Multiculturalisms in Practice

The Politics of Gender, Ethnicity, and Democratization in Malaysia: Shifting Interests and Identities

Maznah Mohamad

The question of whether, and to what extent, divergent gender and ethnic identities can be reconciled to produce common interests has been a subject of considerable study and debate in feminist writings (Siim, 2000; Lister, 1997; Einhorn, 2000; Blacklock and Macdonald, 2000; Dean, 1997; Chhachhi and Pittin, 1996*a*). In Malaysia it is also an important political question because feminist movements have found it hard to create solidarity among women who are ensconced in their exclusive ethnic and religious domains. Why is this so and will this condition, or inability to 'universalize' women's problems and solutions, necessarily be the millstone around cultural and political projects seeking women's empowerment?

In Malaysia's case, the inability of social movements to promote the cause of gender equality as a universal right has become a setback for an overall democratization project. First, social and political movements with active women's participation have been consistently mobilized on the basis of particularistic ethnic interests. Within this premise, while there may be common ground for supporting gender rights, women of the different ethnic groups were impeded from getting together because of the nature of their polarized recruitment. This diluted the sense of common urgency in the push for gender reforms. Second, the absence of a unified multi-ethnic women's voice implied a weakened civil society struggling to exist within the context of a quasi-democracy like Malaysia. Finally, policies within a plural developing country like Malaysia cannot be compared to a developed democracy where feminists need not cooperate across ethnic lines to further gender reforms. This is because in the latter, a universalizing paradigm of a rules-based liberal democracy is fairly in place to allow many groups to pursue their distinctive particularistic interests within a relatively uncontested framework (Kymlicka, 1994). As we shall see in the discussion which follows, a plural society like Malaysia can descend into its politics of diversity in divisive ways. Proponents of the 'Asian values' position often stress that a semi-democratic government does not need to accept a rules-based system as a cardinal obligation, given that the imperatives of public order, political stability, and economic development are more urgent (Kausikan, 1993). In such a situation, while the slogan, 'unity in diversity' is empowering it can also be used at the same time as a divide and rule strategy for the powers-that-be in ensuring dominance.

Nevertheless, in this study I intend to show that the politics of identity and difference, involving gender and ethnicity does not actually remain embedded in any fixed social context. It is capable of transposing itself to fit changing exigencies. The Malaysian experience shows that identities and interests are subjected to a constant state of flux, shifting and changing to fit opportunities and circumstances of historical moments, thus implying either a desirable prospect for women's unified voice or a bleak scenario of heightened division.

This chapter revisits the origins of the Malaysian women's movement by locating it within the (still unfinished) state project, and context of post-colonial nation-building and post-crisis democratization. Previous works on the subject have either fallen short of fully exploring the ethnic dimension in the evolution of feminism (Mohamad, 2001a; Ng and Chee, 1999) or have analysed individual ethnic women's organizations as distinct constructs in isolation from those of other ethnic groups (Manderson, 1980; Dancz, 1987). There is a need to build upon these past contributions. Malaysia's variant of multi-ethnicity locates a specific interconnection between gender and ethnicity, and determines either the delivery or denial of spaces for gender justice, rights and democracy.

Ethnicity is given prominence here because Malaysia is a striking example of a plural society, populated by ethnic Malays and indigenous communities (63 per cent), Chinese (26 per cent), and Indians (7.5 per cent), but in which strong social processes, such as Islamization, have played a distinct role in the construction of the national polity. Most importantly, ethnicity has been the basis upon which political divisions are promoted, while ethnic identity is prioritized over all other identities in the realization of economic, social, and cultural interests. Women's political parties and movements are unproblematically organized along ethnic lines, but feminist movements are formed only when ethnic lines are contentiously traversed.

This chapter looks at Malaysia's three phases of political development and analyses the shifting features of women's movements as they intersect with the politics of ethnicity and democratization. I argue that, after the burst of early feminism through nationalist struggles (in the 1940s and 1950s), gender politics evolved by taking on three main facets—political sponsorship, political division, and political inclusion.[1] What is meant here is that gender politics has been transformed through these vicissitudes in very characteristic ways, with identities and interests shifting to 'selectively respond to economic, social and political pressures' (Chhachhi and Pittin, 1996b: 10). The current phase of political democratization or 'political transition' (post-1998), as some may see it, has specifically brought to the fore many attempts at reworking the notions of gender justice, rights, and equality. This has necessitated critical reassessment and a most pronounced engagement by feminist political actors in their political struggles for gender rights. I contend that in Malaysia's current phase of political reconstruction, conflicting gender interests have the highest chance of being coalesced as ethnic identities and interests are being de-emphasized. However, this process can only be sustained if autonomous feminist movements are able to withstand pressures to succumb to the instrumental agendas of both opposition and ruling political parties in the appropriation of the gender discourse for their legitimacy.

Political Sponsorship, Division, and Inclusion

The initial phase of Malaysia's first post-independent government saw the establishment of an elite ruling 'directorate' which paternalistically established the social contract for interethnic citizenship rights (Von Vorys, 1975). In this is laid the basis for future state evolution. Following this, women's entry into formal politics and subsequent participation in non-party movements were sponsored by their ethnic elites and fed into the overall project of ethnic accommodation, or consociational democracy, designed for the country's post-colonial survival (Milne and Mauzy, 1978: 136). In this early phase of independence, interests and identities were adaptable since there was horizontal political cohesion, albeit fragile, among elites of the various communities. Women's interests and identities were in turn predicated upon this political paradigm of elite sponsorship.

By the 1970s the project of post-colonial nation-building took on a revised dimension, with the assertion of even greater Malay political dominance in 'correcting' inter-ethnic economic disparity. In this second phase, the divide between women's interests and identities became more sharply fractured because of the heightening of race-based politics and the concurrent void in civil society left by its coercion by a state which took on an increasingly authoritarian character. Political divisions, created by hegemonic state processes also became more accentuated among women. Although a second wave feminist consciousness emerged in this period, there were identifiable bifurcations along many lines, for example, between Muslim and non-Muslim interest groups and between modernist-liberals and Islamic modernists.

When the state exhibited signs of weakening in the aftermath of the Asian economic crisis of the late 1990s, and in the concomitant revitalization of civil society, gender politics has taken another peculiar character. Gender became a site for the contestation of populist legitimacy by both the state and opposition forces, thus heralding its political inclusion in the transitional process of power realignment. The incumbent forces now use the 'gender card' to discredit an Islamic opposition and to assuage the representation of opposition female leaders as an icon of an incorruptible and morally untainted new social order. Likewise, civil society tries to consolidate itself by reinforcing gender rights and justice as the sine qua non of a new democracy. In this recent phase of Malaysia's 'post-crisis' restructuring, political processes seem to unravel and blur previously demarcated and even conflicting women's interests and identities.

The First Phase: Nationalist Feminism to Political Sponsorship

The origin of the country's modern feminist movement can be traced to the political struggles against colonial rule. It can be said that Malaysian women of all ethnic origins had their early politicization and leadership training in the tumultuous years of the Second World War, which allowed the flowering of anti-imperialist ambitions when British colonialism was rattled by Japanese territorial expansion. Like elsewhere and like most social processes, women's needs were articulated within a localized discursive space but also in conjunction with a discourse from without. In Malaysia's case, nationalist movements against colonial domination also spawned debates about women's roles in the workplace, their rights to formal education, and their participation in political organizations (Manderson, 1980; Dancz, 1987; Mohamad, 2001a). Such consciousness originated not simply from anti-imperialist mobilization but also from the modernist project conveyed through colonialism itself. Yet without these nationalist movements there would have been no terrain for the gendering of political tensions and resolutions.

The rise of left-leaning Malay political movements soon after the war, such as the Malay Nationalist Party of Malaya (PKMM), created an avenue for Malay women to take up non-traditional roles. PKMM was one of the first political parties to establish a women's wing, known as the Force of Awakened Women (AWAS), ahead of the other non-Malay, more urbanized political parties. Although women were largely recruited for populist mobilization and expediency, strong and outstanding women personalities emerged out of this political strategy, despite its being male-directed. After the Japanese defeat the British Military Administration resumed control over the country, and a few years later the PKMM and its women and youth wings were disbanded because of their pro-Japanese, leftist, and militant bent. Subsequently colonial administrators cultivated the more moderate, nationalist but British-friendly party, the United Malays National Organization (UMNO) in the negotiations for eventual self-rule. The three women leaders of AWAS all took divergent paths after the break-up of the original movement. One went on to lead the women's wing of the Islamic Party, one chose to take the struggle underground by joining the outlawed Malayan Communist Party, while the third went on to join UMNO. The latter subsequently became the country's second woman minister when it achieved its independence.[2] Nevertheless, the early phase of women's involvement in UMNO was not simply marked by their compliance and acceptance of established structures of male dominance. One of UMNO's first female agitators was Khatijah Sidek, who did not waste much time in questioning gender disparities within the party as soon as she was elected leader of the women's wing in 1954. Demands were made that more women be represented in party decision-making bodies, that a separate women's youth wing be formed, and that there be increased nominations for women to contest electoral seats. For this, she was construed as breaching party discipline and finally expelled from the party (Manderson, 1980: 113–14). As UMNO took over the reins of the post-colonial state, any seemingly radical demands made by women, such as reforming *Shariah* laws, were swiftly tempered (Dancz, 1987: 161). Soon, women simply acquiesced or were 'naturalized' to the structure of gendered hierarchy within the party. Even till today, the unspoken norm of UMNO's power structure situates the status of its women's wings below that of its all-male, youth wing.

During this phase of nationalist uprising non-Malay women whose forefathers largely came as immigrants from China and India continued to define their loyalty as belonging to their original homelands.

Citizenship of their new country, British Malaya at that time, was an ambiguous notion. Among Chinese women, it was their schooling experience, moulded after the system in China, which played a pivotal role in influencing their specific political involvements. Some joined the Anarchist Movement and many more became members of the Malayan Communist Party (Khoo, 1994: 1–2). Some of the most active Indian women in the country also joined political movements engaged in struggles in India. In 1941, when Chandra Bose formed the Indian Independence Movement and the Indian Independence Army, Indian women in Malaya were recruited to be part of the Rhani of Jansi Regiment of the Army, and travelled to Burma to make their way into India (Khoo, 1994: 3). Despite having anti-colonialism as a common defining purpose, the mobilization for such a cause was still forged along an uncommon identity-distinct platform. The 'nation' was not necessarily the physical ground upon which one stood.

This helps explain why party politics that downplayed ethnic differences was unsuccessful in attracting adherents. The Independence of Malaya Party (IMP), set up in 1951 with its membership open to all races, specifically promised equal opportunities regardless of sex. However, it barely survived even a year of its formation. Another multiracial party, the Parti Negara was launched in 1954 and even promised equal pay for equal work, equal opportunities as well as emancipation for women. This party too failed to leave a mark in the country's first election. Another non-communal party, the Pan-Malayan Labour Party, which committed itself to ensuring women's equality by including a proposal for a Women's Charter, was also unsuccessful in garnering mass electoral support. Malaysian women's early involvement in formal politics was only successful if it followed the model of the inter-ethnic consociational 'cartel'. Nationalism was based on particularistic ethnic concerns and therefore overrode all other political projects, such as feminism or labour unionism. Even though the nationalists recognized the enhancement of women's rights as an important objective, they could not be universalized and therefore successfully striven for, given that women of the different ethnic groups did not get together.

It was only six years after independence in 1963 that a significant non-governmental multiracial woman's organization, the National Council for Women's Organizations (NCWO) was formed. The formation of the NCWO was spurred by the issue of women's unequal pay, which was first highlighted by the Women Teacher's Union, an organization formed in 1960.[3] Women's unequal pay at that time strongly galvanized women to come together. The impetus for the formation of the NCWO also came from an overall global trend in the 1960s to gain recognition for the rights of working women. International bodies like the Young Women's Christian Association (YWCA) contributed significantly towards the formation of the NCWO. In fact, it was at the YWCA's initiative that a conference of women's groups was organized in 1960 and the NCWO was subsequently formed. In tandem with this development, the NCWO's establishment was further boosted by the close cooperation of the women's wing of UMNO. These women had successfully organized a Women's Day rally on 25 August 1962 by mobilizing the participation of many non-governmental women's organizations. The then woman leader of UMNO saw in the NCWO a formal structure which could serve as an umbrella coalition for the different groups which the party had mobilized (Dancz, 1987: 139–41). Since then, NCWO, together with UMNO has kept alive the annual tradition of celebrating National Women's Day on 25 August.

NCWO's leadership structure mirrored the 'ethnic elite accommodation' model of the ruling party. The leaders of NCWO were 'deliberately' elected among women of the three major ethnic groups of the country.[4] What different ethnic women could not achieve through their membership in the women's wings of their ethnic-based political parties was realized within the NCWO. The NCWO became the vehicle through which legislative reforms granting equal pay, women's equal access to public service jobs, and marital rights were achieved. Several of the chairpersons of the NCWO had also been women ministers in the Cabinet, making the NCWO not only a close ally of the government, but almost a surrogate of the 'consociational-democratic' state.

Although non-partisan, the identification of NCWO with the ruling government was so strong that representatives from two opposition parties, the Socialist and Islamic parties withdrew their membership from the organization in 1965 (Dancz, 1987: 140). The NCWO tried to overcome the contrived divisions with which multi-ethnic elite women were faced at the party politics level, and played a very important role in encouraging cross-party collaboration among women politicians. However, it was no less a sponsored institution. I argue that it was a sponsored entity in the sense that it tied its interests closely to that of the establishment. The NCWO selectively engaged in campaigns which either reflected the interests of a particular class of women or were not politically contentious. For instance, while equal wages for white-collar professionals were fought for, the same rights for equal treatment and remuneration were not sought for women industrial workers, whose numbers in the workforce swelled rapidly during the country's export-led phase of industrialization. The NCWO also steered clear of campaigns demanding the unionization of women workers or welfare provisions for childcare and reproductive health.

The politics of inter-ethnic compromise, accommodation, and bargaining, as levers for successful negotiations with the British for eventual self-rule, had spilt over to affect women's involvement in formal politics after the new nation-state was consolidated. The Alliance party which became the government since independence till today, consisted of three ethnic-based parties, UMNO (United Malays National Organization), MCA (Malaysian Chinese Association), and the MIC (Malayan Indian Congress); all three parties did their part in sponsoring women's entry into politics. The few women candidates fielded in national elections have comfortably succeeded on the strength of their parties (Ramli, 1998). Such a tradition ensured women's unfailing presence in electoral politics but did not allow women leaders to test social limits or to challenge entrenched systems through parliamentary democracy. Since women's wings occupy a subordinate status within their parties, women who were nominated to stand and got elected, were inevitably more beholden to their patrons in the party than to their electorates outside (Ibrahim, 1998). In this quid pro quo arrangement women politicians trod carefully between toeing party lines and appeasing women's rights lobbyists, usually to the disadvantage of women's causes. Thus, women politicians contributed little towards the democratization of gender politics, within as well as outside their parties. Even when women's rights legislation and policies were to be pushed for, it was non-governmental women's groups such as the NCWO which provided the impetus and the gentle pressure or negotiations 'behind-the-scenes' for women politicians to act (Mohamad, 2002). However, even the NCWO avoided pushing for legislation which was considered contentious, such as the reform of *Shariah* laws. The distinctive stance of the NCWO, of which its leaders are still proud today, is that it has always stuck to a 'non-confrontational' approach in advancing women's rights.

Within political parties, internal reforms to break the vicious circle of gender inequality within party structures have also never occurred in post-independent Malaysia. Furthermore, the strength of women voters (in numbers) has failed to translate into a clamour for gender reforms. Thus the issue of women's representation in parliamentary democracies has remained irrelevant for gender empowerment despite the strong perception that women's role in formal politics can lead to a change for the women's constituency (Ramli, 1998). This is a condition which is not unlike that experienced by other Asian countries where women's formal representation in national legislatures has been less important in pushing for women-orientated policies than the role played by autonomous women's groups (Lee and Clark, 2000: 19).

Origin of Hyperethnicity

In 1969 the country's experience with ethnic riots forced a restructuring of national strategies by way of the New Economic Policy (NEP), an affirmative-action instrument for redressing economic inequality based on ethnicity.[5] This policy of social engineering through extensive state intervention was justified on the grounds that Malays and indigenous people had been unfairly disadvantaged by historical circumstances. After three decades of implementation, the NEP delivered both positive and negative changes. The socio-economic disparity between Malays and Chinese has been narrowed, and there has been a rapid rate of urbanization among the formerly rural-based Malay population, thus allowing them to enter the modern workforce. On the downside, the social distributive function of the NEP has been distorted, resulting in the creation of a small class of wealthy Malay capitalists, in tandem with the rise of capitalists from all ethnic groups. Their fortunes were accumulated largely on the backs of patronage politics, leading to the attendant consequence of rampant cronyism and corruption within the system. In a sense, the NEP was the dominant motif upon which all of the country's social, cultural, political and economic priorities were shaped.[6]

With the NEP's implementation from the 1970s onwards, all aspects of Malaysia's political, social, and cultural life became hyperethnicized. The term hyperethnicity is used here to mean an all-encompassing ethnicization whose defenders constantly try to subsume any politics that are outside the interest of the preservation of ethnic particularities. In Malaysia's phase of developmentalism, despite the overarching emphasis on economic growth, there was a heightening of identity politics, acting as a form of boundary closure to mark off the *bumiputra* (indigenous) from the non-*bumiputra* or largely the Malay from the non-Malay. Islam as religion was simultaneously incorporated to lend more definitive authenticity to the identity of the cultural Malay or was used to displace the old, maligned 'Malay' characterizations ('the lazy native'), purported to be the source of the group's backwardness. The new, 'Islamized' identity adopted by Malays was more assertive, forceful, and had strength in a global movement. 'Peripheralized' and 'ossified' by colonial protectionist policy, the only way out of this Malay rut was to reinvent new parameters for its reassertion (Kessler, 1992: 139).

Political causes were also formally and informally identified as the exclusive domain of particular ethnic groups (Islamic women's rights to be articulated only by Muslims, Chinese education rights to be taken up only by Chinese political parties, and estate workers' rights only by Indian political parties). As a result, it was difficult to universalize social problems, and their articulation, qua women's issues, qua labour issues, or as issues of civil liberties, were left to segments of the residual 'civil society' to take up. This residual civil society was essentially the marginalized civil society enfeebled by this situation of hyperethnicization, while the other, bigger, ethnically polarized and 'encapsulated' civil society was reduced to a mere extension of the state (Jesudason, 1996). The inevitable outcome of the NEP was that it could only be implemented through a series of legal instruments which enhanced the repressive apparatuses of the state to limit civil and political freedoms (Munro-Kua, 1996). Hence, people either pragmatically acquiesced to the national project (largely, a disempowered non-Malay constituency), instrumentally accepted it (largely, those who had the capacity to benefit from it), or reinforced identity politics through it for the further assertion of political dominance and exclusiveness (largely, Malays and Muslims).[7] As the cycle of pragmatic acquiescence, instrumental acceptance, and identity reinforcement spiralled and intensified, the residual civil society with its articulation of more universal causes, such as justice, democracy, accountable governance, and human rights struck almost no resonance with this polarized polity. And even if there were to be formidable counterhegemonic dissent, this too had to be fostered within an ethnicized space. The Islamic counter-hegemonic movement, the Darul Arqam was mobilized exclusively among Malays, while at the level of formal representative politics, the biggest opposition party, the Democratic Action Party (DAP), was Chinese-based and Chinese-supported.

The Second Phase: Civil Society Void, Second Wave Feminism, and Political Division

Fifteen years after the country's independence, and through the era of the NEP, Malay women underwent a new phase of weakening, perhaps even more insidious than their experience of being reduced to a sponsored political entity after their engaged participation in nationalist resistance. When Malays reconstituted their identities to stamp their exclusivity and separateness from non-Malays, Islam was used to redefine a new identity. Before this, to be recognized as simply 'Malay' carried with it the connotation of being culturally inadequate. The Malay identity was perceived to be too ambiguous, fluid, and flexible. The cultural 'Malay' was likened to a syndrome of 'backwardness', a condition which opened itself to domination by both colonial and non-Malay forces (Mahathir, 1970). Subsequently, the interleaving of 'Malay political dominance' or *Ketuanan Melayu* (a term which connotes rule by Malay, *male*-masters) as national ideology was used as both the moral and coercive bases for addressing the failed national project of delivering the community from poverty and economic ignominy. It happens that Malaysia's experiment with the NEP coincided in a timely way with the rise of Islamization globally.

Thus, when the global revivalist Islamic movement swept through Malaysia from the 1970s onwards, it was not long before a hyperethnicized feminine identity (the veiled, modest, maternal Malay-Muslim woman) had taken pre-eminence over other identities. Like so many past and contemporary examples elsewhere, women quickly became the touchstone of a new project for recasting ideological foundations (Kandiyoti, 1989; Mostov, 2000). In Malaysia, women's agency was used to 'rebuild Malay-Muslim identity' (Ong, 1995: 179). Mostov elegantly describes shades of a similar project in former Yugoslavia: 'They exaggerate the differences between those on either side of the boundaries and celebrate the common identity among those within, demonizing the ethnic or national Other and denying individual difference among their "own" ' (2000: 90–1).

The liberty to adopt a non-ethnicized feminist identity became a limited option among large numbers of Malay women. Nevertheless, the Islamicized, Malay woman in post-colonial Malaysia was in reality a hybrid of mitigated modernity in fusion with an elusively reconstructed spatial and historical Islam. The spatial and historical Islam was to be found in the authentic past of an Arab world, and not in local traditions and memory. But unable really to counter the inevitable impacts of modernization and the inevitable pressure to reconstitute identity, Malay Muslim women sought psychological as well as pragmatic rationales to justify their choice of clothes, lifestyles, and social behaviour. Minimally, the veil is adopted because the veil is taken to be the undisputed symbol of Islamization even if piety were to be exhibited in a marginal way. Muslim women also don the veil because that eases their public acceptance, largely among Muslim males but also with other Muslim women too (who seek collective reinforcement) as the precondition for strategic career-moves in politics or public management. Much as these women negated the tensions arising from such contradictions, the project to submerge the identity of a universalized woman took full effect and resulted in a division between Islamicized women and other women (both

Malays and non-Malays) who remained outside of the Islamization project, but no less untouched by it. Eventually these contradictions and divisions become naturalized, creating 'other' nations within the 'mainstream/dominant' nation. The enforced dichotomization between Muslims and non-Muslims also led to a pervasive though erroneous perception that unequal gender relations only associated with an Islamized social system and that Islamic practices were highly gendered and non-Islamic practices were more gender-neutral. Such a perception was not difficult to foster, given that more political energies were expended to fortify the *Shariah* and even more cultural attention was targeted to ensure a distinct dress code for Muslims, particularly women. Thus one finds that, in a nation-within-a-nation, robed Muslim men would not bat an eyelid were a scantily clad Chinese woman to cross their path but a modestly dressed but unveiled Malay woman in their way would provoke an angry response.

But the sweep of Islamization was not merely necessitated by an economically induced cultural project. It was reinforced by a political void created by the imperatives of an authoritarian and development-alist state that sought to contain civil society elements, beginning with communist insurgents. Its 'cold-war' fervour of suppressing communist, socialist, left-leaning, and labour movements in post-colonial Malaysia, particularly after the May 1969 riots led to the destruction of a once-vibrant civil society. In such an atmosphere Islam remained as one of the last bastions, if not the only legitimate site, for limited counter-hegemony. Among Muslims the space provided by Islam became the only feasible ambit within which divergent though circumscribed political expressions could find root. Islam was, in actual fact, a two-edged sword. It was a force which the state wanted to contain as well as to co-opt. It served to legitimize the politics of 'Malay domination' but on the other hand it was also the site in which remnants of any Malay opposition or its latent variety could safely be ensconced. As such, even as Islamization was co-opted as a state project, the strongest opposition against this state was the Islamic party.

Non-Muslim Malaysians largely chose the route of compliance because for them, post-independence, post-1969 Malaysian politics spelt 'the end of ideology' or an end to class politics which they could at least previously engage in to countermand divisive ethnic politics and affirm a political role for themselves. But the deployment of draconian measures eventually marginalized dissidents of the left, a majority of whom were Chinese. More than demolishing the ideological presence of the left the state also obscured the nascent project for multicultural democratization. Chinese activists (even among those with leftist traditions) diverted their political energies into fighting for issues within ethnicized rubrics such as Chinese language, education, and cultural rights, often within the safe limits of electoral politics (Heng, 1988; Tan, 1992).

Later, as the developmentalist state with its relentless agenda for economic growth took precedence over the dictates of cold-war politics, a majority of Malaysians simply chose the path of pragmatic acquiescence and became driven by self-seeking economic interests rather than by wider political goals which were becoming elusive and practically intangible. Whatever dissent or sense of dejection they had about the legitimacy of the state gradually transmuted into an instrumentalist acceptance of what the state was able to offer in the form of economic gains and expedient notions of cultural 'freedoms'.[8] This contributed further to the hyperethnicization of the polity, with a culturally and politically engaged Islamized Malay polity on one side, coexisting with an instrumentally depoliticized and pragmatic non-Malay polity on the other. A once oppositional Chinese-based, regional party, the Gerakan, exemplifies the condition of 'instrumental depoliticization' in its decision to join the ruling National Front as a coalition partner during the first national election of the post-1969 period (Von Vorys, 1975: 386–7). Chinese political parties acted upon a perception that they could bargain for their circumscribed rights more effectively within the UMNO-led national coalition than if they were to remain outside of it. But the two Chinese parties, the MCA and Gerakan, have in effect played second-fiddle to UMNO, steering clear of challenging the reified notion of 'Malay dominance' or pushing the limits of Chinese economic or cultural rights beyond the NEP norms. As for the rest of civil society, a small, 'disempowered' non-Malay sector, in unity with a smaller sector of the Malay polity, constituted whatever was left of civil society. This residual civil society, enfeebled by hyperethnicization nevertheless sustained itself through the promotion of movements for labour, environmental, consumer, democratic, human, and women's rights.

Feminism and the Authoritarian State

Despite the overwhelming tide of Islamization, and the reaffirmation of ethnic divides, the feminist movement did manage to take root in the country. Several new women's organizations, all coalescing around the issue of violence against women (VAW) were formed in the mid-1980s. Organizations such as the Women's Aid Organization

(WAO), Women's Crisis Centre (WCC), Women's Development Collective (WDC), and All-Women's Action Movement (AWAM) were initiated by middle-class, urban women, some of whom had returned after receiving their tertiary education in the West. Among the initiators were women activists of the left, especially those disenchanted by the pervasiveness of sexism within movements which prioritized the articulation of class at the expense of gender interests. Feminism as a political project could only gain its adherents among those at the political margins who wanted to articulate their sense of oppression, personal and systemic, through a language of counter-hegemony, moving away from the national project of ethnicization. Thus, the reach of feminism was limited. It had to latch on to issues which were inclusive and away from trammelled sites monopolized by the dominant, ethnicized civil society. The appeal of 'feminism' among some non-Malay and middle-class women was because it had the image of being non-political, enabling them to work in women's organizations without being partisan or the issues ever traversing 'ethnically touchy' boundaries. Many middle-class women were eager to work with the above-mentioned organizations that extended help to battered or abused women. They couched their involvement as 'volunteerism', linking it to acts of altruism and charity, rather than to counter-hegemony. Nevertheless, the underlying principles and philosophy behind the formation of the new women's groups were not simply to confine their activities to extending social services to abused women but also to inject a new ideology of feminism into the conception of the structural origin of women's oppression, such as is manifest in the victimization of women through violence. However, the peculiarity of local political and economic conditions made it difficult for the feminist movement to spread its wings beyond its middle-class, urban, and largely non-Malay enclave. Violence against women (VAW) was the only issue left that was a common denominator in every woman's life, regardless of class and ethnicity. It was also simply the only site not captured or hyperethnicized by the state. Thus, for almost two decades, feminist organizing in Malaysia centred not only strategically but also pragmatically, around the issue of VAW (Tan, 1999).

Alliance with Working-Class Women

The second wave feminist movement which started in the 1980s could also not build any alliances with working-class women, despite the massive and rapid entry of rural women into the industrial workforce (Lim, 1978; Grossman, 1979). The 'horrors' of waged work and cultural dislocation seemed to offer the right conditions for their political mobilization. But this did not happen. First, as soon as the country embarked on attracting foreign investments for its export sector, laws were enacted which prohibited unionization among workers in the foreign-owned electronic sector, where women were largely hired. Second, since a majority of industrial workers were Malay women, this in itself became the social bulwark against their mobilization by unions or feminist groups. In the early years of export-led industrialization, Malay women's involvement in factory work was not kindly looked upon. They were labelled 'morally loose' and considered 'easy sexual prey' by an array of new 'administrative and regulatory mechanisms', employing sexual metaphors and discourses for social control (Ong, 1987: 183). Young, unmarried, rural women were brought out for the first time from their villages and were housed as a group in the cities without parental supervision— a practice which was uncommon at that time. As if to redeem their sullied moral identities, after having been subjected to the slew of cultural admonishments by representatives of their own communities, Malay women workers situated their loyalty even more definitively within their ethnicity rather than class. When they were 'assailed by contradictory, unflattering representations of themselves, factory women often sought in Islam guidance, self-regulation to comply with work discipline and to inculcate an ascetic attitude towards life' (Ong, 1987: 185). Malay women's economic status was changing ahead of their cultural identity. Despite experiencing a tremendous sense of economic mobility, they were pressured to preserve the moral fabric of being 'Malay' and hence women's role in the reproduction of the patriarchal family was reaffirmed.

Alliance with Rural Peasant Women

The feminist movement was also unable to build even the weakest of alliances with rural, peasant women. The rural Malay constituency was a domain that was almost completely hegemonized by Malay political forces, either representing the state or the opposition. The ruling Malay party, UMNO, heavily patronized the Malay peasantry because rural constituencies were delineated so as to increase the number of Malay-majority seats. This gave the greatest electoral advantage to Malay candidates who stood under UMNO. As these constituencies were strategic for UMNO's electoral dominance, the state maintained a tight control over Malay villages. State development committees, although set up and funded by the state, are *de facto* the eyes and ears of the party. Resources and subsidies were

channelled through these committees in exchange for political loyalty
towards the party (Shamsul, 1986). Nevertheless, despite UMNO's
rural hegemony, the main opposition party, the Islamic Party of
Malaysia (PAS) also succeeded in building up its base within the rural
enclave. One reason why PAS was successful was that there inevitably existed various lacunae in UMNO's patronage net, especially
when resources were limited. It is not coincidental that some of the
poorest villages in the poorest Malay states are also the hotbed of
Islamist opposition politics, where economic or social deprivation of
the rural poor are being articulated through the language of Islam.
Islam is used to attack the deficiency of the secular and 'morally
corrupt' government for being unable to prioritize policies on social
redistribution over more materialistic and grandiose projects that
were intended to showcase modernity.

During the pre-independence phase when the state maintained
a weaker hegemony over the peasantry, insurgent movements succeeded in establishing their bases in the rural interior and recruited
peasant women into various nationalist movements including that
of the outlawed Malayan Communist Party. Contemporary feminist
groups, unlike gender activism associated with nationalist movements of the past, have been unable to make any inroads into the
rural Malay heartland. Quite clearly, the feminism that was promoted
in Malaysia's developmental phase was actually ensconced within
a particularistic middle-class and Western-liberal framework. Thus,
the cause of gender rights and equality associated with this group
was also considered biased towards one set of values. Nationalism,
on the other hand had a more 'indigenous' and 'organic' ring to it.
Early colonial resisters had emerged from the ranks of marginalized
rural and religious movements (Roff, 1967).

Alliance with Islamic Women

By the late 1980s, some feminist groups began to make efforts to
engage with Islam. This activity was initially spurred by feminist
international networking, such as initiatives organized by the network of Women Living Under Muslim Laws (WLUML). The WLUML
was one of the most significant networks which began a global project
of feminist dialogue and engagement with Islam (Shaheed, 1994).
In any case, feminist organizations, notably the Women's Crisis
Centre (WCC), the Women's Development Collective (WDC), the
All-Women's Action Movement (AWAM), and Sisters-In-Islam (SIS)
had found it necessary to incorporate an Islamized paradigm in their
engenderment of some versions of an 'indigenous' feminism. SIS was

formed around the early 1990s and sought to reinterpret Islam from a feminist viewpoint. WCC started a research project on Muslim Women and Law in 1995 to study the impact of the *Shariah* on women's rights and status (Mohamad, 2000). By the early 1990s the WCC had also started its programme of social and legal counselling for Muslim women. But there was never any project to challenge the hegemony of Islam *per se*, it was always to *engage* with Islam by entering into dialogue with it, while deploying its discourses within an 'Islamically' acceptable politics. Such efforts did not succeed in breaking down the wall of exclusivity which separated the interests of Muslim from non-Muslim women. Nevertheless, the 'secularized' nature of debates over women's rights created a space for Muslim and non-Muslim feminists to physically converge at fora which deliberated on the various prospects for reforms, from the *Shariah* to the Islamic nation-state.[9]

The large majority of Malay-Muslim, middle-class, and professional women at this time were not directly touched by the feminist project. They were to be found in large numbers within the Islamist organizations which had also flourished under the aegis of the developmentalist state. In line with the NEP's professed objective of creating a large class of professionals and urban workers, scores of *bumiputera*, largely Muslim Malays, were given places in higher education and sent abroad for their studies. Within fifteen years of the NEP's implementation, the number of Malay professionals had risen, along with the rate of urbanization among Malays. But as discussed earlier, a majority of Malays, especially among the youth, was only drawn (either by choice or peer pressure) to Islamic movements. These movements ranged from being fundamentalist-radical, even counter-hegemonic (such as the Darul Arqam), to one which can be characterized as being modernist and having close ties with the ruling party, UMNO (such as the Islamic Youth Movement, or ABIM). There were also NGOs such as the Islamic Reform Congregation (JIM), which drew a large part of its membership among Malay students studying abroad. JIM claims to be a movement of 'reform', or drawing people to the Islamic way of life through charitable acts of providing educational and health services to the community. Many women professionals, such as doctors and teachers, were involved in the provisions of such services.

Malay women who constitute a large membership of these movements, whether the Darul Arqam or JIM, kept clear of secular feminist discourses and organizations. The overall project of Islamic movements was to integrate, not separate, gender interests within the larger rubric of Islamization. Educated, professional Muslim women within these organizations advocated the principle of gender complementarity rather than equality. Even though the VAW campaign during the 1980s and 1990s was engaged in by a wide spectrum of women's groups, ranging from the mainstream to the feminist (largely non-Malay-based), the absence of Malay women's representatives of Islamic groups was striking. But it must also be noted that, with the exception of the Darul Arqam, the main urban Islamic groups which had large women's membership, particularly ABIM and JIM, belonged to the Islamic mainstream. Like the rest of hyperethnicized civil society, they were also an extension of the state (which portrayed itself to be committed to Islamic governance), and did not identify with labour, women, or human rights causes in any prominent way. Even the VAW issue did not provide enough of a bridge to bring middle-class Islamic women and feminist groups together. In fact, when the Domestic Violence Act was passed in 1994, women members from ABIM voiced their concern about this legislation because it did not differentiate the legal jurisdiction of Muslim women from non-Muslim women (Hashim, 1996). Their point was that Muslim women and issues affecting their status within the family could not be governed by a civil act, as only the *Shariah* family law would have jurisdiction over them (Othman, 1996). They argued that the *Shariah* had its own provision to deal with the issue of spousal violence. The choice of language was also a source of contention, with the term 'family violence' preferred over 'domestic violence' and 'violence against women'. Here was an example in which ethno-religious identity was overwhelmingly prioritized over gender identity.

It was as though the rubric of hyperethnicization was resisting the impulse to universalize women's interests and identity. At this time (in the mid-1990s), some years before the political unravelling of the regime, the bulk of the Islamist civil society was a 'captured civil society' performing its role as the purveyor of the ideology of separateness and exclusivity. It was only after the sacking of Anwar in September 1998, that ABIM, founded by Anwar himself in the 1970s, found itself to be on the opposite side of the Mahathir government. JIM which had an image of being non-partisan before the Anwar crisis almost instantly took an active, even partisan role in the *reformasi* movement. The post-crisis period of 1998 saw the active participation of women members of JIM in meetings and programmes planned by feminist groups. Muslim women in Islamic organizations became more open to speaking the language of feminism as part of their wider cause of dissension against the present government, a struggle simply articulated as being the fight for restoring democracy and justice.

The Third Phase: Crisis in Governance and the Politics of Gender Inclusion

The Asian crisis of 1997 was significant in terms of the economic damage that it brought to the formerly prosperous East Asian newly industrializing countries. It was perhaps even more momentous in its ability to unravel entrenched political, social, and cultural institutions of many countries in the region, including Malaysia. It was at this time that Prime Minister Mahathir's rule began to flounder. Mahathir's dismissal of Anwar (his deputy) from office in September 1998, followed by Anwar's torture in prison, a dubious trial to get him convicted of sexual misconduct, and subsequent fifteen-year imprisonment swiftly sparked a *reformasi* (reformation) movement. At first this was expressed as a largely Malay-based outrage against Mahathir's treatment of Anwar. Ultimately, the movement triggered the articulation of a host of other discontents, ranging from government corruption, the emasculation of the judiciary, to questionable racial policies brought about by the abuse of the NEP. The *reformasi* essentially evolved to become the all-encompassing counter-hegemonic, cross-ethnic uprising against a perceived anachronistic order.

Before the precipitation of the crisis favourable economic conditions allowed the state to be both indifferent to as well as tolerant of liberalism as there was a general absence of mass disaffection towards it. The challenge of the women's movement, also associated with liberalism, was considered comparatively benign by the established order when compared to the threat posed by opposition Islamists. Feminist groups or feminist elements within mainstream women's organizations were also marginal, having no popular or mass-based acceptance. Thus, feminists were not obstructed from carrying on with their campaign for gender equity. Even a mainstream group like the NCWO which was close to government collaborated with feminist organizations in the VAW campaign, despite underlying tensions over differences in leadership styles and ideological approaches. Furthermore, large sections of Malay women were mobilized within Islamic-based organizations and preferred to deal with gender issues through a non-ambivalent Islamic framework. Feminism was caught in the middle, between being benevolently ignored and meekly endorsed by the government, since it was an isolated movement and its presence could neither enhance nor damage state hegemony.

The formation of the Alternative Front opposition coalition (the BA) consisting of four major parties, namely the Islamic Party (PAS), the Democratic Action Party (DAP), the People's Party (PRM), and the newly formed National Justice Party (Keadilan), was reflective of this 'rainbow' partnership which seized the situation of a weakening state as an opportunity for rebuilding and reconstituting the strength of counter-hegemonic forces, or a chance for the once residual civil society to stand up to an overpowering state. Out of this, two questions emerged. First, why would Malay elites in general who derived clear advantages from the state's affirmative action policy embrace a cross-ethnic opposition movement after the financial crisis? Second, why would secular feminists as well as the residual but autonomous civil society also find it necessary to participate in this multi-ethnic and multi-sectarian coalition? In addressing these two issues, it must be stressed that it was not the financial crisis *per se* that led to the heightening of *reformasi*. The early stage of *reformasi* outburst was a largely Malay-led movement. Anwar, a charismatic, former dissident Islamic activist was considered an icon of reformist Islam when he was brought on board to join UMNO in 1982. Hence, his dismissal angered a section of the urban-based, Malay middle class who had identified with Anwar's Islamist aspirations. By 1998, the NEP had also created a core of self-assured Malay middle class who were less dependent on government patronage for upward mobility, and thus had few qualms about being more critical towards the UMNO-led government (Mohamad, 2001). Another reason as to why a cross-ethnic opposition movement came about was the impending national election of 1999. There was a strong sense that the ruling National Front government could either be unseated or denied its hitherto unbroken record of winning a two-thirds majority in Parliament, given the level of disaffection that had been generated, both from its handling of the financial crisis and over the Anwar issue. In many ways, forming a united opposition coalition, ranging from Islamic fundamentalists to secular democrats, was largely a pragmatic strategy to try to achieve 'the unthinkable' in Malaysia's electoral history (Khoo, 1999).[10]

Only a few months before the eruption of these new political developments feminist groups were at a loss as to how to redefine their relevance amidst their increasing sense of marginalization within the system.[11] But by 1999, a few months after Anwar's sacking, detention, and assault, and in anticipation of an impending general election, seven women's groups, including an Islamic organization,[12] put together a Women's Charter or a manifesto to be used as a platform of election demands. The manifesto was termed the 'Women's Agenda for Change' (WAC). Meetings to discuss and debate the charter saw an extensive participation of representatives from some thirty organizations.[13] The exception was the women's wing of the

Islamic Party (PAS) which did not want to participate since it did not receive endorsement from the party leadership. On the other hand, another Islamic women's group, the women's division from JIM, saw itself distinct from PAS and readily participated in the preparation of the manifesto.[14] On 23 May 1999, the WAC, which had eleven demands ranging from land rights to rights on sexuality, was officially launched. These 'eleven points' represented some of the more maximal demands made by feminists for an election campaign. One of the most controversial was contained in the section on tolerance of homosexuality and the rights of sex-workers. Yet even Muslim women who represented their respective Islamic bodies did not openly express their disquiet over these contentious points. The other strategy that emanated from feminists was to push for a woman candidate to contest the election on a gender-issues ticket. A group calling itself the Women's Candidacy Initiative (WCI) was formed for this purpose. Zaitun Kasim, a feminist activist, eventually stood for a parliamentary seat as a Democratic Action Party (DAP) candidate but specifically on a 'women's rights' ticket. Her loss was by no means considered disastrous, as the incumbent opponent's winning majority was reduced by 56 per cent from the previous election.

The 'Gender Card' and National Election of 1999

In the general election of 1999 amid more fervent opposition against the Mahathir government, women voters, women's causes and the women's movement of the periphery were elbowed onto centre-stage. Although this may not have led to substantial gains for women's rights in terms of policies and equality, there was nevertheless a visible improvement in terms of women's representation at the legislative level. The outcome of the election saw more women elected into Parliament than ever before, with twenty women parliamentarians, comprising 10.4 per cent of the House of Representatives, as compared to 7.8 per cent in 1995 and 6.1 per cent in 1990. The election also delivered a larger number of women opposition leaders in Parliament compared to previous elections. The four women opposition leaders accounted for 9 per cent of the opposition seats while government women representatives comprised 11 per cent of the seats won by the ruling coalition party.

There were two reasons as to why the run-up to the election saw the marked politicization and co-optation of women's issues. First, from the opposition perspective, it had to do with the entry of Wan Azizah Wan Ismail, the wife of Anwar Ibrahim, as a leading icon of opposition forces. She became the leader of the newly formed opposition party, the National Justice Party, and had quickly become a popular figure in the *reformasi* movement.[15] In a way, her thrust into politics had fired the public imagination about the importance of gender in the politics of change and democratization. There was an irony in this situation. While the *reformasi* movement was rallying behind a woman leader, the strongest force in this solidarity 'front' of diverse social groups and political parties was PAS, whose leaders were often vociferous in dissuading women from taking on any public roles.

Second, from the government viewpoint, faced with mounting public disaffection, only a strategy that could effectively disparage the strongest opposition party, the Islamic party (PAS), would save the incumbent government from possible electoral defeat. PAS's stance on women was also easy to denounce. The party did not even allow its women members to be fielded as candidates for the elections. Furthermore, PAS leaders, such as the popular and unassuming chief minister of Kelantan, were frequently trapped into uttering outrageous public statements. He once told women to leave their jobs as they were needed at home and would be less burdened with only one responsibility instead of two. A case was also voiced for pretty women to give up their jobs in place of their not-so-attractive counterparts as it would be easier for the former to look for husbands as their source of support. Such faux pas on the part of the less savvy PAS leaders were readily exploited by government-controlled media to draw attention to PAS's misogynistic policies. PAS was also discredited through its other stance, its commitment to the setting up of an Islamic state. It was painted as an extremist party bent on establishing a socially repressive and prohibitive state. This stance was perhaps the easiest to exploit as it struck an immediate fear among non-Muslim voters.

Although the BN government was returned to power at the federal level, the above strategies did not succeed in winning back the Kelantan state, a predominantly Malay-Muslim state, for the party. It also lost the state of Terengganu to the Islamic opposition. The 'gender card' was probably more effective among non-Muslim voters because women's rights, as opposed to women's welfare *per se*, were associated with secular politics, doubly acting as a safeguard against Islamic encroachment. This strategy worked in demonizing PAS among liberals and the majority of non-Muslim voters, who ultimately contributed to the BN's electoral victory. On the other hand, in the Muslim majority constituencies, the 'gender card' failed to make any impact.

The BN's 'championing' of women's rights was really meant to mitigate (perhaps successfully) its own record of corruption, mismanagement, and bad governance. In the final reckoning, the BN had calculated that moderate Muslims and non-Muslim voters would be persuaded to vote for the incumbent government because at least it would be 'trusted' to protect women's rights. It would thereby act as the best bulwark against the establishment of an Islamic state, a guarantee more important even than the risk of ousting the BN, with its stain of graft and other wrongdoings. However, given the expedient undertone of the strategy, some sections of the feminist camp could not, and did not, fully back the government's sudden defence of women's rights.

Members within feminist organizations were split as to whether the WAC should be allowed to be co-opted by the BN government or to remain united with the opposition front. Overtures had been made by government women politicians to court some feminists for their side. A few months before the election several selected women from feminist organizations were especially invited to meet with UMNO women leaders, including the deputy prime minister, over issues contained in the WAC. This meeting was not fully approved by all member organizations which had previously endorsed the WAC. Those who did not support the meeting felt that feminists were being made use of to shore up the reputation of UMNO's women's wings which did not have a good record of championing women's rights and was losing its supporters to the *reformasi* movement. On the other hand, those who accepted the invitation felt that they were merely strategically seizing the opportunity to enable the WAC to be taken seriously by those who would be in power to implement it.

Instrumentalizing Gender for Political Survival and Enhancement

As the above episodes have shown, the country's experience with the Anwar crisis and its tenth general election was one of the most significant instances where gender interests were being intensively or fully 'instrumentalized' by political forces.[16] The fact that women's stature could either be enhanced by appreciating the differences in the sexes or by the minimization of these differences (Molyneux, 2000) enabled political forces to play the game of 'pandering' to women's interests and identities by adopting one prerogative over the other. PAS promoted the idea of gender difference which requisitions the institutional protection for women against an 'unsafe' and masculinized public world, thus suggesting their retreat from political participation and ultimately from gainful employment. UMNO, the main Muslim-Malay party within the BN took the opposite stance, stressing the recognition of women's public roles. By obscuring gender difference, UMNO was able to convince liberals and non-Muslims, used to the idea of Islam bearing a heavily gendered cultural ideology (serving as the basis for the ascendance of Islamic fundamentalism) to throw their support behind the party. The expedient tactic of appealing to women's rights helped to repair UMNO's sullied human rights' reputation and deflected its critics from harping too much on its record of suppressing all other forms of civil liberties. PAS, on the other hand, had to focus more extensively on its reputation as a clean, ethical, and just party to win its support among non-Muslims and liberals. Thus, it clamoured for democracy and human rights, hoping to compensate for its disagreeable stance on women's rights and equality.[17] However, even PAS women were eventually forced to address the issues of women's rights when they were egged on by the party's coalition partners to take on a more active stand on many issues. Perhaps it was also the first time that the party and its women leaders were given the opportunity to face the issue squarely and to take a stand that would be subjected to the widest scrutiny by the public. The Islamic party was thrown into a dilemma between upholding strategies that could conflict with its beliefs and the need to abandon ideological differences in order to be unified with the diverse social movements behind *reformasi*. In some instances it threw its support behind women candidates. For example, PAS had to overlook its own conservative stance on women when it helped Zaiton Kassim, the WCI woman candidate, to campaign for her seat. It provided the campaign machinery for her, even though the party itself did not field any woman candidate of its own.[18]

Ever since the burst of *reformasi*, PAS's women members had become more vocal in questioning the party's discriminatory policies. A few months after the country's elections, PAS's women's wing committee member Dr Lo'Lo' Mohd Ghazali questioned PAS leaders as to why women leaders were not allowed to sit with their male counterparts on stage in their General Assembly meetings. She said: 'We see smartly dressed PAS leaders sitting on stage but what happened to us (women), why are we sidelined? If the media wants to play up this issue, go ahead, but I want to speak my mind. Is there women discrimination in PAS, or is it not Islamic if women were on stage with men?' (*Star*, 2001*d*).

Although the situation was not immediately rectified, the party president, aware of prevailing male bias, responded to this enquiry by reminding the party leadership to consider the feelings and proposals of female members rather than rejecting them. The spiral of *reformasi* politicization inevitably pushed Islamist and even PAS women to be more outspoken and more assertive about women's rights than they had ever been before. 'Gender' became a terrain that both government and opposition were keen to have a handle on. It became one of the few remaining bases, after erosion of its economic performance and failure to deliver clean governance, upon which the state could hope to regain legitimacy. Conversely, 'gender' was also the site upon which the Islamist opposition could falter as it forged its electoral ambition of capturing power within a multi-ethnic and multi-religious milieu. It came as no surprise when, two years after the onset of *reformasi*, PAS succumbed to having its women members stand for elections. Early in 2001 the party announced that it would be fielding women candidates in the next national elections because 'it wanted to take a realistic approach as its target was to form the next federal government in 2004' (*Straits Times*, 2001).

The Malaysian struggle for democratization is far from peculiar. The strategy of the state in courting women to shore up its weakening legitimacy had been an oft-used tactic elsewhere and in different historical periods. South Korea's oppressive military regime in the 1960s specifically used women to broaden its legitimacy base (Chin, 2000: 20). Similarly, all forces vying for political power during democratic transitions in Brazil, Chile, and Argentina were strategically compelled to adopt policies which appealed to women (Waylen, 1994). These examples show that there is something universal about the experiences brought about by occasions of democratic transition, particularly in the way that women's interests and identities were instrumentalized. Because of their capacity to shift and be transposed in different political contexts, they are flexibly adopted to accommodate the interests of contending forces in the mobilization of popular support.

Even after more than two years following its return to power, the Mahathir government did not quite succeed in restoring its legitimacy. Its worsening credibility gap allowed opposition forces to persist with their challenge. Perhaps because of this, the government continued to emphasize the women's agenda and tried hard to reap the approval of women constituents. A year after the election, the deputy prime minister announced that mothers would finally be permitted to sign official government forms such as passport applications for their children, consent forms for surgery, and school-related matters. Previously, such a moderate but fundamental right, to recognize women's guardianship status over their children, was deemed too controversial to enforce, for fear of upsetting Islamic conservative and religious forces. The minister justified this move by ambiguously declaring that this did not contravene the *Shariah* as 'it did not touch

on the question of guardianship' (*Star*, 2001*b*). Another concession
to women was the agreement by the prime minister to establish a
committee within the Islamic Affairs Development Department to
monitor all aspects of Islam and gender. The prime minister also
began to officiate at more women's meetings, such as the 'Women's
Conference 2000', a gathering held in conjunction with Malaysia's
Women's Day. The conference was in turn closed by another important male personage, the minister of finance and special functions.
There was also a special meeting, perhaps the first time in the
country, between the prime minister and representatives of a wide
spectrum of women's non-governmental organizations. Before this
new phase of political development, male political luminaries would
not be caught gracing women's functions or conducting dialogues
with them.

Subsequently, in one of the greatest moves to affirm the government's commitment to women's rights, the Ministry of Women's
Affairs was formed in January 2001. However, barely a month after
the announcement of its formation, the name of this new ministry
was quickly changed to the Ministry of Women and Family Development. Not only that, the newly appointed woman minister was
compelled to affirm that her ministry's priorities would be to reinforce women's basic and traditional functions like cooking and caring
for the household. There seemed to be some backtracking on earlier
understandings. The change of name to include 'family development'
was likely to emphasize that *family welfare* rather than *women's liberation* would be the mandate of the new ministry. The reference to
women's domestic chores seems to have been made to avoid upsetting the apple cart of prevailing sexist preference. In the end, the
difference between UMNO's sexism and PAS's was scarcely discernible, not unlike experiences elsewhere. Referring to reforms which
Turkish modernists had sought against Islamic traditionalists in the
early twentieth century, Kandiyoti perceptively noted that reforming
elites were not necessarily consistent as 'retrenchment into conservatism *vis-a-vis* women remained just below the surface' (1989: 131).

The new women's ministry was also set up in haste and without any
definite mandate. When the minister was appointed she did not have
any blueprint or agenda on which to base her activities. There seemed
to be an ad hoc interest in this and that. Some of her press statements
noted that she would look into the housing needs of single mothers,
then later on to include the task of dignifying the status of 'trans-
sexuals', and at some point declared that Muslim women would not
be forced to wear the veil. Besides outrage, there was much cynicism
generated over the formation of this ministry. One feminist stated

that the minister was two-faced, that while wanting 'to mainstream women's issues and bring women to the fore, she also plans to remind women of their traditional functions'.[19] Even the prime minister's daughter, a noted newspaper columnist, joined in the move to disparage the new minister, 'It, of course, doesn't help when the person in charge puts a high-heeled foot into her mouth by saying cooking is a basic function of women (I always thought that having babies was!)' (Mahathir, 2001). Other more straightforward analysis puts the creation of the ministry down to the need for the ruling party to 'secure women's votes at the next general elections' (Tan, 2001).

The ridicule heaped upon the ministry was further fuelled by altercations between two other women's wings of the BN's coalition partners. Their representatives immediately lobbied the prime minister so that important posts within the ministry could be filled by their own members. Since the minister appointed was from the women's wing of UMNO, the women's wing of the Chinese party (MCA) argued that their representative should rightly be given the deputy minister's post because they have 'the largest Chinese women's political membership outside China (*sic*)', and had contributed a great deal to the nation (*Star*, 2001a). But the women's wings of the Indian party (MIC) said that they too deserved an important post because they represented Indian women, who were the poorest class and lagging 'behind their Malay and Chinese sisters' (*Star*, 2001c). The minister proclaimed that the whole matter would be left to the prime minister to decide as he 'will know what to do and when' (Utusan Online, 2001).

Although feminist organizations were cognizant that the 'gender card' strategy was being used to counter and denigrate PAS, some groups did find it equally expedient to 'seize' this 'window of opportunity' to promote women's particularistic, even narrow, interests in the face of a weakening state, desperate for allies and support. Some women's groups saw the government's stance of 'warming up' to women's issues as a chance to bargain for maximum concessions.[20]

The events which followed Malaysia's political crisis and the realignment of ruling and opposition forces marked an important historical watershed. As the government sought to manage the crisis, there was an opening provided by cracks within the system. Opposition forces and the broad spectrum of civil society were able to renew, reorganize, and reassess their roles in affecting the course of possible transformations. Different opposition parties were compelled to bury their varied and contradictory principles in order to form a united front for electoral gain, while the regime was pushed to adopt uncharacteristic measures to counter the concerted challenge. As Jaquette has argued, transitions suggest many possibilities as there is a 'general willingness to rethink the bases of social consensus and revise the rules of the game', thus giving 'social movements an extraordinary opportunity to raise new issues and to influence popular expectations' (1991: 13).

Musing the Divides: Identity/Interest, Local Space/Universal Voice, Masculinized Politics/Feminized Civil Society

As a concluding reflection, this section sums up the essence of discussions above by returning to the question of the 'divides' and the 'differences' used as the basis for framing the analysis of gender politics in Malaysia. What this discussion has tried to show is that identities have taken on various dimensions in the articulation, as well as the suppression, of women's (universalized) interests in a political milieu which is constantly shifting, historically and contextually.

The main point is that the Malaysian feminist project of universalizing women's causes has long been ensconced within a residual segment of the civil society. Given this, the realization of a shared feminism has been constantly undermined. The never-ending and relentless project of state legitimation continues to be dependent on its simultaneous role as bearer of 'Malay-dominance' (with an overarching patriarchal control) and as procurer of economic wealth and welfare. Ling's conceptualization of the notion of 'hypermasculine' development calls this an extension of a 'frightening dual efficiency' of the state, in that women had become instrumental in the propagation of both its economic and political power (2000: 180–1). Women's input into the economy as industrial workers, as foreign domestics, and feminized professionals had always been extensively facilitated and encouraged by the state. At the same time, in the state's project to legitimize itself as patriarch and protector (imbued within the ideology of 'Malay dominance'), it deifies women as the guardians of family values, morals, and culture. The use of ideological apparatuses to convey this conflicting but often unquestioned personification of the exemplary self-sacrificing woman in national development has been pervasive. Such a template has also been used elsewhere. The patriarchs of Brazil's military regimes also 'extolled virtues of traditional womanhood', while thrusting 'millions of women into the workforce' (Alvarez, 1991: 60).

The second point to be emphasized is that the women's movement in Malaysia has also been undermined in its project to universalize due to the prevalence of conflicting interests among women themselves. Women's mobilization on the basis of their class interests has often been more strategic in ensuring their empowerment than the commitment to an all-inclusive feminist solidarity. Women who organize as a class of women bankers, for instance, would be likely to gain more access to specific opportunities than if they were to organize as a general caucus for women in development. In Malaysia, an organization which calls itself Peniagawati (Women in Business), at one time even went to the extent of toying with the idea of setting up a splinter association which would set apart the interest of women in 'big business' from women in 'small business'.[21]

Third, the failure of the feminist movement to instil a sense of collective affinity is due to conflicting identities which women bore, among themselves and within themselves. In Malaysia's case, the NEP syndrome led to the prioritization of ethnic identity over gender interests. Malay women received their preferential privileges not because of their gender status but because of their 'race', hence the importance of belonging to ethnic-based organizations. Muslim women also found themselves torn between upholding the 'group' rights of being Islamic and the 'individual' rights of being woman. Even Islamist feminists had to constantly meander around safe and acceptable precepts of enunciating the language and substance of human rights or seek a 'sensitive internal cultural discourse' so as not to upset prevailing religious and cultural mind-sets (Noraini, 1999: 189).

The fourth point of this chapter is that a relatively united feminist involvement in large civil movements such as the present *reformasi* movement is always in danger of being emasculated because of the prevalence of male-biased, male-defined strategies of mass mobilization. Men assume the frontline roles in political struggles, often because of the pervasive deployment of state violence in suppressing dissent, turning women away from taking undue risks in open confrontations. Yet while women may be just as passionately drawn to the cause of justice and democracy as men, the terrain of political mobilization recycles the same notions of patriarchal responsibility, with men assuming strategic leadership roles. Women's support is usually elicited for ulterior or specific purposes (i.e. to give the resistance movement a broad-based populist character or to use women to mobilize other women in achieving numerical strength).

Finally, in relation to the above, it must also be stated that there has emerged a paradoxical situation in which women leaders have had the greatest chance of ascending during transitional political phases. Perhaps because transitions present possibilities and opportunities to imagine new orders or build bridges between old and new systems, women were readily drawn or cajoled into the process. The *reformasi* in Malaysia catapulted Wan Azizah to prominence as its first symbol of concerted defiance against Mahathir. Her image of inexperience, geniality, and incorruptibility conveys the gentler and feminized face of politics in contrast to the Machiavellian, debased, and masculinized taint of politics attributed to Mahathir by his detractors.

As a matter of fact, across the region, the rise of women leaders in South-east Asia today seems to suggest that the greatest possibility for women's empowerment occurs during a period of flux and uncertainty (Richter, 1990–1). Perhaps they act as the iconic bridge between an ancient but benevolent patriarch and a new order that is in the making. Women leaders at this time are deified as matriarch or guardian angel, and personified as an extension of a revered patriarch. Whether it is Aung San Syu Kyii in Burma, Megawati Sukarnoputri in Indonesia, or Gloria Macapagal-Arroyo in the Philippines, the common denominator among them is fathers who belonged to a romanticized past that is being popularly construed as more glorious than the regime in power. Looked at from another perspective, the participation of women authority figures has been facilitated by the valorization of 'feminization', which Marchand (2000) argues to be the new basis of empowerment for a reconstituted civil society. For all the above reasons, the saliency of 'gender' has become a crucial dimension in democratization movements or in the displacement of old orders for the establishment of new ones.

The discussion above has shown that the issue as to why women cannot be organized within a united feminist movement revolves around their manifold interests and identities. In this regard the distinction between women's interests and women's identities is established so as to understand why women are mobilized differently. Some movements are organized *on* the basis of achieving common interests and others *out of* the basis of the recognition of their members' common identity (Ray and Korteweg, 1999). However, even though women may all potentially be mobilized to seek similar and common interests, their identities prevent them from struggling together in unity. Even more pertinent is the fact that their separate identities have prevented women from recognizing that they are unified by a common and universalized basis of subordination. However, the study has shown that there can exist conditions, no matter how momentary or partial, which enable the reconstruction of identities to support emerging interests, and to a certain extent engender shared visions out of multiple identities. A particular and localized condition such as 'Malay' Islamization did not necessarily mitigate the acceptance of a 'universalized' value, such as human rights and democracy, during the phase of *reformasi*. Values are fluid enough to enable them to be expediently constructed or deconstructed to take on either a universalized or a localized form. However, in grappling with the above issues one may also need to ask how long a 'politics of solidarity in difference' can last in a multi-ethnic and plural society such as Malaysia, especially when the common enemy, in the form of a perceived dictatorial leader, is no longer present? (Lister, 1997: 80).

I noted earlier that Malaysia's basis for ethnicization did not originate from the politics of multiculturalism or positive diversity. State development policies as exemplified by the NEP explicitly set apart the status and interests of one ethnic community from another, leading to the hyperethnicization of political, cultural, and social life. Within this paradigm, women's common causes had a limited chance of being sustained. Furthermore, women articulate their needs and rights differently and sometimes in contradictory ways.[22] However, the pressure for women to converge over common issues began to be felt as soon as the legitimacy of the 'Malay dominant' state was subjected to challenge. In the *reformasi* period a kind of 'social unmooring' from 'stable and hierarchical communal structures' (Mann, 1997: 117–226) was created and, if sustained, may even be enough to set off a reorganization of fixed identities and, ultimately, the development of new forms of agency.

Conclusion

In Malaysia's latest phase of political development both government and opposition have tried to enlarge their parameters for inclusion and political affinities by moving away from a once significant ethnicized and gendered base. Clientelistic politics associated with ethnicity will be slightly undermined and once ethnicity is devalorized as the basis for political mobilization and patronage, other identities will assume a new importance even though this may not necessarily portend the weakening of male domination. In Malaysia's politics of *reformasi,* the slogan of ridding the state of corruption, injustice, and unaccountable governance from the system has become an everyday discourse appearing to dislodge the overhang of hyperethnicity. Out of this, the politics of gender rights has emerged as a crucial site for eliciting popular consensus, transforming women's fragmented identities into universalized interests.

When considering experiences elsewhere the moot question is: would it ever be possible to sustain this state of political inclusion which puts gender rights on a par with other concerns of democratization? If and when the present regime is overturned or a new order is consolidated, will women's voices recede into the background? Even in the comparatively favourable conditions of the *reformasi* movement, women's groups in Malaysia were still not able to exploit fully current 'transitions' to take the more vexing issues such as veiling and the reform of the *Shariah* by the horns. For example, although dissension expressed over the intention of the newly elected state government of Terengganu to impose compulsory veiling succeeded in getting the plan withdrawn, there was no sustained commitment from either government or the Islamic opposition to abandon the instrument of the state to enforce mandatory veiling at some future date.[23] Furthermore, as the effectiveness of opposition and civil society forces in overturning the regime is contingent upon the strength of the Islamic party, the issues of Islamist women's rights as human rights will continue to be dictated by the theocratic authority structure of the party.

Given these uncertainties, perhaps the best lesson that the Malaysian feminist movement can draw from women's democratization experiences in Latin America and Central and Eastern Europe is to remain constantly vigilant against a patriarchal relapse (Alvarez, 1991; Friedman, 2000; Jaquette, 1991; Einhorn, 2000). Most importantly, the agenda for building social equality which Nancy Fraser (1997) asserts to be vital for the democratic mediation and recognition of 'difference' and political pluralities must be absolutely prioritized over other competing agendas. In establishing social equality, gender democratization should not be taken for granted as the natural result of democratization, it must be seen to be the necessary requirement of genuine democracy. Although Malaysia's seeming transition towards democratization may see the flagging of an authoritarian state, this may not necessarily lead to the phasing out of 'hypermasculinized' politics, whether upheld by government or opposition. Thus, if feminist activism is not renewed and consolidated, this inclusive phase of democratic pluralism carries the risk of being overtaken by a new, perhaps less authoritarian, but no less masculinized and ethnicized governance. The question which Kandiyoti (1989) once posed for Turkey rings true here—should women accept being reduced to 'symbolic pawns' or raised to become political actors in their own right, in the country's search for democratization?

As Malaysian feminism goes through its phases of political sponsorship to division and finally towards inclusion there exists, at least, the benefit of retrospection to inform political strategies. Many would like to believe that, had it not been for the triggering of Malaysia's economic and political crisis, the realization of gender justice, rights, and democracy would have become even more remote a prospect. Still, the shifting nature of women's identities and interests leaves open the possibility of new affinities being dismantled and old cleavages reinstated, not forgetting the possible prolongation of repression against civil society by an authoritarian state. Were the latter to occur, women of all identities and interests may find even more of a reason to seek a feminist solidarity in the fight for human rights and democracy.[24]

References

Alvarez, Sonia (1991) 'Women's Movements and Gender Politics in the Brazilian Transition', in Jane Jaquette (ed.), *The Women's Movement in Latin America* (Boulder, Colo.: Westview).

Blacklock, Cathy, and Laura Macdonald (2000) 'Women and Citizenship in Mexico and Guatemala', in Shirin M. Rai (ed.), *International Perspectives on Gender and Democratization* (Houndmills: Macmillan).

———— (1996a) 'Multiple Identities, Multiple Strategies', in Amrita Chhachhi and Renee Pittin (eds.), *Confronting State, Capital and Patriarchy: Women Organizing in the Process of Industrialization* (London: Macmillan Press).

Chhachhi, Amrita, and Renee Pittin (1996b) 'Introduction', in Amrita Chhachhi and Renee Pittin (eds.), *Confronting State, Capital and Patriarchy: Women Organizing in the Process of Industrialization* (London: Macmillan).

Chin, Mikyung (2000) 'Self-Governance, Political Participation, and the Feminist Movement in South Korea' in Rose J. Lee and Cal Clark (eds.), *Democracy and the Status of Women in East Asia* (Boulder, Colo., and London: Lynne Rienner).

Dancz, Virginia H. (1987) *Women and Party Politics in Peninsular Malaysia* (Singapore: Oxford University Press).

Dean, Jodi (ed.) (1997) *Feminism and the New Democracy: Re-siting the Political* (London: Sage).

Einhorn, Barbara (2000) 'Gender and Citizenship in the Context of Democratization and Economic Transformation in East Central Europe', in Shirin M. Rai (ed.), *International Perspectives on Gender and Democratization* (Houndmills: Macmillan).

Fraser, Nancy (1997) 'Equality, Difference and Democracy: Recent Feminist Debates in the United States', in Jodi Dean (ed.), *Feminism and the New Democracy: Re-siting the Political* (London: Sage).

Friedman, Elizabeth (2000) *Unfinished Transitions: Women and the Gendered Development of Democracy in Venezuela, 1936–1996* (University Park, Pa: Pennsylvania State University Press).

Funston, John (2000) 'Malaysia's Tenth Elections: Reformasi, Status Quo or Islam?', *Contemporary Southeast Asia*, 22/1: 23–59.

Grossman, Rachel (1979) 'Changing Role of Southeast Asian Women: The Global Assembly Line and the Social Manipulation of Women', *Joint Issue of Southeast Asia Chronicle/Pacific Research* SEAC 66/PSC, 9/5: 1–27.

Hashim, Rahmah (1996) 'Consider Complexities before Implementating Act, Says Group', *New Straits Times* (11 May).

Held, David (1997) *Models of Democracy* (Cambridge: Polity Press).

Heng, P. K. (1988) *Chinese Politics in Malaysia: A History of the Malayan Chinese Association* (Singapore: Oxford University Press).

Ibrahim, Kamilia (1998) 'Women's Involvement in Politics and the Need for a Paradigm Shift', in Sharifah Zaleha Syed Hassan (ed.), *Malaysian Women in the Wake of Change* (Kuala Lumpur: University of Malaya, Gender Studies Programme).

Jaquette, Jane (ed.) (1991) *The Women's Movement in Latin America* (Boulder, Colo.: Westview).

Jesudason, James (1996) 'The Syncretic State and the Structuring of Oppositional Politics in Malaysia', in Garry Rodan (ed.), *Political Opposition in Industrialising Asia* (London: Routledge).

Kandiyoti, Deniz (1989) 'Women and the Turkish State: Political Actors or Symbolic Pawns?', in Anthias Floya and Nira Yuval-Davis (eds.), *Women-Nation–State* (Houndmills: Macmillan).

Kausikan, Bilahari (1993) 'Asia's Different Standards', *Foreign Policy*, 92: 42–52.

Kessler, Clive (1992) 'Archaism and Modernity: Contemporary Malay Political Culture', in Joel Kahn and Francis Loh (eds.), *Fragmented Vision: Culture and Politics in Contemporary Malaysia* (Sydney: Allen & Unwin).

Khoo, K. K. (1994) 'Malaysian Women's Participation in Politics: A Historical Perspective', in Robert Haas and Rahmah Hashim (eds.), *Malaysian Women Creating their Political Awareness* (Kuala Lumpur: Friedrich Naumann Foundation and Asian Institute for Development Communication).

Khoo, Philip (1999) 'Thinking the Unthinkable: A Malaysia Not Governed by the BN?', *Aliran Monthly*, 19/5: 2–8.

Kymlicka, Will (1994) 'Individual and Community Rights', in Judith Baker (ed.), *Group Rights* (Toronto: University of Toronto Press).

Lee, Rose J. and Cal Clark (2000) *Democracy and the Status of Women in East Asia* (Boulder, Colo., and London: Lynne Rienner).

Lim, Linda (1978) *Women Workers in Multinational Corporations: The Case of the Electronics Industry in Malaysia and Singapore* (Michigan Occasional Papers, 9; Ann Arbor: Women's Studies Program, University of Michigan).

Ling, L. H. M (2000) 'The Limits of Democratization for Women', in Rose J. Lee and Cal Clark (eds.), *Democracy and the Status of Women in East Asia* (Boulder, Colo., and London: Lynne Rienner).

Lister, Ruth (1997) *Citizenship: Feminist Perspectives*, (Basingstoke: Macmillan).

Mahathir, Marina (2001) 'No Place For Timid Women', *Star* (31 Jan.).

Mahathir, Mohamad (1970) *The Malay Dilemma*, (Singapore: Donald Moore Press).

Malaysiakini (2001) 'First Women's Affairs Minister Slammed for Unsupportive Remark', 19 Jan., internet edition, <www.malaysiakini.com>.

Manderson, Lenore (1980) *Women, Politics and Change: The Kaum Ibu UMNO Malaysia, 1945–1972* (Kuala Lumpur: Oxford University Press).

Mann, Patricia S. (1997) 'Musing as a Feminist in a Post-Feminist Era', in Jodi Dean (ed.), *Feminism and the New Democracy: Re-siting the Political*, (London: Sage).

Marchand, Marianne H. (2000) 'Gendered Representations of the "Global": Reading/Writing Globalization', in Richard Stubbs and Geoffrey R. D. Underhill (eds.), *Political Economy and the Changing Global Order* (Toronto: Oxford University Press).

Mohamad, Maznah (ed.) (2000) *Muslim Women and Access to Justice: Historical, Legal and Social Experience of Women in Malaysia* (Penang: Women's Crisis Centre).

——(2001) 'At the Centre and Periphery: The Contributions of Women's Movement to Democratization', in Francis Loh Kok and Khoo Boo Teik (eds.), *Democracy in Malaysia: Discourses and Practices* (London: NIAS and Curzon Press).

——(2002) 'The Unravelling of a "Malay Consensus"', *Southeast Asian Affairs 2001* (Singapore: Institute of Southeast Asian Studies), 208–25.

Milne, R. S., and D. Mauzy (1978) *Politics and Government in Malaysia*, (Vancouver: University of British Columbia Press).

Molyneux, Maxine (2000) 'Analyzing Women's Movements', in *Women's Movements in International Perspective: Latin America and Beyond* (Houndmills: Palgrave).

Mostov, Julie (2000) 'Sexing the Nation/Desexing the Body: Politics of National Identity in the Former Yugoslavia', in Tamar Mayer (ed.), *Gender Ironies of Nationalism: Sexing the Nation* (London and New York: Routledge).

Munro-Kua, Anne (1996) *Authoritarian Populism in Malaysia* (Houndmills: Macmillan).

New Straits Times (1999) 'I Have No Objection to Female Candidate', (28 July).

Ng, C., and H. L. Chee (1999) 'Women in Malaysia: Present Struggles and Future Directions', in C. Ng. (ed.), *Positioning Women in Malaysia: Class and Gender in an Industrializing State* (Houndmills: Macmillan).

Noraini, Othman (1999) 'Grounding Human Rights Arguments in Non-Western Culture: *Shari'a* and the Citizenship Rights of Women in a

Modern Islamic State', in Joanne R. Bauer and Daniel A. Bell (eds.), *The East Asian Challenge For Human Rights* (Cambridge: Cambridge University Press).

Ong, Aihwa (1987) *Spirits of Resistance and Capitalist Discipline: Factory Women in Malaysia* (Albany, NY: State University of New York Press).

—— (1995) 'State versus Islam: Malay Families, Women's Bodies, and the Body Politic in Malaysia', in Aihwa Ong and Michael G. Peletz (eds.), *Bewitching Women, Pious Men: Gender and Body Politics in Southeast Asia* (Berkeley, Calif.: University of California Press).

Othman, Zaitoon Datuk, (1996) 'Constitution Supercedes Proposed Family Violence Act', *New Straits Times*, (27 Apr).

Ramli, Rashila (1998) 'Democratisation in Malaysia: Toward Gender Parity in Political Participation', *Akademika* (July): 72–5.

Ray, R., and A. C. Korteweg (1999) 'Women's Movements in the Third World: Identity, Mobilization and Autonomy', *Annual Review of Sociology*, 25: 47–71.

Richter, Linda (1990–1) 'Exploring Theories of Female Leadership in South and Southeast Asia', *Pacific Affairs*, 63/4: 524–41.

Roff, William R. (1967) *The Origins of Malay Nationalism* (New Haven, Conn.: Yale University Press).

Shaheed, Farida (1994) 'Controlled or Autonomous: Identity and the Experience of the Network, Women Living under Muslim Laws', *Signs*, 19/4: 997–1020.

Shamsul, Amri Baharuddin (1986) *From British to Bumiputera Rule: Local Politics and Rural Development in Peninsular Malaysia* (Singapore: Institute of Southeast Asian Studies).

Siim, Berte (2000) *Gender and Citizenship* (Cambridge: Cambridge University Press).

Star (2000) 'Winds of Change on the Cards' (22 Aug.).

—— (2001*a*) 'MCA Seeks No. 2 Post in New Ministry' (18 Feb.).

—— (2001*b*) 'Mums Okay: They can Soon Sign Government Forms for their Children' (18 Aug.).

—— (2001*c*) 'Wanita MIC Wants Rep in New Ministry' (21 Feb.).

—— (2001*d*) 'Why Can't We Sit on Stage with Men, Asks PAS Wanita' (5 June).

Straits Times (2001) 'PAS Rethink: It Plans to Field Women in Polls' (22 Jan.).

Tan, Beng Hui (1999) 'Women Organizing for Change: Costing the Domestic Violence Act Campaign in Malaysia (c.1985–1996)', *Kajian Malaysia: Journal of Malaysian Studies*, 17 (June): 48–69.

—— (2001) 'Joy Division', *Vox* (weekend magazine of the *Sun*) (28 Jan.).

Tan, L. E. (1992) '*Diongjiaozong* and the Challenge to Cultural Hegemony 1951–1987', in Joel Kahn and Francis Loh (eds.), *Fragmented Vision: Culture and Politics in Contemporary Malaysia* (Sydney Allen & Unwin).

Utusan Online (2001) 'Minister to Give Attention to Plight of Estate Women Too' (1 Mar.).

Von Vorys, Karl (1975) *Democracy without Consensus: Communalism and Political Stability in Malaysia* (Princeton: Princeton University Press).

Waylen, Georgina (1994) 'Women and Democratization: Conceptualizing Gender Relations in Transition Politics', *World Politics*, 46/3: 327–55.

Weiss, Meredith (1999) 'What Will Become of *Reformasi*? Ethnicity and Changing Political Norms in Malaysia', *Contemporary Southeast Asia*, 21/3: 424–50.

National Law and Indigenous Customary Law: The Struggle for Justice of Indigenous Women in Chiapas, Mexico

R. Aída Hernández Castillo

Introduction

During the past two decades official discourse about national identity in Mexico has undergone important changes. By the early 1990s,
a state discourse characteristic of post-revolutionary nationalism
focused on the existence of a mestizo nation[1] was superseded as
legislation was approved which recognized Mexico as a multicultural nation. This was considered by many as a victory for the
Mexican Indian movement. However, this supposed shift to official
acceptance of multiculturalism is far from free of contradictions.
In some cases, 'pro-indigenous' legislation—provisions recognizing
the right of indigenous people to their own norms and practices (*usos
y costumbres*)—has, in practice, worked to the disadvantage of weak
and marginalized groups *within* indigenous communities. In particular, indigenous women now face the dual task of defending their rights
to their own culture *vis-à-vis* the Mexican state, while at the same
time questioning essentialist and static perceptions of 'culture' and
'tradition' within the Indian movement that have negative implications for the full realization of women's rights. This chapter analyses
some of the dilemmas facing indigenous women in Chiapas in their
struggle for rights within the new macro-political context of multiculturalism. Linked to this, it examines the ways in which certain
academic paradigms used to analyse indigenous normative systems
can impede the development of proposals for reform to ensure greater
access to justice for indigenous women.

The political debate over the right of indigenous peoples to cultural
difference, self-determination, and autonomy gathered new strength
after 1 January 1994, when Mayan peasants in the south-east of

Mexico rose up against a national project they considered centralist and exclusive. This indigenous movement, known as the Ejército Zapatista de Liberación Nacional (EZLN: Zapatista National Liberation Army) violently rejected the neo-liberal policies promoted by the government of President Carlos Salinas de Gortari (1988–94).[2] On the same day that the North American Free Trade Agreement (NAFTA)[3] came into effect, the indigenous peoples of Chiapas called the world's attention to the failings of the new economic model. The reality on the ground in Chiapas was sharply at odds with the official version, promoted by Salinas, that poverty and marginality had been eradicated and that Mexico had become a 'first world' country.

Together with mestizo peasants, members of the Tzotzil, Tzetzal, Chol, and Tojolabal ethnic groups declared war on the 'illegal dictatorship of Carlos Salinas de Gortari and his official party [PRI]' (Despertador Guerrillero, 1994: 1). The political discourse of the Zapatistas identified as the immediate cause of the uprising the negative effects of neo-liberal policies on the lives of thousands of indigenous peasants in Mexico. At the same time, they linked their struggle to the 500-year-old resistance movement of indigenous peoples against colonial and post-colonial racism and economic oppression. In later statements, as their specific demands as 'indigenous peoples' became clearer, the Zapatistas began to appropriate and reinterpret the meaning of 'indigenous autonomy'.[4] Their demands for autonomy within the framework of a multicultural nation-state made evident the urgent need to recast the official centralized and culturally homogenizing national project. The Zapatistas took up the demands of other groups in Mexican society, and became the first guerrilla movement in Latin America to advocate and prioritize gender demands within their own political agenda. However, when the EZLN demanded both the right of indigenous peoples to form governments in accordance with their own normative systems,[5] and the rights of indigenous women to hold local posts of authority, inherit land, and have control over their own bodies[6] they entered troublesome terrain. In many cases such rights for women were contrary to the traditional practices of indigenous communities, apparently making demands for indigenous self-government and for recognition of indigenous women's rights mutually exclusive. A new movement of indigenous women, which emerged under the influence of the Zapatista uprising, has taken up the challenge of reconciling these two demands. On the one hand, they have called on the Mexican state to recognize indigenous peoples' rights to self-determination within the framework of a reformed nation-state; on the other, they are struggling within their own communities and organizations for

388 R. Aída Hernández Castillo

a critical rethinking of their prevailing normative systems. This new
women's movement emerged from a long process of organization
and reflection, involving both Zapatista and non-Zapatista women.
In the Selva (eastern lowlands), the Highlands, and the Sierra of
Chiapas, women's lives were transformed in previous decades by
liberation theology, indigenous and campesino organizations, productive projects, and health workshops. These women have now
begun to question their historical exclusion from political spaces
and to advance a platform advocating the construction of democracy
from within the private, family space.[7] In response both to autonom-
ist/Zapatista and government discourses, these organized indigenous
women have pointed out that, while gender inequalities exist within
state law, they also exist within so-called indigenous law (or 'customary law'). They have confronted the essentialist perspectives of some
sectors of the indigenous movement, which glorify certain cultural
traditions, arguing instead in favour of change. As one document
from the organized indigenous women's movement states: 'We want
to find paths through which we may view tradition with new eyes, in
such a way that will not violate our rights and will restore dignity to
indigenous women. We want to change those traditions that diminish
our dignity.'[8]

Such viewpoints were expressed at the negotiating table between
the government and the EZLN, set up twelve days after the Zapatista
uprising. Partly as a result of the pressure applied by the indigenous women's movement, the San Andrés Accords, signed both by the
Zapatista commanders and by representatives of the government (see
n. 5) committed the government to respect indigenous autonomy in
the following terms: 'Indigenous peoples have the right to free self-
determination, and, as the means of their expression, autonomy from
the Mexican government to ... [a]pply their own normative systems
in the regulation and resolution of internal conflicts, honoring individual rights, human rights, and specifically, the dignity and integrity
of women.'[9]

Much of the evidence presented in this chapter derives from an
investigation into the ways in which national law and indigenous
customary law operate in response to indigenous women's demands
for justice in Chiapas within this new political context. Linked to this,
the chapter examines the ways in which certain academic paradigms
used to analyse indigenous normative systems have contributed to
creating an image of customary law as a harmonious space free of
contradiction and in isolation from national law: an image that, it
is argued here, can impede the development of proposals for reform
aimed at ensuring greater access to justice for indigenous women.

With the participation of Tzeltal, Chol, and Tzotzil women, an interdisciplinary research team explored the extent to which both national law and indigenous customary law responded to women's denunciations of sexual and domestic violence.[10] The experiences and concerns of indigenous women that emerged during the course of the research highlighted the dangers of affording primacy to idealized notions of 'indigenous culture' and indigenous customary law. Such dichotomized perceptions tend to understand 'indigenous law' as reflecting a completely different cultural logic to 'national law': the former supposedly being guided by an ethos of conciliation, rather than that of punishment, which is ascribed to the national legal system. However, by idealizing indigenous normative systems, such approaches singularly fail to recognize the unequal power relations that exist *within* indigenous communities, particularly gender inequalities.

Women's experiences with national and traditional authorities have revealed the networks and inequalities of power that exist at the various levels of *both* justice systems. Providing greater autonomy for indigenous communities is not in and of itself sufficient to ensure the 'dignity and integrity' of indigenous women. Proposals advanced by indigenous women to 'reinvent tradition' under new terms signal a need to redefine the traditional debate between cultural relativism—which puts a primacy on the need to respect cultural differences—and universal values, such as human rights and women's rights. Their struggle highlights the need to advance beyond this dichotomy and explore how human rights are understood, translated, and claimed in local contexts, and how the concept of culture is being negotiated and contested by indigenous women. A critical analysis of national law and of customary law can help to develop political and legislative strategies that will ensure the greatest access to justice for those to whom it has traditionally been denied.

Antecedents: The Constitutional Amendment and its Political Uses

On 28 January 1992, the Mexican government approved an amendment to the Fourth Article of the Constitution, which recognized the multicultural character of the nation.[11] This had been preceded by an important amendment to Article 220 of the Federal Penal Procedures Code, which recognized the validity of expert testimonies in reconstructing the cultural context in which a crime is committed. The amendment stated: 'When the accused belongs to an indigenous ethnic group, an effort will be made to follow expert testimony in order that the judge may... better understand [the] cultural difference [of the accused] to the national norm [sic]' (Official Federal Journal, 1991: 15). The revision of the code of penal procedures allowed for certain sentences to be reduced in the light of what are perhaps best called 'mitigating cultural circumstances'. In other words, if an indigenous group's traditional norms and practices were in contradiction with federal law (such as, for example, detaining an offender until they pay compensation or obliging them to carry out community service), then these cultural differences could be taken into account by the sentencing judge.

At the time, proponents of the defence of cultural diversity welcomed this legislative change as a step towards a new relationship between indigenous peoples and the nation-state. However, evidence soon emerged of the contradictory interpretations which could arise. In August 1993, a family of Lacandon Indians came to the Women and Children's Support Centre (Centro de Apoyo a Mujeres y Menores, CAMM) in San Cristóbal de Las Casas, Chiapas, seeking legal support to denounce the murder of a 12-year-old Lacandon girl by her husband, the American anthropologist, Leo Bruce.[12] The victim's relatives recounted a history of domestic violence within the marital home that mirrored the accounts of many women, indigenous and non-indigenous, who came to the centre. However, they maintained they had not intervened on previous occasions because of the husband's 'right' to discipline his wife, a right that was recognized by the Lacandon community as a whole. This same argument was later adopted by Bruce's legal defence, which argued that he had been attempting to 'discipline' his wife according to Lacandon tradition.[13] Taking advantage of the reform of the penal procedures code, Leo Bruce's uncle, the well-known linguist Robert Bruce, provided an anthropological expert testimony in which he demonstrated his nephew's attachment to indigenous norms and practices (usos y costumbres): Bruce had learnt the Lacandon language, changed his clothing and lifestyle to fit those of the Lacandon community, and identified himself as Lacandon. Although no cultural argument could be used to justify the killing, mitigating cultural circumstances could commute the crime from murder to accidental death, or manslaughter. The prosecution also prepared expert anthropological testimonies in order to counter the defence's arguments. However, before the complex legal and anthropological debate could take place, the Ejército Zapatista de Liberación Nacional (EZLN) took the municipalities of Altamirano, Chanal, Huixtán, Las Margaritas, Oxchuc, Ocosingo, and San Cristóbal on 1 January 1994, opening the doors of the municipal jails in the process. Bruce escaped, together with many other prisoners.

Despite the lack of resolution of the case, the expert anthropological testimony made in Bruce's defence provides a clear example of the ways in which affording primacy to 'culture' can disadvantage indigenous women. Another example of the contradictory ways in which anthropological expert testimonies may use the 'cultural argument' against women was seen after thirty-two women and twelve men were murdered by paramilitary groups[14] in the Tzotzil community of Acteal, in the municipality of San Pedro Chenalhó, Chiapas, on 22 December 1997. The government's Comisión Nacional de Derechos Humanos (CNDH: National Human Rights Committee) asked specialists to elaborate expert anthropological reports for the defence of the Tzotzil paramilitaries accused of the massacre, exploring 'the cultural practices of the Tzotzil of San Pedro'. The implicit assumption was that the violence in Acteal, and the mutilations of pregnant women, children, and elders that had occurred in the massacre, might somehow be 'explained' in cultural terms. Many anthropologists refused the CNDH's request and argued instead that, prior to the appearance of paramilitary groups in the region, violence had not been a principal cause of death among the people of San Pedro Chenalhó. Between 1988 and 1993, only sixteen violent deaths were recorded in the municipality. Yet, following the Zapatista uprising and the ensuing militarization of Chiapas, they increased considerably and began to involve firearms. In addition, no previous record exists of mass aggression against women—violent deaths of women had previously occurred only as a result of domestic violence or witchcraft accusations. No mutilations of pregnant women had ever been recorded. In short, there was no evidence of cultural practices that would permit the Acteal massacre to be linked to indigenous worldviews or to indigenous 'rites of war'. Nevertheless, anthropological expert opinion continued to be used in the defence appeal of some of the fifty-seven paramilitaries convicted of material responsibility in the massacre, who were sentenced to thirty-five years in prison. While neither the contents of specialist reports nor the names of those who carried them out have been made public, the defence continued to argue that the massacre took place within a context of 'customary interfamilial fights' among the Tzotzil. Yet in fact the violence in Acteal has little to do with the way conflicts have traditionally been resolved among the highland Tzotzil, and is better explained as a consequence of the broader strategy of 'low intensity warfare' and paramilitarization currently being applied in Chiapas in order to combat the Zapatistas (Hernández Castillo, 1998*b*).

Paradoxically, expert anthropological testimony—originally conceived as a tool for the defence of groups especially vulnerable to the blindness of national law to cultural differences—has become a weapon wielded by powerful elites to protect their wider interests. The way in which the legal teams defending the San Pedro paramilitaries and Leo Bruce made recourse to the amendments to the Fourth Article of the Constitution and the federal criminal procedures code calls into question the utility of such legal reforms, at least when they remain unaccompanied by additional measures to ensure that indigenous women and other vulnerable groups are able to use them to their benefit.

Voices of Women: Challenging Essentialist Visions of 'Culture'

During the 1990s, Zapatista women became some of the most important advocates of indigenous women's rights, through the so-called Women's Revolutionary Law. This charter, created in consultation with Zapatista, Tojobal, Chol, Tzotzil, and Tzeltal women, was made public on 1 January 1994 and has been of great symbolic importance for thousands of indigenous women who are members of peasant, political, and co-operative organizations. It contains ten articles, which enumerate a number of rights of indigenous women. These include, *inter alia*, the right to political participation and to hold leadership posts within the political system; to a life free of sexual and domestic violence; to decide how many children they want to have; to a fair wage; to choose a spouse; to an education; and to quality health services. Although many indigenous women are not aware of the detailed contents of the charter, its mere existence has become a symbol of the possibility of a fairer way of life for women. In a way, the Zapatista Women's Revolutionary Law has helped create what Karl Werner Brand calls a 'cultural climate' which allows the denaturalization of women's inequality and the questioning of existing social and political behaviour (Werner Brand, 1992: 2). Anna María Garza Galigaris has observed this new 'cultural climate' among the Tzotzil women of San Pedro Chenalhó:

During the first months after the armed uprising, the debate in San Pedro Chenalhó about the new law seemed to be taking place in the fields and the hamlets, between relatives, couples, and neighbors: in places where there are no clear boundaries between private and public realms, between the political and every-day activities. Discussions within the community were very different from those carried out in forums, round-tables, and workshops.

While in the forums each article of the law was read and analyzed, and all sorts of proposals voiced and recorded, in the indigenous settlements of Chenalhó the image of revolutionary women and the idea of women's rights were enough to ignite a debate which was very much interpreted in the light of concrete situations and conflicts. In its Women's Revolutionary Law, the EZLN had succeeded in capturing the problematic of the daily lives of indigenous communities, and the need to break with the existing consensus around masculine authority. (Garza Caligaris, 1999: 40)

Since the EZLN uprising, indigenous women have met at local, regional, state, and national gatherings. Under the pressure of their women members, the Indigenous National Congress and the National Assembly for Indigenous Autonomy have instituted national women's meetings. Similarly, special groups for the discussion of problems specific to indigenous women were created within the structures set up for dialogue between the government and the EZLN. Women have used these spaces to claim their rights to change those practices, customs, and traditions that they consider unfair. Many of the documents produced in these fora have vindicated the right of indigenous women to national citizenship and have taken up the national indigenous movement's demand to maintain and recover their traditions. However, they also insist on women's rights to change certain customs and traditions while retaining full membership of their respective ethnic groups.

Although Zapatismo played the role of catalyst in the creation of spaces for reflection and organization for indigenous women, making their demands more visible, it is not possible to understand indigenous women's movements without considering their experiences as part of the indigenous and peasants' struggles of the previous two decades.

In the 1970s, there emerged in Mexico an important indigenous movement that began to question the official discourse on the existence of a homogenous mestiza nation. Together with demands for land, cultural and political demands were made which would later evolve into the struggle for autonomy for the indigenous peoples. During this time there were important changes in the domestic economy, and new spaces emerged for collective reflection—a process in which indigenous women participated.

In the case of Chiapas, the so-called Indigenous Congress (Congreso Indígena) of 1974, in which Tzotzil, Tzeltal, Chol, and Tojolabal people took part, is considered a turning point in the movement's history. Though academic studies of the period make no mention of the participation of women, we know from the accounts of participants that women took charge of the logistics of many of the marches, sit-downs, and meetings documented by these studies. This role of 'helper' continued to exclude them from decision-making and active participation in their organizations, but it did allow them to meet together and to share experiences with other indigenous women from different regions of the state.

Women's active participation in peasant movements was accompanied by some changes in the household economy. These resulted in larger numbers of women being involved in the informal commerce of agricultural or handicraft products in local markets. It is not possible to understand the wider political movements without first considering the local dynamics through which indigenous families were passing. The 'oil boom' of the 1970s, together with the scarcity of cultivable lands, caused many men from the states of Chiapas, Oaxaca, Tabasco, and Veracruz, to migrate to the oil fields, leaving their wives in charge of the family economy. The monetization of the indigenous economy has been seen as a factor which takes power away from women within the family, as their domestic work becomes increasingly dispensable for the reproduction of the workforce (see Collier, 1994; Flood, 1994). However, for many women, the reverse was true, since while their position within the domestic unit was restructured, their involvement with informal commerce led to increased contact with other indigenous and mestizo women, and initiated forms of organization through co-operatives which later become spaces for collective reflection (Nash, 1993).

The Catholic Church, through adherents linked to the Theology of Liberation, also played a very important part in the promotion of these spaces of reflection. Although Liberation Theology, which guides the pastoral work of the diocese of San Cristóbal las Casas, does not promote reflection on gender issues, the analysis in its courses and workshops of the social inequality and racism of mestizo society led indigenous women to begin to question the gender inequalities they experienced in their own communities.

At the end of the 1980s there were some groups who supported this line of questioning. They pointed out the need to open a Women's Area within the diocese of San Cristóbal. Elsewhere I have analysed this meeting between religious and indigenous people, which resulted in the founding of the Diocesan Coordinator of Women (Coordinadora Diocesana de Mujeres, CODIMUJ), one of the principal organizational spaces of Chiapan indigenous women (see Hernández Castillo, 1998b). These women, with their reflections on gender and their organizational experience, played an important role in the wider women's movement.

At the same time, feminist NGOs began to work in rural areas, combining their support for women's productive projects with reflection on gender issues promoting a gender consciousness among indigenous women. Pioneers in this field were the members of the Center for Investigation and Action for Women (Centro de Investigación y Acción para la Mujer, CIAM) and the Women's Group of San Cristóbal (Grupo de Mujeres de San Cristóbal las Casas AC), both founded in 1989. They began working on the issue of violence against women, while supporting indigenous women's organizational processes in Chiapas's Los Altos region. They also worked with women refugees from Guatemala. Discourses centring on women's 'dignity' promoted by the Catholic Church began to be substituted by a discourse centring on women's rights, and by new views on gender. Indigenous women appropriated and resignified these ideas in dialogue with feminists.

Migration, organizational experience, religious groups, feminist non-governmental organizations, and even official programmes of development have all influenced the ways in which indigenous men and women restructured their relations within the domestic unit and reworked their strategies in the struggle. But it was with the public appearance of the EZLN that indigenous women began to raise their voices in public spaces, not only in support of the demands of their male companions, or to represent the interests of their communities, but also to demand respect for their specific rights as women.

Under the influence of Zapatismo, a movement of national dimensions emerged for the first time in Mexico, incipient and full of contradictions as it was, in which the various local forces argue for the incorporation of gender demands into the political agenda of the indigenous movement. In 1997, at the National Encounter of Indigenous Women 'Constructing our History', attended by more than 700 women from different regions of the country, the National Coordinator of Indigenous Women was founded. This was an organizational space at a national level, bringing together representatives of twenty indigenous organizations with a presence in the states of Chiapas, Michoacán, Morelos, the Distrito Federal, Guerrero, Hidalgo, Jalisco, the Estado de México, Puebla, Querétaro, San Luis Potosí, Sonora, Veracruz, and Oaxaca. It has been of critical importance in the promotion of a gender perspective within the indigenous movement. The voices of many of its members were raised in the National Indigenous Congress (Congreso Nacional Indígena) and in the national debate on indigenous rights and autonomy, questioning static representations of tradition, and recovering the right to 'change staying and stay changing'.

The reconceptualization of community traditions and culture from a women's perspective also influenced the political debate around autonomy. Organized indigenous women appropriated the demand for autonomy made by the EZLN and other indigenous and peasant organizations, which proposed the establishment of a new political order to allow indigenous peoples to control their territories and resources. Since 1995, women from one of the oldest national organizations, the National Plural Indigenous Assembly for Autonomy (Asamblea Nacional Indígena Plural por la Autonomía, ANIPA), have played an important role in the reconceptualization of a multicultural national project. In the Final Declaration of the first national women's meeting of ANIPA—which took place in San Cristóbal de Las Casas in December 1995, attended by 270 women from different indigenous groups—women explicitly demanded the inclusion of a gender dimension in proposals to form autonomous, multi-ethnic regions:

We, the Yaqui, Mixe, Nahuatl, Tojolabal, and Tlapaneca women... come from afar to speak in this land of Chiapas... During these two days we have talked about the violence we experience within our communities, at the hands of our husbands, the caciques, and the military; of the discrimination we are subjected to both as women and as Indians, of how our right to own land is denied us and about how we want women's opinions to be taken into account... We want an autonomy with a woman's voice, face, and consciousness, in order that we can reconstruct the forgotten female half of our community. (Cited in Gutiérrez and Palomo, 1999: 67)

The demands of the women at ANIPA echoed those of Zapatista women. The latter have focused their efforts on expanding the concept to include women's autonomy within the larger autonomy of indigenous peoples. Organized indigenous women have referred to economic autonomy (defined as the right of indigenous women to have equal access and control over means of production), political autonomy (their basic political rights), physical autonomy (to have control over their own bodies and to live without violence), and sociocultural autonomy (defined as the right to maintain specific identities as indigenous people).[15]

Indigenous women, in ANIPA, in the EZLN, and the National Coordinator of Indigenous Women, have been pressing for change on two fronts: they claim from the state the right to cultural differences, and within their communities they work to change the traditions which they consider to infringe their rights. Their struggle is not for the recognition of an essential culture, but for the right to reconstruct, confront, or reproduce that culture not on the terms established by the state, but on those set out by their own indigenous peoples within the framework of their own internal pluralisms.

Equality and the Recognition of Difference

Opponents of proposals for greater indigenous autonomy in Mexico have argued that the legal recognition of rights based on notions of cultural difference and tradition is unjustifiable because the colonial origins of many institutions and cultural traditions of indigenous people mean they are not 'authentic'. Adherents to a liberal discourse of universal rights have also opposed proposals for autonomy and the legal recognition of ethnic difference on the grounds that such measures will merely deepen inequalities between mestizo and indigenous societies (Bartra, 1992; Viqueira, 1999). However, indigenous women's efforts to reframe critically 'tradition' and to recast autonomy proposals in such a way that they guarantee the rights of women have demonstrated that liberal criticism of multiculturalism reflects a very limited and static conception of culture.

Throughout the twentieth century the Mexican government's policies towards the indigenous population were influenced at different times by discourses promoting equality and discourses promoting difference. The historical record has shown that the promotion of equal treatment for those who stand on unequal grounds has, in practice, denied the indigenous population's access to justice. Paradoxically, however, the Mexican government's recognition of a different cultural logic has also served to justify the exclusion and marginalization of indigenous peoples in the name of culture.

After the 1917 Revolution, Mexico's political class attempted to build a modern, homogeneous, and mestizo nation. Spanish was imposed as the national language, denying indigenous peoples the right to use their languages. Laws were implemented which did not take the cultural context of plaintiffs and defendants into account, and which indigenous people did not understand. Indigenous political and religious institutions were disempowered, and new mestizo municipal authorities took over the political and economic power of entire regions.[16] All these impositions took place in the name of the 'right to equality': all Mexicans had to be treated equally, despite the cultural, economic, and social differences that characterized this legally imposed citizenship.

However, the much sought-after *de jure* recognition of the right to cultural difference achieved in the 1990s has not meant improved access to justice for indigenous peoples. As indicated above, the practice of anthropological expert testimony by the Instituto Nacional Indigenista (National Indigenous Institute, INI[17]) and by other government institutions such as the CNDH, can prove to be a double-edged sword that disadvantages those with least power within indigenous communities. In the past, the *de facto* recognition of 'culture' in certain regions of Mexico was used as a pretext to justify the exclusion and marginalization of ethnic minorities, and to legitimize pro-government Indian *cacicazgos* and other practices. In effect, only those indigenous institutions useful for ruling elites were recognized as 'traditional'. In the name of 'respect for culture', indigenous women continue to be denied their right to own land, to inherit family property, or to have political power. Today, in the name of 'culture', the existence of paramilitary groups, funded and promoted by mestizo elites, is justified. And in the name of 'culture' a sense of 'otherness' and of 'difference' is construed in order to distort and impede political alliances between indigenous and non-indigenous people. In sum, discourses which emphasize the right to equality and discourses which emphasize the right to difference can be used to hide, reproduce, or deepen the marginalization and exclusion of indigenous peoples. Legal recognition of the right to difference that relies on dichotomized visions counterpoising 'state law' against 'indigenous customary law' can ultimately serve to reinforce such tendencies.

Anthropological Constructions of Law and Custom

The current debates between defenders and detractors of indigenous autonomy are but one expression of the long-running debate over equality and difference which has marked the development of legal anthropology. Malinowski (1926) and Radcliffe-Brown (1952), considered by many to be the 'fathers' of legal anthropology, represent both sides of this debate. Malinowski believed in the universality of law, arguing that every society, including 'primitive' societies, establish rules of behaviour. From his perspective, 'aboriginal' and 'western' normative systems were guided by the same logic, the ultimate goal of which was to respond to the economic and social interests of individuals. By contrast, Radcliffe-Brown, although he did not vindicate cultural relativism (which would not become popular until decades later), referred to different cultural logics and developed the idea of conceptual difference between law and custom. For Radcliffe-Brown, law was a characteristic only of societies with a centralized government and its existence was an indication of a superior developmental level.

The famous debate between Max Gluckman (1955) and Paul Bohannan (1957) mirrored these earlier tensions. Gluckman was of the view that all human beings tend to resolve their problems in a similar fashion. In his opinion, the Barotse judges of Rhodesia (where he carried out his fieldwork) and the judges of Western societies would, if presented with the same problems, tend to create laws based on similar criteria. On the other hand, Bohannan believed in the existence of different cultural logics, which explained why what was considered a crime among the Tiv of Nigeria and what was against the law according to the judges of Western societies was quite different. The political consequences of both discourses within the colonial context in which they were developed were significant. If aboriginal peoples had a legal system, then it could be used by the colonial administration in what was called 'indirect rule': using local indigenous authorities and institutions to control the colonized population. If, on the other hand, it were deemed that indigenous 'customs' could not be considered laws, then the legal system of the colonial power would be directly imposed (see Collier, 1995).

As these early examples indicate, the context of domination from which discourses around equality and difference emerge determines the uses to which they are put, irrespective of the political intentions of those advocating one or the other position. Emphasizing equality can lead to an ethnocentrism, which imposes the Western world-view as the looking glass that colours the social processes, institutions, and cultural practices of other societies. Similarly, emphasizing difference can serve as an instrument to 'orientalize' non-Western societies, to transform these societies into the 'other' and thus permit a definition of Western culture based on discourses of rationality and progress.

The difference between 'law' and 'custom' developed by Radcliffe-Brown, and upon which much of the later development of legal anthropology was based, originated in the eighteenth-century definition of law as a contract between individuals. The religious concept of 'divine law' that prevailed prior to the Enlightenment was replaced by the idea of law as a contract between free individuals that would help overcome the chaos of the 'state of nature'. 'Custom' was subsequently conceptualized as that which opposed the free and rational contract of the 'law'. Other conceptual dichotomies such as savage/civilized (Bartra, 1992), or tradition/modernity (García Canclini, 1995), have been deconstructed by several authors who highlight the mutual constitution which exists between both extremes of the same concept. Just as it is impossible to imagine civilized man without the opposing concept of the savage, so, it could be argued, the concept of law cannot be conceived without the concept of custom. The definition of one depends on the other. Throughout different historical periods, a diversity of cultural practices enforced within different contexts and authority structures were lumped together under the category of 'custom' in opposition to 'law'. In one sense then (after Bartra), 'custom' is the savage seen in the mirror of the 'law'.

In some contexts, the discourse on cultural difference has obscured the relations of subordination that have given rise to and shaped the development of many of the cultural practices of groups considered 'non-Western'.[18] Some of the pioneering works of legal anthropology in Chiapas suffer from this last failing (see Collier, 1973; Hermitte, 1964). The analysis of dispute processes among Zinacantecans carried out by Jane Collier in the 1960s emphasized 'folk' concepts which related conflict to illness, used to explain the Zinacantecan desire for reconciliation between conflicting parties rather than punishment of the offending group or individual. In her later work, Collier (1995) recognized that the prevailing theoretical paradigms of the 1960s did not prompt her to explore either the relationship of Zinacantecan law to state and national law, or the power relations between local leaders and the regional and national power elite.

The functionalist conceptions of 'law' and 'custom' which prevailed in legal anthropology until the 1970s continued to conceive of the juridical realm as a sphere that could be analysed independently of other social and economic processes. Supporters of the analysis of normative systems, following the methodological tradition of Radcliffe-Brown, together with those who, in the Malinowskian tradition, advocated the analysis of juridical processes, effectively ignored the ways in which the systems or processes they analysed functioned within colonial or post-colonial relationships of domination. In Mexico, the influence of Marxism and political economy in anthropology led to a questioning of these theoretical paradigms, and gave rise to a critical anthropology which pointed to the relationship between the analysis of power and the analysis of culture. For example, adopting the process methodology developed by Laura Nader among the Zapotecans (and used also by Jane Collier in her analysis of Zinacatecan law), Teresa Sierra has analysed dispute processes among the Nahuas of Puebla, and contextualized these processes in the framework of relationships of domination with the nation-state. Sierra advocates an approach which analyses the relations between dominant and dominated normative systems, which are articulated through strategies developed by indigenous people when they recur to one or other legal authority (see Sierra, 1993, 1995; Sierra and Chenaut, 1995).

Advocates of alternative theoretical currents who claim to defend indigenous peoples have not only presented their 'cultural logic' as isolated and in opposition to the dominant 'culture', but have often given in to the temptation of presenting indigenous peoples as homogeneous and harmonious. Many well-intentioned anthropologists in Mexico who became personally involved in the indigenous people's struggle thus tended to ignore internal contradictions within indigenous communities and restricted their criticism to the relationships of subordination that indigenous peoples are subjected to within the nation-state (Bonfil, 1987; Bartolomé, 1988; Stavenhagen, 1988; Varese, 1988). This tendency to overlook indigenous heterogeneity and ignore internal conflicts in order to construct a homogeneous and harmonious 'other' was questioned by later studies and is even considered by some to be a new form of colonialism. Said (1978) famously referred to this tendency as 'orientalism', and Mohanty (1991) has called it 'discursive colonialism'. Mystification of the 'other', however noble the overall objectives, merely serves to make the 'other' into a reflection of Western aspirations: indigenous people are thus viewed as ahistorical objects, bearers of immutable 'tradition', rather than understood as historically constructed subjects.

During the 1980s and 1990s, anthropological research developed historical perspectives on indigenous normative systems: for example, Anna María Garza Caligaris (1999) for San Pedro Chenalhó, Jan Rus (1994) for San Juan Chamula, Peter Fitzpatrick (1980, 1992) for New Guinea, John and Jean Comaroff (1991) and Cooper and Stoler (1989) for Africa. Such approaches have contested essentialist representations of indigenous normative systems as some kind of timeless relic of a pre-colonial past.[19] Instead, 'indigenous customary law' is analysed as a social construction which has emerged within the context of power relationships, and which, like state law, has suffered constant modifications as a consequence of complex social processes.

Feminist anthropology has also contributed to a rethinking of the interplay between power, culture, and legality. Many studies have indicated that law is important for women not only because it contributes to the construction of their identities as subordinates, legitimizing patriarchal culture, but also because in certain contexts it can be used by women themselves to construct spaces of resistance (Fineman and Thomadsen, 1991; Lazarus-Black and Hirsch, 1994; Smart, 1989). Through historical investigation, scholars have analysed the ways in which the patriarchal system in Mexico was 'rationalized' with the establishment of laws which prohibited violence against women but justified other forms of control (Alonso, 1995; Varley, 2000). However, while recognizing that national law reproduces inequalities, feminist legal anthropology has also explored the ways in which women have used it to challenge decisions of indigenous customary law they consider unjust (Chenaut, 1999; Moore, 1994). Analysis of processes of dispute resolution in indigenous communities has shown that, while conciliatory procedures may mitigate conflicts, more often than not they reaffirm the subordinate position of indigenous women (Collier, 1995; Garza Caligaris, 1999; Sierra, forthcoming). Many feminist perspectives are characterized by the tension between the analysis of normative systems as reproducers of gender inequality, and the recognition that some of these legal spaces are of strategic value to women for the construction of a more just life.

State Law Versus Indigenous Customary Law? The Many Faces of 'Custom'

An underlying premise of legal reforms to recognize indigenous norms and practices (*usos y costumbres*) is that state law and indigenous customary law are discrete, distinct systems informed by different cultural logics. This separation between 'state law' and 'custom' can be traced back to the very constitution of state law itself. In order to legitimate itself as a symbol of Western rationality, national law has depended on 'custom' to represent backwardness and pre-modernity (see Fitzpatrick, 1992). In the same manner 'custom', when constructed within legal and academic discourses as a homogeneous otherness, can only be imagined as an *alter ego* of Western law. In other words, indigenous peoples' normative practices have been re-framed as 'customary law' in a continuous dialogue with colonial and post-colonial powers in order to legitimize the latter.

However, in contrast to supposed indigenous homogeneity, the politico-legal norms and traditions of indigenous peoples in Mexico are in fact highly heterogeneous. In some regions, they reproduce concepts of justice and morality inherited from colonial religious authorities. In others, indigenous world-views which link crime and conflict with illness, and conciliation and forgiveness with health, are in evidence (see Collier, 1973). Yet, even though broad differences between the cultural logic underpinning indigenous and mestizo society can be discerned, indigenous law and national law are not isolated spheres: rather, the legal strategies of social actors who have recourse to both realms of justice mean they are in continual interplay. Rather than the existence of two independent legal systems, the national and the indigenous, one dominant and the other subordinate, what in fact exists in practice is a mutual constitution of indigenous and national law. Instead of positing the existence of two separate legal systems guided by distinct cultural logics, it would be better to speak of a shared legal map onto which different, overlapping normative systems are traced in an interaction which necessarily affects the very substance of those legal systems themselves.[20]

The Mexican state legal system, represented in Chiapas by the district court of San Cristóbal de las Casas, belongs to the Roman civil law tradition. Complaints are presented before the public prosecutor's office (Ministerio Público), which is charged with representing society and ensuring justice in the enforcement of the law. Once charges have been made, an investigation takes place and the case is prosecuted via written documents without a public trial ever taking place. The accused usually contracts a defence lawyer who presents appeals and petitions. In the case of a guilty verdict, the criminal judge decides the sentence. The central objective of this process is to determine and punish the guilty parties. By contrast, indigenous law is represented by indigenous town councils located in the municipal seats. Here municipal authorities established according to state law are combined with civic-religious authorities in which community elders play an important role. Council meetings to resolve conflicts are public, the parties to a dispute bring their respective witnesses, and an important role is afforded to elders in efforts to secure conciliation. The central object of this process is to arrive at an agreement and reconcile the parties in conflict.

According to the majority of studies comparing the two, the indigenous legal system is based on 'tradition', while the national system is founded on the federal Constitution. The former is administered by authorities appointed and controlled by the community, the latter by paid public functionaries; indigenous procedures are oral and flexible, in contrast to state legal proceedings which are written and schematic; lastly, indigenous law aims for conciliation, state law for punishment.[21] Although these typologies are not entirely without justification, in general they have been used to oversimplify very complex processes. 'Custom' and 'tradition' are disputed terms and are defined differently by different sectors of the community.[22] What is understood by the term 'traditional authorities' in each region ranges from civic-religious authorities to the new autonomous authorities formed by pro-Zapatista communities since 1994, with a multitude of new hierarchies and organizational structures created by Catholic and Protestant groups in between. The problem of recognizing 'tradition' is thus much more complex than the amendment to the fourth article of the Constitution and the expert anthropological testimony of the INI would suggest.

Although a highly heterogeneous range of 'traditional' authorities and dispute-resolution practices exist throughout indigenous communities in Chiapas, the common denominator which links them is the use of 'custom' to denote 'otherness' in contrast to state law. The meaning and content of 'custom' in each region, however, depends on the specific history of each community, their relationship with the state, and the way in which internal power groups have developed. The most striking differences are found between the highlands (Los Altos) and the northern and jungle areas. In most of the highland municipalities, civic-religious hierarchies have long been fused with republican structures of political power. These structures originated in the policies of President Cárdenas during the 1930s, policies which favoured the emergence of a new form of indigenous *caciquismo* ('bossism') merging economic, political and ritual power, as exemplified by the case of San Juan Chamula, thoroughly documented by Jan Rus (1994). In the Chol region of northern Chiapas and the jungle communities, civic-religious authorities have all but disappeared. Where they still exist they have lost political power and their functions are confined exclusively to the ritual realm.[23]

In practice, legal systems and justice administration agencies contribute to the creation of the very identities they are meant to represent (Foucault, 1976; Collier *et al.*, 1995). By legitimizing or delegitimizing certain norms and practices within indigenous communities, the Mexican state has in fact contributed to their creation.[24] By treating cultural identities as essential constructs whose existence precedes their encounter with the legal system, what the law does is obscure the role that its own instruments play in the reproduction of those identities. In the current political context in Mexico, the importance of the state and state law in formulating a discourse on 'custom' and 'tradition' is increasingly evident. The productive capacity of the law is particularly clear in Chiapas. Here state law has been charged with recognizing and so constructing 'legitimate' indigenous law, at the same time as state violence is used against the indigenous Zapatista authorities of the autonomous regions, so creating the idea of an 'illegitimate' and 'unauthentic' indigenous law. Whereas 'traditional' civic-religious based authorities in the highlands are legitimized by the government as part of the *usos y costumbres* recognized in the fourth article of the Constitution, autonomous authorities are persecuted, their members often imprisoned on charges of 'usurpment of functions' or 'kidnapping'.

Clearly traditional authorities and practices are not defined by the temporality of their origin: rather than a descriptive term applied to some kind of 'essence', 'tradition' is an interpretative term used to refer to a process (Handler and Linnekin, 1984). Given that culture is constantly changing, conceptualizing something as 'traditional' affords it a specific symbolic value. As Linnekin states, '[c]ultural categories such as 'tradition' have a reflexive character; we invent them as we live and think about them; people's awareness of them as categories affects their meaning' (Linnekin, 1983: 250). In other words, 'tradition' is socially constructed. Placing these constructions within wider frameworks of power allows us to understand why certain inventions of 'tradition' are legitimized and others are not (see Ulin, 1995). Yet 'tradition' is not only legitimized by the powerful. Some authors have analysed how the past is reinvented in the historic memory of marginalized peoples in order to legitimize their present struggles and diminish the homogenizing power of colonial and post-colonial governments (Price, 1983, 1990; Rappaport, 1990). None the less, such readings are in danger of creating new dichotomies: the traditions invented by 'dominators' to help them maintain their power, counterpoised against the traditions invented by the 'dominated' in order to resist. Perhaps it is preferable to view tradition and custom as concepts born of a dialectic process of resistance and reproduction in which the state and the law have a productive capacity which enables the construction of certain identities, which in turn challenge the very definitions that gave them life.

In this way, autonomous Zapatista authorities reproduce hegemonic discourses, presenting themselves as the bearers of 'millennial traditions' and 'ancestral customs'. Yet through this discourse they vindicate new forms of conflict resolution, which draw on elements of national and international law and reinvent new traditions in which women in particular have a more active role in community life. This process of normative synthesis and critical reflection was described by a member of Tierra y Libertad (Land and Liberty), one of the autonomous Zapatista regions:

When cases of domestic violence came before us, we referred first to the civil code and the penal code. [The cases] were interpreted according to national law, and then compared with our revolutionary indigenous law. We would then determine that national law wouldn't be applied, because the law of the government is almost invariably made against women rather than in their favor. So, we would set things straight, mainly by using the revolutionary law, which speaks of the rights of women. In this way people's knowledge was broadened, they were shown how women have just as many rights as men.[25]

Despite such evidence attesting to the innovative capacity of the autonomous authorities to reinvent 'customary law', in their political discourse indigenous normative systems continue to be labelled as ancestral traditions. In this way, the Zapatista movement continues to uphold the officially engendered dichotomy between national law and indigenous law, although they are using it in furtherance of indigenous demands for self-determination. Evidently, although 'custom', as much as law, is a social construction that legitimizes certain relations of domination, in some contexts it can play the role of resisting dominant powers. None the less, as the case of San Juan Chamula and other highland municipalities indicates, we should not conclude that 'resistance' is always an element of indigenous 'custom' *per se*.

Constructing Subordinated Identities

As indicated above, significant differences exist throughout Chiapas in the way that 'traditional' indigenous authorities and 'custom' (*la costumbre*) deal with cases of marital breakdown and domestic violence. However, in general terms, both state law and custom demand that indigenous women affirm traditionally ascribed gender roles in order to gain legal support. It is all too easy to represent women suffering domestic violence as victims—the fact that many of them decide to denounce their situation is in itself an act of resistance and social agency that is important to recognize. Yet in order to gain access to justice, women invariably emphasize their role as passive victims. In this way the law contributes to the construction of women's identities as victims and subordinates. In their complaints to both the state public prosecutor's office and to community authorities, women try to present themselves as 'good' women who comply with their domestic 'responsibilities'.[26] This signals an attempt to counter the masculine discourse which generally tries to justify violence as a way to discipline women who do not fulfil their domestic tasks or who talk with other men in the absence of their husbands ('bad' women).

A powerful idea exists that there is legitimate violence, violence that has a corrective goal, and that there are individuals who are authorized to exercise it. This idea is present both in state law and custom, and is indeed so widespread that it has become part of women's common sense throughout the region. Article 122 of the Chiapas Penal Code, recently modified to increase the penalization of domestic violence, specifies that there is a 'right to correct, and persons with the ability to enforce it', and that these persons may cause 'unintentional lesions' without being penalized. In the same manner, traditional and autonomous authorities ask men to explain the reason why they resorted to domestic violence, in order to see if its use was justified. Many 'traditional' authorities are of the opinion that women can 'provoke' episodes of domestic violence by not being punctual in the cooking, the laundry, or the house cleaning.[27] In such cases, the indigenous authorities' public trials reprimand the battering husband and the 'irresponsible' wife alike. In other words, the conciliation arrived upon in 'traditional' courts legitimizes gender roles—women are asked to continue complying with their domestic and marital responsibilities, whereas men are asked only not to batter their spouses again. Reanalysing her 1973 work from a gender perspective, Collier realized the profound inequalities that underlay the conciliation process among the Zinacatecans, and began to question the mechanisms she had formerly valued.

[T]he Zinacatecan authorities generally solved matrimonial disputes admonishing both the wife and husband and asking them to behave better in the future. But, whereas women were asked to comply with their conjugal obligations, men were only asked not to hit their wives again. In other words, the Zinacatecan solutions tended to confirm and reinforce the unequal relationship between men and women. (Collier [1973]1995: 10)

The notion that a woman can be 'eloped' against her will, and that this constitutes a minor offence, rectifiable by marriage, is another idea shared by positive law and indigenous customary law. In many cases of 'rape' where legal assistance was sought from women's legal defence NGOs in Chiapas, the parents of the victim asked lawyers to negotiate 'reparation' in the form of a promise of marriage and payment of a dowry. Cases tended to be pursued by the girls' (bilingual) fathers, and legal prosecutions for rape were often dropped if the accused agreed to the proposed settlement. Lawyers slowly came to understand that in many of these cases the feelings of the young victim were valued the least of all, and often her father did not even allow her to speak. In many instances, when they occurred beyond community boundaries, both the rapes themselves and the accusations of rape served as weapons in the hands of quarrelling political groups.[28] The situation, however, is not much better with state law, since Chiapas distinguishes between kidnapping and forced elopement, assuming the latter has a romantic intention in contrast to the former. Legislation regarding elopement was formulated in the nineteenth century, when it was a common practice, and remains on the books. The law describes forced elopement as something that happens to women, whereas kidnapping happens to men. The penalty in cases of elopement is less severe than it is for kidnapping, and can usually be mitigated by 'reparation' through marriage. Significantly, the law does not specify whether the woman needs to declare that she eloped intentionally in order to establish the crime as elopement.

Clearly, with regard to ideas about discipline, maternal responsibility, and the relations between men and women, law and custom overlap and mutually constitute each other. Indigenous women, both within their communities and from without, find themselves controlled and disciplined by both legal discourses. Legislative changes aimed at improving women's rights may have relatively little impact if they are not accompanied by comprehensive structural and ideological transformations. For example, although the new modifications to Article 122 of the Penal Code increase the punishment of domestic violence, as long as they have no possibilities of financial independence, these penalties negatively affect women, because they are left without the financial support of the husband while he is in prison. Alternatively, in the case of customary practices, women may demand their right to choose whom they will marry. But when they override paternal decisions and do not comply with 'tradition' they are cast out from the support network of the family, and their possibilities of receiving support in the face of domestic violence are reduced. Such women may become 'free' from community tradition, but they also lose the protections the community previously afforded them.

In short, legislating for equality or difference will not achieve a more just life for indigenous women if changes are not successfully implemented in the socio-economic and ideological structures that exclude women and construct them as passive victims. The mechanisms that enforce these identities operate within families, in the educational system, the health system, the media, within religious institutions, and other fora. The battle to improve indigenous women's access to justice and exercise of their rights is a battle with many fronts. It is a battle which organized indigenous women are only just beginning to fight.

Conclusions

Discourses of indigenous women collected in workshops and interviews, together with documents produced at the congresses, encounters, and fora which have taken place since the Zapatista uprising, paint a picture of 'culture' as dynamic and changing. In contrast to liberal critiques of multiculturalism, indigenous women in Chiapas do not reject their culture in the name of equality, but rather claim the right to their own culture, at the same time as they fight for the creation of equitable relations inside their families, communities, and organizations.

Many indigenous women's testimonies indicate that community-based justice is marked by relations of gender inequality, wherein women are effectively 'conciliated' with their subordinate situation. These descriptions contrast sharply with the idealized visions of indigenous customary law that the academic world has helped to construct. The multiple normative practices that have been homogenized as 'customary' or 'indigenous' law are being challenged by many women, not only through the use of national law, but also through proposals to transform community-based law, as stated, for example, in the Revolutionary Women's Law, drawn up and promoted by indigenous Zapatista women.

However, indigenous women do not just question their own law. They also tell of a state legal system that shares many of the patriarchal visions of customary law, in which existing gender roles are legitimated and where non-compliance with these ascribed roles is penalized. State law and the official justice system are not a solution to the 'backwardness' of indigenous institutions (as some opponents of indigenous autonomy would have it): rather they are part and parcel of the same legal web that disciplines indigenous women and reifies their subordination. In the great majority of cases, the person charged with representing those women—the public prosecutor's office—does not even speak their language or endeavour to understand or defend them.

The description and analysis presented here of the political uses to which expert anthropological testimony can be put, of the different regional practices and conceptions of legal custom, and of state law as set out in the civil and penal codes of the state of Chiapas, leads us to conclude that the two legal systems—positive, state law and indigenous customary law—are hugely deficient in the defence of indigenous women's rights. Faced with this dilemma, an important sector of indigenous women, led by Zapatista militants, have chosen to fight on various fronts. On one hand, they have lobbied to reform the Constitution on the basis of the agreements between the EZLN and the government and set out in the COCOPA draft bill, so that indigenous peoples' right to autonomy be recognized. At the same time, they are fighting so that an inclusive gender perspective be part of autonomy projects. In effect, this represents a struggle to reinvent tradition on the basis of a culture of equity and justice.

Legislative reform has been the main item on the agenda of the national indigenous movement, including organized indigenous women: the legal recognition of indigenous autonomy is the priority in negotiations between the EZLN and the government. However, our analysis of the uses of legality, be it legality informed by discourses on the right to equality or legality which recognizes the right to difference, indicates that legislative reforms can only have a limited effect if they are not accompanied by additional measures to transform state institutions and a broader political culture which justifies ethnic or gender exclusion. Focusing all the energies of the indigenous movement on legislative battles could prove limiting and politically wearing if it is not accompanied by other efforts to build grass-roots support capable of bringing pressure to bear to ensure that new laws are complied with and that relations of subordination are transformed.

Women within the national indigenous movement seem to share these concerns. In tandem with their struggle for the national Congress to approve the COCOPA initiative, they have focused their energies on forming an Indigenous Women's National Coalition, through which they give training workshops to campesinos, artisans, teachers, and students across the country about their political and cultural rights as women and as indigenous people. This is a painstaking undertaking about which little is known. However, it is within such spaces that indigenous culture is being reinvented from a woman's perspective. And it is here that the grass-roots support is being built which may ultimately mean that new laws are something more than just written documents.

References

Albó, Xavier (2000) 'Derecho Consuetudinario: posibilidades y límites', paper presented at the 12th International Congress of Customary Law and Legal Pluralism, Arica Chile, Mar.

Alonso, Ana María (1995) 'Rationalizing Patriarchy: Gender, Domestic Violence, and Law in Mexico', *Identities: Global Studies in Culture and Power*, 2/1–2 (Sept.): 15–37.

ANIPA (1996) 'Iniciativa de decreto para la creación de las regiones autónomas', mimeo.

Bartolomé, Miguel Alberto (1988) *La Dinámica Social de los Mayas de Yucatán* (Mexico City: Instituto Nacional Indigenista).

Bartra, Roger (1992) *El Salvaje en el Espejo* (Mexico City: Ed. Aguilar).

Bohannan, Paul (1957) *Justice and Judgement among the Tiv* (London: Oxford University Press).

Bonfil, Guillermo (1987) *México profundo: Una Civilización Negada* (Mexico City: Editorial Grijalbo).

CCRI-CG and EZLN Advisers (1996) 'El diálogo de San Andrés y los derechos y cultura indígena: Punto y seguido', *Ce-Acatl*, 78–9 (11 Mar.).

Centro de Derechos Humanos Fray Bartolomé de las Casas (1996) *Ni Paz, Ni Justicia. Informe general y amplio acerca de la guerra civil que sufren los choles en la zona norte de Chiapas* (San Cristobal de las Casas: Ed. Fray Bartolomé).

Chenaut, María Victoria (1999) 'Honor, Disputas y Usos del Derecho entre los totonacas del Distrito Judicial de Panpantla', Ph.D. Dissertation in Social Science, El Colegio de Michoacán, Mexico.

Collier, George (1994) *Ya Basta! Land and the Zapatista Rebellion in Chiapas* (Oakland, Calif.: First Food Books).

Collier, Jane (1973) *EL Derecho Zinacanteco: Procesos de Disputas en un Pueblo Indígena de Chiapas* (repr. Mexico City: CIESAS and UNICACH, 1995).

—— (1995) 'Problemas teórico metodológicos de la antropología jurídica', in V. Chenaut and M. T. Sierra Camacho (eds.), *Pueblos Indígenas ante el Derecho* (Mexico City: CIESAS and CEMCA).

—— (1996) *Research Project on Zinacanteco Law*, (31) Aug, mimeo.

—— Bill Maurer and Liliana Suarez (1995) 'Sanctioned Identities: Legal Construction of Modern Personhood', *Identities: Global Studies in Culture and Power*, 2/1–2 (Sept.).

Comaroff, Jean, and John Comaroff (1991) *On Revelation and Revolution: Christianity, Colonialism and Conciousness in South Africa* (Chicago: University of Chicago Press).

Cooper, F., and A. L. Stoler (1989) 'Tensions of Empire: Colonial Control and Visions of Rule', *American Ethnologist*, 16/4: 609–21.

De Sousa Santos, Boaventura (1987) 'Law: A Map of Misreading. Toward a Postmodern Conception of Law', *Journal of Law and Society*, 4/3: 279–302.

Despertador Guerrillero (1994) 'Primera Declaración de la Selva Lacandona' (1 Jan.).

Fineman, Martha, and Nancy Thomadsen (eds.) (1991) *At the Boundaries of Law. Feminism and Legal Theory* (New York: Routledge).

Fitzpatrick, P. (1980) *Law and State in Papua New Guinea* (New York: Academic Press).

—— (1992) *The Mythology of Modern Law* (London and New York: Routledge).

Flood, Merielle (1994) 'Changing Gender Relations in Zinacantán, México', *Research in Economic Anthropology*, 15: 20–37.

Foucault, Michel (1976) *Vigilar y Castigar* (Madrid: Ed. Siglo XXI).

Gamio, Manuel (1916) *Forjando Patria* (repr. Mexico City: Editorial Porrúa, 1960).

García Canclini, Néstor (1995) *Hybrid Cultures: Strategies for Entering and Leaving Modernity*, tr. Cristopher L. Chiappari and Silvia L. López (Minneapolis: University of Minnesota Press).

Garza Caligaris, Anna María (1999) 'El Género entre Normas en Disputa: Género e Interlegalidad en San Pedro Chenalhó', MA thesis in social anthropology, Escuela de Antropología, Universidad Autónoma de Chiapas (UNACH), San Cristóbal de las Casas.

Gluckman, Max (1955) *The Judicial Process among the Barotse of Northern Rhodesia* (Manchester: University of Manchester Press).

Gutiérrez, Margarita, and Nellys Palomo (1999) 'Autonomía con mirada de mujer', in Burguete Cal and Aracely Mayor (eds.), *México: Experiencias de Autonomía Indígena* (Guatemala City: IWGIA and CECADEPI).

Handler, Richard, and Jocelyn Linnekin (1984) 'Tradition, Genuine or Spurious', *Journal of American Folklore*, 97/385: 273–90.

Harvey, Neil (1998) *The Chiapas Rebellion: The Struggle for Land and Democracy* (Durham and London: Duke University Press).

Hermitte, Esther M. (1964) *Supernatural Power and Social Control in a Modern Maya Village*, Ph.D. dissertation, Anthropology Department, University of Chicago, Chicago.

Hernández Castillo, Rosalva Aída (1994) 'Reinventing Traditions: The Women's Law', *All of Us Akwe:kon A Journal of Indigenous Issues* (Summer).

—— (1998a) 'Between Hope and Despair: The Struggle of Organized Women in Chiapas since the Zapatista Uprising', *Journal of Latin American Anthropology*, 2/3: 77–99.

—— (ed.) (1998b) *La Otra Palabra: Mujeres y Violencia en Chiapas, antes y después de Acteal*, (Mexico City: CIESAS, COLEM and CIAM).

—— (1998c) 'Nuevos Imaginarios en torno a la Nación: El movimiento indígena y el debate sobre la autonomía', *Revista de Estudios Latinomaricanos*, 9 (Jan.–June).

—— (2001) *Histories and Stories from Chiapas: Border Identities in Southern Mexico* (Austin, Tex: University of Texas Press).

—— and Martha Figueroa (1993) 'Entre la Ley y la Costumbre: La Muerte de una Niña Lacandona', *Americas & Latinas* (Centro de Estudios Latinoamericanos, Stanford University), 1/2: 25–30.

—— and Anna María Garza (1995) 'En Torno a la Ley y la Costumbre: Problemas de Antropología Legal y Género en los Altos de Chiapas', in Rosa Isabel Estrada Martínez and Gisela Gonzàlez Guerra (eds.), *Tradiciones y Costumbres Jurídicas en Comunidades Indígenas de México* (Mexico City: Comisión Nacional de Derechos Humanos).

—— and Héctor Ortíz Elizondo (1996) 'Constitutional Amendments and the New Ways of Imaging the Nation: Legal Anthropology and Gender Perspectives on Multicultural México', *Political and Legal Anthropology Review* (POLAR), 19/1: 58–66.

La Jornada (1997a) 'Indigenous Lawyers Defend the San Andres Accords' (9 Jan.): 10.

—— (1997b) 'Legal criticisms to the San Andres Accords' (4 Mar.) 5.

Lazarus-Black, Mindie, and Susan Hirsch (1994) *Contested States: Law, Hegemony and Resistance* (New York and London: Routledge).

Linnekin, Jocelyn (1983) 'Defining Tradition: Variation on Hawaiian Identity', *American Ethnologist*, 10: 241–52.

Malinowski, Bronislaw (1926) *Crimen y Costumbre en la Sociedad Salvaje* (repr. Barcelona: Ariel, 1982).

Mattiace, Shannan (1997) 'Zapata Vive! The EZLN, Indian Politics and the Autonomy Movement in Mexico', *Journal of Latin American Anthropology*, 3/1–2: 32–71.

Millán, Margara (1996) 'Las Zapatistas de fin de milenio: Hacia políticas de autorepresentación de las mujeres indígenas', *Chiapas*, 3: 19–32.

Mohanty, Chandra Talpade (1991) 'Under Western Eyes: Feminist Scholarship and Colonial Discourses', in Chandra Talpade Mohanty, Ann Russo, and Lourdes Torres (eds.), *Third World Women and the Politics of Feminism* (Bloomington, Ind.: Indiana University Press).

Moore, Erin P. (1994) 'Law's Patriachy in India', in Mindie Lazarus-Black and Susan Hirsch (eds.), *Contested States: Law, Hegemony and Resistance* (New York and London: Routledge).

Nader, Laura (1966) *To Make the Balance. Film on Zapotec Courtroom Procedures.* Extension Media Center, University of California, Berkeley.

—— (1969) *Law in Culture and Society* (Aldine: University of Chicago Press).

Nash, June (1993) 'Maya Household Production in the Modern World' in June Nash (ed.), *The Impact of Global Exchange on Middle American Artisans* (Albany, NY: State University of New York Press).

Official Federal Journal (1991) 'Amendment to Article 220bis of the Federal Penal Procedures Code' (8 Jan.).

Ortíz Elizondo, Héctor (1995) 'La Perspectiva Antropológica en Materia legal. La Muerte de una Niña Lacandona', in Rosa Isabel Estrada Martínez and Gisela Gonzàlez Guerra (eds.), *Tradiciones y Costumbres Jurídicas en Comunidades Indígenas de México* (Mexico City: Comisión Nacional de Derechos Humanos).

Price, Richard (1983) *First-Time: The Historical Vision of an Afro-American People* (Baltimore and London: Johns Hopkins University Press).

—— (1990) *Alabi's World* (Baltimore and London: Johns Hopkins University Press).

Radcliffe-Brown, A. R. (1952) *Structure and Function in Primitive Society* (Chicago: Free Press).

Rappaport, Joanne (1990) *The Politics of Memory: Native Historical Interpretation of Colombian Andes* (Cambridge: Cambridge University Press).

Rojas, Rosa (1995) *Chiapas Y las Mujeres Qué?* (Colección Del Dicho al Hecho, 1–2; Mexico City: Ed. La Coorea Feminista).

Rus, Jan (1994) 'The Comunidad Revolucionaria Institucional: The Subversion of Native Government in Highland, Chiapas 1936–1968' in James C. Scott, Gilbert M. Joseph, and Daniel Nugent (eds.), *Everyday Forms of State Formation: Revolution and the Negotiation of Rule in Modern Mexico* (Durham NC, and London: Duke University Press).

—— R. Aída Hernández Castillo and Shannan Mattiace (forthcoming) *The Indigenous Peoples in Chiapas and the State in the Wake of the Zapatista Movement* (Boulder, Colo.: Rowman & Littlefield).

Said, Edward (1978) *Orientalism* (New York: Pantheon).

Sierra, María Teresa (1993) 'Usos y Desusos del Derecho Consuetudinario', *Nueva Antropología*, 13/44 (Aug.).

—— (1995) 'Customary Law and Indian Rights in Mexico: A Study of the Nahuas of the Sierra de Puebla', *Law and Society Review*, 29/2: 227–54.

—— (forthcoming) 'Derecho Indígena y Mujeres: Viejas y Nuevas Costumbres, Nuevos Derechos', in Elena Pérez Gil and Patricia Ravelo (eds.) *Voces Disidentes: Debates Actuales en Estudios de Género*, (Mexico City: CIESAS).

—— and Victoria Chenaut (1995) *Pueblos Indígenas ante el Derecho* (Mexico City: CIESAS).

Smart, Carol (1989) *Feminism and the Power of Law* (New York: Routledge).

Starr, June, and Jane Collier (eds.) (1989) *History and Power in the Study of Law: New Directions in the Study of Law* (Ithaca, NY: Cornell University Press).

Stavenhagen, Rodolfo (1988) *Derechos Indígenas y Derechos Humanos en América Latina* (Mexico City: El Colegio de México).

Ulin, Robert C. (1995) 'Invention and Representation as Cultural Capital', *American Anthropologist*, 97/3: 519–27.

Varese, Stefano (1988) 'Multiethnicity and Hegemonic Construction: Indian Plains and the Future', in Remo Guidieri, Francesco Pellizzi, and Stanley J. Tambiah (eds.), *Ethnicities and Nations: Proceses of Interethnic Relations in Latin America, Southeast Asia and the Pacific* (Austin, Tex: University of Texas Press).

Varley, Ann (2000) 'Women and the Home in Mexican Family Law', in Elizabeth Dore and Maxine Molyneux (eds.), *Hidden Histories of Gender and the State in Latin America* (Durham, NC, and London: Duke University Press).

Viqueira, Juan Pedro (1999) 'Los Peligros del Chiapas Imaginario', *Letras Libres*, 1: 20–8 (Jan.).

Werner Brand, Karl (1992) 'Aspectos cíclicos de los nuevos movimientos sociales', in Russell Dalton and Manfred Kuechler (eds.), *Los Nuevos Movimientos Sociales* (Valencia: Ediciones Alfonso El Magnanimo).

The Politics of Women's Rights and Cultural Diversity in Uganda

Aili Mari Tripp

Introduction

In the 1990s, leading Western political theorists and philosophers grappled with problems relating to the incompatibility between women's rights and multiculturalism (Kymlicka, 1995; Nussbaum, 2000; Nussbaum and Glover, 1995; Cohen *et al.*, 1999; Okin, 1999; Shachar, 2000). Some sought to accommodate both multiculturalism and women's rights by emphasizing the ways in which multiculturalism and feminism both shared the common goal of pursuing more inclusive forms of justice (Kymlicka, 1999). Others argued that cultural and religious impediments posed particular challenges to the struggle for women's liberation in non-Western countries and for minority groups in Western societies (Okin, 1999).

Both general approaches, however, lacked an analysis of many of the political and economic dimensions of the conflicts between women's rights and the rights of religious, ethnic, and other cultural groups. It is useful to examine cases where women have engaged in political struggles with those who focus on ethnic or racial identity and cultural preservation in a way that undermines women's rights. Through studies of such cases we begin to see not only the enormous constraints, but also the possibilities for concrete solutions to competing claims. Ultimately these can only be resolved in real-world contexts. This chapter draws attention to the way in which aspects of the debate around multiculturalism and women have created a false dichotomy between the North and the South. It also shows how, oddly, much of the current debate around multiculturalism and women's rights focuses on culture, side-stepping the material conditions that shape people's lives and underpin cultural justifications for women's subordination. While it is admittedly difficult to combine cultural with economic and political analyses, it seems incongruous to focus so heavily on only one part of the equation, that is, on cultural dimensions of women's oppression, while disregarding how culture and material conditions interact (Hale, 1995: 71).

I make four main points in this chapter, drawing on examples from the women's movement in Uganda, which is one of the strongest and most forceful social movements in Africa and has wrestled for some time with questions of ethnic and religious identity as they conflict with women's demands for equal rights. I argue that those who defend practices that are harmful to women in the name of preserving their religious, ethnic, or other cultural identity are also often seeking to protect certain political and/or economic interests. They have a vested interest in maintaining the status quo and a set of power relations that are tied to certain practices. This is not to say that cultural preservation and identity concerns are not real, but rather that they are often tied to a broader political and economic context that affects their sustainability. This means, ultimately, that practices which hurt women have also to be addressed as a political problem primarily by actors within that society itself. The strategies themselves may not be overtly political. For example, in some cases, education may be a better initial mechanism for change than starting with the pursuit of legislative reform.

Second, those who resist change often make political appeals based on a variety of cultural rationales. It is not only minority groups or certain Third World cultures or religions that make these appeals, as some have implied. Dominant cultures, including dominant Western cultures with long-standing liberal and democratic traditions, do the same.[1] One need not rehearse all the impediments to women's progress in the United States to recognize that many of the obstacles are not only institutional, but cultural as well.

I underscore the cultural dimension of the resistance of the United States to changes in gender relations, because of the *way* some Western feminist theorists have gone about (correctly) challenging the view that cultures should be allowed to exercise group rights and privileges without adequately taking into consideration instances when these group rights undermine women's well-being. While they make an important critique, sometimes they have introduced the debate by making it appear as though there is something unique about minority or non-Western cultures in their disregard for women's rights because of their 'culture'. By culture I am referring to that part of our existence that is not given or natural, but rather is created and constructed, including everything from political, economic, social, communications, and educational institutions and arrangements, to ideology, beliefs, religion, philosophy, and other ways of thinking, right down to family practices and customs.

Susan Okin, for example, points out that

Many of the world's traditions and cultures,... which certainly encompasses most of the peoples of Africa, the Middle East, Latin America, and Asia... are quite distinctly patriarchal. They too have elaborate patterns of socialization, rituals, matrimonial customs, and other cultural practices (including systems of property ownership and control of resources) aimed at bringing women's sexuality and reproductive capabilities under men's control. Many such practices make it virtually impossible for women to choose to live independently of men, to be celibate or lesbian, or to decide not to have children. (Okin, 1999: 14)

She sets Western cultures apart from non-Western ones by stating that

most families in such [Western] cultures, with the exception of some religious fundamentalists, do not communicate to their daughters that they are of less value than boys, that their lives are to be confined to domesticity and service to men and children, and that their sexuality is of value only in marriage, in the service of men, and for reproductive ends. This situation, as we have seen, is quite different from that of women in many of the world's other cultures, including many of those from which immigrants to Europe and North America come. (Okin, 1999: 14)

Such a statement generalizes and homogenizes vastly different societies and experiences to the extent that it provides little if any sociological insight, and is likely to offend non-Westerners who do not share such a vision. It sets up an 'us' versus 'them' world and ultimately misses an important opportunity to find common solutions to seemingly intractable dilemmas.

It is not that Western feminists would have to 'earn' the right to speak out against injustice' in non-Western terrains by 'first demonstrating their track record closer to home', which is what Phillips suggests is at the core of such a critique. Such a demand would certainly close off any meaningful dialogue and analysis. What is at stake is a recognition that the world is not divided into the West versus 'the rest' when it comes to women's rights and that women the world over share common struggles that take varying forms. It is a matter of *how* the issues are framed and not a matter of who is framing them or their credentials.

Certainly it is legitimate to point to the many forms of oppression that women face in non-Western contexts, but the problem comes when certain Western theorists resort to sweeping generalizations that imply that women's subordination in non-Western contexts is a product of their cultures, with the implication that their cultures are 'backward'. Yet, there is no such thing as a unified homogeneous 'Western way of life', any more than one can identify 'an Islamic civilization', 'Hispanic culture', 'African tradition', or 'Asian values'. These characterizations tell us nothing nor can cultural generalizations of this kind be meaningfully contrasted with one other. They oversimplify highly complex and diverse cultures and societies that have either dominated, colonized, sought to convert, and 'develop' others or societies that have been the subject of efforts to dominate, colonize, convert, and 'develop' them for centuries, and in some cases thousands of years. We have all constructed each other, some more than others. This has never been an unidirectional process, in spite of the historical asymmetries of power. Even the colonies transformed the colonizers in their own way. In the contemporary context, transnational influences and interdependencies are greater than ever before. Thus, international human rights and respect for civil and political liberties are not the prerogative of Westerners. Today international rights norms are being shaped by people the world over.

Cultural rationales are used throughout the world to protect the status quo when it comes to advancing women's rights. Even in the United States, which is a democratic country, culture features prominently in arguments against improving women's rights. For example, the United States has not ratified the most important international convention regarding women's equal rights, the Convention on the Elimination of All Forms of Discrimination against Women (CEDAW). Congress cannot ratify CEDAW because if it did it would also have to pass the Equal Rights Amendment, formally granting women equality with men. This puts the United States in the same category as the few predominantly Islamic countries like Saudi Arabia, Iran, Oman, Sudan, and Qatar that have not ratified the convention. Like these countries, the US arguments against CEDAW are frequently premised on the defence of religious freedom and First Amendment rights.[2] Ultimately then, it is religious and cultural arguments that ground the objections to bringing the US law into line with international law, just as it is in the predominantly Islamic countries that resist such reforms (Mayer, 1996). At the end of the day, appeals to cultural identity like religion or ethnicity to justify women's oppression make discriminatory policies no less oppressive to women.

The implication that there are particular tensions between liberal Western and Third World perspectives because Third World countries have greater cultural constraints and group identity concerns confuses issues and mystifies culture. It fails to recognize the locus of the struggle, which is between women's rights advocates in their various countries and those forces who make excuses for and defend women's continued subordination on cultural, religious, historical, genetic, biological, or any other grounds to which they might appeal. I will come back to minority group claims, because this requires further elaboration. Focusing on broad assumptions of cultural difference of non-Western peoples may have the unintended consequence of exaggerating the extent to which civil and political rights are linked to Western culture and underestimate the levels of support for basic human rights, which have become widely accepted worldwide (Mayer, 1994: 383).

This leads me to my third point. Cultures have always been and continue to be changing and malleable. Cultural integrity does not hinge on any one ritual or practice, especially not on ones that hurt women. Cultural practices emerge and become solidified as a result of geographic, environmental, economic, and political factors, but they can also be undone by similar changes. If much is invested in them in terms of political or economic power, they may be more entrenched and less amenable to change. If incentive structures change, cultural identities, practices, patterns, and meanings can be quite fluid, flexible, and open to transformation or reinvention.

Fourth and finally, the debate needs to be seen more as a global struggle between the forces for women's political, economic, and social advancement and those who stand opposed to such change. In other words, there needs to be a shift from thinking about the 'liberal West versus the rest' to seeing the commonality of our problems and solutions, and our common humanity. Phillips (in Chapter 4 above) shows how important it is to have dialogue between the internal critics and external critics because it can lead 'to a different understanding of values and rights'. This is true of women in Uganda who are fighting for women's rights. They have contributed to and learnt from international feminist dialogues and have done so at least since the Second World War when they first became involved with international organizations pushing for women's advancement. This is why, just to take one example, when an Italian court ruled in 1999 that a woman wearing jeans could not be raped, women from the Ugandan Women's Network confronted the Italian ambassador to Uganda and presented him with a large pair of jeans. They were part of a worldwide series of protests to get the ruling overturned. As Seyla Benhabib puts it: 'the issue is less what "our" norms are versus "theirs" but rather the following: what will dominate on a global scale? (Benhabib, 1995: 253).

   For women's rights activists, global norms have emerged very clearly in the past quarter of a century. I emphasize their global nature, because too much has been made of the Western influence on these norms. If one considers how far we have come since the UN meetings in Mexico City in 1975, when the debates tended to be framed to a greater extent by Western feminists, today the picture is dramatically different as debates are now taking place nationally, subregionally, and regionally throughout the world, as well as in international fora. The norms regarding gender, for example, are embedded in documents like the Beijing Plan of Action and various UN conventions. Thus, women need to be seen not only as members of ethnic, religious, national, and regional communities, but also as participants in international communities that are struggling to advance women's rights.

Minority Group Rights

In the Ugandan case as is evident from the case studies, the meaning of tradition, of what constitutes an ethnic identity, of what is legitimately customary, has been contested and reinvented throughout history. I am purposefully flattening out minority group claims pertaining to culture with respect to women's rights, because as much as we share a common humanity, we also share to one degree or another, our own sets of practices, beliefs, and institutions that repress women. Minority groups are no exception. There are different kinds of appeals to tradition, culture, and custom. Some are based on religious, ethnic, clan, and national identities. Other claims to preserve the status quo are more diffuse and pervasive and are not attached to any particular group. But this does not make them any less 'cultural'.

   Generally, appeals for special consideration by various cultural and religious minorities are ultimately pleas for equal treatment (not necessarily to be treated the same). In this sense their claims are similar to those of women, who also want to be treated as equals with men without denying their differences with men. As Anne Phillips puts it in her chapter in this volume: 'Reconceptualizing the claims made on behalf of women and the claims made on behalf of minority cultures as equality claims makes it harder to avoid the parallels between sexual and cultural equality'. Minority appeals for equality apply even to claims aimed at preserving the uniqueness of a particular group and the integrity of its norms and values, as well as its beliefs, mythology, spirituality, and other non-material elements of the culture. The aim is to preserve the group's uniqueness so that it can exist with its different beliefs and practices in the same way that the dominant group upholds its own beliefs and practices. Group appeals for affirmative action in education, economic betterment, or greater political representation are not efforts to give privileges to the minority group, but rather to level the playing field, and institutionalize greater parity in tangible ways. These are generally legitimate claims, even if one might disagree about their implementation and the form these measures take.

But minority claims that then go further to stipulate that another group be deprived of its rights, for example, women or another ethnic or religious group, cannot be seen as essential to any particular group's effort to equalize the score. In fact, the inverse is true, as the examples from Uganda will show. The advancement of women in a minority group is essential to the advancement of the group itself and to furthering its pursuit of equality.

We know that the suppression of women's rights is not essential to the uniqueness of a particular group because cultures have always been variable. The same culture will have attached different meanings to the same practice in different time periods. We also know that societies that plead for practices that repress women have in the past changed the rules regarding many traditions that were once thought to be central and the society did not crumble or disappear. Certain practices and institutions may have been eliminated or transformed, but the integrity of the entire group was not undermined by changes that enhanced women's position.

The Ugandan Case

This chapter addresses the political dimensions of conflicts between women's rights advocates in Uganda and those resisting change who draw on arguments based on 'tradition'. In particular, I examine struggles over laws pertaining to land ownership, female genital cutting among a small minority group, the Sebei, and the fate of a Ganda tradition involving the rape of a young virgin.

As discussed in Chapter 10 by Goetz and Hassim, there was an implicit quid pro quo between women and the government of Museveni when he came to power in 1986. Women gave him their support and votes in return for an expansion of rights, a progressive pro-women's rights Constitution, key positions in government, 30 per cent of local government seats, an expansion of female education, and other encouragements. However, this arrangement began to unravel in the late 1990s as women's rights activists began to assert their political muscle. This became especially evident in the struggles over the Land Act detailed in this chapter.

Women activists in Uganda have made considerable headway in dealing with tensions between individual rights and customary group rights. Women's non-governmental organizations, the media, and members of the Women's Caucus in the Constituent Assembly struggled hard for key clauses in the 1995 Constitution pertaining to this issue. They succeeded in getting a clause that prohibits 'laws, cultures, customs and traditions which are against the dignity, welfare or interest of women or which undermine their status'. Moreover, the 1995 Constitution supersedes customary law so that customs inconsistent with the Constitution are overridden by the Constitution.[3] The Constitution accorded women equal protection and equal opportunities in political, economic, and social activities. Thus customary practices that undermine this guarantee of equality should be unconstitutional.

Spousal Co-ownership of Land

Some arguments to preserve custom in Uganda were tied to clan politics and the preservation of the integrity of the clan. One such conflict involved the heated debates over the Land Act, which was passed 2 July 1998. The debate centred around an amendment to the act regarding women's co-ownership (common property) of land with their spouse. Those who rejected the clause wanted to preserve clan cohesion and power, but not the cohesion of any one specific clan. Since 1996, male parliamentarians, the President, and male ministers had rallied against the co-ownership clause in the Land Act, in defence of 'tradition' and 'custom' in the face of challenges from some women parliamentarians, the women's movement, and the Uganda Land Alliance,[4] all of whom believed customs pertaining to land ownership needed changing. Some male parliamentarians and men in key NGOs supported the women, but the divisions in this debate fell primarily along gender lines, suggesting that men had more invested in the older systems of land tenure.

The stakes were high in this controversy and Museveni's continued popularity in part depended on the resolution of this issue.

The women's movement and women more generally had been extraordinarily supportive of President Museveni and his regime because of his pro-women policies and anti-sectarian politics. However, his defence of 'tradition' in opposing women's right to the co-ownership of land in Land Act angered many women. Women's organizations threatened to withdraw their support from him in early 2000 and urged women to vote against Museveni's Movement. Only a handful of female ministers and parliamentarians ended up siding with Museveni on this issue.

Land is the most important resource in Uganda because much of the population depends on it for their livelihood. In Uganda, as elsewhere in the world, unequal access to land is the most important form of economic inequality between men and women and has consequences for women as social and political actors (Agarwal, 1995). Women provide 70–80 per cent of all agricultural labour and 90 per cent of all labour involving food production. Yet they own only 7 per cent of the land (Kawamara, 1998). They are generally responsible for providing for the household, therefore their access to land is critical. But women are dependent on men to access that land. Moreover, women who are childless, widowed, disabled, old, separated/divorced, or with only girl children often have little or no recourse to land since they cannot even rely on men for access to land. In addition, the country's food productivity is determined in part by women's ability to access land and have control over their produce. In Uganda, a woman may have jointly acquired land with her husband and may have spent her entire adult life cultivating it, but she cannot claim ownership of the property because the land titles are registered in her husband's name. If he dies, the land generally goes to the sons, but even if he leaves it to both sons and daughters, he may leave the wife with no land and therefore no source of subsistence. It is not uncommon for a man to sell off part of his land to settle a debt without even consulting with the wife, let alone informing her. In both cases, the woman has no basis for contesting those claims.

The insistence on the co-ownership clause stems from the fact that current legislation, given customary practices, provides limited possibilities for women to own land. In patrilineal societies, women generally do not inherit land from either their fathers or their husbands. Their fathers often do not bequeath land to their daughters because daughters marry outside the clan, and will therefore take the land with them to another clan. Husbands often do not bequeath land to their wives for the same reason: they need to ensure that the land remains in the clan because they worry that the widow might sell the land to non-clan members. In some societies in Uganda, if the

Aili Mari Tripp

husband dies, the wife and children are inherited by the husband's brother so that he may provide for them. This practice is dying out, raising fears that if a widow remarries outside the clan, the clan land she has acquired is lost.

The arguments that have been raised to oppose co-ownership of land have, for the most part, been red herrings. Some have said that, with such a clause, women will start marrying old men so they can inherit their land. Others have suggested that they will marry men and then divorce them for the sole purpose of acquiring their land. 'Can't we as a clan do something about this? The women are misusing the land', asked an elderly man, Eugenio Oluk Ogwang, in a public meeting led by the Uganda Land Alliance over the co-ownership clause in Otuke county in Lira district (Wamboka, 1999). He was concerned that with the co-ownership clause women would acquire clan land through inheritance and then sell it.

These disputes over land tenure laws reflect a conflict between the older values of a culture based on communal property ownership controlled by men and a newer notion of individual private property that would allow women access to private property. Culture is integrally tied to political and economic changes. These tensions thus arise in a context of changes in the system of land tenure, in gender relations, and in the structure of the society. Where pressures for land have become intense, for example, in Kigezi (western Uganda), the conflicts between men and women over land have also heightened and women, almost all of whom are poor peasants, have increasingly taken their land claims to court, especially since women won the right to own land with the 1998 Land Act (Khadiagala, 1999, 2001; Achieng, 1998).

Clan-owned land is diminishing and individually owned property is becoming more common (Troutt, 1994). This has undermined the power of the clan and the male control within the lineage. As Sylvia Tamale (2000), a leading legal scholar in Uganda, put it: 'Sad as it is, the fact is that the extended family is quickly disappearing and with it, the social security and mutual support arrangements (e.g. communal land) that they once provided'. For some, urbanization and the increase in non-agricultural incomes have lessened dependency on clan-controlled land. While it has been argued that the shift from clan-held land to privately owned land has not always benefited the poorest women in many African contexts (Tsikata and Whitehead, 2001), the legal right of women and wives to own land has never been disputed. In the Ugandan context, recent studies have shown that women are increasingly seeking ownership of land, regardless of class (Troutt, 1994; Khadiagala, 1999).

These tensions between clan politics and women's rights were epitomized in the well-publicized conflict over the burial of a prominent lawyer, Silvano Melea Otieno, in Kenya (Cohen and Odhiambo, 1992; Stamp, 1991; Otieno, 1998). There have been several such high profile cases in other parts of East Africa in recent years. In the case of S. M. Otieno, his body laid unburied for 155 days as his rural Luo clan members fought a court battle with his widow, Wambui Otieno, over who had the right to bury him and where. Wambui Otieno was an urban, professional, Kikuyu woman who argued that her husband shared with her 'modern' nationalist values that differed from the clan and tribal values of his family and for this reason he should not be buried in his home area, where the clan wanted to bury him. In the course of this High Court case, the meaning of tradition, modernity, ethnicity, and lineage were fought out as the litigants tried to interpret the meaning of Otieno's life. Otieno's Umira Kager clan, which also wanted to lay claim to the Otieno's joint property, won the case. Underlying the struggle, as April Gordon points out, was a conflict between two different systems of land ownership. Partially commercialized agricultural production, the privatization of land, land scarcity, sharpening class divisions, and rapid population growth had put enormous pressures on the kinship-based systems of land ownership and production. Women had to access land through their husbands, sons, and fathers because only males could inherit land. These patriarchal tendencies of the lineage system became even more pronounced as competition over shrinking land and other resources intensified (Gordon, 1995).

Many of these same tensions are evident in Uganda, similarly giving rise to conflicts over the issue of spousal co-ownership of land and to differences over issues of clan control. Individual ownership of land by women challenges revered notions of communalism and is resisted by those who see it is as promoting an ideology of individual autonomy apart from the community. There are even some women landowners who oppose spousal co-ownership out of fear that when their sons inherit their land, it may go to their daughters-in-law should their sons die, thereby being removed from clan control. Women activists, in contrast, are concerned about the vulnerability women face economically when they cannot inherit their own land that is their source of livelihood.

Women activists see some gains made by the Uganda Land Alliance with the Land Act of 1998. Section 28, for example, guarantees that decisions regarding land held under customary tenure either individually or communally shall be taken 'in accordance with the custom, traditions and practices of the community concerned' unless they deny women ownership, occupation or use of land (Government of Uganda, 1998). During the debate over the Land Bill, however, key clauses regarding co-ownership of land were moved by Hon. Miria Matembe and they were agreed to by the House. When the Land Act was redrafted, the House Speaker, James Wapakhabulo, did not pose the question of acceptance to the members, creating a furore among women leaders. The Act was passed without this key clause.

In February 2000 when the Minister of State for Lands brought the Amendments to the Land Act before Cabinet, it was the President, by his own admission, who decided to remove the co-ownership clause. As he explained, he foresaw trouble and advised them to go slow or pass the clause along for consideration with the pending Domestic Relations Bill. 'When I learnt that the Bill was empowering the newly-married women to share the properties of the husbands, I smelt a disaster and advised slow and careful analysis of the property sharing issue', Museveni said (New Vision, 2000a). Women activists argued that moving the clause to another bill was unconstitutional because the decision should not have been taken unilaterally by the executive, but rather it should have been put to the House. It was believed that the President's decision was intended to save face so that the government would not appear anti-woman.[5]

After noticing that the clause had not been incorporated, the Uganda Land Alliance (ULA) immediately asked the government to amend the Act. Winnie Byanyima, an outspoken member of Parliament and leader in the women's movement, called on fellow activists to join the struggle, saying that 'Women are the voters and the Movement will lose their vote unless the co-ownership clause is brought back on board'. Donors also had their say, like the British Overseas Development Agency (ODA), which was coordinating donor assistance for implementing the Land Act. The ODA at one point threatened to stop supporting the land reform programme if the amendment was not adopted. Clearly the donors played a role, which meant that at times the ULA was accused of fronting for Western interests, a charge the activists deeply resented as a diversionary tactic of their opponents. The agenda was set by the ULA and they felt they had complete control of it.[6]

A coordinator of the ULA, Rose Mwebaza, said during a press conference in December 1998 that, with the dropping of the co-ownership clause, 'Women lost one major revolutionary clause that was to be the basis to challenge the very foundations of a patriarchal system... its effects would be a tool for social change, a provision for protection and security for women on land'.

The omission was raised on numerous occasions, and the Cabinet promised to amend the Act, but failed to do so. After over a year of government footdragging, women activists announced that they would mobilize rural women widely to vote against Museveni if the clause on co-ownership was not included in the Land Act. 'Should government become adamant, we can mobilise women and pressurise it. We have the vote. It is not fair for us to be used only when our votes are required. We have the strength being 51% [of the total population], we can boycott these elections', Hon. Abu Dominica, (MP Moyo) chairperson Uganda Women Parliamentary Association, told a press conference (*New Vision*, 2000b). The government all of a sudden woke up and took note. Frantic consultations began, according to the *Monitor* newspaper between Betty Okwir, Minister in the Vice President's Office, the Vice President (who is a woman and former Minister of Women and Development) Specioza Kazibwe, and the then Minister of Gender, Labour and Social Development, Janat Mukwaya (Bakyawa, 2000a). The Minister of Gender and the Vice President, under orders from the President, called leaders of the ULA and told them to cool down.[7]

The Land Act put Museveni's most loyal female supporters to the test, especially those who both championed women's causes and were in power because Museveni had appointed them. The Minister of Gender, Labour and Social Development had always been more loyal to Museveni than to women's causes. She explained, 'As a woman activist, I don't buy blackmail'. She attacked the activists by saying that they were acting like men and in so doing were defeating their own cause. Other ministers like Miria Matembe argued fiercely with Museveni and the Cabinet in defence of the co-ownership clause and had championed it vigorously in Parliament.

The women involved in this struggle did not believe that traditions were irreversible. The head of one of the leading women's rights organization, Action for Development (ACFODE), Edith Natukunda, argued that the government had implemented other challenging programmes like Universal Primary Education, therefore there was no excuse not to implement this provision (Bakyawa, 2000b). Even the *Nabagereka* (Queen) of Buganda, Sylvia Nagginda, weighed in on the debate, in spite of the fact the monarchy is a thoroughly clan-oriented institution (Olupot, 2000). In her International Women's Day statement for 2000, the *Nabagereka* criticized the gender gap in decision-making at the national and community levels, and pointed out that the power balance was worse at the household level where decision-making is by the man who owns and controls wealth.

As she put it, 'There is still much need for more advocacy work and new strategies to be designed to balance the powers'. In particular, customary rights deprive women of ownership of property, especially land and other fixed assets, even in statutory law, in case of death of the husband, the woman is entitled to only 15% of the property, (Olupot, 2000).

In response to such criticisms, the Cabinet announced they would shift the debate over the clause to the Domestic Relations Bill, on the grounds that land has to do with family relations. Women activists accused the President of once again trying to confuse and divert the issue by saying that he hoped that the Domestic Relations Bill would allow women to share properties where they are born rather than where they are married. He argued that women should limit themselves to the law of inheritance and succession, which is covered by the Domestic Relations Bill (DRB). However, as the ULA leaders pointed out, this would do nothing to address properties that women shared with their husbands for the duration of their lifetime (Kameo, 2000). Moreover, over thirty-five years various Ugandan governments had talked about family law reform, but nothing had been done to change substantially the family law, which dated back to 1904. 'The DRB is already riddled with controversy over marital rape, regulation of polygamy, declaring the payment of bride price as no longer necessary in contracting a customary marriage, even the age of marriage... And so we saw it as dangerous to add another clause that in essence would lock debate on the whole bill', explained ULA leader Jacqueline Asiimwe.[8] For this reason ULA members saw the Cabinet's decision as a diversionary tactic to remove the issue from the agenda altogether. Moreover, Jacqueline Asiimwe, pointed out that the co-ownership clause could not be referred to the Domestic Relations Bill because land had never been a domestic issue (Bakyawa, 2000*b*).

All of these tactics indicated government reluctance and unwillingness to incorporate the key clause that would transform women's land rights in Uganda. Meanwhile the land coalition in Tanzania, inspired by the Ugandan efforts around co-ownership, was able to get such a clause put into their Land Act, which was passed in February 1999.

Women activists were demoralized by this setback. Nevertheless, they were enthused by the 6 per cent increase in women parliamentarians in 2001 and were determined to start on a new footing with the opening of the new parliamentary session. They met with the women parliamentarians and made clear their expectations of them regarding the Land Act amendment. The struggle had galvanized women in ways they had not anticipated. As the ULA chair put it:

One thing I appreciate about this whole struggle is that women NGOs are now learning to work in coalitions and to respond to such issues in a more timely and aggressive way. For example, when Hon. Baguma Isoke announced the shifting of the co-ownership clause to the Domestic Relations Bill, we quickly held a press conference, and stated in the strongest of terms our disappointment at the Cabinet decision, and we declared International Women's Day (March 8th) a day of mourning.

Grass-roots women mobilized themselves at the Women's Day celebrations in Rukungiri district, and women held placards demanding the right to land at Women's Day celebrations in Rukungiri where the President spoke, forcing him to devote most of his speech to the subject of co-ownership.[9]

The struggle united women across political, ethnic, and class divisions, although the organizational linkages were sometimes weak because they were only recently established and suffered a shortage of resources. The movement was spearheaded, as is generally the case with legislative reform, by urban educated women. While not all issues in Uganda draw cross-cutting support from all classes, this campaign did achieve broad support, even if it was sometimes difficult to mobilize supporters to assert themselves. In this respect, the movement parallels the struggles for legislative quotas for women in Argentina in the early 1990s (Bonder and Nari, 1995: 188) or the struggles for reproductive rights for women in India. Historically, struggles over education and violence against women in many parts of the world have similarly drawn widespread support cutting across class differences.

The conflict over the Land Law showed how women's organizations took their struggles to transform deeply entrenched customary practices and institutions into the political arena and directly challenged economic and political constraints blocking them. 'Cultural' rationales to maintain the status quo were inextricably linked with economic structures that protected male control over land resources.

Female Genital Cutting in Kapchorwa

While the battle over land ownership had mixed results, the struggle against female genital cutting[10] met with greater success. Unlike the land conflict, in which the opponents of the clause were defenders of a more diffuse clan-based notion of tradition, the struggle over cutting was over a more specific Sebei identity. Cutting is not practised elsewhere in Uganda except among this small group (numbering around 116,702) in the eastern Kapchorwa district. The Sebei sincerely believed that their particular identity, culture, and values would be undermined by the abolition of female genital cutting. The cutting was part of Sebei initiation ceremonies into womanhood, in which the clitoris and labia minora of girls and women aged 15–25 were cut. Girls were forced into the practice through strong social pressures and the intimidation of older women. Cutting was seen as an act of purification and as a status symbol (*Monitor*, 1994). Community by-laws forbade women from milking a cow, fetching water, or grinding corn in front of uncut women. Moreover, they would be treated like children and therefore could not attend clan meetings or speak in public (Landman, n.d.).

The Ugandan government had been silent until the 1990s on the practice of female genital cutting and its harmful psychological and physical side effects. When Museveni came to power with a policy of promoting women's advancement, educated women in the Kapchorwa district saw this as an opportunity to campaign against the practice of cutting and to link it to broader concerns regarding women's equality. The Kapchorwa Council of Women petitioned the government to take measures to bring an end to female genital cutting. In response, the government sponsored a study carried out by women leaders and academics in 1990 to investigate the impact of the custom. The study found many young women who wanted to resist the practice in Kapchorwa, but were under severe pressure from mothers and grandmothers who teased and mocked the girls, saying they would not find husbands or be real women if they were not cut (IPS, 1992). The Cheyoshetap-Tum, the elderly women who carried out the cuttings and profited from them, campaigned to promote cutting (Etengu, 1992). Meanwhile, opponents of cutting worked with the World Health Organization to launch a major campaign to fight for the eradication of this practice, primarily emphasizing the health hazards involved.

Initially, the elders dug in their heels and accused outsiders and foreigners of interfering in their local culture and judging it negatively, even though the leading advocates were Sebei women themselves. The District Council went as far as passing a law in 1988 making female cutting compulsory, threatening to cut women by force if they refused. It was clear that powerful local male elders felt their authority and leadership of the community was being threatened, and had vested interests in the practice that needed to be addressed.

At this point the struggle became intensely political. Jane Frances Kuka, a Sebei teacher at a teacher's training college, was one of the most vocal opponents of the practice. As women were being seized by local authorities to be cut, she was caught up in the fray but escaped under police protection and contacted the then Minister of Women and Development, Joyce Mpanga. In a dramatic rescue mission Kuka and Mpanga boarded a helicopter and flew to Kapchorwa to rescue women who had been taken against their will to be cut. As Kuka explained:

I came away from this battle convinced that those in power will never voluntarily relinquish that power. Women from the grassroots needed to effectively organize, or they would continue to suffer with no voice in their own governance. FGM would not be eliminated from above, by decree. Our efforts along such lines had actually backfired. Instead, a strategy of persuasion and grassroots political activism was required.[11]

She ran for Parliament in 1989 and was defeated because of her activism and, in particular, because of the helicopter incident. In 1994, Kuka ran to be a member of the constituent assembly (that debated the Constitution) and lost again due to election rigging.

As a result of pressure from women's groups, the national government began to pay attention and put pressure on the Sebei to change. Moreover, local political authorities began telling the Sebei to desist from cutting on the grounds that it was detrimental to women's health (Kissa and Muzungyo, 1993). Sebei leaders became even more defensive. As Getrude Kulany, parliamentarian representing Kapchorwa, explained in 1993 in the midst of the campaigns to eradicate cutting: people must be persuaded because they consider any effort to change this practice an infringement on their culture. According to Kulany, the Sebei felt intimidated by other Ugandan societies because every dignitary who went there talked of nothing but the circumcision of women. 'Why should it be our culture being attacked all the time?' she asked (Luganda, 1994: 4).

Although many women activists saw the issue as a human rights concern, not all women in Kapchorwa were persuaded that cutting belonged in this category and preferred to see it more as a health concern (Egunyu, 1989, 1994). As the previous parliamentarian from the area put it: 'Culture which violates fundamental human rights and antagonises national unity, should be discarded away. But all other aspects of culture should be left to the people concerned' (Egunyu, 1989, 1994). This implied that cutting was not an issue of rights. Such views persuaded activists in the area to pursue a tactical approach that focused on the health consequences of the practice, showing in particular how it affected reproductive health, which was a priority for Sebei women.

Jane Kuka continued her campaign and worked with a variety of local women's groups, forming a community-based programme called the 'Reproductive, Educative and Community Health' (REACH) that had funding from the United Nations Population Fund (UNFPA). Many other groups were also active around these issues, including the Women's Federation for Peace in Uganda (WFPU), the Family Federation for World Peace, the Association of Uganda Women Doctors, Action for Development, Association of Women Lawyers in Uganda (FIDA-U), Uganda Women's Credit and Finance Trust, along with Women's Global Network on Reproductive Rights.

It took only one year for the elders to start to back down. REACH began working with the Sabiny (Sebei) Elders Association (SEA), which was one of the most powerful organizations in Kapchorwa and included district elders from 161 Sabiny families. The SEA had been hostile to REACH until 1996, at which point they began to support the programme. The earlier government tactics had been too heavy-handed. As Jackson Chekweko, a REACH leader, explained: 'The problem with the previous attempts to stop the practice was that they were coercive and it undermined the community's ability to reason for themselves' (Eliah, 1999).

REACH worked to promote Sebei values underlying the practice of cutting without supporting the actual cutting. In other words, they separated the practice from the idea behind it, which was to bring girls into adulthood and into the Sebei community. Moreover, they did not criticize Sebei culture or call it into question. REACH and other groups successfully worked to transform the initiation ceremonies so that the spirit of the practice was maintained, but without performing the actual cutting. They also incorporated education on cutting, AIDS, family planning, and income-generating strategies into the initiation ceremonies. In 1998 the Uganda's Sabiny Elders Association was awarded the United Nations Population Award for its work in combating genital cutting.

The SEA chairman, William Cheborion, explained his rationale for changing his thinking regarding female cutting in this way: 'When I was a young man growing up, still young, I used to support circumcision of girls very much. When I grew up and became a teacher, I found out that circumcision was a wrong practice' (Eliah, 1999). Appeals based on the health of his girls had convinced him. 'We all love our children. Does anybody want to do any harm to his or her children, particularly the girls? Neither will any man wish to see his wife suffer or die of labour complications if he is aware of the cause' (Eliah, 1999).

Kuka ran again in 1996 for Parliament. This time she won by a landslide, claiming over 80 per cent of the vote. She saw her victory as not just an individual victory, 'but also a victory for the women of Kapchorwa and a victory against the strong cultural base of FGM'. Soon after her electoral victory, Kuka was appointed Minister of State for Gender and Cultural Affairs.

In the span of a decade, the practice of female genital cutting had diminished considerably and was on its way out. Organizations like Women's Federation for Peace in Uganda (WFPU) continued to work with girls in schools and to educate them about cutting. They also trained them to start and run small businesses like tailoring, rabbit-keeping, farming, as well as bookkeeping. Erina Rebecca Rutangye, who was president of WFPU, explained:

I think it's going to be eradicated. That's for sure; how long (it takes) is the question. So far we see a lot of hope with young girls; most have agreed to reject it. But with the older generation we really have to push, some of them think FGM should stay. There had been a proposal to make a law banning FGM like some nations are doing, so that offenders are imprisoned. But government opted for education so that it becomes a give-and-take affair. I think that's a better way even if it may take longer. (Gawaya-Tegulle, 1999)

There is, however, continuing pressure on the government to ban female genital cutting even though the strategy of education and persuasion has been highly successful. Those who argue for the banning of the practice point out that governments shy away from such measures because they do not want to lose political support and votes. Even an editorial in the government-owned *Sunday Vision* pointed out that 'worst of all, female genital mutilation is not only still going on but government, being a political institution, does not have the heart to unequivocally outlaw this dangerous, violent assault on little girls... in Africa, governments would rather see little girls mutilated for life than lose the votes of the mutilators. Activists, please stay alert' (*Sunday Vision*, 1999).

The Sebei example illustrates, on the one hand, how important the practice was to Sebei identity, but it also shows how malleable cultures can be. When confronted with a little political pressure, it took the elders only a year to come around. Health education, the modification of the initiation ceremony, combined with new economic incentives for the women who carried out the cutting, produced a cultural transformation that protected the integrity of both the Sebei as a people as well as its girls and women. Were culture really so fixed and impermeable, the Sebei never would have changed their initiation ceremonies willingly as a result of internal pressures and outside influences. The reforms were more easily incorporated because the agents of change were primarily Sebei who understood their problems and priorities.

The King's Virgin Wife

The Sebei were not the only ones who were willing to change deep-rooted customs with surprising speed. Within half a year of protests by women's organizations and Ganda women, a practice that had been a cornerstone of Ganda identity became a tradition that was of 'no consequence in modern times', according to its former advocates in the Ganda monarchy.

The Ganda are the largest ethnic group in Uganda out of more than thirty-four groups, making up almost one-fifth of the population. Anthropologists and historians have shown that the Baganda have historically engaged in self-conscious debates over how to shape their customs in the past and continue to do so today. Many Baganda leaders are very aware of the malleability and construction of the practices and beliefs that they adhere to as a people, as evident even in recent debates related to kingship.[12]

In the 1910s and 1920s, partly in response to missionary influences, the Ganda elite engaged in major debates and decided that they needed sweeping cultural reforms because they felt Ganda culture was anachronistic. Their Parliament, called the Lukiiko, started issuing directives to abandon numerous rituals, such as ceremonies pertaining to twins. Lineage succession rituals practised at night were shifted to the daytime. They banned forms of sexual imagery from various rituals, eliminated some forms of marriage, and called for the rejection of certain witchcraft practices. This was part of a very conscious effort to carry out a wholesale transformation of Ganda culture after much debate on which aspects of their culture they would retain and which they would eliminate or transform (Karlstrom, 1999, 2000). The Ganda were therefore experienced in dealing with challenges to particular traditions when in 1999 a controversy erupted as the Ganda king was preparing for his wedding.

The conflict erupted over a tradition that required a young virgin, called a Naku, to serve as a ceremonial wife before the wedding and perform certain cultural rites, which historically had involved having sexual relations with the king. A 13-year-old girl was selected from one of the fifty-two Ganda clans to be the Naku.[13] When the house of the Naku was thatched, a reigning king had to break the ground by putting the first bundle of grass at the house. Although some Nakus did not marry because of cultural beliefs, in recent years they had married and had children, including Dorotiya Naku, Ludiya Naku, and Siribasanga Naku.

When the controversy first broke, the Ganda *Katikiro* (Prime Minister), Joseph Mulwanyamuli Ssemwogerere said that the Naku was very important in Ganda culture and that it was impossible for the kingdom to do away with her in spite of protests from several women's rights groups (Kibirige, 1999). Women belonging to fifteen women's organizations, including the Uganda Women's Network (UWONET), let it be known they took issue with the custom because they believed this was tantamount to condoning the rape of a minor, who had little choice in the matter. Major protests had already been launched over some years by the women's movement which had focused on government inattention to problems of rape and defilement (rape of under-aged children). These concerns had been heightened by the AIDS crisis Uganda had been facing, as some men were preying on younger girls in the belief that they were not HIV positive. Ganda women activists were, in effect, challenging a culturally sanctioned act of defilement.

Many Baganda women wrote letters to newspapers protesting the custom. One, for example, addressed the king:

With due respect to you sir, and to Ganda's culture, my humble request is that you spare the virgin girl. Advise your people not to bring her to you. If they insist, don't touch her even when she is at your disposal. You will definitely win the admiration of most Ugandans—particularly women and child rights activists—plus all right thinking people of this country and beyond. Short of that, the law should take its course. Not even kings are supposed to be above the law. The Police should be on the look out. These are the '90s. I stand to be corrected on this. (*Monitor*, 1999)

Prior to the wedding, the *Katikiro* (Prime Minister) of Buganda, Joseph Ssemwogerere told me he had met with women activists from fifteen different organizations who protested the mock marriage with the Naku. He assured them that the Naku would not be expected to have sexual relations with the *Kabaka* (king) and that she was free to marry whomever she chose. Women's groups were not about to take any chances. They took out a notice in the *New Vision* newspaper, saying that 'these are some of the outdated cultural practices that subordinate women and can no longer fit in modern times'. Ssemwogerere was outraged by the notice and wondered why women's groups did not protest when young Catholics were taken to become nuns and priests before they were adults. He was adamant

that the Naku custom be continued, especially at a time when the
Buganda kingdom was trying to re-establish itself and build itself as
an institution after having been sidelined and suppressed by every
government since independence.

Nevertheless, by the wedding day, half a year later, the palace
announced without warning that it was going to drop the Naku tradition. Its own research showed that the ritual was outdated and of
no consequence in modern times. 'Should the abolition of the Naku
tradition affect the well being of the kingdom in any way, I hope
the spirits guide us to put things right', the Ganda paper *Bukedde*
quoted Ssemwogerere as saying. Newspaper editorials commended
the Ganda Prime Minister. One editorial commented: 'Culture must
be dynamic enough to change with times. Mengo should be commended for reading the public mood and doing away with what is
not fashionable' (*New Vision*, 1999). It is interesting and revealing
that what was primarily a protest from women activists came to be
interpreted as 'the public mood'. But even more striking was how a
custom that was ostensibly fixed and essential to Ganda tradition was
dropped within the span of a few months with no fanfare or popular
resistance.

Conclusions

Ultimately, the struggles for gender equity are political and need to
be addressed directly by the people most affected by the practices
that harm and discriminate against them. Societies are especially
receptive to change when the political, economic, and social conditions no longer serve the practice or have begun to erode. When those
conditions are in flux, cultural practices need to be dealt with politically because they will not simply fade away of their own accord.
In Uganda, the male-dominated clan structures underlying the land
tenure system have begun to crumble, but they are still present.
The gender and clan related ideologies that once were supported by
the clan system have lingered and are now clashing with the new
women's movement that has a different vision of land ownership
and gender relations.

People often continue practices because they believe they benefit
from them, in terms of status, money, or other advantage. They do
not continue practices simply because they are preserving an abstract
culture or tradition, even if this is the verbal rationale for maintaining the status quo. This means that incentive structures need
to change as well. For this reason, Ugandan women activists found

themselves waging their struggle over land co-ownership primarily on the political battlefield.

The co-ownership of land amendment to the Land Act remains a difficult struggle. Although economic and political changes have diminished the power of the clans since the nineteenth century, they are still a vital part of society. The very fact that there are forces advocating change in women's ability to own land is, however, a reflection of other fundamental changes in society and in gender relations. Political and economic changes within society have opened the door to changes in thinking. These changes include the rise of an educated class of women, the growth of women's independent economic clout through business and income-generating activities, the encouragement of the Museveni regime for women's advancement, and the political appointment of women to key positions, in addition to the rise of new autonomous women's associations separate from the state. It was the growth of new independent associations since 1986 that made it possible for the coalition of associations, the Uganda Land Alliance, to threaten to lobby for women to withdraw their support from the government.

Legal reform may not be the only political battleground, depending on what is at stake. Abolishing a practice through legal instruments is not the same as abolishing it in practice. In the case of female genital cutting in Uganda, women activists will no doubt continue to press for the legal abolition of the practice, but only after the practice has been almost completely eradicated through other means. They avoided starting with legislative reform because they did not want to put the Sebei on the defensive, given that they already felt under siege as a minority group. Persuasion, education, and providing new sources of income for those who performed the cuttings proved critical. But none of this could be carried out without the political support of the local authorities and elders and it was also at that level that the battles had to be waged.

Ugandan women's rights activists have been successful where they have resisted caricaturing, oversimplifying, and exaggerating offensive cultural practices. They have not taken the worst elements of a culture to characterize an entire religion or peoples. As the women themselves are members of a particular ethnic or religious community or work with women activists from that community, they are not as prone to make homogenizing assumptions about the culture. They know that there is a whole spectrum of opinion within a community that cannot be defined simply by what its elders or most conservative elements have to say. They have also succeeded where they have bargained in good faith, where they have treated their adversaries with respect and on the assumption that they also want what is best for women. They have done well when there has been some understanding of the culture in question and the different meanings vested in certain practices. They have been most effective when they have not made unfounded presumptions about cultural practices. Even then there is bound to be resistance to such change. Women activists in these three examples promoted what have become increasingly universal values regarding women's rights, while simultaneously maintaining a respect for diversity and what it signifies to people themselves.

Yet it is sometimes difficult to avoid imposing laws that affect particular communities more than others. This raises some very difficult issues, which Ugandan women activists have been trying to work through. The Muslims in Uganda, who make up 16 per cent of the population, already feel singled out and persecuted by the government, which has been intimidating and harassing their members as part of its efforts to eradicate terrorism involving some extremist Islamic groups. At the same time, women activists have been pushing for a Domestic Relations Bill, which would curtail if not outlaw polygamy and other practices that are seen as harmful to women. Some Muslim leaders are saying that such a bill would further alienate the Muslim community, which will never again trust that they are safe with legislation. The bill therefore has political implications well beyond the gender issues at stake that will complicate the passage of this bill.

In Uganda, women's organizations have succeeded in promoting women's rights in the context of an ethnically and religiously diverse society because they have not mystified culture. Women activists do not see culture as entirely immutable and impermeable. Ugandan cultures have always changed; rituals and symbols have come and gone; and their meanings have been transformed over time, often becoming divested of their original meaning or taking on different significance. Broader economic and political changes have often set the stage for many of these changes in thinking and practice.

Cultural integrity has never hinged on any one ritual or practice, most certainly not on ones that hurt women. To the contrary, the strengthening of women's rights and status generally leads to increased development and improvements in standards of living. Appeals to preserve practices that have proven to be harmful to women on the grounds of custom, tradition, ethnicity, or religion are still appeals to do harm to women.

Finally, the Ugandan case suggests that we need to think of individuals not just in relation to their communal or confessional groups, or their nationality, but also as members of even wider international communities who are susceptible to international influences and ideas as well. Some of these influences, for example, come from international religious communities like the Vatican or Islamist movements. Others pertain to the marketing of popular culture or to the spread of various forms of consumerism more generally, and still others have to do with social movements and non-governmental organizations. Ugandan women activists see themselves as connected to international women's movements advocating for women's advancement. The dialogues with feminists throughout the world have been important to domestic struggles. Societies should not be seen as homogeneous, self-contained, culturally coherent entities, but rather as constituting people with varying allegiances. Advocates of gender equality worldwide are involved in this process together. Across the globe, women activists struggle with cultural constraints that keep women from moving forward. This is not the prerogative of Third World cultures or minority groups. We share a common humanity that makes these struggles belong to all of us.

References

Achieng, Judith (1998) 'Uganda: Fighting Tradition, Landless Widows Win Major Court Test', *IPS* (1 Sep.).

Agarwal, Bina (1995) *A Field of One's Own: Gender and Land Rights in South Asia* (Cambridge: Cambridge University Press).

Bakyawa, Jennifer (2000a) 'Cabinet May Review Co-ownership—Okwir', *Monitor*, 7 Mar., internet edition <www.monitor.co.ug>.

—— (2000b) 'Women Threaten to Vote Against Movt Over Land', *Monitor*, 22 Feb., internet edition <www.monitor.co.ug>.

Benhabib, Seyla (1995) 'Cultural Complexity, Moral Interdependence, and the Global Dialogical Community', in Martha Nussbaum and Jonathan Glover (eds.), *Women, Culture and Development: A Study of Human Capabilities* (New York: Oxford University Press).

Bonder, Gloria, and Marcela Nari (1995) 'The 30 Percent Quota Law: A Turning Point for Women's Political Participation in Argentina', in A. Brill (ed.), *Rising Public Voice: Women in Politics Worldwide* (New York: Feminist Press).

Buergenthal, Thomas (1988) 'The United States and International Human Rights', *Human Rights Law Journal*, 9: 141–4.

Cohen, David William, and E. S. Atieno Odhiambo (1992) *Burying SM: The Politics of Knowledge and the Sociology of Power in Africa* (Portsmouth: Heinemann).

Cohen, Joshua, Susan Moller Okin, Matthew Howard, and Martha C. Nussbaum (eds.) (1999) *Is Multiculturalism Bad for Women?* (Princeton: Princeton University Press).

Egunyu, Fiona (1989) 'Letter to the Editor', *New Vision*, 17 Aug., internet edition, <www.newvision.co.ug>.

—— (1994) 'Circumcision: Leave it to Kapchorwa', *Sunday Vision*, 21 Aug., p. 5, internet version, <www.sundayvision.co.ug>.

Eliah, Elaine (1999) 'In Uganda, Elders Work with the UN to Safeguard Women's Health', *UN Chronicle*, 36/1: 31.

Etengu, Nathan (1992) 'Girls Pay for Circumcision', *New Vision*, 30 Sept., internet edition, <www.newvision.co.ug>.

Gawaya-Tegulle, Tom (1999) 'Female Circumcision is on the Way Out', *Monitor*, 19 Jan., internet edition, <www.monitor.co.ug>.

Gordon, April (1995) 'Gender, Ethnicity, and Class in Kenya: "Burying Otieno" Revisited', *Signs*, 20: 883–912.

Government of Uganda (1998) *Land Act 1998* (Entebbe: Government Printers).

Gray, John Milner (1934) 'Early History of Buganda', *Uganda Journal*, 2/4: 259–70.

Hale, Sondra (1995) 'Gender and Economics: Islam and Polygamy—A Question of Causality', *Feminist Economics*, 1/2: 67–79.

IPS (1992) 'Women Leaders in Uganda Fight Against Female Circumcision, Kapchorwa' (31 Jan.).

Kaggwa, Apolo (1971) *The Kings of Buganda (Basekabaka be Buganda)* (M. S. M. Nairobi: East African Publishing House; 1st publ. 1901).

Kameo, Elizabeth (2000) 'Land Group Irked', *New Vision*, 11 May, internet edition, <www.newvision.co.ug>.

Karlstrom, Mikael (1999) 'The Cultural Kingdom in Uganda: Popular Royalism and the Restoration of the Buganda Kingship', Ph.D. thesis, Anthropology, University of Chicago.

—— (2000) 'Deja vu: Social Reproduction and Responses to Transformation and Crisis in Colonial and Postcolonial Buganda', paper presented at the conference on 'The Politics of Social Reproduction in Neoliberal Africa', Wilder House, University of Chicago, 2 Dec.

Kaufman, Natalie Hevener (1990) *Human Rights Treaties and the Senate: A History of Opposition* (Durham, NC: University of North Carolina Press).

Kawamara, Sheila (1998) 'Uganda: Women are Still Not Secured', *Global News* (Jan.).

Khadiagala, Lynn (1999) 'The State and Family Law in Uganda', Ph.D. dissertation, University of Wisconsin-Madison, Madison.

—— (2001) 'The Failure of Popular Justice in Uganda: Local Councils and Women's Property Rights', *Development and Change*, 32/1: 55–76.

Kibirige, David (1999) 'Monitor Features', *Monitor*, 28 Apr., internet edition, <www.monitor.co.ug>.

Kissa, Ben, and Rachid Muzungyo (1993) 'Female Circumcision Decried', *New Vision*, 14 July, internet edition, <www.newvision.co.ug>.

Kymlicka, Will (1995) *Multicultural Citizenship* (Oxford: Clarendon Press).

—— (1999) 'Response to Okin', in J. Cohen, S. M. Okin, M. Howard, and M. C. Nussbaum (eds.) *Is Multiculturalism Bad for Women?* (Princeton: Princeton University Press).

Landman, Ruda (n.d.) 'Commentary: Female Circumcision', *Phoenix Television*, internet edition, <www.phoenix-tv.net/html/orange/video/africa/ugandacir1.htm>.

Luganda, Patrick (1994) 'Sabiny Feel Intimidated', *Women's Vision* (6 Dec.), 4.

Mayer, Ann Elizabeth (1994) 'Universal versus Islamic Human Rights: A Clash of Cultures or a Clash with a Construct?', *Michigan Journal of International Law*, 15: 307–401.

—— (1996) 'Reflections on the Proposed United States Reservations to CEDAW: Should the Constitution be an Obstacle to Human Rights?', *Hastings Constitutional Law Quarterly*, 23/3: 728–823.

Monitor (1994) 'The Disappearing Knife of Cheyoshetap-Tum', 11–14 May, internet edition, <www.monitor.co.ug>.

—— (1999) 'Letter from Asiimwe Robina Akiiki', 1 Mar., internet edition, <www.monitor.co.ug>.

New Vision (1999) Editorial: 'Culture Must be Dynamic', 6 Sept., internet edition, <www.newvision.co.ug>.

—— (2000*a*) 'Share Parents' Property, Museveni Tells Women', 10 May, internet edition, <www.newvision.co.ug>.

—— (2000*b*) 'Uganda Land Alliance Threatens Referendum Boycott', 22 Feb., <www.newvision.co.ug>.

Nussbaum, Martha C. (2000) *Women and Human Development: The Capabilities Approach* (New York: Cambridge University Press).

—— and Jonathan Glover (eds.) (1995) *Women, Culture, and Development* (New York: Oxford University Press).

Okin, Susan Moller (1999) 'Is Multiculturalism Bad for Women', in Joshua Cohen, Susan Moller Okin, Matthew Howard, and Martha C. Nussbaum (eds.), *Is Multiculturalism Bad for Women?* (Princeton: Princeton University Press).

Olupot, Milton (2000) 'Nabagereka Decries Gender Imbalance', *New Vision*, 8 Mar., internet edition, <www.newvision.co.ug>.

Otieno, Wambui Waiyaki (1998) *Mau Mau's Daughter: A Life History*, ed. with an introduction by Cora Ann Presley (Boulder, Colo.: Lynne Rienner).

Ray, Benjamin C. (1991) *Myth, Ritual, and Kingship in Buganda* (Oxford: Oxford University Press).

Shachar, Ayelet (2000) 'Should Church and State be Joined at the Altar? Women's Rights and the Multicultural Dilemma', in Will Kymlicka and Wayne Norman (eds.), *Citizenship in Diverse Societies* (Oxford: Oxford University Press).

Stamp, Patricia (1991) 'Burying Otieno: The Politics of Gender and Ethnicity in Kenya', *Signs*, 16: 808–45.

Sunday Vision (1999) 'Opinion—Nakku: Good Ending!', 20 Apr., internet edition, <www.sundayvision.co.ug>.

Tamale, Sylvia (2000) 'When Girls can be Heirs to Fathers', *Monitor*, 9 Jan., <www.monitor.co.ug>.

Troutt, Elizabeth (1994) 'Changing Land Markets in Buganda (Uganda)', Ph.D. dissertation, Agricultural Economics University of Wisconsin-Madison, Madison.

Tsikata, D., and A. Whitehead (2001) 'Policy Discourses on Women's Land Rights in Sub-Saharan Africa', UNRISD, mimeo.

Wamboka, Nabusayi L. (1999) 'Land Act: Lira Men Grumble, Women Grin', *Monitor*, 9 Apr., internet edition, <www.monitor.co.ug>.

....
Notes
....

Chapter 1

The authors are grateful to Yusuf Bangura and three anonymous referees of OUP for their comments on an earlier draft.

1. The United States however has not signed up to CEDAW. See Tripp in Ch. 13.
2. For a discussion of the impact of the women's movement on policy change in the Latin American region see Molyneux (2000*b*); Craske and Molyneux (2001). For a global synopsis of the situation regarding women's entry into politics see Jaquette (2001).
3. See UNIFEM, 2000, for a full report on progress.
4. Feminists criticized the androcentric bias that made universalism appear to be 'false' in its taking of the masculine norm as the subject of liberal contract theory, in its neglect of the social conditions that make its universalist principles meaningful, and in its 'erasure of difference'.
5. See Yuval-Davis and Werbner (1999) for elaboration from a gender perspective of the view that 'abstract' universalism is not *'intrinsically exclusionary'*.
6. Citizenship was bound up with the capacity to bear arms and hence serve the nation; women argued that the capacity to bear children was at least of equal importance and should be recognized as worthy of citizenship.
7. This applies to all the Muslim countries that have signed up to CEDAW but other states including New Zealand and Great Britain have also entered reservations, albeit less extensive.
8. See e.g. Pateman (1988) and Phillips (1991, 1993).
9. Rawls does qualify his universalism in *Law of the Peoples*.
10. For a gendered analysis of poverty and well-being and the methodological impact of the capability framework see Razavi (2000).
11. The 'missing woman' phenomenon refers to the excess mortality and artificially lower survival rates of women in many parts of the world.
12. See Wade (2001) on the neglect of inequality in the debates on globalization.
13. See Hirst (1994) for an argument in favour of non-state provision through self-governing associations.
14. This is particularly notable in Latin America where in the 1980s and 1990s six states with indigenous populations altered their constitutions in this manner.

442 *Notes*

15. Iris Marion Young (1990) has argued the case for group rights for women and minorities as the best way to guarantee justice.
16. Advocates of multiculturalism are divided over this issue of culture most evidently because poststructuralists oppose essentialist arguments of this kind.
17. This debate cannot be entered into here but poststructuralist defenders of some version of universalism include Judith Butler (1995) and Robbins (1998).
18. The superiority of private pensions was argued on several counts: expansion of coverage; competition; administrative cost of the system; and its impact on capital markets, national savings, and investment. Yet, contrary to the claims and predictions of those promoting privatization, the reforms appear to have proceeded on the basis of assumptions the existing data do not substantiate (Huber and Stephens, 2000; Mesa-Lago, 2001).
19. For discussions of this 'demobilization' phenomenon see *inter alia* the collections by Alvarez *et al.* (1998); and Chalmers *et al.* (1997).
20. In reality, no country can live up to the ideal view of democracy, and it is also widely appreciated that democratization is a cumulative process. But in many of the new emerging democracies of East and South the liberal component is vastly underdeveloped, rendering them 'illiberal democracies' (O'Donnell, 1993, 1998).
21. On the challenges of pursuing transformative change while dealing with the constraints imposed by working within bureaucracies in both state institutions and international development agencies see Miller and Razavi (1998).
22. As is well known, by 'de-personalizing' the vote, the PR system with party lists helps to override traditional sentiments against candidates due to their gender, ethnic affiliation, or other personal characteristics.
23. This is Stuart Hall's formulation, one that seeks to distance itself from the idea that there is *one* 'multiculturalism'; rather in Hall's view, there are many multiculturalisms, and many possible answers to the multicultural question—a view endorsed here.
24. For example contrast Iris M. Young's (1990) advocacy of group rights as the most effective mechanism to ensure equality; with Seylah Benhabib's (1995) endorsement of 'a global dialogical moral community'.
25. Amerindian, Indian, and indigenous are all terms used in Latin America to describe the descendants of the people who inhabited the Americas prior to Spanish colonialism. Terminology raises many questions of politics as well as of who is considered by whom to belong to this category, given four centuries of intermarriage.
26. Opinion has been divided in Mexico over the move towards multicultural policies. Opponents claim that the legal recognition of rights-based notions of cultural difference and tradition is unjustifiable because the colonial origins of many institutions and traditions of indigenous people mean they are not 'authentic'. Others fear that indigenous

autonomy and difference can only deepen social and ethnic inequalities, and risk strengthening indigenous elite rule which is subject to limited democratic sanction.

Chapter 2

The present chapter is closely related to the arguments of my book *Women and Human Development: The Capabilities Approach* (2000*a*): Introduction and ch. 1; those who would like more extensive versions of my arguments (and more empirical material, focusing on India) can find them there. The book also contains detailed discussion of Sen's views and differences between his version of the approach and my own. For earlier articulations of my views on capabilities, see Nussbaum (1988, 1990, 1992, 1995*a*, 1997*a*, 1997*b*); 'Non-Relative Virtues: An Aristotelian Approach', in Nussbaum and Sen (1993); 'Human Capabilities, Female Human Beings' in Nussbaum and Glover (1995*b*: 61–104); and 'Women and Cultural Universals' ch. 1 in Nussbaum (1999).

1. For examples of these inequalities, see Nussbaum (2000*b*: ch. 3; and 1997*c*, 1999).
2. Among the four countries ranking lowest in the gender-adjusted development index, GDI (Niger, Ethiopia, Burkina Faso, and Burundi—no ranking being given for Sierra Leone because of insufficient data), three are among the bottom four on the Human Poverty Index, HPI, a complex measure including low life expectancy, deprivation in education, malnutrition, and lack of access to safe water and health services (the bottom four being Sierra Leone, Niger, Ethiopia, and Burkina Faso—Burundi is fifteen places higher) (UNDP, 1999: 140–1, 146–8); among the four developing countries ranking highest in the HPI (Barbados, Trinidad and Tobago, Uruguay, and Costa Rica), all have high rankings on the GDI (Barbados 27, Uruguay 36, Costa Rica 42, Trinidad and Tobago 44).
3. On India, see the special report on rape in *India Abroad*, (10 July 1998). According to the latest statistics, one woman is raped every fifty-four minutes in India, and rape cases increased 32% between 1990 and 1997. Even if some of this increase is due to more reporting, it is unlikely that it all is, because there are many deterrents to reporting. A woman's sexual history and social class are sure to be used against her in court, medical evidence is rarely taken promptly, police typically delay in processing complaints, and therefore convictions are extremely difficult to secure. Penile penetration is still a necessary element of rape in Indian law, and thus cases involving forced oral sex, for example, cannot be prosecuted as rape. Rape cases are also expensive to prosecute, and there is currently no free legal aid for rape victims. In a sample of 105 cases of rape that actually went to court (in a study conducted by Sakshi, a Delhi-based NGO) only seventeen resulted in convictions.

4. Sub-Saharan Africa was chosen as the 'baseline' because it might be thought inappropriate to compare developed with developing countries. Europe and North America have an even higher ratio of women to men: about 105/100. Sub-Saharan Africa's relatively high female/male ratio, compared to other parts of the developing world, is very likely explained by the central role women play in productive economic activity, which gives women a claim to food in time of scarcity. For a classic study of this issue, see Esther Boserup (1970). For a set of valuable responses to Boserup's work, see *Persistent Inequalities* (Tinker, 1990)

5. The statistics in this paragraph are taken from Drèze and Sen (1989; and 1995: ch. 7). Sen's estimated total number of missing women is one hundred million; the India chapter discusses alternative estimates.

6. Personal communication, Viji Srinivasan, Adithi, Patna, Bihar.

7. See Kittay (1999); Folbre (1999); Harrington (1999) and Williams (1999).

8. On this see Nussbaum (1998*a*,1998*b*, 2000*a*).

9. The terms 'political liberalism', 'overlapping consensus', and 'comprehensive conception' are used as by Rawls (1996).

10. See 'Women in Informal Employment: Globalizing and Organizing', publication of a public seminar, Apr. 1999, in Ottawa, Canada; the steering committee of WIEGO includes Ela Bhatt of SEWA, and Martha Chen, who has been a leading participant in discussions of the 'capabilities approach' at the World Institute for Development Economics Research, in the 'quality of life' project directed by Amartya Sen and myself, see Chen (1995, 1983).

11. See the excellent discussion of these attacks in the essay 'Contesting Cultures' in Narayan (1997).

12. For one fascinating example of this point, together with a general critique of communitarian fantasies of cultural peace and homogeneity, see Kniss (1997).

13. For a general discussion, with many references, see Nussbaum and Sen (1989).

14. Cited by Amartya Sen, in a speech at the conference on 'The Challenge of Modern Democracy', University of Chicago, Apr. 1998.

15. The initial statement is in Sen, 'Equality of What?' in McMurrin (1980, repr. in Sen, 1982); see also various essays in Sen (1984; 1985*a*, 1985*b*, 1992); 'Capability and Well-Being' in Nussbaum and Sen (1993: 30–53); 'Gender Inequality and Theories of Justice' in Glover and Nussbaum (1995). See also Drèze and Sen (1989, 1995).

16. *Human Development Reports* (UNDP, 1993, 1994, 1995, 1996). For related approaches in economics, see Dasgupta (1993); Agarwal (1994); Alkire (1999); Anand and Harris (1994); Stewart (1996); Pattanaik (1998); Desai (1990) and Chakraborty (1996). For discussion of the approach, see Aman (1991) and Basu *et al.* (1995).

17. See the discussion of this example in Nussbaum and Sen (1993: 'Introduction').

18. Nussbaum (2000*b*: ch. 2), gives an extensive account of economic preference-based approaches, arguing that they are defective without

reliance on a substantive list of goals such as that provided by the capabilities approach. Again, this is a theme that has repeatedly been stressed by Sen in his writings on the topic.

19. Obviously, I am thinking of the political more broadly than do many theorists in the Western liberal tradition, for whom the nation-state remains the basic unit. I am envisaging not only domestic deliberations but also cross-cultural quality of life assessments and other forms of international deliberation and planning.

20. For some examples of the academic part of these discussions, see the papers by Roop Rekha Verma, Martha A. Chen, Nkiru Nzegwu, Margarita Valdes, and Xiaorong Li in Nussbaum and Glover (1995).

21. The 1994 International Conference on Population and Development (ICPD) adopted a definition of reproductive health that fits well with the intuitive idea of truly human functioning that guides this list: 'Reproductive health is a state of complete physical, mental and social well-being and not merely the absence of disease or infirmity, in all matters relating to the reproductive system and its processes. Reproductive health therefore implies that people are able to have a satisfying and safe sex life and that they have the capability to reproduce and the freedom to decide if, when, and how often to do so.' The definition goes on to say that it also implies information and access to family planning methods of their choice. A brief summary of the ICPD's recommendations, adopted by the Panel on Reproductive Health of the Committee on Population established by the National Research Council specifies three requirements of reproductive health: '1. Every sex act should be free of coercion and infection. 2. Every pregnancy should be intended. 3. Every birth should be healthy'. See Tsui *et al.* (1997: 14).

22. See the fuller discussion in Nussbaum (2000*b*: ch. 1).

23. Chapters 3 and 4 in Nussbaum (2000*b*) confront the difficult issues raised by religion and the family for this approach.

24. See Nussbaum (1999: ch. 3 and 4).

25. See the varied proposals in the works cited above n. 11, and also my 'The Future of Feminist Liberalism', a Presidential Address to the Central Division of the American Philosophical Association, 22 Apr. 2000, and to be published in *Proceedings and Addresses of the American Philosophical Association*, 74/2 (Nov. 2000: 47–79).

26. Rawls (1996) a frequent phrase. For detailed discussion of Rawls's views on this question, see my 'Rawls and Feminism' (forthcoming); and also 'The Future of Feminist Liberalism'.

27. See the excellent argument in Kittay (1999).

28. Not all political approaches that use an Aristotelian idea of functioning and capability are freedom-focused in this way; thus Aristotle was an inspiration for Marx, and also for many Catholic conservative thinkers. Among historical approaches using Aristotle, my approach lies closest to that of the British social-democratic thinkers T. H. Green in the latter half of the 19th cent. (pioneer of compulsory education in Britain) and Ernest Barker in the first half of the 20th.

29. Sen (1994: 38). Compare Rawls (1996: 187–8), which connects freedom and need in a related way.
30. The material of this section is further developed in Nussbaum (1997*b*).
31. On both India and China, see Sen (1997*a*) and Taylor (1999).
32. See Sen (1997*a*). On Tagore, see Sen (1997*b*) and Bardhan (1990. 'Introduction'). For the language of rights in the Indian independence struggles, see Nehru (1990: 612).
33. That is my account of the political goal: one might, of course, retain the capabilities approach while defining the goal differently—in terms, for example, of complete capability equality. I recommend the threshold only as a *partial theory of justice*, not a complete theory. If all citizens are over the threshold, my account does not yet take a stand on what distributive principle should govern at that point.

Chapter 4

1. The phenomenon in contemporary Britain of white youths 'talking black'—adopting what they see as the street-culture of their African-Caribbean peers—is one rather weird illustration.
2. Though I will not address it here, I find this distinction between voluntary and involuntary incorporation far from convincing; and in its suggestion that migrants cannot later complain about the laws and practices of their 'chosen' country, it edges too close to John Locke's infamous argument about citizens demonstrating their 'consent' to the laws of their country whenever they enjoy the security that is provided by those laws.
3. Her extended discussion of this is published as Okin (1998). An abbreviated version, with a number of critical and supportive responses came out in *the Boston Review*, (Oct.–Nov. 1997), and this was later published, with some additional contributions, as Susan Moller Okin with respondents (Okin *et al*., 1999).
4. In one recent assessment, not discussed here, Shachar (2001) takes her to task for setting up a stark either/or between cultural identities and gender equalities, and argues for forms of 'joint governance' as an alternative solution.
5. Saharso (2000) argues for a modified understanding of autonomy that is worthy in Western liberal eyes but also compatible with what she sees as a different kind of autonomy characteristic of Asian cultures. Parekh (2000) makes a stronger claim, arguing that when liberals set up autonomy as the central moral norm, they deny the authentic otherness of non-liberal cultures. See also his 'A Varied Moral World' in Okin *et al*. (1999).
6. I develop this further in Phillips (2001).
7. For a good discussion of the tensions these posed between sexual and cultural equality, see Deveaux (2000). See also Phillips (1995: ch. 5).
8. E.g. in Phillips (1995).

9. In her discussion of these matters, Martha Nussbaum defends a political liberalism that respects different religious conceptions, even when these entail metaphysical positions about the superiority of men over women, or individuals choosing to live non-autonomous lives. See 'A Plea for Difficulty' in Okin *et al.* (1999).

Chapter 5

1. In some, these rights are simply ignored, as in the case of political rights in Loukatchenko's Belarus or Koutchma's Ukraine.
2. According to Marshall (1992), citizenship has three facets: civil, political, and social. Civil citizenship includes rights connected with individual liberties: personal liberty, freedom of expression, the right to owner-ship, and the right to justice. Political citizenship involves the right to participate in political power as a voter or elected official; social citizen-ship encompasses the right to well-being and economic security, but also relates to societal norms.
3. As a number of critical analyses have pointed out, Marshall's theoret-ical framework is based on a history of rights created for men in several countries. The sequence of events that he cites—the emergence of civil rights in the 18th cent. political rights in the 19th cent., and social rights in the 20th cent.—is not universally valid (in Germany, the first forms of social protection were introduced by Bismarck in the 19th cent.). But even more importantly, this categorization by periods takes no account of women. Almost everywhere, women have obtained certain social rights (including maternity leave and a prohibition on night work) *before* gain-ing the right to vote, while many civil rights (notably those related to marriage) continued to be denied them as late as the 1970s (Del Re, 1994).
4. The analogy should not be carried too far. Welfare in the West, after the Second World War, implied the establishment of systems of social compensation, major wage increases, and a net increase in the level of consumption at one and the same time—a situation far different from what occurred under 'real socialism'.
5. In the same vein, in Hungary assistance is only available to 'needy' families (Haney, 1997).
6. On the tendency of Central and Eastern European countries to conform to the neo-liberal model, see, in particular, Ferge (1998).
7. On the notion of social status, see Fraser (2000) who uses the term in her discussion about the link between recognition (of specific group identities) and redistribution (of resources and wealth).
8. Let us also recall that a movement like Solidarność, which resisted mar-tial law under the authoritarian regime, would not have been able to do so without strong roots in the private sphere, as shown by the accounts of activists who described their struggles and the importance of family solidarity for those opposing the reigning bureaucracy.

9. Specifically, shortages in housing led to several generations having to live under one roof. The situation was so bad that divorced couples were often forced to continue living in the same house while awaiting relocation.

10. Though striking, such opinions are not unique to Poland, as shown by a number of surveys in other Eastern European countries (Heinen, 1999*a*).

11. Nurses earn between 800 and 1,400 zlotys. The poverty line in 1999 was 950 zlotys (IPISS, cited by *Polityka*, 24 Feb. 2001).

12. *Robotnik* (Spring 2001).

13. In 1992, three-quarters of the Polish population were less confident in Solidarność than four years earlier and 40% of them considered that no trade union understood their problems (Heinen, 1995: 31). Only 14% of Polish workers are members of trade unions, in private firms it is 6% (*Wprost*, 22 Apr. 2001, p. 30).

14. Economic restructuring has not only led to extremely high unemployment rates in a country where unemployment was previously unknown, but to a very marked weakening of private-sector unions. These unions even disappeared in many cases where multinationals succeeded in imposing labour relations every bit as draconian as those prevalent under the wild capitalism of the late 19th century.

15. Although various clubs of female entrepreneurs have emerged, women represent a very small proportion of employers heading enterprises of some importance. However, it is worth noting that the president of the very active Polish Confederation of Private Employers is a woman (Henryka Bochniarz) and that, in recent years, some women have reached top positions, as, for example, Hanna Gronkiewicz-Waltz, vice-president of the BRD, or Maria Wiśniewska and Henryka Pieronkowicz, presidents of important Polish banks.

16. Constitution of Poland available on the website <www.sejm.gov.pl>.

17. Conventions 100 and 111 of the International Labour Organization (ILO); the United Nations Convention on the Elimination of All Forms of Discrimination Against Women (ratified in 1981); the European Social Charter (1989); the Beijing Platform of Action (1995); and lastly, the final document of the Copenhagen Social Summit (1994).

18. Council of Minister of the Republic of Poland, National Programme of preparation for membership in the European Union, 26 Apr. 2000, available on the website <www.kie.pl>. Article 11-2 says 'Workers enjoy equality of rights based on carrying out duties that are of equal value ... This relates specifically to equal treatment of men and women in regard to work' (ch. 13, pp. 20–38). Article 11-3: 'All discrimination in work relationships is unacceptable, particularly based on gender, age, handicap, race, or nationality' (ibid.).

19. In June 1993, the European Council of Copenhagen defined the criteria for membership for candidate countries. One is the obligation to implement fully the *acquis communautaire*. On 31 Mar. 1998 negotiations concerning Poland's membership began. These negotiations are based on an annual screening of the harmonization process in

the economic, social, and juridical fields. However, each of these chapters are not treated equally. Most of the negotiations concern economic issues. The social dimension, including equal opportunities for men and women, appears to be marginal. But, among intergovernmental bodies, the European Union has a privileged position because of the compulsory character of the implementation process. Poland will implement the following directives: 75/117/EEC on equal pay, EEC/76/207 and EEC/86/813 on equal treatment in the field of employment, 79/7/EEC, 86/378/EEC, 96/97/EC on occupational social security schemes, (97/81/EC) on part-time work, and 96/34/EC on parental leave.

20. The concept of indirect discrimination is defined in Article 2 of the directive (dated 15 Dec. 1997), concerning the burden of proof in cases of discrimination based on gender, which reads as follows: 'Indirect discrimination exists when a provision, criterion or practice that is apparently neutral clearly affects a higher proportion of persons of a given sex, unless the provision, criterion or practice is appropriate and necessary and can be justified by objective factors independent of the sex of the interested parties' (97/80/CE).

21. Occupational segregation is measured as the proportion of women and men who would have to shift occupations in order to create an equal gender distribution.

22. In Poland women have traditionally held 80% or more of the jobs in education, health, and social services, while fewer than one-third worked in construction, transport, and communications. Vertical segregation is very high as well—only about 6% of women hold higher positions of responsibility. The gender profiles of employment have been quite stable during the transition. Stereotypes preventing girls entering so-called 'masculine' jobs have been and still are very strong (Heinen, 1995).

23. Among blue-collar workers, twice as many women as men earn less than half the national wage, while women in the higher wage brackets earn one-third less than men. In 1996, women with a university education received, on average, only 72.5% of what males in the same category received, compared with 82.5% in 1989 (GUS, 1998).

24. Women represent a little over one-third of private sector employees, whereas they constitute 46% of the total workforce.

25. Financial establishments are much more reluctant to lend money to women than to men. Even when women do have access to borrowing, it is much harder for them to raise the amount of seed capital that most banks require (up to 30%) before they are prepared to lend.

26. For more details concerning the changes in various social fields (health, housing, education), and how they affect the very content of social citizenship, including its gender dimension, see Heinen (1995, 1999*b*).

27. In the 1980s, 90% of women who had the right to take leave took all or part of their leave, while barely 1% of fathers took leave.

28. Law of 17 Dec. 1974, amended Mar. 1995; law of 1 Dec. 1994, concerning social services for families caring for children; law of 25 June 1999, regarding maternity and health insurance benefits.

29. In Eastern European countries, childcare provisions directly linked to factories constituted 30–50% of the provision, depending on the country. It should be noted that, in most of these countries, pre-school services—at least, in terms of quantity—were clearly better than in the West, since, except in Poland, 70–90% of 3- to 6-year-olds were cared for by collective establishments in the 1980s, though the proportion of 0- to 3-year-olds cared for in day-care centres was only between 15–20%—except in East Germany, which is a separate case.

30. As far as pre-schools are concerned, the daily per-child cost is now in the order of 15–50% of the minimum wage, and recent surveys find numerous cases of children who have nothing to eat during the day because their parents are unable to pay for a meal.

31. UNICEF (1999) considers the poverty line to be 40% of the average salary. If the overall economic situation has improved in Poland, the standard of living has deteriorated: the poorest 20% of the population claimed 9% of total income in 1989; by 1997 this share had declined to 7%. Among these are the unemployed, and especially low-skilled workers, pensioners, farmers, members of large families and of single-parent families. In all these groups, women form the majority.

32. Also, they constitute a category that is growing quickly: the proportion of households headed by women rose from 27 to 30% in the short period between 1995 and 1996.

33. During the 1980s, the number of abortions performed officially ranged between 120,000 and 150,000, depending on the year. These figures, however, represented only one-third or one-fourth of total terminations, i.e. 400,000 to 600,000, according to the estimates of gynaecologists questioned in 1989. At the time, the practice of voluntary termination of pregnancy constituted a real substitute for contraception, and the choice of going to private doctors, despite the high cost involved (ranging from half to twice the average salary) was, for most women, as much due to inadequate hospital capacity as to a concern for discretion, i.e. the desire to escape the opprobrium of the Church.

34. In 1997, only 43.2% of women and 44.5% of men stated that they favoured abortion (Domanski, 1999: 112), the percentage being much lower among those under the age of 20 (CBOS, 1999).

35. In addition, the pill is extremely difficult to obtain, and only two types are reimbursable—both intended for dermatological purposes.

36. The term was taken up again by the bill sponsored by the Catholic Church in 1988.

37. Komitet Integracji Europejskej

38. European Commission (1999: 36).

39. See European Commission (2000).

40. Immediately after 1989, the proportion of women deputies fell to 13% of the total and women comprised only 6% of senators. In 1991, women constituted 9% of members of Parliament and 8% of the Senate. In the elections of 1997, 13% of deputies' seats and 12% of senatorial seats went to women (Siemienska, 2000*b*).

41. Interview by *Wysokie Obcasy* (supplement to *Gazeta Wyborcza*; 7 Oct. 2000).
42. A similar decline was seen in all the Eastern European countries after the implosion of the communist system (Heinen, 1997, 1998; Siemienska, 2000*b*).
43. This system provides a humiliating caricature of democracy. While members of both sexes served as members of Parliament, women were treated as mere figureheads, as illustrated in numerous official POUP speeches of the time.
44. Similar figures are presented by a survey of 1,388 respondents carried out on 22 Apr. 2001 by the Centre of Electoral Studies (OBW): 69.7% of female respondents and 52.97% of male respondents indicated they were in favour of reserved seats for women.
45. With regard to changes in attitudes towards employment, as well as to the trend, particularly among young women, to seek professional status and regard themselves as independent individuals who wish to provide for their own needs, see Heinen (1995), Domanski (1999), and Siemienska (2000*a*).
46. In the 1997 legislative elections, 81% of men and 72% of women with university education voted, as compared with 52% of men and 50% of women with only elementary education (Siemienska, 2000*b*).
47. During the first years of the decade, before the law was adopted in 1993, numerous women's demonstrations protested against the project of the Church. Later, the signs of discontent became less visible, but one can interpret the drop in the fertility rate as a sign of resistance against the situation imposed by the law.
48. The social group to which the majority of Polish feminists belong—generally, the intelligentsia—has certainly favoured this choice.
49. Among the most distinctive measures in the bill are the establishment of quasi-parity (a minimum of 40% women) in all public deliberative bodies; a prohibition on mentioning gender in offers of employment; combating gender stereotypes in school textbooks; and the establishment of an agency on gender equality.
50. Interview by *Wysokie Obcasy* (supplement to *Gazeta Wyborcza*; 24 Mar. 2001), 40.
51. See A. Kwaśniewski, 'O wyższości moich kobiet' (About the Superiority of my Women), *Polityka* (6 Sept. 2001), 32.
52. The figures, cited in *Wysokie Obcasy* (21 July 1999), 26, are based on a survey, and, indeed, they appear more optimistic than the figures cited earlier, in terms of a continuing and strong distrust of women's ability to engage in politics.

Chapter 6

The research on which this paper is based was funded by grants from IDRC (International Development Research Centre of Canada), from SSHRC

Notes

(Social Sciences and Humanities Research Council of Canada), and the University of Western Ontario. I want to thank Leonora Reyes for her valuable assistance with the research in Chile, Linzi Manicom for thoughtful contributions to an earlier draft, and Maxine Molyneux and Shahra Razavi for their useful editorial suggestions. I am grateful to Malcolm Blincow for his generous and detailed comments on various versions of this text.

1. My approach to the state, or more accurately state formation, has been influenced by Foucault's work on governmentality and on bio-power and the government of populations, and by analyses of the impact of culture on state formation and public policy (Foucault, 1991; Steinmetz, 1999; Rose, 1999; Corrigan and Sayer, 1985). I borrow here Nikolas Rose's notion of rationality of government to characterize political power as a dominant discursive field, which offers not only a particular political grammar and vocabulary within which 'problems' are defined, but also the ethical principles and explanatory logic which are proper to it (Rose, 1999: 28). Having said this, I maintain with Corrigan that the question of the state is central in analyses of contemporary political power. State agencies may not be the only means for governing populations, but as this study illustrates they continue today to be central to it (Corrigan and Sayer, 1985; Corrigan, 1990).

2. This redefinition of the role of the state is echoed in the reforms introduced by the British Labour Party under Tony Blair, and by the Democratic Party under Bill Clinton. Moreover, these recent experiences with state reform formed the basis of inspiration for the World Bank's new manifesto, *World Development Report 1997: The State in a Changing World* (1997). For a critical appraisal of this document, see Orford and Beard (1998).

3. According to Fernandez, 'years of statism, totally contrary to the principle of subsidiarity, the inordinate extension of the state often meant the destruction of legitimate areas of action for the individual, the family and the municipality' (quoted in Austin, 1998: 314).

4. This modification of the neo-liberal 'subsidiary' state has come to be known as 'neo-structuralism' in recent debates in the economic development field. Structuralism refers back to the basic premise proposed by ECLA under the Argentine Raul Prebisch in the 1950s that poverty in Latin America is ultimately rooted in the unequal distribution of assets in the international economy. This approach provided the ideological underpinning for significant state intervention in the national economy to promote inward-oriented capitalist development. Neo-structuralists have abandoned this basic premise and see no contradiction between export-oriented capital accumulation and the unequal distribution of wealth in particular countries. Moreover, they see transnational firms as the means for modernization and innovation. The key difference between neo-liberalism and neo-structuralism appears to be premised on whether or not unencumbered market forces can guarantee development, that is, on the issue of what role the state plays in development.

For neo-liberals state intervention leads to unnecessary inefficiencies, while for neo-structuralists, the state has a crucial consensus-building role to play in rallying the support of various and competing segments of society behind the project of neo-liberal modernizations and intensified global competition (Leiva, 1998; Petras and Leiva, 1994: 62–73).

5. The commitment to the principle of universality in social provisioning did not, of course, necessarily translate into meaningful gains in all domains for the majority of the population in all Latin American countries. It is important here to recognize the specificities of particular cases. Uruguay, with its early and well-developed welfare state and predominantly urban population is, for example, the exception to generalizations about the lack of effectiveness of the region's post-Second World War welfare states. Moreover, in Chile, the decade of profound social reforms (e.g. the agrarian reform, educational reforms, and extension of the already entrenched universal health coverage) associated with the Revolution in Freedom by Eduardo Frei Montalva (1964–9) and backed heavily until 1967 by the Alliance for Progress, followed by the unconcluded socialist experiment of the short-lived Popular Unity government (1970–3), meant important social and political gains for previously excluded segments of the population, including those in the rural and marginal urban areas. See Austin (1998); Vergara (1990); and Montecinos (1994).

6. See Montecino and Rossetti (1990) for the proposals articulated by the Concertación de Mujeres por la Democracia. The decision of this prominent group of feminists to pursue an agenda of women's rights through institutional means introduced a fundamental divide in the movement. For a discussion of this, and of the ambiguous and contradictory legacy of the option to work for women's rights within the neo-liberal state, see Schild (1998*a*, 1998*b*).

7. For an elaboration of this agenda, see Gobierno de Chile (2000).

8. I borrow the notion of the individualized ethos of neo-liberal politics from Nikolas Rose (1999: 249). For a more detailed elaboration of the crafting of gendered 'market' citizenship in Chile, see Schild (1998*a*, 1998*b*).

9. For an elaboration of how, and why, this has occurred, see Schild (1998*b*, 2000).

10. The report is discussed in Mujer/Fempress (1999*a*).

11. See SERNAM (2000: 71).

12. For a discussion of the polling results, see Mujer/Fempress (1999*c*).

13. Interview with Ana Pichulman, President of REMOS, 7 July 2000.

14. See, e.g. Molina (1998). This frustration is increasingly echoed in other parts of Latin America. For a discussion of Argentina, see Di Marco (2000). More recently, it was expressed by several panelists in the Ford Foundation-sponsored International Conference on Civil Society and Democratic Governability in the Andes and the Southern Cone, held at the Catholic University of Peru, Lima, 31 Aug–1 Sept. 2000.

15. Important elements of these legacies are: unelected 'institutional senators'; the quorums needed to reform the constitution; an electoral system which facilitates the over-representation of conservative sectors in congress; and the guardianship role of the institutional order assigned to the armed forces. See Galleguillos (1998: 162).

16. In his analysis of the transformations of the Conservative neo-liberal project of the Thatcher regime to its present modified form associated with Blair's New Labour Party, Nikolas Rose offers the neologism 'advanced liberal' (see Rose, 1999: 137–42). Beyond its deployment in economic development and policy debates, neo-liberalism has come to stand in critical political analysis for the new dominant discourse with its emphasis on individualism and its reduction of all domains of public/social life to the terms and rationality of the economic field. In this text I deliberately preserve the term neo-liberalism when referring to Chilean liberal democracy in its present form, in order to insist on the cultural-political continuities with the earlier, radical form of neo-liberalism, and on the significant break with earlier forms of liberal democracy.

17. Figures from SERNAM (2000: 11).

18. See e.g. the comprehensive study, Fundación and UNDP (2000); and the two recent ECLAC reports (2000*b*, 2000*c*).

19. For a summary of ECLAC (2000*b*), see ECLAC Press Release (2000*b*).

20. One of the recommendations ECLAC makes is that 'social policies go back to offering some degree of universal access' as a means to reduce poverty and social vulnerability.

21. Chile has recovered very slowly from the impact of the Asian meltdown. Growth rates fell from 7.1% in 1997 to 4% in 1998 to 2.8% in 1999. Moreover, the price of copper—still the main export commodity—reached a fifty-year low in early 1999 (IWRAW, 2000). ECLAC projections suggest an optimistic picture for 2000, with a growth rate of 5.5% and improving copper prices in the international markets (ECLAC, 2000*a*).

22. Lourdes Beneria (1996) uses this term for the narrow, market-defined focus of social policy in her excellent overview of the legacies of neo-liberal reforms in Latin America.

23. For a discussion of the new social policy, see Bienefeld (1997).

24. Lagos has captured the imagination of the international media, which has hailed him as representing the Blair/Clinton 'Third Way' in Latin America. He is a socialist, it is often remarked, but 'more Keynesian than Marxist'. See, e.g. Krauss (2000).

25. For a more extensive discussion of the new discourse of social policy in Chile, see Schild (2000). For a very positive view of the so-called innovative social policy in Chile, see Graham (1995). A sympathetic overview of strengths and weaknesses is offered by Raczynski (1995). For incisive critiques of the new social programmes, see Salazar (1995) and Leiva (1995). See also Vergara (1994); and Petras and Leiva (1994).

26. A recent expose of the 'hidden poverty' in the wealthy Santiago commune of Providencia has dramatized the limitations of surveys like CASEN which measure poverty in terms of income levels. Although the survey indicated that there was a 0% of low-income people in the commune, the social assistance spending by the municipal government tells a very different story. Food baskets, passes for subsidized medical attention in health clinics, and emergency housing (*mediaguas* or one-room lean-tos), in addition to assistance with refinancing utility debts for people whose water and electricity services had been cut off, are key areas of social spending for the municipality. As Marcia Munoz, a social worker for the municipal government, puts it: 'We have another type of poverty here. These are not people who are poorly dressed because they wear the same clothes they have had for thirty years, and they find it hard to ask for help. . . . These are people who lived well, bought a home through the *Caja de Empleados Particulares* (the Private Employees' Fund), but once they retired, their pensions are so low that they don't manage to subsist on them.' The income-based CASEN survey, then, fails to measure the hidden poverty which affects many, especially the elderly, according to municipal sources (Gutiérrez, 2000).

27. The conclusion of critics like Bob Deacon and others is that without such support 'services for the poor become very poor services' (Deacon, 2000). I am indebted to Maxine Molyneux and Shahra Razavi for alerting me to this critique of the targeting approach.

28. For a discussion of FOSIS, see Schild (2000); and Petras and Leiva (1994).

29. For a description of the creation of SERNAM and the difficulties it has faced, see Matear (1996).

30. The demands of the Concertación de Mujeres por la Democracia are discussed in Montecino and Rossetti (1990). For a discussion of the split in the women's movement between those wanting to remain autonomous (the *autónomas*), and those choosing to work for institutional reform (the *políticas*), see Schild (1998b). Also, Gaviola *et al.* (1994).

31. The Catholic Church and parties of the left (indirectly) played a fundamental role in the post-1973 period, in setting up and offering protection to NGOs and grass-roots initiatives.

32. For an historical overview of NGOs in Chile, see Loveman (1995). For an account of the involvement of international funding agencies in supporting NGO activities in Latin America in general, see Mayer (1999).

33. Initially the Ford Foundation and the Inter-American Foundation played a leading role in financing research centres and NGOs involved in social action. Eventually, a large and diverse group of foreign donors, including the International Research Development Centre of Canada, the Netherlands Organization for International Development Cooperation, the Swedish Agency for Research Cooperation with Developing Countries, as well as a variety of European governments, and myriad

church-based and other private agencies, subsidized the work of NGOs in Chile.

34. Feminists engaged in research in mixed NGOs, and those women who were engaged as popular educators, social workers, and nurses whose work in the field convinced them that women needed special attention, often found allies in the donor agencies to legitimize their agendas in these organizations. For a more detailed discussion of this, see Schild (1995).

35. The contribution of foreign aid to social spending was important, as a study conducted by Alvaro Garcia (1993) suggests. In a country with an estimated 44% of its population living in poverty, addressing the 'social debt' while building on the prevailing economic system became a priority for the incoming government and sympathetic foreign governments.

36. See Schild (2000) and Petras and Leiva (1994); for a detailed analysis of NGOs' new functional relation to the policy agenda of Concertación governments, including the role many play as executors of innovative social programmes. For an official view of the role of NGOs in the new policy framework, see Garcia (1993). See also Brian Loveman's account of the debate among the political elites begun in 1989 about the need to articulate the NGO sector to the future government social agenda (1995: 138–40).

37. For a discussion of this symbolic network and the patterns of popular education with a feminist content which emerged from it, see Schild (1998*b*).

38. See Schild (1998*a*), for fuller discussion of this point.

39. For a more detailed discussion of women's NGOs, their links to the women's movement, and their fate after the return to civilian-elected politics, see Schild (1998*b*). Sonia Alvarez (1999) suggests that the developments affecting NGOs, and the fate of these organizations, are part of a region-wide transformation affecting the women's movement and feminist agendas.

40. For a discussion of the limitations in the design and implementation of these programmes, see Matear (1996: 233–56).

41. See Lechner and Levy (1984) for a description of these volunteers. For a discussion of the Secretaria, see the memoir, Aguayo's de Sota (1982).

42. Some estimate the number of employees hired in these conditions as 300. Interview with representative of a solidarity NGO, Oct. 2000.

43. See Schild (2000) for a detailed description of the work of *promotores* in the implementation of social programmes in the 1990s.

44. Many *promotoras* rose through the ranks, as it were, through their contacts with, and training from, NGOs during the 1980s. Today, however, many of these women without proper accreditation have lost out to a new generation of social science graduates for whom the basic income, and if lucky, minimal health coverage, constitutes the only choice of employment.

45. Quoted in Franklin (1999).

46. Figures from the latest census, cited in SERNAM (2000). In fact, by 1995, the rate had reached 32.1% and 'was growing at a 4.1% annual rate, while the workforce as a whole was growing at a 3.0% annual rate' (Riesco, 1999: 107).
47. Recent estimates by SERNAM placed the figure for women's unemployment in the region of Santiago and surrounding areas at 11.9% and concluded that it was much higher than male unemployment. See SERNAM Press Release (2000).
48. This study concluded that, in terms of work conditions, Chile had stagnated in relation to other Latin American countries. See Mujer/Fempress (2000a).
49. See Barrera (1998: 135, table 6.4.). A recent ECLAC/CEPAL report acknowledged the 'important gains' seen in urban minimum wages in Chile between 1990 and 1992. However, it also indicated that the purchasing power achieved by this recovery only reached 1980 levels, (quoted in Boron, 1998: 48).
50. Date on the variation of the index of real wages per hour compiled by Instituto Nacional de Estadísticas (INE), offers an indication of this. Taking April 1993 as base = 100, the variation in percentages is as follows: Dec. 1994, 5.2; Dec. 1995, 5.1; Dec. 1996, 2.7; Dec. 1998, 2.9; Aug. 2000, 1.7 (variation in relation to Aug. 1999). For details, see <www.ine.cl>. I am grateful to Fernando Leiva for this information.
51. Overview and conclusions of ECLAC (2000c) in ECLAC Press Release (2000a).
52. Secretaria Técnica de la Mujer (1992) 'Análisis encuesta: Proyecto multinacional de promoción de la mujer sindicalista', Central Única de Trabajadores (CUT), mimeo, Santiago, cited in Matear (1996: 186–7).
53. Under this much touted scheme, employers do not contribute anything, while workers are expected to contribute 10% of their wages to the Administradoras de Fondos de Pension (AFPs) for investment in funds, plus an additional 3% of their wages which go towards a disability insurance premium and commission fees. A study by Stephen J. Kay of the performance of the private pension system from its inception in 1981 to 1998, suggests that the actual returns for workers are 'considerably lower' than the impressive levels of average annual returns on investment. According to Kay, while returns averaged 11% between 1982 and 1998, workers' actual annual return, after deducting commission fees, would have been 5.1% and this means 'that workers would have received a higher return had they invested in a bank savings account invested in 90-day certificates'. He concludes that 'when charges are factored in, an average worker entering the system after 1990 received negative annual average returns through 1998' (Kay, 2000: 198).
54. Without differentiating by gender, the report *Social Panorama of Latin America, 1999–2000* has found that for the region as a whole, already 'from 40% to 60% of senior citizens (60 years of age and over) receive no

income from pensions or jobs and therefore must rely on their extended families' (ECLAC Press Release, 2000*c*).

55. The region-wide study of pension reforms by Huber and Stephens (2000) highlights the same gender-based discriminations of the private scheme.

56. Cited in IWRAW (2000). As Arenas de Mesa and Montecinos point out, under the old public health service, 'men and women of all ages and equal salaries had the same benefits' (1999: 28).

57. A recently proposed labour reform (Nov. 1999) promised to give unions greater power to negotiate better conditions for workers, including seasonal workers. Unlike earlier attempts, this reform bill was narrowly passed in Congress. However, after considerable pressure from powerful business lobby groups and economic experts in Chile and on Wall Street, outgoing president Eduardo Frei Jr. caved in and vetoed it. The most contentious aspects of this bill were making illegal the hiring of workers during a strike, and creating a system for joint collective bargaining by inter-firm unions and unions of seasonal workers. Ultimately, the spectre of Chile's loss of economic competitiveness, raised by those opposing the bill, won the day. Chile, it is worth remembering, has yet to ratify the 1987 and 1998 ILO agreements which call for the strengthening of unionization and of collective bargaining.

58. According to Pearson, countless studies demonstrate that when ' "cheap" labour is deconstructed beyond the absolute wage levels to include employee protection, employers' contribution to the social wage, taxation, investment and working conditions in combination with non-militancy, docility, manual dexterity and conscientious application to often monotonous production process, women are almost invariably the preferred labour force' (Pearson, 1998: 173).

59. The functional relation of the vast informal to the formal sector of the economy at different moments of capitalist development in Latin America has, in fact, been the subject of long-standing debate since the 1960s. For more recent discussions see Portes *et al.* (1989); Beneria and Roldan (1987).

60. For a detailed discussion of labour flexibilization in Chile, see Martinez and Diaz (1996). For a useful, albeit gender-biased, overview of changes in labour structure and labour relations in Chile, see Barrera (1998). For a discussion of the feminization of flexibilized labour and the implications for women workers, see Schild (2000).

61. e.g. employment in the commercial sector increased from 12.1% in 1970 to 20.4% in 1985, and in the service sector from 30.8 to 34% during the same period. These upward trends continue today (Barrera, 1998: 132). The overall number of employed persons has increased by 95% since 1970, or from 2.7 million to 5.4 million in 1997. The population grew from 9.3 million to 14.7 million during the same period (Riesco, 1999: 104).

62. Community and labour leaders have for some time registered their concerns about this widespread economic activity in poor neighbourhoods.

SERNAM's newly appointed director recently suggested that home work is work that today enjoys no protection whatsoever and 'we don't even know how many women are engaged in that type of work'. Speech by Adriana Delpiano in connection with the start of the campaign 'Mujer con Derechos, Mujer Ciudadana', Santiago, 5 May 2000.

63. Self-employment comprises 27% of the employed workforce, or 1.4 million, while waged workers constitute 3.6 million, or 70% of the active workforce, including 274,000 persons employed mainly in domestic services (Riesco, 1999: 111).

64. SERNAM, Documento de trabajo, 19, Seminario de Mujer y Microempresa en los 90 (Santiago, 1993), cited in Matear (1996: 243).

65. This account of the garment industry and the 'maquilization' of poor women's work is based on an interview with Miriam Ortega, director of Centro Ana Clara, an NGO operating on a shoe-string budget whose focus is women and labour issues, and on interviews with working-class women activists in Santiago's poor southern periphery, all conducted in Dec. 1997.

66. For an excellent account of early working-class feminism, see Hutchison (1995).

67. Interview, 12 Oct. 2000.

68. One of the goals of organizations like Centro Ana Clara, the NGO specializing in women's labour issues, is precisely to reach those women. So far, there has been little interest on the part of the labour movement and of SERNAM in this sector of workers. Interview with Miriam Ortega, director of Centro Ana Clara, Dec. 1997.

69. The effects of neo-liberal restructuring on people's quality of life are being felt throughout Latin America, not just in Chile. For a region-wide discussion, see Beneria (1996).

70. According to an evaluation of recent welfare changes in Latin America conducted by Stephen J. Kay, 'In Chile, spending on pensions reached a high of 10% in 1984, then dropped almost by half to a low of 5.8% of GDP in 1994. Health spending declined from 1982 to 1990, but increased in the 1990s. Housing reached a high in 1983, then fell off dramatically and remained low throughout the 1990s. Education hit a high of 5.4% of GDP in 1982, before dropping almost by half and reaching 2.8% of GDP in 1994' (2000, 187–8).

71. Although no studies of police corruption in poor areas have, to my knowledge, been conducted to date, the anecdotal evidence is overwhelming. Stories of policemen insisting on free meals at local restaurants, stopping taxis in the downtown and poorer areas of the city under false charges, or legitimate ones, and then demanding cash, a lunch, or whatever form of bribery, from the drivers, are fast becoming part of the lore that greets the returning visitor to *poblaciones* in Santiago. Invariably, the reasons given highlight the poor salaries of the police and their class-based contempt for people of poor areas, very often their own people.

72. The study listed the following communes as the most affected areas: Renca, Conchali, Huechuraba, Cerro Navia, Lo Barnechea, El Bosque,

La Granja, La Pintana, San Joaquin, San Ramon, La Reina, Macul, Penalolen, Puente Alto, San Bernardo, and Penaflor. See Espinoza (1999).

73. The paltry results in terms of sustained economic growth, income distribution, and reduction of poverty of the nearly two decades of macroeconomic policies pushed by the World Bank and the International Monetary Fund have given rise, even among erstwhile supporters, to a call to critically re-examine this policy package also known as the Washington Consensus. For a critical evaluation of the World Bank and International Monetary Fund macroeconomic policy claims, see Weisbrot *et al.* (2000).

74. Interview with Alejandro Ferreiro, Superintendent of ISAPRES, quoted in Muñoz (1999).

75. As it turns out, then, the overstrained, underfunded public health system has been subsidizing the privatized health scheme all along, as Waitzkin and Iriart (2000: 30) point out.

76. See Schild (2000: 278–82).

77. After fourteen years of regular visits to La Pintana, Santiago's poorest commune, I have been struck by the steady decline in women's organizing and by the inordinately long working hours kept by women friends and acquaintances. I am also saddened by the potential implications of their necessary options, for example, a loss of the rich organizational experiences they had accumulated over a period of ten years or more. The anthropologist Julia Paley has noticed the same decline in organizing in a nearby commune (2001).

78. Interview, 16 Jan. 2000.

Chapter 7

The author would like to thank Shahra Razavi, Maxine Molyneux, and anonymous referees for helpful comments on an earlier draft.

1. Targets for international cooperation, also known as the International Development Targets, specify a focus on eliminating gender based disparities in education in relation to eliminating world poverty: 'Progress towards gender equality and the empowerment of women should be demonstrated by eliminating gender disparity in primary and secondary education by 2005' (DFID, 2000). See McMahon (1999) for an account of the policy rationales for investing in female education.

2. See, for instance, the discussion in Goetz and Jenkins (1999) on the importance of rights to information in relation to the right to survival and sustainable livelihoods.

3. The distinction between literacy and education is important to uphold, as both these terms can be defined and discussed in numerous ways. While literacy can be narrowly discussed in terms of the ends of reading, writing, and numeracy skills, more radical approaches such as

REFLECT stress the importance of processes of challenging power relations in the course of acquiring these skills, indeed more radical than conventional approaches to formal education in schools, for example. Further, education can be discussed in terms of a lifelong approach, or in terms of specific stages of institutionalized learning occurring through childhood, adolescence, and early adulthood. In this chapter, education will be discussed as the basic provision of institutionalized learning opportunities in terms of elementary education, defined in India in terms of the age-group 6–14. When literacy is referred to, it is largely in terms of skills and programmes aimed at adult women who were denied opportunities for schooling in their childhood.

4. Though what is meant by basic education continues to be a matter of some debate (see Bennell and Furlong, 1997; Malhotra, 2000).

5. See Colclough (1991) for an introduction to the basic 'neo-liberal' doctrines that were influential in promoting the virtues of free markets and the vices of excessive state interventionism.

6. India's economic reform period is formally recognized as starting in the early 1990s, though it is argued that the trend towards the types of reform such as market liberalization were started much earlier, and through stealth rather than public debate (Shah *et al.*, 1999).

7. Many commentators, most notably Tilak (1995) have pointed out that education in India has never been 'free', despite policy rhetoric—not just on account of the direct and indirect costs associated with formal schooling, such as uniforms, hidden fees, text books, etc., but also on account of the opportunity costs of children's schooling. However, on paper, private schools can charge fees; public schools do not (although that does not preclude them from charging for additional elements).

8. See Deacon (2000) for a discussion on this debate in the context of global social policy.

9. The increasing focus on 'community' working in partnership with the state has seen a proliferation of village-based bodies in rural India, charged with the responsibility of promoting universal education at local level (Subrahmanian forthcoming). Critics point to the 'neoconservative' roots of such a shift, and in particular the ahistorical way in which community is presented, sanitized of all the power relations that have traditionally upheld social hierarchies and inequalities (Kumar *et al.*, 2001).

10. Cornwall and Gaventa (2000) note that this shift entails viewing people as 'users and choosers' in contexts where services are being handed over to communities for design, delivery, and maintenance of projects, rather than as 'active' citizens who can 'make and shape' their own development trajectory.

11. Issues of the relative efficiency and greater accountability of private versus public schools need far more detailed empirical study. However, as Sudarshan (2000) notes, private schools pay teachers less and recruit less qualified teachers than public schools. Yet teacher attendance is observed to be far better in private schools.

12. Based on a household survey of 32,230 rural households from sixteen states conducted by the National Council for Applied Economic Research, New Delhi, in 1994 (Sudarshan, 2000: 77).

13. 'Caste' in India refers to a social system of differentiation, resulting in particularly inequitable outcomes for those groups clustered at the bottom of the social hierarchy, those previously considered 'untouchable'. The term 'Scheduled Caste' is used to denote the (in a legal sense) 'ex-untouchable' castes based on a Schedule promulgated by the British in 1936, which is a list of castes that are entitled to special educational benefits, parliamentary seats, and public employment (Mendelsohn and Vicziany, 1998). 'Scheduled Tribes' refer to the large number of indigenous communities speaking their own languages and following cultural practices relatively distinct from the mainstream (Nambissan, 2000).

14. I use the term 'occupation' rather than 'class', to move away from thinking about educational disprivilege in terms of income classifications. In the Indian case, there is plenty of evidence to argue for an occupation-based approach to understanding economic factors underpinning education deprivation.

15. For more recent data from different states of the country, see Vaidyanathan and Nair (2001). They note the limitations of data in going beyond the most generalizable findings to explain the huge variations across villages even within one district.

16. NCAER data presented in Haq and Haq (1998: 40).

17. See Fine and Rose (2001) and Subrahmanian (2000b) for more detailed discussions of the limitations of conventional human capital theory and its application to the case of female education.

18. In addition to asking 'what change' forms the basis of our evaluations, we need to ask 'whose version of change'? The relationship between autonomy and the achievement of 'quality of life' is complex. As Jeffery and Basu (1996b) argue, the definition of 'autonomy' itself is highly contested, particularly in cultural contexts where the idea of 'autonomy' as directly translated from English can have negative connotations even amongst women. They emphasize the importance of sensitivity to localized understandings as developed by women in taking forward the debate on how 'autonomy' may be achieved.

19. Preliminary findings from the Census 2001 reinforce Erwer's broad point about the gender paradox. States like Haryana and Punjab which are performing better than many other states in female education have witnessed a decline in juvenile female–male sex ratios, largely, it is speculated, on account of the widespread availability of technologies such as amniocentesis that are used to reinforce and promote sex-selective abortions (see related article Dugger, 2001).

20. The title of a recent study by Dasgupta et al. (2000) on juvenile gender ratios in India.

21. See also data from Dreze and Murthi for the strong effects of regional location on fertility, with the southern region displaying 'distinctly lower'

fertility than their (northern) control states, and eastern and western states (2000: 18).

22. Mukhopadhyay and Seymour are careful to note that the patrifocal family is one of many kinds of family form, and that they do not intend to present a monolithic or static model of household form and relationships. However, they note that it is a 'very prominent and culturally sanctioned system of ideal relationships and beliefs to which most Indians have been exposed and that provides a set of guidelines for social action' (1994: 7).

23. *Sangha* or group, refers to the women's collectives organized within the Mahila Samakhya programme, a donor-supported government programme operating in seven states of India.

24. See Subrahmanian (2000a) for a discussion of the links between livelihoods and education aspirations and prospects; see also Aruna (1999) for a discussion of the ways in which social networks shape access to employment, often requiring that children forgo education at a young age to forge apprenticeships with potential employers. As a strategy for job security in the context of high competition for jobs, employment at early ages creates disincentives for completion of elementary education.

25. Sudarshan refers to this as a 'standardization of aspirations, for schooling followed by salaried/secure employment' (2000: 57).

26. The link between gender, education, and employment can be studied from several perspectives. First, we need to understand the link between education and employment opportunities in India; second, understand how the labour market operates in terms of entry requirements and other considerations in different segments, formal and informal; third, assess the link between education investment and *aspirations* for employment. The last category entails also understanding what information exists about job availability, how social networks function in shaping access to employment. There is tremendous potential for research on the links between education and employment for women, especially as both figure strongly as potential catalysts for transforming women's unequal status.

27. See also Kabeer (2000) for compelling evidence on the impact of access to wage employment in the garment sector on women's agency within the household in Bangladesh.

28. A particularly significant finding was that employed daughters stayed on longer with their parents, thus allowing for the formation of close bonds with their natal families that continued after marriage (Seymour, 1995). Such a change in the nature of intra-family relations would constitute a big challenge to the gendered expectations and intergenerational bargain issues raised earlier in the discussion.

29. i.e. enforceable in a court of law.

30. Mehendale (1998) argues that the Supreme Court judgment discussed above provides a legally enforceable rights framework, as the Constitution deems law declared by the Supreme Court to be the law of the

land. Taken together with India's international commitments to various conventions, a climate has been created whereby the 'right' to education can be taken as granted. Of course the constitutional stamp will imbue it with more significance and weight, given the difficulty of holding states accountable through international treaty obligations, or arguing on the basis of legal precedent.

31. As Mehendale (n.d.) notes, these are also defined in specific ways. For instance, the rights of students refer to protection from abuse, discrimination, and maltreatment; in many states this is achieved through legislation prohibiting 'ragging'. Teachers' working conditions are regulated through a body of administrative rules that are revised intermittently. The quality of education is protected through stand-ard setting, regulating admissions, examinations, and syllabi. Although there has been litigation on these aspects, this has not addressed the broader question of the right of citizens to demand a particular quality of education, treating all education quality issues as the responsibility of the state.

32. In Subrahmanian (forthcoming), I argue that the levy of penalties through community bodies such as panchayats or Village Education Committees will be extremely difficult, where communities see decisions to invest or not invest in education as the 'private' decisions of a household, and not a matter of public concern.

33. A related dimension is what is referred to in economics as the 'principal–agent' problem, as parents are charged with the responsibility of making decisions on behalf of their children.

Chapter 8

This chapter is based on joint work with Afsaneh Najmabadi sponsored by UNRISD for its Beijing +5 workshop in New York in June 2000. I would like to dedicate it to Afsaneh Najmabadi in appreciation of her tremendous support with thinking it through and accessing reference material. Elahe Rostami-Povey (Maryam Poya) also assisted me with reference material, for which I am thankful. I would also like to acknowledge the valuable editorial comments from Shahra Razavi and Maxine Molyneux.

1. The chapter concentrates on the first four years of the presidency of the reformist President Mohammad Khatami who came to power in June 1997. The chapter was completed before the presidential election of June 2001 and does not take its result into consideration. The 2001 elections resulted in a major victory for President Khatami who was re-elected with a higher proportion of the votes than he achieved in his first term.

2. See Razavi (2000) and Molyneux (1998, 2000) for an overview of the debates on women's movements in the international context and trends affecting them in democratization processes.

3. In the Islamic Republic of Iran *hejab* consists of a scarf, a loose and long overcoat, with trousers and thick socks underneath, but some women

put on the more strict optional form of it that is a thick head-to-toe veil which only leaves hands and parts of the face visible. The hard-line clerics have pushed for the strict version to become the norm for women working in government offices but have not succeeded thus far in making this the norm.

4. The women's newspapers, magazines, and periodicals that have played an important role in raising awareness inside and outside the country about women's rights and sufferings in the Islamic Republic include: *Zanan* (editor Shahla Sherkat); *Payam Hajar* (editor Azam Taleghani); *Zan* (editor Faeze Hashemi-Rafsanjani); *Hoghugh Zanan* (editor Ashraf Geramizadegan); *Jens Dovom* (editor Nooshin Ahmady-Khorasany); *Farzaneh* (editor Mahbubeh Abasgholizadeh); *Zan Ruz* (different editors); *Nimeye Digar*, 1983–2000, (editor Afsaneh Najmabadi); *Nashriyeh Bonyad Pazhuheshhaye Zanan Irani* (editor Goli Amin). On *Zan* newspaper, see Hashemi-Rafsanjani (1999). On *Farzana* periodical, see Abasgholizadeh (2000).

5. To place women's citizenship role in Iran in the international context see Razavi (2000).

6. The only international convention on women's rights that the Islamic Republic has acceded to is the 1996 Covenant on Civil and Political Rights (with two reservations). Nevertheless the state has been under international pressure to defend its record on women's rights, particularly since the UN Fourth World Conference on Women in Beijing (Tohidi, 2001).

7. Personal communication with Mrs Shojai.

8. See *Peyvand's Iran News* (2000) and *Hoghugh Zanan* (2000) about the internationalization of the women's movement. See also various issues of *Farzaneh* and interview with its editor in Abasgholizadeh (2000), and *Foreign Policy Journal* (1995).

9. Body of Islamic jurisprudence and rules governing the lives of Muslims.

10. See *Bad Jens* (www.badjens.com) for examples of such collaborations. Also see the works cited in n. 4.

11. This was rejected by Islamist feminists as we shall note later.

12. Mir-Hosseini (1999) is the most comprehensive work in English so far on dynamic jurisprudence. These clerics are under state censorship and some like Saidzadeh and Yusofi Eshkevari have experienced prison and been banned from preaching. On Mojtahed-Shabestari, see Vahdat (2000) and interview with him in *Zanan*, 57 (Oct. 1999: 18–22). On Yusofi Eshkevari, see Yusofi Eshkevari (2000*a*, 2000*b*). On Kadivar, see the account of his defence in the court in Kadivar (1999*a*, 1999*b*).

13. The main sources used in English on the views of Abdolkarim Sorush are Vakili (1996), Boroujerdi (2001, 1994), and Mir-Hosseini (1999). These works give reference to Sorush's original works in Farsi.

14. See the Islamist feminist criticism of this in *Zanan*, 64 (June 2000: 2–5).

15. This part of the chapter has particularly benefited from discussions with Afsaneh Najmabadi.

16. This part of the chapter is based on a series of interviews with prominent reformists published in the women's magazine *Zanan* in 1999 and 2000.
17. On Abbas Abdi, see roundtable discussion in *Zanan*, 33 (Apr. 1997: 12–18), and interviews in no. 58 (Dec. 1999), 38.
18. See interview with Baghi in *Zanan*, 57 (Nov. 1999: 23–4).
19. See interview with Sorush in *Zanan*, 59 (Jan. 2000: 32).
20. For interview with Mohammadi, see *Zanan*, 58 (Dec. 1999: 39–41).
21. See Paidar and Tabari (1982) and the introduction in Paidar (1995) for a critique of the theoretical positions of socialists and monarchists on 'Islam versus feminism', 'universalism versus cultural relativism', and the concept of patriarchy.
22. The public positions of Islamist feminists are reflected in the women's magazines mentioned in n. 4. On works in English that discuss the positions of Islamist feminists, see the items listed in the reference section of Najmabadi, Paidar, Afshar, Haeri, Mir-Hosseini, Rostami-Povey, Tohidi, Hoodfar, Kian-Thiebaut, Keddie, and Nakanishi.
23. See also, as an example, the editorial of the *Hoghugh Zanan*, 18 (Oct./Nov. 2000: 4–5).
24. As an example, see the profile of Faeze Hashemi-Rafsanjani in Price (2000) and interview with her in *Zanan*, 28 (Apr. 1996).
25. See the works listed in the reference section under Molyneux, Razavi, Miller and Razavi, Jackson and Pearson, Jakobsen, Mohanty, Perseram, UNRISD; and Phillips (Ch. 4).

Chapter 9

The author wishes to thank Stephanie Rousseau for her comments and assistance in the final editing of this piece.

1. Definitions of Fujimori's regime have fluctuated over time and remain a matter of academic and political debate. Democratically elected in 1990, it was later categorized as 'authoritarian' after Fujimori's 'self-coup' (*autogolpe*) in 1992. Fujimori recovered some of his democratic credentials in the 1995 elections, but increasingly behaved in an authoritarian fashion until the fraudulent elections of 2000.
2. The Ministry of the Presidency was created during the government of President Alan Garcia (1985–90). However, it was during Fujimori's presidency (1990–2000) that it became the regime's most powerful ministry, accounting for more than 30% of the nation's budget. Its programmes focused on poverty alleviation, promotion of development, infrastructure works, and overseeing the government's—and the President's—propaganda.
3. After two consecutive terms President Fujimori assumed the presidency for a third time following a fraudulent and unconstitutional election. However, after three months, domestic and international pressure in the wake of corruption scandals forced him to resign.

4. The system of 'psychosocial' control, as it was called, consisted of different strategies that allowed the government to manipulate people's fear. Fujimori warned that disaster would ensue if his conditions were not met, evoking the memory of dramatic moments of terrorist violence (through videos shown during peak television viewing hours), resorting to military skirmishes on the borders, threats of invasion, and even raising the possibility of the withdrawal of foreign support and the loss of the country's precarious economic stability.

5. Interview with Rosa Angeles, Sarita Colonia community kitchen.

6. The addition of this law to existing electoral legislation meant a mandatory minimum of 25% of female or male candidates in the lists of political parties running for the Congress. For the 2001 elections, the minimum was increased to 30%.

7. One month before the elections the female candidate, Lourdes Flores Nano, received a surge of female support. As pointed out by Manuel Torrado, Director of the polling firm DATUM, in the journal *Caretas* (8 Mar. 2001), she enjoyed an advantage of more than 20 points among women voters in Lima over Alejandro Toledo, the leading candidate at the time. In other words, half of Lima's women favoured Lourdes Flores Nano. At a national level, the discrepancy was not so great: Alejandro Toledo held 27% of the female vote and Lourdes Flores 30%. However, the difference increased when voters were presented with the question of a second electoral round between the two candidates. In such a scenario, women gave Toledo 37 points (men 45), while Lourdes Flores scored 53 (men 43). If Lourdes Flores had won, she would have had a considerable support base among women. This is particularly interesting if one considers that Lourdes Flores did not wage a campaign particularly targeted at women, nor did she make gender-related demands a focus of her platform.

8. In the context of research being carried out at the Institute of Peruvian Studies to establish the acceptance of women's leadership and the initial reactions to the new Quotas Law, a series of questions was prepared and subsequently posed to a sample of 800 persons by the polling firm IMASEN in Dec. 1997. This survey gathered opinions from Lima residents of various ages and differing social classes on issues regarding women's participation in politics.

9. These observations were subsequently confirmed by the behaviour of the electorate in the 2001 elections, in which the leading candidate Lourdes Flores Nano ran unopposed.

10. However, these opinions appear to be shifting. The dramatic events which beset Peru during the first half of 2001, in which corruption and immorality extended indiscriminately to politicians, business people, judges, and journalists, led many people to turn to women in the search for new faces in politics, thus reinforcing the stereotype that women are more honest.

11. By way of analogy, after the flight of President Fujimori in Nov. 2000, women from his inner circle dedicated themselves to justifying his actions and protecting him from the attacks of the rest of the population. They proved his most loyal defenders, even when there was convincing evidence of his complicity with Vladimiro Montesinos, the National Intelligence Service adviser who had managed to gain control over all branches of government. In other words, like the Aprista women and communists of the 1930s, those supporting Fujimori remained loyal to him until the end. However, compared to women activists in the past, Fujimoristas women were forced to assume political responsibility in the face of serious charges of corruption against their colleagues.

12. And, more specifically, of Vladimiro Montesinos, 'presidential adviser' and Head of the National Intelligence Service. According to evidence presented by congressional investigations and the judicial branch during the transition government of President Paniagua, Montesinos effectively ran the country, controlling the judicial branch, the Congress, the media, and the armed forces through bribes, special privileges, or blackmail directed at high officials in those institutions.

13. The group Women for Democracy (Mujeres por la Democracia, MUDE) was founded in 1997. It includes women from various social groups, from NGOs concerned with development benefiting lower-income women, and from different feminist groups. Its objective is to debate and define a position in defence of democracy and women's rights, within a framework of law and order. Along with youth and human rights organizations and associations of intellectuals and artists, the women from MUDE and from other feminist groups became civil society's most combative force in the defence of democracy. The conspicuous participation of women in the streets of Peru's cities helped to reaffirm the 'common sense' regarding the public participation of women, while balancing authoritarian images of women in government. Among this sector of 'opposition' women were, for example, Susana Villaran, the current Minister of Women's Affairs, leader of MUDE and of the national human rights umbrella NGO, the Coordinadora Nacional de Derechos Humanos.

14. President Fujimori was able to run for a third term of office through an anti-constitutional measure called the 'Law of Authentic Interpretation', passed by Congress in Aug. 1996.

15. In the context of the economic crisis which began in the late 1970s and became acute during the 1980s and 1990s, women in poor neighbourhoods created and led the so-called 'subsistence organizations', such as community kitchens, Mothers' Clubs, and 'Glass of Milk Committees' to provide for the basic sustenance needs of their families and communities.

16. In the most recent elections of 2000, the use of women's subsistence organizations in support of Fujimori and the government's parliamentary candidates was blatant. The manipulation carried out by the office of the National Food Aid Programme (PRONAA)—which made support for Fujimori a precondition for receiving food aid—was clearly

demonstrated. The same was true of other national public assistance offices.

17. While these powerful women remained close throughout the entire regime, none has been 'burnt' by the painful end of Fujimori and his allies. They withdrew in good time and maintained their distance during the last, fatal year of the regime. And while they still participated in the government, they were not of the corruption extravaganza that affected many. Despite their loyalty to the President, a few months after his demise they already occupied technical posts in the transition government. Their experience in power and their link to international organizations provided them with a more mature 'gender awareness' and many have run for Congress with a subtly feminist rhetoric—enough to gain the support of the youngest women voters.

18. Most women politicians remained loyal to President Fujimori, even after his flight from the country. In the 2001 elections, they ran on a slate under the banner of the Fujimori party, *Cambio 90-Nueva Mayoría*, despite the bad reputation it acquired when evidence of corruption surfaced.

19. Opposition Congresswomen played an important role during the Fujimori regime and the transition process. This sector of female politicians was partially revitalised in the elections of 2000, with many young politicians entering Parliament. While many did so under the banner of Fujimori's party as an expression of support for pro-feminist policies, they abandoned the Fujimori ranks at the first signs of corruption, forming the group of 'independents' together with other members of Congress. In many cases they became the accusers of the regime.

20. The judicial branch and the Public Ministry played a critical role in promoting the interests of government leaders in the Fujimori regime, filing complaints or initiating trials despite lack of evidence as a means of manipulating and extorting businesspeople or opposition members. The former Attorney General of the Nation, Blanca Nelida Colan, was unquestionably an ally of the system. Once the transitional government assumed office she was replaced by another woman, the new Attorney General, Dr. Nelly Calderon, who has played a prominent role in trials of those involved in the 'Fuji-mafia'. The Prosecutor, Ana Cecilia Magallanes, has acted courageously and efficiently in one of the most difficult and important trials in recent Peruvian history, ordering the apprehension of high-level officials, judges and members of the military involved in corruption.

21. The Mesa Directiva del Congreso, or Bureau of Congress, is the governing body of the legislature, charged with organizing its agenda and schedule.

22. After Sept. 2000 Peruvians became accustomed to a context in which truth and lies and fiction and reality become indistinguishable. On a daily basis the scandalous scenes of corruption painstakingly recorded on video by the National Intelligence Service revealed the impunity with

which Peru's leaders acted in order to gain absolute control of state institutions and society. The media, the armed forces, the judicial branch, the electoral system and the national Congress were all involved. Citizens seem perplexed and ashamed by their own passivity, forced by a morbid curiosity to confront the trafficking in values and principles which had come to characterize Peru in recent years, as revealed by over a thousand videos.

23. 'At the End of the Battle' is taken from the collection of poems, *Masa* by Cesar Vallejo, one of the greatest Peruvian poets. It is also the title of the International Conference of the Interdisciplinary Andean Studies Seminar (SIDEA), Nov. 2001.

24. Taken from the title of Degregori (2000), *La década de la antipolítica*.

Chapter 10

1. See for example articles in Basu (1995).

2. Although we agree with Anne Phillips (1995) that these strategies may be based on vastly different and contradictory assumptions about the nature of the political system, and the roles and capacities of women to impact on the underlying values and institutions of democracies.

3. Although nationalism was not completely abandoned, it appears to have taken a benign form. The new Constitution is popularized through the slogan 'one law for one nation', for example.

4. This interpretation of the clause remains a contested issue. Traditional leaders have organized against a local government framework that reduces the extent of their powers in traditional areas. The Constitution accords the Council of Traditional Leaders strong advisory powers relating to reform of customary law.

5. The male leadership of these parties nevertheless held to more minimal definitions of democracy. The tension between these two conceptions remains within all political parties in South Africa.

6. This was despite the ground-breaking 2 May 1990 Statement of the NEC of the ANC, which called on women to begin a debate on a Charter of Women's Rights 'which will elaborate and reinforce our new constitution, so that in their own voice women define the issues of greatest concern to them and establish procedures for ensuring that the rights claimed are made effective' (ANC, 1990).

7. Interview with Thenjiwe Mtintso (Mar. 2000).

8. We do not mean this in the pejorative sense, but in the sense of grasping clearly the nature of opportunities presented by the transition.

9. This discussion is based on unpublished archival research and interviews conducted for Shireen Hassim's thesis.

10. Although their primary *concern*, to varying degrees, was the advancement of women's position.

11. Of course, such powers can also be used to advance the narrow interests of party elites. For this reason, the PR system has been criticized for undermining vertical accountability.

12. The adoption in 1993 of the quota for electoral lists appears to be a response by the ANC leadership to the failed quota proposal for party positions at the ANC's 1992 Conference. Following this failure, gender activists within the ANC continued to lobby for a quota. When the internal procedure for deciding on electoral lists was discussed, women activists successfully included the following clause: 'Affirmative action for women will be a central part of being representative and we need to ensure that no less than one third of the lists are made up of women (They are 50% of the electorate). The ANC policy has been consistent in supporting the need for affirmative action and gender equality. The people we elect to represent us in government will be responsible for representing the people of South Africa, not the ANC, and this makes it even more important that we ensure that no less than one third of the lists are made up of women' (ANC, 1994: 4).

13. In 1996, women won 28.2% of the PR seats and 10.87% of the ward seats.

14. Many male MPs, even within the ANC, saw women's presence as token gestures to equality. One male MP commented to Thenjiwe Mtintso: '[Men] don't think that this woman comrade is there because in her own name and right she deserves to be there. What also happens is that because of the quotas even in delegations abroad some women comrades go ten times more even before some male comrades have ever had a single chance to go. Some of these women comrades are almost like flowers that must decorate every delegation' (Mtintso, 1999: 52).

15. 'Linda', a woman MP interviewed by Mtintso, commented in 1995 that 'this place gives me the creeps. It is unfriendly and unwelcoming. It was meant to make the people feel the power, even in the building itself. I feel overwhelmed and completely disempowered. I cannot see myself making any input never mind impact here. I feel lost. I do not think I will even finish my term of office' (Mtintso, 1999: 56).

16. Feminists who spoke up in the National Assembly were laughingly called 'that lot who went to Beijing' (Vos, 1999: 108).

17. This committee was initially established as an *ad hoc* committee to oversee the implementation of CEDAW. Skilful lobbying by feminists within the ANC resulted in its upgrading into a proper standing committee, able to command parliamentary resources (such as a researcher) and regular slots on the parliamentary timetable.

18. Govender was the project manager of the Women's National Coalition and a leading union and women's organizer.

19. Interview with Sheila Camerer (NNP MP), 1999.

20. In the most recent example, MP Andrew Feinstein, ANC representative on the parliamentary committee on public accounts, was removed from his position as head of the ANC's study group after pushing for an investigation into the government's R3 billion arms deal, against the

wishes of the President. Justifying this 'redeployment', the ANC's parliamentary whip said the study group was being 'strengthened so that the ANC, from the President downwards, could exercise political control' (*Sunday Times*, 4 Feb. 2001). The *Sunday Times* journalist noted that 'nothing would go from the committee to the plenary of the National Assembly without first going through the caucus and any leaks would be investigated'.

21. For example, the highly effective and independent first chairperson of the Commission for Gender Equality, Thenjiwe Mtintso, was 'redeployed' early in 1999 to the post of Deputy Secretary-General of the ANC. The Commission did not fully recover from the loss of an experienced and critical leader at a crucial stage in the organization's development.

22. Parties are allowed to exist in name, but prohibited from opening and operating branch offices, holding delegates' conferences, public rallies, and, above all, campaigning for a candidate in any election.

23. The problem of mediating ethnic conflict has been dealt with through patronage—e.g. restoration of the Kabakaship (the aristocracy and throne of the Baganda people)—plus new rules on parties—that they should have a national base and a non-sectarian character.

24. The label 'National Resistance Movement' is no longer used. The term 'movement', particularly used in lower case, implies an embracing of all forms of associational life, all social movements, in the country, and is part of the government's efforts to generate a sense of a national social project (or if this cannot be generated, then to control and co-opt all opposing social movements in the country).

25. Increasing opposition to Movement candidates has, however, prompted the beginnings of a concern to set in place candidate selection procedures. The most spectacular challenge to the policy of not screening and selecting candidates came when, during the late 2000 National Conference, Colonel Kiiza Besigye, a veteran of the bush struggle, announced his candidature for presidency alongside the predictably unanimous call for Museveni to stand for a second time as presidential candidate. The National Executive Committee promptly declared that Museveni was the sole Movement candidate, making policy on the spot about formal endorsement of a sole candidate: 'Where a constituency is under threat from multipartyism, full support should be given to one Movement candidate that would have to be identified' (*Monitor*, 2000).

26. Interview with a member of the Movement Secretariat (Feb. 2000). No names are cited for interviewees due to promised anonymity.

27. Interview, Movement Director (Feb. 2000).

28. Interview with a woman MP (23 Feb. 2000).

29. Interviews with members of the Uganda Women's Network and the Forum for Women in Democracy, as well as feminist lawyers (Feb. and Dec. 2000).

30. Interview, Dec. 2000.

Chapter 11

1. The analysis of early nationalist feminism deserves a study on its own; I will focus here on the post-colonial phase of nation-building.

2. Aishah Ghani, AWAS's first leader, joined the Kaum Ibu (KI: Mothers Community), and became its fifth president and later a Cabinet Minister in the UMNO-led government. Sakinah Junid who led the six-mile protest march on the first anniversary of the Angkatan Pemuda Insaf (API: Awakened Young Men Front), joined the Parti Islam Se Malaysia (PAS) and became president of its Women's Section. Shamsiah Fakih, joined the Communist Party of Malaya (CPM), carried on the struggle underground, went into exile in China, and was only allowed back into the country in the early 1990s.

3. This information was given by F. R. Bhupalan in 1995. My speculation is that the Women Teacher's Union must have been one of the earliest associations which had a multiracial women's membership. To date there is a dearth of study on this association.

4. The pro-tem committee of NCWO which was initiated by YWCA in 1960, with Mrs F. R. Bhupalan as chairperson, had, as its members, Datin Kamsiah Ibrahim, Mrs Ruby Lee, Mrs Rani Elizir, Mrs Lakshmi Navaratnam, and legal adviser, Miss P. G. Lim. The composition of this committee reflected its multi-ethnic representation (interview with F. R. Bhupalan, 12 May 1995).

5. In Malaysia, the identity of 'race' is virtually predetermined. Being Malay also means being Muslim, according to its constitution. Further, Malays and other indigenous communities are conferred the status of *bumiputra*, literally, 'sons of the soil'. Under the aegis of the NEP, which was promulgated in 1972, *bumiputra* are then entitled to special privileges or subsidies ranging from places in higher education to preferential credit access.

6. The NEP was replaced by the New Development Policy (NDP) in 1990. The NDP focuses more on maximizing the growth potential of the economy. It is also not coincidental that this policy was in tune with the global neo-liberal phase of free-market emphasis. The NDP did not in practice replace the NEP since preferential social and economic policies continued to be put in place. Today, under the political mood of 'democratization' there has been more forceful questioning of the NEP, especially calls for it to be dismantled or remodified to shift development priorities away from race. Debates over this issue which used to be downplayed because of fear of reprisal through the Sedition Act, are now being freely aired through the internet medium. See, for example, P. Ramasamy, 'Diabolical Game of the Malay Hegemonic State', 28 Feb. 2001 (www.malaysiakini.com); Nik Nazmi Nik Ahmad, 'Saying Yes to Non-Racial Affirmative Action' (www.geocities.com/niknazmi/).

7. The concepts 'pragmatic acquiescence' and 'instrumental acceptance' are borrowed from Held (1997: 182).

474 *Notes*

8. It is sometimes jocularly said that 'freedom' among non-Muslims is now reduced to having the social and legal licence to drink, eat pork, gamble, and dress as one pleases. For example, one letter writer to the internet newspaper, *Malaysiakini*, dated 17 Jan. 2001, had this to say, 'Years away from its socialist origins, DAP is more immediately concerned about such issues as the right to be agnostic, to gamble and to drink liquor. These were the nuts and bolts for playing racial politics, a ploy that has long been successful.' The freedom openly and publicly to practise religious and traditional rituals, such as religious processions, is considered to be one of the highest tests of the state's ability to accommodate ethnic rights. The ruling National Front government uses these indicators of 'tolerance' in election campaigns to affirm its credentials as the only legitimate arbiter of inter-ethnic relations.
9. In 1992, the WCC and the WDC jointly organized and sponsored an international workshop entitled, 'Women and Islam: Towards a New Approach'. SIS also organized a workshop entitled, 'Islam, Women and the Nation-State', in 1994. Both events were attended by Muslims and non-Muslims.
10. For accounts of the 1999 Malaysian election see Funston (2000) and Weiss (1999).
11. The author attended a meeting in early 1998, organized by the Women's Development Collective (WDC), one of the leading feminist organizations in the country. Some of the leaders expressed a sense of fatigue or of having outlived their usefulness, as Malaysian feminism then seemed like it was in the doldrums. It had no mass base, nor the prospect of replenishing their corps of feminist advocates and leaders among younger women.
12. The Women's Development Collective, the MTUC Women's Section, the All Women Action Society (AWAM), Friends of Women, Jemaah Islah Malaysia (JIM), Sisters-in-Islam, and the Selangor Chinese Assembly Hall Women's Section as well as several key individuals.
13. Some thirty-four organizations participated in meetings held in Jan. 1999.
14. When the political crisis broke out, leaders of JIM played a key role in the formation of the new opposition party, the National Justice Party (Keadilan). The founders of this new party came from various ethnic, religious, class, and professional backgrounds. JIM itself was politicized almost overnight, providing the party with its grass-roots base with its network of branches and membership spread throughout the country.
15. She later stood for the parliamentary seat previously occupied by Anwar and won it with a convincing majority.
16. The concept, 'instrumentalized' by political forces, is after Molyneux (2000).
17. Nik Aziz himself did not consistently argue for women to retreat into the private realm. In fact he even made statements to support the fielding of women candidates in the then coming elections. However, this

was conditionally premised upon women protecting themselves against violence and men being able to continue giving protection to them (see *New Straits Times*, 1999).

18. Being Muslim she was often cajoled during the campaign period to put on the veil when she had to address a crowd together with other male Islamic party speakers. She refused but was not rebuked in any way, perhaps because the campaign period was too short and critical to allow for any dissension to develop.

19. Ivy Josiah, executive secretary of the Women's Aid Organization (WAO), quoted in the newspaper *Malaysiakini* (2001).

20. Among the changes proposed by women's groups was the setting up of a Ministry for Women's Affairs, Children and Family Development and the placing of the current Women's Affairs department (HAWA) under the purview of a full minister. It was also proposed that HAWA set up offices in districts, parliamentary constituencies, and states. Another proposal was to upgrade the National Action Council for the Integration of Women in Development (NACIWID) to become the National Council for Women's Advancement (*Star*, 2000).

21. Interview with secretary of organization in 1996.

22. Although there have been attempts by Tan (1999) to show that an alliance among many diverse Malaysian women's groups was possible in the case of lobbying for the country's Domestic Violence Act, the mobilization of women in this case was still limited to an exclusive segment of civil society, namely middle-class feminist groups with the backing of the country's oldest, mainstream women's organization.

23. In 2000, the PAS government of Terengganu (a predominantly Muslim state) announced that it was imposing a law to make veiling compulsory for women in the state. This immediately received prominent coverage by the media, which also prompted statements and condemnations from women's groups. The DAP, a political party in the Alternative Front coalition, threatened to withdraw from the front if the PAS government did not reverse its stance. The pressure did work, forcing the state Islamic government to retract its intention. However, many Muslim women were torn over this issue, preferring to couch their statements differently, with emphasis on the notion of 'no compulsion' but nevertheless endorsing any 'educational means' to persuade Muslim women to veil of their own accord.

24. In Apr. 2001, eight *reformasi* leaders, mostly Malays were arrested under the Internal Security Act (ISA), a legislation which allows for the detention of anyone unfriendly to the regime (in unknown cells) without recourse to a trial in court. The most prominent group organizing for the release of these recent detainees is their wives and families. In the past women did not always take on an active role to secure their spouses' release. This time, the Islamic party organized a rally on 19 Apr. in which wives of the detainees reportedly gave fiery speeches to condemn the action of the government. As an internet report, 'Wives of

Detained Activists Vow to Fight until ISA Abolished', states in assessing the longevity of the Mahathir government, 'when you turn innocent housewives and children into fire brand orators and activists, you must have transgressed human decency well beyond the limit!' <www.freeanwar.com>.

Chapter 12

Research for this project was partly funded by a grant of the Sistema Benito Juárez del Consejo Nacional de Ciencia y Tecnología (SIBEJ-CONACYT) and by CIESAS. I am grateful to all the Maya women who participated in the legal workshops, and to the research team of Guadalupe Cárdenas, Martha Figueroa, and Anna María Garza. Valuable comments on earlier versions of this article came from Jane Collier, Teresa Sierra, Maxine Molyneux, and Shahra Razavi.

1. The nationalism promoted by the state in post-revolutionary Mexico upheld the mixed-blooded Mexican as the foundation of national identity. In this official discourse the mestizo nation was the result of the union of two cultural traditions: the European, represented by Spain, and the Mesoamerican, represented by the Aztecs. This dichotomy reduced the spaces for indigenous peoples to engage in political action, and their presence was subsequently formulated as a national 'problem', to which anthropologists set to work to find a solution, creating the integrationist state policy known as *indigenismo*. Manuel Gamio, who studied with Franz Boas at Columbia University, was the first exponent of this movement, and is recognized as the pioneer of modern anthropological practice in Mexico. His book, *Forjando Patria* (Forging the Fatherland 1916), set the ideological foundations for official nationalism. For an analysis of the transition from a mestizo to a multicultural Mexico, see Hernández Castillo and Ortíz Elizondo (1996).
2. The term *neo-liberalism* is used in the Mexican context to refer to a set of policies based on the diminished importance of the state, privatization, and economic and financial deregulation, together with the promotion of exports. This economic model replaced the statist model, which was protectionist and based on import substitution industrialization, prevailing from the 1930s to the beginning of the 1980s. In the economic terminology of international organizations, these policies have also been called 'structural adjustment programmes' and became generalized throughout the developing world at the beginning of the 1980s.
3. NAFTA, known in Mexico as the TLC (*Tratado de Libre Comercio*), was one of the main initiatives promoted by Carlos Salinas's government in order to lock in economic reforms, especially commercial and financial liberalization. It is the first agreement of commercial liberalization in the world signed between two developed countries, the USA and Canada, and a developing country, Mexico.

4. For a detailed analysis of Zapatista and non-Zapatista autonomy demands, see Mattiace (1997). The history of the EZLN and its impact on the lives of indigenous communities in Chiapas can be found in Collier (1995); Harvey (1998); Rus *et al.* (forthcoming).

5. This demand is central to the *Acuerdos de San Andrés* (San Andrés Accords) that were signed by representatives of the federal government and the EZLN on 16 Feb. 1996. These were converted into a draft bill to be presented to the legislature by delegates of the different parties forming a body called the *Comisión de Concordia y Pacificación* (COCOPA: Concordance and Pacification Commission). On 19 Dec. of the same year, President Ernesto Zedillo rejected the agreements that his own representatives had reached with the Zapatista command. This arbitrary decision closed the dialogue between the parties and meant that the threat of war hung over south-east Mexico. In Jan. 2001, President Vicente Fox sent the COCOPA draft bill to Congress, in an effort to re-establish the peace dialogue with the Zapatistas. Two months later, twenty-five commanders of the EZLN marched to Mexico City, together with representatives of the National Indigenous Congress (CNI), in order to promote the approval of the COCOPA bill in the national Congress.

6. These demands are contained in the *Ley Revolucionaria de Mujeres* (Revolutionary Law of Women). For a description of this law, see Hernández Castillo (1994).

7. The *Ley Revolucionaria de Mujeres* was symbolically important in the formation of a broader organization of women in Chiapas, in that it began to articulate the demands of indigenous women *qua* indigenous women with the demands of *zapatista* women. The issues raised by this broader women's movement gained a wider audience during the National Democratic Convention (CND), held during August 1994 in the heart of the Lacandon rainforest, in a community renamed as Aguascalientes. The objective of this meeting was to form a broad-based civic movement that would work to democratize Mexican society. Prior to the convention, women from NGOs, productive co-operatives, and campesino organizations held a preparatory meeting to draw up a document listing the specific demands of the women of Chiapas. This was the basis for the Chiapas Women's State Convention in Sep. 1994. The term 'organized indigenous women' in this chapter refers to women who have been involved in this movement. For a history of the process of organization of indigenous women in Chiapas, and of the national indigenous women's movement that emerged in 1994, see Hernández Castillo (1998a); Millán (1996); Rojas (1995).

8. 'Propuestas de las Mujeres Indígenas al Congreso Nacional Indígena' (Proposals of the Indigenous Women to the National Indigenous Congress), seminar *'Reformas al Artículo Cuarto Constitucional'* (Reforms to the Fourth Article of the Constitution), Mexico City, 8–12 Oct. 1996.

9. A comparative analysis of the *Acuerdos de San Andres*, and the COCOPA draft bill with the counter-proposal the government offered after breaking the signed agreements can be found at <www.laneta.apc.org>. Much of the government's rejection of the agreements was based on the way in which recognizing autonomy compromised the central power of the state. Government speakers argued that autonomy threatened 'national unity' and that autonomy would represent a step backwards in 'civilization'. The racist prejudices of government consultants were reflected, for example in a statement that there was a danger of indigenous peoples reverting to 'human sacrifices' if they were given autonomy (*La Jornada*, 1997*b*). The Zapatistas and the indigenous independent movement declared on several occasions that they did not want to separate from Mexico, but rather to have a measure of autonomy within the nation. Adelfo Regino, an Oaxacan indigenous leader, stated: 'Politically speaking, the concepts of autonomy and sovereignty are radically different. It has been understood traditionally that sovereignty is an attribute of states ... whereas autonomy is the ability of communities within the framework of the state—not outside it—to determine, together with agencies of the state and federal government, their general living conditions. When the indigenous peoples of Mexico claim our right to free determination in pursuit of autonomy, we are not challenging sovereignty' (*La Jornada*, 1997*a*). For a detailed analysis of official speeches and of the indigenous movement towards autonomy, see Hernández Castillo (1998*c*).

10. The project was carried out in the framework of an agreement between the *Grupo de Mujeres de Sant Cristobal* (COLEM), a non-governmental feminist organization formed of indigenous and mestiza women, and CIESAS, an anthropological research centre. The collective project is entitled 'Positive Law and Customary Law in the Face of Sexual and Domestic Violence: A Co-Participative Investigation in the Search of Legal Defense Alternatives for Indigenous Women'. The members of the research team were the lawyers Martha Figueroa and Guadalupe Elizalde, the pedagogue Guadalupe Cárdenas, and the anthropologists Anna María Garza and R. Aída Hernández.

11. The first paragraph now reads: 'The Mexican nation has a pluricultural composition sustained originally on its indigenous peoples. The law shall protect and promote the development of their language, culture, ways, customs, resources and specific systems of social organization; it shall grant their members effective access to state law. In the trials and agrarian procedures in which they participate, customary law and practices shall be taken into account as prescribed by law'.

12. For a detailed analysis of this case, see Hernández Castillo and Figueroa (1993); Ortíz Elizondo (1995).

13. In his initial statement, Bruce admitted to having argued with his wife and to having struck her with a bamboo cane, although he played down

the severity of the blows. He subsequently retracted this first statement and presented his marital relationship as a harmonious one.

14. Paramilitary groups are formed of armed groups of civilians who receive training from active army members. Their links with the official party and with local power elites have been denounced by human rights organizations (see Centro de Derechos Humanos, 1996).

15. See 'Propuestas de las Mujeres Indígenas al Congreso Nacional Indígena', seminar 'Reformas al Artículo Cuarto Constitucional', Mexico City, 8–12 Oct. 1996.

16. For a detailed analysis of the political and cultural implications that the national post-revolutionary project had for indigenous peoples, see Hernández Castillo (2001).

17. The National Indigenous Institute is the government institution in charge of public policy towards indigenous peoples.

18. I do not mean to imply that culture and power are always mutually exclusive concepts; much has been written based on the works of Michel Foucault about the way in which discourses reflect culture and the relationships of power that exist in the context from which they spring. Nevertheless, many functionalist studies from the 1950s and 1960s that highlighted cultural analysis did so without recognizing how the construction of meaning is marked by power relationships.

19. In 1989, *History and Power in the Study of Law*, ed. June Starr and Jane Collier, was published, marking a new direction in North American legal anthropology. This volume highlighted the importance of considering power and historical perspectives in the analysis of any legal system.

20. I take the term 'legal maps' from Boaventura de Sousa Santos, who refers to legal pluralism as 'different legal spaces superimposed, interpenetrated and mixed in our minds as much as in our actions, in occasions of qualitative leaps or sweeping crises in our life trajectories as well as in the dull routine of eventless everyday life. We live in a time of porous legality and legal porosity' (De Sousa Santos, 1987: 289).

21. This contrasting characterization is present in the classical works for Oaxaca and Chiapas by Nader (1966, 1969) and Collier (1973), and continues to hold sway in the anthropological debate, as shown in a recent paper by the Bolivian anthropologist Xavier Albó (2000).

22. The way in which various political sectors struggle for control of the 'authentic' tradition has been analysed by George Collier (1994) in the case of the Zinacantán Tzotzil.

23. In some areas, such as Simojovel, the Catholic Church, through its Indigenous Pastoral, created a new religious structure, which reinvented traditional posts, taking up such terms as 'principals' and 'elders' councils'. In contrast to pre-existing civic-religious authorities, women can occupy public office (although only married women occupy them together with their husbands).

24. Anna María Garza Caligaris (1999) has traced the formation of 'traditional' spaces for justice administration in the highland municipality of

San Pedro Chenalhó and has noted the important role played by the Mexican government in the legitimization of some concepts of 'tradition' and the negation of others.

25. Interview of Aureliano López by R. Aída Hernández Castillo, 8 May 1999.

26. In her analysis of 19th-cent. judicial records from Chihuahua, Ana María Alonso (1995) has shown how legal reforms of the time aimed at penalizing domestic violence in fact served to 'rationalize patriarchy' by reinforcing gender roles. Only 'decent and obedient' women could count on the law to protect them from domestic violence, others could not.

27. Both customary law and state law define the domestic space as a female space par excellence. Until 1998 the Chiapas State Civil Code established in its Articles 165 and 166 that the wife was responsible for the upkeep of the home, and could only have a job if it did not affect her domestic responsibilities. The same code established that wives required conjugal permission to work outside the home or to travel. These articles were modified in 1998 partly in response to an initiative presented to the state Congress by the lawyer of the San Cristóbal Women's Group (COLEM).

28. One of the cases reviewed was that of a girl raped by the Municipal President of Chenalhó (in 1991) whose parents denounced the rape with the help of the COLEM lawyers, only to retract the charges later after a conciliation between the parties (see Garza Caligaris, 1999). Several indigenous women expelled from San Juan Chamula also denounced the use of rape as a form of punishment used against their parents or husbands who confronted local political bosses (*caciques*).

Chapter 13

1. Only recently has domestic violence against women been taken seriously in the USA. Over 2.5 million women per year suffer from violent crimes in the USA, and two-thirds of these women are attacked by people they know. Yet it was not until 1994 that a Violence Against Women Act was passed that declared domestic violence a federal crime. There are whole topics that are not even up for discussion in the United States, like national paid maternity leave, let alone paid paternity leave. Given the lack of popularity of affirmative action in the United States, it is not surprising that many balk at the idea of positive measures to improve the number of women in the legislature, yet 13% of Senate seats held by women is a long way from the 50% mark and rates of increase in female representation are slow. Meanwhile, Mozambique, Uganda, and Namibia are shooting for the one third mark and South Africa is already there. While the welfare culture of Finland and Sweden maintains poverty levels of single mothers at 3–4%, we, in the USA, seem to be able to tolerate a 60% level of poverty for single mothers.

2. The religious right and conservative opponents of CEDAW are concerned that the convention will threaten First Amendment rights, individual

privacy, and freedom from government interference in private conduct. They want to ensure that freedom of religion supersedes gender equality in the Constitution. As Republican Senator Nancy Kassebaum of Kansas explained to the Senate Foreign Relations Committee on 29 Sept. 1994: 'I'm going to vote no on this convention ... I don't know that it serves the United Nations well to somehow, somehow [sic] to be engaging in a convention that doesn't allow for differences in cultural, different cultural (pause) principles, more or less, mores, religions' (Mayer, 1996: 813). Although there have been many politicians, officials, and administrations (e.g. Kennedy, Carter) that have supported international human rights, the USA has a history of being reluctant to ratify international human rights conventions, e.g. Genocide Convention, because of a fear among Senate conservatives that international human rights will undermine the Constitution of the United States. Opposition to civil rights for Black Americans was at the basis of the arguments against international human rights in the 1940s and 1950s, although the arguments against international human rights were cast in terms of undermining the superior protection of rights in the USA (Mayer, 1996; Buergenthal, 1988; Kaufman, 1990). Today, it is the law in the USA that does not meet the standards of international law when it comes to the treatment of women. Because the Constitution does not explicitly provide for the principle of equality between men and women, the law in the USA is not in compliance with CEDAW, which requires parties to pursue appropriate policies to eliminate discrimination against women (Mayer, 1996).

3. (1) This Constitution is the supreme law of Uganda and shall have binding force on all authorities and persons throughout Uganda. (2) If any other law or any custom is inconsistent with any of the provisions of this Constitution, the Constitution shall prevail, and that other law or custom shall, to the extent of the inconsistency, be void' (Constitution of the Republic of Uganda, 1995: ch. 1, art. 2). Earlier quotation comes from ch. 4, art. 33, cl. 6.

4. The Uganda Land Alliance is a consortium of non-governmental organizations (NGOs), funded by the British charity, Oxfam International. It includes the NGO Forum, Uganda Law Society, and Legal Aid Project, in addition to women's organizations like Uganda Women's Network (UWONET), Association of Women Lawyers in Uganda (FIDA-U), Action for Development (ACFODE), the Uganda Media Women's Association (UMWA), Akina Mama wa Afrika.

5. Personal communication, Jacqueline Asiimwe, 27 Sept. 2000.

6. Personal communication, chair of ULA, Jacqueline Asiimwe, 14 Jan. 2001.

7. Personal communication, chair of ULA, Jacqueline Asiimwe, 19 Feb. 2001.

8. Personal communication, 27 Sept. 2000.

9. Personal communication, Jacqueline Asiimwe, 27 Sep. 2000.

10. I use the term Female Genital Cutting for the reasons Jane Frances Kuka of Kapchorwa gives: 'Within Uganda the procedure practiced by the Sabini is officially referred to as "Female Genital Cutting" (FGC). The term "Female Genital Mutilation" (FGM) sounds too harsh and fosters too much defensiveness. On the other hand, "Female Circumcision" (FC) does not adequately describe the magnitude of the operation nor the gravity of the effects associated with the practice. It implies a degree of acceptability which is inappropriate and misleading' (www.un.org/womenwatch/news/kuka.htm).

11. Hon. Jane Frances Kuka, Ugandan Minister of State, Gender and Community Development Program, 'Culture, Education and Female Circumcision', speech given 15 June 1998 to United Nations, 'Ugandan Government Official Creating Healthy Alternatives to FGM for Women and girls' (www.un.org/womenwatch/news/kuka.htm).

12. Baganda is plural for Ganda people, and Muganda is the singular for Ganda person.

13. In the 13th, 14th, and even 15th cents. women are said to have ruled as *Kabaka* (king). One Ganda historian, Sir John Gray, claims that there is abundant evidence of this, although much of this early history is semi-mythological. One such ruler was Naku, the daughter of Mukibi, the founder of the Lugave clan. She married Kimera, who is credited with having established Buganda as a kingdom during the 13th or 14th cent. (Kaggwa, 1971; Ray, 1991: 98). However, Gray argues that she was *de facto* ruler because Kimera's only claim to authority was the fact that he had married the daughter of a king. In fact, she eventually had her husband killed, suspecting that he was to blame for her son's death. Naku was so powerful that every king that followed Kimera took a wife from her clan and called her Naku (Gray, 1934: 267; Kaggwa, 1971 : 16–17). Thus Naku became the title for any woman performing her role. The *Kabaka* treats a Naku with high esteem because it was the original Naku who saved the kingdom.

Index

Index